The Law and You

The Law and You

General editor: Marcel Berlins

Published by Consumers' Association and Hodder & Stoughton

Which? Books are commissioned and researched by
The Association for Consumer Research
and published by Consumers' Association
14 Buckingham Street, London WC2N 6DS
and Hodder & Stoughton
47 Bedford Square, London WC1B 3DP

Designed by Trevor Vincent
Illustrations by John Holder

First published in 1986 as *You and the Law*

The law and you.
  1. Law—England
  I. Berlins, Marcel
  344.2   KD665.C6
ISBN 0 340 41512 6

Typeset and printed in Great Britain at the Alden Press Ltd,
Oxford

Bound in Great Britain by Butler & Tanner Ltd, Frome and
London

Contents

Contributors

John Barlow
Solicitor; Senior Lecturer, College of Law

Diana Brahams
Barrister

Madeleine Colvin
Barrister

Kathryn Cronin
Barrister

Chris Davey

Clare Dyer
Solicitor; journalist

Louise ffoulkes
Deputy Editor, Legal Action Group

Godfrey Gypps
Solicitor; Senior Lecturer, College of Law

Jennifer Levin
Solicitor; Head of Law and Government, Polytechnic
of the South Bank

Robert Lowe
Solicitor in private practice; lecturer;
conference organiser; Commercial Editor of *Litigation*

Walter Merricks
Solicitor; legal affairs writer; broadcaster

David Pannick
Barrister

Kevin Slevin
Taxation consultant

Peter White
Solicitor; taxation consultant

Geoffrey Woodroffe
Solicitor; Director of the Centre for
Consumer Law Research, Brunel University

Introduction

Never before has the law played so important a part in so much of our lives. There is today scarcely one human activity that is not controlled, regulated, directed or fundamentally affected by law. The unhappy paradox is that the more law pervades our day-to-day existence, the more complex it becomes and the less chance we have of knowing and understanding it. Lawyers complain that they cannot keep up with the legal avalanche. What hope, then, for the non-lawyer?

This book aims to provide consumers of the legal system – and that means all of us – with a comprehensive guide to the main areas of law which may affect them in their normal lives. Its scope takes us from before birth to after death, with stops along the way for children and education, marriage and divorce, jobs, homes, consumers' rights, health and a host of other topics of importance and relevance.

For the most part, we have used a question and answer format because it allows us both to answer the kind of specific queries that a lot of people ask about the law and to explain the general principles that lie behind those answers. The intention is to give the reader not just information but understanding as well. The text has been written by a large team of lawyers, all of them with personal practical experience of the issues that people who are not legal experts worry and ask about. As far as possible we have tried to avoid legal jargon, and we have shunned the kind of issues that may be of great interest to lawyers but are of little practical importance to the average person.

Even a book of this size cannot cover every relevant facet of the law relating to a particular set of circumstances. Almost every legal principle is subject to exceptions, provisos, extensions and a myriad of detailed rules that govern its application. We have not been able to lead you down every by-way. No single book can do that – legal textbooks on even narrow subjects can run to thousands of pages. What we can do, though, is to lead you through the impenetrable legal maze towards a clear statement of the parts that matter – those aspects of the law of greatest practical relevance to most of us.

It is not our aim to provide a 'do-it-yourself' service. Certainly we hope that the content will enable you to understand the law better and therefore to use it to more effect without the need to go elsewhere, but space has not allowed us to give full details of, say, how to do your own conveyancing or how to obtain your own divorce without the help of a solicitor. At various points throughout the book, in some areas of the law more than others, we emphasise that it would be wise to take your problem to a solicitor or to one of the agencies specialising in a particular field. No two cases are identical, and legal solutions often depend on particular facts and circumstances. No book, however comprehensive, can completely take the place of an expert applying his or her mind to an individualised problem requiring a specific response or immediate action.

Reluctantly, we have been compelled to restrict the ambit of this book to the law of England and Wales. The law of Northern Ireland and, in particular, Scotland differs from English law so considerably in a number of areas that to have covered the two countries would have made the book impossibly long.

The law is a constantly changing beast. We can try to trap it on a particular day – in our case in August 1987 – but it will not stay still. We have sought to incorporate future changes of which we are aware, but readers should bear in mind that Parliament, the courts and the various bodies that make rules and regulations will start nibbling at the content of the book almost as soon as it is printed.

Marcel Berlins

Family and personal

Living together

Property

1 | *My girlfriend and I may get married eventually, but for the moment we are happy just living together. Are there any special considerations for unmarried couples buying property jointly? What would happen if we decided to go our separate ways?*

There are two types of joint ownership; you and your girlfriend will have to decide which is the best for you. One type of joint ownership is a joint tenancy. Joint tenants together own the whole house or flat rather than each owning a share of it. So when one of them dies, the whole house or flat automatically becomes the property of the other.

The other form of joint ownership is used by those who don't necessarily want their share to go to their co-owner – for example, two friends buying a property together. They own their home as 'tenants in common'. Each owns a share of the property – the shares can be unequal – and can leave his or her share by will to anybody. If the person dies without making a will, it goes to whoever is entitled to that person's property according to the intestacy rules (see WILLS, DEATH AND INHERITANCE, Q18). A joint tenancy can be changed into a tenancy in common at any time. This involves giving a written notice to the other owner. You should also notify the Land Registry if the title of your house or flat is registered (see YOU AND YOUR HOME, Q170). It's best to get legal advice about this.

What you really have to decide is whether you would like your partner to have your share of the house in the event of your death. You could, of course, achieve the same effect by holding the house as tenants in common and leaving your shares to each other in your wills. Or you could make a will leaving it to someone else, but giving your partner the right to live in the house for life. You can always make a new will if you change your mind.

The most important consideration, however, when an unmarried couple buy a house together is what share of the property each owns and what should happen in the event of a break-up. If one of you is contributing more than the other, you may want this to be reflected in the size of your shares. The size of your respective shares – for example, whether half and half or one-third and two-thirds – should be clearly spelled out in the deeds (see YOU AND YOUR HOME, Q172) or in a separate agreement or deed drafted by a solicitor.

Whether you own your home as joint tenants or tenants in common, it is a good idea to have an agreement in writing setting out how the outgoings are to be paid and what should happen in the event of a sale. Your agreement might stipulate, for instance, that if either partner wishes the property to be sold, the other partner will be given, say, six months to raise the money to buy his or her share.

In most cases when a relationship breaks down, either the house or flat is sold and the proceeds split, or one partner buys the other out. If one co-owner refuses to co-operate, the court can be asked to order the sale. Going to court can be expensive, so it is much better to tie everything up in advance.

2 | *My girlfriend and I bought a house in joint names. A few years later, I moved out. She stayed on in the house and now another man has moved in with her. I want the house sold so that I can get my share of the money, but she refuses to move. Is there anything I can do?*

Since both your names are on the deeds, you will not be able to sell the property without your girlfriend's consent. If she cannot be persuaded, you will need a court order to sell the house. The court will usually make an order for sale in these circumstances. One possible exception is if you have children. In one such case, the Court of Appeal refused to order a sale until the youngest child reached 16. In one recent case involving an unmarried couple, where the man and his new wife were living in the house, the Court of Appeal postponed the sale for four months to give

him time to raise the money to buy his ex-girlfriend's share. Sometimes a court will also order the joint owner who stays on to pay the joint owner who moves out a rent for the use of his or her half share.

3 | *I know that a married couple buying a home together can get tax relief on a mortgage of up to £30,000. Is the position the same for unmarried couples?*

No. This is one of the tax advantages of remaining unmarried for those who need and can afford a large mortgage. Every individual is entitled to tax relief on up to £30,000 as long as the house is his or her main residence. A married couple, however, are treated as one individual for this purpose, while an unmarried couple still count as two separate individuals for all tax purposes. Therefore, if you buy a house together you each have a £30,000 entitlement to tax relief, or a joint £60,000.

4 | *Ten years ago, the man I was living with bought a house for us, but put it in his name. I worked while we were living together and bought furniture for the house and paid for housekeeping, but I did not contribute anything towards the deposit or the mortgage. Two years ago we split up and I left. Recently I saw a newspaper report about a woman in a similar position who won a share of her ex-lover's house. It made me wonder if I would be entitled to anything. If so, how much would I be likely to get? I would estimate that the house is worth £40,000.*

In a very similar court case recently, a woman won a one-fifth share of the value of her ex-partner's house. But every case depends on its own particular facts, and you should not assume that this would necessarily apply in your case. The court will look at what your intentions and your partner's were when you set up home together, and how substantial your contributions were (see Q6). Certainly you should take legal advice on the strength of your claim.

5 | *My boyfriend is the tenant of our flat. If he left, would the landlord be able to evict me as long as I kept paying the rent?*

The landlord may be happy for you to take over the tenancy. But it is very unlikely that you will have any

legal rights against him, and if he wants to do so he will probably be able to turn you out. In some circumstances he would have to go to court to get you out if you refused to go. However, landlord and tenant law is complicated, and you would be well advised to take a solicitor's advice if you found yourself in this situation. See YOU AND YOUR HOME, Q18.

6 | *I have lived with a man as his wife for 20 years. We never married because he never got round to divorcing his legal wife. I stayed at home looking after our children and running the house, which is in his name. Now he has found someone else and wants me to leave. He says I have no legal claim on him. Is this right?*

Certainly he has no obligation to maintain you. Nor has he any automatic obligation to support his children, though you have the right to apply to the magistrates' court for affiliation orders to claim maintenance for any children under 18 (see Q17).

You might have a possible claim for a share of the house. But in a recent case, the Court of Appeal held that a woman whose only contributions during most of a 19-year relationship were looking after the home and children (though during the final years of the relationship she paid the rates and telephone bills and bought some fixtures and fittings) was not entitled to a share of the house. In all the successful claims so far, the woman has made some contribution to the home apart from doing housework and raising children. Examples include helping with the mortgage payments, contributing part of the deposit, paying for 'furnishing and housekeeping', and doing substantial improvement work on the house.

You have made no financial contributions, but perhaps you have done some heavy DIY work. In one case, a woman won a third share of the bungalow she helped her ex-partner to build. Another successful claimant stripped wallpaper and painted woodwork and cabinets, broke up concrete and helped demolish a shed and build another. The contribution has to be substantial; a spot of decorating would not be enough.

Yet another possibility is to try to convince the court that there was an implied agreement between you and your partner giving you a right to stay on in the house after the breakdown, though this is not an argument that has been successfully advanced in many cases. In any event, you should not simply leave. The best thing to do is to see a solicitor as soon as possible and explain your circumstances.

7 | *I have not lived with my wife for 10 years, although we were never formally divorced. She has never asked for any maintenance from me, but I'm worried that when I die she may try to claim a share of my assets. I'd like them all to go to the woman I live with. Is there any way I can prevent my wife from getting anything? I'm particularly anxious about our home, which is jointly owned by myself and my new partner. Is there any chance that my wife would be able to turn her out of her home?*

You should certainly make a will in your new partner's favour if you have not already done so. If you and your new partner own the house as joint tenants rather than tenants in common (see Q1), then your new partner will automatically inherit your share of the house whether there's a will or not. But in the absence of a will, any property that belongs solely to you will go either mainly or entirely to your wife, depending on the size of the estate and whether you have children (see Q9).

Even if your will leaves everything to your cohabitee, your wife would still have the right to make a claim under the Inheritance (Provision for Family and Dependants) Act 1975 for a share of your estate, just as your cohabitee would (assuming she was at least partly dependent on you) if you failed to make a will and your property went to your wife (see WILLS, DEATH AND INHERITANCE, Q54).

If your wife were to apply, how much she would get would depend on the circumstances of the case. Among the questions the court would ask are: How long did you and your wife live together? How long have you and your present partner cohabited? Did your wife get anything when you separated? How much is there to share out? What are your wife's and your cohabitee's needs and resources?

If your wife were to make a successful claim, there is a possibility that your house might have to be sold to raise the money, if the rest of the estate was insufficient. But you may be worrying unnecessarily. Since your wife has made no claims on you for 10 years, she may not think of putting in a bid on your death. If you have lost contact, she may not even be aware of it.

Finally, to safeguard your partner's interests, consider insuring your life so that the policy monies will be payable direct to her.

8 | *I have no relatives or dependants apart from the woman I live with. Would she inherit my assets if I died without making a will?*

If you have no relatives at all, and you were to die without leaving a will, your estate would go to the Crown (see WILLS, DEATH AND INHERITANCE, Q31). It would be administered by the Treasury Solicitor's Department, who would have a discretion, but no obligation, to give all or part of it to anyone with a convincing moral claim. Normally, in these circumstances, they would exercise their discretion in favour of a long-standing cohabitee.

If you were wholly or partly maintaining your partner at the time of your death, she could apply to the court for a share of your estate (see Q9). But obviously the safest way of making sure she inherits your property is to make a will (see WILLS, DEATH AND INHERITANCE, Q1).

9 | *The man I lived with for 30 years died recently without making a will. He was married and, though he lived with his wife only briefly, he never got round to divorcing her. They had one child. Who inherits his property, his wife or me? Are our three children entitled to anything?*

You are not automatically entitled to anything. The intestacy rules (see WILLS, DEATH AND INHERITANCE, QS 27 to 32) say that if his estate is worth £75,000 or less, his wife will inherit everything. Half of anything over that will go to his four children (including your three), with each child getting a quarter share. His wife will be entitled to the income from the other half for her life; the administrators will see to this. After her death the capital would go to the children equally. However, any property which you and he owned as joint tenants (see Q1) will not count as part of his estate and will pass automatically to you.

These rules will take effect unless you apply to the court for a share of the estate. Your children can apply in any event. So can you if your partner was wholly or partly maintaining you when he died. The benefit you got from him could be a benefit in kind, such as free housing. You need not have been totally dependent on him; you may, for instance, have a job of your own. The courts look favourably on cases such as yours where there has been a marriage in all but name, as opposed to a businesslike expense-sharing arrangement.

You should see a solicitor straightaway. Normally, a claim must be made within six months of the grant of letters of administration (see WILLS, DEATH AND INHERITANCE, Q22).

You would also have the right to apply to the court if your partner had left a will, but made inadequate provision for you.

10 | *The man I lived with has recently died. Our flat, which is rented, was in his name. Now the landlords want to sell the flat and have given me notice to quit. Do I have to go?*

You should certainly not go without taking legal advice. If your partner had a regulated tenancy (see YOU AND YOUR HOME, Q19), you may well have the right to step into his shoes as the new tenant. You would have to show that

- you were living together at the time he died
- you had been living together for at least six months immediately before his death, and
- you were a member of his family.

Unfortunately, the Rent Act 1977 does not define 'member of the family'. But recent cases show that if a relationship is a long-standing and stable one, and has the appearance of marriage, the court will normally consider the couple a family even if there are no children and even though they did not pretend to be married. If your partner acquired the regulated tenancy on the death of a member of his family, you will still be able to take it over from him. The Rent Act allows two successions.

Had your home been a council tenancy, you would have had an easier time proving your entitlement. For the purposes of taking over a secure tenancy (see YOU AND YOUR HOME, Q19), the Housing Act 1980 defines 'member of the family' as including someone living with the tenant 'as man and wife'; a 12-month period of living together is required. For secure tenancies only one succession is allowed. So if a tenant takes over the property on the death of a member of his family, he cannot pass it on when he dies.

11 | *When my husband and I divorced, the court gave me the right to live in the family home. Is there any danger that I might lose that right if I asked a man to move in with me?*

If the ownership of the family home was transferred outright to you on your divorce, then the home is yours to use or sell as you wish. But if you were given only a right to live in it, then the court order will spell out the terms under which you can continue to stay in the house. If you have children, it may say, for instance, that the house will be sold and the proceeds divided once the youngest child reaches 18, or earlier if you remarry or if you leave the house of your own accord.

Some court orders in the past provided for the house to be sold if the former wife cohabited with a new man, but such orders are unusual nowadays.

However, in addition to the three events mentioned above which might trigger a sale, orders often conclude 'or until further order'. If so, an ex-husband might apply to the court for the house to be sold if his former wife started to cohabit. In deciding whether to order a sale, the court would consider both the husband's and the wife's circumstances. The children's need for a home would be a particularly important factor.

12 | *I bought out my husband's share of our home when we divorced, and now it belongs entirely to me. I have formed a relationship with another man and I am thinking of asking him to move in. What are the chances that he might have a legal claim on my house if we split up?*

It is possible for someone to become entitled to a share of property which legally belongs to someone else. There have been a number of court cases in which a woman who has been living with a man outside marriage has won a share of the value of their home, despite the fact that it was in the man's name. The reasoning behind the decisions in these cases is that the house was intended to be a joint home, and that the woman earned a share by her contributions.

In your case, since the house was obviously not acquired as a joint home, the court would look at what your intentions were when you started living together. If your new partner shares the mortgage payments or does minor improvements to the house, this will not necessarily entitle him to a share. It is more likely to be seen as a contribution to expenses in return for the accommodation provided.

To avoid any possible claims, however, it would be wise to spell out exactly the terms on which your new partner occupies your house. You could, for example, give him a written licence to live there in return for

SIGN HERE, HERE AND HERE.

sharing the household expenses, specifying that the licence can be terminated on, say, three months' notice. The licence could be a separate document signed by both of you, or you could incorporate it in a cohabitation contract. To be safe, have a solicitor draw it up.

13 | *My boyfriend owns his own home and has asked me to move in with him. However, I'm reluctant to give up my council flat. What rights would I have if I moved in with him and things didn't work out?*

This would depend on what you agreed at the beginning. If you just moved in without any specific agreement, then legally you would probably be your boyfriend's licensee. This means that you would be really only a guest, and entitled to stay only as long as he wanted you there, though he would have to give you reasonable notice if he wanted you to go. Four weeks would generally be considered enough notice, unless there were special circumstances – for example, if you had lived together for a long time or had children.

If you decide to make the move, there are steps you can take to put yourself on a firmer footing. Your boyfriend might be prepared to give you a written licence allowing you to stay for a fixed period of time, or for an initial fixed period then continuing until terminated by, say, three months' or six months' notice. Or you could become your boyfriend's tenant, though his mortgage, if he has one, will almost certainly require him to get permission to take in a tenant. You would have to pay rent and have the right to the exclusive use of at least one room. This would put you in the same position as any tenant whose landlord lives on the premises (see YOU AND YOUR HOME, Q 2 3). You would not have a fully protected tenancy and would have to leave eventually if your boyfriend wanted you to go. But he would need a court order if you resisted, and you could ask the court for a six-month extension.

The most secure arrangement from your point of view, however, would be to have a stake in the ownership of the house. You and your boyfriend should see a solicitor if you and he decide to do this.

If you have in mind keeping on your flat for an experimental period, paying the rent even though you no longer live there, so that you have a chance to change your mind, examine the council's letting conditions carefully. It's probable that the council forbids this, and you'll lose the flat if it finds out. Certainly, moving out means you will lose the chance to exercise your right to buy your council flat (see YOU AND YOUR HOME, Q 1 0).

14 | *If my boyfriend were a council tenant or the tenant of a private landlord and I moved in with him, how secure would my position be?*

Again, in the absence of any specific agreement, you would probably be considered just a guest, and would have to leave if your boyfriend ordered you out. Your best bet (if your boyfriend agrees) is to ask the landlord or the council to grant a new joint tenancy to you both. Whether you'll get one is up to the landlord or council, though many councils are willing to grant a joint tenancy if the relationship seems stable. This would give you both equal rights to live in the house, and neither could get the other out without a court order. If your partner left, you could remain. As a guest, you would have no right to stay once your partner, the tenant, left.

Not all tenants are allowed by their tenancy agreements to have people living with them. If your boyfriend needs his landlord's approval to your moving in and does not get it, the landlord could oblige him to get you out or force you both out. A council tenant is always entitled to take in a lodger, but cannot sublet without consent.

Children

15 | *My baby's father and I are not married. He has not seen the baby for three months, and has given me no money towards his keep. Now he's decided he wants to re-establish contact and take him out regularly. I am afraid this could upset things with my new boyfriend. Does the baby's father have the right to insist on seeing his son?*

If parents are married, both have equal rights as far as their child is concerned. But in the case of unmarried parents, the mother has sole say over the child. You are legally entitled to deny your ex-boyfriend access to your child.

However, he will be able to apply to the court for an order allowing him to see the child. In deciding whether to grant the order, the court has to consider whether it would be in the child's best interests to maintain contact with its father. A father who is a stranger to the child is less likely to be allowed access than one who has played a real part in the child's life. The fact that your baby's father has not been supporting him will not necessarily disallow his claim, though it will be one of the factors the court will weigh up in the balance. On the other side of the scale will be the child's need for a father figure. If the mother is in a stable new relationship which provides the child with a surrogate father, this could weaken the real father's chances. But courts have become more reluctant in recent years to sever the father–child tie. As a judge put it in a 1977 case, 'the court should always be slow to deprive either parent of access to a child and should have, when refusing a father access to his illegitimate child, positive and compelling evidence that access is not in the child's best interest, particularly when they have lived together under the same roof'.

16 | *My boyfriend and I live together, but we have decided not to marry. We have two small children. A friend has told me that their father might not be allowed to look after them if something happened to me. Is this really the case?*

Since you and your children's father are not married, your children are illegitimate in the eyes of the law. This means that as their mother all the parental rights and duties belong to you. Their father has no legal right to play a part in decisions about where they live, their religious upbringing or schooling, or whether they should be allowed to marry under 18, for example. This is the strict legal position, even though you and your boyfriend probably jointly make the decisions about your children.

If you die while your children are under 18, their father will not automatically become their legal guardian, that is, the person who takes over the rights and responsibilities of a parent. But you can take steps to make sure that he becomes their guardian in the event of your death. The simplest way is by appointing him guardian in your will. If you want your partner to inherit your property, you should make a will anyway, because the inheritance rules which come into play when someone dies without making a will take no account of unmarried relationships.

If you die without appointing a guardian, your boyfriend (or anyone else, such as your parents) can apply to the court to be appointed one. The court will decide on the basis of the children's best interests. The court would be likely to agree that a satisfactory father who has been living with the children and helping to care for them should become their guardian.

A new law, the Family Law Reform Act 1987, which was passed in 1987 but has not yet come into force, will give the fathers of illegitimate children greater rights. A father will have the right to apply to the court for an order allowing him to share the parental rights and duties with the mother, as married fathers do. If the father has such an order he will be able to carry on caring for the child if the

mother dies. As of August 1987, no date had been fixed for bringing the Act into force.

17 | *I am an unmarried mother with a six-month-old son. The baby's father and I are separated. He has a good job, but he has never given me any money. Is there some way I can make him contribute to the baby's keep?*

You can ask the magistrates' court to make an affiliation order declaring your former boyfriend to be the baby's father and requiring him to pay a regular weekly or monthly sum for the child's support. You can also ask for a lump sum of up to £500. The size of the payments will depend on how much he earns. Most orders are for fairly low sums – around £10 a week – but this is mainly because most fathers who are taken to court are young and not well off.

Unless your former boyfriend admits that he is the baby's father you will need to produce some proof that he is – for example, the fact that you were living together when the child was conceived, or the fact that your boyfriend agreed to be named as the father on the birth certificate. Blood tests can be ordered if you or your boyfriend asks for them. No one can be forced to take a blood test, but the court can draw its own conclusions from a refusal.

Regular payments under an affiliation order count as part of a mother's resources and reduce her entitlement to Supplementary Benefit, so if you are on Supplementary Benefit you may feel that affiliation proceedings are not worth the effort. It is official DHSS policy not to force a mother on benefit to take proceedings against the father. The DHSS can take a father to court if it knows who he is, but it cannot force a mother to give them the information or deny her Supplementary Benefit if she refuses to name him.

It is often a good idea to get an affiliation order while the baby is young even if the father is not well off or the mother is on Supplementary Benefit because the payments can be increased later if the father's circumstances change. Application must be made before the child reaches the age of three, unless the father has contributed to the child's maintenance in the first three years.

An affiliation order will be more valuable to you if you have a job. For tax purposes you can ask the magistrates to word the order so that the payments count as the baby's income and not as yours.

When the Family Law Reform Act 1987 comes into force, affiliation proceedings will be abolished, and either parent (not just the mother) will be able to apply to the court for financial support for the child from the other parent. Possible orders will not be limited to monthly or weekly payments and lump sums up to £500. Unlimited lump sums may be ordered, and a parent could be ordered to transfer property to the child, though obviously this would happen only if the parent were very well off.

18 | *My daughter's father and I are not married. Would she be able to inherit our property if we died without making a will?*

If you or her father should die without leaving a will, your child (together with any brothers or sisters she may have) will be entitled to inherit your property in accordance with the intestacy Rules (see WILLS, DEATH AND INHERITANCE, QS 27 to 32) just as if she were legitimate. Illegitimacy makes no difference to the right to inherit on a parent's intestacy.

19 | *What are the rights of our illegitimate daughter when it comes to inheriting her grandparents' property?*

This is one of the few areas of the law where a distinction is still made between children born inside and outside wedlock. If her grandparents made a will leaving something to your daughter by name, or to their grandchildren generally, your daughter would be entitled to that gift. But if her grandparents died without making a will, the fact that she was illegitimate would prevent her from inheriting a share of their property. In practice, this would matter only if you or your partner died before your respective parents, because your child would become entitled to a share of your parents' estate only if you were no longer living at the time of their death. Similarly, if her brothers or sisters or any other relative – apart from you and her father – dies intestate, she gets nothing.

Once the Family Law Reform Act 1987 comes into force, your daughter will have the same rights of inheritance from all her relatives as a legitimate child would have.

20 | *Can my boyfriend's name appear on our baby's birth certificate as her father, or is this allowed only if the parents are married?*

Your boyfriend may be named on your baby's birth certificate as her father if you both wish it. About half the illegitimate births in England and Wales are registered by both parents. As an unmarried mother, the decision is yours to make. The baby's father has no right to insist that his name appear on the birth certificate against your wishes. Conversely, you can

name him as the father on the birth certificate only if he agrees. If he wants to be named on the birth certificate, he should go along with you when you go to register the birth, or provide you with a statutory declaration (a formal written statement witnessed by a solicitor) which you can take with you. The only circumstance in which an unmarried father can be named without his agreement is if the mother gets an affiliation order from the magistrates' court (see Q17).

Having his name on the baby's birth certificate will not give your boyfriend any extra parental rights, though it would strengthen his position if he were to apply for an order for access to the child and your position if you decided to take affiliation proceedings. As the mother of an illegitimate child, you will still have the sole right to make all the decisions about your child's upbringing.

21 | *My girlfriend and I have been living together for five years and we are not in any hurry to get married. We would like to have a child, but we don't want our child to suffer any disadvantages. Are illegitimate children worse off than those born in wedlock?*

Whether or not your child would suffer any *social* disadvantages from being born illegitimate is for you to decide. But as far as the law is concerned, very few distinctions remain between children born inside and outside marriage. The differences which still exist concern inheritance, nationality, and the right to financial support.

As explained in Qs 18 and 19, an illegitimate child can inherit from a parent who dies without making a will, but not from a grandparent or any other relative who dies intestate. He or she can inherit from other relatives only if there is a will to that effect.

A legitimate child can claim British nationality through either parent, an illegitimate child only through the mother.

Married fathers are legally liable to maintain their children. Unmarried fathers have no obligation to support their children (in the absence of an affiliation order or a legally binding agreement). The courts have wide powers to provide for the support of legitimate children when their parents divorce or separate. Magistrates' courts, which make affiliation orders (see Q17) for the support of illegitimate children, can order only maintenance (usually weekly or monthly) and/or a lump sum of up to £500.

Under the Family Law Reform Act, when it

becomes law, all children, whether their parents were married or not, will have the same rights of inheritance and financial support.

22 | *If a child is born to unmarried parents, does he always remain illegitimate, or is there any way he can become legitimate?*

An illegitimate child becomes legitimate if his parents marry each other at any time after his birth. If he is adopted by anyone, he becomes the legitimate child of his adoptive parents.

23 | *My son, aged five, lives with his mother. She and I were never married. I see him regularly and we are quite close. He often says he would like to live with me. Is there any chance I could get custody of him?*

Even when parents are married, and therefore start off with an equal claim to custody, the courts still slightly favour mothers over fathers when it comes to choosing with whom a young child should live. Where the child is illegitimate, the mother's claim is much stronger and the father has no legal rights as far as the child is concerned. The mother has all such rights (see Q 1 6), including the right to have the child live with her.

You can apply to the court for custody, but the chances of success are slim unless the mother agrees to transfer custody to you or if there are very exceptional circumstances – if she is an unfit mother, for example. Apart from the mother's stronger legal position where the child is illegitimate, courts are always reluctant to move a child from one home to another without very good reason.

Cohabitation and the law

24 | *I've heard that if a woman lives with a man as a common-law wife for a certain number of years, she acquires all the rights of a legally married wife. Is this true? If so, is it three years or seven? I've heard both.*

This is a widespread belief, but one which has no basis in fact, and the phrase 'common-law wife' has no meaning in English law. No matter how long a woman may have lived with a man, she cannot achieve the status of a wife without going through a formal marriage ceremony. This means that any

children born to her will be regarded as illegitimate. Unlike a wife, she has no right to be supported by the man she lives with, either while the relationship continues or when it breaks up. Should the man die without leaving a will, she will not automatically be entitled, as would a wife, to a share of his estate (though she can ask the court to give her something). Nor will she be entitled to the state benefits reserved for widows.

25 | *Surely the law gives some special protection to a woman who has lived with a man for a long time?*

In recent years the law has given increasing protection to 'unmarried spouses' of both sexes. For example, the legal remedies against domestic violence apply to couples who live together as well as to husbands and wives (see Q 30). A cohabitee who has helped to buy or made some other substantial contribution to a home in the other partner's name may be entitled to a share if the relationship breaks down (see Q6). A long-standing cohabitee can take over a partner's council tenancy or regulated private tenancy on death (see Q 1 0) and, if dependent in some way on the dead partner, can apply for a share of his or her estate (see Q9).

26 | *I believe that some couples who live together have cohabitation contracts to deal with everything from who does the washing up to what happens to the home in the event of a split-up. Have these contracts any legal force, and are they a good idea?*

Cohabitation contracts are by no means common, but a few couples have them. It is not absolutely certain that they would be legally enforceable, because no cohabitation contract has yet been tested in the English courts. Just possibly the courts might consider such contracts to be immoral or against public policy. But the likelihood is that at least the parts of a contract which dealt with property and child support would be upheld.

Certainly no court would enforce an agreement about who does the domestic chores. If you want to put something in writing about your domestic arrangements and your personal relationship, it would be wise to put them in a separate document rather than including them with the cohabitation contract that deals with your property and financial arrangements. That way, if you did have to go to court, you would stand a better chance of having the court take the latter arrangements seriously.

A cohabitation contract can be a good idea, because cohabitation, unlike marriage, carries no clearly defined rights and obligations. While you may not want to accept the assumptions of marriage, you may both prefer to know where you stand in the relationship, and what rights and obligations you would have if you split up. Having this sort of thing clearly spelled out in writing could save you from an expensive court battle.

27 | *What points are usually included in a cohabitation contract?*

If you are buying a house together, you may want to lay down how you will share the bills and what will happen to the house and your other belongings if you decide to part. For example, will one of you have an option to buy the other out, and how much time will he or she have within which to exercise that option?

Provision for the support of any children you may have is another possibility. However, any agreement you might make about sharing rights over your children will not be legally binding. The mother of an illegitimate child has all parental rights and cannot voluntarily share them with anyone else, even the child's father. But any agreement you make for the children's support will probably be enforceable.

Some cohabitation contracts are designed to prevent the parties from making any claims on each other, particularly where one has moved into the other's house. On the other hand, you may agree that the non-owning partner should have some protection in these circumstances. For instance, he or she may be given a licence to stay in the house, and the agreement can spell out how much notice should be given to terminate the licence (see Q 1 3).

When the Family Law Reform Act becomes law, unmarried fathers will be able to apply to the court for an order allowing them to share parental rights with their child's mother. The new law will also allow unmarried parents who are separating to make agreements about how parental rights will be exercised, though the courts will not enforce such an agreement unless it is to the child's benefit, in the court's opinion.

Compensation

28 | *The man I lived with was killed recently in a collision with a drunken driver. Can our children and I, as his dependants, claim compensation from the other driver's insurance company?*

Until recently, you would not have been able to get compensation, since your partner was not your lawful husband, and only your children would have had a claim for the loss of their father's support. But the Administration of Justice Act 1982 includes a provision allowing a cohabitee of at least two years' standing to claim compensation for the loss of a partner killed in an accident through someone else's fault.

The amount of compensation for fatal accidents depends on the man's age, earnings and prospects. But a court could award you less than a wife would get because your partner had no legal duty to support you.

Change of name

29 | *I'm living with a man I hope to marry when his divorce comes through. In the meantime I'd like to change my name to his. How do I go about it?*

It is possible to change your name without formality simply by starting to use the new name. But for official purposes – for example, applying for a passport – you are likely to have to produce evidence of your change of name.

The most usual formal method of changing a name is by deed poll. You can draw up your own simple deed poll. But if you intend to have it 'enrolled' – filed with the Central Office of the Supreme Court in London – you should have it drawn up by a solicitor. Enrolment, which costs £34, is not necessary, but it does mean that you can get official copies of the deed to use as proof of your name change.

A common alternative to a deed poll is a statutory declaration. You can draw it up yourself or have a solicitor do it. If you do your own, you will still need to sign it in front of a solicitor, who will charge a fee of £3 for witnessing your signature.

A less formal alternative is simply to advertise your name change in a local newspaper, keeping copies of the advertisement as proof of the change.

Violence

30 | *The man I live with has been mistreating me for some time. Recently he has come home drunk on several occasions and been violent towards the children. We live in a council house which is in his name. I have nowhere else to go. What can I do?*

There are two types of court orders – or injunctions (see SEPARATION, Q 1 3) – which may be of use to you. A non-molestation order is one possibility. This will order your partner not to molest you or the children. If he breaks the order, you can have him committed to prison for a short period for contempt of court. In cases of serious violence, you can ask the court to attach a power of arrest to the non-molestation order, so that the police can be called to arrest him if he breaks the order. Being taken to court is a salutary lesson for some men who are inclined to violence, but it has to be said that in many cases, probably most, the violent behaviour recurs. In most cases, a non-molestation order is of little practical effect if your partner is still living with you.

If you have made up your mind that your partner is not likely to change, and your relationship has come to an end, you can ask the court for an exclusion order, also called an ouster injunction, banning him from the family home. If the order is granted, it will normally be for only a short period to allow you to sort out your living arrangements on a more permanent basis. For example, if you were married you could file for a divorce and apply to have the tenancy transferred to you. Because this option is not open to an unmarried partner, the courts have been willing in some cases to make longer-term ouster orders in cases involving cohabiting couples, depending on what seems reasonable in the circumstances of the particular case. However, recent Court of Appeal cases show a certain inconsistency. In one case involving an unmarried couple the Court approved an exclusion order lasting for five years; in another where the man had broken three previous injunctions it agreed that an order for an indefinite period was right. But in a third case the woman was allowed only one month; the Court said that that was sufficient time for the council to rehouse her.

Your first step is to consult a solicitor. Legal Aid (see page 490) is available if you qualify financially. If you are obliged to leave your home because of violence, your local council has a duty to rehouse you. But few councils have enough spare accommodation to fulfil their duty, and you may have to wait for permanent housing. Your solicitor may be able to bring some pressure to bear on your behalf.

Supplementary Benefit

31 | *My children and I live on Supplementary Benefit. I have a man friend who stays the night two or three times a week. He takes me out and sometimes buys small presents for me and the children and gives me gifts of money. Is there any danger that I might lose my Supplementary Benefit?*

In contrast to the tax system, which treats an unmar-

ried couple as two unconnected individuals, the social security system treats a couple 'living together as husband and wife' as if they were married. This means that a woman living with a man as his wife cannot claim Supplementary Benefit as if she were a single person. The couple are treated as a unit, so if the man is working full-time the woman will not qualify for Supplementary Benefit.

Therefore, if a woman who is receiving benefit starts cohabiting with a man, her benefit will normally be withdrawn. The question is: what counts as cohabitation? The legislation does not define what it means by 'living together as husband and wife'. The Supplementary Benefits Handbook sets out the criteria which the DHSS uses in deciding whether a couple are cohabiting. These include such factors as whether they have a common household, share expenses, have children together, are publicly acknowledged as husband and wife, and have a sexual relationship. It can be difficult to distinguish between a simple flat-sharing arrangement and cohabitation. What the benefit officers look for is evidence of sharing a common life: do the couple have meals together, go out together, sleep together, and so on? The presence or absence of sexual intercourse is not conclusive; neither is the sharing (or not) of household expenses.

In cases like yours, where the man has a separate home where he normally resides, you should not be regarded as cohabiting with him and benefit should not be withdrawn. However, this does sometimes happen. If it should you can appeal to the Social Security Benefits Appeal Tribunal (see BENEFITS, Q15). If you lose, there is a possibility of a further appeal to the Social Security Commissioners.

The chances of success are reasonable, particularly if your case is put by someone who knows the ropes. The Child Poverty Action Group (address on page 509) is a good source of help and advice with difficulties over benefits.

Tax

32 | *I've recently read that there can be tax advantages for a couple in remaining unmarried. How does this work?*

This is an incidental side effect of the fact that couples who live together unmarried are treated as two unrelated individuals for tax purposes, whereas a wife is considered largely as an appendage of her husband. By treating a husband and a wife for the most part as a unit, the tax system can actually penalise couples for marrying.

Two unmarried people, for example, qualify for tax relief on a joint mortgage of up to £60,000. A married couple is limited to £30,000.

Couples with children are particularly likely to be better off unmarried than married, especially if the mother stays home to look after them. Although the man cannot claim the married man's tax allowance, this is more than offset by other possibilities for tax saving:

● If there are two or more children, each parent can claim the single parent's additional personal allowance of £1,370 on top of the single person's allowance of £2,425.

● The man can enter into a deed of covenant (see TAXES, Q65) transferring some of his income to the woman, resulting in a lower tax bill for the family.

● A father who supports an illegitimate child under an affiliation order can claim tax relief on the payments, in the same way as a divorced father claims relief on maintenance payments under a court order; the fact that the parents live together makes no difference.

33 | *Surely there must be some tax advantages to marriage?*

Couples with no children who are both earning, but not enough to afford a mortgage of more than £30,000 (see Q3), will usually be better off married. They are entitled to a total of £6,220 in personal allowances, the married man's allowance of £3,795 and the wife's earned income allowance of £2,425. Unmarried couples get only £4,850, two single person's allowances. However, if a married couple between them earn at least £26,870 a year, they may be better off electing to be taxed as two single persons on their earned incomes (see TAXES, Q32). If the woman has substantial unearned income the couple could well be better off single. Also, single partners are both entitled to income tax relief on a mortgage of up to £30,000 each, giving them a joint tax-deductible mortgage of £60,000.

When it comes to inheritance tax – the tax on gifts made on death or within seven years before death (see TAXES, Q38) – married couples have a clear advantage. Anything given away or left on death to a husband or wife is totally free of inheritance tax, whereas tax is payable on gifts and bequests to a cohabitee, or anyone else – apart from exempt gifts (see TAXES, Q45). Because the exemptions are quite generous and are frequently revised and because the tax begins to bite only over £90,000, most people

escape this tax altogether. But as a cohabitee, you would have to think about inheritance tax if, for example, your partner was planning to leave or give you a house or a share of a house, and that house or share was worth more than £90,000.

Pensions

34 | *The pension scheme which goes with my job provides for a widow's pension if I die before my wife. She would also get a lump sum if I died before retirement. The trouble is that we are not legally married. Does this mean she is not entitled to these benefits?*

Occupational pension schemes vary, and you should ask to see a copy of your particular scheme's rules. The widow's pension provided by an occupational pension scheme would normally go only to a lawful widow. But in some schemes the trustees would have a discretion to pay all or part of the pension to someone other than a widow, for example a cohabitee.

The rules for the death-in-service lump sum benefit vary as well. Often, the employee may nominate a person to whom he wishes the money to go on his death. It may be that the rules of your scheme will allow you to nominate your partner. Some schemes define the categories of people who may be nominated, and if your scheme is one of these you may well find your cohabitee excluded.

For tax reasons, you cannot insist that the money go to a particular person. The trustees of the pension scheme have the final say. But generally they will observe your wishes as long as there is no breach of the scheme's rules.

Marriage

1 | *The engagement ring I want to give my fiancée is a family heirloom, and I've been told by a friend that she wouldn't have to return it if we split up. Is that true? Is there anything I can do about it?*

What your friend has told you is generally quite correct. The law treats the gift of an engagement ring as an 'absolute' gift unless you can show that you intended something else – that a condition of the gift was that you got married, say. If you can show no such condition, your fiancée can keep the ring if the engagement is broken off.

People generally act honourably, and rings are usually returned, very often as the symbol of the break. But if you want to make sure this will happen the best thing to do is to have a document drawn up – a letter will do – to the effect that the ring is not being given but only lent and that it will not become your fiancée's property unless and until you marry. She should sign that document, and you should keep it. Quite how you tell your fiancée that you don't trust her and that you want this agreement in writing is a matter for you, not a lawyer!

2 | *My girlfriend and I have been living together for a year. She's pregnant and we want to get married, but she's only just 17. Her parents are divorced. Whose consent do we need to get, and what if it's refused?*

Your girlfriend, being under 18, is a minor and she cannot marry without the appropriate consent. If her parents were living together they would both have to give consent, but as they are divorced (or if they were separated) then only the parent with custody needs to give it. You therefore need to find out who was given custody at the time of the divorce. If one parent were dead the consent of the surviving parent would be needed.

If the parent with custody refuses to give consent, a court can give its consent instead. The High Court or a county court can do this, but it is easier to apply to the magistrates' court. You and your girlfriend should visit the nearest magistrates' court; the Clerk to the Justices' Office will explain everything to you.

Since your girlfriend is pregnant and your relationship seems stable, you should get the court's consent fairly easily. However, you have no right of appeal if the court refuses its consent, and you would then need to wait until your girlfriend is 18 before getting married.

3 | *My fiancée and I aren't regular churchgoers, but we'd like a Church of England wedding. Is this possible?*

Yes, everyone is entitled to be married 'according to the rites' of the Church of England, the established Church. There are only two real exceptions to this. First, you cannot insist on a church wedding if either of you has been divorced, and, second, you cannot go to any clergyman and demand to be married in his church: there are rules as to which parish or parishes you can choose to have your wedding in, and generally it is only the parish in which either or both of you live or worship.

4 | *My fiancée and I are getting married in church. Do we have to go to hear our banns being read?*

No, there is no legal requirement that you should, although most people like to do so.

Unless a licence of some sort is obtained (see Q6), a Church of England wedding cannot take place unless the banns – the notice of the marriage – have been read in the church where the wedding is to take place and, if either or both parties live in another parish, in that church as well. There are special rules too where, for example, one of the couple lives in Scotland or Northern Ireland, or is at sea with the Royal Navy.

Banns are 'published' on three consecutive Sundays, the priest reading out the names of the parties and calling for any person to declare it if he or she knows of any 'just cause or impediment why these two persons should not be joined together in holy matrimony'. He will say that this is the first, second or third time of asking.

5 | *My fiancée and I are university students. Must we get married at the nearest church? We'd prefer a wedding at my home village church or in our college chapel.*

A lot of people would prefer not to marry in their local church, especially if it is a forbidding and unattractive building. You should speak to the priest of the church or the chapel where you want to be married to find out exactly what your position is, but broadly speaking it is as follows.

A Church of England marriage can take place only in a church, or authorised chapel, and it can only be that church for the parish in which either or both of the parties has resided for 15 days or which has been his or her regular place of worship. Depending on the facts, the vicar may accept that your term-time address can be ignored and treat you as having resided at your parents' home in the village, especially if you have returned for vacations and weekends; alternatively he may ask you to spend some time there in the weeks leading up to the wedding. If you have been a churchgoer there during your stays at home, he may treat his church as your regular place of worship.

The chances are that the college chapel is not authorised as a place in which marriages can be performed even though there may be a full-time chaplain and other services are held there. The easiest solution will probably be to have a Register Office wedding first (see Q8) to make you legally husband and wife and then to have a subsequent service in the college chapel; it can follow the usual Church marriage ceremony but has no legal effect.

While it is possible to apply for a special licence (see Q6) so as to be married anywhere else, such as at your college chapel, such a licence is unlikely to be granted simply because you do not happen to like one particular church and fancy another.

6 | *What is the difference between a 'common licence' and a 'special licence'? Who grants them and why?*

A common licence is granted by or on behalf of the bishop of a diocese, and has the effect of enabling a Church of England marriage to take place without the publication of banns (see Q4). The wedding can still take place only at the parish church of one or both parties or at the church which was the regular place of worship of one or both; fifteen days is still the qualifying period of residence too. For most practical purposes, such a licence is sought only where there has been some mishap over the reading of the banns

– say, where one party forgot to see the vicar to arrange them or had the banns read in the wrong church.

A special licence, on the other hand, is granted on behalf of the Archbishop of Canterbury, and it alone can authorise a church marriage to take place at any place (or time) such as at a chapel, a private house or in a hospital. In practice special licences are granted only in exceptional circumstances or grave emergencies, for example where a person is very ill and unable to get to a church.

In either case you should ask the clergyman whom you want to perform the marriage about the need for such a licence and how to get one.

7 | *Neither my fiancée nor myself were brought up as Anglicans and we want a wedding ceremony in our own religion. Does that mean we need to go to the Register Office to be legally married?*

No. People can generally be married according to their own rites in their own places of worship. In most cases, other than in the Anglican faith marriages can be performed in places of worship registered for the purpose by the Registrar General provided that either a registrar is present or an authorised person – usually a minister of the faith in question. The function of the registrar or authorised person is to ensure that the due formalities have been satisfied and that the marriage certificate is issued.

8 | *My girlfriend and I want to be married in a Register Office. What is the normal procedure?*

It is very straightforward. You will need to go to the Register Office and give notice, by completing a form and making a declaration. The details are entered into the notice book and a copy is displayed on a board in the Register Office for 21 days, after which the marriage can take place. This must be at the office for the registration district (check in the telephone directory under Registration of Births, Deaths and Marriages) in which the parties have lived for at least seven days before the notice is given; if one of you lives in a different district notice must be given to the registrar for each one, and you can choose where you want to be married.

The ceremony itself is quite short. The parties must declare that they know of no impediment to the marriage and repeat the form of words 'I call upon these persons here present to witness that I, [man-/woman], do take thee, [woman/man], to be my lawful wedded [wife/husband]'.

There must be at least two witnesses who, in addition to the couple themselves, will sign the register. They are usually friends or relations, but complete strangers brought in off the street are not unknown!

No religious service may be used in a Register Office, but there may be a separate one elsewhere if the parties want.

9 | *My partner and I have lived together for many years. He has developed terminal cancer and his dearest wish is that we should marry. He cannot leave hospital. Can we get married there?*

Yes. Although the general rule is that a marriage can take place only in church or in a Register Office or other authorised building, in cases such as yours arrangements can be made for it to take place elsewhere. Of course, your partner must be conscious and able to give his consent and approval to what is going on.

If you want a Church of England wedding, you will need a special licence (see Q6); your clergyman will help you to get one. If not, you will need to get a Registrar General's Licence, and your local Superintendent Registrar will advise you how to go about it (look in the telephone directory under Registration of Births, Deaths and Marriages). The Registrar General (the chief registrar in London) will need to be satisfied that the person concerned is seriously ill and unlikely to recover, and that he or she cannot be moved to a place where a marriage could take place in the usual way.

10 | *My husband and I need our marriage certificate to get a joint passport, but we seem to have lost it. Can we get another copy?*

Yes, you can. If you married in a Register Office you can get one from the office in question. If you married in church you can get one from the Register Office for the district in which the church is located.

Alternatively, you can get one from the office of the Registrar General at the General Register Office in London (address on page 510).

However you obtain the copy, unless you go in personally to collect it you should telephone first to check the current amount of the fee payable.

11 | *Is a woman legally obliged to use her husband's name when she marries, or can she keep her own name for all purposes? If I wanted to change back to my own name after marriage, would I need my husband's consent?*

Any adult is free to use any surname he or she wishes to use, except for the purposes of fraud. So you are perfectly entitled to keep your own surname for all purposes after your marriage, or to use your husband's name for private purposes and your own for business or professional uses. If you do adopt your husband's name, you can revert to your own surname at any time without his consent.

12 | *My husband and I met and married while we were working abroad. Is our marriage valid in English law?*

The answer is almost certainly yes, and there is no real reason why you are not just as legally married as if you had married here, provided of course that the marriage was valid according to the law of the country in which it took place.

If either or both of you was 'domiciled' in England and Wales at the time of the marriage, which means broadly the place that you regarded as your real or permanent home even though you were abroad for a while, then some of the more fundamental English marriage laws will apply to your marriage: a court would not, for example, uphold a marriage to which either party was under 16.

13 | *My ex-husband is American. We were married in England, but our marriage lasted for only a short time before he returned to the States and divorced me there. I now want to remarry. Am I free to do so?*

Yes, you are. A divorce obtained abroad will usually be accepted as valid or 'recognised' by the English courts, and if so the marriage will be treated as having been dissolved by that divorce. There are one or two minimum requirements: first, the divorce must be valid according to the law of the country in which it was obtained, and second it must generally (though not necessarily) have been obtained in a place where one of the parties was a national or habitually resident.

Assuming that you have a copy of the American divorce decree, the best thing to do is to take it along to your local Register Office, or the one at which you intend to marry, and explain the position. Your new marriage should be perfectly straightforward.

14 | *I married my husband years and years ago. We bought a house and then he just walked out one day. I've not seen or heard from him since, and I don't know if he's alive or dead. I've lived with someone else for a long time now and I want to marry him. What should I do?*

The short answer is to go and see a solicitor; you have quite a tricky legal problem here largely because you do not know if your husband is dead or alive.

If he is still alive, you cannot validly remarry because you already have a spouse and a second marriage would be bigamous and void, even though you might not actually be prosecuted for bigamy. To be able to remarry you would need to get a divorce, not that that would be much of a problem because your husband deserted you many years ago, and also you have been living apart for over five years (see DIVORCE, Q I).

If he is dead and you can prove it by producing a death certificate, then you are free to remarry because you are a widow.

The snag is that you do not know either way. You may be able to find out by making searches for a death certificate and by contacting friends and relatives, or by enquiring at the DHSS records at Newcastle upon Tyne. The DHSS will tell you if he is alive or dead, to their knowledge, and will pass on a letter to his last known address, although they will not give it to you; it will help them if you can give his National Insurance number.

Once you or your solicitor have followed up all available trails and have still come to no definite result, the only step remaining will be to apply to the court to presume him to be dead; this can generally be done after seven years where there are people who would be expected to have heard from him but who have not done so.

The thing to take up carefully with your solicitor is that there are in fact two separate applications you may need to make: not only do you want to remarry but there is also the house to consider. Unless he made a will leaving his property to someone else, you are entitled to his property on his death as his widow, and the first step will be to get a grant of Letters of Administration (see WILLS, DEATH AND INHERITANCE, Q22) to wind up the estate and get the house vested in your name. Having done that, you will apply to a divorce county court for an unusual order, called a Decree of Presumption of Death and Dissolution of the Marriage, to enable you to remarry. You must get these in the right order, because once your marriage is dissolved you will no longer be his widow and you could have great trouble with the house.

Separation

Financial aspects

1 | *My husband has left me and I can't work because of the children. What state benefits am I entitled to claim?*

You should apply at once to the DHSS for Supplementary Benefit. This provides an income for those not in full-time work (which is 30 hours per week, usually) whose 'requirements' exceed their 'resources'. Single lump-sum payments are also available to meet special needs such as to replace essential furniture. You should also get other help, such as free school meals for the children, free prescriptions, and so on.

Even though you might consider getting a maintenance order against your husband (see Q24), the procedure will take several weeks at least. You can claim Supplementary Benefit immediately.

Other benefits to which you could be entitled are:

● Child Benefit. This is basically payable to anyone responsible for a child under 16 irrespective of means. Where he or she is a 'lone' parent there is an additional One-Parent Benefit payable for the first (or only) child.
● Housing Benefit. This provides help with rent and rates and in most cases a Supplementary Benefit claimant will get a hundred per cent rebate or an allowance to cover the whole of these items; in the case of a mortgage Supplementary Benefit will cover the interest part of the repayments.
● Family Income Supplement. This provides top-up income for a household with at least one child where the wage-earner is in low-paid but full-time work (30 hours per week, or 24 for a 'lone' parent).

See also BENEFITS, page 393.

2 | *My husband has deserted me. Who is responsible for paying the rent of my flat?*

If the flat is rented in your husband's sole name, he is responsible for paying the rent even though he has moved out. If he refuses to pay, the landlord could go to court to evict you. However, you always have the right yourself, as a spouse, to pay the rent to continue living in the matrimonial home. The law, under the Matrimonial Homes Act 1983, gives you this right; the landlord cannot refuse to accept the rent from you.

If the flat is rented in joint names (or if you are the sole tenant yourself), you will both be responsible for paying the rent. You will also be responsible for paying any arrears that may arise; you will have no liability for arrears if the flat is in your husband's sole name, and the responsibility for them will then be his.

If your income is too low to take over the rent, you should apply for Supplementary Benefit; this will automatically also give you Housing Benefit which will cover the rent of a private tenancy, or give you a rebate is you live in a council house or flat. As this may take a little time you should explain the position to your landlord, especially if you are a private tenant.

3 | *My husband has left me. Is he still responsible for paying the mortgage or must I take over? What will happen if it isn't paid?*

The best place to start in answering this question is to look at the building society's position. A mortgage represents two things. First, it is a contract under which the society has lent money which the borrower agrees to repay with interest. Second, the mortgage 'pledges' the house to the society, as you might pledge a watch to a pawnbroker, so that it can sell the house if the loan is not repaid.

If the repayments fall into arrears the society could simply sue the borrower or borrowers for the debt. If the house (and therefore the mortgage) is in your husband's name alone, only he is responsible and can be sued; if the house is in your joint names you could both be sued. That is not altered by the fact that he has moved out.

In practice, though, building societies rarely just sue for the debt; if they have to take steps to protect themselves they will usually go to the court for what is called a possession order. This evicts the occupiers of the house so the society can sell it with vacant possession and clear the whole balance of the loan, plus interest and costs, out of the proceeds of the sale; anything left over is returned to the borrower or borrowers. Again, this is not affected by the fact that your husband has gone, and you are just as much at risk of eviction if the house is in joint names or not. If you want to stay on in the house, you must ensure that the repayments are made. Your husband may do so direct, or he may pay you maintenance (see Q24) to let you do so, or you may have income yourself enough for the purpose.

The building society's main concern is that if the instalments are not paid the mortgage debt will keep getting bigger because of the interest that keeps accruing, and eventually it will get so big that a sale would not clear it. The manager will usually be very sympathetic in a case such as yours, and if the position is explained to him or her it may be possible to allow interest only to be paid for a while, with nothing being paid off the capital. This will at least stop the debt from rising.

If your husband refuses to make the payments or to give you money to do so, and if you have little or no earnings or other income, then you should apply for Supplementary Benefit (see Q1). If you are eligible, the DHSS will then provide enough to cover the interest part of the repayments and you will keep your home.

4 | *I've left my wife. Can I still be sued for the rates on the house?*

Yes. Almost certainly the council can still treat you as the 'rateable occupier' even though you have left the house and even though the council may know you have gone. This liability can last up to the end of the marriage on divorce, and the council could enforce payment from you if your wife does not pay.

5 | *Is my husband, who's deserted me, liable for the gas and electricity bills?*

Yes. If he signed the contracts with the boards in the first place he remains liable to them under those contracts. Even though he has moved out, and even though you may have said that you will pay the bills out of any maintenance (see Q24) he pays you, as far as the boards are concerned your husband is the person liable.

Your husband can stop being liable only if he goes to the boards and gives notice to terminate his contracts. Once they are terminated he will not be liable for future supplies, but any arrears to that date are still his responsibility. It is no good at all his saying that you had agreed to pay them if in fact you had not paid them. Whatever arrangement your husband and yourself came to is a matter between the two of you and has no effect on your husband's position with the boards.

The family home

6 | *My husband has left me. Do I have the right to stay on in the family home?*

The short answer is: 'Yes, at any rate for the time being.' A married person always has the right to occupy the matrimonial home unless and until a court says otherwise. If the house is owned or rented in joint names (or in your sole name) you have that right because you are an owner or tenant yourself. But even if the property is owned or rented in your

husband's sole name, the law (under the Matrimonial Homes Act 1983) still gives you the right to remain in it. If your husband tries to throw you out or harasses you to make you go, you can apply for an injunction (see Q13) to stop him.

In the long term, if there is a divorce or the separation becomes clearly permanent, a court might decide that in all the circumstances an owner-occupied home should be sold, but that is far from always the case, especially where it is needed as a home for the children.

If neither of you owns or rents the home in the usual way, then you could have a problem; a common example is the case of a house or flat that goes with the husband's job. His employers could have the right to evict the wife should the husband leave her, but even then a court order is necessary and eviction would not be immediate.

7 | *Can my husband, who's left me, sell the family home? It's owned in his sole name, but my children and I are still living in it.*

If the house were owned in joint names your husband would not be able to sell because your signature would be needed on the conveyancing forms. But as the house is solely in his name, only his signature is needed, so he could try to sell. You can stop him quite easily by getting a solicitor to take a simple step called registering your rights under the Matrimonial Homes Act 1983. This shows up on the searches made by a purchaser's solicitor (see YOU AND YOUR HOME, Q140) and the transaction would not go through unless you agreed to remove the registration. The same applies if he tried to mortgage the house to raise money.

While you stay in the house you are probably safe anyway because of a House of Lords ruling recently which said that in some cases a wife's rights can be binding on a purchaser or lender even if there is no registration. It has made solicitors who do the conveyancing on property very cautious over the rights of anyone in the house. Even so, the safe course is to register straightaway.

8 | *Our house is in our joint names. Does that mean we own half of it each?*

As a general rule one would say yes, the law will usually come to that conclusion. There may be other facts to be taken into account, though.

For example, if it went to court a judge could find that the shares are unequally owned where one party has carried out substantial improvements at his or

together, friends or relatives who join forces to buy a holiday bungalow, partners who run a shop together, and so on.

The general rule is that unless both (or all, if there are more than two) the co-owners agree to keep the property it will be sold. But that is subject to an overriding consideration in family law cases that where the house was bought for a family home to bring up the children and the children are still there and, being young, need the home, then it will not usually be sold. So if you are a mother with dependent children it is most unlikely that the house would be sold while they need it.

If there are no such children – they have grown up or the marriage was childless – then there is a strong chance that the court would order a sale, though not necessarily immediately. If you are in this second situation it is one of the cases where you should consider a divorce or at least a judicial separation. The divorce court operates under a rather different set of rules (see DIVORCE, Q 3 5) in which the needs of the parties rather than property law play the bigger part, and if in all the circumstances you need the house to live in then your husband would be ordered to let you do so. It is even possible that he might be ordered to transfer it to you outright.

her own expense, though this is unlikely to be applied where this happened while the parties were still living together.

A rule that is commonly applied concerns the mortgage repayments made by the party after the other has deserted. The repayments will have reduced the mortgage debt and thus increased the 'equity' in the house. The court will usually say that the party who stayed on is to be given credit for the *capital* repayments (but not the interest) made since the separation. In other words, if the house is sold the capital repaid will be refunded to him or her before the balance of the sale proceeds are divided between both parties.

Where there is a divorce, the court can override these rules altogether by transferring the home to one party outright or by giving one a larger share if that is just and fair, although the commonest outcome is still an equal division.

9 | *My husband, who is separated from me, wants a divorce. He says that if I don't agree he'll sell the house. Can he do that? It's in our joint names.*

Your problem is in a very difficult legal area because it is on the fringes between normal property law on the one hand and family and divorce law on the other.

Since the home is jointly owned your husband cannot sell it without your signature. But if you do not agree to a sale he can apply to a county court to have one ordered. Whenever two or more people own property together and one wants a sale, he or she can apply to the court; that is so for any type of property and any type of person – friends who buy a flat

10 | *My wife has left me for another man and has taken the children. She says she wants the house sold; it's jointly owned. Can she force me to sell it?*

The legal position is that where a house is in joint names and there is no divorce or judicial separation, strict property law applies. This says that the house should normally be sold if one spouse wants it sold. The usual exception is that it will not be sold if it is needed as a home for the children, but this does not apply in your case because your wife has taken them. Unless there is some other very good reason for your keeping it – such as the fact that it is a shop where you trade as well as its being a home – if your wife went to court, the court would probably order it to be sold.

You can probably assume that your wife wants her share in cash of the value of the house rather than to force a sale as such. If she went to court, you would probably be given the option either of selling the house or of paying her her share (assuming you want to keep the house) if you can raise the money. Decide what you want to do and then ask your building society if you can borrow the money to buy her out, or raise the money from some other source.

The other thing to bear in mind is that your wife probably wants the cash fairly quickly and taking you to court and waiting for a sale could take time and cost her money in legal fees. To get a quick settlement she may be prepared to accept less than her full share if it can be paid quickly, especially if it is all you can raise. So you will probably find you can settle by negotiation. Bear in mind too that as she may be keen to marry her new partner and needs you to agree to divorce her, a complete 'package' involving the house, a divorce, custody, costs and so on could probably be worked out. It would be sensible for you, because if you have a divorce and as part of the settlement she agrees to forgo all rights to maintenance for herself (the so-called 'clean break') (see DIVORCE, Q46) she can never come back to you with any financial claim, whereas if she and her new partner separate before that your wife could try to get back into the old home, claim maintenance from you and perhaps make other claims.

I I | *Our family house is in my husband's name. Would I have a share in the value if we separated?*

These days, not many houses are bought in the name of one partner only, so this question doesn't arise often. Where the marriage ends in divorce what happens over the house is usually decided on the basis of the general needs and resources of the two parties and the children rather than that of who owns it, so ownership does not matter much. At first sight the position in property law is that you are not entitled to a share because it is not in joint names. But having said that, there is a strong chance that in the modern marriage you will have a share. You will have one if you can show that you have made a 'substantial direct or indirect contribution to the purchase or improvement of the property'.

A direct contribution to purchase might arise where you had provided all or part of the deposit, or had paid off part of the mortgage out of your own money; an indirect contribution might be where you went out to work so that the house could be bought. If you bought only the groceries or paid other bills out of your wages and your husband could not have paid the mortgage had you not done so, you may also have helped to buy the house.

A direct contribution to improvement would come from paying for an extension or something similar or from your carrying out physical work which would otherwise have had to be paid for, and an indirect one from taking care of other bills so your husband could pay for the improvement.

Any such contribution must be substantial, so very slight financial help or routine do-it-yourself or decorating work would not be enough. In particular, this branch of the law, which goes back over a hundred years, does not regard being a good wife and raising and caring for a family as a relevant contribution at all – an omission now remedied on divorce, but not yet in the property area.

I 2 | *Although the family home is in my husband's name, I contributed enough towards it financially to justify having a share in it should we split up. How would my share be assessed?*

It would depend on all the circumstances. The main factor is the amount of your contribution towards the value of the whole property, and a court would assess the size of your proportion on that basis. In most cases it is impossible to unscramble all the family finances back over the years to work out exactly the wife's share, so a broad fraction would usually be arrived at – a quarter, a third, a half, or in very few cases even more.

If you get divorced, however, the court applies different rules, and you could end up with a larger or a smaller share than your actual contribution.

Injunctions

I 3 | *My husband has been violent towards me in the past, and on those occasions the social services department has put me up in temporary accommodation for a few days until I recovered and my husband calmed down. But after this last outburst, when my husband cracked my ribs and blacked my eyes, I don't think I can take any more. My GP suggested I get an injunction. What is this, and will it stop my husband from abusing me again?*

An injunction is an order of the High Court or a county court requiring a person to do or not to do a particular act or acts. In your case the injunction should order your husband not to assault or molest you, and if necessary it might order him to leave the family home (see LIVING TOGETHER, Q30).

The most important feature of an injunction is that if it is not obeyed, the person concerned commits contempt of court and can then be fined or sent to prison. The court order itself has a notice printed on it warning that this may happen.

An example of an injunction is given on page 30. Injunctions have become increasingly common in

IN THE BARCHESTER COUNTY COURT
No. of Matter 1234

In the Matter of Section 1 of the Domestic Violence and Matrimonial Proceedings Act 1976, and
In the Matter of 9 Sycamore Street, Millstone
BETWEEN

MARY JANE CITIZEN   Applicant

and

JOHN JAMES CITIZEN   Respondent

Before His Honour Judge Swallow sitting at the Shire Hall Barchester this 11day of January 1986

Upon hearing the Solicitors for both parties
and upon hearing the oral evidence of
the parties and reading their affidavits

NOW IT IS HEREBY ORDERED

1. *That the Respondent be restrained from molesting assaulting interfering or communicating with the Applicant save through a solicitor for a period of three months or until further order.*

2. *That the Respondent do before 12 noon on the* 15 *day of* January *1986 vacate the property known as*

    9 Sycamore Street, Millstone

    and before four o'clock in the afternoon of that day deposit all keys in his possession to the said property with the solicitors to the Applicant.

3. *That having vacated the said property the Respondent be restrained from entering the said property or coming within 100 yards thereof for a period of three months or further order.*

P.C. Swallow   JUDGE

TAKE NOTICE THAT UNLESS YOU OBEY THE DIRECTIONS CONTAINED IN THIS ORDER YOU WILL BE GUILTY OF CONTEMPT OF COURT, AND WILL BE LIABLE TO BE COMMITTED TO PRISON.

matrimonial cases in recent years. They are usually issued to deal with violence or the occupation of the family home, and occasionally to stop a party squandering the family savings at the time of a divorce.

In your case you could visit a Citizens Advice Bureau or a Law Centre as soon as possible to find out what your best course of action would be; your GP and the social services department will obviously help too, but getting an injunction is a job for a solicitor.

14 | *My husband has always been violent. He walked out last week, but last night came back and there was a dreadful row. He kicked and punched me and said that he'd return at the weekend and if I was still here he'd throw me and the children out. What can I do?*

You will have to apply for an injunction to protect yourself. Since this is a case of serious violence and you need *immediate* protection your solicitor will probably advise an application for an '*ex parte* injunction' (see q16). This will order your husband not to molest you and to keep away from the home on a temporary basis. There will then be another hearing about a week later when the judge may grant an injunction lasting indefinitely. At that stage the judge may also order your husband to hand over all his keys to the house and make a court order for you to have custody of the children.

15 | *How long does an injunction last, and what happens when it comes to an end?*

An injunction lasts for as long as the judge says it will. The general rule is that an injunction granted where there is a divorce pending will last until the divorce is made final on decree absolute (see page 54); in other cases the usual period is three months. An injunction can be ended earlier if the parties become reconciled or if there is some other change in the circumstances. It can also be extended if it expires after three months, say, and there is still a need for protection; a further hearing is needed.

The effect of an *ex parte* injunction is only temporary, to afford immediate protection for a limited period. There is then a second hearing about a week later, when the judge will decide whether to continue the order – even indefinitely – or to change it.

When an injunction expires it obviously ceases to have any effect.

16 | *I have made an appointment to see a solici-*

tor to get an injunction against my husband. What will I have to do, and what will happen exactly?

When you see the solicitor, the first thing to happen will be that he or she will take a statement from you to find out exactly what has happened and to see what needs to be done. He or she will also ask you whether you have started divorce proceedings yourself or whether you want a divorce, because this affects the type of documents the solicitor has to prepare. If you have not made up your mind about the future of your marriage and hope that this is just a crisis that may pass, you will not have to start divorce proceedings now just to get an injunction (this used to be the law, but is not any longer).

The solicitor will then probably make a number of telephone calls straightaway, especially where an injunction is needed very urgently. One call will be to the court to find out where and when a judge can hear your case; another will be to the Legal Aid office to get emergency Legal Aid cover (see page 490).

Quite what happens next depends on the amount of time available before the court hearing, but the solicitor will usually prepare a number of documents for you to sign. Some will be Legal Aid forms, and one will be an affidavit – a sworn statement by you about what has happened and why you need the injunction. If you have decided to start divorce proceedings now, there will be several others, including the divorce petition (see page 80).

If you need an *ex parte* injunction (see Q14), you will go straight to court and before a judge, who will read your affidavit and perhaps ask you some questions before granting the injunction. '*Ex parte*' means that your husband is not told about your application. The first he will know about the case is when he is served with the injunction.

Most of the rest of the work is done by your solicitor, who will also arrange to have the necessary documents handed personally to your husband.

About a week after the case started there will be a hearing before the judge with your husband present. If you went for an *ex parte* injunction this will be the second time you have to go to court, otherwise it will be the first time. What happens depends on your husband's attitude. If he refuses to be reasonable, both of you may have to give evidence and be cross-examined by the other partner's lawyer. In most cases, however, the husbands agree to behave themselves and then give a solemn promise, called an 'undertaking', to the court to that effect; where this happens you will not have to give evidence at all.

17 | *How quickly can I obtain an injunction? Will my husband have to be told in advance so he can argue his case?*

The general rule is that if you are going to apply for an injunction, your husband must be told in advance and given copies of the court papers several days before the hearing itself; this is so that he has time to see a solicitor, get Legal Aid (see page 490) and prepare his case. The number of days' notice he must have depends on the sort of injunction you are asking for and the particular way in which you are applying. Usually, the minimum period is two clear days (so he must get the papers by a Tuesday if the hearing is to be on the Friday) in a case where you have already started divorce proceedings, or four in any other case. It may sometimes take a little longer because a hearing has to be fixed before a judge, and occasionally it may not be possible to get an appointment as quickly as the applicant would like.

If the case is extremely urgent, and telling the man that in two or four days' time a judge is to be asked to evict him from his home would invite another attack in the meantime, an *ex parte* injunction will be granted (see Q14). In this case the husband is not informed at all, so that the judge hears only the applicant's evidence. An *ex parte* injunction can ban molestation, harassment or violence, and it can order the husband to keep away from the home if he has already left (although it cannot order him to leave if he is still there). It will also be temporary only; he will be ordered not to molest you, etc. for only about a week, when there will be a second hearing at which the judge will hear both sides and decide whether to continue or change the order. An *ex parte* injunction will not be necessary when the woman is safe in a refuge or elsewhere for the time being.

An experienced solicitor will be able to get an *ex parte* injunction within a matter of hours of first seeing the client. The courts make arrangements very quickly for a judge to deal with such an application, which takes only a few minutes.

18 | *I got an injunction yesterday which ordered my husband to stay away from the home and not to try to contact me. Last night he came round and yelled threats at me through the letterbox. He said if I don't get it cancelled and take him back he'll cut me up. What should I do?*

You must get in touch with your solicitor immediately. If you wish, he or she can take the matter back before the judge to ask for your husband to be sent to

prison because your husband has broken the injunction and is in contempt of court. You were granted the injunction because you needed protection, and the protection it gives is this right to apply for your husband to be committed.

In fact, the chances are that he will not be sent straight to prison, or at least not for very long. Although the judge could imprison him for two years, he or she is far more likely to tell your husband what could happen, in no uncertain terms, and then make what is called a 'suspended committal order' – an order imprisoning him for, say, 28 days, which will not take effect provided that he obeys the injunction in future.

Your solicitor may also apply for a 'power of arrest' to be attached to the injunction (if there was not one attached already), which means that any repetition of his molestation could result in his immediate arrest by the police.

19 | *A friend's husband was very violent and threw her out of the house. She went to her solicitor, who took the case to the magistrates' court to get a court order instead of applying to a judge for an injunction. Is that common?*

It is not as common as going to a county court judge for an injunction, but it can certainly be done. A magistrates' court has the power to make orders banning the use or threat of violence and dealing with the occupation of the matrimonial home, and to imprison or fine a man who breaks such an order.

There are a number of things that a judge can do which magistrates cannot, and these are important in practice because they give the wife much better protection. For example, a judge can and usually does

not only ban the use or threat of violence but also any form of harassment and any communication other than through a solicitor; if the man is banned from the home he will usually be forbidden to enter the area of the home as well. The magistrates can do neither of these.

Having said that, it is cheaper and can be quicker to get an order from the magistrates' court. In many cases their powers are adequate, too, especially bearing in mind that it is often the psychological fact of getting an order which counts rather than the legal terms of the document itself.

A solicitor will normally explain the choice that can be made between the courts and advise as appropriate. There are only two cases when the magistrates cannot be used. One is where the parties are not married to each other, and the other is where there is already a divorce pending and an injunction is being sought as part of the divorce.

20 | *My husband and I had a blazing row a few nights ago and he started to beat me – and not for the first time. A friend has said that there's no point in calling the police on such occasions because they wouldn't interfere in a domestic argument. Is this right, and, if so, would it make any difference if I had an injunction or some other court order?*

The police will always answer a call for help, and they will always step in to stop violence going on no matter who is involved. Having said that, the police are often reluctant to prosecute in cases of domestic violence between members of the same household unless it is a serious case of injury: the victim, after a few days' calm and the violence has stopped, may refuse to attend court, say, or if she does she may claim that the bruises were caused by a fall rather than an attack.

In practice, it often makes a difference if there's an injunction or a magistrates' court order (see ǫ 1 9).

First, where the injunction or magistrates' order is obtained because there had been violence which has caused an injury, and this is likely to happen again, the court can attach a further clause to it, the effect of which is to give the police a power to arrest the man if the order is broken. The police must then take him straight before the court, where he can be dealt with by committal to prison if necessary. Where this clause is attached, the court will tell your local police station so that if the police are called out they know about it and will act firmly at once.

Second, even if there is no such clause to the

injunction, if it is clear that the wife has taken legal proceedings herself for her own protection, the police are far more likely in practice to take the view that this is more than a mere domestic argument and may well be readier to arrest the man and prosecute him.

It is good practice among solicitors, provided that their clients agree, to tell the police if any injunction or order of this sort is obtained.

21 | *My husband has never been violent but we just can't get on, and last month I felt I had to get away for a while because of the atmosphere in the house. I took the children and we went to stay with my sister. Now my husband refuses to let me back in. What should I do? Can I get an injunction to put* him *out?*

Since you are husband and wife, each of you has a right to live in the matrimonial home. That is so whether the home is owned or rented in joint names or in the sole name of one of you. Neither of you should be excluded from it without a court order, and since your husband is refusing to let you back in you can apply to a county court for a court order to make him do so. You should have no difficulty about getting one, although taking your husband to court is bound to cause a lot of friction between you. If necessary, the court can lay down rules about which partner can use which rooms.

Since your husband has not been violent, your chances of getting him put out are pretty slim, at least in the short term. Until the middle of 1983 it was common for wives in your sort of position to be able to get their husbands ordered out where the children were living in overcrowded conditions, and even wives who had left to live with other men were able to get their innocent non-violent husbands out. Some judges justified this by saying that it was in the best interests of the children and that that was paramount. In 1983 the House of Lords decided that this was wrong; they said that the court must look at all the circumstances, not only the interests of the children but also the needs, resources and conduct of the parties, none of these being automatically paramount over the others. So unless you can show some serious risk of violence, or some mental or physical harm to the children if you and your husband share the home, your husband is likely to be allowed to stay.

Your only real prospect of getting your husband out would be if something serious happened after your return. Alternatively, if you got a divorce the court would look at the long term and it might then give you the sole right to live in the family home with the children. In the short run you are likely to be there together.

22 | *My wife and I haven't been getting on for some time, and our rows often erupt into violence. I concede that our marriage is probably over, but she's now had me served with some injunction papers. What should I do?*

Your wife is presumably applying for an injunction to ban any further molestation, threat or violence, and to put you and keep you out of the matrimonial home. Because of the history of violence she will probably succeed.

The first thing you should do is to look carefully at the papers you have been given to see if there is an *ex parte* injunction among them; this is a temporary order which your wife can obtain without your knowledge (see Qs 14 and 16). You must obey the *ex parte* injunction if there is one; if you don't you could be sent to prison.

Second, you should see a solicitor without delay and ask him or her to represent you. The papers you have will tell you when your wife's application will be heard by the judge, and you can and should be present. You can apply for Legal Aid (see page 490).

Because of the apparent strength of your wife's case, you must expect to have to leave the house and be restrained from further violence, threats, and so on. There are two ways in which this can be done. Subject to whatever advice your own solicitor gives you, the best thing will be to give an undertaking to the court not to molest your wife and to vacate the property by a certain time. In most of these cases the parties and their lawyers meet in the court corridor before the hearing to discuss matters. Giving an undertaking to the court in terms agreed by the lawyers has the same effect as a court order: if you break it you are in contempt of court. Giving an undertaking also means that neither of you will have to give evidence in court of these unpleasant matters. Further, you will have some room to negotiate about how long you have before you must move out, and it is often possible to make arrangements for access to your children, if any, and sometimes even to get an agreement that you will not have to pay all the costs if you are not legally aided. The alternative to an undertaking is that the case will be heard in full by the judge. Both of you will then have to give evidence and be cross-examined. The outcome from your point of view will not be much affected, except that the terms of an injunction will be imposed on you, the experience will probably make your future relationship with your wife all the more difficult, and you may well finish up paying all the costs.

23 | *Since we separated my wife has made a perfect pest of herself, ringing up and telling lies about me to my boss and ringing me up in the early hours of the morning too. Can I do anything to stop her?*

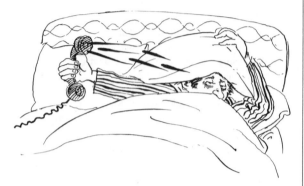

This sort of behaviour sometimes happens when a marriage breaks down, and it can be very distressing. A solicitor's letter is usually enough to end it, and after speaking to your wife and asking her to stop that should be your next step.

If she carries on you can get an injunction to stop her, or in legal terms to restrain her from molesting you (which is what it amounts to). Molestation is difficult to define, but it covers anything that interferes with someone's physical or mental comfort and well-being. In one case similar to yours it consisted of parading up and down outside the other party's place of work with scurrilous posters.

You can seek such an injunction whether or not you are applying for a divorce.

Strictly speaking, some of her lies might amount to defamation, which will give you a right to sue for damages. However, as that would be expensive and you would probably not do yourself any good in the long run, there's little point in pursuing that.

Court money orders

24 | *My husband deserted me recently, leaving me to look after our young children. A friend has advised that I should apply to the magistrates' court for a court money order. What money orders can the magistrates make?*

The magistrates' main power is to make orders for maintenance, legally called 'periodical payments'.

Orders can be in favour of the spouse who applies and the children of the family. These would be weekly or monthly amounts depending on how your husband is paid by his employers.

The child maintenance can be worded as payable to the parent for the child's benefit or direct to the child. This makes no difference to who will actually get the money, but it will be better from a tax point of view to have it worded so that the money is payable to the child so it is the child's income (see TAX AND DIVORCE, page 386).

The court can also order the payment of lump sums of up to £500 per person, so that a mother with two children could in theory get £1,500. In practice such sums are rarely ordered, and when they are they tend to be much smaller sums designed to meet particular needs, such as debts or the cost of a bed to replace an outgrown cot for a child. They can be payable by instalments, as they will have to be if the person paying lacks the money to do so in one go.

25 | *I've left my husband. Can I expect him to pay me maintenance?*

The first questions to ask are whether you need maintenance and, if so, whether your husband can afford it, and whether you have any children. If he cannot afford anything, the matter ends there. If you have no children and are self-supporting from a job or are being kept by another man, then you would not need anything from your husband and you would probably not apply.

If you do need maintenance and your husband can afford to pay some, the next question is whether there is anything in your conduct which might affect the issue, in particular the fact that you have left your husband. The reasons why you left could be especially important. If he drove you out by his behaviour, there is nothing relevant in the fact that you left him.

If, on the other hand, you walked out for no good reason, that is to say you deserted him, or you left because he found out about an affair you had been having, things might well be very different. The magistrates' court must have regard to conduct in deciding what, if any, order to make 'if that conduct is such that it would in the opinion of the court be inequitable to disregard it'. That form of words has only recently been introduced, and it remains to be seen what the magistrates make of it. It looks as if wives may find that their conduct in walking out could reduce the amount they would have got otherwise, or that they receive nothing at all.

Where the wife has the children, the court may decide to make a full order in her favour regardless of her conduct because the court's first consideration is the welfare of any child under the age of 18. If the court were to make an order for the children but none for the wife, that would adversely affect the children so she would probably get some maintenance.

26 | *On what grounds can I apply for a maintenance order? Will I have to take my husband to court?*

There are four grounds on which you can apply for a maintenance order. Two of them, that your husband has deserted you or that he has behaved in such a way that you cannot be reasonably expected to live with him, are borrowed from divorce law. The others are that he has failed to provide reasonable maintenance for you, or to pay or make a proper contribution towards reasonable maintenance for a child of the family. It is necessary to show only one of these four to enable the magistrates' court to make maintenance orders.

These grounds are the ones on which you would rely if you had to take your husband to court because he is not paying you maintenance (or very little). If you and he are agreed about the amount, you can seek an order by consent (see Q36) without the need to show any of these grounds. Your husband will get a summons (see Q27) and should come to court, but a maintenance order can be made whether he is present or not.

Even if the court does not make an order in your favour for any reason, it can still make orders for maintenance for the children.

27 | *What procedure must I follow for getting a maintenance order against my husband, who's left me?*

First, you, 'the applicant', will sign a form called a complaint either in your solicitor's office or at the magistrates' court office which sets out the grounds under which you are claiming. The court then prepares and issues a summons which is sent to your husband, the 'respondent', usually by post, ordering him to come to court on a particular day when you must also attend. Both of you will usually be asked to fill in a court form about your income, outgoings, savings, and so on; often you will be asked to do so in the corridor at the court before the hearing, but sometimes it is well in advance.

The hearing takes place in private, and although it is usually in one of the ordinary magistrates' court-rooms it will be on a morning or afternoon separate from the rest of the crime, traffic, licensing and other sorts of case magistrates deal with. Some magistrates' courts are very informal and everyone remains seated except when they swear the oath before they give evidence. There will be three magistrates, of whom at least one must be a woman and one a man. They are members of the Domestic Panel, experienced magistrates who have received special training in family cases. Apart from them, their clerk and a court welfare officer, the two parties and their solicitors will usually be the only people present.

After the applicant takes the oath, her solicitor leads her through her evidence, usually concentrating on the financial side rather than on the breakdown of the marriage, and she can then be asked questions by the respondent or his solicitor, and sometimes by the court. Then the respondent gives his evidence on oath and is questioned in the same way. There are usually no other witnesses, and the court will make its order. The whole matter is normally over in under an hour, but it can take longer of course.

28 | *Can I get Legal Aid if I apply for a maintenance order?*

Yes. You can get preliminary advice under the Green Form Scheme (see page 490), and if you decide to apply to the magistrates' court that Scheme will cover you. Under special arrangements that apply only to 'domestic proceedings' in that court, your solicitor can apply to the Legal Aid office for what is called 'approval for assistance by way of representation'. This is not strictly Legal Aid, but it amounts to exactly the same thing in terms of paying for your solicitor; it is easier for you too because you will not have to undergo the assessment by the DHSS which Legal Aid applicants have to go through.

Approval is normally granted quite quickly and easily, but it can be refused if it would not be reasonable to take the proceedings, for example where a husband has obviously no money to pay maintenance.

There are a few people who may have to apply for ordinary Legal Aid. The figures for financial eligibility are a bit different, and someone could be outside the limits for the Green Form Scheme but inside those for Legal Aid depending on their income and outgoings.

29 | *How much maintenance would I get?*

The magistrates work to much the same guidelines as the divorce court (see DIVORCE, Q44), and the amount will largely be decided on the basis of the needs and resources of the parties and those of the children.

In practice, cases coming before the magistrates tend to be from people at the lower end of the income scale, and the court's main job is to see how much the payer, usually the husband, can afford. He must be left with at least enough to keep himself or his new household at no less than the level he would be at if he drew Supplementary Benefit. He will usually be left with a few pounds more than that as an incentive to stay at work and pay the maintenance rather than to give up his job and claim Supplementary Benefit for himself.

In these lower-income cases the court will share out between the wife and children whatever they think the husband can afford. In middle- or upper-income cases, the court should arrive at the same sort of figure the divorce court would, and the magistrates may use the same 'one-third starting-point' (see DIVORCE, Q43) in their calculations. Nevertheless, it is generally accepted that the sums of money arrived at by magistrates' courts tend to be lower than the divorce courts'.

30 | *My husband, who left me recently, pays maintenance on a voluntary basis. Should I try to get a maintenance order through the magistrates' court?*

As a matter of common sense, the best way to arrange for maintenance is on the basis of whatever suits the parties best. If you've come to an arrangement with which you are both happy you might as well leave it as it is. Voluntary maintenance is probably the most regularly paid, simply because the husband has agreed to pay it and because it is not something imposed on him by a court. Access to the children seems to work better, too, with such an arrangement, and if the wife runs into a cash problem the husband may be readier to help.

Having said that, there are two reasons why it might be sensible to try to get an order from the magistrates' court. First, from a tax point of view, having maintenance paid under a court order – including one for an agreed amount made by consent – can cut the tax bill for the family as a whole, especially where there are children. That saving can be shared, making both of you better off (see TAX AND DIVORCE, page 387). Second, it may be that what your husband is prepared to pay you on a voluntary basis is too low and a court might order him to pay more. When you look at what he pays you, though, remember to take into account the rent or mortgage or any other bills he is paying; a court cannot order him to pay bills separately but must ensure only that the amount of maintenance you get is enough to allow you to do so.

31 | *I live on Supplementary Benefit and also get Child Benefit. Should I apply for a maintenance order against my husband, who's now living with another woman?*

This is always a difficult question to decide. The thing to do is to ask yourself whether you would really be better off if you did.

As things are, you have a secure source of income for your family, with the rent or mortgage interest paid and the rates met. You get various other benefits like free school meals. If you have not been on Supplementary Benefit for long, you will find that your money goes up after a year when you go on to the long-term scale. You may not have needed one yet, but you might need to claim a single payment – a lump sum paid to replace some essential item of household equipment or repairs – to which claimants of Supplementary Benefit are entitled (see Q1).

Would maintenance from your husband keep you at least as well off? If not, there is no real advantage to you in applying for a maintenance order. On the other hand, some of the state benefits might continue to be paid even if you also received maintenance. You could still draw Child Benefit and the One-Parent Benefit, and you might well still get Housing Benefit to help with rent and rates. These will need investigating.

But bear in mind too that a maintenance order is only a piece of paper with words on it. It is not as good as money in your hand. Will your husband pay regularly? An unpaid order, or one which is sporadically paid, is not worth much.

32 | *I'm a working mother and get Family Income Supplement and Housing Benefit. Should I apply for a maintenance order?*

The same considerations apply to you as they did in Q31. You must ask yourself whether you would be better off. Will the maintenance be paid regularly? By how much will your state benefits be reduced to take into account your increased income? Since you are at work you would get little or perhaps even no maintenance for yourself anyway, although you would get it for the children.

33 | *How is maintenance paid under a court maintenance order?*

Maintenance orders in the magistrates' court usually provide that the money is to be paid through the court. This means that your husband will take or send the maintenance to the court office from where you will collect it (unless you are on Supplementary Benefit and the order has been 'signed over' to the DHSS; see Q35). If you want your husband to pay the money to you direct (and if you trust him to do so) you must so inform the court. This will be unlikely if you have had to fight for the maintenance, but if you have agreed the amount and are having a consent order made you might prefer payment direct or by bankers' standing order.

34 | *What will happen if my husband does not pay me my monthly maintenance, as he is obliged to under the order?*

If he does not pay, the order can be 'enforced' against him. You should visit the magistrates' court office or write in to draw the clerk's attention to the arrears. A summons will be issued ordering your husband to reappear before the court; you will be present too. The court can make an 'attachment of earnings' order if he is employed (but not if he is self-employed); this means that the maintenance will be deducted from his pay by his employers. The court can also send him to prison. Very few men are sent to prison for non-payment – the threat is usually enough – and of course a man in prison cannot pay anything at all. If the non-payment was due to the fact that he could not pay because his income has dropped – his firm has gone on short time, for instance, or stopped overtime – or his expenses have escalated – his rent has gone up dramatically – the court can wipe out the arrears and reduce the future amount of the order.

35 | *A friend of mine has a maintenance order but she has to 'sign over' the full amount of the maintenance to the social security office. Why is this?*

The proper term for your friend's signing over her maintenance to the DHSS is the 'diversion procedure'. It is used where a person has a maintenance order and also receives Supplementary Benefit.

The amount of Supplementary Benefit paid is calculated by examining the person's needs or 'requirements' on the one hand and his or her income or 'resources' on the other. The amount of any resources reduces the amount of the Supplementary Benefit paid. Maintenance is a resource, so if your friend receives £10 a week under a maintenance

order her Supplementary Benefit will drop by £10. Since maintenance is often paid badly or sometimes not at all, your friend could frequently find herself short of £10 a week. Because of this, the DHSS is prepared to let people 'sign over' the maintenance order to the DHSS. The court then sends the DHSS whatever your friend's husband pays for maintenance and she will get her maximum Supplementary Benefit week by week. She thus has a secure source of income without having to worry about whether her husband will pay.

36 | *My husband and I have agreed the amounts of maintenance he is going to pay. Do I still have to go through the procedure of getting a maintenance order?*

No, you needn't. The maintenance could be paid voluntarily (see Q30) or you could get a maintenance agreement drawn up by your solicitor (see Q40).

But a court order for maintenance is usually better from a tax point of view than voluntary maintenance or a maintenance agreement, especially where there are children, and the tax savings can be split between both parties, making them both better off (see TAX AND DIVORCE, page 387). Where the two parties agree the amount to be paid, the magistrates' court can make an order for that amount without any of the four grounds (see Q26) having to be proved. This is known as a 'consent order'. The parties will need to agree who is going to be the applicant for the order. He or she will sign a complaint (see Q27) and the other will receive a summons. Only the applicant will need to go to the court hearing provided that the other signs a form giving brief details of his or her financial position and consent to the making of the order. The court hearing is short, quite informal and in private.

The magistrates' court is not bound to rubber stamp the agreement reached by the two parties and can refuse if it would be contrary to the interests of justice, as where one party has misled the other.

37 | *My husband and I have agreed that he is going to leave. I have a job and don't need maintenance for myself, but I feel that he should pay it for the children. What is the best way to arrange it? Can I force him to pay?*

The best way to arrange for the maintenance to be paid, if your husband agrees, is to have a consent order (see Q36). Alternatively, a maintenance agreement (see Q40) could be drawn up by your solicitors, but since you have an income yourself this is unlikely to save much tax, if any.

Typically, you will be unlikely to find that your husband refuses to pay maintenance for the children, since most fathers pay quite happily. If, however, he should prove difficult you can apply to the magistrates' court (see QS 24 and 27) for a maintenance court order. The magistrates can make an order for child maintenance whether the wife is herself entitled to any or not.

38 | *The maintenance I pay my wife is crippling me financially. What steps should I take to get the amount reduced?*

Either party can always apply to have a maintenance order varied. The magistrates' court will decide by how much if at all the maintenance is to be reduced or increased, assuming of course that the parties cannot agree for themselves. You can go direct to the magistrates' court office and explain what you want to do. The clerks will supply you with the forms needed to make the application. It may be sensible to see a solicitor first to get some preliminary advice.

An order is likely to be reduced where either the husband cannot afford to pay the original amount, as in your case, or where his wife's needs have dropped. Things to look for from his side are a fall in his income – redundancy, short-time working, or the like – or a rise in his outgoings – his responsibilities to his new partner and family, say. The wife's circumstances too might change – by her taking a job or working full time instead of part time, or by moving in with a new partner or by the new partner moving in with her.

The court must always look at the case as if it were fixing a new order rather than just compensating for a particular change in the circumstances – a 10 per cent drop in the husband's income will not automatically mean a 10 per cent drop in the maintenance. The court must also take account of child maintenance and arrive at a correct 'package'.

You can either make your own application for a reduction or, if your wife tries to enforce the original

order because there are arrears, you can make a 'cross application' at the same time to apply for a reduction. Whoever starts the ball rolling, the court has the power to remit or wipe out any arrears that the husband obviously cannot pay.

The court has been known to make an order in the opposite direction from the one requested. If a party applies for a variation, the court can increase or decrease the order, and husbands who unreasonably try to get a reduction can find that there is a rise instead.

39 | *My wife and I have just separated. I'll be paying her maintenance, but I wonder if I should pay the household bills myself or give her more maintenance and let her pay them?*

There are two points to deal with here.

The first is about income tax. If you pay maintenance under a court order you will get tax relief on it, so that every pound you pay costs you only 73p, or less if you are a higher-rate taxpayer. If you pay household bills on top of that you will not get tax relief on the bills (except on the mortgage interest).

The second is about making sure you don't have to pay twice. If you are the person who signed the supply contract with the gas or electricity boards, then you are the person who is liable to pay the bills; you cannot refuse to pay them because you gave your wife the money to do so and she spent it on something else. She will probably pay them, because she will not want the supplies cut off, but you cannot be sure.

The best course all round is for the maintenance to include the cost of these various bills, and for your wife to assume responsibility for as many as possible by signing new contracts herself with the electricity and gas boards.

Maintenance agreements

40 | *My husband and I have parted. He's agreed to pay maintenance for me and the children. Should we have a maintenance agreement drawn up?*

If you are separated but are not going to get a divorce yet, you certainly could get a maintenance agreement drawn up by your solicitors, but when you see them they will probably tell you that it is not necessary in most cases, and if the object of the exercise is to try to save some tax there is a better way of going about it, especially since you have children.

The best way of providing for the maintenance to be paid is to have a consent order made by the magistrates' court for whatever amount is agreed between you (see Q36). It will usually have the effect of making the amount of the child maintenance tax free in a way that a mere agreement cannot do (see TAX AND DIVORCE, Q1).

Any other terms you and your husband might want to include in an agreement can just as effectively be set out in a simple exchange of letters between your solicitors; these might include custody of and access to the children, occupation of the home, and so on.

Custody and access

41 | *If I apply to the magistrates' court for a maintenance order against my husband, who's left me, can I at the same time apply for an order giving me custody of the children?*

Yes. In fact, magistrates cannot finally dispose of a financial application – either by making a maintenance order or dismissing the case – unless they have at least considered whether or not to make a custody order and at the same time considered an access order on behalf of the other parent. In most cases they will give legal custody to one parent – the one with whom the child will make his or her home – and give access to the other. They can do other things, though, including giving custody to a grandparent or some other third party if neither parent can provide a proper home.

If there is a dispute about custody or access, the court will adjourn the case and ask a court welfare officer to produce a report before making a decision.

Legal separation

42 | *What is a 'legal separation'?*

This is a commonly used expression, but it has no real meaning in law unless what is meant by it is a decree of judicial separation (see Q43). Otherwise people say they have a legal separation when what they really mean is that they are separated and some legal steps or proceedings have been taken, perhaps a maintenance agreement, for instance (see Q40).

43 | *What is the point of getting a decree of judicial separation rather than a divorce?*

A decree of judicial separation is a decree, or order, made by the divorce court stating that the parties are separated in the eyes of the law. From a practical point of view it is the same as a divorce except that as the parties remain married to each other neither can remarry.

The advantage of a judicial separation is that you do not have to wait at least a year before petitioning for the decree (see DIVORCE, Q19) and you do not need to prove that the marriage has irretrievably broken down. Most of the rest of the law and the procedures are the same as for divorce though. In fact, the court's powers to deal with property and finance are the same as they are on divorce, so the court can make whatever orders are fair between the parties.

If one partner dies, while the other will still be his or her widow or widower if that partner dies intestate – without a will – the survivor will not be entitled to anything from the estate as a surviving spouse would in the normal way (although a claim may be made under the Inheritance (Provision for Family and Dependants) Act 1975 for provision out of the estate; see WILLS, DEATH AND INHERITANCE, Q54). Widows' pension rights are usually unaffected, though.

The fact that a decree of judicial separation has been made does not prevent either party from seeking a divorce later.

Nullity

44 | *I've read about marriages being annulled. What does this mean?*

Just as the court can end a marriage by a decree of divorce (see page 54), so it can end it by a decree of nullity in certain circumstances. The marriage is then said to be annulled. The proceedings are less common than those for divorce, because for a nullity decree to be granted there must have been something wrong with the marriage itself.

In some cases the defect in the marriage is so fundamental that the law regards the marriage as never having taken place at all and the marriage is said to be 'void'. This can arise where, for example, one of the partners marries bigamously, or the partners are closely related, or one partner is under 16. Strictly, no decree is necessary in such a case, but it is 'tidier' to have the piece of paper showing that the marriage is void.

In other cases the defect is less substantial and the marriage is valid unless and until one partner gets a nullity decree. Such a marriage is said to be 'voidable' and the law regards the marriage as having taken place. The grounds here include the fact that the marriage has not been consummated because either partner was unable to do so or the respondent refused to do so, the fact that the wife was pregnant by someone else at the time of the marriage and the husband did not know, or that the respondent was suffering from a venereal disease. Certain types of mental illness existing at the time of marriage can also provide grounds.

The law of nullity is more complicated than that of divorce, and so is the procedure. Unlike divorce, which can be dealt with through the post, a nullity petition must be heard by a judge in court. The court has the same powers to deal with finance and property after a decree of nullity as it has on divorce. But now that a divorce petition can be filed after a year of marriage (see DIVORCE, Q19), the small number of nullity petitions will probably drop even further.

Divorce

Grounds

1 | *I've heard that the only ground for divorce is the irretrievable breakdown of the marriage. What is this, and how would I prove it?*

The sole ground for divorce is that the marriage has broken down irretrievably – in other words, it cannot be saved – and if that is not so and there is a reasonable chance of a reconciliation no divorce can be obtained.

The law, in the Matrimonial Causes Act 1973, lays down five 'Fact situations', any one of which must be proved to exist before a court can decide that the ground for divorce exists. In other words, these 'five Facts', as they are known, represent the only ways of proving irretrievable breakdown. If one of them is proved the court must hold that the marriage has broken down, unless it can be shown not to have done so, and grant the divorce.

The five Facts are:

● Fact A: that the respondent has committed adultery and the petitioner finds living with the respondent intolerable;
● Fact B: that the respondent has behaved in such a way that the petitioner cannot reasonably be expected to live with the respondent;
● Fact C: that the respondent has deserted the petitioner for a continuous period of at least two years immediately preceding the filing of the petition;
● Fact D: that the parties to the marriage have lived apart for a continuous period of at least two years immediately preceding the filing of the petition and the respondent consents to a decree being granted;
● Fact E: that the parties to the marriage have lived apart for a continuous period of at least five years immediately preceding the filing of the petition.

Only Facts A and B allow a divorce promptly after separation; Facts C, D and E require lengthy periods of life apart.

2 | *I've found out that my wife has been having an affair with another man. I'm so distressed that I can't bear living with her. What would I have to prove to get a divorce?*

You have to prove what is stated under Fact A (see Q1). There are two elements to this Fact, first her adultery and second that you find it intolerable to live with your wife. The courts have decided that the two

elements do not need to be connected, so that it need not be the adultery that led to the intolerability. In practice, if you state that you find living with your wife intolerable that is an end of the matter.

Adultery means an act of sexual intercourse between a married person and a person of the opposite sex who is not his or her spouse. It must be voluntary, so that while a married rapist commits adultery his victim does not. Drunkenness is no defence unless it was such as to make the person concerned unable to know what he or she was doing or (in theory) that it was wrong. There must be some sexual penetration; other intimacy or 'heavy petting' is not enough.

One act of adultery is always enough, although, as in your case, there is usually a continuing affair.

3 | *How would I prove my wife's adultery?*

In the vast majority of cases, adultery is proved by the respondent making a written and signed admission. The petitioner identifies his or her spouse's signature on the document and the court accepts that as sufficient evidence.

Although a letter admitting adultery would be good enough, the more usual way of going about it is for the respondent to sign a 'confession statement' prepared by his or her own solicitor which is then sent to the petitioner or his or her solicitor. Alternatively, the respondent answers 'yes' to a question on the acknowledgement of service (see page 84) which the respondent receives with the petition. The question asks: 'Do you admit the adultery alleged?'

No one is ever obliged to admit to adultery, and if your wife refuses to do so you will need other proof. The well-known old chestnut of the enquiry agent (appointed by a solicitor) keeping watch on a bedroom window can still apply – the agent may show proof of 'a guilty passion and an opportunity to gratify it', as old law books phrased it, from which adultery can be inferred. Less colourful methods are more commonly used, such as proof that a wife has had a child of whom the husband cannot be the father, a finding against a man in certain legal proceedings brought by the mother of an illegitimate child, catching a venereal disease outside the marriage, and so on.

In practice, the easier it is to prove the adultery by

● *Divorce procedure*

Until the middle of the 1970s no divorce could be obtained without a hearing before a judge in court in public. Even if there were no children and the case were based on two years' life apart, the petitioner had to go into the witness box and give evidence on oath. In cases of the respondent's behaviour or adultery, it was a strain for the petitioner to have to tell the judge aloud and in the unfamiliar atmosphere of a courtroom what had happened in the marriage, and it was really rather pointless because all the evidence did was to confirm what was already set out in the petition the judge was reading at the same time. If the respondent did not deny the grounds for divorce, the case was undefended and the outcome in little doubt.

Because there was such a hearing it was necessary to have lawyers appearing as advocates, and the result was a high emotional and financial cost to all concerned. As a result, the 'special procedure' was introduced, allowing undefended divorce (and judicial separation) to be dealt with through the post in the vast majority of undefended cases. Although the term 'special procedure' is still used, there is nothing 'special' about it; only defended cases or those involving some serious doubt are actually heard before a judge with one or both parties giving oral evidence.

This recognises the reality of modern society that the divorce itself is no longer a matter of major difficulty, but that the real issues of concern are those affecting the children's welfare and the family's financial future. Where there are children involved there will be a hearing of some sort before the judge, but in private and usually in an informal atmosphere, and if necessary there may be a private hearing to sort out money and property questions.

other means the more easily the reluctant respondent can be persuaded to give a signed admission. Where it is plainly going to be difficult to prove adultery, it may be easier instead to forget it and to rely on behaviour (which comes under Fact B; see Q1).

4 | *My husband is divorcing me on the grounds of my affair with another man. I don't mind admitting adultery but I don't want to involve the other man. Can I avoid doing so?*

Yes. Because you, as the respondent, are not obliged to admit the adultery at all, what, if any, detail you choose to give about it is up to you. Sometimes confession statements admit to adultery 'with a person whom I decline to name' or 'with a person whom I will name only as Chris' ('Chris' being the person's true forename), perhaps adding some justification such as that the person is married.

However, if your husband, as the petitioner, knows the identity of the other person, he will have to name the other man in the petition. The other man will be a co-respondent in the divorce and served with a copy of the petition. The fact that the other man is named in the petition still does not mean that either you as respondent or he as co-respondent is obliged to answer the question admitting the adultery.

5 | *I knew my husband was having an affair with another woman, but I carried on for the sake of the children. Am I too late to get a divorce on the grounds of adultery? He stopped seeing the other woman about eight months ago.*

Yes, you have stayed together for too long and will now be prevented from getting a divorce based on adultery. The law is that if you continue to live with your spouse for more than six months after you come to know that he or she has committed adultery, you cannot get a divorce based on that particular adultery. One period of six months or two or more periods making up that time have the same effect. Notice that it is the time when you *knew* of the adultery which counts, not when it happened.

The words 'that particular adultery' are important, and make this quite a tricky rule. Suppose that your husband committed adultery once with each of two women, Ann and Brenda, and that he told you about Ann but you did not know about Brenda. After six months of staying together you cannot file a petition relying on adultery with Ann, but you can do so using the adultery with Brenda so long as you do not stay together for six months after you discover it. Taking another example, suppose that he committed adultery with Christine on holiday last year and you stayed with him for six months after you found out; you cannot rely on that adultery. But if he also committed it with her after the holiday this will be a separate act of adultery with a fresh six-month time-limit starting to run from the time you find out about it.

If you know your spouse is an unfaithful person in general and you stay together for six months you will not lose your right to complain in future as long as you complain of a specific affair you did not know about at the time.

6 | *When I discovered that my husband was having an affair I had a short relationship with another man. I don't see him any more, but I know my husband still sees the other woman. Does the fact that I committed adultery make any difference if I divorce my husband?*

No. The mere fact that the petitioner in a divorce has committed adultery does not mean that he or she cannot petition on the fact of adultery committed by the other spouse. The only practical consideration really, assuming that both spouses know of each other's adultery, is that there is a choice to be made as to who is going to file the petition – the wife relying on her husband's adultery, or vice versa.

7 | *My husband is often violent with me, and a friend has advised that his treatment of me is so bad that it should be enough to get me a divorce. Is this the case?*

If you can prove, under Fact B (see Q1), that your husband's behaviour is such that you cannot reasonably be expected to live with him, you should have good grounds for divorce.

Lawyers often refer to the behaviour of a partner as grounds for divorce as 'unreasonable'. This is only a shorthand and not an accurate term, and the test used to prove Fact B situations was laid down in one of the important decided cases some years ago. 'Would any right-thinking person come to the conclusion that this respondent has behaved in such a way that this petitioner cannot reasonably be expected to live with him or her, taking into account the whole of the circumstances and the characters and personalities of the parties?'

Thus, it is a matter of an ordinary person looking at the situation of the individual parties. Accordingly, it is impossible to draw up two lists of types of conduct and to say that one consists of those that will always be sufficient grounds for divorce and the other which

will never be so. What is enough in the case of one couple might not be in another.

Nevertheless, the following are likely to be behaviour within Fact B: violence, alcoholism, refusal of sex, excessive or perverted sexual demands, constant nagging and criticism, public belittling and humiliation, neglect, associations with others of the opposite sex even if there is no adultery, and so on. In most cases there will be allegations of more than one of these. Anyone can readily imagine that the sort of person who is prone to one will be prone to others too, especially in the context of a breaking marriage and the vicious circle that often develops.

In the petition itself you will have to give examples or incidents of what actually happened in your marriage, usually with exact or approximate dates and short particulars of words used and things done. In the way of things such a petition is an unpleasant document both for the petitioner to prepare and for the respondent to receive.

8 | *I'm sure my husband is mentally ill and it's that which makes him behave so intolerably towards me. Can I get a divorce if he is mentally ill?*

There are bound to be some cases where the behaviour complained of is due to some mental illness or to the psychological effects of a physical illness. There is no specific provision about this in the law, but there have been a number of cases before the courts in which it has been held that where the behaviour is within the definition quoted in Q7 a decree can be obtained even though the respondent had no intention to hurt and could not help what he or she was doing. Indeed, in one case a wife was suffering from an irreversible condition of the nervous system which was leaving her bedridden and unaware of the world and completely unable to be a wife in any real sense of the word; her husband got a decree. If, however, the behaviour is comparatively slight and the evidence is that it arises from a condition that is likely to be temporary – a minor nervous breakdown, say – then it may be that the other spouse can reasonably be expected to weather the moderate storm and a divorce may be refused. From a practical point of view, then, the behaviour and not the cause will be what is relevant.

9 | *I've been putting up with my husband's violent behaviour for years now. Does that mean I've left it too late to divorce him because of it?*

No, certainly not. There is a six-month bar rather like the one in adultery cases (see Q5) if you live together

for more than six months after the last incident complained of. But even if your husband was violent towards you more than six months ago, the bar is not an absolute one and can be overridden by the court.

The only real problem and one that would be likely to arise only in the unlikely event of your husband's defending the divorce, would be that you might find it hard to show that you now cannot stand what you had stood for years. But the answer to that would be that things are harder to bear the longer they go on, so a court should be sympathetic.

10 | *What is the legal definition of desertion?*

Desertion arises where one spouse ceases to cohabit with the other without good reason, without the other's consent and with the intention of deserting. Desertion is rarely used as the basis for divorce nowadays.

Strictly speaking it is not necessary for a spouse to walk out and leave the other, since ceasing to live together as one household even under the same roof amounts to ceasing to cohabit (see Q14).

Having good reason for living apart prevents desertion, and this may flow from the conduct of the spouse who remains (a battered wife who is driven out is not in desertion), or from business, health or other causes.

If the parties agree to separate neither will be in desertion; the agreement can consist of a formal written separation agreement or be an entirely informal agreement to go their own ways.

11 | *Why is desertion so rarely used these days as grounds for divorce?*

The main reason is simply that where the parties have been apart for at least two years it is usually possible to get the other party to agree to a divorce by consent based on two years' separation (Fact D; see Q1). It does not matter how and why the separation came about, and in practice it is not uncommon for the party who deserted to persuade the other to consent to a divorce and for the deserter to then be the petitioner.

Another reason is that in most cases perfectly good spouses do not suddenly walk out. There will usually have been some odd behaviour and a breakdown in the relationship beforehand, and a divorce on that basis under Fact B can be obtained without a two-year wait.

12 | *My wife first left me three years ago, then came back for a few months last year and then left again. Can I divorce her on the grounds of desertion?*

It depends. To qualify as the basis for a divorce the desertion must have been running for at least two years and be continuing when the petition is filed.

Fact C, quoted in Q1, refers to the desertion being continuous, so you would think that if you get back together again for a while you have to start the two years running again from when she walked out the second time.

To prevent hardship, and indeed to encourage people to try again, there is a provision which says that a six-month period, or two or more periods not altogether exceeding six months, does not make you start all over again, although the time you were together cannot count as part of the two-year period. Suppose that a husband left on 31 December 1983 and came back on 1 January 1985, staying until 31 May 1985, when he left again for good. Since he was back for less than six months, his wife would not have to wait until two years from May 1985 to petition. But she cannot count that period January to May 1985 as a period of desertion, so she must wait two years and five months from his first departure.

The days on which your wife left and returned each time will not count as part of the period either, so for safety where the timings are close most solicitors will wait for an extra week or so to make sure that the two years have clearly passed.

13 | *My wife and I split up just over two years ago and we both want a divorce. On what grounds can we get one?*

Now that you have lived apart for over two years, the

easiest and least messy course is to use Fact D (see Q1). It is necessary only to show that you and your wife have been living apart for at least two years. As each of you has agreed to a divorce, one of you should file the petition and the other should give his or her consent to the decree being granted. The respondent gives consent by signing the acknowledgement of service to that effect and returning it to the court office. This is the nearest thing there is to a joint petition, and of course it depends entirely upon the agreement of both parties.

There are, however, two complications that need to be watched, apart from the continuity of the two-year period, which is the same as for desertion (see Q12). These complications are, first, whether you have in fact been 'living apart' (see Q14) and, second, what either of you thought about the future of the marriage during the separation – the so-called 'mental element' (see Q15).

14 | *How does the law define 'living apart'?*

There is a provision in the Matrimonial Causes Act 1973 which says that a couple will not be treated as living apart unless they have been living as 'two separate households'. It applies to Facts C, D and E (see Q1) and to the six-month bars in Facts A and B (see Qs 5 and 9).

Where the parties have been living in separate buildings under separate roofs there is no problem at all – they can be seen to be and can prove that they have been living apart. The difficulties arise when they claim to have been living separate lives under one roof as two households rather than one. In the way of things, when a marriage breaks down the parties will have less and less to do with each other and may sleep apart, rarely speak and go increasingly their own ways. But the chances are that in legal terms there is usually one unhappy household rather than two.

If the matter of two separate households has to be decided by the court, the court will look at all the facts to see what the domestic arrangements really are, and sleeping arrangements and sex will be only one factor. If the couple have slept together this strongly suggests one household, but on the other hand separate bedrooms are not much indication of two households.

Financial and other mundane matters are often much more indicative. The arrangements for buying, cooking and eating food are very relevant, as will be those for laundry and cleaning. The use of rooms in the house would be considered, especially in practice the sitting-room or another room containing the television. Holidays, going out and other entertainment arrangements frequently will be examined so the court gets a complete picture.

The importance of proving that a couple have been living apart is that it may mean (in Fact C, D and E

CASE A

Anne and Bill are both in their late twenties and have been married for four years. They have no children. They live in a small house which they jointly own. They have a building society mortgage. Both have good jobs. The marriage has not been going well for some time and there have been frequent rows. Anne wants to end the marriage and thinks she could probably get a divorce based on Bill's behaviour if she wanted to. Bill agrees that the marriage is finished, but sees no point in a divorce yet as neither of them has any intention of remarrying or setting up home with anyone else. At the moment they are still living together.

PROBABLE OUTCOME *In this sort of case the only two questions that really apply are whether to have a divorce yet and what to do about the house. Because there are no children, and because Anne has a good job, it is most unlikely that she will seek maintenance.*

Since neither of them has any real reason for wanting to be divorced, so as to remarry for example, they might just as well separate and seek a divorce by consent two years later. If either of them finds a new partner and wants to remarry in the meantime the other would probably agree to petition relying on adultery with that new partner. But if Anne has grounds and wants a divorce now to get everything out of the way she is quite entitled to go ahead.

The house should be easy to deal with. The choice is either to sell it and divide the proceeds or for one party to buy out the other's share. Which is chosen will depend upon whether either of them wants to carry on living in the house and, if so, whether he or she can afford to raise the necessary money to pay to the other.

There should be no question of this case going to court for a decision about the home or anything else. If and when a divorce is obtained, an order by consent for a 'clean break' should be sought.

cases) that the divorce can be obtained sooner than two or five years from the date one of the partners physically left the home. The courts are well aware of this importance, and will require very clear evidence that two single households actually existed.

15 | *A friend has told me that apart from having to prove grounds for divorcing my husband, a 'mental element' is also involved. What is this?*

Although there is nothing in the Matrimonial Causes Act 1973 about it, the Court of Appeal decided in a case several years ago that before the two-year period in Fact D cases (see Q1) could start to run, not only must the couple be living apart but one or other of them must have come to the conclusion that the marriage was in fact dead and had no future. This is the 'mental element'. There is no need for the other party to be told that this was what he or she thought, and it need not strictly be the person who is now petitioning for divorce who first came to that conclusion – he or she can only just have come to it so long as the other had done so earlier.

In most cases there will be little difficulty in proving the mental element. The separation may come after a series of rows, or be because one party has moved out of the matrimonial home to live with someone else, or takes a job away from home and the other decides not to move but to lead a fresh life alone. Such facts as these can be put before the court to satisfy it that the necessary mental element exists; the facts are stated on the affidavit of evidence (see page 86).

The court might be suspicious, though, if the party who left has returned to live at the home from time to time, for example when he is a husband who has been working abroad but who has returned home for Christmas and other holidays. Even this can be met quite easily if the truth is that he came back to stay at the house for reasons of economy and to enjoy better access to the children, or something like that.

16 | *My wife and I have lived apart for over two years and both want a divorce. Does it matter which of us is the petitioner?*

Because you and your wife are in agreement and because there is no question of showing fault on either side, it is up to you to decide who will file the petition, and from a legal point of view it does not much matter who does so.

The person who is the petitioner will have the task of dealing with a bit more paperwork and will be liable to pay the solicitor's fee (unless conducting the case without one, or getting Legal Aid). This is not

likely to be very much in a simple case, and it is usually possible to agree between the two parties that they will share the costs, or if one party is keener on divorce than the other that person may agree to pay them all anyway and put up the money in advance.

The other consideration is purely psychological, in that there are some people who are prepared to have a divorce but only if they can be the petitioner and be seen as the person who got the divorce 'against' the other party, unrealistic though this attitude may be.

Generally, it is not very sensible to file a petition based on Fact D (see Q1) unless you are pretty certain that consent will be given, and as a matter of common sense the parties should agree as much as possible right at the start. The best thing is to approach your spouse and make it clear that everything is open to agreement, including the fact that you do not mind who divorces whom.

17 | *When is the five-year separation period used in practice as the grounds for divorce?*

It is used only where the partner who wants the divorce cannot get one on the basis of any of the other Facts (see Q1) and his or her spouse refuses to agree to a divorce. The classic example arises where one partner leaves his or her spouse for a new partner and wants a divorce to be able to remarry. If the deserted spouse has not committed adultery or not behaved in a manner to warrant divorce and refuses to file a petition or to consent to a decree after two years apart, the other partner will have to wait until five years have passed from the separation, when he or she can seek a divorce.

It is not only necessary to show five years' life apart

to obtain a divorce. The party seeking the divorce must also show that he or she regarded the marriage as dead throughout the period (see Q15) and that the period was continuous (see Q12).

18 | *My husband and I have been living apart for over five years. He says he can divorce me now whether I like it or not. Is this true?*

Yes. The whole idea of Fact E (see Q1) is that it allows a dead marriage to be ended even against the wishes of a completely innocent party once five years have passed since the separation. In a good many cases the refusal to agree to a divorce is for emotional rather than practical reasons, often pure spite in fact, and the law provides for the 'guilty' party eventually to be able to get a divorce and be able to remarry if he or she wants.

The law does provide an exception, though. There is a special 'defence' in Fact E cases which enables a person to fight the divorce if the dissolution of the marriage would cause 'grave financial or other hardship' and that it would be wrong to dissolve it. If that defence succeeds, there will be no divorce and the parties will remain married. It is the *dissolution* of the marriage – the divorce itself and the ending of the married state – which must cause the hardship, not just the fact of separation. In other words, some legal right which exists only because the parties are married must usually stand to be lost. The most common example of this is of a woman who, as a result of divorce, would lose her right to a widow's pension under her husband's employer's pension scheme. Women in this position have successfully defended their husband's divorce proceedings.

19 | *We have only been married for eight months but it's a disaster. When can we get a divorce?*

You can get divorced once you have been married for at least a year, but not before. Until recently there was a three-year time-limit which could be waived only by a judge to allow an earlier divorce in cases of exceptional hardship or depravity. The new one-year limit is absolute and cannot be overridden in any circumstances. Though the petition cannot be filed within the first year it can be based on allegations of adultery or unreasonable behaviour which occurred during that time; also, the period of living apart can start during this first year. See Q1 to see if you have any grounds for divorce.

20 | *My wife left me a year ago. I'd like a divorce, but I don't know what her reaction will be. Can I*

get one and should I speak to her before going ahead?

The first point to tackle is whether either of you has grounds for a divorce (see Q1). Since you have been separated for only a year, you will have to wait another year before you could file a petition based on her desertion, or before either of you could file one based on two years' life apart with the other party consenting to the decree. If you want to be divorced before that, it would have to be on the basis of adultery or behaviour, either of which could be yours or hers. Has either of you committed adultery? If she has you could file a petition; if you have she may agree to file a petition based on it. That would be preferable to a divorce based on behaviour, although you may need to think whether you behaved in such a way that your wife could not reasonably be expected to live with you; if your behaviour drove her away she may be prepared to file the petition.

You should certainly speak to your wife about a divorce. You may decide to wait a year and get one by consent at that time if neither of you is in a hurry. If you want to go ahead earlier, discuss with her a divorce on the grounds of behaviour or adultery.

Before you speak to her it would be a good idea to think out what you want to do about the other important matters – maintenance, the home, the children, the costs of the divorce, and so on – because her attitude may well be affected by them. It would also be sensible to approach her on the basis that while you want to dissolve the marriage, you do not mind who divorces whom. She may be happier to go ahead if she can be the petitioner.

21 | *I am American, my husband English. We were married in America but have always lived in England, and I propose to stay in this country. Can I get a divorce in England?*

Yes. For the English courts to have jurisdiction to grant a divorce one of the partners must have been either 'domiciled' or have been 'habitually resident' in England for at least 12 months immediately before the petition is filed. Thus, your circumstances make it clear that you can file your petition in the English courts.

'Domicile' is quite a difficult concept to get to grips with. A person is said to be domiciled in the place that he or she regards as his or her true or permanent home. You would be regarded as being domiciled in England. In the case of people born here who have never settled abroad there will be no question but that they are domiciled here, and immigrants intending to stay permanently will also acquire domicile. Similarly, people working abroad will not lose their English domicile unless they intend to settle permanently in that other country.

'Habitual residence' is applied in the case of people from other countries who have been here more or less continuously for some time, but who have not yet decided to settle permanently so as to be domiciled here.

It is enough in law if just one party can show domicile or a year's habitual residence. A Dutch wife, for example, who has never been in England could petition if her husband has become domiciled here or has the necessary 12 months' residence.

See also MARRIAGE, QS 12 and 13.

Defending the petition

22 | *My wife left me and went to live with her mother three months ago. I've now received a divorce petition saying all sorts of things that are lies or half-truths. Should I fight it? I'm not taking all this lying down!*

The first thing to realise is that fighting the divorce itself – defending the petition – will not save your marriage. If, and it is a big 'if', you prevent your wife from getting a divorce, that only means the legal shell of the marriage is not ended; it will not make her come back to you to live happily ever after. If you want to save your marriage you should talk to your wife about trying again, and consider marriage guidance.

If you accept that your relationship is at an end, then the sensible thing to do is to end the marriage with as little bitterness and acrimony as possible. You should probably let your wife's petition go through undefended, even though you find that some of the things she says are hurtful, exaggerated, taken out of context, and so on. Lawyers have a saying that in husband and wife cases there are always three sides – his, hers and the truth. An undefended divorce petition is not made public so no one will know what your wife has said apart from you, your lawyers and the court.

What really counts for the two of you and your children (if any) is the future, and the most obvious things to affect you are money and your home. Defending a divorce is an expensive business, and whatever you spend on legal costs will simply cut down the amount that could be used to provide for the family.

23 | *Surely there are some cases when it is sensible to defend a divorce?*

Yes, there are, but really there are only two.

The first arises in cases where the divorce is being sought on the basis of five years' life apart and the respondent thinks that the ending of the marriage itself will result in grave financial hardship. This usually occurs because a middle-aged or older wife will lose her right, when divorced, to receive a widow's pension under her husband's employer's pension scheme (see Q 18).

The other arises in cases based on behaviour where what is alleged is so serious that it is likely to affect the outcome of other aspects of the divorce, in particular the financial and property side. Only the most extreme conduct by a party will affect who gets what by way of money or property, very serious violence being one of them. As a matter of law, if something is alleged in a petition and it is not successfully challenged, by way of defending the divorce, it is too late to deny it for other purposes later.

To take a simple example: suppose that the wife's petition alleges that the husband deliberately ran her down in his car, breaking her legs and ending her working life. His story is that it was an accident and that she stepped out in front of him in a dark driveway. If the wife's version is true, she will probably be far better off when the property and finance arrangements come to be dealt with. If the husband simply lets the divorce go through undefended, he will be taken to accept that his wife's version is true. He should defend the divorce, deny her allegations, disproving them if he can, and give his own version of the truth.

The respondent can avoid defending a divorce even in these two cases if both parties agree on a financial settlement acceptable to them both or if technical steps can be taken by the solicitors whereby the issue of conduct can be left out of the financial side of the divorce by agreement.

24 | *My wife is divorcing me, but I've told my solicitor to defend the petition I've received. What will happen now?*

The first thing to happen is that your solicitor will probably try to talk you out of defending the divorce. If that fails, and you cannot get Legal Aid (see page 62), he or she will probably ask you for quite a lot of money on account of costs, because you are embarking on what can be an expensive business and your solicitor will want to be sure of getting paid!

Although your solicitor will take the following steps on your behalf, for simplicity they are described as if you were doing so yourself.

When you receive the petition, it has with it the acknowledgement of service. You must answer 'yes' to the question 'Do you intend to contest the proceedings?' and complete the rest of the form. The form then goes back to the court. Within three weeks you must send another, which the court does not supply, called an Answer; it is a complicated and formal document in which you set out exactly what you are saying by way of denying your wife's allegations and those you are making yourself. Often there follows a series of similar documents with further allegations and cross-allegations.

There will be a short private hearing before the court registrar to make sure the case is ready for trial, and then the hearing itself takes place before a judge sitting in public. You and your wife will both have barristers to present your cases, you will both give evidence and be cross-examined, and there will usually be other witnesses too – in a 'behaviour' case there may be friends or neighbours who saw certain incidents, and often a doctor to give evidence about the effect of what happened on a party's health. The case can get very sordid and go on for several days. Eventually, the judge will pronounce a decree nisi (see page 54) in favour of one or other party, or dismiss the case. Whatever the judge says when summing up can be reported by the press, so you could find yourselves in the newspapers.

Although you are determined to defend the divorce, and you may go part way towards doing so, it is fair to say that very few defended cases actually arrive in court. If they do not settle earlier, the parties generally come to terms in the court corridor, with a deal being done on finance and property as well as who will have the decree. But by then money and anguish have been wasted.

25 | *I agree I behaved pretty badly when we were married, but so did my husband. Surely I'm not going to be branded as the only wrongdoer? I want to have my say as well.*

Very often both parties share the blame for the breakdown of their marriage. Each could put up a case for getting a divorce because of what the other has done. In the present state of the law, though, only one person petitions for divorce and the other generally has to let the divorce go through undefended unless he or she defends the petition or perhaps 'cross-peti-

tions' for a divorce based on what he or she says the petitioner has done.

Because the vast majority of divorces these days are undefended and dealt with through the post, neither party goes into court to give oral evidence and has his or her 'say'. Only undefended divorces where the grounds are very weak and defended ones are actually heard by a judge in court.

While it is technically possible for a respondent to file a 'cross-petition', this is rare, it costs money and serves no useful purpose in most cases because it may simply mean that the divorce is granted to both parties on the strength of their respective allegations rather than those of one alone.

Basically, either you swallow your pride, or, to have your say, engage in a fight with all that that involves.

26 | *I've decided that I want to defend my wife's divorce petition. Can I get Legal Aid?*

That depends on the circumstances, although you can certainly apply for it if you want to. To get it you will not only have to show that you are financially eligible (see page 493) but also that it would be reasonable to grant you Legal Aid for your purpose – and that may very well be your difficulty. If you have no good reason for defending the divorce other than what is really personal pride, it would not be a proper use of public money and Legal Aid would probably be refused.

Procedures

27 | *Getting a divorce sounds quite straightforward. Do I really need a solicitor or can I do it myself?*

The procedure for getting a divorce, as set out on pages 79 to 87, is straightforward and a sensible person should have no difficulty in managing it without a solicitor. If you should decide to go it alone an excellent booklet is available free of charge from the court. This is *Undefended divorce – a guide for the petitioner acting without a solicitor*, and it takes the petitioner through the procedure step by step. The court also provides all the forms you need, again free of charge.

Having said that you *can* do it yourself, whether you *should* do so is another matter. As the booklet itself makes plain, the court staff are not allowed to give legal advice. The booklet gives examples of matters on which a solicitor should be consulted, including:

• whether or not grounds for divorce exist, and if so which Fact should be used (see Q1);

• what effect divorce will have on financial matters, such as maintenance, the home, and pension and inheritance rights;

• what to do if there is or is likely to be a dispute over the children.

These are the most difficult and important areas of marriage breakdown, and it would be wise to take expert legal advice about them before embarking on a divorce.

There is no reason why you should not see a solicitor to find out where you stand, at least to set your mind at rest, and to ask whether yours appears to be the sort of divorce which you could then handle on your own. Any sort of do-it-yourself work in the law can be a false economy, and divorce is no exception.

28 | *Are the various documents provided by the court difficult to complete?*

No, not really. They are intended to be simple enough for an ordinary person to understand. All the necessary forms (see pages 79 to 87) are supplied by the court, and the booklet (see Q27) also supplied by the court explains how to complete them. If you consult a solicitor he or she will complete them on your behalf. If you should start by doing your own divorce and then get into difficulties with the forms, you can still go to a solicitor. In fact, you would probably have to because the court staff are not allowed to fill in forms for people.

29 | *If I decide to see a solicitor about my divorce, can I get Legal Aid?*

Yes, you can. You might see a solicitor to get some preliminary advice, intending to handle the divorce on your own, or you might decide to ask the solicitor to deal with the entire divorce for you. In either case the Green Form Scheme (see page 490) is there to meet the cost if you cannot afford it.

Provided that you are financially eligible, the solicitor will give you all the advice and help you need, both with initial advice only, if that is all you want, and with preparing the documents and dealing with the whole case throughout. The same help is also available to the respondent.

A point to bear in mind here is that when a solicitor is consulted under the Green Form Scheme, he or she will assess whether or not a financial contribution is required from the client according to means. If you have no contribution to pay, or very little, it will cost you no more in most cases to let the solicitor deal with the whole job than it would just to get initial advice.

If there are other matters to be dealt with, such as

● *If I want a divorce, which court do I apply to?*

All divorces start in a divorce county court. Most towns outside London have county courts, even quite small towns, but only those in the big cities and larger towns will be divorce county courts. If you go to a solicitor, he or she will know which is the nearest one, and if you decide to deal with the divorce yourself you can find out which it is from a Citizens Advice Bureau or by telephoning the nearest county court (the number is in the telephone directory under Courts).

Slightly different rules apply in London. Many of the London county courts deal with divorce, and the Principal Registry of the Family Division of the High Court (address on page 509) is also treated as a divorce county court.

It is generally best to use the court nearest to where you live because, although the divorce itself will almost certainly be dealt with through the post under special procedure (see pages 79 to 87), it will be necessary for you to attend court at least once if there are children; if there is a dispute over the children or maintenance and property there would be further hearings at that court.

If you would prefer not to use your nearest court, perhaps because you are on the point of moving to another area or you know someone who works at that court and you would rather he or she did not see the file, you can apply to any other divorce county court or to the Principal Registry of the Family Division.

financial negotiations or hearings or a dispute over custody, the solicitor will probably advise you to apply for a Legal Aid certificate to cover them (see page 492).

30 | *Someone has told me that I may not have to pay the court fee. Who is exempt from paying it?*

Three types of petitioner are exempt from paying the court fee, which is at present £40 and is payable when the petitioner files the petition. The people exempt are those who draw Supplementary Benefit, those who draw Family Income Supplement, and those who are being helped with their divorce by a solicitor under the Green Form Scheme (see Q29). The third category is a good reason for letting a solicitor deal with your divorce under the Green Form Scheme; because the Scheme enables you to claim exemption from the fee, all you will pay is your contribution to the solicitor and this could well be less than the £40 court fee.

31 | *Must I send my marriage certificate when I petition for divorce? I'd like to keep it. Won't a photocopy do instead?*

A photocopy will not do. The court must be satisfied that you and your spouse are in fact husband and wife, and only an official certificate will provide the evidence. The court will not return it. If you want to keep the one you were given when you got married, or it has been lost or destroyed, you will have to get a duplicate. You can obtain one from the Register Office where your church marriage was registered –

normally the one for the area where your wedding took place – or from the Register Office at which you were married. Your local Register Office will tell you how to go about obtaining a copy even if you married somewhere else; look it up in the telephone directory under Registration of Births, Deaths and Marriages. Alternatively, you can obtain a copy from the General Register Office (address on page 510).

32 | *How is a divorce petition served?*

The normal way of going about things is just to have the petition and the other documents sent to the respondent by post (see page 79). The court will do this. The respondent then returns the acknowledgement of service to the court, and service is proved by the petitioner identifying his or her signature in the affidavit of evidence later (unless a solicitor has signed on the respondent's behalf, when this is not necessary). If no acknowledgement of service is returned to the court, the next step would usually be for another copy of the petition and the other documents to be prepared and served personally on the respondent; this means that they are physically handed to him or her. Sometimes this is done by the bailiff, who is an officer of the court, or by an employee or agent of the petitioner's solicitors. Anyone can do it except the petitioner himself or herself. If someone other than the bailiff serves the documents, an affidavit of service must be prepared and sworn to prove that due service has taken place.

33 | *I want a divorce but I don't know where my husband is. What procedure will be followed?*

You have a problem here, because you will not be able to give an address to which the petition can be sent, nor a place where your husband could be served personally. You should first make some enquiries among friends and relatives to see if you can trace him. Former employers may know the name of the firm he moved to, and you could try there.

If neither of these steps works, you can write to the Department of Health and Social Security, whose records department at Newcastle upon Tyne will tell you if, to their knowledge, he is alive or dead, and they will also forward a letter for you, although they will not give you his address.

If you are drawing Supplementary Benefit and have a solicitor handling your divorce, the DHSS will usually give your husband's address to your solicitor to enable the case to proceed; they do this so that a maintenance order can be sought against him. The court itself has certain powers to get information from the DHSS, and if you draw blanks with all other efforts you or your solicitor can ask the court to help.

34 | *I've tried everything, but I still can't trace my husband. What should I do now?*

If you and your solicitor really have tried everything without success, you should apply to the court for a special order, of which there are two types.

The first is an order for 'substituted service'. This means that if you can prove that by taking certain steps the petition will come to your husband's attention, then, if you take those steps, he will be treated as duly served. This is normally used these days only where the petitioner knows that his or her spouse is in regular touch with someone else or with someone who knows where he or she is. A letter you have from his mother, say, stating that she knows where your husband is, but refusing to give the address, could be enough to get an order for substituted service on her.

The second is an order that 'service be dispensed with'. When it is plainly impossible to serve the petition the court can direct that the case may proceed without your husband being served at all.

In both these cases it would generally be necessary to consult a solicitor to ensure that all lines of enquiry have in fact been exhausted and to have the necessary documents prepared to apply for the orders from the court.

Financial aspects

35 | *What does 'strict property law' mean in the context of marriage breakdown? It's a phrase my solicitor used.*

This is a term lawyers use to describe the legal rules that are applied to decide who owns assets and property and in what proportions. Lawyers may find it

---

CASE B

Don and Carol are both in their early thirties. They have been married for six years and have a daughter, Elise, who is four. The matrimonial home is a detached house on a modern estate, bought in joint names with the aid of a mortgage. Don has a well-paid job; Carol has not worked for some years.

Two years ago Carol began having an affair with Frank, a divorced man, and six months ago she discovered she was pregnant by him. She trusts Frank, who says he wants to marry her, so she recently left Don and took Elise to live with Frank. She wants a divorce so that she can remarry before the birth of her child. Don realises that there is no future for the marriage but is unsure what to do. His pride has been hurt and he feels inclined to refuse to divorce as quickly as she wishes. He accepts that Elise is better off with her mother, and will not contest custody.

PROBABLE OUTCOME *Don's solicitor would probably advise him to agree to petition for divorce on terms that the value of the house should be divided, and that Carol would relinquish her claim to maintenance for herself. Don would pay maintenance for Elise.*

That advice would be given because the risk for Don is that if Carol's new relationship breaks down, as things stand she could seek maintenance for herself and seek an order to get back into the former home. A divorce would give Don certainty.

Don's solicitor would probably recommend the following package:

● *that Don will divorce Carol on the basis of her adultery which she will admit;*

● *that the home is sold and the proceeds divided equally, or that Don will buy out Carol's share for an agreed amount, depending on whether he wants to stay in the home and can raise the money;*

● *that Don will pay maintenance at an agreed figure for Elise, but that Carol's right to seek maintenance for herself would be ended by an order of the court made by consent. In other words, as far as she is concerned there would be a 'clean break'.*

Carol's solicitor would advise her to accept this package as being the only way to get a divorce quickly (unless she has grounds against Don); the solicitor would also point out that she is really losing nothing by giving up her own claim to maintenance from Don, because the payment of any maintenance would cease anyway on her remarriage. The main risk Carol runs is that Frank might refuse to marry her after the order ending her rights against Don has been made.

The only outstanding financial matters concern costs, and an agreement would probably be reached that these should either all be paid by one party or be shared, the latter being the more common in practice.

necessary sometimes to look at the property and savings and any other assets and to find out whether they are the husband's or the wife's, or if both partners own them what the respective shares are. The divorce courts now have the power to make orders transferring property from one to the other partner or changing their existing ownership rights in accordance with the partners' needs, resources, and so on, to achieve a just balance between them, taking particular account of the needs and welfare of any children.

The power to redistribute property rights arises only on a court's decree of divorce (see page 54), judicial separation or nullity (see SEPARATION, QS 43 and 44) and if there is no such decree the court can be asked only to make orders on the basis of 'who owns what?'; in other words, on the basis of strict property law. So if the house is in the husband's sole name he is presumed to own it outright unless the wife can show she contributed to its purchase or improvement. This can plainly be most unjust in many cases, and a decree of divorce or judicial separation should usually be sought to give the court its wider and fairer powers.

Those rules of strict property law can also be relevant in other situations, for example on the death or bankruptcy of a spouse in cases where it may be necessary to decide what is the husband's or wife's and what must go to the beneficiaries or creditors; the other partner's property will not pass to them.

36 | *Are the financial aspects of divorce always settled by the court?*

No, far from it. Just as most claims for damages after an accident are settled out of court, so in most cases the parties to a broken marriage will be able to agree what is to happen about the home and money. Often this will happen before the divorce petition is even filed, so the whole divorce proceeds on an agreed basis. Usually the negotiations are handled by the parties' solicitors.

When negotiating, the solicitors will bear in mind what sort of decisions a court would be likely to make on the particular facts, and they will advise their clients accordingly.

It is always necessary to have a decree of divorce from the court to dissolve the marriage, but as far as the financial and property side is concerned it is not strictly necessary to have anything from the court at all. Even so, it is usually sensible to have the terms of the agreement drawn up and made into a court order, in this case a consent order. The main reasons

for this are to get tax relief on any maintenance payments in the best way, and so that there can be no dispute in the future about financial and property matters. A consent order can be made without any hearing at all; the document is drawn up by the solicitors who then simply send it to the divorce court office where it is stamped with the court's seal to make it binding.

If the parties cannot agree, then it will be necessary for the court to decide about maintenance, the home, and so on, and for that purpose there will have to be a hearing (see Q 37).

37 | *If my wife and I can't agree how the value of our assets is to be apportioned between us, does the court have the power to deal with our money and property on our divorce?*

Yes, the court has a very wide range of powers open to it to deal with the resources and assets of the parties on divorce. It is concerned to share out whatever is available by way of income and capital between the parties in accordance with what each has and what each needs, putting first the needs of any children.

The incomes of the parties are resources, and the court can deal with them by making an order for maintenance against one party (invariably the husband) in favour of the other (invariably the wife) and/or any child of the family, as appropriate. It can also make whatever orders are needed to deal with the capital assets of the couple, and these take a variety of forms depending on the asset concerned and the circumstances of the case. The court can make a 'property adjustment order'. This can direct that the property is sold and the proceeds divided, or transferred by one party to the other or from joint names into one party's sole name. Orders can also be made for one party to pay to the other a lump sum of cash if that is the most convenient way to divide things up. These powers have to be wide to achieve the flexibility the court needs.

38 | *Does the court consider property, income and other assets separately if the two parties in divorce cannot agree how they should be split?*

No. The object of the exercise is to arrive at a complete package to dispose of all the financial and property aspects of the divorce in one go. In most cases the court will decide what is to happen about the home and other assets, and fix any maintenance at one and the same time.

The capital and income sides are so closely involved that they must be considered together. To take a very simple example, if the court is thinking of ordering the house to be kept to provide a home for the wife and growing children, it must at the same time consider the amount of maintenance she would need if she is to take over paying the mortgage and running the home, and whether the husband can afford to pay that much as well as support himself in his new home. Solicitors work in exactly the same way when negotiating an agreed settlement – they always consider capital and income together.

39 | *In divorce cases, I gather that the court's decisions do not depend on who earns the money or owns the property. Is that correct?*

Yes, it is. On divorce all the assets of both parties go into the melting-pot, and they are all available for the court to use as it sees best. Although it would be a very extreme case indeed, even if the husband owned the home long before he met and married his wife and she put nothing into the family funds at all, the court could make him transfer the home to the wife outright. When he has built up a large and successful business, say, allotting the house to the wife may be the most appropriate course. Thus, while existing property rights will be considered by the court before it decides what to do, no property of either party is totally immune from the court's reach.

It can work both ways though. While a husband who has a 'windfall' inheritance at the time of the divorce might find himself losing part of it to the wife, a wife who gets a 'windfall' might well get less out of the family assets and less by way of maintenance because she now needs less.

40 | *Can court orders be made against a wife as well as against a husband if the parties themselves can't agree how to divide up their property and assets?*

Yes. The law does not discriminate between them; it just refers to a party to the marriage.

Having said that, in the way of things the court is more likely to make a maintenance order against the husband simply on the basis of needs and resources in the two common cases of the younger wife who is not working because she is looking after young children, and the older wife who has stayed at home to raise a family and has forfeited her career in the process. But if these roles were reversed and the husband had little or no income while the wife could and should afford maintenance, an order against her could be made. By

● *What's the difference between a 'decree nisi' and a 'decree absolute' of divorce? Why have two decrees?*

The effect of a decree absolute is to change the legal status of the parties. They cease to be married to each other with all that entails by way of legal rights and duties.

The decree nisi means that the marriage will be dissolved (by the decree absolute six weeks or so from the decree nisi) *unless* something happens in the meantime (*nisi* is the Latin for *unless*). Usually nothing does, but suppose, for example, that the divorce itself has been defended and the judge eventually pronounces a decree nisi at the end of a court hearing. The respondent might want to appeal against the decision, and if this were successful the marriage would not end in a decree absolute as expected. Similarly, there have been cases where the parties have lied in order to get a divorce; a neighbour has seen the decree nisi announced in the local newspaper, has realised this and reported the facts; the decree nisi has been cancelled and the parties remain married.

It is chiefly to cover these admittedly remote possibilities, and for other technical reasons, that the two-stage process exists. It prevents the absurd possibility of 'now you're married, now you're not, now you're married again', and enables the parties to know that the decree absolute is completely final. In most cases today there is no real need to have two decrees and one would be quite enough; it is to cater for unusual cases that the distinction exists.

the same token, the capital assets of both parties can be redistributed if need be.

Of course, if both parties have adequate incomes, and there are no children, neither would need support from the other.

41 | *How final are the orders the court makes on divorce when the parties are in dispute? Can they be varied later?*

Maintenance orders can be varied, but the basic rule in dealing with orders for the payment of lump sums, property transfers and other orders dividing the parties' capital assets is 'one bite at the cherry': they are final.

Once the court has made a lump sum order, the amount cannot be increased or decreased, and nor can another lump sum order be made or even applied for if the recipient now thinks the amount is not high enough.

By the same token, once the court has ordered property to be transferred or to be sold and the proceeds divided, or to be retained by one partner for the growing family for a period of time, the parties' shares in the proceeds being fixed, then that is the end of the matter, and the court has no power to change the shares or order the property to go outright to one party. The order cannot be varied, and neither party can apply for another.

The only exceptions to this otherwise hard-and-fast rule are that the court can vary the time by which a lump sum is to be paid if it is payable by instalments, and it can also vary the original provisions about the time and manner of a sale of property.

42 | *When we got our divorce six months ago I agreed to a consent order which gave me half the value of the house and £30 a week maintenance for our daughter; my own claim for maintenance was dismissed. I've now lost my job and can't manage financially. Can I go back and ask for more from my ex-husband?*

All you can do is to apply to the court for the maintenance for your child to be increased, which the court has the power to do. You cannot get any more money out of the value of the house, and nor can anything be done about getting maintenance for you because the order dismissed your claim, creating a 'clean break' (see Q46).

The law is perfectly clear in this area. Once an order has been made on divorce the only thing that can be changed is maintenance: while a maintenance order is still running the court can increase or reduce it. So as far as the family capital is concerned, the rule is 'one bite at the cherry' and all you can claim is the half share of the home that the order gave you; the share cannot be increased or decreased. As far as maintenance for yourself is concerned, if an order *had* been made requiring some to be paid to you, the amount could have been changed. Since there is no such order in force there is nothing to change, and as your claim was dismissed you cannot revive it and try to get maintenance now.

The fact that the order was made by consent rather than fixed by the court after a fought hearing does not affect this at all. Unless you can show that you were misled into agreeing to the consent order in the first place, which might get it cancelled, there is

nothing else you can do. A change in your circumstances is quite irrelevant.

43 | *I've been told that if there's a dispute between husband and wife on divorce, and the decisions about income and assets are made by a judge, the wife always gets a third of everything. Is this true?*

No. There is not and never has been any such rule, although many people think there is. It is never possible to apply some fixed fraction in an arbitrary way – it would be completely unjust in most cases because there are so many variables. The court's duty is to make an order that is fair in all the circumstances of the particular case before it. The wife may get nothing at all, either because she does not need anything or because the husband can afford nothing; in other cases she may get a lot more.

What you've been told about the wife receiving a third comes from a decision made by Lord Denning, then Master of the Rolls, in an important case in 1973. He said that a convenient *starting-point* in the process of deciding what order to make would be to consider allotting to the wife a third of the assets and awarding her maintenance so as to bring her income up to a third of the combined gross incomes to see where that would leave the parties. It is quite clear that it was never more than a starting-point, or 'ranging-shot' as one distinguished judge put it, in the process of working towards a final order.

Today the one-third is not used at all in deciding what to do with the home and capital assets, nor is it regarded as useful in dealing with maintenance at the low or very high ends of the income scale. In middle-income cases it is still helpful, but again very much as a ranging-shot in assessing maintenance, and the court must look very carefully at the result and decide what, if any, adjustments should be made to see exactly what the respective positions of the parties' households will be.

44 | *How does the court decide how much maintenance to award a divorced wife?*

The practical answer to that question is that it is an educated form of trial and error with a series of calculations being made until a figure that is fair to both sides is arrived at.

In recent years the courts have come to recognise that what the order does is to dictate to the parties what their respective standards of living are to be. Maintenance paid reduces the income of the husband's household and improves that of the wife's. Achieving the right balance is a matter of detailed calculation, looking as closely as possible at what income is to be left in the husband's household and what outgoings it has to meet and mouths to feed, doing the same for the wife's, and trying to balance the two.

Not only will the court need to look at things like housing costs, travel to work, and so on, but account must be taken of income tax and the entitlement of the parties to the various state benefits, both of which will be affected by the making of an order. A series of calculations will usually be required to get to the right set of figures.

Child maintenance will also have to be taken into account because, assuming that the wife has custody, whatever is paid to them will be an outgoing for the husband and a source of income for the wife's household.

The term that is used to describe this process is the 'net effect' approach, and lawyers presenting a case in court should produce a calculation of the 'net effect' of any set of proposals they are arguing for. Programs for mini-computers are now available to help them, but not yet to the courts.

45 | *Does the divorce court always award maintenance to the wife?*

No, it depends on the needs and resources of the parties, mainly whether the wife needs maintenance and whether the husband can afford to pay any.

A wife who is self-supporting from her own earnings will not need maintenance, and if she is living with another man who is keeping her she is most unlikely to get any. She would probably not ask for any anyway in either of these two cases. If she has remarried she will not be entitled to apply for any from her first husband, and if she was already receiving any her remarriage would automatically terminate it.

If the husband has such a low income or such high outgoings and obligations that he cannot afford to pay maintenance, the wife will again get none.

The court can cut off a wife's right to maintenance whether she likes it or not if the court thinks it just to do so. If on the other hand the court cannot make a worthwhile order in her favour now – her husband is a student, say, with very little income – but because there are children of whom she has custody her own right to apply in the future should be preserved, the court will make an order for purely nominal payments, usually 5p per annum, just to keep her rights alive and to enable her to apply for an increase should the husband's circumstances change.

46 | *I would like to put my marriage behind me and forget about it. Someone mentioned that I should try for a 'clean break' divorce. What is this?*

A 'clean break' divorce is one where an order of the court is made making it impossible for either party to apply ever again for any sort of financial provision from the other. In particular, the wife's application for maintenance for herself is dismissed, so that not only will she get no maintenance now, but her right to ask for it in the future is destroyed once and for all.

Such an order may be made in three main types of case:

● where the parties are already self-supporting – after a short childless marriage, or where the children have grown up and both parties have jobs, for example;
● where the wife intends to remarry shortly. In many such cases she will want a divorce so she can marry the man with whom she is living. The husband may well be advised by his solicitors to agree to divorce her, but only on the basis that she forgoes her right to maintenance, just in case her new relationship founders and she tries to get maintenance from him in the future;
● where there is enough capital around for the wife to be given sufficient to live on for the rest of her life; this occurs only rarely.

47 | *Can there be a clean break where there are young children?*

Yes, there can. But two points need to be explained.

First, the court can never destroy the children's right to maintenance in the same way as it can that of a spouse. Even if the court were to dismiss an application for child maintenance (which would be very unlikely indeed), a fresh application can always be made should the circumstances change and should the need arise.

Second, bearing in mind that the court's main duty in deciding what to do about finance and property is to secure the welfare of the children under 18, it would not be sensible in most cases to destroy the wife's right to maintenance completely, because, if she has custody, she might need to apply for maintenance for herself in the interests of the children. Even if she is self-supporting at the moment and needs no maintenance other than for the children, she might lose her job or have to give up work to look after a sick or injured child, and she would then need maintenance so as to provide a proper home, and if the husband can provide it she should have it. Only if there were plenty of capital around or if she were remarrying would it be safe for the court to cut off her right entirely.

48 | *Is a court order needed for a clean break?*

Yes, at any rate for safety. An agreement not to apply for maintenance does not prevent an application being made later (although it might well affect the outcome). But once a court order has been made ending the wife's rights by formally dismissing her application, that is final. Until recently, such an order could be made only with the consent of both parties, but now the court can impose a clean break if it thinks it right to do so.

The order in which the dismissal is made will usually contain various other provisions – maintenance for the children, for example – so that between the spouses it effects a complete and once-and-for-all disposal of all their claims.

49 | *A wealthy friend of mine pays his wife 'secured maintenance'. What is this?*

The first thing to say is that secured maintenance appears only in very 'big money' cases. It is a way of ensuring that the maintenance is paid whether or not the husband wants to pay it, without the need to enforce payment against him through the court, and it has the further effect of enabling the payments to continue after his death. Both spouse and child maintenance can be ordered to be secured.

The mechanics are rather complicated. In essence the husband is usually ordered to transfer income-producing assets, such as stocks and shares, to trustees. They will pay the income produced to him if and so long as he continues to pay the maintenance as

ordered. If he fails to do so or dies, then the trustees pay the same amount of maintenance to the wife or children out of the investment income.

The proper term for this is a 'secured periodical payments order', and it is clearly possible only where there is enough free capital for the purpose.

50 | *My wife and I have just divorced, and I've agreed to pay her maintenance. For how long will I have to pay it?*

The maximum length of an order is until the death of either party, or until the wife remarries. So if your wife remains single the order can continue until one of you dies. The husband's remarriage will not affect the order as such, but hers terminates the maintenance order automatically.

Most orders are drafted so they are indefinite in this way, but sometimes the court may fix a shorter period – what is coming to be known as 'rehabilitative maintenance'. This might be done where there has been a short but disastrous marriage leaving the wife unable to work for a while; she might get payments limited to a two-year maximum, for example, to tide her over until she gets back on her feet. It can also be done where the wife is studying at the time of the divorce to finance the rest of her studies which will then enable her to be self-supporting. It would usually be inappropriate where there are children to be provided for, as she might need help up to the time they are off her hands.

Where secured maintenance is ordered (see Q49), the payments can go on beyond the payer's death unless again the payee remarries.

A maintenance order can be suspended or brought to a premature end or an application can be made for a variation if circumstances change (see Qs116 and 117).

51 | *My husband and I divorced recently and he's going to pay me maintenance. I'm sure he'll pay me regularly. How should we best arrange for the maintenance to be paid?*

The best arrangement is for your husband to pay it by bankers' standing order from his bank account into yours. The main advantage of this method is that there are independent records kept by the banks so there is no room for argument about what has and has not been paid. It also takes care of the practical difficulties of the payer forgetting or being unable to send a cheque or to call with the money on the due day.

If you, the payee, receive Supplementary Benefit,

the DHSS may require the order to be registered in a magistrates' court so it can be 'signed over' to them (see Q65 and SEPARATION, Q35).

52 | *My ex-husband is living with another woman. Will that make a difference to the amount of maintenance I get?*

Yes, it may well do.

Assuming that the maintenance is paid for you and/or the children, one of the chief factors in deciding the amount is what your ex-husband can afford to pay, and the fact that he is sharing a household with someone else will have an important bearing on the amount of maintenance.

If the other woman contributes to the cost of their household this will increase what he can afford to pay you because he will not be alone in shouldering the financial burden of that household. Although the income of your ex-husband's new partner cannot be treated as his as such, by relieving him of expenses or sharing them she is freeing more of his income for his former family.

If, on the other hand, she is being kept by your ex-husband – and if she has no income she will be unable to claim Supplementary Benefit as she is cohabiting so he will have to keep her – then this is again taken into account in deciding what he can afford to pay by way of maintenance. Her existence means that his income is having to support more than himself alone, and the court can therefore order less maintenance. The court will never make an order which will reduce your ex-husband's household to living at below subsistence level, that is, the standard of living his household would have were he to receive Supplementary Benefit.

These rules do not apply just where there is a new partner of the opposite sex. A homosexual relationship would have the same effect. Completely non-sexual arrangements are also treated in the same way. For example, if the ex-husband had adult children living with him who contributed to the household bills he would be able to afford more maintenance; this would also apply were he sharing a flat with a friend or living with his parents.

53 | *My husband, whom I divorced recently, runs his own business. Does that make any difference to the amount of maintenance and capital he should pay me?*

No, not really. The court's powers are the same as in all other cases, and the factors it must consider in

deciding how to use those powers are always the same too.

However, there are a few purely practical considerations that apply in your case which do not apply to the salaried or wage-earning person.

First, it may be more difficult to establish exactly what he earns. There will be no pay slips to look at, and in many cases business accounts do not exist or are downright misleading. You can call in an accountant to advise you if necessary, or the court can draw inferences about what he earns from the standard of living he enjoys.

Second, maintenance is notoriously difficult to enforce against a self-employed person because it is not possible to get an attachment of earnings order (see SEPARATION, Q34) to have it deducted from his pay.

Third, in deciding what to do about the value of the business, the special nature and problems of business assets must be taken into account. There is always the risk of killing the goose that lays the golden eggs: the business may be run from valuable freehold property and have valuable machines or hold valuable stock; their total value must be taken into account in deciding how to share the capital of the family, but the court cannot order much of it to be sold without damaging the business and perhaps crippling it. The courts have said in many cases that they must look less at the value of such assets than at what can in fact be turned into cash, or 'realised'. Judges have spoken of the world of difference which exists between money in the bank and money locked up in farmland, say, or in business property. In most cases the court will see what can be sold without undue damage (perhaps a few acres of a farm) or what the husband can afford to borrow and repay, and order a lump sum to be paid accordingly.

54 | *My wife is the only daughter of elderly wealthy parents. Surely that should be taken into account when the court assesses the maintenance I'm going to pay her and the proportion of the family home she's entitled to?*

This is a difficult question to answer briefly. The starting-point is that among the factors to which the court is bound to have regard are the resources that each party has or 'is likely to have in the foreseeable future'. If, therefore, money or property has already been put into your wife's name it will be a relevant asset.

Similarly, if you can prove that she is likely to come into money in the foreseeable future, that is relevant, especially in deciding what to do about capital assets you jointly own. The problem is one of proving what she will receive. If there is a family trust which provides that she will get money on her parents' deaths, then the court will know what is coming to her. But it will not be good enough if all you can say is that, being an only child, her parents would probably leave their property to her. Furthermore, the court will not order the parents to state their financial resources and what they intend to do with them.

What your wife may inherit is only one of the various factors the court must consider; it must look at all the other facts of the case. If your wife is now living with her parents and has a secure home with low living expenses, or is living with another man, she may not get much from you anyway, at least by way of maintenance.

55 | *My husband works for his father. He receives a low salary and has no assets, but his father's a wealthy man and in time my husband will take over the business. How will this affect the question of maintenance and provision of capital when we divorce?*

The court will have to look at all the circumstances to decide what to do, putting the welfare of any children first and having regard to all the other facts of the case.

To take maintenance first, assuming that you need it, your husband has a low salary and will not be able to afford much. The court will look at both his outgoings and his benefits in kind – free meals at work, a car supplied by his father, and so on – in deciding what he needs to be left with.

As far as capital is concerned, you say that he has no assets at present but is likely to take over his father's business so that he may come into money later. The courts on occasions in cases like yours adjourn the applications for capital and property orders, so that if and when your husband does have some assets you would be able to re-apply. Such a course is rare and would not be taken if you intended to remarry or are self-supporting. If you are in neither position all the court can do now is to safeguard your and, more importantly, the children's financial interests. Whether you would get anything at that future date would depend on all the circumstances at that time.

56 | *My wife and I are getting a divorce and we're negotiating a settlement. I don't think my wife knows about some money I've tucked away in a building society. Must I tell her about it?*

The short answer is that you should tell the whole truth. If you conceal assets or understate your income you might persuade her to accept a lower figure than she should, but the risk is that if a settlement is reached, even if it is embodied in a consent order (see Q36) made by the court (as is usual), it can be overturned on the ground of non-disclosure or misrepresentation. She would then get whatever would have been the correct settlement, and the costs of all this would fall on you.

57 | *My husband left me six years ago, but I've always refused to give him a divorce, mainly because, as I'm now 58, I wanted to feel I would get the widow's pension I'm entitled to under his employers' pension scheme on his death. He's now divorcing me on the grounds that we've been separated for five years. Is there anything I can do?*

Yes. Cases where divorce based on five years' life apart would cause 'grave financial or other hardship' are often defended successfully by women in your position, and the judge may well decide that it would be wrong to dissolve your marriage. Your husband's solicitor will probably advise him of this. To guarantee getting his divorce, your husband should make financial provision for you equivalent to what you would get as his widow. This means he would probably need to take out life insurance which would be payable to you on his death to ensure that any financial hardship would be removed.

It should be said that young wives, who would probably be able to work (at least once the children were old enough) and could provide for their own old age, and wives who are working and building up pensions of their own, are unlikely to be in a position to defend a divorce on the grounds that they would suffer 'grave financial hardship'.

58 | *I agreed with my husband that I would have half the value of the house and no maintenance. Now I want to change my mind and claim more of the house. Can I do that?*

Yes, you can, in that it is always possible to withdraw from an *agreement* and to ask the court to fix who gets what. The trouble is that although the court can and may order something different from what you have agreed, it may take the view that what was agreed is in fact fair and make an order in similar terms. It may also say that where a bargain has been negotiated freely between the parties, with nothing concealed or lied about and no abuse, the agreement should be followed in any event. So don't make an agreement unless you are happy to keep it. Once an agreement about the house – or any capital assets – has been made into a court *order*, as most are on divorce, then it is generally too late to change your mind (see Q41).

59 | *Who will pay the costs of applications for court orders?*

Each party is liable to pay his or her own solicitor's bill in full (unless he or she is legally aided; see Q66). As far as the court is concerned, it may make orders that one party is to pay the other's costs (although each party is responsible for actually paying his or her own solicitor's bill whatever the court orders), and in the usual case of the wife applying for orders against her husband he will have to pay her costs if she succeeds. These 'party and party' costs, as they are known, are almost invariably less than the full amount payable to her solicitor, so she will have a shortfall even assuming that he pays what he is ordered to.

A less obvious but crucial point is that whatever is spent on legal fees will reduce the amount of cash available to the family as a whole, so both parties may be worse off, and indirectly perhaps both sides will be paying. That is always a point to bear in mind in deciding whether to fight or to settle out of court.

60 | *My husband and I have agreed the terms of my financial settlement. Who pays my solicitor's fees, myself or my husband?*

The question of costs should be taken into account as a term of the settlement. If, say, a wife is to receive a lump sum to enable her to buy another house it should be enough to do just that. If she has a large bill to face from her solicitor in connection with the divorce, her solicitor should advise her of the likely amount and ensure that the total sum she will receive is going to cover that as well; if it will not do so she will not be left with enough after paying the bill for the money to do what was intended.

Equally, the husband may be going to increase his mortgage to pay the lump sum, and he will want to know what he has to borrow to raise it and to settle his solicitor's bill.

Thus, both parties should check carefully with their solicitors what the costs position is, preferably getting the answer in writing, so that they know just where they stand before making or accepting any offer. Costs are easy to overlook and can have devastating results if a lot of legal work has been done.

61 | *My husband and I haven't yet agreed the amount of the financial settlement I feel I should get when we divorce. If the matter goes to court, will witnesses be called to give evidence at the hearing?*

Yes, though they will not usually be necessary. Sometimes accountants have to be called where a business is involved to speak about its value and how much money can sensibly be raised without crippling it. In other cases there may be a dispute about the value of the matrimonial home or the cost of an alternative home for one or other party, and surveyors might have to give evidence. Usually, though, that sort of evidence is agreed by the parties and affidavits (sworn written statements) by those experts can be used in court.

62 | *My husband, whom I'm divorcing, is living with another woman. Can I make her swear an affidavit or give evidence about her income and property?*

Presumably you have in mind arguing as part of your case that your husband can afford to make generous provision for you on the basis that his new partner is earning or has capital, so he needs to be left with less of his income or capital than he otherwise would. If he has remarried or the relationship is permanent your argument would be a good one. But the court will not order your husband's new partner to swear an affidavit against her will, and it has no power to do so. Your husband's affidavit will probably give some information and he can be ordered to say what, if any, contributions she makes to his household.

However, she can be ordered to attend court to give evidence under a witness summons in the usual way, though this is rare and there are restrictions on the way in which she can be questioned. As a general rule she cannot be cross-examined by the lawyer for the party calling her, so if you make her come under a witness summons you will have to be satisfied with whatever answers she chooses to give.

63 | *My husband and I are getting a divorce. If we can't agree a settlement and the divorce court has to make a financial or property order in my favour, what will the procedure be?*

There are three main stages in a contested case.

First, the applicant sends to the court an application form, drawn up by a solicitor, together with an 'affidavit of means' – a sworn statement of the applicant's income and other assets; the affidavit is often a standard printed form of questionnaire. Copies of these will be sent to the other party. The other party will then complete and swear a similar affidavit, sending it to the court with a copy to the applicant. The object of these affidavits is to let each party see what the other says he or she has by way of income and assets; copy payslips, business accounts, bank statements, and so on, should be attached.

The second stage consists of each side making enquiries of the other about the contents of the affidavits, requesting further information, copies of other documents, and so on. If information is not supplied in answer to a written request, or if no affidavit is filed at all, an application to the court can be made for an order directing that this be done.

The third stage is the hearing, which takes place in private before the registrar of the court, at which each side may give evidence and be cross-examined by the other party's solicitor or barrister. Each party's lawyer will address the registrar, arguing for a particular type of order – say, for maintenance. Lastly, the registrar will give judgment and make the order.

64 | *Is it ever too late to apply for court orders on divorce? What if I were to remarry?*

The basic rule is that it is never too late to apply as long as the applicant has not remarried. Provided that the party has made a formal application before his or her remarriage the court can hear the case after the remarriage and make orders then, though only orders for capital and for maintenance for any children – not maintenance for the ex-spouse who has remarried.

The formal application made by the petitioner will usually be in the 'prayer' of the divorce petition (see page 81), so provided that nothing is deleted from the printed form the necessary step will have been taken. A respondent who does not defend the divorce will have to use a special form, called a 'notice of application', of which a copy will be sent to the court and the other party. Should he or she remarry without having done so it will be too late to apply, and what lawyers call the 'remarriage trap' will have sprung.

Even though a party may still be able to apply, or may even have made the formal application, the court may decide that it would be unfair to make orders if too long a time has passed before the application is taken to the stage of a hearing. Where several years have gone by and it has not looked as if the applicant was going to do anything, the other party may have been lulled into a false sense of security and planned his or her life accordingly.

65 | *My neighbour and I are both divorced. She says her maintenance order has been 'registered' in the magistrates' court. What does that mean? Why has it been done in her case and not in mine?*

To deal first with why it has been done: it is probably because either she is having problems with her ex-husband paying the maintenance or she is drawing Supplementary Benefit, or quite possibly both.

When maintenance is ordered on divorce it is an order of the divorce county court and payment is made directly from one party to the other either in cash, by cheque or standing order. The money does not go through the court. If the maintenance is not paid, the payee can take enforcement steps in a county court, but the procedure can be expensive and awkward, and it may be difficult to get Legal Aid. Also, if the payee is claiming Supplementary Benefit, the maintenance to which she is entitled counts as income and may cut her weekly Benefit pound for pound, whether the maintenance is paid regularly or not.

Registration of the order in a magistrates' court simply means that the order is transferred there by the county court; it is just a matter of form filling. Once that happens, the enforcement and Benefit problems are much reduced. The effect of the registration is that your neighbour's ex-husband must now pay the maintenance to the magistrates' court rather than to his ex-wife; the court will pass on what he pays either to her or, if she is drawing Supplementary Benefit, to the DHSS (see SEPARATION, Q35).

If the ex-husband stops paying, the clerk to the justices will issue a summons for him to come to court. Payments can be then enforced by an attachment of earnings order (see SEPARATION, Q34) or by committal to prison (or at least the threat of it). The payee should draw the court's attention to the arrears for this to happen, and the procedure is much easier than it is in a county court; it does not usually need a solicitor.

Legal Aid and the statutory charge

66 | *Can I get Legal Aid to cover the financial and property aspects of my divorce?*

Legal Aid (see page 490) is available for the financial and property sides of a divorce, provided of course that you are financially eligible. Your solicitor will advise you whether you are eligible and will provide you with the necessary form; he or she will help you fill it in.

The general rule is that application should be made as soon as possible. It is not necessary to wait until a hotly contested dispute breaks out, because a Legal Aid Certificate covers trying to negotiate an agreed settlement as well as the hostile and determined steps that may have to be taken later.

67 | *I've applied for Legal Aid to claim maintenance and a share in the value of the house. A friend has warned me to watch out for something called the 'statutory charge'. What is this?*

If a legally aided person succeeds with his or her case and 'recovers or preserves' cash or property as a result of work done under a Legal Aid Certificate, the Law Society, as custodians of the Legal Aid Fund, has a duty to recoup the Fund's expenditure from that cash or property in the form of the 'statutory charge'.

Cash or property will be 'recovered' if it has been claimed and won by the assisted person. Property is 'preserved' if it has been claimed by the opponent and that claim has been successfully resisted in whole or in part by the assisted person. Accordingly, one must look at who claimed what and at the final outcome of the case. The formal court documents are the main place to see what the claims were, and the outcome can be seen from the terms of any court order made or from the terms of any agreed settlement.

The amount covered by the statutory charge is the Legal Aid Fund's 'deficiency' under the Legal Aid Certificate. The procedure is as follows:

The Fund pays to the lawyers of the person claiming Legal Aid an amount of costs assessed by the court in the process known as 'taxation'. This is the Fund's outlay. The Fund receives the assisted person's contribution to Legal Aid (if any) and whatever the opponent pays by way of party and party costs (see Q59). The difference between these two is the Fund's deficiency, which is repayable by the assisted person out of what was recovered or preserved.

Suppose that a wife who has paid a contribution of

£100 towards her Legal Aid recovers a lump sum of £10,000 from her husband, who also pays £150 costs, and her solicitor is paid £850 from the Legal Aid Fund. The deficiency of the Fund is:

costs paid to her solicitor		£850
less		
her contribution	£100	
costs paid by her husband	£150	
		£250
		£600

The wife will therefore receive £10,000 less £600 – £9,400.

Most commonly, the statutory charge bites into the value of the family home, which is likely to be in dispute at some stage in the case.

68 | *Are there any exemptions from the statutory charge?*

Yes. Maintenance is not subject to the charge at all, and the first £2,500 of any capital, whether cash or a share in the home or any other asset, is also exempt in a matrimonial case.

Where a parent has a Legal Aid Certificate, money or property going to the children is outside the charge because it is not 'recovered' by the assisted person (see Q67), but the courts will not allow this rule to be used by a parent to avoid the charge by his or her asking for everything to go to the children.

69 | *Is the statutory charge payable if there is no cash recovered?*

If there is no cash recovered, or not enough to meet the charge, the charge will be applied to any property, which in most cases means the matrimonial home.

Taking the figures given in Q67, had the wife recovered or preserved a £10,000 share in the value of the home, that share is subject to the charge as if it were cash. The Law Society will not insist that the house be sold at once to pay off the charge, but if and when it is sold the £600 charge will be paid out of her share of the proceeds of the sale. The Society will put a notice with the title deeds (and sometimes take other steps) to ensure that this will happen.

70 | *I had Legal Aid and lost part of my share in the house to my wife, so I'm worse off. Surely the statutory charge will not bite into what I have left?*

Yes, it can. The charge does not only apply when the assisted person has actually gained from the proceed-ings. Even if you have just preserved something as a result of legally aided proceedings, the charge can apply to that.

Suppose that the family house is jointly owned and that each spouse has an equal share in the value before the case starts. If the wife seeks an order to give her the house outright but gets only three-quarters of the value, the husband will have 'preserved' a quarter and the statutory charge will bite into that.

71 | *Does the statutory charge apply only to the costs of the financial and property applications themselves?*

No. The charge applies to *all* work done in the same proceedings. If there is a divorce pending, there may be custody or access disputes or injunctions sought and these will usually be dealt with as part of the divorce case. If so, they will all be covered by the same Legal Aid Certificate as the one that provides for the financial and property aspects. That being so, all the costs from all the various matters dealt with in the divorce will be added together and, if cash or property is recovered or preserved by work done under the Legal Aid Certificate, it will be subject to the charge accordingly.

This can cause some nasty shocks. In one well-known case a Mr Jones received a divorce petition from his wife, and she at once sought an injunction to keep him away from the home. Her divorce petition claimed an order transferring the jointly owned home to her. He applied for Legal Aid to oppose both the injunction and her financial and property claims. His solicitors did several hundred pounds' worth of work in connection with the injunction. The house was dealt with on the basis of an easily reached agreement that she would buy out his share for less than half the value. The result was that his costs for the injunction work were taken out of the lump sum he received, although very little work was actually done to arrive at the settlement regarding the property. He had 'preserved' part of the value of the house, and accordingly the cost of *all* the work done under the Certificate came out of it.

In practice, it is usually injunction or custody and access dispute costs that cause large sums to be payable under the charge.

72 | *Can anything be done to reduce the impact of the charge?*

The thing to think about all the time is the Fund's deficiency. The lower that deficiency can be kept, the less will be the charge.

First, do not take unnecessary proceedings. Custody and access disputes, injunction applications and fighting for a small advantage on the financial side all add to the costs and increase the Fund's outlay. Try to find out from your solicitor the likely cost of such steps before you decide to take them so you can weigh the pros and cons.

Second, try to agree as much as possible with your spouse. This will keep down costs by avoiding expensive disputes.

Third, think carefully about costs before you make or accept an offer of settlement. If the other party agrees to pay costs this will reduce the deficiency. In any case, ask your solicitor what the charge is likely to be.

Lastly, although it will not affect the size of the charge, its impact can be reduced by taking property in the shape of the home, or maintenance rather than a lump sum of cash. Maintenance is exempt, capital over £2,500 is not; the charge applies to property, but the Law Society has a discretion not to enforce its payment until the property is sold.

73 | *Does the statutory charge apply even if we agree how to allocate our property and assets under a negotiated settlement?*

Yes. It does not matter whether the case ends after a fight in court or if there is a negotiated settlement. Money or property will be 'recovered' or 'preserved' just the same. The obvious difference is that the charge will be less in most cases where there is a settlement because the Legal Aid Fund's outlay will be less, the lawyers having had less work to do.

74 | *My house is subject to the statutory charge but I'd like to move. Will I have to pay off the charge?*

The Law Society has a discretion to allow the original house to be sold and another bought, with the charge being transferred to the second house. The charge will then be paid when the second house is sold.

This will be allowed only if consent is sought before the sale and hardship would result from a refusal. Among other conditions, the Law Society must also see that there is sufficient 'equity' in the new house for the charge eventually to be paid, and that the house will be lived in by the assisted person with dependent children or that the move is needed for reasons of health, disability or employment.

You must seek the Law Society's consent before you take the matter of selling very far.

Children: maintenance, custody and access

75 | *When I went to see my solicitor about a divorce, he mentioned something about a conciliation service. What is this, and what does it do?*

Conciliation schemes are found in most parts of the country. They exist to try to settle the differences between the parties to a divorce and to achieve sensible and civilised arrangements between them. Most are organised by the courts themselves, in particular the courts' own welfare officers who carry out most conciliation work, with the legal profession and other bodies such as the probation service. While the welfare officers accept that the marriage is at an end, they discuss with the parties the parties' difficulties and disagreements to encourage them to compromise and to avoid the bitterness and distress which fighting things out in court is bound to cause. The conciliation service is especially valuable in the case of disputes about the custody of and access to children.

There is no nationally financed conciliation service, and no formal court rules apply to insist that parties attend for conciliation interviews. Nevertheless, if there's a disagreement about custody and access the court may adjourn the case for conciliation to take place to try to settle it. Solicitors should alert their clients to local schemes and also to the National Family Conciliation Service, which can supply a list of affiliated services. The financial arrangements differ, and in some places people may be asked to pay a small fee towards the costs of the service.

76 | *My husband and I are considering getting a divorce. Will the court automatically take our children into account?*

Yes. To ensure that young children are not overlooked and that their well-being is safeguarded, the court cannot make the decree absolute of divorce, finally dissolving the marriage, until the judge has considered the arrangements that exist for their welfare under Section 41 of the Matrimonial Causes Act 1973. That Section number is specified because it is a vital provision, and also because 'Section 41' is a convenient shorthand expression to refer to types of hearings before the court, and so on.

The children to whom Section 41 applies are children under the age of 16 or under the age of 18 if still in education or in vocational training. Children over 18 are not covered unless the court so directs – in the case of disability, for instance, or very occasionally if they are in full-time further or higher education.

The judge must usually declare either:

● that there are no children of the family within Section 41, that is, there are no children at all or they are over the ages mentioned in the preceding paragraph, or
● that there are children within Section 41, naming them, and that in respect of each one the arrangements for his or her welfare are satisfactory or the best that can be devised in the circumstances, or that it is impracticable for the parties to make such arrangements.

Unless and until such a declaration is made, the decree cannot be made absolute, and if by mistake it is made absolute that decree is void.

77 | *How does the court satisfy itself about the arrangements for the children?*

The petition (see page 80) will show whether or not there are children within Section 41 (see Q76). If there are, the petition will have been accompanied by a statement signed by the petitioner setting out the financial and custody and access arrangements, and the respondent's acknowledgement of service of the petition enables him or her to indicate what, if any, dispute there is.

The registrar of the court will consider these arrangements at the same time as deciding whether the petition is proved and whether a decree nisi can be granted. If there are no children within Section 41, the judge can so declare without more ado.

If there are children within Section 41, the registrar will look at the papers to see if the proposals are clear and undisputed. If they are, an appointment will be fixed for the petitioner to come before the judge in private so that the judge can talk to him or her about the children and make the Section 41 declaration, all being well. The respondent can attend too, and this is encouraged. The judge will usually make the necessary custody and access orders, and may make an order for child maintenance if the amount has been agreed. If the judge is not happy with the arrangements, the case can be adjourned to obtain a welfare officer's report or for conciliation (see Q75) if a dispute has arisen.

The Section 41 appointment with the judge is quite an informal occasion. It usually takes place on the day the decree nisi is pronounced, and the judge will usually spend 10 or 15 minutes talking to the parents about the children and how the arrangements are working, especially over access. The judges are always friendly and understand what the parties are going through.

78 | *How does the court go about assessing child maintenance?*

The Matrimonial Causes Act 1973 lays down factors to which the court is to have regard, and they are very similar to those regarding the case of spouses (see Q44); needs and resources are the main ones.

The amount will usually depend mainly on the age of the child (children get more expensive as they grow older) and the financial position of the family. At the lower end of the income scale the courts tend to think in terms of ordering the amount that would be payable for the child by way of Supplementary Benefit, assuming of course that the father can afford even that much. If there are several children he may not be able to do so. In the middle range most courts have an informal tariff scale depending upon the age of the child. In the upper range the amount of maintenance may take account of school fees.

In practice, where both spouse and child maintenance is to be paid it is quite common to pitch the child maintenance on the high side and to cut the wife's because this can produce a better income tax result, especially if the wife has some income of her own. This is all part of the 'net effect' approach described in Q44.

79 | *For how long will I have to continue to pay maintenance for my children?*

Maintenance for children is payable at least until the

children reach 17 years of age, the age that marks the end of compulsory education. This can be extended to age 18 and even beyond, depending on the age of the child when the order is made. If the order is made at 16, say, and the child looks certain to stay on at school to 18, the order will run until the child's eighteenth birthday. An order may run beyond the eighteenth birthday if the child is in full- or part-time higher or further education. So even though a child may be over the age of majority, new orders can be made or former orders extended if he or she is a student or apprentice of some kind.

80 | *I remarried immediately after my divorce. While my ex-wife has custody of our children, I feel my new wife and I would have got custody if I'd fought for it. What does the court pay attention to in deciding a custody or access dispute?*

The court's duty in deciding any question about the upbringing of a child under the age of 18 is to follow Section 1 of the Guardianship of Minors Act 1971, namely that 'the welfare of the child is the first and paramount consideration'.

This rule applies in all courts and in all types of proceedings, whether on divorce, in wardship cases (see Q98) or where custody or access is the only issue between the parents (or third parties, such as grandparents, seeking access to a grandchild). It applies not only to custody and access disputes, but in disputes on other matters too, such as a change of name (see Q118).

The child's welfare therefore takes clear priority over the so-called rights of the parents, and indeed justice between them as such. Custody or access will not be regarded as a reward for good 'spousely' conduct, nor will they be refused as a sort of punishment for bad behaviour.

An example much beloved by law students concerned a clergyman whose wife was having an affair with a youth club leader, with whom she intended to set up home. She applied for a custody order in respect of the two young children before she left, and she succeeded. The father took the case to the Court of Appeal, which said that however bad her conduct as a wife might have been she had never been anything but a good mother, and looking at all the facts the children's welfare would be best served by giving custody to her, unjust though this might seem to the completely innocent father.

81 | *What is the procedure if there is a dispute between the parents over custody or access?*

The practice here differs a bit between individual courts, but the judge will still have to make a Section 41 order (see Q76), and in addition the dispute will have to be dealt with. If necessary the judge himself or herself will have to decide who is to have custody or what the access arrangements shall be.

The registrar will have seen the existence of the dispute from the papers before him or her, and will have decided that the judge could not deal with the matter in the few informal minutes of a normal Section 41 appointment. The parties will therefore not usually be given such an appointment but will be told instead that they must make a formal application for a hearing before the judge to deal with the matter. At this stage the parties should definitely see solicitors if they have not done so already, because such a hearing is a formal trial with major issues at stake. Legal Aid is available, subject to the means of each party.

At that hearing, which will be in private, evidence on oath will be given in the normal way, with cross-examination by the parties' lawyers, and there will be a court welfare officer's report on the circumstances of both the parents and the child. The judge will reach a decision and make a Section 41 declaration as well as the order for custody or access which had been fought out. The decree absolute can then go through.

The differences between the courts centre around the use that may be made in such cases of any conciliation service operating locally (see Q75). In some areas the parties may be referred to a conciliator to see if the matter can be settled by negotiation and counselling before a hearing is fixed.

CASE C

Michael and Helen are in their early thirties and have two children, Ian and Jane, aged eight and six. Michael has a supervisory job at a local factory. The matrimonial home is a modern, semi-detached, three-bedroomed house bought in Michael's sole name with a mortgage three years ago. Were the house to be sold, there would be about £8,000 left after paying off the mortgage and sale costs. A year ago Michael left Helen, saying he was fed up with married life, and moved in with his younger brother. Since he left he has paid the mortgage and other household bills and has sent Helen money for the children each week. After drawing Supplementary Benefit for several weeks, Helen took a part-time office job with hours that fit in with the children's school times. Helen now wants a divorce, and has filed a petition based on Michael's behaviour. She has no intention of remarrying and has no new partner.

PROBABLE OUTCOME *The main problems here are housing and maintenance. It is clear that the house cannot be sold to provide two homes. The present home seems to be the minimum size appropriate for Helen and two children, who as a boy and a girl should not share a room as they grow older. Thus, the likely outcome is that the home will be retained unsold until the children have both finished their full-time education (or reached 18, if later), though the court would be likely to say expressly that the house should be sold earlier if Helen remarries, dies or moves out in the meantime. An order for an equal division of the eventual sale proceeds would be likely, even though the home is in Michael's sole name, because it was bought during the marriage probably as a result of joint efforts. Such an order would provide a secure home for the children while they need it. Michael has a home with his brother, and even if that does not last the court's opinion will be that a single man can find housing quite easily and that his needs are far less than the family's.*

Helen will also need maintenance. Michael is already paying the household bills and sending money for the children. Although Helen earns, her income is small, and she will need help if only of an amount similar to the present payments he is making because she is unlikely to be able to pay the mortgage and other bills out of what she earns. She might be happy with an order for maintenance of the same amount as he now pays. On the other hand, Michael can probably afford more, depending on his income and outgoings, because he is not keeping anyone else and by sharing a flat with his brother he is presumably paying only half the bills.

Helen should ensure that she claims all the state benefits available to her, including One-Parent Benefit, Family Income Supplement and Housing Benefit. It appears that she is not eligible for Supplementary Benefit since she no longer claims it, although she should check again once the order is made.

82 | *In a custody dispute, what factors do the court take into account in deciding what is in the child's best interest?*

The court must look at all the circumstances of the case. It will place great reliance on the reports produced by the court's own welfare officers, who will have interviewed both parents, their new partners, if any, the children, and sometimes their school teachers, grandparents and anyone else who can give relevant information. These reports are prepared because the court will want to reach a decision based on as much evidence as can be gathered away from the artificial atmosphere of the court room. The court itself will usually want to hear evidence from the parents and others, and may want to talk to the children too.

There are two rules of thumb which are often applied, these being that a young child, especially a girl, usually needs the care of the natural mother, and that it is generally wrong to split up brothers and sisters. These rules are not absolute, though.

Continuity of care is very important, too. The court will never take a child away from an established home unless there is very good reason for doing so, especially where this would also involve loss of friends and a change of school. Similarly, the court will want to see that there are arrangements for the child to be looked after all the time; a non-working mother is usually better than a working father helped by a grandparent or child-minders.

Other factors include the characters and personalities of the parties and their new partners, their relationships with the child, the child's own expressed wishes if he is mature enough to know his own mind and these are not against his own long-term interests, the quality of the home environment each claimant can provide, occasionally religious or ethnic or social considerations, and the past conduct of the parties as parents – a parent who has abandoned the family for some time for no good reason may find that counting against him or her, and child abuse or certain sexual criminal convictions may be decisive.

83 | *I have a daughter of 14 by my late husband and two sons by my current husband. If my husband and I get divorced, can the court make orders for custody and maintenance for my daughter as well as my two sons?*

Yes. In all cases the court is concerned with a 'child of the family', which is a term that covers more than just the legitimate offspring of the parties. The court's powers and duties can extend to other children provided that they fall within that definition.

A child of the family may be either

● a child of both parties to the marriage, including their adopted child, or
● any other child (other than a foster child placed with them by a local authority or voluntary organisation) who has been *treated* by them as a child of their family.

The court will almost certainly regard your daughter as falling within the second category; your sons fall within the first. Who has been treated as a child of the family and included as a member of the family will be decided as a matter of pure fact by the court's looking at the behaviour of the couple towards the child.

There is nothing in the second category to require true paternity to be known, so that if a wife has a child by an adulterous relationship and the husband treats that child as a child of the family, it will be a child of the family whether or not he knew it was not his.

A child of both parties born after they separate will be a child of the family within the first category. A child born to the wife after separation which is not the husband's cannot be a child of the family because it is not the child of both parties and nor has the husband treated it as a child of the family.

Special factors apply where the court is contemplating making a maintenance order against a party in favour of a child who is not the child of that party. The court will look at whether he knew the child was not his, the basis on which he assumed responsibility, and whether anyone else (such as the real father, if still alive) is liable to maintain the child.

84 | *Does the court ever refuse access?*

The court certainly has the power to refuse access altogether, but it very rarely does so. Access is not regarded as a right of a parent but as the right of the child to know and to have a continuing relationship with both his or her parents, and maintaining that relationship will almost invariably be in the best interests of the child's welfare.

Thus, only if access would militate against the child's interests would the court withhold it completely. Reasons for this may include the fact that the parent concerned is a positively bad influence on the child or is a danger to him or her, perhaps because of a drug addiction or convictions for child abuse or sexual assault on that child or others.

Access can be difficult for the child to cope with emotionally, and some children are so completely upset by access that it has to be stopped for that reason alone. This is very rare indeed, and when it happens it is generally a symptom of the relationship between the parents. Most cases can be dealt with less drastically by counselling and conciliation (see Q75).

85 | *What is the difference between 'custody' and 'care and control'?*

That is a very difficult question to answer briefly. Custody, in its everyday sense, carries with it the idea of the possession of something – a man might be in police custody, or you might leave your coat in the custody of a cloakroom attendant. In most cases the same idea applies to custody of a child – the parent with custody has possession of the child in the sense that he or she has the child living with him or her.

As a matter of law, though, custody is a much wider term and really means the whole bundle of rights that a parent has over a child – the right to decide the child's education, medical treatment, marriage under the age of 18, religious upbringing and a whole range of others as well as the right to possession itself.

The right to physical possession can be called the right to care and control, and consequently where one person has custody he or she will have care and control if nothing else is said. The term 'care and control' needs to be used only where the bundle of rights called custody is split up in some way so that the child is to make his or her home with a person who does not have sole custody. This most commonly happens where the order of the court gives custody to both parents jointly, but with care and control to one. The child lives with that one, but both parents have a joint say in all major matters affecting the child.

86 | *What are the most commonly made custody orders?*

There are two types that are commonly made. The most common is an order that gives custody to one parent and access to the other. The custodial parent will have care and control by implication, and the child will therefore make his or her home with that parent. The other has the right to see the child by virtue of the order for access.

The other is what is normally known as a 'joint custody order', which gives custody to the parents jointly, with care and control to one parent and access to the other. The day-to-day effect is just the same, but the order gives the parent with whom the child is not living an express right to a joint say in major matters affecting the child.

A joint custody order should usually be made only where the parties are both good parents and are likely to agree on questions affecting the child. The court would be unlikely to impose such an order against the wish of either party.

87 | Is there any real difference between an ordinary custody order and a joint custody order?

No, not really. If a dispute arose between the parents, the court would decide what was in the best interests of the child and act accordingly, whatever the order made on divorce might originally have said.

The theoretical difference is that under a joint order both parents expressly have an equal say in matters affecting the child's welfare, whereas if one party has sole custody he or she has the rights alone. However, the Court of Appeal has said several times that a parent who does not have custody still has a right to be consulted by the other parent on major matters, and he or she has an undoubted right to take any question back to the court for a decision.

So the difference is in reality largely psychological – the parties may recognise that the breakdown of the marriage does not affect the parent–child relationship, and, apart from an order directing with whom the child shall live, the court is not disturbing their equal concern and rights by making a joint order. Put another way, no one has 'won' or 'lost' custody.

88 | Are there any other types of order the court can make regarding children?

Yes, although they are very rare.

A 'split order', as it is sometimes known, can be made. This will give care and control to one parent with custody and access to the other. The parent given care and control will provide the child's home, but the other will take the major decisions. These orders are made only when one parent can provide a home while the other cannot and the former is not a particularly responsible person compared with the latter. There will usually be a 'supervision order' made to back it up, which involves a social worker keeping a careful eye on things.

The court can make orders giving custody or care and control to persons other than the parents themselves if it is in the child's best interests. Where a marriage between a very young couple breaks down and neither is mature or capable enough to provide a home, a grandparent may be the best person to do so, or a brother or sister of one party.

If there is a need for it the court can make a supervision order, imposing on the local authority or the court's own welfare officers a duty to keep in close touch with the family and to report back if there is anything amiss, and if there is no one to whom the child can be safely entrusted the court can place him or her in the care of the local authority.

89 | Are there any standard terms contained in custody orders?

A custody order on divorce is produced on a printed form with the names of the parties and the individual provisions about custody and access filled in. That form has two paragraphs printed on it which are standard terms (unless the court has agreed to delete one because, for example, one parent is emigrating).

The first refers to the child's surname, and provides that no step is to be taken which would result in the child being known by another name without the consent of the other party or an order of the court. It is not a criminal offence to change the child's name, but if the wife, say, remarried and registered the child at school under her new married name, the father might apply to the court for an order for a change back (see Q118).

The second deals with removing the child from the country. It says that the child should not be removed without the consent of the other party or the court, with special provisions about short trips for holidays. If there is a serious threat by a parent to snatch the child and to go abroad permanently, other steps are taken to deal with this (see Qs98 and 99).

90 | At what stage in the divorce are these various orders made?

By far the majority are made on or after the grant of the decree nisi, and most are made at the short informal Section 41 hearing before the judge at the time when the declaration of satisfaction with the arrangements for the child's welfare is made (see Qs76 and 77). The court cannot make a decree absolute without a Section 41 declaration.

The court's powers arise as soon as the petition is filed, though, and where there is a dispute about the child, or where the court grants an injunction (see SEPARATION, Q 13) to protect one party from violence or threat, it may make an order for custody or care and control or access at that stage. This is usually only on an interim basis to cover the short term.

9 1 | *Can a custody or access order be changed later?*

Yes, indeed it can. It is never possible to prevent a parent from taking a question affecting a child back before the court if he or she feels it is necessary.

At one end of the spectrum the court certainly has power to take a child away from the parent who was given custody and to give custody to the other parent, or even someone else if the circumstances demand it. This is very rare, but it can be done.

At the other end, a parent with an order for access who changes his or her job and as a result works different shifts or at weekends can if necessary ask the court to redefine the arrangements.

Since custody includes all matters affecting the child's welfare, other matters can be brought back to the court as well, such as a dispute about schooling, or medical treatment where there is a dispute about blood transfusions and the like, although these are uncommon.

9 2 | *My ex-wife has custody of our daughter and I have an order for reasonable access. I usually take her out every Saturday and have her to stay over*

the weekend. Now she's saying I can only see her every other week and never overnight. Can she do that?

When the court made your order for 'reasonable access' it was saying two things: first, that you have the right to see your child and spend time with her, so access must not be refused altogether by your wife, and, second, that the amount and frequency of that access is to be left to you and her to agree. You would have agreed on set times each week or month which would be kept to, or you might agree changes to fit in with your other commitments, holidays, and so on. The order lays down nothing rigid. You are also free to agree that your daughter stays with you, as you have done.

In such a case, if the parents have an access dispute, where access is being refused or the parties are at loggerheads over the amount and times, or over whether a particular person is or is not going to be brought into contact with the children, then an application can be made to the court for it to 'define' the access. Such disputes are increasingly being settled by conciliation (see Q 7 5), but if this fails the court will lay down a rigid timetable providing exactly when and by whom the child is to be collected and when he or she is to be returned. There is then no flexibility at all.

'Staying access' simply means that the child will be away overnight, often for a weekend or for several nights on holiday, with the non-custodial parent. This is very often agreed by the parents as part of reasonable access, but it can also be ordered as part of defined access after a dispute. Staying access is generally good for all concerned, especially the child, who maintains a closer relationship with the other parent than day visits allow. Staying access is nearly always to be encouraged, and the courts are becoming readier to order it expressly when defining access.

9 3 | *I don't mind the children seeing their father, but I don't want them anywhere near the woman he now lives with. Can I prevent it?*

This is a common feeling where the husband has left to live with another woman, or, the other way round, if the wife left for another man and the father has custody. Emotionally it is very understandable because there is probably very real resentment for the interloper on the part of the deserted spouse.

But it is most unlikely that the court would see it as a good reason to refuse access or to impose any restrictions to keep the children from seeing their parent's new partner. Unless he or she is an obviously bad influence on the child – say, by being a drug taker or a person with convictions for child abuse – the court will probably take the line that he or she is a part of the parent's life and household and that the children should not be kept away.

If you've withheld access to your children for some time, the court might order, or at any rate suggest, that when access to their father is resumed his new partner should not be present for the first few occasions. Also, if a welfare officer is producing a report or trying to conciliate (see Q 7 5) before a court hearing, the same suggestion would probably be made as a matter of common sense. A long-term ban is really out of the question in most cases.

94 | *My son's marriage has broken down. Can I demand to see my grandchildren?*

The chances are that you will continue to see them, because if your daughter-in-law gets custody your son should get access and can bring them to visit you. That is the way most grandparents keep in contact with their grandchildren.

If that does not happen for any reason, you can apply to the court for an access order in your own favour. Where there is a divorce or other court proceedings between the parents of the children and a custody order is made, a grandparent can apply for an access order more or less as part and parcel of those proceedings. If not, you would have to take the rather large step of making your grandchildren wards of court (see Q 9 8), and this is very rarely done. In either case, such an application to the court will need a solicitor

The court deciding the case would put the grandchildren's interests first, and, where there has been a close relationship between you which the children's welfare dictates should continue, an access order would probably be made. Your own distress at being kept from seeing them would not be a very important factor.

Although you can apply for your own access order, you would probably do better to support your son's application for access, in particular staying access for them to stay with him. You could then either go to stay with them or have them to stay with you.

95 | *I'm 19 and I'm just going to start my university course. Now my parents have parted and are getting a divorce, I'm worried that they won't pay their contribution towards my grant. What is the position?*

First, your parents should contact the local authority which pays your grant to see if their contribution can be reduced because of their changed circumstances: now that they are living as two households, life is more expensive for them than it was before. Then whoever actually pays the parental contribution should make sure that he or she gets income tax relief on the payments; this can be done by means of a deed of covenant under rules that apply in all cases, not just on marriage breakdown.

Since there is a divorce the court can make orders for maintenance. Even though you are over 18, because you are a student an order can be made for you.

It is unlikely that your parents will refuse point blank to pay their contribution, but if that happens you can yourself apply for maintenance orders against either or both of them. You would have to apply to the court which is dealing with their divorce and you would need to see a solicitor because this is a difficult and technical procedure. Very few people ever take the step of suing their own parents – which is what this really means – but a few years ago a woman student, the daughter of divorced parents, did so and the court established that the right exists.

96 | *My ex-wife, who had custody of the children, has died. What happens now?*

As the surviving parent you now regain sole custody of your children. The custody order the court made had effect only while both you and your ex-wife were alive. Even if she had remarried so that the children had a stepfather, he has no legal rights as such.

There are only two possible complications here (assuming that there is no local authority care order) and neither is at all likely.

First, the divorce court can declare a parent unfit to have custody, in which case the automatic regaining of custody would not apply, although the law is strangely silent about what then happens. Such orders are very rare indeed and are made only where a parent has been guilty of child abuse of a serious kind.

Second, your ex-wife might have made a will appointing her second husband or someone else as a 'testamentary guardian'. Since you are still alive that has no real effect, other than to make it easier from a purely procedural point of view for that person to apply to the court for custody against you.

It is possible for anyone with a sufficient interest to bring a question affecting a child before the court, so a stepparent or a relative could apply for custody, though this is very rare, and the court would make whatever order was in the best interest of the child.

CASE D

Ken and Lorna are both in their fifties. The marriage had been unhappy for many years but they decided to stay together for the sake of the children. The children are now independent and Ken has decided that the time has come to part. He is head of department at a local school; Lorna does not work and has not done so for many years. Their home is a large Victorian semi-detached house in quite a good area; the mortgage has been paid off. Both could probably make out a case to get a divorce on the other's behaviour, but they would prefer to get a decree by consent in two years' time.

PROBABLE OUTCOME *Again, housing and maintenance are the main problems. The present house appears to be too big for one party to occupy alone; it is also expensive to heat and to run generally. The sensible course would be to sell it, and that would produce a good amount of cash.*

Lorna is in the weaker financial position, having no job or apparent earning capacity. Her prime need is a home, and it would be sensible to think of using some of the proceeds from the sale of the house to buy a property for her which she would own outright – something convenient and cheap for her to run. Money will be needed to furnish and carpet it, and the costs of the purchase must not be overlooked either. If she drives and now has the use of the family car, it might be reasonable for her to have some money to buy a car of her own. Lorna will also need maintenance, the amount depending in part on her reasonable needs. The lower outgoings from having a smaller house would reduce those needs.

Ken would expect to get some of the proceeds from the sale of the house, which he could use to put down on a small property for himself. He would probably need a mortgage, but he should have a high enough income to pay it and he can probably also look forward to a lump sum from his pension scheme when he retires, which should pay off the balance of the mortgage. They will thus both own their own homes outright by the time Ken retires. Any savings are resources which can be used in the same way as the value of the house – to go towards providing homes for the couple.

Lorna's main fear will be for the future. What will happen if Ken dies or retires? When he retires he will have a pension and will continue to pay maintenance, although it will be reduced because he will be able to afford less. When he dies, though, Lorna would not be his widow after a divorce – just a surviving ex-wife. As such, she would not be entitled to draw a widow's pension from his job, just a state retirement pension. Because there is not enough capital around to provide Lorna with an income for life, she might think about refusing to have a divorce. But if Ken can divorce her, as seems likely, relying on her behaviour, she cannot stop him. She would at least have a secure home, which is also a capital asset that she could use to provide an income from a lodger or to take out an income contract with an insurance company which will pay regular amounts and will be repaid out of the value of the house on her death. Lorna should not rely on a promise that Ken might make to leave her anything in his will, because he can always revoke it. She could, however, make a claim for provision out of his estate on death under the Inheritance (Provision for Family and Dependants) Act 1975.

As a natural parent you would probably have the strongest case.

One other point arises, and that concerns the children's maternal grandparents. Now that their daughter has died they can seek an order for access to their grandchildren if they wish. If your children have a close relationship with their grandparents you would presumably want it to continue in the children's interests in any event, but were you to refuse to let them see each other the court could make an access order in the grandparents' favour, principally for the benefit of the children.

97 | *We got a divorce last year and I have custody of our 10-year-old twins. I'm now going to marry an American, and we'd like to settle in the States, taking the children to live with us. My ex-husband says he'll stop the children going. Can he do that?*

If you look at the custody order the court made when you got your divorce, you will see that it contains a clause saying that the children must not be taken out of England and Wales under the age of 18 without the permission of the court, except for fixed periods with the consent of the other parent. It also has a note saying that your husband can request the Passport Office not to issue passports for them without his knowledge. These are standard terms appearing on all divorce court custody orders.

Your correct course is to go back to the divorce court and apply for an order giving permission for what you want to do. The judge who hears the case will reach a decision on the basis of whatever is in the best interests of the children, and if you will provide a secure and loving home for them in America you will probably get what you want. Be warned, though – your ex-husband may try to get custody himself if he can provide properly for them here. Everything will depend on the particular facts.

You would be well advised to try to agree with your ex-husband what is to happen so that the court can be asked to make its order by consent. In particular, try to come to an agreement with him about access, perhaps for the children to visit him for holidays once a year so that his natural fear about never seeing his children again is overcome.

You should certainly not just take the children abroad. If your ex-husband finds out you are leaving he could take steps very quickly to prevent the children from going, and you could prejudice your chances in the long run. Equally, even if you got to America with the children, your ex-husband might follow you and apply to the American courts for the return of the children. You could then finish up with a long and expensive period of uncertainty.

98 | *What is a ward of court?*

A ward of court is any child under 18 who is the subject of wardship proceedings brought in the Family Division of the High Court. All matters affecting a ward of court are entirely subject to the direction of the High Court – in effect, it is as if the ward is the child of the court. The court appoints a 'guardian' – normally a parent – for the ward; the guardian has day-to-day care and control of the ward.

A child becomes a ward as soon as the originating summons papers are taken to the court office, but this immediate effect is only temporary and the wardship will lapse after 21 days unless an application is made for the court to continue it. The other parent is sent a copy of the originating summons; if he or she does nothing about it the case can proceed without his or her appearance.

Wardship proceedings need not be brought only by parents. One of the special features of such proceedings is that they can be taken by any interested party in respect of any child. Thus, grandparents have made their grandchildren wards of court, as have social workers and local authorities to prevent violent parents from trying to see their children in care.

Finally, once a child is a ward of court certain things become contempts of court without a specific court order being made. These include marrying a ward, giving publicity to his or her affairs, and removing a ward from England and Wales without the permission of the court. This last one is particu-larly important in the context of the snatching of a child by a non-custodial parent where there is a risk that he or she may be taken abroad.

See also page 91.

99 | *When my husband received my divorce petition last week he rang me up in a furious temper and said he'd snatch our son and probably take him abroad. He's now been seen outside the school. I'm very worried. What should I do?*

A lot of people make this sort of threat at some stage in a divorce; usually it is no more than a threat made to hurt the other person. You know your husband best and you are the only person who can really assess the risk.

If you think he may be serious, you can apply to the divorce court for an injunction (see SEPARATION, Q13) ordering him to stay away from the child and from the area of the school. If he were to break that injunction he would be in contempt of court and could be sent to prison. The court can also make an order that the child should not be taken out of the country and that no passport should be issued.

You should also contact the school and explain the position to the headmaster or headmistress to try to make sure that you are told at once if your husband tries to take your son. Of course, you should make sure that you or some other reliable person takes your son to and from school.

If the worst happened and your husband did take the boy, you must contact the police at once. Kidnapping a child or attempting to do so can now be a criminal offence even if the abductor is a parent. The police have recently introduced a nationwide system to alert the ports and airports very quickly so that a watch will be kept to prevent a child's removal abroad, and your husband may be arrested if he is found.

You should also see your solicitor straightaway to apply for a court order to get the boy back. His or her advice will probably be to apply to make your son a ward of court (see Q98), which places him under the direct control of the High Court. The judge may issue a 'seek and find' order telling the court's own officers and the police to try to find the child. The court may also ask the press for assistance by making an appeal to the public to help find him. Photographs of your son and husband will be very useful.

The police keep a list of solicitors who are on call overnight and at weekends if you cannot find one yourself quickly, and the solicitor will know how to contact a judge out of hours via the Royal Courts of Justice in London.

The family home

100 | *On divorce, what does the court try to achieve as far as the home is concerned?*

The court should always try to ensure that both partners, and more particularly any children, are properly and securely housed. Sometimes this is not possible because there is just not enough money around to do so – the home itself is heavily mortgaged, for example, a common situation where the marriage breaks down early on while there are young children.

The owner-occupied home represents two things. First, it is a 'roof' that can go over someone's head if it is kept and not sold. Second, however, it represents a valuable capital asset, in most cases the only one the partners have.

The court must have regard to both these aspects and work accordingly. It will usually start by considering how the capital value might be used to house, or help house, both partners, but if that is impossible it will have to look at the home mainly as a 'roof' and order it to be kept and lived in by one or other of the partners, normally the spouse who gets custody of the children. If the marriage is childless and the wife self-supporting, the court may well decide that the home should be sold and the proceeds divided between the two partners equally or otherwise. Alternatively, the court could order the husband to pay a lump sum to buy out the wife's share, or vice versa. Exceptionally, the court may order the home to be transferred outright to one partner with no payment being made in return, though this is very rare.

These are all things that the partners may agree in any case. In particular, the couple may decide to sell the house and share the proceeds, or that one will buy out the other, shortly after the marriage breaks down, without waiting for the divorce or an order.

101 | *My wife and I have split up and we'll be getting a divorce. I'd like to buy her out of our family home. How will we decide how much she should get?*

There is no universal answer to this, and your decision will depend on all the circumstances.

The most common amount would be half the value of the 'equity' in the property, that is, the market value (which can be assessed by a professional valuation) less the amount of the mortgage debt. This is especially so where the wife has left and the husband wants to carry on living in the house and they agree to have a divorce. This may be the quickest and cheapest way of dividing the value.

The usual problems of needs and resources apply, though, and the main practical question is: 'How much can the purchaser afford to raise?' It will usually be a matter of increasing the mortgage to find the money, and a husband may find that he cannot borrow enough to pay half the equity. If that is so, the wife will have to settle for less or the house will have to be sold. If she wants a divorce to be able to remarry, it is quite common for her to accept a smaller amount in order to get things sorted out quickly.

If the court made an order it could itself decide that the wife should receive more or less than half the equity. More than half could be given to the wife where it can be shown that because of her age or low income she needs more, for example to buy a house for herself.

102 | *If the family home is sold, will the two partners get half the proceeds each?*

No, not necessarily, although this is the most common split where both parties agree to sell.

The solicitors or court must look at the amount of money that a sale will produce after paying off the mortgage and the expenses of the sale, and the position of both parties generally. If, say, both parties are independent, having formed new relationships or being self-supporting from their own incomes, an equal division might well be fair. That could also be so if only the wife has found a new partner.

Otherwise one partner could well need more than half. A common example of this occurs where partners are middle-aged or older and the house is large and expensive with a small mortgage, or none at all. Selling that house and giving one partner, usually the wife, more than half could allow her to buy a new smaller house outright. The reduced outgoings would mean that less maintenance (if any) would be needed and the husband might well be able to put down his share of the money as a deposit on a new home for himself and afford a mortgage more easily. Both parties would then have secure homes, which is something the court tries to achieve if possible.

103 | *When is the court likely to order the house to be kept as a home for one of the partners?*

The court, and no doubt the parties, will prefer to see the house sorted out if possible by the sale and the division of the proceeds or by one party buying the other out. But it is not always possible.

The main reason for this arises where there are young children, and the parent who has custody of them is living in the home with them. Unless the equity is sufficient for that parent to buy another house or that person can raise a mortgage to buy another, or there is other capital available (all of which are uncommon) the former matrimonial home will have to be kept. The usual court order (lawyers call it a '*Mesher*' order, after the names of the parties to the Court of Appeal case in which the first one was made) will be for the house to be kept until all the children have ceased their full-time education, when it will be sold and the proceeds divided between the parties.

Other cases have led to similar orders being made which give one party an indefinite right to occupy, for example, in the case of a middle-aged but childless wife who was in a modest home, the husband having left her for another woman. She was not able to support herself and the value of the home was low. She was given the right to stay for the rest of her life unless she remarried or moved out of her own accord.

104 | *If the court orders that the wife can live in the family home until the children have finished their full-time education, can it be sold before then?*

Yes, it's possible.

First, of course, the wife might want a sale, in which case the husband would no doubt be happy to agree as he would get his share of the sale proceeds.

Second, the order itself may say that the house is not to be sold until all the children have finished their full-time education *unless the occupying spouse dies, remarries or voluntarily leaves the property in the meantime.* If any of these occurs the other spouse can call for a sale and the proceeds of the sale will be split.

Third, even if neither of these two things happens, the non-occupier can apply to the court for an earlier sale if the circumstances change markedly. The occupier might cohabit there for a long period without remarrying, or might inherit a lot of money so as to be able to buy another house, or the non-occupier might regain custody of the children after a dispute. Any of these might make the court say that the property should now be sold and the proceeds split.

105 | *When the house is sold once the children have grown up (or even earlier), how are the proceeds divided?*

They will be divided in the proportions that the court laid down when it made the original order. They cannot be changed later. Most commonly, the shares will be equal, but the court looks at the facts of the particular case and other fractions are not unusual. Sometimes, for example, while a roomy house is still needed to be kept for the children to grow up in, two-thirds of the sale proceeds given to the wife when they leave might enable her to buy another one outright. This could be fair in the case of an older mother who has little or no earning capacity to be able to rehouse herself, especially if the husband has capital or a pensionable job with a lump sum on retirement to look forward to, which would pay off any mortgage he might take out to buy a house for himself.

106 | *If one partner has the use of the house until the children are grown up, who is responsible for the outgoings?*

The order itself will make it clear. In most cases it will be the occupier, and where the wife is receiving maintenance the order will usually say that the maintenance has been calculated to enable her to pay the bills. Sometimes the husband will undertake to pay these items himself, and as a result the maintenance he will have to pay will be reduced. It is usually better for the occupying wife to make the payments, because she knows what has and has not been paid in respect of her own home, and the husband will get income tax relief on the maintenance.

107 | *When might the matrimonial home be given outright to one party?*

This is very rarely done by the court in practice, although it is not so uncommon as part of an agreed settlement. Such a case might arise in the middle- or upper-income bracket where the parties are middle aged and the husband wanted a divorce, perhaps to remarry; the wife might reasonably demand security as the price of her co-operation and accept the house to provide some of that security.

In very high-income or high-capital cases the court might take the same attitude, and it could be a convenient approach to the problem of dividing the family's capital assets of which the home forms only a part.

Otherwise the courts make such a Draconian order, depriving one party of what is probably his or her only valuable asset, only where it is really necessary. In one such case, for example, the husband attacked the wife so viciously that she was unable to work again, and giving her the house outright was the only way to provide any future security for her. In another the husband was not only violent but was a hopelessly persistent maintenance defaulter who simply would not provide for his family. Very occasionally, the court may also give the house to the wife outright and in return order the husband to pay little or no maintenance.

108 | *What can the court do when the family home is rented?*

The first point to notice is that, unlike the owner-occupied home (whether freehold or held under a long lease), the rented home has no capital value to the parties and represents only a roof that can go over the head of one or the other. On divorce the court has the power to decide whose head that is to be and to make orders transferring the tenancy. That is so whether it is a council tenancy or a private letting.

Although it may not seem like it, the question of a rented home, especially where there is a private landlord, is one on which legal advice should be taken at an early stage. It may not be good enough just to agree that one person will stay on after the divorce and hope to carry on paying the rent.

109 | *What happens about the contents of the home on divorce?*

The court can make orders for the transfer or sale of any property, but the contents of the home are rarely worth enough to fight about and most people agree on how to divide them, especially where 'heirlooms' from his family or hers are concerned.

If the home is to be retained for the children's

benefit the bulk of the contents will need to stay there. In other cases many solicitors, exasperated with the obstinacy of one or both parties, will suggest that either everything be put in a saleroom for auction or that one party should divide everything into two lots and the other can chose which to have. This usually brings about a settlement, especially when the parties realise just how little second-hand furniture and carpets are worth.

Maintenance non-payment and changes in circumstance

110 | *My ex-husband has stopped paying the maintenance ordered on our divorce. What should I do?*

The first point to note is that nothing will happen automatically, and the court will do nothing unless you ask it to. You will have to take the initiative.

Ask him why he has stopped paying. He may not have the money because he has lost his job or there has been some other change in his circumstances since the order was made. In that case you and he might agree to a lower figure which he can afford and apply to the court to have the order changed to that.

Assuming that you are going to try to enforce the order, you will need to know whether the order was registered in a magistrates' court (see Q65). If so, all you will need to do is to contact the clerk to the justices at that court and ask for a summons to be issued.

If not, you will either need to have the order registered at the magistrates' court now so that you can apply to the magistrates, or you will have to apply to the county court that made the maintenance order to take one of the measures open to it to try to compel payment.

111 | *My ex-husband has stopped paying me maintenance. How will the court force him to continue paying?*

There are three main possibilities.

First, if your ex-husband is employed (as opposed to self-employed), the court can make an attachment of earnings order. This means that his employers will deduct the maintenance from his pay and send it to the court for transmission to you. This is usually the best method where he has a regular job.

Second, the court can make an order which will have the effect of sending him to prison if he continues to default. The threat of this may make him pay, but if he still does not pay and actually goes to jail this will not benefit you at all.

Third, the court can make one of a number of orders to get at the value of his assets: seizing and selling goods, or selling land or getting at money in a bank or other savings accounts. These orders may clear arrears, but will not get you future payments as they fall due.

As far as arrears are concerned, only 12 months' worth are usually enforceable, and you should think carefully before having business assets sold or a business bank account emptied to pay them, because this may put him out of business and end your chances of getting any more maintenance.

112 | *Which court should I apply to if my ex-husband stops paying the maintenance due under a maintenance order?*

You can apply to the county court that made the order, or to a magistrates' court if the order has been registered there (see Q65) or if you now take steps to register it, which is just a matter of form filling.

County courts can make all the orders mentioned in Q111, but magistrates can make only attachment of earnings orders, orders for committal to prison, and orders to seize and sell chattels; they have no powers over either land or money in accounts. The magistrates' procedure is simpler and cheaper, with far less paperwork, and it is quicker too in most parts of the country. It is often acknowledged, though, that they are readier to reduce the amount of an order.

113 | *The court ordered my ex-husband to pay me a lump sum when we divorced, but he hasn't done so. What can I do?*

You will have to seek to enforce payment by applying to the county court (there is no question of applying to the magistrates' court). The county court has wide powers to enforce payment, and where a lump sum is concerned you will want it paid promptly, not in dribs and drabs under an attachment of earnings order. The usual order under these circumstances is for property to be sold and the lump sum paid out of the proceeds of the sale. That property can be land, including your ex-husband's home if he owns it, or anything else, such as business assets, stocks and shares, a car, boat, and so on.

114 | *The court ordered my ex-husband to transfer the house to me when we got divorced, but he's refusing to sign the deeds. What can be done?*

There is a short answer here. If he refuses, the county court can order someone else to sign the deeds on his behalf; the court registrar will usually sign himself.

115 | *I can't afford to pay my ex-wife the maintenance the court ordered me to. What should I do?*

You should first explain the position to your ex-wife and try to agree a lower figure which is fair. If you do reach agreement, you can then change the order by writing to the court; there need be no court hearing. Most courts will provide the necessary forms for you both to complete and sign.

If you cannot agree you should apply to the court to have the amount reduced. If you can afford to pay nothing, the amount can be reduced to a purely nominal sum or even suspended. You would make your application to the county court unless the order has been registered in a magistrates' court (see Q65), in which case you apply there. You cannot get the order registered yourself; only your wife as the payee can apply to register.

Although you are applying to reduce the order, it is possible for the court nonetheless to increase the amount, and it will be looking at spouse and child maintenance together, so the one might be reduced and the other increased.

Legal Aid (see page 490) is not always granted in cases of variation of maintenance, and while you could get advice from a solicitor under the Green Form Scheme you might not be given cover for a solicitor to represent you in court if the argument is just on the arithmetic of what you can afford. The same may apply to your ex-wife.

116 | *My ex-wife has remarried. What legal effects may this have on me?*

The first and most obvious effect is that her right to maintenance from you ceases from her wedding day. Any maintenance order in force in her favour ended automatically, and if you made any payments not knowing of her remarriage you can apply to the court to get them back.

Although her own right to maintenance is ended, her remarriage has no effect as such on the maintenance orders for the children, which continue as before.

If the home was subject to an order giving your ex-wife a right to stay in the house until the children were grown up, it may have said expressly that the house should be sold if she were to remarry, in which case you can now ask her for a sale. Even if the order did not cover the point it may now be fair to have a sale, and you should take legal advice on the point.

117 | *My ex-wife is living with someone else. What effects will that have on me?*

As such, none, unlike the position were she to remarry (see Q116), but the change in her circumstances may enable you to make a number of applications to the court, assuming that she does not agree to alter the existing arrangements between you. The position will depend upon the permanence or otherwise of her new relationship, and we will assume that it appears to be pretty permanent.

First, you could apply for a variation or discharge of any maintenance order in her favour on the basis that she is now cohabiting. The court could end her rights altogether, although it would be more likely to suspend them when there are young children of yours living with her in case her new relationship came to an end.

Second, if the former matrimonial home was subject to an order giving your ex-wife the right to live in it until any children were grown up, the court might order a sale if she no longer lives there or if her new partner has moved in and now shares it with her. Sometimes the order will expressly cover these contingencies, but if not you can still apply to the court for an early sale.

Third, you might want any child maintenance reviewed if the new partner is contributing towards the costs of bringing them up or if your ex-wife might now be expected to contribute towards their upkeep.

Change of name

118 | *As well as changing my own name to my new husband's name, I should also like to change the surname of my two children by my previous marriage (I have custody). I'm afraid my children will be embarrassed at school if their name is different from their new father's and my name. Is there any objection to this, and how do I do it?*

A standard clause in the custody order made on your divorce states that you will need to get your former husband's consent before you change your children's surname. You cannot even register them at school in your new husband's name without their father's consent. If he will not agree, you will have to get permission from the court. This applies while your former husband is alive; the custody order is terminated on death, and you can then change the children's surname.

The Court of Appeal has laid down guidelines for the courts to follow in deciding whether to override a father's objections. The most important consideration is whether the name change would be in the children's best interests. The factors the court will take into account include possible embarrassment to the children, the strength of their links with their father, and the stability of the mother's new relationship. In the Court of Appeal case, though the children were going to live in Australia with their mother and her new husband, the Court refused the mother's application to change their surname, disregarding possible embarrassment to the mother and her new husband. The Court said that it was right that the children should keep the name of their father, with whom they had strong links. Other Court of Appeal judges in earlier cases, however, have attached less importance to names.

In the case described above, the mother had remarried. If instead she had been living with a man in a stable but unmarried relationship, the Court might well have been even less inclined to allow her to change the children's name.

119 | *I'm divorced, and would like to go back to using my pre-marriage name. Can I just start using my old name, or are there any legal formalities?*

As a divorced woman you are entitled to continue using your married name or to revert to your maiden name, just as you wish. No formalities are necessary, but you should notify the tax and national insurance authorities, your bank, and any other bodies whose records may need to be altered.

If you used your former husband's name for a number of years, you may wish to have formal evidence of your change of name. The most common means of changing your name is by deed poll; an alternative is a statutory declaration. See LIVING TOGETHER, Q29, for details of these.

THE MAIN STAGES IN GETTING A DIVORCE BY SPECIAL PROCEDURE

Those involved
PETITIONER The party applying for the divorce
RESPONDENT The petitioner's spouse
CO-RESPONDENT The third party (as in an adultery case)

The procedure

1. THE PETITIONER prepares and sends to THE DIVORCE COURT:
   ● the petition – the formal document that starts the court procedure (see page 80) – with a copy for the respondent and co-respondent (if any); plus
   ● a statement of the proposed arrangements for any relevant children (see page 82), with a copy for the respondent.

   Blanks of these forms are available from the court office.

   The petitioner also sends the marriage certificate and will either pay the court fee or apply for exemption from it (see q77).

   The court proceedings start from the day the petition is received, or 'filed', by the court office; this is what is meant both by 'filing' the petition and by the 'presentation' of the petition.

2. THE COURT acknowledges receipt of the papers, and posts to THE RESPONDENT:
   ● a copy of the petition
   ● a copy of the statement about the children
   ● a form of 'notice of proceedings', which amounts to notes for guidance and instructions
   ● a form of 'acknowledgement of service' (see page 84), on which the respondent can indicate his or her stance.

   Any co-respondent gets similar forms (except a copy of the statement about the children).

3. THE RESPONDENT (and CO-RESPONDENT) completes the acknowledgement of service and returns it to THE COURT within eight days.

4. THE COURT then sends THE PETITIONER:
   ● a photocopy of the completed acknowledgement of service
   ● a form of 'affidavit of evidence' (see page 86)
   ● a form of 'request for directions for trial', which is no more than a formal request to the court to proceed to decree nisi (see page 54).

5. THE PETITIONER completes these last two documents and returns them to THE COURT.

6. THE REGISTRAR OF THE COURT reads the file carefully. If he or she is satisfied that the petitioner has proved the grounds for divorce, a certificate to that effect will be given. The registrar must also consider the position of the children, if any. He or she must decide whether the judge can satisfy himself or herself about their welfare at a short informal hearing, or whether there is a dispute about custody or access, in which case a longer hearing to resolve it must be fixed later.

7. THE COURT informs BOTH PARTIES of the registrar's decision. They are told the date when the decree nisi will be pronounced by the judge, and they are also told that they need not be present. Assuming that there is no dispute about the children, they are informed when the judge will consider the arrangement for their welfare; the petitioner must attend that appointment. (If there *is* a dispute, see q141.)

8. THE JUDGE pronounces the decree nisi in open court, and a copy of the decree is sent to BOTH PARTIES.

9. THE COURT appointment about the children takes place (often on the same day as the decree nisi is pronounced) and the judge will usually make an order for custody and access as agreed by the parties. Copies of these orders, and a declaration that the judge is satisfied with the arrangements for the children, will be sent to BOTH PARTIES.

10. Six weeks after the decree nisi the THE PETITIONER applies for the decree absolute (see page 54) by completing and returning a form supplied by THE COURT.

11. THE COURT makes the decree absolute, thus finally dissolving the marriage, and sends copies to BOTH PARTIES.

Many of the steps listed here will be taken by the solicitors acting for each party; for convenience, the parties themselves are referred to.

Petition

IN THE   **BARCHESTER**   COUNTY COURT

No. 1234

1) On the **15** th day of **August** 19 **78** the petitioner was lawfully married to

    ANGELA MARY SWIFT

    PAUL MICHAEL SWIFT (hereinafter called 'the respondent')

at

Saint Mark's Church in the Parish of Saint Mark Barchester in the County of Barsetshire.

2) The petitioner and respondent last lived together at

14 Oak Drive, Barchester

3) The petitioner is domiciled in England and Wales, and is by occupation a

journalist

and resides at

14 Oak Drive, Barchester

and the respondent is by occupation a

lecturer

and resides at

The Garden Flat, 82 Beech Road, Barchester

4) There are no children of the family now living except

Giles Martin Swift, who was born on the 23rd day of April 1980.

5) No other child, now living, has been born to the petitioner/~~respondent~~ during the marriage (~~so far as is known to the petitioner) except~~

6) There are or have been no other proceedings in any court in England and Wales or elsewhere with reference to the marriage (or to any child of the family) or between the petitioner and respondent with reference to any property of either or both of them ~~except~~

7) There are no proceedings continuing in any country outside England or Wales which are in respect of the marriage or are capable of affecting its validity or subsistence ~~except~~

8) ~~No agreement or arrangement has been made or is proposed to be made between the parties for the support of the petitioner/respondent (and any child of the family) except~~

9) The said marriage has broken down irretrievably.

10

The parties to the marriage have lived apart for a continuous period of at least two years immediately preceding the presentation of the petition and the respondent consents to a decree being granted.

11) PARTICULARS

Unhappy differences having arisen between the parties, the respondent left the former matrimonial home to live elsewhere on the 2nd day of January 1985. Since that date the parties have continued to live separate and apart.

PRAYER

The petitioner therefore prays:—

1) That the said marriage be dissolved.

2) That ~~the petitioner may be granted~~ the custody of **Giles Martin Swift** may be granted to the petitioner and the respondent jointly, with care and control of the said child being granted to the petitioner.

3) That the **respondent** may be ordered to pay the costs of this suit.

4) That the petitioner may be granted the following ancillary relief:

   a) an order for maintenance pending suit
   a periodical payments order
   a secured provision order
   a lump sum order

   b) a periodical payments order
   a secured provision order
   for the children of the family
   a lump sum order

   c) a property adjustment order

Signed *A.M.Swift*

The names and addresses of the persons to be served with this petition are:—

Respondent:—   PAUL MICHAEL SWIFT,

The Garden Flat, 82 Beech Avenue, Barchester.

~~Co-Respondent (adultery case only):—~~

The Petitioner's address for service is:—

care of Messrs. Larch and Pine, Bank Chambers, 13 High Street, Barchester.

Dated this **4** th day of **February** 1987

Address all communications for the court to: The Registrar, County Court,

The Court office at **BARCHESTER**

is open from 10 a.m. to 4 p.m. (4.30 p.m. at the Divorce Registry) on Mondays to Fridays.

Statement as to Arrangements for Children – Matrimonial Causes Rules Form 4

1) *Delete as appropriate.*

IN THE **BARCHESTER** COUNTY COURT[1]

No. of Matter 1234

~~IN THE DIVORCE REGISTRY[1]~~

Between **ANGELA MARY SWIFT** Petitioner

and **PAUL MICHAEL SWIFT** Respondent

~~and~~ ~~Co-Respondent~~

State in respect of each child

The proposed arrangements for the children of the family under 16 and those over 16 but under 18 who are receiving instruction at an educational establishment or undergoing training for a trade, profession or vocation are as follows:—

State where the child is to live, with particulars of the accommodation, what other persons (naming them) live there and who will look after the child; and, if it is proposed that the child should be in the immediate care of a person other than the petitioner, state whether or not that person has agreed to this arrangement.

1) residence

Giles will continue to live with the petitioner at 14 Oak Drive, Barchester. It is a three-bedroomed semi-detached house with the usual offices. No one lives there but the petitioner and Giles. Although the petitioner works, she does so from home and is always there to look after Giles when he is not at school or with the respondent.

State the school or other educational establishment which the child will attend or, if he is working, his place of employment, the nature of his work and details of any training he will receive.

2) education etc.

Giles attends Mill Grove County Infants' School, a state school within a few minutes' walk from his home. He is happy there and his teachers are pleased with his progress.

He will almost certainly continue to attend local state schools.

3) financial provision

Since the separation the respondent has not paid maintenance as such but has paid all outgoings on the home and has bought most of Giles' clothes, the petitioner keeping herself and Giles from her earnings. It has been agreed that the respondent will provide at least the same level of support but by way of maintenance orders to be made after the decree in favour of the petitioner and Giles. The amounts are likely to be agreed.

State who is at present supporting the child or contributing to his support and the extent thereof, and whether it is proposed to make any application to the court for the financial support of the child and, if so, what support is to be applied for.

4) access

Giles normally sees his father for one whole day each weekend, which is spent at his father's flat or his grandparents' house nearby. He has also spent weekends and short holidays away with his father, and both parties are keen that these amicable and flexible arrangements should continue.

State any arrangements which have been agreed for access and the extent to which access is to be given.

State, in respect of each child so suffering, the nature of the disability or illness and attach a copy of any up-to-date medical report which is available.

The said child[ren] is [are] [not] suffering from serious disability or chronic illness or from the effects of such illness [namely;

Give details, and state the date of any order for care or supervision and the circumstances which gave rise to its being made.

The said child[ren] is [are] [not] under the care or supervision of a welfare officer, or officer appointed by a local authority or other person or organisation [namely;

Dated this 4 th day of February 1987

Signed *A.M.Swift*
petitioner

Address all communications for the court to: The Registrar, County Court

The court office at   BARCHESTER

is open from 10 a.m. to 4 p.m. (4.30 p.m. in the Divorce Registry) on Mondays to Fridays.

Acknowledgment of Service – Respondent Spouse

IN THE **BARCHESTER** COUNTY COURT

No. of matter 1234

BETWEEN ANGELA MARY SWIFT   *Petitioner*

AND   PAUL MICHAEL SWIFT   *Respondent*

~~AND~~   ~~Co-respondent~~

IF YOU INTEND TO INSTRUCT A SOLICITOR TO ACT FOR YOU, GIVE HIM THIS FORM IMMEDIATELY
READ CAREFULLY THE NOTICE OF PROCEEDINGS BEFORE ANSWERING THE FOLLOWING QUESTIONS
PLEASE COMPLETE USING BLACK INK

1. Have you received the petition for divorce delivered with this form?   **yes**

2. On which date and at what address did you receive it?

   On the **7th** day of **February** 19 **87**

   at

   The Garden Flat, 82 Beech Road, Barchester.

3. Are you the person named as the Respondent in the petition?   **Yes**

4. Do you intend to defend the case?   **No**

5. Do you consent to a decree being granted?*   **Yes**

6. In the event of a decree nisi being granted on the basis of two years' separation coupled with the respondent's consent, do you intend to apply to the Court for it to consider your financial position as it will be after the divorce?   **No**

7. ~~Even if you do not intend to defend the case do you object~~
   ~~to paying the cost of the proceedings?~~

   ~~If so, on what grounds?~~

8. Even if you do not intend to defend the case, do you object to the claim in the petition for custody of the children?   **No I agree with her application**

9. Do you wish to make any application on your own account for:

    a) custody of the children? *Just joint custody as she proposes.*

    b) access to the children? *Yes, Reasonable access has been agreed,*

10. *(In the case of proceedings relating to a polygamous marriage)*
    If you have any wife/husband in addition to the petitioner
    who is not mentioned in the petition, what is the name and
    address of each such wife/husband and the date and place of
    your marriage to her/him?

    N/A

Dated this **7th** day of **February** 19 **87**

If a solicitor is instructed, he will sign opposite on
your behalf

*but if the answer to Question 5 is Yes, you must also
sign here.*

Signed *Paul Swift*

Address
for service *The Garden Flat,*
82 Beech Road,
Barchester.

I am/We are acting for the Respondent in this matter.

Signed

Address
for service

Unless you intend to instruct a solicitor, give your place of
residence, or if you do not reside in England or Wales, the
address of a place in England or Wales to which documents
may be sent to you. If you subsequently wish to change
your address for service, you must notify the Court.

Affidavit by petitioner in support of petition under section 1(2)(d) of Matrimonial Causes Act 1973

MATRIMONIAL
CAUSES RULES
Rule 33(3)

No. of matter   **1234**

IN THE   **BARCHESTER**   COUNTY COURT

Between   ANGELA MARY SWIFT   *Petitioner*

and   PAUL MICHAEL SWIFT   *Respondent*

QUESTION	ANSWER

1. Have you read the petition filed in this case?

Yes

2. Do you wish to alter or add to any statement in the petition?
   If so, state the alterations or additions.

No

3. Subject to these alterations and additions (if any),
   is everything stated in your petition true?

   If any statement is not within your own knowledge,
   indicate this and say whether it is true to the best
   of your information and belief.

Yes

4. State the date on which you and the respondent separated.

2nd. January 1985

5. State briefly the reason or main reason for the separation.

Our marriage had become increasingly unhappy for about a year and we decided that we could not live together any more. We agreed that my husband should leave and get a flat.

6. State the date when and the circumstances in which you came
   to the conclusion that the marriage was in fact at an end.

We both came to the conclusion that it was at an end over Christmas 1984 when we took the decision to separate.

7. State as far as you know the various addresses at which you and the respondent have respectively lived since the date given in answer to Question 4, and the periods of residence at each address.

Petitioner's address *14, Oak Drive, Barchester.*

From *January 1985*

to *The present.*

Respondent's address *The Garden Flat 82 Beech Road, Barchester.*

From *January 1985*

to *The present.*

8. Since the date given in the answer to Question 4, have you ever lived with the respondent in the same household?

No

If so, state the addresses and the period or periods, giving dates.

I, *ANGELA MARY SWIFT* (*full name*)

of *14, Oak Drive, Barchester Barsetshire.* (*full residential address*)

Journalist (*occupation*)

make oath and say as follows:

1. I am the petitioner in this cause.

2. The answers to Questions 1 to 8 above are true. *Paul Swift*

3. I identify the signature appearing on the copy acknowledgment of service now produced to me and marked "A" as the signature of my husband/~~wife~~, the respondent in this cause.

4. I ask the Court to grant a decree dissolving my marriage with the respondent on the grounds stated in my petition

A.M. Swift

Sworn at *Barchester*

in the County of *Barsetshire*

this *11* th day of *Feb 87*

Before me *Tom Sawyer*

Officer of a Court appointed by the Judge to take Affidavits.

Children

General parental rights and duties

I | *What are my legal responsibilities as a parent towards my children?*

While there is a lot of legislation covering the custody of children and the removal of parental rights, it is generally thought that decisions about a child's behaviour or the degree of freedom a child should be allowed are private family matters that should be left to the parents. Although legislation protects children from serious parental abuse or neglect, the law does not lay down exactly how you should bring up your children or what you have to do to be a good parent.

However, generally as a parent you are expected to provide for your children's physical and emotional needs and to exercise proper control over them. The law will intervene if you ill-treat or neglect your children or if you do not send them to school. You can also have your rights over your children removed if, for example, you do not care for them properly or if you do not exercise sufficient control.

The law does state that you generally cannot pass your duties and responsibilities towards your children to someone else, though children may be removed from a parent's care by a court order or may be placed in voluntary care, and parents are allowed to arrange who shall have custody if they separate. Otherwise you have a duty to care for your children and cannot just hand that responsibility to other people.

2 | *My 11-year-old son is quite unruly and the neighbours often complain about the noise and his destructive behaviour. How far am I expected to have control over my child?*

It is generally accepted that parents have a duty to exercise control over their children's behaviour. Obviously there are limits to how far you can go to control your child: if you try to do so by keeping your child locked in, for example, you could find yourself accused of ill-treatment. But as a parent you are expected to exercise 'reasonable' control.

Parents can be held liable if their child causes an accident that results in damage, loss or injury to someone else, but only if this happened because they did not exercise proper control. For example, if you let your child have an air rifle and he or she injures someone while playing with it in the park, you may be held liable if you didn't give proper instructions as

to how, when or where the air rifle should be used. In most cases where parents are held liable, this means having to pay damages. The courts do not, however, expect parents to watch over their children every second of the day: when deciding whether a parent is in some way responsible, a court would take into account the age and maturity of the child and the circumstances surrounding the accident.

Your child may be taken into care (see Q56) if you fail to exercise proper control. This would not normally happen as a result of just one incident; care proceedings are usually brought when it is thought that a child (in most cases a teenager) is totally beyond parental control. You may also be punished by being ordered to pay a fine or compensation if your child commits a criminal offence.

3 | *Can I choose how to discipline my children, and am I allowed to smack or cane them?*

The law specifically allows parents to administer reasonable punishment to their children. It does not define what methods of punishment a parent should or should not use, so it is up to you to decide what standards of behaviour you expect from your child and what forms of punishment you use for any mis-behaviour as long as it is reasonable.

In court cases it has been held that parents may use corporal punishment upon their children. But you can be prosecuted for assault if you hit your child too severely. It is also a separate criminal offence to ill-treat your child in a way that is likely to cause him or her unnecessary suffering. The term 'ill-treatment' not only covers hitting your child but also generally covers all forms of neglect. If, for example, you deprive your child of food or clothing, or lock him or her up for long periods of time, this could constitute ill-treatment. Your child may be taken into care (see Q56) if the punishments you use against him or her are considered to be abuse.

4 | At what age can I leave my child alone or with a babysitter?

The law does not state an age at which your child may be left alone or with a babysitter (nor does it state that someone below a certain age cannot babysit). It is basically left up to you to decide at what age your child is able to take care of him or herself, and whether a particular person will look after your child responsibly.

There are, however, a number of offences relating to ill-treatment which you should be aware of. It is a criminal offence to neglect, abandon or ill treat any child under 16 in a way likely to cause unnecessary suffering or injury, or to cause or allow this to happen. If a child under 12 is injured as a result of being allowed in a room with an open fire or another heating appliance which is not properly guarded, the person responsible may be charged. In both these offences charges may be brought against a person who has custody or is looking after the child even temporarily, such as a babysitter, when the injury or suffering occurred, but only if that person is over 16.

Frequently in such situations, rather than punishing the parent, steps will be taken to protect the child. Suspicion of ill-treatment can lead to the involvement of a social worker and your child's name being placed on a child abuse register (see Q5); more serious cases can lead to proceedings to remove your child from your care.

5 | Who decides whether a child is being abused, and what can happen?

The two main agencies that deal with allegations of child abuse are local authority social services departments and the National Society for the Prevention of Cruelty to Children (NSPCC) (address on page 511). Child abuse is usually thought of as parents using physical violence against their children, but it can also mean neglect, or emotional or sexual abuse. Literally anyone can report a suspicion that a child is being abused at home: a doctor, a teacher, a relative, a neighbour or someone acting anonymously.

If a suspicion of child abuse is reported to the NSPCC, officers of the society will investigate the case. If there is evidence that the child is being abused, the NSPCC can itself start care proceedings to have the child removed from the parental home or may hand the case over to the social services department for further action.

All social services departments operate child abuse registers. If there is an allegation or evidence of abuse, a 'case conference' may be called of all the professionals, such as social workers and teachers, who may have contact with the family. Where there is firm evidence that a child is in danger, the social services department may seek authority from a magistrate to remove him or her to a place of safety immediately (see Q55) and start care proceedings (see Q56). If this is not the case but it is still believed that the child is at risk, his or her name may be placed on the child abuse register. All kinds of professionals have access to the child abuse register. They are supposed to keep careful watch over families where a child's name has been entered on it.

Social services departments do not have to tell parents that their child's name has been placed on the child abuse register, and there is no easy legal process by which they can challenge the entry. Parents who suspect that there has been a wrongful allegation concerning their treatment of their child should take advice from a solicitor.

6 | At what age do my children have the right to decide about their own medical treatment?

Medical or dental treatment can constitute an assault unless valid consent to the treatment is given. In relation to young people, normally the consent of one of the parents is required. However, in an emergency, particularly when necessary to save the life of the child, a doctor may treat your child without your consent.

The law remains somewhat unclear about what age your children must be before they can give a valid consent to treatment in their own right. What is clear is that at 16 young people have the right to choose their own doctors and dentists, and can give proper consent to medical, surgical or dental treatment (see HEALTH, Q12). But the fact that your child is under 16 does not automatically mean that she or he cannot give consent. Whether those under 16 are considered capable of consenting to their own treatment depends upon their maturity and understanding and the nature of the treatment in question. See also HEALTH, QS 11 to 14.

7 | *My son of seven has to go into hospital for an operation. Can the hospital dictate how much time my husband and I can spend with him?*

Although the situation has much improved in recent years, conflict can still arise between parents and hospital authorities over visiting children. The DHSS has advised all hospital authorities that when young children have to spend time in hospital, access by parents should not be restricted unless, for example, there is danger of infection or the treatment may be disrupted. So you should be able to spend as much time with your son as you wish.

Many hospitals will now also arrange for you to stay overnight with your child, particularly if she or he is very young. It is also worth noting that if your child is of school age and going into hospital for some time, the local education authority (LEA) should make arrangements for alternative schooling during the hospital stay.

The National Association for the Welfare of Children in Hospital (NAWCH) (address on page 511) offers advice and information to parents with children in hospital. If you experience problems with the hospital authorities you should certainly contact the Association.

8 | *Can I prevent my daughter of 16 from having a relationship with someone I disapprove of?*

There is no set age at which your children become entitled to make their own decisions about personal relationships, although the law does make age restrictions with regard to sexual relationships.

While your daughter is under 18 and living at home, she is in theory still in your custody, care and control. In that sense you may try to make stipulations about whom she does and does not see. However, it must be acknowledged that trying to control your daughter's personal relationships can be a source of great conflict, and this is the kind of family situation in which the law will not generally intervene.

A girl under 16 cannot legally consent to a sexual relationship. Although she cannot be charged with a criminal offence herself, the boy or man involved can be charged with unlawful sexual intercourse if he is over 16 or with assault if he is between 14 and 16.

9 | *Can I decide whether my son of 16 may drink or smoke?*

If you give any kind of intoxicating liquor to a child of under five, you are committing an offence (though a doctor can give alcohol to a child of under five for medical reasons). Between the ages of five and 16 your child may drink alcohol, but only on private premises such as your own home. In this sense it is up to you to decide whether your child may drink.

Children under 14 are not allowed in bars selling alcohol during licensing hours, though a pub may provide special facilities for them. Young people aged between 14 and 16 are allowed into a bar, but they do not have the legal right to be there and a licensee can exclude them.

Children over 16 may have beer, cider or perry with a meal in a hotel or restaurant, but cannot drink alcohol in a bar. Only when your child reaches 18 and is legally an adult can he or she buy alcohol, whether in a pub, shop or off-licence.

Cigarettes and tobacco cannot legally be sold to children who are or appear to be under 16, even if the cigarettes or tobacco are for someone else. If a child under 16 is found smoking in a public place, a uniformed police officer or a park-keeper is allowed to confiscate any tobacco or cigarette papers. However, in theory a child may smoke in private at any age, and it is largely your decision whether your child may smoke.

10 | *My son of 14 wants to take on a paper round in the mornings. What is the legal position?*

Children under 13 are not generally allowed to work at all, the only exceptions being children employed by their parents in light agricultural or horticultural work, and child performers for whom parents must normally obtain a special licence (the local authority should be contacted for information).

Children of between 13 and 16 may take a part-time job, but for no more than two hours on any schoolday or on Sundays. This work must not be during school hours, unless it is part of a school work experience scheme, and should not begin before 7am or finish later than 7pm on any day of the week. This age-group can be employed only in light work and is specifically excluded from certain types of work such as in building and demolition.

Your local authority may also have by-laws that further restrict the employment of those under 16. The local authority is also entitled to stop your child working altogether if the work is felt to be interfering with his or her education or general welfare. Employers who employ children illegally may be prosecuted.

Children and young people who work part time are not protected by the laws and regulations on minimum wages, so many are exploited by employers and paid only a pittance. There are few remedies against such exploitation, but it may be worth seeing whether the relevant union is interested in taking up the matter.

11 | *At what age are my children entitled to have their own passports?*

Children can have their own passports at any age, though until they are 18 parents must sign the relevant forms to signify their consent. However, the Passport Office advises that only in exceptional circumstances should an application for a separate passport be made for a child under five years of age.

The application for a passport for a child can be made by either parent (the mother's consent is always required if the child is illegitimate). The child's birth certificate, *not* a photocopy, must be submitted in all cases.

Children who travel abroad on their own must have their own passports. When children are taken on group trips abroad, for example by schools, normally a collective passport is obtained for all those involved; again, the parents' consent will be required.

12 | *My daughter of 14 has been given a few thousand pounds by her grandfather. What is the legal position?*

Legally, any money, such as pocket money, or other gifts given to your children, and any money they earn, actually belongs to them. If the children are very young, parents can hold any money until they are mature enough to decide how to spend it. You may be able to use money given to your children, but

● *Wards of court*

Any minor – someone under the age of 18 – may become a ward of court. Wardship may be used where the care or property of a minor, or a matter relating to his or her upbringing, is in dispute. Wardship may be useful where disputes between adults involve removal of the child from the country or abduction to this country.

There are no absolute restrictions on who may apply to have a young person made a ward of court. Very often the applicant is a parent, but any other relative or someone else with a special interest in the young person's welfare may apply. In recent years local authority social services departments have increasingly used wardship as a means of applying for children and young people to be committed to care. Young people may also apply themselves to become wards of court, using an adult, who is known as a 'next friend', to act on their behalf.

The court retains custody of a ward of court while ordering who shall have care and control on a day-to-day basis. But wardship is not only used to sort out who should have the care of a child or a young person. The court may be asked to decide upon disputes over such matters as access, the payment of maintenance, the most appropriate school, religious upbringing, and whether a particular form of medical treatment should be given.

Once a child or young person is a ward of court, the wardship continues until he or she becomes an adult at 18 unless the court decides it should cease earlier. So although wardship may be an effective way of sorting out an immediate problem, it may have longer-term consequences since the court's involvement in the young person's life does not necessarily cease at that point. For example, if a young person remains a ward, he or she may not marry or go outside England and Wales without the court's permission. In addition, there may be other important decisions, such as those relating to schooling, for which the court's consent remains necessary.

See also DIVORCE, Q98.

this must be for their benefit – to assist with their education, say.

You can open a bank account in your child's name to deposit money given to her. Young people may themselves open deposit accounts at a bank at any age as long as they can give a signature. However, banks very rarely allow anyone under 16 to open a current account and have a cheque book; children of

16 and over must be working or in receipt of a student grant before a bank will allow this.

The law states that young people under 18 cannot own houses or land. If your children are left such property this must be held on trust for them until they are 18.

13 | *Our daughter of 16 has just left school and has now declared that she's going to leave home and move in to a flat with some friends. Can we prevent her from going?*

The law does not stipulate an age at which children may leave home of their own accord. Generally it is accepted that young people cannot leave home until they are over 16 and are financially independent by working or by claiming Supplementary Benefit. However, those under 16 do sometimes leave the parental home, for example to live with another relative.

It can be difficult for a parent to stop a child leaving home, particularly if that child is 16 or over and no longer needing financial support. You may ask the social services department to intervene to try to help resolve conflicts within the family, whatever the age of your children. In extreme situations social services departments can take care proceedings if your child is 17 or under and deemed to be beyond your control.

Parents may make their children wards of court (see page 91) to prevent them from leaving home. However, normally the court will not intervene if a young person is 16 or over and can look after him or herself. The only exception to this may be if, for example, a 16-year-old wishes to leave home to live in a situation which is thought to be very unsuitable, and if the court is convinced that the young person requires protection it may order that he or she should continue to live at home. If the child is under 16 the court is more likely to intervene, but the court may decide that the parental home is not the best place for the young person. Day-to-day care and control can then be given to someone other than the parents, or to the local authority, though the parents may still be liable for maintenance.

If your child actually runs away, a missing person report can be made to the police. If the police are able to trace your child, they will either bring her home or inform you of where she is staying, or perhaps ask the social services department to deal with the situation. The action the police decide to take tends to depend both on the age of the child and on the circumstances of the case.

14 | *My daughter's father and I never married*

and we split up soon after she was born. Someone has told me that I am solely responsible for her. Is this true?

Yes. A child is legally defined as illegitimate if the mother and father are not married at the time of the birth (and do not subsequently marry), and the law states that the mother has all the parental rights and duties in respect of an illegitimate child. Thus, you can choose your daughter's name and take all the decisions about her care and upbringing. The father has no legal rights even if he is living with you (though when the Family Law Reform Act 1987 is brought into force, he will be able to apply to the court for parental rights and duties). See also LIVING TOGETHER, QS 15 to 23.

Education

15 | *At what age will my children start to attend school, and what is the school-leaving age?*

All children have a right to start school at the beginning of the term following their fifth birthday, although some LEAS arrange for some or all children to start school earlier, for example when they are four and a half years of age. You can find out the policy of your particular LEA by writing to the office of the Chief Education Officer.

LEAS also have the power to establish nursery schools or nursery classes and to support other forms of pre-school provision, such as playgroups. But they are under no legal duty to do so; even if they make such a provision your children are not required to attend. If, however, a child who is under school age is assessed as having special educational needs (see Q19) the LEA is under a duty to make relevant pre-school provision.

There are two alternative dates for leaving school, depending on the date of the child's birthday. Young people whose sixteenth birthdays are between 1 September and 31 January may leave school at the end of the Easter term following their birthdays; those whose sixteenth birthdays fall between 1 February and 31 August may leave on the Friday before the last Monday in May. LEAS have a duty to provide education in schools and colleges of further education up to the age of 19 for those who wish to continue their education.

16 | *My LEA has only comprehensive schools at the secondary level. Do I have any legal right to send my child to a grammar school? The nearest one is eight miles away in a different LEA.*

You do have the right to apply to a grammar school in another LEA if you are not satisfied with the comprehensive schools provided in your area. Parents can express a preference for a particular school and it does not have to be a school in the LEA within which you are living (see Q17). There is, however, no guarantee that your child will be accepted; for example, that particular grammar school may be oversubscribed and have no available places, and your child will have to satisfy the entry requirements in any case.

17 | *Do I have a choice about which school my child goes to within my LEA?*

The law gives you some choice about which primary and secondary school your child goes to.

You have a right to state a preference for a particular school you wish your child to attend, and this can be a school in a neighbouring LEA rather than your own. Very often the LEA, when it sends you the relevant papers before your child is due to start at primary or secondary school, will ask you to list a number of schools in order of preference, but you are under no legal obligation to name more than one school. If the LEA does not accept your choice of school, you should be informed in writing and given reasons for this decision.

Information about all LEA schools (including voluntary-aided schools – those provided by voluntary bodies, most often the Roman Catholic and Anglican Church) must by law be made available to you by the schools themselves and by the LEA; public libraries are another source. This information must include the curriculum of the particular school, the school rules and some details of examination results. You will need to assess each school on the basis of this information – and also by asking other parents, of course.

If you do not accept the LEA's reason for not allocating your child a place at a particular school or do not wish to accept an alternative, you may appeal against the decision to a local appeals committee. All LEAS must explain their appeals procedures in the information leaflets available from the schools and the LEAS. You must appeal in writing and setting out your reasons for wanting a particular school and for not wanting any alternative school which has been offered. You should be given at least 14 days' notice of the appeal hearing, and you may attend and state your case. The appeals committee's decision is binding on the LEA. If you are not satisfied with the outcome of the hearing, you can make a further

appeal to the Secretary of State for Education and Science (though the Education Secretary is very unlikely to intervene). For more information, read *School Choice Appeals*, a handbook published by ACE (address on page 509).

18 | *Can I educate my child at home?*

The Education Act 1944 states that parents have a duty to ensure that their children receive suitable education 'either by regular attendance at school or otherwise'. The inclusion of the words 'or otherwise' means that you can arrange for your child to be educated at home if you choose.

Normally, your child will be registered as a pupil at a particular school, so you will have to de-register the child by writing to the head teacher in order to educate your child at home (otherwise you could be in trouble for your child's non-attendance; see Q21). Even if your child has not been registered at a school, the LEA will undoubtedly require you to explain what is happening about your child's education; it has a duty to check on all children in its area.

You will need to satisfy the LEA that you can provide efficient education suitable to your child's age, ability and aptitude within your home. LEAS have tended to establish their own criteria as to what will be accepted as proper and suitable education.

The attitudes of LEAS to parents wishing to educate their children at home vary, some being more sympathetic than others. Although educating children at home is quite legal you will need to convince the LEA that you are serious in your intention and capable of providing proper education for your child at home: parents have been taken to court for failing to provide proper alternative education. The organisation Education Otherwise (address on page 509) provides advice and support to parents wishing to educate their children at home.

● *Challenging decisions about your child's education*

If you have a complaint about some aspect of your child's education – the curriculum or discipline, for example – you should discuss it initially with the head teacher, and also raise it with the school's Parent–Teacher Association if appropriate. Complaints about school rules or management may be made to the school governors. All school governing bodies must have at least two parent governors (one in the case of voluntary-aided schools).

If your complaint is not resolved you can take the matter to the LEA by writing to the Chief Education Officer. In some cases the problem may in any event be caused by a decision of the LEA rather than of the school. You could also write to the councillor who chairs the local authority's Education Committee.

The Education Act 1944 allows parents in England and Wales to complain directly to the Secretary of State for Education and Science (address on page 509) if an LEA or a school governing body is acting unreasonably or is failing to carry out its duties. The Education Secretary is under an obligation to investigate complaints. The Advisory Centre for Education (address on page 509) has prepared an information sheet about making complaints.

If a formal complaint does not meet with success, in exceptional situations you may be able to take the matter to court; some cases taken to court have been successful. You should seek legal advice about this, perhaps approaching a local law centre before seeing a solicitor. Alternatively, contact the Children's Legal Centre (address on page 509).

The Local Government Ombudsman (address on page 510), officially called the Commissioner for Local Administration, can investigate complaints of maladministration by an LEA but not internal school matters. Forms telling you how to make a complaint to the Ombudsman should be available from your local library and Citizens Advice Bureau.

---

19 | *My daughter of nine is at primary school. Her headmistress recently said she may have 'special educational needs'. What is meant by this?*

The term 'special educational needs' is used to refer to children who are deemed to have educational problems or difficulties and to those with physical disabilities. Chidren under five are also included if they would be likely to fall into either of these categories if special provision were not made for them. The Education Act 1981 places a duty on LEAS to integrate such children in ordinary schools and provides significant new rights for parents.

If the LEA and the school believe your child has special needs – say, because she is performing less well than average, or perhaps has a possible hearing problem – they can insist on a formal assessment being made. This assessment involves tests and examinations by various professionals, such as doctors and educational psychologists. Following the assessment, the LEA may then make a statement of the special educational needs, setting out your child's particular needs and how it is proposed they should be met. Parents also have the right to request an assessment of their children, and as long as their request is reasonable the LEA has a duty to arrange the assessment.

The legislation gives parents the right to be consulted throughout this process, so you can be present at the examinations, receive all the reports prepared for assessment, and comment on the draft statement of special needs. If you disagree with the decision the LEA makes about your child, you may appeal to a local appeals committee. This committee cannot change the authority's decision, but it can recommend that it is reconsidered. If you are not satisfied with the result of your appeal to this committee, you can make a further appeal to the Secretary of State for Education and Science (address on page 509). For further information, read *Special Education Handbook*, published by ACE (address on page 509).

20 | *Does a child who is assessed as having special educational needs have to go to a special school?*

Over 150,000 children with special needs attend segregated 'special' schools, whether their needs result from physical or mental disability or severe learning difficulties. In many cases this means that the children are denied educational opportunities and become isolated from their peers. The Education Act 1981 provides that children with special needs should be educated in ordinary schools as long as their needs can be met, this will not interfere with the education of others, and is compatible with the efficient use of resources. Although all LEAS are now under this duty to integrate, few are taking active steps to speed up the process. It is worth checking how your LEA has responded to this situation – whether, for example, teachers are being given appropriate training or access is being provided in schools for children in wheelchairs. Your LEA should provide you with this information.

In deciding whether your child should go to a special school or be integrated into an ordinary school, the LEA must take your views into account. If you do not agree with the LEA's proposal to send your child to a special school, you may appeal against the decision. The Children's Legal Centre (address on page 509) will advise parents whose children have been assessed as having special needs.

21 | *My neighbours' 11-year-old son is around so often during the day that I'm sure he's not attending school regularly. Aren't his parents obliged to ensure that he attends school?*

Yes. Parents have a legal duty to ensure that their children receive proper education between the ages of five and 16. This means that parents must make sure that their children attend school regularly, though it is possible for a child to be educated at home (see Q 18). Absence from school is allowed for particular religious observances, for instance, or when your child is ill.

If a child's attendance has been poor or there has been a prolonged absence, the school will get an educational welfare officer to contact the parents to discuss the situation. The LEA may give them a specified time (which must not be less than 14 days) to show that their child is receiving adequate education. If the parents cannot do so, the LEA may serve them with a school attendance order which requires them to ensure that their child attends a particular school. If they fail to comply with this order the LEA may take the parents to court.

If the LEA takes them to court and they can give no satisfactory explanation for their child's absence from school, the court will find them guilty of an offence and order them to pay a fine. Care proceedings can also be taken on the grounds that the child is not receiving proper education and is in need of care and control. Ultimately the child could be removed from his parents' care as a result of frequent or prolonged absence from school.

22 | *I'm firmly against any form of corporal punishment. Do I have any control over how my child is punished at school?*

Following a recent decision by the European Court of Human Rights, parents may now decide whether they will allow corporal punishment to be used against their children in school. If you do not wish corporal punishment to be used, you should inform the head teacher and your child must be exempted from it.

The head teacher of a school determines internal school rules and disciplinary measures under the general direction of the governors. You should find out what forms of punishment are used in your child's particular school; write to the head teacher. The school's policy may be something you wish to consider when initially deciding which school your child should go to (see Q 17).

Schools are also subject to any general rules determined by the LEA, many of which stipulate that schools in their area may not use corporal punishment on pupils in any circumstances. You should check whether your LEA has laid down any rules about corporal punishment or other forms of disciplinary measures by writing to the office of the Chief Education Officer.

23 | *My son has been suspended from his secondary school, it seems to me for the flimsiest of reasons. Can I appeal againt the suspension?*

A child may not be suspended from the school unless there are 'reasonable' grounds for doing so, and only the head teacher has this power. The head must notify the school governors and the LEA of all suspensions. The law does not lay down a general system for suspensions which all schools must follow. Generally, any rules about suspensions are included in the articles of government of individual schools, so you should find out from your child's school or from the LEA what the rules are about suspension. Some articles of government include a right of appeal against suspension, often to the school governors.

Whatever rights the particular school does or does not allow you as a parent, if you believe that your child has been suspended unreasonably you should make a formal complaint to the governors and to the LEA. If this does not resolve the situation you should make a complaint to the Secretary of State for Education and Science (address on page 509).

Your child cannot be permanently excluded from school because whatever the situation the LEA has a legal duty to provide full-time education for any child who is between five and 16 years of age. If your child is excluded from one school he must be offered a place at an alternative school, and tuition should be provided during any interim period.

24 | *Can I insist that our LEA provides transport*

to get my daughter to and from her secondary school?

LEAS are required to make arrangements for the provision of transport, or to pay for transport, for school pupils or students in further education where they consider it necessary or as directed by the Secretary of State for Education and Science. This allows the LEA considerable discretion as to whether it provides or pays for transport. However, parents are entitled to free transport if the nearest school is two miles away for pupils under eight years of age and three miles above that age. The LEA can, however, avoid having to provide transport by offering your child a place at a nearer school, if there is one.

It is not uncommon for parents to find themselves in dispute over the provision of school transport. Sometimes the distance involved may be very close to the two- and three-mile limits; in other cases LEAS measure the distance along a route parents feel is unsafe. The law does not say that LEAS may not provide transport if the child's journey is less than the maximum walking distance; it says only that they should provide transport if it is more. Parents should therefore argue their case with their LEA. If there is no agreement they may take their case to the Secretary of State for Education and Science (address on page 509).

25 | *Does my child have to wear school uniform?*

The law does not state that if a school has a uniform all pupils must wear it. However, parents generally accept that this is one of the internal school rules which they and their children should follow. If your child does not obey the rules about uniform, the head teacher may send him or her home. If this happens repeatedly, you can be taken to court for failing to ensure that your child is receiving proper education (see Q21). In one case parents were convicted for failing to send their daughter to school when she was repeatedly sent home for wearing earrings contrary to the school rules.

If you object to the school's policy about uniforms, or to any other rules about dress, you should discuss the matter with the head teacher. You may also raise the matter with the governors and the LEA. There may yet be some changes in the legal position relating to school uniform: for example, it is argued that schools which forbid girls from wearing trousers are breaking the Sex Discrimination Act 1975, although as yet no case has been brought before the courts.

LEAS can give parents assistance with the cost of a school uniform. In most LEAS this is a standard grant according to the age of the child and the parents' income. LEAS may also provide clothing if it is considered necessary for the child to enable him or her to take advantage of a particular educational opportunity, for example a sports kit so the child can participate in games lessons.

26 | *Does my child's school have to provide proper meals at lunchtime?*

No. The Education Act 1980 states that LEAS generally have complete discretion as to whether to provide food at schools. If the LEA does provide lunches, the LEA may decide what the meal should consist of and what to charge parents. Food must, however, be provided for children whose families are on Supplementary Benefit or Family Income Supplement (see BENEFITS, QS 1 and 6), but the LEA may serve whatever food seems to be 'requisite', which may not be what parents would call a 'proper' meal. The LEA must also provide free of charge adequate facilities for pupils to eat food brought from home.

LEAS no longer have a legal obligation to provide children with free milk in school, as they once used to. If milk is provided, the LEA may charge for it unless it is part of the midday meal for children whose families are on Supplementary Benefit or Family Income Supplement.

27 | *Do I have any say in the amount of teaching my child receives and in what subjects are taught?*

Children up to the age of eight in nursery and primary schools should receive at least three hours of secular, that is, non-religious, education each day;

children over eight should have a minimum of four hours' education each day. Schools should normally be open for at least 200 days a year, less up to 10 days for special holidays like religious festivals.

These periods are the minimum amount of education your child should receive. If you are dissatisfied with the amount of teaching your child is getting at school you should make a complaint to the LEA.

The law states that an LEA has a duty to provide 'suitable' education in primary and secondary schools, which must be 'sufficient in number, character and equipment to afford all pupils opportunities for education'. While decisions about which subjects are included in the curriculum are the responsibility of the LEA and the school governors, in practice they are usually delegated to the head teacher. Schools are obliged to publish details of the curriculum, so you should check this very carefully when deciding to which school you would like your child to go. However, the problem may not arise until later, when your child develops an aptitude for a particular subject. If you are not satisfied that your child is receiving a suitable education and you are concerned about the omission of a certain subject, you should discuss this with the head teacher. He or she can, for example, arrange for your child to attend another school for a particular subject. If the problem cannot be resolved you should complain to the LEA and even beyond it, if necessary, to the Secretary of State for Education and Science (address on page 509).

28 | *My son of 12 is outstanding at mathematics and is so far in advance of the rest of the class that he should receive special teaching. Can I insist that the school provides special facilities for him?*

Your LEA is under a duty to provide education suitable to your child's age, ability and aptitude. If you think your child's aptitude for a particular subject is not being catered for, you should discuss with the head teacher whether other arrangements can be made. It may be possible for your son to join a higher class for that particular subject within the school or at another school.

If you are not satisfied with the LEA provision, you will have to seek private tuition or special courses outside the school system. It may be helpful to contact the National Association for Gifted Children (address on page 511); the Association organises weekend and week-long summer courses and has local groups that run Saturday morning classes. These classes and courses do not in the main cover school syllabus subjects – they are aimed at enriching the child's educational opportunities rather than duplicating the school curriculum. However, a group may also be able to provide you with helpful advice from other parents as to how to best cater for your child's special ability.

29 | *Does my child have to attend assembly and receive religious instruction in school?*

No. You have the right to withdraw your child from any form of religious worship and from religious instruction in school.

Some schools now hold assemblies in the mornings which have no religious content (though they are breaking the law by doing so); these assemblies are used mainly for general announcements, disciplinary matters, and so on. If the assembly is purely non-religious, you do not have the right to withdraw your child. However, if the assembly is used wholly or in part for the purpose of religious worship – and most are – and you do not wish your child to participate, you should notify the school.

In LEA schools religious education is taught according to a locally agreed syllabus that should not favour any particular denomination. Again, if you do not want your child to have religious education, you should inform the school of your wishes. You can also request special lessons for your child in a particular religion if, for example, your child's religion is different from that of other children in the school, although the school will not necessarily meet your request.

30 | *I do not want my daughter to attend any sex education lessons at school as my wife and I prefer to explain everything ourselves. Do I have the right to withdraw her from these lessons?*

You do not have the legal right to withdraw your child from this part of the curriculum, but if you discuss the situation with the head teacher he or she may be sympathetic towards your point of view and could allow you to withdraw your child. Many schools will in any event consult parents before sex education classes begin.

If you do not get a satisfactory response from the school you may make a complaint to the LEA. Ultimately the only solution may be to move your daughter to another school, although many schools now include sex education as part of the curriculum.

31 | *My son is having violin lessons, for which his school has asked me to pay. When I complained to a friend about this, she said she was expected to*

buy books for her son. Are schools right in expecting parents to pay in this way?

You do not have to pay for lessons or for books or other equipment required for study if the particular subjects are part of the school's curriculum, that is, they are taught during the school day.

But as a way around this, some LEAS designate particular subjects, especially instrumental music tuition, as being outside the curriculum.

LEAS have a duty to provide without charge 'sufficient' schools, which must be 'sufficient in number, character and equipment'. The law does not, however, lay down minimum standards in relation to, for example, the number of teachers or books. Many schools find it difficult to maintain the standard of education which ought to be provided because of reductions in expenditure. As a result, parents are sometimes asked to contribute, by purchasing textbooks themselves, say. This practice obviously penalises children whose parents cannot afford to pay and can cause difficulties for many families.

You cannot be required to pay for lessons that are part of the curriculum, so you can merely refuse to pay. If you feel the necessary resources for your child's education are not being provided, you should make a formal complaint to the governing body and to the LEA. Ultimately, if the LEA does not provide 'sufficient' educational resources and the Secretary of State does not press the LEA to do so, such lack of provision may be challenged in the courts.

32 | Our local education authority is planning to close the primary school my son goes to. Is there anything I can do about this proposed closure?

LEAS are required to give two months' public notice of any proposal to establish a new maintained or voluntary school or to close or significantly alter any existing school. The LEA must also state the time when they intend to carry out the changes and the number of pupils to be admitted to any new or altered school.

The approval of the Secretary of State for Education and Science used to be required for all such proposals, but this is no longer the case. The Education Secretary now has to assess a proposal and give approval only if a local objection has been made. If you wish to object to the closure of your child's school, you must register your objection with the LEA, which will pass it on to the Department of Education and Science. For more information and advice about opposing school closures contact ACE (address on page 509).

33 | Do I have the right to see my child's school records?

Parents have no legal right to see their children's school records; pupils have no legal right either. Very often parents are completely unaware that such records are kept. In fact, all schools keep records about individual pupils. The record is started as soon as a child begins nursery or infant school and is passed on as he or she changes school. The record includes information about educational attainment and predictions of future potential. It may also contain medical details, psychological and other reports, and comments about your child's family background, and his or her behaviour and personality.

Your child's record will be kept at the school, and there may also be a copy at the LEA offices. Normally, it is left to the head teacher to decide what information should be included and who should be given access to it. In addition to the teaching staff, other professionals such as educational welfare officers and social workers (in some cases even the police) may be given access.

If you wish to see your child's school record, you should ask the head teacher. You may be refused, as you do not have a legal right to access, but it is worth trying. If you are refused you could raise the matter with the school governors. Some LEAS have a policy to allow parents limited access to their children's school records. You should try to find out if your particular LEA has such a policy; if it hasn't, try to get the Education Committee to discuss it, perhaps after canvassing a member of the Committee who may be sympathetic.

34 | *My 16-year-old daughter wants to continue her education to A-level, either at school or at college. I realise that the school-leaving age is 16, but does she have the right to stay on at school after 16?*

Yes. LEAS must provide continuing education for young people aged between 16 and 19 if it is requested. This can be at school or at a college of further education, and a number of LEAS have now also established sixth-form colleges. The right to continuing education to the age of 19 applies equally to young people with special educational needs, however serious (see Q19).

LEAS also have a duty to establish careers services to advise and assist young people attending educational institutions. (This does not include university, where advice need be given only at the student's request.) LEAS may provide work experience for pupils in their last year of compulsory education, too, though they are not obliged to do so.

35 | *Can I get any financial assistance from our LEA towards my child's education?*

LEAS can make various grants to enable pupils to take advantage, without hardship to themselves or their parents, of any educational facilities available to them. It is up to the individual authority to decide what financial assistance to give and to whom to give it. You should find out from your LEA offices what schemes operate in your particular area.

Most LEAS have uniform and other clothing grant schemes (see Q25). LEAS may also give grants to cover all or part of the costs of transporting your child to and from school (see Q24), and can give you a grant for fares incurred in visiting your child if he or she is at a special school some distance away. Financial assistance may also be given for pupils who cannot otherwise afford to take part in an organised school trip, though if the trip is part of the curriculum, for example a geography field trip, no charge should be made in any event.

If you have a child who is remaining at school after 16, you may be eligible for a maintenance allowance. Again, it is up to the individual LEA to decide whether you are eligible and how much it should pay.

LEAS have to provide mandatory grants, in accordance with national rules, for students who are accepted for a first degree course; this applies also to those studying for most vocational courses and for teaching qualifications. These grants are based on a parental means test unless the student is over 25 or has been self-supporting for three years. The LEA also has the discretion to give grants to students for other courses. You should ask at your LEA offices for a copy of the Department of Education and Science booklet *Grants to Students* and for the LEA's own grant regulations.

Fostering and adoption

36 | *My wife and I are interested in fostering a child (we have three children). How would we go about it, and are any people disqualified?*

Fostering is the temporary care of children by people who are not their natural parents and who do not have legal custody of them. Foster parents do not take over parental rights, as they do in adoption, though they have actual day-to-day custody of the child.

Foster placements can vary greatly in length. A child may be fostered for only a matter of days, for example when the mother has had to go into hospital. But long-term foster placements can involve caring for a child from a very young age until he or she is ready to leave home. This may happen where, for example, a young child is taken into care and adoption is not considered to be appropriate.

The law states that certain people are disqualified from acting as foster parents (unless the local authority gives specific consent). This category includes parents whose own children have been taken into care, anyone convicted of an offence against children, and any child-minder whose registration has been refused or cancelled. Apart from this, the law does not place any general restrictions on who may act as foster parents.

Natural parents may arrange 'private' fostering with another relative or a friend of the family – for example, if one of the parents is taken into hospital or the parents are working abroad for a time. But the majority of foster placements are arranged by local authority social services departments. The departments will know of children who need fostering – those who have been removed from their natural parents, say, or whose parents are temporarily unable to look after them. Each local authority has its own criteria for deciding whether someone will be a suitable foster parent, and applicants will be required to go through some form of assessment. Many local authorities now accept single people of either sex and couples living together as well as those who are married.

You will need to contact the social services department of your local authority (or a neighbouring authority) to find out whether you will be considered and to obtain information about the assessment process. The National Foster Care Association (address on page 511), an independent voluntary organisation, will also provide information to people interested in fostering.

37 | *Is local authority approval required for a private fostering arrangement?*

You may arrange for your child to be fostered by *another relative* for any length of time without any form of outside approval. The local authority social services department must be informed if:

- your child is under 16, and
- the proposed private foster parent is not a relative or guardian, and
- your child will be staying for more than 27 days with a person who is not a regular foster parent or for more than six days with someone who is a regular foster parent; a regular foster parent will have already been checked by the local authority.

The private foster parent must give the local authority at least two weeks' prior notice of the proposed arrangement, unless the child arrived in an emergency in which case the authority must be notified within 48 hours. Failure to notify the authority is an offence.

Following notification, a social worker should visit to assess the private foster parent and the home. The local authority may prohibit a private foster placement if it is considered to be unsuitable. It may also lay down conditions regarding, for example, the accommodation provided. The social services department may continue to supervise the placement on a regular basis.

38 | *What help and support will my local authority give me if I become a foster parent?*

When a local authority is notified that you are fostering privately (see Q37), a social worker will visit you to ensure that the arrangement is suitable for the child. You may receive further visits from time to time to check that everything is going well and to offer you advice if it is needed. However, the support and supervision of private foster parents varies from one authority to another.

When a local authority places a child with foster parents, it remains under a duty to ensure that the child is well cared for and to give the foster parents support. During the first two years of a foster placement, a social worker should visit at least once every two months, and after these two years at least once every three months. This is only a minimum requirement, and many authorities recognise that more frequent visits, particularly in the early days of a placement, can be very important both for the foster parent and for the child.

A local authority has a duty to review the situation of every child in its care at least once every six months. The review meeting is generally used to discuss long-term plans as well as to discuss the present situation. In many authorities foster parents are automatically included in this review. If, as a foster parent, you are not invited and you wish to attend you should ask the social services department.

In many areas there are independent foster care groups that give foster parents the opportunity to meet each other to give mutual support and to share information. The National Foster Care Association (address on page 511) will supply details of local foster care groups.

39 | *Can foster parents choose which children they wish to take?*

There are a considerable number of factors that local authorities must take into account in arranging foster placements for children. These include the age, ethnic origins and background of the child and whether a short- or long-term placement is required. In some cases efforts are made to have brothers and sisters fostered in one home. There are children who are regarded as needing particular care because they have 'special needs': this term is used to include children with disabilities, those with educational difficulties and adolescents with criminal records.

When you are assessed as a potential foster parent,

this will include consideration of what type of foster placement would be most suitable for your particular situation. Your own personal interests and preferences will be of great importance in this process of assessment.

As a matter of good practice, local authorities should give foster parents and children an opportunity to spend time together – perhaps a trial period of a weekend – to try to ensure they will get on before the placement is actually finalised. But the practice does vary from one authority to another, and it is important to find out how your authority operates in this respect. As a foster parent you should feel able to say no if you think a particular placement will not work well for the child or for your own family.

40 | *What are the responsibilities of a foster parent?*

Foster parents do not actually take over parental rights; these rights remain with the natural parents or with the local authority, depending upon the situation. But basically foster parents are required to take care of the children placed with them as if they were their own.

There are basic duties that local authority foster parents must undertake, including:

● allowing a social worker to visit;
● notifying the social worker if anything serious happens to the child, such as an accident or getting into trouble with the police;
● ensuring that the child has adequate medical and dental treatment;
● making sure that the child is brought up in a particular religion if this has been agreed between the parents and the local authority.

However, the law does not detail the day-to-day responsibilities of a foster parent, though local authorities may make their own requirements and sometimes ask foster parents to enter into a form of contract with the local authority when a child is placed.

41 | *Does the local authority need the natural parents' permission before placing a child with foster parents?*

A local authority's powers to make decisions about a child vary according to the legal basis upon which the child is in care.

If a child is in voluntary care, that is, he or she has been received into care at the parents' request, the parents still retain their parental rights. This probably means that the local authority should consult the parents about any proposed placement, though the law does not state that the parents' permission is required. In practice, if the local authority places a child who is in voluntary care with foster parents and the natural parents do not agree with this, they can demand their child's return at any time (though they will have to give 28 days' notice if the child has been in voluntary care for more than six months).

When a child is in care under a care order or a parental rights resolution (see page 106), the local authority has complete discretion as to where that child should live and a fostering placement can therefore be made even if the natural parents oppose it.

Natural parents sometimes lose contact with their children when they are in care, and the local authority can try to prevent access in some cases. But the majority of children in care maintain some form of relationship with their natural parents. It is important to ensure that arrangements about parental access are properly worked out and understood by all those involved at the start of any fostering placement.

In any decision a local authority makes about a child in its care, the child's own wishes and feelings should be taken into account. The local authority should also consider the Code of Practice on access to children in care.

42 | *Do foster parents get paid?*

When private fostering is arranged (see Q36) it is up to the natural parents and the foster parents to reach an agreement about the maintenance of the child and whether any payment is to be made to the foster parent.

Local authorities make a payment to foster parents for the maintenance of each child placed; the amount depends upon the age of the child. There is no national rate, the sums involved varying slightly from one authority to another. Additional payments may also be made direct to the foster parents to cover birthdays and Christmas.

If the particular child has special needs, for example he or she requires specialist medical treatment, the foster parents may be paid an additional amount for the extra expenditure involved. In some areas, foster parents may now be paid an enhanced allowance to take on children who need particular care, such as those with some form of disability or adolescents who are considered to be difficult or disturbed.

Anyone wishing to foster should find out from the local authority social services department what payments are made and what these payments are intended to cover. It is also important to be clear about the position regarding insurance. Not all local authorities insure foster parents against any loss or damage they may incur as a result of fostering children, and this may be something they have to arrange themselves.

43 | *As a foster parent, can I eventually adopt a child placed in my care?*

When a local authority places a child with foster parents, it should have a clear plan about the purpose and likely duration of the placement. If the plan were for adoption from the start, then as an adoption agency the authority would be obliged to place the child in accordance with the provisions set out in Q44, below.

Sometimes a placement may for a variety of reasons continue longer than originally planned. In such cases foster parents may then wish to be considered as adopters and they will have to go through the same procedures as if they had originally applied to adopt.

Once they have had a child five years, foster parents may give the local authority notice of intention to adopt, and if they then within three months apply to the court for an adoption order no one may remove the child without the consent of the court.

Foster parents should never take on a foster child in the hope that it will lead to adoption, because they are likely to be disappointed and will not be able to act in the child's interests.

A booklet on adoption by foster parents is available from the National Foster Care Association (address on page 511).

44 | *How are adoptions arranged and who decides whether someone is suitable to adopt a child?*

The law states that every local authority must run an adoption service which should include facilities for assessing children and prospective adopters and for placing children for adoption. In addition, there are a large number of officially approved adoption societies which assess prospective adoptive parents and can place children with someone they consider suitable. These agencies are governed by statutory regulations which lay down their duties in making arrangements for adoptions.

The law imposes very basic rules about who is and

who is not allowed to adopt. If a couple wish to adopt they must be married, not just living together, and must be over 21. The law states that single people over 21 can adopt, but it is still fairly unusual for a single person to be accepted as an adoptive parent.

Adoption services and agencies make their own general rules about who they will accept as suitable to adopt a child. Usually, couples are expected to have been married for at least two or three years and to be under 35 (or sometimes 40) if they are adopting a first child. This would apply to married couples who are applying to adopt because they are unable to have children of their own. Age is generally not such an important factor in relation to married couples who already have children of their own. People who have been divorced and remarried now stand a much better chance than previously of being accepted as prospective adopters.

Whatever the situation, adoption services and agencies will thoroughly check to make sure that someone wishing to adopt is suitable and can provide a good home. Prospective adoptive parents have to undergo interviews and home visits. Medical examinations and references are also required. The process of assessment may vary somewhat from one agency or service to another, as may the criteria for deciding whether someone is suitable. British Agencies for Adoption and Fostering (BAAF) will provide advice and information to people interested in adoption and a list of the various agencies; BAAF's address is on page 509.

Unless the prospective adopters are relatives or the placement is made abroad (in the latter case there may be immigration restrictions), a child may not be legally placed for adoption without the arrangements being made by an adoption agency. Where an orphaned child cannot be cared for within the family, he or she may be placed with adoptive parents by an adoption agency or service.

Children who are available for adoption are generally those whose natural parents are unable or unwilling to provide them with a home or whose natural parents are dead. The natural parents may decide for themselves that they wish their child to be adopted. In other cases the child may have been removed from their care by a court order and social services have decided that adoption is the best answer to the child's needs.

Many couples, and particularly those who are unable to have children of their own, decide they would like to adopt a baby. The number of prospective adoptive parents who wish to adopt a baby or a very young child exceeds the number of children who are available for adoption. The limited numbers and the fact that many prospective adoptive parents of babies have not had the experience of looking after children of their own means that it is much more difficult for such people to be accepted, and if accepted there can be a long delay until a suitable child can be placed with them. In many cases it is easier to get accepted as an adoptive parent if you are willing to accept an older child or a child with special needs, such as some form of disability. There are many such children awaiting adoption.

45 | *As a stepparent, may I adopt my stepchild?*

In recent years the law has discouraged adoption by stepparents where the natural parents are divorced. The law states that the court should dismiss applications to adopt by stepparents where it is satisfied that the situation can be better dealt with under matrimonial provisions. In many cases, therefore, stepparents should consider applying for a variation of whatever custody order has been made. As a stepparent you may apply for a joint custody with the child's natural parent.

The courts may still consider making an adoption order in respect of stepchildren in some cases. This may happen, for example, where the first marriage ended when the child was very young and the child thinks of the stepparent as his or her 'real' mother or father, particularly if the child also has little or no contact with the natural parent. This is a matter upon which you need to get detailed legal advice.

It is usually a lot easier to adopt as a stepparent where the child is illegitimate or where one parent has died.

46 | *I had a breakdown after my baby was born and he went to foster parents. They now want to adopt him. Can I prevent this from happening?*

The law states that generally an adoption order cannot be made unless the parent or guardian of the child has consented, and most adoptions are by consent. However, if the natural parent does object an adoption order may still be made in adoption proceedings if the county court considers there are grounds for setting aside this consent. The court may do this if the parent or guardian:

● cannot be found or is incapable of giving consent;
● is withholding consent 'unreasonably' – say, when he or she has had no contact with the child for a considerable time but refuses consent;
● has persistently failed, without reasonable cause,

to discharge parental duties in relation to the child;
● has abandoned or neglected the child;
● has persistently ill-treated the child;
● has seriously ill-treated the child and is unlikely to rehabilitate the child into the household.

If a child is illegitimate only the mother's consent is required unless the father has been given custody under a court order. However, in this situation the father may be able to put his views to the court, and, if he is paying maintenance, he must be made a party to the application so his views can be heard.

The natural parents may attempt to remove a child from the care of prospective adoptive parents, and generally they may do so if they still have parental rights. But a natural parent who has agreed to the making of an adoption order may not remove the child from prospective adopters after they have filed their adoption application without the consent of the court. Where the child has lived with the prospective adoptive parents continuously for five years and they give notice of intention to adopt to the local authority, neither the authority nor the natural parents may remove the child without the consent of the court, provided application to the court is made within three months of service of the notice.

There is also now an alternative procedure by which a child may be freed for adoption before an adoption application is made. An adoption agency may apply to a court for an order freeing a particular child for adoption. This order has the effect of transferring the parental rights and duties to the adoption agency. The natural parents may object to a 'freeing' order, but their consent may be dispensed with on the same grounds as outlined above. If the court makes the order the natural parent will have no further involvement in the child's adoption. However, if after a year following the order the child has not been adopted, not placed for adoption, the natural parents may apply to have the order revoked so they can resume parental rights, provided they have not signed a declaration that they do not wish to be further involved.

47 | *What is the procedure for adopting a child?*

An adoption becomes legal only once an adoption order is made by the court. Where the applicant is a stepparent or a relative of the child, or the child has been placed by an adoption agency, the court cannot make an order until the child has had his or her home with the applicants for at least 13 weeks; the first six weeks of a baby's life cannot count towards this period. If the prospective adopters do not fall into this category, an adoption order may be made only if the child is at least 12 months old and has lived with the applicants during the preceding 12 months.

If the child is placed with a couple by an adoption agency, they may make the adoption application to the court straight away. Although an adoption order cannot be made until the child has lived with the couple for the 13-week probationary period, there will in any event be some delay before the court hearing. During the probationary period the adoption agency will supervise the placement and ensure that the child is being well cared for. The agency will also prepare a report for the court.

The procedure is slightly different where a child is not placed by an adoption agency – a relative who wishes to adopt an orphaned child, say; or a step-parent. In this kind of situation the prospective adopters must give three months' notice to the local authority that they have the child in their care and intend to adopt. Again, application papers may be lodged at the court during this period. After the local authority has been notified, a social worker will visit during the probationary period.

Once the application to the court has been made, the court will appoint an officer to report. If the natural parents agree to the order, the court will appoint a 'reporting officer' to discuss their agreement and obtain a formal signature. If the parents do not agree, the court will appoint a 'guardian *ad litem*' (see Q56) who will investigate the case and interview all the parties.

Adoption cases are heard privately at the court – usually a county court – which means that only those directly involved are present. In reaching its decision the court must consider all the circumstances but give first consideration to the need to safeguard and promote the welfare of the child. The court must be satisfied that the natural parents have agreed to the adoption or that there are grounds for dispensing with their consent or that the child has been freed for adoption. Where there is no opposition from the natural parents, legal representation at the hearing may not be necessary, but if there are any difficulties involved legal advice should be sought.

Normally, the court will make an adoption order if it is satisfied that the conditions are complied with and that the order will be in the child's best interests. If the court refuses the adoption order there is a right of appeal available to the applicants. In cases where the child was not placed by an adoption agency, the court can make an interim order of up to two years where a further probationary period is thought necessary.

48 | *What is the legal position of the child and his or her adoptive parents once the adoption order has been made?*

Once a couple or a person adopts a child the law treats that child as if he or she were born to that couple or person: the adoptive child has the same rights in relation to the adoptive parents' property as a natural child (see WILLS, DEATH AND INHERITANCE, Q16), and if the adoptive parents separate or divorce the same arrangements must be made about custody and access as with their other children.

When the adoption order is made, the adoptive parents take over all parental rights, duties and responsibilities in relation to the child. The order ends all the natural parents' rights over the child. In exceptional circumstances it may be suggested that the adopters should allow a member of the family of origin to continue seeing the child occasionally after adoption, but this would normally be at the discretion of the adopters.

49 | *Can my adopted son, who's 12, find out who his natural parents are?*

The law gives adopted children certain rights in relation to finding out about their natural parents but only once they reach 18. At that age an adopted person has the right to see a copy of his or her original birth certificate which gives the names of one or both of the natural parents. This can be done by writing for an application form from the General Register Office (address on page 510).

Anyone adopted before 12 November 1975 must have an interview with a counsellor from the Registrar General's office (address as for General Register Office) before seeing the birth certificate. Alternatively, the adopted person may choose to see a social worker from the local authority. Those who were adopted after 12 November 1975 can decide whether they wish to have counselling before they are given access to their birth records.

Adopted children are entitled to their original birth certificates at 18, but an adopted child who is under 18 and wishes to marry is entitled to ask the General Register Office to check to ensure that the marriage is not prohibited because of some blood tie.

Adoptive parents are advised to tell their adopted child that he or she was adopted and to discuss his or her adoption and origins at an appropriate age.

Children in care

50 | *I'm a widow with a 12-year-old son and no other family. I have to go into hospital for a minor operation. Can I place my son in care temporarily?*

Yes. If you are ill or for some other reason feel temporarily unable to look after your child (if he is under 17), you can ask the social services department of your local authority to look after your child instead. If the department agrees, your child will be received into voluntary care. Sometimes, social services departments themselves suggest to parents that it may be best if their child is placed in voluntary care for a short period.

Before deciding to place your child in voluntary care, it is worth remembering that local authorities have a duty to help and support families to avoid the need for a child to be in care. The kind of help that may be given depends on the circumstances and on the decision of the particular local authority. It could be financial assistance, by helping with the rent or paying off arrears, or it may be arranging for someone to help you in the home for a few hours each day. Although you cannot demand that the social services department helps you in a specific way, it is worth asking – particularly if you prefer that your child stays at home.

When your child goes into care, generally the local authority has complete discretion as to where he or she should live, though you may be consulted – and you should be if your child is only in voluntary care. Children in care may be placed with foster parents or in a community home. Community homes vary enormously in terms of size, age-group and organisation; the term covers all types of homes from small 'family' establishments to large hostels. Children in long-term care may also be placed in some kind of special boarding-school.

While a child is in care a social worker will take overall responsibility for him or her and any decisions which need to be made. But on a day-to-day level the child will be cared for by the foster parents or by residential social workers within the home in which she or he is living.

51 | *If my son does go into voluntary care, how will that affect my rights as his parent?*

Unfortunately, the law does not say precisely how your parental rights are affected when your child is in voluntary care. However, it is generally accepted that as the arrangement is entirely voluntary on your part you retain the right to make certain major decisions concerning your child – the right to consent to your child's non-emergency medical treatment, say. In practice, though, the social services department decides such matters as your child's schooling. It will also decide where your child lives; when doing this it has a duty to ensure that your child stays near your home if at all possible.

You have the right to see your child when he is in voluntary care, and it would be most exceptional for parents to be refused access. The question of when and where this access will occur is a matter for discussion between you and the social worker.

Before you make any decision about your child, you should first discuss the matter with a social worker; he or she will take your views into account. You should say so if you are worried or dissatisfied with any of the arrangements, and if the problem persists you can write to the Director of Social Services. (In a few local authorities a special complaints procedure exists.) If none of this works to resolve any problems, or if you are unsure of your legal position, you could get legal advice from a Law Centre or from a solicitor. You could also contact the Family Rights Group (address on page 509), an organisation that advises and assists parents who have children in care.

● *Ways in which a child may go into local authority care*

A child may come to be in the care of the local authority (acting through the social services department) by various routes. The major ones are:

VOLUNTARY CARE This occurs when the local authority 'receives' a child into its care, usually at the request of a parent and with parental consent. The local authority has a duty to receive a child who is under 17 into voluntary care if the parents are dead, or the child has been abandoned, or if the child's parents are incapable because of illness or for any other reason to provide 'accommodation, maintenance and upbringing'. Before receiving a child into voluntary care, the local authority must first consider whether it would be better if another person, such as a relative or a friend, should look after the child and whether it is in the child's best interests to be in voluntary care for the time being.

PARENTAL RIGHTS RESOLUTION Where a child is already in voluntary care, the Social Services Committee of the local authority may in certain circumstances decide to pass a parental rights resolution, the effect of which is to vest the parental rights over the child in the local authority and to keep the child in care even against the parents' wishes. If the parents object to the resolution, the matter will be decided by a juvenile court.

CARE PROCEEDINGS These proceedings are held in the juvenile court and are usually initiated by the local authority. If the court makes a care order the child will be placed in the care of the local authority which then holds parental rights. Care proceedings may be preceded by the child already having been removed from his or her home under a place of safety order (see Q55). Care proceedings may be taken in relation to any child of 17 or under.

WARDSHIP PROCEEDINGS Instead of passing a parental rights resolution or taking care proceedings, the local authority may decide to make the child a ward of court. This is an increasingly common route into care, particularly in an emergency, since an interim order can usually be granted within a day or two. Where a child is warded, the court has custody but may place him or her in the care and control of the local authority. The department must, however, refer all major decisions concerning the child to the court, and parents may apply to the court for a direction on any major matter affecting their child – how frequently they may see their child, say.

MATRIMONIAL CARE ORDERS A court which is deciding a custody application made by one or both parents may in exceptional circumstances decide that it is 'impracticable or undesirable' for either parent to be granted custody. In such cases the court can order that the child be received into care by the local authority. The court may also make directions on matters such as where the child should live and access by parents either when it first makes the matrimonial care order or later if an application is made to resolve a dispute over such matters.

CARE IN CRIMINAL PROCEEDINGS A juvenile court in criminal proceedings may order a child or young person to be in local authority care in the following ways:

● When the court refuses bail it may order a remand to care.
● On finding a child or young person guilty of an offence the court may make a care order.
● Where a child or young person is already subject to a care order made in criminal proceedings and then commits another offence the court may make a residential care order.

---

52 | *Can I get my child out of voluntary care whenever I want?*

If your child has been in voluntary care for less than six months, he or she should be returned to you as soon as you ask. However, in practice, it is not always so simple. Social services departments may decide that it is not in your child's best interests to return home, and may take steps to try to prevent this happening. They may either make your child a ward of court (see page 91) or, if they have the time and reasons for doing so, pass a parental rights resolution (see above). Alternatively, if you have already taken your child home, the social services department may ask a magistrate to grant a place of safety order (see Q55).

If your child has been in voluntary care for more than six months, you must give the social services department of the local authority 28 days' notice in writing that you wish to have your child home. Once the 28 days are up (or before if the local authority agrees) you may take your child home. You will be committing a criminal offence if you remove your child from care during this period without the consent of the local authority.

The period of notice is intended to give the social services department time to make a decision on what they think is best for your child. Again, if it decides that it is not in your child's best interests to return home, it may take the same steps as mentioned above to try to prevent this happening.

If you are worried that the local authority may stop you from having your child home when you ask, or if it takes legal proceedings to prevent your child from returning home, you should get legal advice and assistance as soon as possible either from a Law Centre or from a solicitor. The Family Rights Group (address on page 509) may also be able to help.

53 | *How does the local authority take a parental rights resolution and can I object to this happening if it should try to do so in the case of my son, who is in voluntary care?*

If your child is already in voluntary care, the social services department may decide at some point that it should take over your parental rights by passing a parental rights resolution (see page 106). It may do so when it is satisfied that one or more of the following reasons apply:

● your child has no parent or guardian (though this obviously does not apply in your case);
● you have abandoned your child (for example, you have been out of touch and your address has been unknown for a year or more);
● you are unfit to look after your child because of a serious physical or mental illness or a serious disability;
● your way of life makes you an unsuitable parent or you have regularly failed to act as a proper parent;
● your child has been continuously in voluntary care for the past three years or more;
● parental rights have already been taken away from your child's other parent and he or she is likely to be living in the same home with you and your child.

Before the resolution is passed, a social worker should tell you why the local authority has reached this decision and should explain the procedure. A meeting of elected councillors on the local authority's Social Services Committee will be asked, after reading reports and perhaps asking further questions of the social workers, to pass the resolution. Before this meeting takes place you should ask for copies of the reports. Although the social services department is not obliged to give them to you, it should at least provide you with a statement of its reasons in writing.

If you wish to attend the council meeting, you should ask the social worker to obtain permission for you to do so. Whether or not you will be allowed to attend depends on the practice in your particular local authority. Local authorities have been generally advised to allow parents to attend at least part of the meeting either alone or with a friend or an adviser like a solicitor so as to enable them to put their own views directly to the councillors who are making the decision. If you do not wish to attend, or your local authority does not permit it, you should write to the Social Services Committee giving your views.

It is important that you seek legal advice and assistance from a Law Centre or from a solicitor as soon as possible after you have been told that the social services department intends to pass a parental rights resolution. If your local authority allows you to attend the council meeting, you may well want your solicitor to go with you and speak on your behalf.

54 | *I've been told that if my local authority passes a parental rights resolution on my child, the matter will be referred to a court. Is this true?*

It depends on whether or not you object to the resolution. When a parental rights resolution is passed by the Social Services Committee, you will be notified of the decision in writing. You then have 28 days in which to decide whether to object to the resolution. If you wish to object, you must write to the social services department telling it this within 28 days of receiving the letter.

If you do object the department may agree to let the resolution lapse. However, this does not usually happen. More commonly the social services department will decide that it wishes to continue the resolution. If so, within 14 days of receiving your letter it must make an application to the juvenile court asking the court to decide who should have the parental rights of your child. If it fails to do this, the resolution will automatically end after the 14 days.

You will be told of the date, time and place of the court hearing. While you wait for the case to come to court, and while the case is being heard, the social services department keeps parental rights over your child, who must therefore stay in care.

As the case is between you and the social services department, you are entitled to have your own solicitor represent you; depending on your means you may get Legal Aid (see page 490). Your child is not automatically entitled to have his or her own solicitor, but the court may decide that this would be best. The court may also decide to appoint a guardian *ad litem* (see Q56) to represent your child's interests.

Before the court can decide to confirm the resolution and therefore allow the social services department to retain parental rights over your child, it must be satisfied on the following three matters:

● that one or more of the grounds for a resolution (see Q53) existed when the resolution was originally passed; and

● that one of those reasons still exists at the time of the court hearing; and

● that the parental rights resolution is in the best interests of your child.

You may appeal against the court's decision within 28 days of its making that decision; a Law Centre or your solicitor will advise you of the procedure, and the Family Rights Group (address on page 509) will help too.

55 | *My neighbours often treat their 10-year-old son with extreme violence, and after one episode when I saw the child with a black eye, a friend said I should have applied for a place of safety order. What is this?*

It is an emergency order granted by a magistrate at any time during the day or night which allows a child to be removed from home (or wherever he or she is) and be taken to a 'place of safety'. The order lasts for a specified period but must not exceed 28 days. The place of safety could be a children's home, a police station, a hospital, a foster home, or any other suitable place. Usually, it is a social worker from the social services department who asks for the order, but in fact anyone may apply. You should not apply direct to a magistrate but elicit the advice and help of a social worker or an NSPCC officer.

Nobody need tell the parents that a place of safety order is being sought. In fact, parents usually come to know about it only when their child is actually removed. They will be told the reasons for it, but not necessarily where the child has been taken. There is very little that parents can do to challenge the order. They have no right of appeal, nor can they apply for it to be removed. Nevertheless, the parents should seek legal advice.

Additionally, a child may be removed from home by a police officer and taken to a place of safety for a period of up to eight days. The police officer does not need an order from a magistrate. When this happens, a senior police officer must investigate the circumstances giving rise to the child's removal, and in practice the police will ask the social services department to step in. During the eight-day period the child (or the parents on behalf of their child) may apply to a magistrate for the detention to cease.

Technically, the child is not in care but is merely being detained during the time that he or she is in a 'place of safety'. This should mean that parents retain their parental rights. In practice, though, the social services department (or the police) will make the decision as to where the child lives. The parents have no automatic right to see their child, but it is important that they contact the social services department to try to arrange visiting.

If the social services department considers that the child should be in care, it must apply to the juvenile court for a care order (see Q56) before the period of the place of safety order has ended.

56 | *What are care proceedings?*

This is the name for the legal process by which the juvenile court can order that a child be taken into the care of the local authority. The proceedings are usually started by the social services department and may be taken in relation to any child under the age of 17.

The parents will be sent a summons stating that they should attend court on a particular day. It is important that they go to court; if they don't, the court can order them to attend.

Technically, these proceedings are between the local authority and the child. This means that the child has an automatic right to apply for Legal Aid (see page 490) for his or her own solicitor. The court sometimes appoints the child's solicitor, but there is nothing to stop the parents from doing so at the outset of the proceedings. The child's solicitor *cannot* also represent the parents. Although the parents are entitled to have their own solicitor, they are not entitled to Legal Aid unless the court makes a 'separate representation order'. It will do so when it considers that there is or may be a conflict between the parents' interests and the child's. Under enacted provisions still to be brought into force, if the court makes such an order the parents will have full party rights. If the court does not make this order, the parents can still get legally aided advice and assistance from a solicitor, and some Law Centres and private solicitors may agree to represent them in court free of charge. The Family Rights Group (address on page 509) may be able to help too.

If the court makes a separate representation order, it may also appoint a guardian *ad litem* to represent the child's interests. This person is usually a social worker who is independent of the social services department in the case, that is, he or she works for a different local authority. The guardian *ad litem* must, among other things, investigate the circumstances of the case (which may include interviewing the parents) and write a report for the court. He or she must also ascertain the child's wishes and feelings and report these to the court.

It is usual for the case to be adjourned at the first hearing (and possibly subsequent hearings). This occurs if anyone taking part in the proceedings is not ready to go ahead or if the court has insufficient time to hear the full case. An adjournment may last for a period of up to 28 days on each occasion. If the court considers that the child should remain in care during this time, it will make an interim care order. The parents are entitled to oppose this order being made.

Strictly, in law parents may participate in the proceedings only to the extent of answering any allegations made against them. However, most courts recognise the importance of parents taking a full part in the proceedings and allow them or their solicitor to cross-examine witnesses and to call their own witnesses, and so on.

Before the court can make an order at the full hearing it must be satisfied that at least one of the following reasons exists for the child to be taken into care:

● either the child is not making the progress – physically, emotionally, mentally – he or she should, or the child's health has been damaged or neglected, or the child is being ill-treated;
● one of the above things *may* happen to the child because a court has already found this to be the case in respect of another child in the family, or a person who lives or may live with the family has been convicted of a criminal offence concerning children;
● the child is in moral danger – the child's sexual behaviour is disapproved of, or the parents' life-style;
● the parents cannot control their child;

● the child is of compulsory school age and is not receiving proper education;
● the child is guilty of a criminal offence.

In addition to one of these reasons, the court must also be satisfied that the child is in need of care or control which he or she is unlikely to get unless an order is made.

If the court decides that the local authority has not proved its case, that is the end of the matter and the parents can take their child home. If the court decides that the case is proved it must then decide what to do. The magistrates will probably look at any reports that have been prepared about the child. Although there are several orders that a court may make, in practice the decision is usually between making a *care order* or a *supervision order*. A care order gives the care of the child to the social services department. This means that almost all parental rights are taken over by the department (see Q57). A supervision order means that the child can go home but that he or she will be supervised by a social worker or a probation officer. The child should have regular contact with the person, who will advise, assist and befriend him or her.

Parents have no legal right themselves to appeal against the court's decision. They may appeal on behalf of the child, unless the court has appointed a guardian *ad litem* for the child.

57 | *Do I have any parental rights if my child is taken in care under a court order?*

In general terms, when your child is in care following a court order or a parental rights resolution the local authority takes over almost all your parental rights, so generally it may make all the decisions about your child's life. For example, it is entitled to decide matters of education; it may also decide where your child should live – either in a community home, with foster parents or even at home with you – as far as possible, however, placing your child near to your home.

There are some restrictions on these powers. Although it can arrange for your child to be placed for adoption with prospective adopters, it cannot give parental consent to the adoption (see Q46); nor can it consent to your child's emigration without the consent of the Secretary of State for Social Services. Also, your child cannot be brought up in a religion different from the one he or she had on going into care.

While looking after your child, the local authority

is under a duty to give 'first consideration to the need to safeguard and promote' your child's welfare. When taking decisions the department must find out your child's wishes and feelings and take them into account.

If you are worried or dissatisfied with any of the arrangements made for your child, you should discuss them with the social worker. If this does not resolve the problem, you should write to the Director of Social Services and the councillor who chairs the Social Services Committee of the local authority. There are very few situations in which a decision of the social services department can be taken to court, so it is often difficult to take problems any further. Your child's six-monthly review (see Q58) may offer the opportunity to have the issue more widely discussed. If writing to the Director of Social Services and to the chairman of the Committee gets you nowhere, contact a solicitor, the Family Rights Group or the Children's Legal Centre (addresses on page 509) to see if they can help.

58 | *What rights does my child have while in care?*

Your child is entitled to all the rights that any other child has: the right to education, to receive necessary medical treatment, to be cared for, and so on. There is also an important addition for children in care: the social services department is under a specific duty to 'ascertain the wishes and feelings' of the child and to 'give due consideration to them' (which depends on the child's age and understanding). Recently, a group of young people in a children's home successfully took their local authority to court to stop the department from closing the home until it had listened to them and considered each of their individual needs.

The local authority is under a duty to hold a 'review' of your child's circumstances at least every six months. This review must specifically consider whether the care order can or should be discharged. Some local authorities actively encourage or, at least, permit children (or parents) to attend the review. This will allow your child (and possibly you) to raise matters about his or her treatment.

Some local authorities now publish a guide for children in care, setting out their rights.

Frequently, children in care feel isolated and unable to bring about any changes to their situation. This highlights the importance of such organisations as the National Association of Young People in Care (NAYPIC) (address on page 511) and the local WHO

CARES? groups (details should be available from Citizens Advice Bureaux). NAYPIC is an independent organisation run by and for children in care and is concerned specifically with the rights of children in care. WHO CARES? groups are organised locally by young people in care and by concerned adults; they hold meetings and social functions to which your child may wish to go. If your child needs legal advice about his or her rights, the Children's Legal Centre (address on page 509) will help.

59 | *Can the social services department prevent me from seeing my child, who is in care?*

Generally, social services departments decide whether you may see your child, where this is to take place, and how frequently. Until recently, parents had no way of challenging such major decisions even when social services departments refused to allow them to see their child at all. Now, however, if you are refused access totally or your access is stopped, social services departments must first serve a notice on you telling you that this is happening. You may then apply to the juvenile court for an access order; you will need legal advice to do this and the Family Rights Group (address on page 509) should be able to help too. If the court decides that it is in your child's best interests that you should have access, it can say how often access should occur, where, with whom, and how long for.

Unfortunately, the right to apply for an access order is applicable only to situations where you are not allowed to see your child at all, and if the social services department severely restricts your access to, say, once every four months you are not entitled to go to court and there is little you can do to challenge the decision. Likewise, social services departments are entitled to change the arrangements for access without your consent, and may even postpone access 'for such reasonable period' as allows the department to consider future arrangements. Again, you are not able to go to court to challenge this.

Once the court has made an access order, either you or the social services department may apply to the court for it to be varied. In an emergency, the department may apply to the magistrates (without your necessarily knowing) for an order suspending access for a maximum of seven days. If the department then wants to continue to deny you access, it must apply within seven days for a full court hearing.

There is a Code of Practice on access to children in care which provides guidance to the local authority.

If you have a child in care you should ask to be shown this.

If you experience any problems over the question of access to your child you should take legal advice either by going to a Law Centre or by seeing a solicitor. If you want to have your child home at some later time, it is crucially important that you keep in regular contact with the child by visiting him or her and also writing and telephoning.

60 | *My nephew, who was in trouble with the police, is in care, but recently a social worker warned me that he should be in secure accommodation. What is this?*

'Secure accommodation' is a home specifically designed to restrict liberty. Social services departments may now place children in such accommodation only in specific circumstances for a maximum period of 72 hours; after that, the juvenile court must authorise any further period.

Before the social services department may place a child in secure accommodation, even in an emergency, it must be satisfied that one or more of the following reasons applies:

● the child has a history of absconding, is likely to abscond from other kinds of accommodation and be 'at risk' normally of getting involved in offences;
● the child's behaviour is such that if kept in any other kind of accommodation he or she is likely to cause injury to himself or herself or others.

There are additional reasons applicable to children who are remanded to care in criminal proceedings (see page 115).

Parents or guardians should be informed as soon as their child is put into secure accommodation. They will also be told if the local authority decides to take the matter to court for authority to keep the child there beyond the 72-hour period.

Once the court is satisfied that there are grounds for keeping the child in secure accommodation, it will make an order authorising this. On the local authority's first application the authorised period must not exceed three months, and on subsequent applications the period must not exceed six months. The child is entitled to a solicitor on Legal Aid (see page 490) and can oppose any order being made.

The social services department is under a duty to review the child's circumstances at least every three months while the secure accommodation placement continues. The parents' and the child's views must be

taken into account during this process. If at any time the reason for keeping your child in secure accommodation no longer exists, your child must be removed to other accommodation that does not restrict liberty.

61 | *My son of 12 is in care under a court order and living in a community home. He's now run away. What will happen to him?*

By absconding from care, a child does not automatically commit a criminal offence, although he or she may be arrested by the police and returned to care. If a child persistently absconds, he or she runs the risk of being kept in secure accommodation (see Q60).

A person who either encourages or assists a child to run away, or who harbours, conceals or in any way prevents a child from returning to care, is committing an offence. As a parent you are not obliged to inform the social services department where your child is while 'on the run' if you know, but on the other hand you might be committing a criminal offence if you mislead the department by telling a lie. If it is thought that you know where your child is and that you are able to produce him or her, the juvenile court may order you to attend court with your child. A search warrant may also be granted to search premises where your child is believed to be.

If your child absconds because he is unhappy in care, you should try to persuade the social services department to make changes that would help your child – by moving him to another home, say, or allowing him more contact with the family. You would need to get legal advice from a Law Centre or from a solicitor if you feel that an application to discharge the care order is necessary.

62 | *Do I have to contribute to my child's upkeep when he's in care?*

Depending on your means, the social services department may ask you to contribute towards your child's maintenance so long as your child is under 16. Young people in care who are 16 and over and who are working, receiving Supplementary Benefit or a training allowance may be required to contribute themselves.

If you are asked to contribute, the social services department will send you a notice stating the amount of the contribution. If you think that the amount is too much or you fail to pay it on two or more occasions, the matter will be taken to the magistrates' court for a decision as to whether you should contribute and, if so, how much. Your local authority is entitled to fix a flat-rate contribution for all children in care; it can alter this as it thinks reasonable in individual cases. The upper limit of the parents' contribution must not exceed the allowance paid by the local authority to a foster parent for a child of the same age.

You are not liable to pay contributions if you receive Supplementary Benefit or Family Income Supplement. Social services departments also have a discretion whether to charge you at all; they need not do so where this would be unreasonable because of your particular circumstances. In fact, they may even help financially – for example, by paying parents' fares to and from visiting their child.

63 | Does the social services department keep written records about me and my son, who is in care, and can I see them?

Social services departments keep some kind of personal case record about most people who come to them for help. If your child is in care, the department will certainly keep a case record which states the reasons why he or she is in care and includes details of your family circumstances. Sometimes this is only a family case record – one that deals with your whole family – or there may be a case record about the individual child as well.

Local authorities are now encouraged to reveal information held on their files, although social services departments are still entitled to withhold disclosure of certain information which may of course be what parents or children particularly want to know. For example, they will not show you any part of the file that records information given to them in confidence by a neighbour, say, or by a GP. Similarly, if a social worker has expressed an opinion and this is recorded in the file, you are unlikely to be able to see it. From what you are allowed to see, if you feel that anything is inaccurate you should try to persuade the social services department to amend the record or, at least, to record your version of events as well.

If your child does not wish you to see his or her case record, it is unlikely that the social services department will go against these wishes, although this obviously depends on the age of the child and whether he or she is old enough to be consulted by the social services department.

64 | Does my child have to stay in care until 18?

Both court care orders and parental rights resolutions automatically end when the person reaches 18

(or 19 if the child was 16 or over when the court care order was made). The order will also cease if your child is adopted.

However, a child may leave care before reaching this age if a successful application is made for the removal, or 'discharge', of the original order. How this application is made and what the court must decide varies slightly according to the kind of order that placed your child in care. Legal advice should be obtained from a solicitor or Law Centre or from the Family Rights Group (address on page 509).

If your child is in care following a care order made by the juvenile court (see Q56), strictly it is your child who applies for the discharge. You may, however, sign the application form on his or her behalf. The local authority may also make the application if it considers that your child no longer needs to be in care. After the court has heard the evidence, it may decide either that the care order should continue, or that it should be substituted by a supervision order (see Q56), or that it should cease totally. Before ending the care order, the court must be satisfied that your child is no longer in need of the kind of care and control that can be provided only by a care order or a supervision order.

If your child is in care as a result of a parental rights resolution (see Q53), social services departments may decide to ask the Social Services Committee to pass another resolution giving back your parental rights. If at any time you think that your child no longer needs to be in care under a parental rights resolution, you can suggest this to the social services department. Otherwise, there are two ways in which you may apply for its discharge. First, if for some reason you did not formally object when the resolution was originally passed by the Social Services Committee (and therefore the matter did not go to the juvenile court for a decision at that stage; see Q54), you may apply to court for its discharge within six months of the date on which the Committee made its decision. In order to succeed with this application, you have to prove to the court that there were no good reasons for passing the resolution in the first place. Second, you may at any time apply to the juvenile court on the grounds that it is in your child's best interests that it be removed.

In order to prevent parents from making repeated unsuccessful applications, no new application may be made within three months of a previous application that failed. This restriction applies to both applications to discharge a care order and a parental rights resolution.

If your child was placed in care in wardship proceedings (see page 106) or a matrimonial care order (see page 106), you may make a similar application to end the care order to the court that made the original order.

Children in trouble

65 | *If my son were ever to get into trouble with the police, would I automatically be told?*

The law states that when the police arrest a juvenile, that is, a young person under 17 years of age, they must take all practicable steps to inform at least one of the parents. This means the police should try to contact you as soon as they have discovered your child's name and address. Where a juvenile is on a supervision order (see Q56), the person responsible for the supervision – usually a social worker – should also be informed.

This notification of parents is in addition to the right available to any person who is arrested to have a friend or a relative informed of the situation. Thus, your child may ask that someone else be informed about his or her detention, though the police must still inform the parents.

66 | *Can the police detain my child for questioning?*

The police may hold any person for questioning only if he or she has been arrested. Otherwise attendance at the police station is voluntary: anyone asked to help the police with their enquiries may refuse to answer questions and may leave at any time unless he or she has been arrested.

See also YOU AND THE CRIMINAL LAW, Q13.

67 | *What should I do if my child is arrested and is held by the police on a suspicion of stealing, say?*

When you are informed that your child is being held by the police, it is important that you go to the police station as quickly as possible. You should then find out as much information as you can, including why, when, and where your child was arrested and whether the police have already started questioning your child. You should ask to see your child immediately.

Guidance on police practice imposed by the Home Office states that juveniles should be interviewed in the presence of a parent or another responsible adult

who is not a police officer as well as an interviewing police officer, only one of whom is permitted to conduct the interview. The police are allowed to ignore this guidance if they consider that the delay will involve serious loss or damage to property or an immediate risk to other people.

Research published by the Policy Studies Institute in 1983 (*Police and People in London*) indicates that children are in fact often questioned by the police before a parent has arrived, or separately from the parent even when he or she actually is at the station. The report acknowledges that the presence of a parent can be very important, 'since officers tend to be more restrained in their manner and questioning method when an adult is present than otherwise'. Whether your child is innocent or guilty, he or she has the right to be treated fairly by the police. Your presence may help to ensure that this happens.

Anyone held by the police has a right to remain silent and you may be best advised to tell your child not to answer questions or to make a statement until you can obtain legal advice. Generally, any person who is detained by the police has the right to see a solicitor – the police may delay this only where a serious arrestable offence is involved (see YOU AND THE CRIMINAL LAW, QS 14 and 15). But young people are often unaware of their right to legal advice, so you should ensure that a solicitor is contacted. Where possible, you should get in touch with a solicitor before you go to the station or otherwise ask to telephone a solicitor from the station. The police should provide names of solicitors who operate emergency schemes and who will be prepared to come along whatever the time of day or night.

● *Juvenile offenders – principal forms of sentencing*

ABSOLUTE DISCHARGE A juvenile offender may be discharged absolutely, but this is not very common and is used only for very trivial offences.

CONDITIONAL DISCHARGE A juvenile offender may be discharged on condition that he or she commits no further offence for a period of up to three years. Someone (usually a parent) may have to give security for the young person's behaviour during this period. If a further offence is committed during that period, the court may pass sentence for the original offence as well as the subsequent one.

BINDING OVER The parents of a young offender may with their consent be ordered to enter into a 'recognisance' of up to £1,000 for a period of up to three years to take proper care of and exercise proper control over their child. If this is breached and the child commits a subsequent offence the parents have to forfeit the sum stipulated. This sentence is often used where the child is young and the offence relatively trivial.

FINES, COMPENSATION AND COSTS The maximum fine a magistrate can order on 10- to 12-year-olds is £100 and on 14- to 16-year-olds £400. The parents (or in some cases their child) may be ordered to pay the fine. Compensation of up to £2,000 may be ordered for injury, loss or damage resulting from the offence – one involving vandalism, say. The court may also order that the costs of the case be paid.

SUPERVISION ORDER A young offender may be placed on a supervision order for up to three years. The supervisor is usually a social worker, but in some areas it may be a probation officer. Generally, this entails the young person visiting the supervisor once each week or every couple of weeks, or the supervisor may visit the young person at home. The supervisor will discuss any difficulties the young person is experiencing at home or at school and help to resolve problems that may have led to the offence.

SUPERVISED ACTIVITY ORDER Within a supervision order the court may direct that the young offender complies with any directions the supervisor may make. Alternatively, the court may itself order particular requirements. The requirements in a supervision order may include living at a specified place – such as the parental home if the young person has been staying elsewhere – for specified periods; participation in specified activities such as groups run by social services or the probation services; attending a specified place on certain days for group activities, say. No requirement may exceed 90 days. If the court itself makes directions, it can order that the young offender refrains from particular activities, such as attending football matches, for up to 90 days. It may also include a night restriction or curfew, requiring the young person to be at home for specified periods of up to 10 hours between 6pm and 6am; curfews may last for up to 30 days and must be within the first three months of the supervision order.

68 | *Can I refuse to allow the police to photograph or fingerprint my child?*

It has become an increasingly common practice for the police to photograph any person they detain following arrest. Guidance governing police practice states that parental consent is required before a photograph is taken of any child aged between 10 and 14 (children under 10 would not be photographed). Juveniles aged 14, 15 or 16 must themselves consent *and* the permission of a parent is required. However, the police may photograph without consent if:

● the child has been charged with an offence for which a conviction would be recorded in the national police records which involves virtually any criminal offence; or

● the child has been convicted of an offence and his or her photograph is not already on record; or

● where a number of people have been arrested and a photographic record is necessary to establish who was arrested, at what time and in what place.

Similar provisions apply to fingerprinting. If your child has reached 10 years of age but is under 14, your consent is required; if your child is aged 14, 15 or 16 both your consent *and* that of your child are required. Again, there are situations where the police may fingerprint without consent: see YOU AND THE CRIMINAL LAW, Q18.

69 | *On what grounds can the police refuse to release my child?*

The police may detain your child only if there has

DEFERRED SENTENCES The court may defer sentencing a young offender for up to six months. When the sentence is finally given the court will take into account the young person's conduct during that period and any change in circumstances.

ATTENDANCE CENTRE ORDER Normally, an attendance centre order will be for between 12 and 24 hours, with a maximum of three hours per day. Attendance centres are usually run by the police and involve the young offenders in physical activity.

COMMUNITY SERVICE A community service order may be made on anyone of 16 or over for anything between 40 and 120 hours. Community service involves unpaid socially useful work usually carried out over a period of up to a year at weekends. The work often involves physical labour, such as decorating a church or an old people's home, but can involve helping to run community groups, for example.

CARE ORDER A care order may be made in criminal proceedings if:

● it is appropriate because of the seriousness of the offence, and
● the young offender is in need of the care or control he or she is unlikely to receive unless the court makes a care order.

During the care order the local authority determines where the young person should live, which may be in a community home, with foster parents or even with the natural parents. In the last case, however, if a young person who is in care as a result of an offence commits another offence, the court may impose a 'charge and control' restriction on the care order for up to six months. This means the court may order the local authority that the young person must not be placed at home, or, if there, must be removed from it.

DETENTION CENTRE The sentence is normally for between 21 days and four months and may be imposed on only *male* offenders of between 14 and 20 years old. Detention centres generally operate a very strict regime with the young people having various tasks of physical labour to perform and compulsory involvement in drill and physical exercise. Those under school-leaving age must also receive education.

YOUTH CUSTODY Male *or* female young offenders aged 15 or over may be sentenced to youth custody. The maximum sentence for 15- and 16-year-olds is 12 months; normally, the sentence will be for at least four months, although shorter sentences can be given in some cases. Youth custody centres are in theory intended to give young offenders some kind of training in terms of work and education. In practice the provision of such facilities has diminished: educational opportunities are limited and work experience tends to be confined to physical and manual labour within the institution.

been an arrest. If your child is arrested and taken to a police station, a particular officer must be designated as 'custody officer'. This officer must decide as soon as practicable whether your child should be released or charged for committing a crime.

The police may detain a person without charge for questioning or to 'secure and preserve' evidence, but the law lays down certain limits: see YOU AND THE CRIMINAL LAW, QS 16 and 17.

If your child is charged, in the majority of cases he or she will be released (see Q70). But the police may continue detention if:

● they believe the detention is necessary to prevent harm, or
● they are not satisfied that the name and address given are correct, or

● they believe your child may not appear in court, or
● they have grounds for believing detention is in your child's own interests.

If the police do decide to detain your child for one of the above reasons, he or she must be transferred to the care of the local authority. However, 15- and 16-year-old boys may be detained in penal establishments, generally remand centres, if they are considered to be 'unruly'. Where a juvenile is charged and detained, he or she must be brought before a court 'as soon as practicable'.

70 | *Will I be asked to stand bail before my child can be released? And what would this entail?*

After arrest, your child will be allowed to leave the station only if the police decide to release him or her unconditionally or on police bail. Your child may be released unconditionally if the police are not going to proceed with a charge or if the offence involved is a relatively minor one. Bail may be required where your child has been charged or has been told to return to the station at a future date to be charged. This procedure applies to everyone, not just to juveniles.

The police can release a juvenile on his or her own surety – a pledge that he or she will turn up at the station or at court – but will often demand that someone else, normally a parent, stands as surety to guarantee the child's appearance. A surety must enter into a 'recognisance', the amount of bail specified by the police or by the court. This sum may have to be surrendered if your child does not appear in court or fails to return to the police station at the stipulated date. You do not actually have to hand over any money to the police when you agree to stand bail, but you may have to show that you are able to if required.

The police should generally allow bail, but there are situations in which your child's detention can be continued (see Q69). If the police refuse bail, a bail application may still be made to the magistrates when your child appears in court, and if the magistrates refuse bail an appeal may be made against their decision to a judge of the High Court in chambers.

71 | *At what age can children be charged and taken to court if they should commit a criminal offence?*

Children under 10 cannot be charged with a criminal offence; only children aged 10 and over may be charged and taken to court. Children aged 17 are considered to be adults and will be treated as such for the purposes of any criminal offence.

Although the law presumes that a child under 10 is incapable of committing an offence, this does not necessarily mean that nothing will happen to a child who is under 10 and is caught committing an offence. In most such cases the police may informally reprimand the child, but they may also – particularly where it is a serious offence – arrest the child. The child will then be taken to the police station, where the circumstances of the offence will be investigated. If the police consider that it is in the child's interests, or because of the seriousness of the offence, they may detain the child in a 'place of safety' (usually a local authority children's home) for up to eight days. During this time the police normally ask the social ser-

vices department of the local authority to become involved. The social services department will then decide whether your child should be taken into care or not. The child has the right to apply to a magistrate for his or her release at any time during this eight-day period.

If the child is aged between 10 and 14 and is taken to court, the police must prove not only that the child committed an offence but also that he or she knew that what he or she was doing was wrong. This should be an additional protective measure for children who are taken to court.

72 | *When children commit offences, must they always appear before a magistrate?*

The police decide whether or not a child must go to court for a criminal offence. In the case of serious offences, the police will usually charge a child or young person with the offence while he or she is still at the police station following arrest. Once the child is charged, he or she will have to go to court at some later time. Your child does not have to be taken immediately before the court once charged unless he or she has not been released on bail. Very often, the first court appearance will happen some months after the charge.

Alternatively, the police may release the child from the police station without charging him or her. In these circumstances the child may be told that the Juvenile Bureau will be in touch, which means that the police will refer the matter to the Juvenile Bureau for a decision on what is to happen. The Bureau (or Liaison Scheme as it is sometimes called) is run by the police in liaison with other agencies such as the local education authority and social services department; these agencies will be asked to say what they know about the child. A police officer from the Bureau may go to talk to the parents and the child at home. After making these investigations, the Bureau will deal with the matter in one of three different ways. It may:

● prosecute the child, which means that a summons will be sent to the parents saying when the child is to attend court;
● caution the child;
● take no further action.

A caution is an oral warning given to the child by a police officer and is formally recorded on the child's police record. The child is warned about his or her conduct and about the possibility of a future prosecution if any other offence is committed. However, before the child may be cautioned, three conditions must apply:

- the child must admit the offence,
- the parents must agree that the matter can be dealt with in this way, and
- if there is a 'loser' or 'victim' to the child's offence, that person must also agree to the caution.

If a child is offered a caution, the parents should seriously consider whether this is a good idea. Some young people admit an offence merely for the sake of getting a caution rather than having to go to court. This is seen as the best way of getting the matter over and done with. However, it is not as simple as that because if the child commits another offence and is taken to court, the court will be told of the caution and will regard it as little short of a finding of guilt. It is therefore important that if the child did not commit the offence he or she does not agree to a caution.

73 | *How do juvenile courts differ from other courts?*

Proceedings in the juvenile court are dealt with in a more informal way than would be the case in an adult court. The juvenile court generally consists of three lay magistrates, that is, non-professionals, one of whom must be a woman, although it is also possible for juvenile cases to be heard by a stipendiary magistrate – a full-time professional – who sits alone. The rules that govern the procedure of a juvenile court require that the language be simpler and easier to understand than in other courts. In addition, the court must give more explanation as to what it is doing or what it is about to do.

In exceptional circumstances a child and/or his or her parents may be asked to leave the court. This happens only after a child has been found guilty of an offence and the court is discussing the home background before deciding on the sentence. However, if this does happen the child and parents must be told the broad substance of what has been discussed and be given an opportunity to put their own point of view.

Juvenile courts are not open to the public and only certain people are authorised to be in court. These usually include an officer from the Juvenile Bureau (see Q72) and representatives from the social services department, the local education authority and the probation service. Although members of the press are allowed to be present, any report of the proceedings must not reveal the name, address, or school or any other fact that may lead to the identification of the child.

74 | *Does my child have the right to be legally represented in court?*

Yes. Your child may be represented by a lawyer in court whatever the nature of the charge. However, whether you will have to pay or whether the costs will be met by Legal Aid depends upon the case and the particular court – generally Legal Aid in criminal proceedings is discretionary and practice varies from one court to another. But Legal Aid must be granted in certain criminal proceedings. These are:

- if the child has been refused bail and was not legally represented at the first hearing;
- if the child is remanded to custody or care before sentencing;
- if the child is charged with murder;
- if the court is considering making a care order or a detention or youth custody order (see page 115).

In other situations the court will consider both financial eligibility and whether 'it is in the interests of justice' to grant Legal Aid. Parents of children under 16 must normally submit a statement of means to the court. There is no upper limit above which the child will be refused Legal Aid, but if the parents' disposable income and capital are above a particular amount they will be required to make a contribution.

An application for Legal Aid may be made at the first court appearance. Very often there is no right of appeal if the court refuses, but a further application may be made at each court appearance.

It can be very important for parents to obtain legal advice before the case comes to court, to discuss the case, the court procedures, whether the child should be legally represented, and other matters. Some solicitors now operate a fixed-fee interview system, that is, they will give a half-hour interview for £5 whatever the client's means (see page 482).

Alternatively, depending upon financial eligibility, it may be possible to get advice and assistance under the Green Form Scheme (see page 490). Under this scheme a solicitor may take action costing up to £75 on your child's behalf; this can sometimes be extended. The Green Form application must be made at the solicitor's office by you or your child, depending on whether he or she is working. The costs of this preliminary advice and assistance may be met totally under the Green Form Scheme although parents may have to make a contribution according to their means. Information sheets on the various types of Legal Aid can be obtained from solicitors or the Children's Legal Centre (address on page 509).

Parents should attend court with their child both to give support and to demonstrate that they are responsible parents. In fact, the court can order them to attend where it is thought necessary.

75 | *As a parent, for what am I liable if my child should commit an offence?*

If your child is fined, you, as his or her parent, will have to pay the fine unless the court is satisfied that this would be 'unreasonable'. The law does not specify the circumstances that might make it unreasonable, but factors such as whether you have contributed to the offence by failing to take proper care and control of your child, your financial means, and so on, are relevant to the court's decision. In the same way you are liable to pay any compensation ordered by the court (see page 114).

You must be given the opportunity of putting your views to the court before being ordered to pay the fine. You can also appeal to the Crown Court about the order.

Paying the fine and any compensation is the full extent of parents' financial liability should their child be found guilty of a criminal offence.

Custodianship

76 | *I've been looking after my grandson for two years since he was born. Can I obtain any legal rights in respect of him?*

A new legal provision which came into force on 1 December 1985 enables relatives (such as grand-parents, aunts and uncles), stepparents (where the child has not been referred to in divorce proceedings; see Q45) and foster parents to apply to the court for what is known as a custodianship order. This gives them legal custody of the child, which includes some of the parental rights and duties acquired by adoption but not all (see Q48). A custodian may not change the child's name and requires permission (of the parent or the court) to take the child out of the UK. The order may be revoked by the court, and parents and grandparents may seek access orders.

As a relative (or stepparent), you will be able to make an application after the child has had his home with you for three months, if you have the consent of a person having legal custody. This could be the parent or, in certain circumstances, a local authority. A foster parent may apply, with the consent of the person having legal custody, once the child has had his home there for a year. Custodianship applications by foster parents are thought to be more appropriate for older children who retain substantial links with their family of origin. If the person having legal custody of the child does not wish to consent to the application, it cannot be made until the child has had his home with the applicant(s) for three years.

A local authority has discretion to pay a custodianship allowance similar to a boarding-out allowance.

Seven days' notice of an intended application must be given to the local authority where the child resides. The local authority will appoint a social worker to see the applicants, the child and his or her natural parents and to report to the court. In deciding whether to make the order the court will regard the welfare of the child as the first and paramount consideration. Where an application has been made to the court in respect of a child who has had his home with the applicants for three years, no one may remove the child from them without the consent of the court.

Health

Abortion

1 | *I've just found out that I'm pregnant, but I don't want to have a baby. Can I have an abortion?*

The law does not allow abortion on demand. The Abortion Act 1967 lays down the criteria that doctors use to decide whether or not women qualify. Unless an abortion is immediately necessary in an emergency (in which case one doctor's opinion is needed), two doctors have to be of the opinion *either* that if the child were born it would be seriously handicapped (physically or mentally) *or* that continuing the pregnancy would risk the mother's life or either injure her health (physically or mentally) or the health of any other children in the family. The risk has to be greater than the risk would be of having the abortion.

Doctors' opinions vary very widely. Some doctors interpret the Act liberally, and are ready to agree to an abortion in most cases on the grounds that if a woman wants an abortion her mental health will to some extent suffer if she has to have the baby. Other doctors are far more strict.

The sooner an abortion is carried out, the simpler and safer the operation. After 28 weeks' pregnancy the foetus is deemed capable of being born alive and it is too late for an abortion under the Act. In practice, abortions are not usually performed after about 20 to 22 weeks.

2 | *I want an abortion, but my GP refused to help because he said I don't meet the requirements of the law. I then went to another GP who said he didn't believe in abortion at all and wouldn't even discuss it with me. I'm sure I'm entitled to an abortion under the 1967 Act. What should I do now?*

There's nothing you can do about the attitude of these two doctors, who acted within their rights. Your own GP has perhaps interpreted the Act too rigidly, but you cannot force him to come to an opinion that suits you. The other doctor is in a different position because the Act specifically exempts doctors – and others, like nurses, who may be involved in the operation – with conscientious and moral objections from performing abortions, which means they have no legal obligation to help you.

If direct approaches to other GPs get you nowhere, contact the FPC (see Q39) who may be able to help, or an NHS family planning clinic. Alternatively, get in touch with one of the non-profit agencies like the Pregnancy Advisory Service (address on page 511), or the British Pregnancy Advisory Service (number in the telephone directory; address of main office on page 509). These agencies can sometimes help to arrange an abortion under the NHS, although it is more likely to be private. In some parts of the country women may have to pay privately in any case, because the provision of such a service under the NHS is patchy.

Age

3 | *I'm a 72-year-old widow and I find that I can't keep my flat as clean as I'd like to simply because old age is making me weaker. Am I entitled to home help?*

The social services department of the local authority must by law provide domestic help where it is needed. However, it is up to the department to decide who needs a home help and who can manage without. This decision will be influenced by the resources available. Priority will be given to certain people, and your age may make you one of them. It will probably help, however, if you have something to support your application for a home help, such as a letter from your GP. Send your application to the home helps organiser at the social services department, who will visit you to decide how much help you need. There will probably be a charge for the service according to your means.

4 | *I'm a 68-year-old widower who finds it difficult to get out of the house. Am I entitled to Meals-on-Wheels?*

The social services department of the local authority must provide meals in the home or elsewhere, such as at a lunch club, if they are needed. As with home helps (see Q3), this department decides who needs to have a meal delivered. Meals-on-Wheels are not generally delivered every day in any case. There will probably be a standard charge for each meal. If the social services department turns down your application, and there is no other way you'll be able to get a hot meal, try to get someone to support your application (see Q5).

5 | *I'm severely arthritic, especially in my hips, and find the stairs a real problem. My late husband used to help me, but I was widowed two months ago. As I'm reluctant to move to a flat (this is the family home), I wonder if my local authority will pay for, or subsidise, installing a small bathroom and converting part of the kitchen for it?*

If the social services department of the local authority is satisfied that such an adaptation is necessary, the department must provide it under the Chronically Sick and Disabled Persons Act 1970. There are, however, often long delays in having such work approved and carried out. There is no legal definition of precisely when an adaptation is deemed 'necessary'. The social services department will decide this, and the decision will, to a certain extent, depend on what resources are available in your area.

If your application is refused, and you feel that you really cannot manage without this adaptation, ask someone to help you press your claim – your GP or health visitor, for instance. The local Age Concern office or Citizens Advice Bureau may also be able to advise you; look them up in the telephone directory. If you are still dissatisfied you could put your complaint to your local councillor and ask if he or she will help you.

6 | *My 84-year-old mother is now too frail to live alone. I live a long way away and there are no relatives able to care for her. She cannot afford a full-time nurse. Can I insist that she be housed in a home with proper facilities?*

If your mother does not need medical treatment or nursing care, but simply the sort of care which a relative would be able to provide, she should apply for a place in a home run through the social services department of the local authority. Because these homes are provided under Part III of the National Assistance Act 1948, this is often called Part III accommodation. Local authorities are obliged to pro-

vide accommodation for elderly people who need care and attention – the problem lies in defining 'need'. Priority is usually given to those who live alone. Your mother probably also stands a better chance of getting a place if she can no longer cope with everyday tasks, even with, say, a home help and Meals-on-Wheels. On the other hand, local authority homes may refuse to accept residents who seem to need more care than they can supply because there may be no nurses on the staff.

An application for a place should be sent to the social services department of the local authority. You could ask your mother's GP to write a letter supporting the application. If the application is turned down, ask the local Age Concern office or Citizens Advice Bureau if they can help; their numbers should be in the telephone directory. You cannot *insist* on a place being found for your mother immediately. The social services department may not consider that she needs to be in residential accommodation, and there may well be a waiting list. Residents in local authority homes have to contribute towards the cost of their accommodation according to their means.

If a place cannot be found, the local authority may be able to advise you on local rest homes or private homes run by charities, voluntary organisations or profit-making concerns. Sometimes the social services department will help with the cost of accommodation, or you mother may be entitled to a supplementary pension.

If your mother requires nursing care, a private nursing home will be more appropriate. These are registered with health authorities. The local authority will not help with the charges, but again your mother may be entitled to a supplementary pension.

Should your mother need medical treatment and hospital facilities, she would be admitted under the NHS to a geriatric or general hospital.

Alternative medicine

7 | *I don't approve of taking a lot of modern drugs. Can I see a homoeopathist under the NHS?*

You would have to register with a GP who gives homoeopathic treatment on the NHS – but very few do. A list of doctors who practise homoeopathy is available from the British Homoeopathic Association (address on page 509). If your GP doesn't use homoeopathy (and there isn't a suitable GP locally with whom you could register), your GP may be prepared to refer you to one of the few NHS hospitals where you can receive homoeopathic treatment, such as the Royal London Homoeopathic Hospital.

Another form of alternative medicine which a few GPs and hospital doctors practise on the NHS is acupuncture. Your local FPC should have received a list of medical acupuncturists. Contact the FPC (see Q39) to find out if there is one in your area. If you can't find an NHS doctor who practises acupuncture, write to the British Medical Acupuncture Society (address on page 509). The Society will send you a list of members which you should pass on to your GP to make a referral.

Treatment can only be under the NHS if it is from the GP with whom you are registered (or a partner), or if your GP refers you to a hospital doctor for NHS treatment, and generally you will find that NHS doctors who practise homoeopathy or acupuncture are so few and far between that you will need to have private treatment in any case – either from a doctor or from a non-medical practitioner. All other forms of alternative treatment, such as osteopathy and herbalism, are available only privately. The Institute for Complementary Medicine (address on page 510) has lists of practitioners.

Artificial fertilisation

8 | *My husband and I have been married for three years. I came off the pill a year ago, when we decided to have a baby, but nothing has happened yet. Does my GP have to refer me for infertility treatment on the NHS if I ask for it?*

There is no absolute right to infertility treatment under the NHS. It is for your GP to decide whether you are a suitable case for referral, and for the clinic to which he refers you to decide whether to take you on. However, a GP will normally refer a patient who has been trying to conceive for a year, though he may want to do some initial investigations himself.

The more usual types of infertility treatment – artificial insemination by husband or by donor, fertility drugs, and surgery on the fallopian tubes – are widely available on the NHS, though there are waiting lists. A newer treatment for women with blocked fallopian tubes – *in vitro* fertilisation (IVF) – is still at an experimental stage and available on the NHS in only a few centres. This treatment involves removing a ripe egg from the woman's ovary, fertilising it with her partner's sperm, and then reimplanting it in the uterus. The success rate is still fairly low.

You may be referred to one of these centres even if you live outside the area they cover, but the clinic itself will decide whether to accept you for treatment.

Some will only accept patients who are from a certain catchment area or who are under a certain age.

For advice on infertility treatment and its availability around the country, contact the National Association for the Childless (address on page 511).

Birth

9 | *I want to have my baby at home. Can I insist on this?*

Most women have their babies in hospital, where there is access to all the specialist facilities should they be needed. However, you are entitled to have your baby born at home. If your GP agrees, he or she may make the necessary arrangements and attend the birth. But it is up to the GP to decide whether he or she will provide maternity services and, if so, up to which stage in your pregnancy. Those GPs with particular experience or specialist training are on the Obstetric List within the Medical List (see Q39).

If your GP is unwilling to take charge of a home delivery, then either your GP or the health authority will arrange for a midwife to attend the birth. A registered midwife, or a recognised medical practitioner, must attend a woman in childbirth; except in cases of urgent necessity it is a criminal offence under the Midwives Act 1951 for an unqualified person to help deliver a child, and a father who excluded professional assistance was prosecuted under the Act.

In the first instance, consult your GP about where to have your baby. The National Childbirth Trust (address on page 511) will provide helpful information and ante-natal and post-natal instruction for both you and your partner. The Society to Support Home Confinements and the Birth Centre, London (addresses on pages 511 and 509), will give you advice if you decide to have your baby at home.

10 | *I am shortly going into hospital to have my first child. Must I have my baby induced if the hospital says I should?*

No. You can refuse to have the birth induced, as you can refuse any medical treatment. The rational thing, of course, would be to discuss a matter like this with the doctor in charge.

Children

11 | *My son, who is 13, does not like our GP. Can he insist on changing doctor without my consent?*

Such a case has never been tested in the courts, so it would seem that he can't. It is normal for children under the age of 16 to accept their parents' choice of doctor. However, from practical and therapeutic points of view, if your son does not like your family doctor you might be advised to let him see another doctor with whom he has more rappport.

12 | Can my child of 16 receive medical treatment without my or my husband's consent?

Yes. While in law your child reaches the age of majority at 18, statute provides that he or she can give his or her consent to medical treatment from the age of 16 and can therefore accept and refuse treatment, though in practice this consent is usually implied. How far a child under the age of 16 must consent to medical treatment or an operation with or without your approval is less certain. It will depend on all the circumstances, the age and maturity of the child and his or her capacity to understand what the treatment involves and the issues and risks at stake. It will also depend on how radical or dangerous the treatment is. For example, an intelligent girl of 15 could consent to a tonsilectomy or the removal of her appendix and a younger child could consent to the dressing of a wound.

13 | Can my 15-year-old daughter obtain contraceptives or advice on birth control without my knowledge or consent?

If your daughter is a mature, intelligent girl, she may be able to receive contraceptive advice and treatment without your knowledge or consent if that is her express wish. When a child of under 16 consults a doctor unaccompanied by a parent (or an adult *in loco parentis*), the doctor should satisfy himself that the child has sufficient maturity and understanding to appreciate what is involved in relation to her emotional development, family relationships, problems associated with the impact of pregnancy and/or its termination, and the potential health risks arising from sexual intercourse and certain forms of contraception (e.g. the pill) at an early age. Further, the doctor must try to persuade the child to involve her parents in the consultation. However, if the girl refuses to allow the parent to be told, then the doctor will have to decide whether or not it is in the girl's best medical interests for her to receive the advice and treatment she wants. He should, however, respect the rules of professional confidentiality.

14 | I have strong religious convictions that it is wrong to interfere with God's will and I do not want my children to be treated by doctors. Can I prevent this if they are ill?

The answer depends, in part, on how seriously ill your children are. The law does insist that you, as parent or guardian, provide proper medical care for your children up to the age of 16. If you refuse to consent to an operation necessary to save your child's life, the doctor could obtain a written second opinion from another practitioner and then perform the operation. You would be very unlikely to succeed in any legal action against the doctor, since he would have the defence of necessity.

If a child urgently needs treatment, but it is not a matter of life and death, a doctor would do everything he could to try to persuade you to consent to treatment. In an extreme case he could refer the matter to the local authority social services department. This department would hold a case conference and might decide to apply for a care order. The local authority would then be able to consent to treatment for the child.

Alternatively, the child could be made a ward of court, and the court would then decide whether the child should be treated. In one case, a baby girl with Down's syndrome (sometimes called mongolism) needed an operation to remove an intestinal blockage. Her parents refused to consent to the operation, and a social worker had the case brought before a court. In the case in the High Court the judge concurred with the parents' wishes. However, the Court of Appeal ordered that the operation be performed to save the baby's life.

There is nothing in law to say that a child under 16 cannot give consent to his or her own treatment. Depending on the child's maturity and understanding, and the nature of the consent required, the child may be held capable of giving the necessary consent. So, in certain circumstances, if your child consented to treatment by a doctor, you could not prevent this going ahead.

In short, if your child is not very seriously ill, and is incapable of giving his or her own consent, then if you withhold consent to treatment, your child should not be treated by a doctor.

Complaints

1 5 | *My GP refused to come to the house to treat me when I was too sick to travel to the surgery. How should I register my complaint?*

In case your grievance has arisen due to a misunderstanding between you and your GP, or through his receptionist, you should first discuss the matter with your doctor. If you still wish to make a formal complaint, put this in writing to the FPC (see Q 3 9) within eight weeks of the incident. It is worth contacting the FPC for advice on how to proceed with your complaint. The local Community Health Council (see Q 1 6) and the Patients Association (address on page 5 1 1) will also help. The address of your FPC is on your NHS Medical Card, or it may be listed in the telephone directory under 'Family'.

Other causes for complaint to the FPC would be if your doctor failed to refer you to a specialist when this was necessary, or if he charged you for a service which is free under the NHS.

The FPC cannot look into complaints concerning a GP's manners, attitude or remarks, but if the incident is serious you can complain to the General Medical Council (address on page 5 1 0) which decides on matters of professional conduct and health problems affecting a doctor's fitness to practise.

1 6 | *I'm not satisfied with the medical treatment I received in hospital. How can I complain?*

If you wish to question the treatment you received or a doctor's clinical judgment, you should first contact the consultant under whose care you were treated. Explain your complaint, and ask to see him, and any other medical staff involved, to discuss the matter. After the meeting you should receive a written reply to your complaint.

Should you find the consultant's reply unsatisfactory, write to the Regional Medical Officer (RMO). He may ask the consultant to see you again, and should also answer your complaint in writing.

If you still consider that you received inappropriate treatment, or that your treatment was not performed to a proper standard, there can be an independent review of your case – a 'second opinion'. The RMO asks two independent consultants practising in the same field of medicine (at least one of whom comes from a different health authority) to discuss the clinical aspects of your case fully with you and with the medical staff involved. You may bring along a relative or friend to this meeting. If these consultants think that the medical staff exercised responsible clinical judgment, they should try to reassure you. If they uphold your complaint, steps should be taken to prevent the problem re-occurring. The consultants will report to the District Administrator, who will write to you.

The procedure for other types of complaint following a stay in hospital is different. If a discussion with the person concerned, or with the consultant responsible for your case, does not resolve the matter, write to the Hospital Administrator or District Administrator within a year.

If you are dissatisfied with the reply to your complaint you may write to the Health Service Commissioner (NHS Ombudsman) at the addresses on page 5 1 0. He can investigate only certain types of complaint, however.

Complaints about the ethical, personal or professional conduct of a doctor – such as abusive or insulting behaviour – may be sent to the General Medical Council (address on page 5 1 0).

Community Health Councils (CHCS) offer advice on how to make a complaint, and may even agree to take on a case for you. There is usually one CHC for each District Health Authority (DHA). Ask at the GP's surgery, a hospital, post office or the Family Practitioner Committee office (see Q 3 9) for the address. It may be in the telephone directory; look up 'Community' or the name of the DHA.

Confidentiality

1 7 | *During a time when our marriage was going through a bad patch I confided a lot of what went on between us to our GP. I wouldn't want my wife to know what I revealed. Is my doctor likely to tell my wife and what can I do if he does?*

Your doctor, whether he's your GP or works in a hospital or clinic, must treat anything you tell him as confidential. Even though any information you give him is likely to be entered on your medical records, it should be disclosed only to others involved in your treatment, and they too are obliged to keep the information confidential. If your GP disclosed your confidential information without your consent you would be entitled to sue him for monetary compensation for any damage suffered as a result of the disclosure. Further, you may complain to the General Medical Council (GMC) (address on page 510) as the GP would have been acting unethically.

18 | *Are there any circumstances in which a doctor should divulge confidential information?*

Yes, there are:

● A court of law can order a doctor to testify and divulge confidential information in the witness box.
● A doctor is required by law to inform the local authority if you are suffering from a notifiable disease, such as measles or tuberculosis, or food poisoning. There is a list of diseases which are always notifiable, but local authorities may add other diseases to it.
● If a doctor considers that a patient is addicted to one of the drugs specified in the Regulations under the Misuse of Drugs Act 1971, he must notify the Chief Medical Officer at the Home Office of the patient's particulars (see Q37).
● A doctor must notify the Chief Medical Officer of the Department of Health and Social Security if he carries out an abortion.
● A doctor must help the police to identify drivers who are suspected of certain driving offences (specified in the Road Traffic Act 1972). Requests for information should be made by senior police officers to the doctor himself, and not to staff or administrators.
● There are other circumstances in which a doctor may feel that he has a moral duty to reveal confidential information. For example, if a doctor were aware that his patient had committed manslaughter, but could not persuade the patient to give himself up, he might feel duty-bound to report it to the police.

19 | *What can I do if my confidential records have been disclosed without my permission?*

Doctors and other health workers have professional codes placing a duty on them to keep information about patients confidential. In general, the patient's permission should be sought before disclosing any information. Exceptions to this duty are described in Q18, and there are other situations in which information may legitimately be divulged. For example, a GP would not need permission to describe a patient's current medical condition to the district nurse who was to treat him.

Any *wrongful* disclosure of your medical records is a breach of the duty of confidentiality, and there are two possible courses of action. You could complain to

the General Medical Council (address on page 510) about a GP's unethical conduct in disclosing the information. If a hospital record is disclosed, write to the District Administrator of the health authority.

You might also be able to take legal action against the GP or, in the case of hospital medical records, against the health authority. In this case you would need to demonstrate that harm had been done by disclosure of the information. For example, if your doctor gave information from your medical record, without your consent, to a company that was considering you for a job, and you then failed to get that job, you might be able to take legal action.

20 | *If my child tells the family GP something in confidence, can I be sure our GP will tell me?*

No, though the younger the child the greater the responsibility shouldered by the GP. In practice, the GP is always likely to try to involve the parents in view of a child's limited ability to consent to treatment. However, the GP will probably use his or her judgment and try to act in the best interests of the patient. Where circumstances require, the GP may disclose what he has learned from the child, though he should first tell the child that he is going to tell a parent.

Contraception

21 | *I am a single woman of 26. Can I insist on my GP providing me with contraceptives under the NHS?*

No. Not all NHS GPs provide contraceptive services. To find out whether your GP does or does not, simply ask the receptionist. There is no absolute entitlement to be provided with contraceptives, and the decision of which, if any, are available rests with the doctor. If your own GP doesn't provide contraceptive services, look at the Contraceptive Services List, appended to the Medical List (available normally from libraries, main post offices and Citizens Advice Bureaux), to find one who does.

Death

22 | *My daughter of 12 was badly injured in a car accident. At first the doctors kept her on a life-support machine but then they took her off it. Though she's remained deeply unconscious she can breathe without assistance. The doctors say she will never get better, and now that she's developed pneumonia they don't want to treat her. Without treatment she will inevitably die. Can I insist they keep her alive by treating the pneumonia?*

In such a difficult case you should discuss your daughter's condition with the doctors and perhaps another sensible person you feel you can trust. If the doctors are sure that your daughter's condition cannot improve and that pneumonia is nature's way of providing a merciful end, you should probably accept it. However, though the doctors can advise, the decision as to whether to go on treating your child will be yours. The doctors' basic duty is to preserve life, and there is no rigid code by which such considerations as 'quality of life' can be considered when deciding appropriate treatment. You can insist that treatment be given, but although doctors have a duty to care for their patients, where they feel that maintaining life at all costs is not in the patient's interests they may suggest withdrawing treatment. If the patient is suffering, they may also prescribe drugs to alleviate the pain even if this shortens life expectancy. In such a difficult situation you may well be advised to take a second opinion, which in the circumstances you have a right to ask for under the NHS.

23 | *My 14-year-old son is in a coma from which I believe he cannot recover. He has now developed pneumonia, but my husband and I do not wish him to be treated but to be allowed to die with dignity. The doctors at the hospital want to go on treating him. Can I refuse the treatment?*

Yes. However, if the doctors are not satisfied that your decision is in your son's best interest they could make him a ward of court which removes him from your care. You and the local authority can then argue the matter before the court (if necessary taking it to the Court of Appeal) and the court will have to make the decision on the evidence before it. In practice this would be most unlikely in the circumstances you describe, and your wishes would almost certainly be respected.

24 | *My son was seriously injured in a car crash and since then has been in a coma. He is on a life-support machine which helps him breathe and carry out other bodily functions. The doctors now say they want to take him off the machine because in reality he's already dead. How can I be sure they have properly diagnosed his death when he is still breathing?*

There is no legal definition of death, and it will be a matter of medical judgment. Traditionally, death was always recognised as the moment the heart stopped beating, and in most cases this is still true. However, where, as in your son's case, modern life-supporting techniques are used, doctors should establish that 'brain stem death' has occurred. The brain stem, which is at the base of the back of the brain, regulates the basic functions of the body, in particular breathing. A lack of oxygen will lead to varying degrees of 'brain death', which can range from the diminishing of intellectual functioning (an example may be the loss of memory, speech or co-ordination) right up to the loss of all bodily functions save the ability to stay alive in an irreversible coma in a persistent vegetative state. The body is not dead unless the whole brain is dead, including the brain stem. Doctors have now firmly established that brain stem death can be diagnosed while the heart is still beating. Once they've done so, the life-support machine is not maintaining life at all.

Careful tests must be made before brain stem death can be established. Doctors have to show that the patient's coma is a result of irremediable structural brain damage and does not arise from some other cause. Tests must be carried out to demonstrate that all brain stem reflexes are absent and that there are no signs of breathing when the patient is taken off the life-support machine. The tests should be repeated and the diagnosis made by two doctors.

25 | *My friend and I went out to a restaurant for lunch and then on to do some shopping when suddenly my friend collapsed on the pavement. She was dead before the ambulance arrived. The funeral has had to be postponed because the hospital notified the coroner and he wants a post-mortem. My*

friend's husband is very upset and distressed that the coroner has been involved without his permission. Can he complain?

No. A referral to the coroner leading to a post-mortem – a medical examination of the body to ascertain the cause of death – is normal in a case where death occurs suddenly and without explanation. The coroner, who is normally a lawyer or doctor and is appointed by the local authority, under the Coroner's Rules has to be informed of the following deaths:

● when no doctor has treated the deceased in his or her last illness
● when the doctor attending the patient did not see him or her within 14 days before the death
● when the death occurred during an operation or before recovery from the anaesthetic
● when the death was sudden and unexplained or attended by mysterious circumstances
● when the death might be due to industrial injury or disease or to accident, violence, neglect or abortion or to any kind of poisoning.

Other deaths that are always reported to the coroner include those taking place while the deceased is in legal custody, those of people receiving an industrial disability pension or war pension and any cases where negligence (medical or other) has been alleged to have contributed to the death. It is also usual for the coroner to request that he be notified of deaths occurring within 24 hours of a patient's admission to hospital.

26 | *If there's a post-mortem, is there then an inquest?*

No, there's not necessarily an inquest, which is an inquiry into the cause of death. If after the post-mortem the coroner considers that as a result no further investigation is needed, he himself may certify the cause of death as indicated by the post-mortem (and this certificate will invalidate any previous medical certificate as to the cause of death). If the post-mortem reveals that the death was a result of a natural illness and there were no suspicious circumstances, then that will be the end of the matter.

27 | *Under which circumstances would an inquest be heard before a jury?*

Once the coroner has decided that an inquest is necessary, he can either hear the case alone or can summon a jury. In some circumstances he is obliged by law to summon a jury, which must consist of no fewer than seven people and not more than 11. These circumstances are where it is suspected that the death

● occurred in prison
● was due to a traffic or industrial accident
● was due to poisoning or any disease that must be notified to any government department.

The coroner is in fact restricted in cases of murder, manslaughter, infanticide and death caused by dangerous driving, and must notify the Director of Public Prosecutions (DPP) who may then adjourn the inquest and tell the police to investigate. The coroner must also not frame his verdict so as to suggest criminal or civil liability on the part of a named person, and if evidence is adduced that he should do so the case must be adjourned and the DPP informed.

28 | *Reports of an inquest often say that the jury returned an 'open' verdict. What does this mean?*

An open verdict is given when the jury cannot decide exactly how the deceased met his or her death, because there is not enough evidence pointing firmly towards one particular cause of death. Quite often, for instance, a jury will be unable to decide whether a drug overdose was accidental or suicide.

The other main inquest verdicts are:

● unlawful killing. The jury is not allowed to name a particular person as the killer (see Q27);
● suicide. This verdict is sometimes accompanied by the phrase 'while the balance of mind was disturbed' or something similar. This phrase has no special meaning in law;
● death by natural causes;
● accidental death or death by misadventure. The two terms mean much the same and are listed as the same category in the official records.

Dentists

29 | *Our local dentist won't treat me and my family under the NHS. What can I do about it?*

Not very much! Dentists are quite free both to refuse and to accept patients for treatment under the NHS. You will have to shop around to find a dentist who is happy to treat you and your family under the NHS. Be sure you make it clear that he *is* treating you as an NHS and not as a private patient, and do so for every course of treatment: even if your dentist treated you under the NHS in the past, he is not obliged to continue to do so in the future. You will need your NHS number (it's on your Medical Card; see Q39 if you don't have one) on your first visit, and you will have to sign a form saying that you consent to pay the required charges for NHS treatment. These charges will include examinations, x-rays, fillings and extractions, and may include dentures. Other specialist work will need referral to another dentist or a hospital and may involve further fees. The NHS lays down a scale of charges. The current maximum for a course of treatment is £14.50, but some types of treatment, such as dentures and crowns, could be higher, to a maximum of £110.

30 | *I'm expecting my second child. Will I receive dental treatment under the NHS free of charge, as I did with my first?*

Yes. All pregnant women receive free dental treatment under the NHS. Women who have given birth are entitled to free treatment for a year from the date of birth.

31 | *My daughter is 17. Do I have to pay for her dental treatment under the NHS?*

No. Children under 18 are entitled to free dental treatment under the NHS, and treatment and dentures are provided free to age 19 for students in full-time education. Generally, the rules covering exemption from dental charges are similar to those applying to prescription charges (see Q85).

32 | *I recently visited a dentist for the first time. I needed four fillings but three of them fell out within five weeks and I had excruciating toothache. Despite the toothache, he refused to see me for a further two weeks. I was in such agony that I feel I should complain about the distress he's caused me. How would I go about it?*

Anyone who feels he or she has been mistreated can complain about a dentist. You should write as fully and as promptly as possible to the FPC (see Q39) for the area in which your dentist practises.

33 | *I am confined to a wheelchair and more or less housebound. Can I expect a dentist to visit me at home?*

Some but not all dentists may be willing to visit a housebound person at home as long as this is not more than five miles from the surgery (and under the NHS there's no charge for the journey). However, home visits are not common. Ask your GP or social services department about the possibility of transport to take you to the dentist.

Deputising services

34 | *My husband had a heart attack at 2am. I rang my doctor's number and was referred to a deputising service. The deputy took two hours to arrive. My husband was admitted to hospital, where he died the following morning. Do I have grounds for complaint about the delay, or could I sue my doctor for the deputising service?*

Your doctor is responsible under his terms of service for his deputising service. If you wish to complain about the deputising service's competence and speed in arrival, you should report the matter in writing to the FPC (see Q39) within eight weeks. If you leave it any longer your case will not be heard, though exceptions can be made if there are special circumstances.

If you can prove (and this will depend on the evidence available) that your husband would not have died but for the delay you may have grounds to sue the deputising service (and/or locum) for negligence (see Qs 72 to 80) and perhaps even your own doctor as well if he knew or should have known that the deputising service he was providing was unreliable or inexperienced. If you feel you have a claim you should consult a solicitor.

Disability

35 | *After a bad fall I can no longer walk properly. Can I get a walking aid or wheelchair under the NHS?*

If your doctor feels that you need a walking aid he will refer you to a hospital department where the correct aid will be selected for you. If you are recovering in hospital from your accident this may be arranged before you are discharged. Wheelchairs are provided when needed by those with permanent disabilities. Again, your doctor will refer you to the relevant department.

Local authority social services departments also provide some aids, though not wheelchairs. If for some reason you cannot get a walking aid through your doctor, try the occupational therapy service at this department.

36 | *Last month I had an epileptic fit for the first time. My doctor advised me that I had to inform the Licensing Authority, and my driving licence was suspended. How long must I wait before I can apply to have my licence restored?*

Epilepsy is one of the 'prescribed' disabilities – those that are likely to be a source of danger to the public (see below). An applicant suffering from epilepsy must satisfy certain conditions before a driving licence will be restored. These are:

● he must have been free from epileptic attacks during the preceding two years, or
● any attacks must have taken place only while he was asleep for the preceding period of three years, and
● he must not be a source of danger to the public while driving.

More stringent provisions apply to vocational drivers, such as drivers of public service vehicles like buses, and heavy lorries and so on, which will exclude anyone who suffers from epilepsy and various other notifiable conditions.

Apart from epilepsy, disabilities for driving are:
● severe subnormality under the mental health legislation
● mental deficiency
● liability to sudden attacks of disabling giddiness or fainting
● liability to sudden attacks of disabling giddiness or fainting caused by any disorder or defect of the heart
● acute poor eyesight.

The application form for a licence asks the question: 'Have you now or have you ever had epilepsy?' If there is a history of seizures, however minor, the answer 'yes' must be given. The applicant then receives a further form asking questions about dates and details of the seizures and treatment. He will then be asked for the address of doctors who have treated him, and his consent will be sought for the Licensing Department to contact them.

If the Licensing Department's Medical Adviser is satisfied that the applicant can comply with the regulations, he will normally recommend the issue or re-issue of a licence.

After this it will be the responsibility of the licence-holder to report to his family doctor any recurrence of fits. If the doctor confirms that these symptoms are epileptic in origin, the licence-holder must inform the Licensing Authority.

Drug addiction

37 | *Recently, I discovered that my son, who lives away from home, is addicted to heroin. He said he would like to come off it, but he's afraid to see his GP because he says the GP will notify the police. What is the position?*

The law regarding dangerous drugs is found mainly in the Misuse of Drugs Act 1971 and Regulations made under it. The Act classifies drugs according to their relative harmfulness; under the classification, heroin is one of the most dangerous. If you can persuade your son to see his GP, and the GP considers that he is addicted to heroin, the doctor must by law notify the Chief Medical Officer at the Home Office within seven days. He must give the addict's name, address, sex, date of birth, NHS number, the date on which he saw the person and the name of the drug concerned. However, neither the GP nor the Home Office should contact the police.

There are specialist NHS centres for drug addiction, though they are not numerous, and there are waiting lists of at least two to three weeks. A GP's referral is not necessary for most of them, and you can obtain the address of the nearest centre from the Standing Conference on Drug Abuse (address on page 512).

Voluntary organisations such as Release, Narcotics Anonymous and Families Anonymous can supply advice and support (addresses on pages 509 and 511).

38 | *Can our GP prescribe drugs for my son, who is an addict?*

Some, but not all, GPs are licensed by the Home Office to prescribe drugs 'controlled' by the Misuse of Drugs Act 1971. If your GP is not licensed to do so he will probably refer your son to one of the specialist NHS drug centres (see Q37).

GPs

39 | *Two months ago I returned to live in England after many years living and working abroad. My local NHS GP, recommended by friends, refused to accept me and my family as patients. Does he have the legal right to refuse us, even though we're British subjects? And how do I go about finding a GP who will accept us?*

All doctors have the right to refuse to accept patients and they need not give reasons for refusals (though there may well be a straightforward reason – the practice may be too large already, say).

You should consult the Medical List, published by the Family Practitioner Committee (FPC), which contains the names, addresses and phone numbers of all GPs in the area; the List should be available at libraries, main post offices and local FPC offices (the address is in the telephone directory). The FPC will find you a doctor if you keep getting refused. Once a GP does accept you, you will need to produce a Medical Card. As you've been living abroad, you may not have yours. Apply to the FPC for new Medical Cards: until you produce the Card you could be refused NHS treatment and be charged a fee (reclaimed from the FPC once the card is issued).

If you want to know whether any GP has any particular qualification – in paediatrics, say – you will need to refer to the Medical Directory, available at most larger reference libraries. The Medical Directory may also give you an idea of the doctor's age if you particularly want a younger – or an older – doctor, as it may specify the year in which he or she qualified (normally at about 23). The Directory is in alphabetical order by doctors' surnames, so you'll need to note the names of your local GPs from the Medical List before you consult it.

40 | *My family and I registered at a group practice with a particular doctor in whom we have confidence. Now, whenever we need to make an appointment, the receptionist offers us a different doctor. What can I do?*

If you wish to see the same doctor each time, and many people find it helpful, either explain this to the receptionist and the doctor with whom you are registered, or if this does not produce results because your doctor is too busy or only there part of the time, consider whether another doctor in the practice may fulfil your needs. You have no right to always see the same doctor. If you can't work out a satisfactory

solution, you may have to look elsewhere at a practice differently organised and run.

41 | *When I ring up for an appointment with our GP, the receptionist always offers a date several days ahead. Can I insist on seeing the doctor the same day?*

A GP must provide all necessary and proper treatment, and if he has stated surgery hours he must see you within them at his surgery unless he operates an appointment system. If he does run an appointment system then he need not see you at once as long as he offers you an appointment within a reasonable time. It is the GP who is supposed to decide whether a consultation should be deferred, and not the receptionist, but in practice it is the receptionist who will often make decisions, particularly on non-urgent matters.

When your case requires urgent attention, an offer to see the doctor should be made immediately, or, if it can wait so long, until the next surgery. If there is a real problem, you should contact the GP personally so that he can agree to see you.

42 | *I had a row with my doctor who now refuses to treat either me or my family. Can I insist on his continuing to treat us?*

In the long term, the answer is no. Your GP is an independent contractor and he cannot be forced to treat patients whom he does not want on his list. However, if you are being treated for a particular condition, you are entitled not to be immediately abandoned. Your doctor may notify the FPC that he wants you and your family removed from his list, but your removal will be effective only when you are accepted by or assigned to another GP, or on the eighth day after the FPC is asked to remove your name. If you are receiving treatment at intervals of less than a week, your GP must notify the FPC, and you will remain his responsibility until you have been accepted by another doctor as his patient, or until the end of the eighth day after the FPC has been notified that the treatment is concluded. In this way you will not be left needing regular medical treatment with no GP to administer it.

43 | *I have difficulty getting out of the house. Can I insist on my doctor visiting me at home?*

If you are too ill to visit the surgery or incapacitated in some way, your doctor will normally visit you at home. However, a GP does not have to agree with every request for a house call. If, after he is told about your illness – a bout of flu or tonsillitis, say – or your incapacity, he decides that no visit is necessary (or that it can wait, or that you should see him at the surgery) he will be behaving reasonably provided that subsequent evidence proves that his interpretation was well founded.

44 | *My job takes me all over the country. Can I get NHS treatment from any local GP?*

Anybody who is away from home for a short while is entitled to be treated by any available local GP as an 'emergency' patient. If you find yourself staying in one place for longer spells (but for less than three months), you can register with a GP in the neighbourhood where you are staying. You will need to contact the doctor and to fill in a form. If he refuses to accept you, contact the local FPC (see Q39) so that you can be assigned to a different GP.

If you are likely to be away from home for more than three months you should get yourself on the list of a local GP and then, when you return home, you should rejoin your doctor's list.

When you change doctors for any reason, your Medical Card must be surrendered and the FPC will issue a new one in due course. If you move within the same area without changing your doctor (though some operate a 'catchment' area, so check with the surgery to make sure you're in the same catchment) send your Card direct to the FPC for your new address to be added to the Card. If the Card is lost, the FPC will issue you another one free of charge, though this may take a little while. There is a duty on you to present your Medical Card to a doctor from whom you seek NHS treatment.

45 | *I've been seeing my GP regularly but my condition doesn't seem to be improving. I'd like to see a specialist. Can I insist on this?*

No. It is your doctor's decision whether or not you need specialist advice. You should discuss your condition carefully with your GP, and explain why you are anxious to have specialist advice. If, however, your GP is still of the opinion that you should not be referred to a specialist you cannot of right insist on a referral. The only alternatives open to you in such a situation are:

● change your doctor
● see another doctor privately
● write to the FPC (though this is hardly likely to improve your relationship with your GP and may cause him or her to ask you to remove yourself from his or her list).

46 | *My GP referred me to a specialist, but I had no confidence in him and didn't like him as a person. Can I insist on a second opinion?*

No, no one can insist on a second opinion without the agreement of his or her GP. Even paying for a private second opinion is at the discretion of a GP. Explain your problem to your GP and if he or she doesn't respond sympathetically you could consider changing your GP. Alternatively, it may be possible to find a specialist – asking friends, enquiring at special hospitals, or even ringing up your local hospital to find out who its consultants are – and then approaching him or her to see if he or she will accept you as a private patient. Most, though, will prefer to see you with a letter from your GP.

Hospitals

47 | *My doctor thinks I should go into hospital for 'tests' and if necessary an operation and drug treatment. Must I go into hospital? If I do go into hospital and have the tests, must I have the operation if the tests indicate that one is necessary?*

Apart from admission as a compulsory patient under the Mental Health Act 1983 or as an emergency patient when unconscious (when consent is deemed to have been given), your admission into hospital is entirely voluntary. You can take the doctor's advice and go into hospital for the tests, and leave after the tests have been made even if discharging yourself before the operation is against the advice of the doctor (in which case you will be taking the responsibility on yourself). Similarly, as with a visit to your GP, a medical practitioner who examines a person against his or her will and a surgeon who carries out an operation without that person's consent will be liable to trespass and battery and may be sued. Thus, if after the tests you decide not to have the operation you may refuse your consent to any further treatment and leave the hospital.

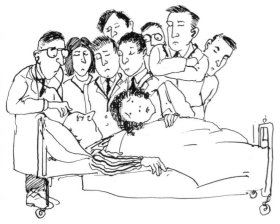

48 | *When I was recovering from an operation in hospital, the doctor came round with a group of students. Can I refuse to be examined in front of so many people?*

Yes. It is open to you to refuse, and your treatment will not be affected in any way. The doctor will explain the reasons for the students' attendance and will ask for your co-operation. You can then withhold your consent to be examined in the presence of the student doctors if you wish.

49 | *When I was in hospital I didn't object to students watching the doctor examine me but I didn't like them all touching me. Could I have refused?*

Yes. You should be asked if you mind being examined by a student, or indeed more than one, and you are entitled to refuse permission. If, despite your refusal to be examined, a student examines you, this amounts to a trespass to your person and it is also an assault actionable as such in law.

50 | *I am very worried about an operation my GP says I should have, and I don't really understand what is involved. Will the hospital doctors have to explain the implications?*

Yes – within limits. Before the operation is performed you must be given a consent form to sign. This states the name of the operation, followed by a phrase along the lines of 'the nature and purpose of which have been explained to me'. If nothing has been explained, and you have some questions, ask to discuss the operation with a doctor before you sign the form. You should be in a fit state for such a discussion when you are given the form. If a nurse comes to administer a pre-med tranquilliser before you've consented to the operation, say that you haven't yet been given a form to sign and tell her if you wish to speak to a doctor. An example of a consent form is given on page 132.

Doctors have a duty to explain what is involved in an operation and to inform you of the alternatives open to you – for example, the likely consequences of not having surgery. A doctor may use his discretion to decide exactly how much to tell a patient; he does not have to detail every conceivable risk involved in having the operation. His decision must be reasonable, however, and in accordance with rightly accepted medical practice prevailing at the time of the incident complained of. In a case before the Court of Appeal in 1984, the judges held that a surgeon did not have to warn the patient of a one to two per cent risk inherent in an operation. Other surgeons testified that withholding this piece of information was in line with medical practice.

You do not have to wait until you go into hospital for an explanation of the operation. If you are worried, ask the consultant at an out-patient appointment, or your GP, what will be involved.

51 | *I had to have a Caesarian for the birth of my first child. The doctor who performed it says that he found tumours on the uterus, making it dangerous for me to have another child, and decided to sterilise me. I didn't know anything about it at the time, and I'm very angry and upset. I think he should have discussed it with me first. Can I sue him?*

Many hospital consent forms have a phrase along the lines of: 'I also consent to such further or alternative operative measures as may be found necessary during the course of the operation . . .' This doesn't give the doctor the right to do what he likes, but it does allow him to take emergency measures if, during an operation, he unexpectedly finds something else wrong with you. The question is whether or not it is necessary for him to carry out the second operation immediately. If it isn't urgent, he should wait until he can discuss it with you and get your specific consent.

In your case, it doesn't seem as if there was any urgency and you may have a claim for damages

HMR 10 (90–595)

CONSENT FOR OPERATION

Smalltown HOSPITAL

UNIT NO. *12*

I *Margaret Smith* of *12 Windsor Drive, Smalltown.*

hereby consent to

undergo the operation of   VEIN STRIPPING

the nature and purpose of which have been explained to me by Dr. *Jameson*

I also consent to such further or alternative operative measures as may be found necessary during the course of the above-mentioned operation and to the administration of general, local or other anaesthetics for any of these purposes. No assurance has been given to me that the operation will be performed by any particular practitioner.

Date *11 · 1 · 85*   Signed *M. Smith*

(Patient/~~Parent/Guardian~~)

I confirm that I have explained the nature and purpose of this operation to the patient/~~parent/guardian~~

Date *11 · 1 · 85*   Signed *Dr. Jameson*

(Medical/~~Dental~~* Practitioner)

ANY DELETIONS, INSERTIONS OR AMENDMENTS TO THE FORM ARE TO BE MADE BEFORE THE EXPLANATION IS GIVEN AND THE FORM SUBMITTED FOR SIGNATURE.

†THIS FORM IS NOT SUITABLE FOR CONSENT TO PROCEDURES SUCH AS ELECTROPLEXY, STERILISATION OR VASECTOMY

*Delete as necessary

against him. There have been court cases where patients in similar circumstances have been awarded compensation. But if, say, he found a cancerous growth that threatened your life unless it was removed immediately, he would be justified in operating even without your specific consent. This would apply even if you hadn't signed the type of consent form mentioned above.

52 | *I need an operation and I would prefer it performed at one of the large teaching hospitals. But I've been told that as my case is not urgent I might have to wait a long time for a bed. Can I insist that the operation be performed sooner?*

No. If your case is not acute and there is a shortage of resources, there is little you can do but wait. The only alternatives to waiting are going privately or being more flexible in your choice of hospital: your GP could

try a few different hospitals to see whether any of them have a shorter waiting list for your type of surgery.

53 | *I've been in hospital for several weeks with cancer, and am being treated with drugs that have very unpleasant side-effects. I've decided that if I'm going to die I'd prefer to die at home. The doctors say that if I leave hospital and no longer continue with the drugs treatment, I'll lose any chance I have of recovering. I've thought about it and still want to leave hospital. Have the doctors the right to keep me in?*

No. Treatment in hospital is voluntary, and the fact that you may have a serious, even terminal, illness makes no difference to that principle. You are entitled to refuse treatment if you want and you can discharge yourself at any time. The only exceptions to the rule that treatment is entirely voluntary are cases of admission as a compulsory patient under the Mental Health Act 1983 and people who are incapable of deciding for themselves – when unconscious after an accident, say.

54 | *If a kidney patient is rejected as a candidate for dialysis because there are not enough kidney machines to go round, is there any way he or she can challenge the decision in the courts?*

There has been no such case in the English courts as yet, but in theory legal action could be a remedy in a situation like this to force a health authority to carry out its duty to treat the sick. A body with a duty laid down by Act of Parliament can be compelled by a court order – known as mandamus – to carry out that duty.

However, it seems likely that a court would take the view that the duty is one that must be carried out within the available resources and would be reluctant to interfere with an authority's discretion as to the allocation of resources.

In a 1980 test case on behalf of four orthopaedic patients whose treatment was delayed by a shortage of facilities, the Court of Appeal judges said that the Secretary of State for Social Services had a discretion as to how resources were used, and he would fail in his duty only if he exercised his discretion in a way in which no reasonable Secretary of State would have done. Financial constraints must be a factor in the exercise of public duties, said the court, and such constraints would probably be considered by any court in a similar case.

Mental health

55 | *My husband is very depressed although there is no apparent reason for this. How would he set about seeing a psychiatrist?*

Your husband should make an appointment to see his GP, and it might be an idea for you to accompany him if he's willing. If the GP thinks your husband should see a psychiatrist, he will refer your husband to one under the NHS just as he would refer him to any other specialist or consultant.

56 | *What does the law regard as mental disorder?*

The Mental Health Act 1983 defines mental disorder as 'mental illness, arrested or incomplete development of the mind, psychopathic disorder and any other disorder or disability of mind'. Basically, Sections 2 and 4 of the Act, by which people enter hospital compulsorily either for a 72-hour period of assessment in emergency (Section 4) or for assessment possibly to be followed by treatment for a maximum period of 28 days (Section 2), operate by reference to this definition.

Four categories of mental disorder are further specified:

● mental illness, which the Act does not define
● severe mental impairment, 'a state of arrested or incomplete development of mind which includes severe impairment of intelligence and social functioning and is associated with abnormally aggressive or seriously irresponsible conduct'
● mental impairment, which is defined exactly the same as severe mental impairment except that it covers 'significant' rather than 'severe' impairment
● psychopathic disorder, defined as 'a persistent disorder or disability of mind (whether or not including significant impairment of intelligence) which results in abnormally aggressive or seriously irresponsible conduct'.

Section 3 of the Act operates by reference to these four definitions. This Section covers longer-term detention in hospital, for an initial period of six months, renewable for a further six months and then for periods of one year at a time. Nobody can be detained under Section 3 unless they are suffering from one or other of the four conditions. This means that mentally handicapped people (see Q57) can no longer be detained under Section 3 unless their disability results in 'abnormally aggressive or seriously irresponsible conduct'.

57 | *What does the law regard as mental handicap?*

The term 'mental handicap' is understood to be a permanent and irreversible mental disability. The Mental Health Act 1983 (see Q56) defines mental disorder as including 'arrested or incomplete development of mind', and this definition is taken to encompass the mentally handicapped. Under the Act, mentally handicapped people can be detained under Section 4 (for a maximum of 72 hours) and Section 2 (for a maximum of 28 days) but cannot be held under Section 3 unless their condition is associated with 'abnormally aggressive or seriously irresponsible conduct'. Very few mentally handicapped people are detained under the Mental Health Act.

58 | *I've always looked after my mentally handicapped son but he's now getting too much for me. Can I insist he be admitted into a hostel or home?*

There are some 13,000 places for mentally handicapped people in homes and hostels provided by the social services and housing departments of local authorities. Their distribution varies from one area of the country to another, as does the level of vacancies. If your son is not a suitable candidate for a local authority hostel or sheltered accommodation, or there is no vacancy in one, you cannot insist on his admission and he may have to be admitted into hospital. Contact your GP and MIND or MENCAP (addresses on pages 511 and 510) who, apart from helping you generally, will give you advice and information on how best to get your son into suitable accommodation.

In any event, if your son needs constant attention he will be entitled to claim an 'attendance allowance' and probably other benefits as well; enquire at your social security office. Some of these benefits could be spent on paying for outside help to care for your son at home. There are also day centres that your son might attend if he does not already do so, which would help relieve some of the burden and may enable you to continue looking after him at home.

59 | *I have a mentally handicapped son who set fire to a local barn. He was admitted as an emergency case to our local mental hospital and has since been detained, as he is likely to set fire to other buildings if he is not closely supervised. Are the doctors entitled to compulsorily detain my son?*

Yes. Your son would be eligible for detention under the Mental Health Act 1983. It would seem that your son falls into the category of either severe mental impairment or mental impairment (see Q56 for definitions), depending on his mental condition. Patients in both these categories can be compulsorily detained in hospital if their mental impairment is associated with abnormally aggressive or seriously irresponsible behaviour. This is covered by Section 3 of the Act, not by Sections 2 and 4.

Section 3 authorises longer-term compulsory stays in hospital of six months, renewable for a further six months and then a year at a time. The patient has to be suffering from one of the four categories of mental disorder (see Q56) which needs treatment in hospital, and has to be detained for the sake of his own safety or health or for the protection of others. Application and recommendation must be made in the same way as under Section 2 (see below).

However, if he was an emergency case he was most likely admitted to hospital under Section 4 of the Act. This covers cases where it is of 'urgent necessity' for a patient to be compulsorily admitted for assessment. The maximum duration is 72 hours, and application has to be made by you as the nearest relative or an approved social worker (ASW) (who must have 'appropriate competence in dealing with persons who are suffering from mental disorder') plus one doctor's medical recommendation.

He may also have been compulsorily admitted under the provisions of Section 2. Section 2 specifies that the patient should be admitted for assessment, or for assessment followed by treatment, for a period of up to 28 days maximum and that he should be detained in the interests of his own safety or health or with a view to the protection of others. Application again has to be made by you as the nearest relative or an ASW plus two doctors' medical recommendations.

60 | *Is violent or irrational behaviour resulting from alcohol or drug addiction treatable under the mental health legislation?*

No. The Mental Health Act 1983 states that a person may not be treated as suffering from mental disorder under the Act by reason of behaviour arising only from dependence on alcohol or drugs, sexual deviancy, promiscuity or other immoral conduct. If, however, the alcoholic or drug addict had an accompanying mental disorder, then use of the Mental Health Act could be considered.

61 | *My son has been suffering from acute depression for some time. Our GP has recommended that he should be admitted to hospital for assessment. What does this mean and what does it*

involve? Will my son be free to leave if he's taken into hospital, or can he be made to stay there?

If your son is willing to be admitted as an informal patient (that is, voluntarily) then his status will be exactly the same as that of any patient admitted to any hospital. He can then refuse to be treated if he so wishes, and will be free to leave the hospital whenever he wants. He should be aware, however, that doctors and some nurses do have the power to detain a departing informal patient in certain circumstances.

If the GP considers that your son should be admitted as a compulsory patient, your son would have to be suffering from a mental disorder of a degree which warrants detention in hospital 'for assessment (or for assessment followed by medical treatment) for at least a limited period' of up to 28 days, and must be so detained in the interest of his own health and safety or with a view to the protection of others. Your GP alone is not in a position to recommend your son's attendance at hospital on this basis: recommendation must be made by two medical practitioners (one of whom must have special experience in the diagnosis of mental disorder) plus the application of an approved social worker (see Q59) or you if you are the nearest relative.

62 | *My mentally disordered son has been detained compulsorily in hospital for a 28-day period of assessment. I think this is far too long. Can he leave any earlier?*

If you are the nearest relative you can discharge the patient, assuming he's been admitted under Section 2 (see Q59), by giving the hospital managers (see Q69) a minimum of 72 hours' notice in writing. Within that period, the doctor in charge, known as the 're-sponsible medical officer' (RMO), can report to the hospital managers that in his opinion the patient if discharged 'would be likely to act in a manner dangerous to other persons or to himself'. Your notice to discharge the patient would become void if the managers accepted the report. Perhaps you should first get in touch with MIND or MENCAP to ask their advice; addresses on pages 511 and 510.

The patient himself can appeal to a Mental Health Review Tribunal (MHRT) within the first 14 days. There is a MHRT for all the Regional Health Authorities in England and one for Wales, with four MHRT offices to whom application should be made. The addresses of the MHRT offices are given on pages 510–11. The Tribunals are independent bodies composed of doctors, lawyers and lay people with know-ledge of social services or other appropriate qualifications. The Tribunal will hear your son's case and decide whether he should continue to be detained or be discharged.

63 | *My sister is mentally handicapped and recently she has deteriorated so much that she doesn't understand much of what is happening about her. She is a voluntary patient in a mental hospital. She has developed cataracts over her eyes, but she would not understand enough to have the procedure of an operation explained to her. Does she have to give her consent to an operation to remove the cataracts, or can I as her nearest relative consent on her behalf?*

As an informal (or voluntary) patient, your sister can consent to or refuse treatment just like a patient in any hospital. But the difficulty in her case is in her lack of ability to understand and therefore to give a proper informed consent to any medical treatment. Efforts should be made to explain the nature and purpose of the operation, but if real understanding and consent by your sister is just not possible, then technically, unless the treatment were an urgent necessity, the doctors might be committing an assault if they were to go ahead with the operation. Normally, however, if you as her closest relative were to agree (though in law this has no relevance to her ability to consent), and everyone were agreed that it is in your sister's best interests to have the operation, the staff would probably feel it legally safe and ethically right to proceed, as there is nobody likely to bring any objection and therefore to sue them for assault and battery.

Generally, English law on mental health treatment seems to assume that mental patients admitted informally and voluntarily are capable of consenting validly to medical treatment, when in many cases they are not. There is no legal procedure equivalent to that available for children whereby a parent or guardian consents to treatment on behalf of a child under the age of 16, or for the patient to be made a ward of court in order for a difficult decision to be taken.

64 | *My brother is seriously mentally ill and potentially dangerous, but he refuses to have any treatment or to go into hospital. What steps could be taken?*

If the situation is *urgent*, or becomes so, your brother could be detained in hospital under Section 4 of the

Mental Health Act 1983 for up to 72 hours, during which his condition would be evaluated. Your brother could be admitted as a compulsory patient under this Section of the Act on the recommendation of a doctor and an application by you as his nearest relative (or another equally close relative), or by an approved social worker (see Q59). It must be an *urgent necessity*, with any delay 'undesirable'; other than in such an urgent situation, the normal admission procedure is under Section 2 for a 28-day period. For the emergency 72-hour admission, the medical recommendation should if possible be made by a doctor who is familiar with your brother's health, probably his GP, and he must verify the statement made on the application for your brother's admission to hospital. It should be signed on or before the date of the application. Your brother must be admitted to hospital within 24 hours of the time he is medically examined or the application, whichever is earlier.

65 | *My brother, who is severely mentally ill, has been detained as a compulsory patient. What treatment can he be forced to undergo? He has lucid intervals and is generally not willing to be treated.*

Where possible, your brother's consent should be sought during his lucid intervals. However, if this is not practicable, the position is as follows:

● Certain very severe and potentially hazardous treatments such as psychosurgery (operations on the brain) and surgical implants of hormones cannot be carried out without your brother's consent, and if he should consent to these severe treatments the doctors must still gain an independent confirmation of valid consent and a second medical opinion within the detailed safeguards of the Mental Health Act 1983 (see Q66).
● Electroconvulsive therapy (ECT), in which an electric current is passed through the brain, may be given only if your brother consents or a second opinion (by an independent doctor appointed by the Mental Health Act Commission; see Q71) agrees that it will alleviate or prevent a further deterioration of your brother's condition. There must be consultation with the patient, as laid down in the Act.
● Your brother can be given medication with or without his consent (as a compulsory patient) for a period of three months, but after that the treatment may not be given without his consent or the agreement of a second independent doctor.

Treatment can be given to your brother without his consent or a second opinion in matters of urgency, such as saving life, or provided the treatment is not irreversible or hazardous, if it is to prevent serious deterioration of your brother's condition or to alleviate serious suffering. If can also be given to prevent your brother from behaving violently or being a danger to himself or others.

As the provisions of the Act are both detailed and complex, you would be well advised to contact one of the major organisations concerned with mental health, such as MIND or MENCAP, and ask for advice; their addresses are on pages 511 and 510.

66 | *My brother has been admitted as a long-stay compulsory patient in a mental hospital. He is very severely depressed and the doctors have recommended psychosurgery, but he has so far refused to give his consent. Can he be forced to undergo this psychosurgery?*

No, your brother will have to consent to such drastic treatment as psychosurgery, which involves an operation on the brain, the results of which are irreversible. The Mental Health Act 1983 sets out safeguards for certain kinds of very serious and irreversible treatments, including psychosurgery. If your brother agrees to this treatment, his consent must be confirmed by a doctor and by two other people, not doctors, who are appointed by the Mental Health Act Commission (MHAC) (see Q71) and they must certify in writing that the patient understands the nature, purpose and likely effects of the treatment, and has consented to it. These three people must also get the opinion of another doctor also appointed by the MHAC, who must consult two other people who are concerned with the patient's treatment: one of these must be a nurse, the other neither a nurse nor a doctor (a member of the therapeutic team at the hospital, for instance). Only after this second opinion can the operation be carried out.

These provisions apply to both compulsory and informal patients.

67 | *Although I have been in a mental hospital for many years I could be discharged if I were given family or community support in my daily life. Unfortunately, none of my family is prepared to shoulder the responsibility of helping and providing for me, and I cannot cope alone. At the last yearly review of my position my discharge was turned down. Is there anything I can do?*

Section 117 of the Mental Health Act 1983 lays a

duty to provide after-care services on the District Health Authority and on the social services department of your local authority. This provision would apply to a person like yourself who may need a home, some help in looking after it, and continuing medical and nursing care after discharge.

Social services departments generally have some residential accommodation for the mentally disordered. Housing departments may also provide a range of accommodation, and the Housing (Homeless Persons) Act 1977 specifically states that people 'vulnerable as a result of mental illness or handicap' are priority cases.

Speak to your doctor at the hospital. You, or a member of your family, should also explain your circumstances to MIND or MENCAP (addresses on pages 510 and 511) and you could also contact the National Association of Voluntary Hostels (address on page 511) whose aim is to help the single homeless to find accommodation in hostels.

68 | *My father has been compulsorily detained in a mental hospital for several years. Recently I thought he had improved and really ought to be discharged. If the doctors won't listen to me, is there a tribunal which can review his case?*

You will need to discuss your father's case with his doctor (legally known as the 'responsible medical officer' (RMO)) at the hospital. If he agrees that your father's condition has improved sufficiently for your father to be discharged, he will take the necessary steps. Alternatively, you can give the hospital 72 hours' notice in writing that you intend to discharge your father. During that 72-hour period the RMO can submit a report to the hospital managers (see Q69) advising that the patient should not be discharged on the grounds that he would be a danger either to himself or to others.

Only if the RMO thus overrules your request for your father's discharge can you yourself approach an MHRT. See Q62 for details of the MHRTs. Alternatively, your father can apply to the MHRT once within any renewal period, which in this case is once annually (see the details given in Q56 about Section 3 renewals).

If both a request to the RMO and an appeal to an MHRT fail, there's very little further you can do. Under the Mental Health Act 1983, patients detained under Section 3 (which presumably includes your father) have to be automatically referred by the hospital to an MHRT. This happens once in the first six months of their detention if they do not apply them-

selves, and then every three years if in the meantime they have not applied themselves. An MHRT considers each case individually. It would seem that unless your father's condition improved only in the very recent past, an MHRT must have examined his case within the past three years and concluded his condition warranted continued detention in hospital.

69 | *Who can detain a patient in a mental hospital? Must it be a doctor? My father is a potential danger to himself and to others. What if he tries to leave hospital?*

Section 5 of the Mental Health Act 1983 makes provision for detaining an informal mental patient when it is deemed necessary. Generally it would be a doctor in charge of the patient's treatment who would make a report and the patient then could be compulsorily detained on this basis for up to 72 hours from the time of the report. However, when an informal patient who is receiving treatment for mental disorder as an in-patient is so mentally disturbed as to constitute a danger to himself or others, and it is not practicable to secure the immediate attendance of a doctor, then a 'first-level' nurse (one qualified in nursing mentally disordered or mentally handicapped people) may detain a patient for up to six hours. The first-level nurse must make a written report which must be delivered to the hospital managers. These are: the District Health Authority in the case of NHS hospitals, Secretary of State for Social Services for special (mental) hospitals, and the registered managers in the case of mental nursing homes. Once the doctor arrives, the nurse's holding power lapses (even if the six hours have not expired), and the doctor can decide what should next be done and whether to detain the patient for 72 hours or not.

In the case of patients compulsorily detained in hospital under Section 3 of the Act, the responsible medical officer will make a report to the hospital managers recommending that the patient be detained for a further period of six months or a year.

70 | *I feel my father is being maltreated by the staff of the mental hospital where he has been detained for many years. I'm worried that if I complain to the staff they'll take it out on him. What should I do?*

You should first try to talk to your father and establish the facts. If this is not possible you should very carefully note all the available evidence. To stop the suspected maltreatment you should then contact the hospital administrators as soon as possible. You may find it easier to do this if you have the support and help of an independent organisation like MIND or MENCAP.

You then have to decide what steps to take in the long term not only to protect your father but possibly also to stop other people being maltreated. The alternatives are:

● Section 127 of the Mental Health Act 1983 makes it an offence for staff to maltreat patients, which means you could refer the matter to the police, and indeed the hospital may do this itself.
● Either you or your father could file a formal complaint with the hospital managers (see Q 69). If your father does this and he is dissatisfied with the result, he can refer his complaint to the Mental Health Act Commission (MHAC), an independent body set up by the Mental Health Act to oversee the rights and welfare of all detained patients; the MHAC's addresses are on pages 510–11.
● Either you or your father could complain direct to the Mental Health Act Commission.
● Either you or your father could file a complaint with the Health Service Commissioner (NHS Ombudsman) who has a parliamentary duty to investigate certain complaints; the Commissioner's addresses are on page 510.

71 | *My husband is an informal patient in a mental hospital. He is interested in politics and wants to vote in the next general election. May he vote, and what address should he give if he can?*

As an *informal* patient your husband is entitled to vote, but he cannot use the hospital as an address for voting. He must without assistance and in the presence of a member of staff sign a declaration (though he can receive help in filling in the declaration, he must sign it without assistance) saying that he is an informal mental patient, giving the UK address where he would be resident if he were not at hospital. If a patient cannot give such an address, his last UK address before he moved into hospital is acceptable. It does not matter that this former address no longer exists perhaps because of redevelopment. The declaration, once completed, will result in your husband's name being added to the electoral register and he will be entitled to vote by post or in person.

Negligence and compensation

72 | *I had a hysterectomy a year ago. Since then my back hasn't been right and I've had to cope with constant, acute pain. I'm always extremely exhausted and depressed. Surely I'm entitled to compensation for whatever went wrong?*

It depends. You are not automatically entitled to compensation just because an operation has gone wrong. To succeed in a claim, you would have to show that the surgeon was negligent, in other words that he fell below the standard of care that could be expected of a reasonably competent gynaecologist, and that his negligence caused the damage.

Most operations have built-in risks of one sort or another. For instance, if surgery involves delicate work in the region of the spinal cord, some spinal cord damage may happen in, say, one per cent of cases even if the surgeon's performance on that occasion is up to the accepted standard of competence.

You will need to establish what went wrong with your operation and, since a judge cannot be expected to know the ins and outs of gynaecological procedures, you will need to produce other gynaecologists who will say that a reasonably skilled gynaecologist should not have done what yours did.

Your first step is to see a solicitor experienced in medical negligence claims. The organisation Action for the Victims of Medical Accidents (address on page 509) will put you in touch with one. Your solicitor will try to obtain your hospital notes to see if there are any clues as to what went wrong with your operation. The court can order these to be handed over to a patient's solicitor even before legal proceedings have started.

He will arrange for you to be examined by another gynaecologist, who will also see your notes. On the basis of the gynaecologist's report a barrister will probably be asked to advise whether your case is worth fighting.

Another factor that will obviously influence your decision is whether or not you qualify for legal aid. Even if you qualify on financial grounds, you will not get legal aid if the committee of lawyers which makes the decisions feels (usually on the basis of a barrister's opinion) that your case is not strong enough.

Medical negligence cases have a considerably lower success rate than other personal injury claims, such as road or work accidents, and losing such a case (unless you have legal aid) could be very expensive.

73 | *I was never warned before having a hysterectomy that back pain might result from the operation. If I'd known I would never have gone ahead with it. Isn't it negligent of the doctor not to give a*

proper warning of risks and possible complications?

Even if a doctor performs an operation competently, he could be held to be negligent if he fails to inform a patient properly about the risks, so as to enable the patient to make a rational decision about whether or not to undergo the operation. To succeed in a negligence claim on this basis, you would have to convince the court that you would not have gone ahead with the operation had the risks been properly explained.

However, a doctor is not obliged to tell a patient of every possible risk; for instance, awareness of all the risks might put a patient in an unsuitable frame of mind for an operation and might prejudice the operation's chances of success, or cause the patient to forgo a necessary operation. If a doctor acted reasonably in withholding information on these grounds – and it would be up to the court to decide this, if a case came to court – then he would not be negligent.

Another possibility is that the court might decide that whatever went wrong was such a remote risk that the doctor was not negligent in not warning of it. This is the line that the courts have taken in several recent cases.

74 | *I fell down some steps at work and hurt my arm and ankle. The doctor who saw me at the hospital casualty department said there were no signs of a fracture and he didn't send me for X-rays. More than a month after the accident, I still couldn't move my arm properly. My GP sent me to a consultant, who said my arm had been fractured and that it is now permanently disabled. Have I got a case against the casualty department doctor, who seemed quite young and not very experienced?*

A doctor has to use the same care in diagnosing what is wrong with a patient as in performing operations, prescribing drugs, and undertaking any other medical procedures. Not every misdiagnosis will be negligence – no doctor is infallible. But a doctor will be negligent if he fails to conduct tests which a reasonably competent practitioner would have performed in the circumstances, or if he misses a condition which a reasonably competent practitioner would have spotted. The fact that the doctor is young and inexperienced, or suffering from flu, or exhausted from a long spell on duty is no excuse if he falls below a reasonable standard.

A case similar to yours was settled out of court a few years ago, with the doctor admitting negligence and the patient getting damages for her disablement.

HMMM.... WELL, YOU DON'T LOOK TOO BAD.

75 | *If I want to bring a claim for medical negligence, whom should I sue, the hospital or the doctor?*

In the case of NHS treatment you can sue either the doctor or the health authority that runs the hospital. In most cases both are sued. In rare cases it is not clear which member of the hospital staff was negligent, and in these circumstances you would sue the health authority alone. The health authority is responsible for the negligent acts of all its medical, nursing, and other staff. But if you engage a surgeon to perform an operation privately, the surgeon alone can be sued. Even if he performs the operation in an NHS hospital, the health authority is not liable for his negligence. Similarly, a negligence action against a GP would have to be brought against him personally.

76 | *My husband and I have three children, and I was sterilised under the NHS a year ago. Six months later I started getting terrible pains in the abdomen and bleeding from the vagina. The problem turned out to be an ectopic pregnancy. Even though I've not had an unwanted baby, have I any right to compensation for my pain and suffering? The surgeon didn't warn me there was a possibility of my becoming pregnant after being sterilised.*

Women occasionally become pregnant after sterilisation even though the operation was properly done, so the fact that you became pregnant does not mean that the surgeon was negligent when he carried out the operation. However, an examination might show that the operation was negligently done. For example, if it was a sterilisation using clips to seal off the fallopian tubes, the clips might have been put in the wrong place. But it is very likely that the effects of the ectopic pregnancy on the tubes will make it difficult to work out whether your pregnancy could have been due to a negligently performed operation.

A surgeon's failure to warn a patient about the risks of an operation may in some circumstances be negligent. In a recent case involving a vasectomy, where the vas deferens spontaneously rejoined some time after a properly performed operation, the surgeon was held to be negligent in not warning of this possibility. But in that case the damage suffered – that the man's wife did not realise she was pregnant until it was too late to have an abortion – resulted from the surgeon's failure to give the warning.

In your case it would be difficult to argue that your damage – the pain and suffering associated with an ectopic pregnancy – resulted from the surgeon's failure to warn. In order to succeed you would have to convince the court that you would not have agreed to be sterilised had you known of the small risk of an ectopic pregnancy, which in itself is unlikely, and that the ectopic pregnancy was caused by the sterilisation.

In any event, you could see a solicitor (see Q72), who will look into your case and advise you whether a claim would be worth pursuing.

77 | *Suppose, after being sterilised, I became pregnant and my pregnancy resulted in a healthy child. Could I claim the cost of bringing up the child?*

First, you would have to establish that the doctor was negligent and that his negligence led to your having an unwanted child. Despite the vasectomy case (*Thake* v. *Maurice*) mentioned in Q76, you cannot assume entitlement to damages in every case where a doctor fails to warn the patient about the possibility of pregnancy, and an unwanted child is born. If a respectable body of medical opinion would not have warned of the possibility of pregnancy at the time, and in the circumstances of your case, then you would be unable to prove that your doctor had acted negligently because he would not be said to have fallen below an acceptable standard of medical care, which is the test to be applied.

However, assuming that negligence can be estab-

lished, either on the basis that the doctor negligently failed to warn you or because the operation was not completely performed, you may claim compensation which would include a sum for the cost of your child's upbringing. The amount of the award will be tailored to the individual household's living standards. In *Thake* v. *Maurice* the Court of Appeal did not interfere with the trial judge's award of damages for the cost of bringing up the baby, which totalled £6,677. However, the Court did allow an appeal against his refusal to award damages for 'pain and suffering' on the basis that this had been set off by the joy the parents had received from the baby. The Court of Appeal said that although in assessing damages arising from the birth of a healthy child any sum in respect of the future trouble and care involved in the upbringing was to be set off against the joy occasioned by the birth, an award for normal ante-natal pain and suffering should not be extinguished by the happiness of events after the birth of the baby. The parents were awarded an additional sum of £1,000. The mother was also awarded £2,000 for loss of earnings. In another Court of Appeal case damages were awarded to the mother of a baby born with severe handicaps following a negligently performed sterilisation operation.

It remains to be seen whether damages for private education and holidays abroad would be awarded in appropriate circumstances.

78 | *After my baby's birth I found that I had lost normal control of my bladder. The doctors told me that such a complication of childbirth was not unusual. I had an operation to put it right, but that operation and two further ones were unsuccessful. The result is that I now suffer permanently from incontinence whenever I laugh, sneeze or cough, which is very embarrassing. Can I sue for compensation?*

As in other medical negligence cases, you will have to show that the doctor failed to live up to the standard of a reasonably skilled medical practitioner. To establish this, you will need to produce evidence from other specialists in the same field.

In one case like yours, the surgeon performed the first operation a month after the baby's birth, even though it was normal practice to wait three months before performing the operation in order to prevent a haemorrhage from occurring which might cause the repair to break down. Though the two further operations produced some improvement, permanent damage had been done. The judge said that in cases where a doctor departs from normal practice, it is up to the doctor to show that the departure was justified. In that case, the judge ruled that it was not justified and the mother won damages of over £11,000.

As the judge put it: 'A doctor owes a duty to his patient to observe the precautions which are normal in the course of the treatment that he gives. But where there are two schools of thought as to the right course to be followed, he may not be charged with negligence simply because he chooses one course rather than another. Where, however, there is but one orthodox course of treatment and he chooses to depart from that, his position is different.'

If your first operation was not performed too early, your solicitor (see Q72) will look for other indications that the surgeon fell short of accepted medical standards.

79 | *When I was pregnant I had a mild attack of German measles (rubella). I told my GP that if the baby were likely to be born handicapped I would prefer to have an abortion. He said the baby would be all right and that I shouldn't worry. My daughter was born blind. Have either my daughter or I a right to sue the doctor?*

Firstly, not all physical (or mental) handicaps are caused by rubella, the German measles virus, and you need to be sure that your daughter's blindness was indeed the result of rubella by seeking the opinion of another doctor. If that doctor confirms your belief, consult a solicitor (see Q72).

If you can show that your GP was negligent in failing to diagnose the likelihood of risk to the foetus in being born handicapped, and that had you been told of this likelihood you would have elected for an abortion, then you may be able to sue the GP. You could then claim for the extra cost involved in bringing up a handicapped child – loss of earnings, nursing, adaptation of the family home, and any special equipment needed. The baby herself may have a claim against the GP for loss of amenities, enjoyment of life and loss of earnings. What the baby cannot do is claim for compensation on the grounds of 'wrongful birth' – that in her handicapped state she should not have been born at all – because such a claim does not exist in English law.

80 | *My little daughter has recently been diagnosed as brain-damaged. I believe it must have been the result of the vaccinations for whooping cough, tetanus and diphtheria she had between six and twelve months. She seemed a normal baby before she had the vaccinations, but after the second injection she began to get fretful and her movements seemed uncontrolled. I let her have the final vaccination because the doctor said it would be in her best interests and I was being over-anxious. Can I get compensation if it was the vaccine that caused the brain damage?*

There is a statutory scheme to compensate children who are brain-damaged by vaccine. To qualify for compensation, you will not have to prove that the vaccine was negligently administered, but you will have to show that the vaccine was more likely than not to blame for your daughter's brain damage. Only children who are at least 80 per cent disabled qualify for compensation, and your child must be at least two years old before you can apply.

If you believe the vaccine caused the brain damage, the first stage is to make a written claim to the DHSS vaccine damage unit at Blackpool (address on page 509). The DHSS form HB3 will tell you how to go about it. Only 13 per cent of applications succeed at this stage; most fail because there is insufficient proof of the link between the damage and the vaccine.

If you are rejected at this stage, you can ask for your case to be re-examined by a vaccine damage tribunal. The DHSS will refer you to your nearest tribunal. A solicitor's help (see Q72) will make your task easier. You will probably need to obtain the hospital notes of your daughter's birth and child health clinic notes, including the records of her vaccinations, and to have your daughter and her records examined by a consultant, who will give an opinion on whether the vaccine was to blame for her condition. If the tribunal accepts that it was, your daughter will receive a lump sum of £20,000.

The fact that your doctor failed to follow the manufacturer's directions will, however, not necessarily entitle you to succeed in a claim for negligence in the courts. Recently a Scottish court refused to accept that the plaintiff's brain damage was caused by vaccination even though he had already been compensated on that basis by a vaccine damage tribunal. A recent attempt to test the matter in the English High Court had to be abandoned because of discrepancies in the mother's evidence.

Opticians

81 | *Do I have the right to a sight test under the NHS?*

Yes, under the NHS you can have one sight test a year free of charge. Most sight tests are made by ophthalmic opticians, though there may be a local medical eye centre you could go to. Look in Yellow Pages and telephone to enquire whether your local optician provides NHS services. Alternatively, the FPC Opticians List gives details of those who do NHS work; you can consult the List at main post offices or at the FPC office (address in the telephone directory).

82 | *Are NHS spectacles free?*

Since July 1986 NHS glasses are no longer available. Instead, if you qualify, you will be given a voucher which you can use to pay for glasses bought privately. Vouchers are available if you are:

● under 16
● under 19 and in full-time education
● getting Supplementary Benefit (including Housing Benefit Supplement) or Family Income Supplement (see BENEFITS)
● on a low income (get DHSS leaflet G11 from your post office or local DHSS office). Children aged 16 or over can claim help on low income grounds: it's their income that counts, not that of their parents.

Prescriptions

83 | *If I see a GP as a private patient, can I ask him for a prescription under the NHS?*

No. If you see a doctor privately, he is not allowed to issue you an NHS prescription and you must pay the full price for any prescription he writes for you. There is nothing to stop you having two doctors if you wish,

one private and the other under the NHS, but you must choose the basis on which you consult them.

84 | *Does everyone pay prescription charges, or are there some exemptions?*

Those exempt from prescription charges, and the procedures they should follow, are:

● all children under 16, men over 65 and women over 60: fill in the box on the back of the prescription before handing it to the pharmacist
● pregnant women: applications for exemption certificates are available from GPs, midwives and health visitors
● mothers of children under one (or for one year after a stillbirth) and those who didn't claim while pregnant: complete form FP91, attached to leaflet P11 and obtainable from post offices and social security departments
● people and their dependants on Supplementary Benefit or Family Income Supplement: an exemption certificate should arrive with the order book; if not, ask the pharmacist for form FP57
● people in low income groups, including young people of 16 and over who are at school or college: complete form FP91 (see above)
● people suffering from various conditions requiring regular medication (including epilepsy, diabetes, a colostomy) and those permanently disabled and housebound: complete form FP91 (see above)
● war or service disablement pensioners requiring medication specifically for their disability: if an exemption certificate is not issued automatically, write to the DHSS war pensioner branch at Blackpool (address on page 509).

Apart from these exemptions, those who need more than 15 prescriptions a year can buy in advance pre-payment certificates lasting four or 12 months. These certificates, known as season tickets, give a discount to those not exempt from the full prescription charges. Use form FP95, available from post offices, social security departments and pharmacists.

Private medicine

85 | *What is the advantage of having private medical treatment from a legal point of view?*

For most people the main advantage is the right to select a specialist and buy his (or her) time to discuss their case fully with him and to be treated personally by the specialist and not simply by the hospital's departmental staff. Once a specialist has accepted you under his care privately, you have an individual legal contract with him personally. Apart from a more direct and, for many patients, a more satisfactory relationship, this means that should anything go wrong you are entitled to sue the doctor for breach of contract as well as for his breaking his duty of care. You also have a contract with the hospital (which will have to be separately paid). Under the NHS you have no direct contract with the doctor or the hospital, though they both still owe you a duty of care under which you will be entitled to sue should this be broken and cause you damage.

86 | *If I am treated privately, can I choose the specialist I'd like to see?*

Some specialists will see a patient privately without a referral from a GP but most prefer a GP's letter, and a proper liaison between GP and specialist is in the patient's best interests. If you wish to nominate a specialist, speak to your GP, though he is unlikely to refer you to a specialist of whom he does not approve or in whom he has no confidence. The main advantage of being a private patient is that you will be treated by the specialist designated by your GP, whereas under the NHS you may be treated by the registrar or some other doctor in the specialist's department.

87 | *I broke my nose in a car accident and it's now a very ugly shape. My husband tells me I'm silly, but I'm so self-conscious of it I'd like to have it remodelled. My breathing and sense of smell are not impaired. Can I have such plastic surgery under the NHS, or will I have to pay as a private patient?*

Your GP is unlikely to recommend an operation under the NHS because, as you point out, any remodelling would be on cosmetic, not medical grounds. But do discuss the matter with your GP because if the psychological reasons for the remodelling are strong enough he may recommend an NHS operation. Failing that, if you are prepared to pay as a private patient your GP should be able to recommend a reputable plastic surgeon. Anyone considering plastic surgery would also be well advised to check the surgeon's qualifications in the Medical Directory (available at larger reference libraries) because there's a world of difference between the skilled plastic surgeon and a 'cosmetic' surgeon.

There's a possibility that any private medical insurance you have may cover you for voluntary, non-essential treatment, so check your policy carefully. Bear in mind that you will be responsible not only for the surgeon's fee but for the anaesthetist's, and for the hospital's charges, bandages, drugs and so on, so find out first what the operation will cost.

Suicide

88 | *My life is useless and I want to end it. I would like a doctor or a friend to help me out of my misery, but would they get into trouble if they do?*

Although suicide is no longer a crime, by the Suicide Act 1961 it is an offence to aid and abet, counsel or procure a suicide, and if your doctor knowingly prescribes or anybody else gives you any drugs to help you to end your life he or she could be guilty of a criminal offence.

89 | *I am a helpless invalid with incurable cancer. If I could physically get hold of the means to end my life I would commit suicide, but the doctor and my family are keeping me alive at great trouble and expense because they say to accede to my wish for an overdose would be to commit a crime. What can I do? My plight is intolerable.*

If you have honestly and carefully made up your mind that you do not wish to prolong your life, you may refuse any medicines and treatment, and any food or drink, and this is perfectly legal. Your doctor may give you drugs to relieve pain and distress but he may not force you to submit to treatment against your will.

Transplants of organs after death

90 | *I want to donate my body to medicine after my death. How can I be sure that my wishes are carried out?*

The Human Tissue Act 1961 permits the removal of parts of the body of a deceased person for medical purposes if the person has requested in writing that his body or any part of it should be so used or the person has made such a request orally during his last illness in the presence of two or more witnesses. Alternatively, the persons lawfully in charge of the body – the hospital administrators, say – may authorise the removal of any part of the body for medical purposes if after making all reasonable enquiries they have no reason to believe that the deceased had

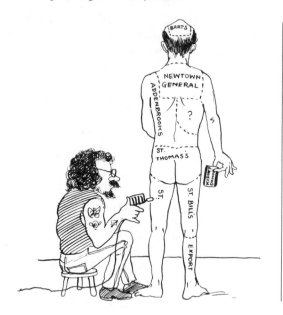

expressed an objection to his body being so dealt with and there's no objection from any surviving spouse or any surviving relative.

However, you can't be absolutely sure that your wishes are respected. Basically, you have very limited rights to enforce the disposal of your body after your death in accordance with your wishes, and in practice the wishes of your next of kin will normally be upheld in preference to your own however you had expressed your intentions. But there are steps you can take to make your wishes clear and therefore more likely to be followed after your death. Mention your plans to your closest relatives and accustom them to your ideas, which may not accord with their own. Confirm them in writing and include them in your will. There are also cards you can carry for kidney and corneal donations.

Wills, death and inheritance

Wills

1 | *What do I have to do if I want to make a will?*

You have two choices. Either you can go to a solicitor or you can make your own 'home-made' will.

Most firms of solicitors have a department which prepares wills for members of the public. The fees for this type of work are quite modest and, if you cannot afford to pay, the Green Form Scheme (see page 490) is available under which your fees may be paid. If you have a solicitor already you will probably want to go to his or her firm; otherwise you should approach several firms to find out what they charge so you get the best price. The solicitor will prepare the will for you, and will supervise its signing and witnessing. Once that is done you can be confident that your will is valid (if it is not the solicitor will be liable to pay compensation for his mistake).

If your wishes are very straightforward – for example, you might want to leave everything to your spouse – you could make a home-made will. *Wills and Probate*, published by Consumers' Association, takes you through the required procedures step by step. An example of a simple home-made will is given on page 146.

You should always make a will by typing it or by writing in ink – a pencil is not acceptable. Apart from dating and signing the will, you will need it witnessed by two people when you sign. Neither these witnesses nor their spouses should benefit from the will; if they *are* beneficiaries, the will is still valid but the witnesses lose their right to inherit.

Printed forms of wills are available from stationers, but it is generally not advisable to use them as they can be difficult to adapt to the individual's particular circumstances and have been known to contain printer's errors.

2 | *What are the advantages of making a will?*

The most important advantage is that you can determine now who will inherit on your death your personal possessions, your property like your house or flat, and your money and investments (all these may commonly be referred to as your 'assets' or 'property'; what you leave behind when you die is known as your 'estate'). If you do not make a will certain Rules laid down by Parliament will apply, and these may well not correspond with your wishes. QS 26 to 32 deal with the distribution of property after death when there is no will.

If you make a will you can and should choose what is known as an executor to administer your estate; this is someone who will deal with your property when you are dead and follow the instructions in your will. If you do not make a will one or more of your family will administer your estate (when there's no will they are known as administrators) and you will not be able to choose who does the work. In this case, often the administrator will be your spouse, who may not wish to take on the responsibilities involved at a time of bereavement.

If you make a will and have young children you can appoint 'testamentary guardians' to look after your children should you and your spouse die together (see Q19). While there's no guarantee that the persons you choose will become your children's guardians, your wishes will be taken into account and will usually be respected.

Finally, you can use a will as a means of making known your wishes as to the disposal of your body for transplants or medical research (see HEALTH, Q90) and whether you want to be buried or cremated.

Once you've made a will, remember to keep it under review. If your family or financial circumstances change you should consider changing your will as well.

3 | *Whom should I choose to be my executor?*

The most common choices of executor – a person appointed by your will to deal with your property after your death – are: relatives or friends, a solicitor or a bank. It is up to you to choose when you make your will. One executor is sufficient, but many people appoint two so that the work does not all fall on to one person.

If you have friends or relatives whom you think would be able to do the work involved in paying your debts and dealing with your property as well and as quickly as a professional person, then they would be ideal. This is particularly so as friends and relatives will not charge for their work. Bear in mind, however, that if the person you have chosen is unable to do the work he or she will probably consult a solicitor who will do most of the work and will charge a fee which will be paid out of the estate. In this case it might have been as well to appoint a solicitor in the first place. It is unwise to choose people who are your contemporaries as executors (particularly if you are yourself elderly) in case they die before you. In some cases it is also unwise to choose relatives, as they may

THIS IS THE LAST WILL AND TESTAMENT
of me JOHN SMITH of 1 West Street
Newtown Blankshire.

1. I hereby REVOKE all former wills and testamentary dispositions made by me.

2. I APPOINT George Brown and Jean Smith both of 10 East Street Newtown Blankshire to be my executors.

3. I GIVE the grandfather clock which my mother gave to me on my 21st birthday to Michael Smith.

4. I GIVE to Nigel Smith of 20 North Street Newtown Blankshire the sum of one thousand pounds (£1,000) and I DIRECT that if he has not attained the age of 18 years at the time when the said legacy is payable my executors may pay the said legacy to his parent or guardian whose receipt shall be a full discharge to them.

5. I GIVE all the rest and residue of my estate both real and personal whatsoever and wheresoever SUBJECT TO the payment of all my debts and funeral and testament expenses (hereafter called my Residuary Estate) to my wife Elizabeth Smith absolutely PROVIDED THAT if she shall fail to survive me by 28 days then I give my Residuary Estate to my mother Nora Smith of 30 South Street Newtown Blankshire absolutely.

IN WITNESS whereof
I have hereunto set my hand
this 14th. day of January 19 87.

Signed by the said John Smith *John Smith*
in our joint presence and then *Jean Smith*
by us in his *George Brown*

NOTES

Clause 1 *revokes all former wills. This should be done just to be on the safe side even if it is thought that no previous will exists.*

Clause 2 *appoints two individuals to be executors of the will.*

Clause 3 *contains a 'specific legacy', that is, a gift of a particular asset. The description should be sufficient to describe the item so as to make it easy to identify.*

Clause 4 *contains a 'pecuniary legacy', that is, a cash gift. As the gift is to a minor (a person under 18) provision is made for payment to the parent or guardian. Without such a provision the executors would have to hold the money until the minor was 18 or pay it to trustees.*

Clause 5 *contains the gift of 'residue', that is, the gift of all the rest of the property apart from what is specifically given away; the person who receives the residue is the 'residuary beneficiary'. In this case the gift is to the testator's wife if she lives longer than 28 days after the testator's death. If she dies first or dies very soon after the testator there is a 'substitutional gift' to his mother. The 28-day period is laid down so that if husband and wife are both killed at the same time – in a car crash, say – his property will go to his mother rather than under the wife's will.*

Date: *It is very important that the will is dated so that if another will is made there is evidence as to which is the latest. This is important because normally only the latest will is valid.*

Signature: *The will must be signed by the testator and then by the witnesses. The witnesses must be present when the testator signs and must not be, or be married to, anyone who will benefit from the will.*

find dealing with your estate disturbing at a time of bereavement. However, the spouse is normally an executor when more than one is appointed.

Most firms of solicitors have experts in this type of work who are willing to act as executors provided, of course, that they are authorised to charge for their services. A clause must be added to the will to allow the executor to charge the estate; without such a clause, solicitors are not entitled to a fee from the estate.

Each of the large banks has a trustee department which is willing to act as executor. The bank will usually accept appointment only if the words of appointment in the will follow the bank's own prece-

dent (which your bank manager will provide on request). Banks also charge for their services, usually at a higher rate than most firms of solicitors.

4 | *How should I sign my will to ensure that it is valid?*

There are strict rules about the signature of wills which must be complied with if the will is to be valid. You should sign the will with your usual signature. (In fact, any mark which is intended to be your signature and which you make personally is, strictly speaking, sufficient. In one case the court held a will to be valid which had the words 'your loving mother' written at the end by a woman giving instructions to dispose of her property. The usual signature is, however, preferable as then there are unlikely to be any problems with proving that the signature is the correct one.) The signature should come at the end of the will to show that it is intended to authenticate the whole of the document.

The person making the will should write his signature in the presence of two witnesses; it's not enough to sign a will and take it to witnesses later, even if they know the signature. The witnesses must not be people who will get any benefit from the will when the person making the will – the 'testator' – dies, nor must their spouses be beneficiaries. The witnesses must sign their names in the presence of the testator.

When you choose witnesses, try to find people who are likely to be easy to contact should any dispute arise. Neighbours who are well settled in the area are often suitable, and so are professional people (for example, doctors and accountants) as they can be contacted through their professional organisations if necessary.

5 | *I made a will some time ago and now want to change it. Can I do so?*

Yes. One of the essential features of a will is that it is 'revocable' – that is, it can be cancelled by the testator, who is then free to make a new will. The only exception to this is that a person may become too ill to make a will (see Q7), in which case he is also considered too ill to revoke an existing will. A will can be revoked, according to the Wills Act 1837, by 'burning tearing or otherwise destroying the same' or by making a new will or codicil (see Q6).

A will is revoked by destruction only if there is a physical act of destruction; crossing out words with a pen is not sufficient. The physical act of destruction must be performed by the testator or by someone else 'in his presence and by his direction'. In addition to the physical act, the testator must have intended to revoke it. Accidental destruction, therefore, does not revoke a will. (If a will is accidentally destroyed it may be difficult to prove what it said, but if the will was drawn up by a solicitor a copy should be available and may be sufficient proof.)

The making of a new will or codicil nearly always has the effect of revoking the old will in whole or in part. The new will may actually say that the whole of the old will is revoked, and the usual method of doing so is to include words such as: 'I hereby revoke all former wills and testamentary dispositions heretofore made by me and declare this to be my last will.' If the new will does not specifically revoke the old will it is

nevertheless considered to revoke the old will to the extent that its terms are inconsistent: for example, if the old will said 'I leave my piano to my daughter' and the new will says 'I give my piano to my son', the son and not the daughter will inherit the piano. Because a later will usually revokes an earlier will it is important that the will should be dated to show which is later.

A will may also be wholly or partly revoked by the marriage or divorce of the person who made it (see Qs 12 and 13).

6 | *I've made a will and left most of my property to my children. I've now decided that I'd like to leave a close friend a valuable painting I own. Do I have to revoke my will and make a new one?*

No. You can add a codicil to your will. A codicil is a supplement to a will. It may be more convenient to make a small change to an existing will by producing a short codicil setting out the intended change rather than by making a complete new will. The codicil should be dated and must be signed and witnessed in the same way as a will if it is to be valid. Great care must be taken in preparing a codicil to ensure that it is compatible with the will it supplements and that it does not accidentally revoke parts of the will which are intended to continue to be effective.

A codicil to the effect that you wish to leave a particular item – say, 'I bequeath the Constable painting in the dining-room to my dear friend Mrs Lucky' – takes precedence over any more general provision in the will itself – such as, 'I leave all the contents of my house to my daughter' – without affecting the validity of the more general provision.

When a codicil is added to a will, the will is usually considered to have been remade on the day the codicil is made. This can affect the legal meaning given to the will. For example, in one case a will made a gift to 'my cousin's wife'. A codicil was later added, also making a gift to 'my cousin's wife'. It was held on the death of the testator that the gift should go to the woman who was married to the cousin at the date of the codicil, not at the date of the will.

7 | *An elderly relative wants to make a will but I'm not sure whether he understands what he's doing. Are there likely to be any problems with the will?*

A will is invalid if the testator did not have 'testamentary capacity'. Testamentary capacity is present if the testator understands:

8 | *My will specifies that a friend is to inherit my car when I die. But the car's now worn out and I need a new one. Will he get anything if I should change cars?*

That depends on the precise wording of your will. A gift of a particular piece of property (other than land) is called a 'specific bequest' (a gift of a particular piece of land is a 'specific devise' and a gift of cash is a 'legacy'). For example, if the will says 'I leave my car to Jim Driver' that is taken to be a specific bequest of the particular car you own at the time when you make the will. If you sell, give away or destroy the subject-matter of a specific bequest the gift is 'adeemed', which means the beneficiary is entitled neither to the property nor to a replacement for it nor to any money to compensate for the lack of the gift.

On the other hand, if your will says 'I give any car which I may own at the date of my death to Jim Driver', you have made it clear that if you sell your present car he will get the one that you own when you die.

9 | *My son, who is 17, wants to make a will. Can he do that? If he can't, what would happen to his savings in the event of his death?*

No one can make a will until his or her eighteenth birthday. The only exception to this rule allows seamen and military personnel either at sea or involved in actual military service to make wills even though they are under 18.

If someone under 18 dies, his or her property will be distributed according to the intestacy Rules (see QS 26 to 32). This usually means that it will all go to the spouse if he or she is married or to his or her parents if not.

10 | *I want to leave some money to a friend of mine. What will happen if there's not enough money in the bank when I die?*

Your friend will still be entitled to be paid. A gift of money in a will takes effect whether or not money is readily available at the time of death. If there is insufficient money available your personal representatives (see Q 22) will have to sell something of yours to raise the money. The personal representatives cannot, however, sell something for this purpose which you have specifically stated should go to someone else. For example, if your will leaves 'my stamp collection' or 'my house' to one of your friends and some money to another, neither the stamp collection nor the house will be sold to raise the money. This means

● the nature of the act of making a will,
● the value, or 'extent', of the property he is disposing of, and
● the claims to his estate he ought to consider. This means that the testator must be aware of who are his relatives and others whom he should consider, although there is no obligation on him to leave his property to these people, and as long as he is capable of making a proper judgment he can choose to give his property to anyone he likes.

Once the testator is dead the people who apply to have the will put into effect may be called on by the court, on an application for a Grant of Representation (see QS 22 to 25), to prove that the testator had testamentary capacity. However, if the will appears to be rational those who wish to challenge the will must produce some evidence as to incapacity before capacity needs to be proved. To avoid difficulties it may be a good idea in cases of doubt to get the opinion of a doctor at the time the will is signed as to whether the testator knows what he is doing.

In certain cases a will can be made on behalf of a person 'who is incapable by reason of mental disorder of managing and administering his property and affairs'. An application for the making of such a will is made to the Court of Protection, which is part of the High Court and meets only in London (address on page 509); the person applying need not be a solicitor but the applicant would be well advised to see a solicitor.

that the friend to whom you left the money will get nothing if the stamps or the house are the only valuables you own when you die. If you have left money to two or more persons and when you die they cannot all be paid in full, each will get the same proportion of what you intended to leave them. Thus, if you leave £10,000 to friend A and £20,000 to friend B and when you die you are worth only £15,000 (after payment of debts and after any items of property and belongings specifically given away have been distributed), A will get £5,000 and B will get £10,000 – they will each get half of what you wished them to have as that is all that is available for apportionment between them.

11 | *I want to leave some money to my sister and if she dies before me I want her children to have it instead. Can this be arranged?*

Yes, this can be arranged quite easily. Your will must state specifically that if your sister does not survive you then her children are to have the money divided equally between them. If you do not include this 'substitutional clause' – so called because it substitutes other parties for the specified legatee – then your sister's children would not get the money that you want to leave their mother. This is because a gift in a will 'lapses' when the person to whom it is given dies before the testator.

Where a gift lapses and there is no substitutional clause, the property passes to the residuary beneficiary (see page 146) or, if there's no will, it passes to the relatives entitled to receive it on intestacy (see QS 26 to 32).

There are a few exceptions to this rule about lapse. The main one provides that if you leave something to your *own* child or another descendant, such as a grandchild, and that person dies before you leaving children or grandchildren living when you die, even without a substitutional clause that person's children will get the gift between them unless your will states otherwise.

12 | *I'm about to get married. Should I make a new will?*

Yes. A will is automatically revoked when the person who made it gets married. The law lays down this rule because it is assumed that the old will is unlikely to cover what the testator would now want to do with his or her property. As the will will now be void, the intestacy Rules (see QS 26 to 32) will apply unless a new will is made.

There are, however, two important exceptions to the revocation-by-marriage rule:

● The will itself may show that the testator did not intend it to be revoked by marriage *and* that the testator was contemplating marriage to a particular person when the will was made. This is usually done by naming the intended spouse in the will, although that is not essential. The whole will then remains valid if the testator gets married to the particular person contemplated; marriage to anyone else revokes the will.

● The will itself may show that the testator did not intend a particular gift to be revoked by marriage *and* that the testator was contemplating marriage to a particular person when the will was made. For example, the will may specify that a sum of money should go to the testator's children and the residue of the estate to the person he or she subsequently marries. In this case the particular gift remains valid if the testator gets married to the particular person contemplated, and the rest of the will also remains valid. Again, marriage to anyone else revokes the whole will.

A person who is about to get married should always consider making a new will or making a will for the first time. If he or she does decide to do so there are two courses open. First, he or she may decide to make a will 'in contemplation of marriage', in which case professional help is especially advisable to ensure that the person to whom the testator is getting married will be a beneficiary and to ensure that the marriage will not revoke the will. Second, he or she may decide to make a will after the marriage has taken place. While this avoids the problems of revocation on marriage, there will be a gap between the marriage and making the new will and if the testator dies during that gap the intestacy Rules will apply.

13 | *My will specifies that everything I own goes to my wife when I die. What would happen if we ever got divorced?*

On divorce any gift that you have made to your former spouse in your will fails, and your ex-wife will be treated as if she had predeceased you. This means that the property given to your former spouse will go instead to some other specified beneficiary, such as your children, or to those people who are entitled to your estate if you died without making a will (see QS 26 to 32). If you have appointed your former spouse to act as your executor, this appointment will also be void. These rules do not apply if your will specifically provides to the contrary by stating that your spouse is to be entitled to the gift or is to be an executor even if you get a divorce.

It is very important to realise that the rules excluding the former spouse apply only when you die after actually obtaining a divorce. If you are only separated from your spouse you should think about making a new will immediately in case you die before your divorce is finalised.

14 | *My mother died last week. I know she made a will but I can't find it. Is there anything I should do?*

The first thing to do is to check with relatives and friends who may know where it is. You should also check with your mother's bank, as she may have left it there in the safe deposit, and with her solicitor (if you know that she has used a number of solicitors you should check with all of them). There is also a procedure whereby people who have made wills can deposit them with the Principal Registry of the Family Division of the High Court at Somerset House, London; while this procedure is little used, it is worth enquiring if nothing turns up elsewhere – telephone the Court to find out how to check.

If it is known that your mother had a will in her possession and yet the will cannot be found after her death, there is a presumption that the deceased revoked the will. If, however, there is evidence that she did not revoke the will or if the will was not kept by your mother herself and has been lost it may be possible to use a copy as proof of what the will said. If a solicitor prepared a will he should have a copy even if he returned the original to your mother.

15 | *My 10-year-old daughter lives with her mother, whom I never married. Does she have the same rights to inherit my property as the children of my present marriage?*

Yes. Your illegitimate daughter has the same rights to your estate as any of your other children. If you die without making a will her entitlement is the same as your other children's (see Q30). If you make a will leaving property to 'my children' this expression will include your illegitimate daughter, and if you exclude her from your will and fail to make provision for her then she can make a family provision claim (see Q54).

16 | *If in my will I specify that I want to leave £500 to each of my four grandchildren, I assume that will be enough to cover the eldest, who was adopted?*

Yes. An adopted child is treated as the child of the couple who have adopted him and not of his natural parents, and the adopted child will be regarded in the same way as your other grandchildren as far as your estate is concerned. Adopted children also have the same rights to their parents' estates as the children of the marriage.

17 | *My wife and I have three children of our own and we've fostered a young girl for the past three years. I'd like to make provision for our foster child in my will. Must I mention her separately?*

Yes. Foster children are not regarded as your own children for the purposes of entitlement to your property. If you wish to provide for your foster daughter you must do so specifically in your will. The only right that a foster child may have is to make a family provision claim as a dependant (see Q54).

18 | *I want to leave some money to my children when I die but I don't want them to be able to spend it until they are at least 21. Can this be arranged?*

Yes, you can provide for this in your will. If you make a gift to a minor (someone under 18 when you die) he or she cannot spend the money until reaching the age of 18. You can extend this to 21 or even an older age by making express provision in your will. Normally the beneficiary will be entitled to any income produced by the gift once he or she is 18 even though not entitled to the gift itself, but again you can make express provision to the contrary if you wish. There are technical problems involved in such gifts, particularly in relation to taxation, so you would be wise to get the advice of a solicitor before making provisions of this sort in your will.

19 | *I have two young children and am worried*

about who will be responsible for them if I die. Can I put anything in my will about this?

Yes. If you alone die then your husband or wife will, of course, remain responsible for the children, although you can appoint a guardian to act jointly with him or her under the Guardianship of Minors Act 1971 if you wish.

More commonly, parents want to specify in their wills 'testamentary guardians' to be responsible for their children in the event of the death of both parents. You should discuss this with your spouse so as to ensure that you both appoint the same person or persons in your wills. This does not absolutely guarantee that the persons appointed will be guardians to your children as the High Court, if the matter goes to law, always has the right to appoint someone else. But if you and your spouse both agree then it is very unlikely that the Court would choose someone else. You should consult the people you have in mind before making your will.

20 | *I took out an insurance policy on my life some time ago. How will this be dealt with on my death?*

First, check whether the policy is a term policy or a whole life policy. If it is a term policy then you are insured only for a particular period of time, for example, for 10 years after you enter into the policy. If you do not die within that time there will be no capital sum payable on your death. If the policy is a whole life policy a capital sum will be payable whenever you die. Second, check to make sure that any premiums due under the policy have been paid; if you are in arrears you are probably no longer insured. Some policies require a lump-sum premium when you take out the policy, while others require premiums to be paid regularly – every year, say. In the latter case the policy will become void (and so nothing will be payable on your death) if the premiums are not paid on time. Usually, the policy allows a little leeway as to when premiums should be paid and may give you the right to 'revive' the policy by paying premiums late.

If the policy is still valid when you die, the capital sum paid by the insurance company will be treated as part of your estate for the purposes of inheritance tax (see Q49). This may result in a payment of tax if your estate is large enough, although to the extent that you leave your property to your spouse you will be exempt in any case.

If you take out the policy on your own life but assign it to another person who will receive the capital payable on your death, the insurance company will pay the sum to that nominee and the amount will not be treated as part of your estate.

21 | *I'm a member of my employers' pension scheme which also gives me life insurance cover should I die while in my job. I've been asked to specify to whom the insurance money is to be paid if I die. Why is this? I've already made a will and nominated my wife as my sole beneficiary.*

Your employers' pension scheme is run by independent trustees who have the power, under the conditions that established the scheme, to pay the lump sum due on your death to anyone *they* choose. This means that you cannot leave the money to anyone in your will, as you are not entitled to decide to whom the money is to go as it is not part of your estate. Nevertheless, the trustees have asked you to state to whom the money is to be paid, and you can be confident that your wishes will be respected unless the circumstances are very unusual.

At first sight you might feel that the scheme would be better if it gave you an absolute right to dictate to whom the money due on your death is to be paid. However, if you had such a choice the money would be treated as part of your estate and so, depending on the size of your estate, might be liable to inheritance tax (see Q49). Because, technically, it is the trustees and not you who make the choice, no inheritance tax is payable on this money whoever it is paid to.

Grants of Representation

22 | *I'm not quite clear who deals with the property and assets of a person who has died. Is it always the executors of the will? If not, who is it?*

If the will specifies an executor (see Q2), he or she is the person who is entitled to deal with the property and assets. If the will appoints more than one executor, each of them is entitled to act. If there is no will, the property and assets are dealt with by an 'administrator'.

In both cases, an executor or administrator has to apply for a Grant of Representation (see Q23) shortly after the deceased's death. This is an official document issued by the Family Division of the High Court which proves that someone is legally entitled to deal with the affairs of the dead person.

In the case of an executor this document is known as a 'Grant of Probate', and it confirms the powers of the executor appointed by the deceased in his or her will to deal with the deceased's property and assets. In practice, a Grant of Probate is needed before certain steps (such as selling land owned by the deceased) can be taken. Where the Court considers that the executor appointed by the will is unsuitable – if the person is known to be dishonest, say – it can refuse to make a Grant in his favour.

If the deceased died intestate (see Qs 26 to 32), the Grant of Representation is known as 'Letters of Administration'. These grant the same powers to the administrators as a Grant of Probate does to executors. Normally the administrators will be the deceased's next of kin.

A third type of Grant of Representation exists in cases where the will appoints executors but they are unable or unwilling to act – through illness, perhaps, or because they had a blazing row with the deceased shortly before death. It also applies if the testator appointed no executors or if the executors have predeceased the testator. This type of Grant is known as Letters of Administration with will annexed. Rules imposed by Parliament specify who is entitled to such a Grant. The rules are complicated, but in most cases the person who is left the bulk of the deceased's property and assets is the first person entitled. Others will be able to take such a Grant only if that person chooses not to.

Executors and administrators, both of whom 'administer' an estate, are often referred to as 'personal representatives'.

23 | How do I apply for a Grant of Representation?

You can apply for a Grant of any of the three types referred to in Q22 either by making a personal application or by asking a solicitor to help you. To make a personal application you have to contact an office of the High Court called a Probate Registry or Subregistry (addresses in the telephone directory under Probate or Court). You don't have to use any particular Registry but can apply at whichever is most convenient for you. If you telephone, the Registry will send you by return a questionnaire about the deceased and his or her property (see Q24). You will have to complete the questionnaire (as you will see when you get it, this is not an easy task because a great deal of information is required about all the deceased's assets) and send it back to the Registry. Some time later you will be asked to attend at the Registry so that the officials there can go through the questionnaire and make sure it is accurate. Once they are satisfied with the questionnaire and that you are

entitled to act, a Grant of Representation will be made in your favour. If any inheritance tax is payable on the deceased's estate (other than on land and business assets) you will have to pay that before you get the Grant (see Q52), and you will also have to pay a court fee if the estate is larger than a certain amount, the size of the fee depending on the size of the estate.

24 | I've asked my solicitor to apply for a Grant of Representation on my behalf. What procedure is involved?

Your solicitor will apply on your behalf at one of the Probate Registries. He will prepare an Inland Revenue Account and an oath for you to sign. These documents together fulfil the same functions as the questionnaire does in the case of a personal application (see Q23).

The Inland Revenue Account sets out details of all the property owned by the deceased and any deductions for debts and funeral expenses. It also sets out your assessment of any tax (see Qs 38 and 49) payable on the estate (the Inland Revenue can, of course, challenge this if they do not agree the figures). An Inland Revenue Account is not usually required where the deceased's estate is below a certain value (the figure is currently £40,000).

The oath states why you are entitled to apply for a Grant of Probate (if you are an executor) or Letters of Administration (if you are an administrator). It also contains a promise by you that you will administer the estate properly. The oath must be sworn to or affirmed by you in the presence of an independent solicitor – that is, a solicitor who is not from the same firm as your own solicitor. Your own solicitor will make arrangements for the swearing of the oath.

Once the Account and oath are finalised your solicitor will send them together with the tax payable, if any, the court fee, if any (see Q23), and will (where there is one) to the Probate Registry. If the documents are in order the Grant will then be made in your favour.

25 | Many years ago I agreed to be a friend's executor. He died a week ago but I'm not sure that I want to take on the responsibility, as his affairs seem very complex. Can I now refuse?

Yes, you can, as long as you decide fairly quickly. You are entitled to 'renounce probate' by writing to inform the Probate Registry (see Q23). Once you have renounced you cannot change your mind later unless a Probate Registrar agrees.

There are two ways in which you can lose your right to renounce probate. First, if you have actually taken out a Grant of Probate (see Q22) you cannot later simply renounce it, although you may be permitted to give up the executorship if the Probate Registry agrees – if you are ill, say, or about to emigrate; the procedure involved is called a 'revocation of Grant'. Second, you cannot renounce probate once you have taken substantial steps to deal with the estate of the deceased, such as paying and collecting debts or selling belongings or property. However, you do not lose the right to renounce probate if all you have done is to arrange the funeral of the deceased or taken steps to protect his belongings, for example by moving them to a safe place.

If you do not make up your mind fairly speedily as to whether you want to take or renounce probate you are likely to be put under pressure by the deceased's family. It is also possible that the family will bring proceedings against you at the Probate Registry to force you to make up your mind.

Where two or more people are appointed executors, between one and four of them can take a Grant of Probate. Any who do not take a Grant are said to have 'power reserved' and can take a Grant later if necessary.

Intestacy

26 | If I die before I've made a will, who will handle my estate?

A person who dies without leaving a valid will is said in legal terms to die intestate. The intestate's property is dealt with by an administrator (see Q22). The administrator divides the deceased's property between his or her relatives according to certain statutory Rules which are summarised in Qs 27 to 32. He is also responsible for paying any debts, funeral expenses and tax, if any, on the deceased's estate.

Certain types of property and assets are dealt with according to different procedures and are not handled by the administrator at all. This includes property jointly owned by the deceased and someone else, normally the husband or wife, and some insurance policies and pension rights (see Qs 20 and 21). In the latter case, the insurance and pension companies will pay direct to the beneficiary on production of the certificate of registration of death (see Q34).

27 | Will my wife get everything I own when I die if I do not make a will?

Not necessarily. It depends on how much you leave, whether you have any children and whether you are survived by a parent, brother or sister. The property of a person who dies intestate is divided among his or her family according to Rules of the Administration of Estates Act 1925. These Rules give the surviving spouse of a marriage an entitlement to the deceased's estate. The Rules apply to anyone whose 'domicile' – permanent home – at the time of death is in England or Wales regardless of where he or she actually dies. The Rules apply equally well to the death of both a husband and a wife.

The Rules state that if a husband's possessions are worth less than £75,000, the widow inherits everything. If he leaves more than £75,000-worth of possessions, the widow receives all the husband's 'personal chattels' – the household effects, the car and so on – together with £75,000-worth of the estate (plus interest from the date of the late husband's death) which includes the house, stocks, shares, bank accounts, etc. What is left above £75,000 is divided into two equal halves; one half goes to the husband's children equally (and 'children' means the husband's issue, which includes children by a previous marriage and any illegitimate children), and the widow gets a life interest in the other half. This life interest means that she cannot touch the capital but receives an income from it in the form of interest payments, dividends, rents and so on. On her death, the assets from which she's been receiving an income are divided equally among the children. If there are no children of the marriage, the widow gets the personal effects and up to £125,000 and half the rest of the estate (not just the income from it); the other half is inherited by the deceased's parents (if living) or brothers and sisters.

If the wife is the sole surviving relative, she gets everything. If there are children and the wife is dead, the estate is divided up equally among the children. If the wife predeceases the husband and there are no children, the estate is divided among the nearest surviving relatives. See Q31 for the order these take.

28 | My husband died recently without making a will. He left the house (in his name and worth £75,000), various personal items (worth £4,000) and £20,000 in building society accounts. I understand from my solicitor that I'm entitled to the house and the personal items and that the children (who are grown up now) will get £10,000 immediately and that I will get income

*from the other £10,000. Can I take a cash lump
sum instead of this income?*

As your husband died intestate you are entitled to the
personal items, £75,000 (which you can take in the
form of the house if you wish; see Q29) and income
from half the rest of the estate – as you say, income
from the £10,000 (see Q27). If you prefer you may
insist on taking a cash lump sum instead. The
amount you get depends on how old you are; the
older you are the less you will get. If you want to take
a lump sum you must write to your husband's administrator. If you are the sole administrator you
must write to the Senior Registrar of the Family
Division of the High Court at the Probate Registry
(address on page 509).

29 | *If my husband were to die without leaving a
will, is there any guarantee that I'll be able to
carry on living in our house?*

This depends on a number of factors.

If your house is owned jointly by yourself and your
husband (see LIVING TOGETHER, Q1), your husband's
interest in it will pass automatically to you on his
death.

If your house is in your husband's sole name and
he dies intestate, you will inherit all his possessions if
their total value – including the value of the house –
is less than £75,000.

If your husband's estate has a value of more than
£75,000, whether you will have to sell the family
house depends on the actual size of the estate and
whether he has any children – and children from a
previous marriage and any illegitimate children must
be taken into account. If there are no children, you
are entitled to receive up to £125,000 (see Q27),
included in which is the value of the house. If there
are children and the estate is worth over £75,000,
you are entitled to all his personal chattels plus
£75,000-worth of the estate. If the house itself is
worth more than £75,000, you are entitled to
continue living in it but will have to pay to the estate
the difference between £75,000 and the true worth
of the house.

If, say, your house is worth £79,000 and your
husband leaves cash of £8,000 (apart from personal
chattels like the car which you will inherit anyway),
you will inherit only £75,000-worth of the total
estate. That means not only that you will inherit no
cash but also that to continue living in the family
home you will have to raise £4,000 to pay to the
estate – which could of course involve selling the
house anyway.

30 | *Will my children get anything when I die if I
don't make a will?*

It depends on your family circumstances and the
value of your estate when you die. If you are married
when you die your spouse will be entitled to part of
your estate (see Q27). The rest of your estate will go
to your 'issue' – your children – and if any of your
children are dead it will go to their children. The part
of the estate available to issue where the spouse also
survives is half the value of the estate after the
spouse's share of £75,000 plus the personal chattels
are deducted; this share is available immediately and
the rest when the spouse dies. This means that your
children get nothing if you are worth £75,000 or less
when you die.

If you are not survived by your spouse when you
die and have made no will your issue will get the
whole of your property.

Where issue become entitled to some or all of the
estate it is divided between the children equally. If a
child has predeceased the parent his share goes to his
children equally, or to the other children of the parent equally where the deceased child had no children
of his own. Where any of the children are under 18
and are unmarried their portions of the estate are
invested by trustees and not paid to them until they
are 18 or get married, whichever is sooner.

31 | *I'm not married. Who'll inherit my property
when I die if I don't make a will?*

AS FATHER McGUIGAN DID NOT MAKE A
WILL HIS ESTATE WILL BE DIVIDED BETWEE.

Assuming that you have no children and remain unmarried, your property will be distributed equally among your closest blood relatives. There is a statutory order of the relatives who are entitled to your property on death:

1. Parents (or the surviving parent if one dies before you)
2. Brothers and sisters 'of the whole blood' – people who have *both* parents in common with you
3. Half brothers and sisters – people with *one* parent in common with you
4. Surviving grandparents (equally if more than one)
5. Uncles and aunts 'of the whole blood' – people with two parents in common with one of your parents
6. Half uncles and aunts – people with one parent in common with one of your parents.

If there is one person surviving in any category, no other relative in a lower category takes anything. For example, if there is no surviving parent but there is one brother he will take everything and half brothers and sisters and grandparents and so on will get nothing.

A person (other than a parent or grandparent) who dies before you is replaced by his own children, if any, rather than by relatives in a lower category. For example, if you have a brother and sister and when you die the brother is alive but the sister is dead having left three children, your brother will get half the property and your sister's children will each get one third of the other half.

Only blood relatives are included (but see Q32), so that your mother's brother's wife is not an aunt for these purposes.

If there are no surviving relatives in any of the above categories, your property goes to the Crown and not to more distant relatives.

32 | *If I die without making a will, is there a chance that my ex-husband, whom I divorced only a year ago, can get his hands on my money?*

Very little. Under the intestacy Rules, none of the property or assets of a divorced man or woman who dies intestate will go to the ex-wife or ex-husband. An ex-spouse can apply for maintenance out of the estate under the Inheritance (Provision for Family and Dependants) Act 1975 (see Q54), but the courts are very reluctant to award maintenance to ex-spouses after death as the court will already have decided what should be provided at the time of the divorce.

Death

33 | *When someone dies, who supplies the certificate stating the cause of death?*

A 'registered medical practitioner' – a doctor – who attended the deceased during his or her last illness must sign a 'certificate of the cause of death'. Sometimes the doctor himself sends the certificate to the Registrar of Births and Deaths and gives a 'notice of the cause of death' to a close relative of the deceased. However, much more commonly the doctor gives the certificate of the cause of death to a relative of the deceased who then takes it to the Registrar when he or she registers the death (see Q34). Where it is intended that the deceased's body will be cremated a certificate of the cause of death from a second doctor is required confirming the opinion of the first doctor. In practice, the undertaker will organise this.

See also Q36.

34 | *I know that a death has to be registered, but I'm not sure what this means. What is the procedure?*

By law, every death in England and Wales has to be registered by the appropriate Registrar of Births and Deaths. For the purposes of registration the country is divided up into districts and sub-districts. Registration must be in the Registry for the sub-district in which the death occurred, which may be a different sub-district from the one in which the deceased lived. If you are in any doubt as to which is the appropriate Registry you should telephone first (look up the number under Registration of Births, Deaths and Marriages).

The law defines who may register the death. A 'notice to informant', attached to the certificate of the cause of death (see Q33), lists the people who may act as informants. Where the deceased died in a house (in his own or someone else's), the informant should be the nearest relative present at the death or in attendance during the last illness or, if none, any other relative who lives in the same sub-district or, if none, some other relative or the occupier of the house in which the death occurred. Where the deceased did not die in a house but in a hospital, say, any relative or any person present at the death can supply the particulars.

The informant must attend personally at the Registry. The registration process is a brief question-and-answer interview between the Registrar and the informant. The informant must supply the certificate of the cause of death (unless it has already been supplied by the doctor; see Q33). The informant should also take details of the deceased's full name and full address, place of death and if possible the deceased's NHS medical card.

Registration must normally be dealt with within five days of the death. The Registrar will supply one copy of the certificate of registration free of charge; this is needed for claiming any National Insurance benefits. Other copies may be needed to deal with other aspects of the deceased's estate, like bank accounts, and these copies can be obtained for a small fee. Further copies can be supplied later if necessary.

35 | *What are the legal rules relating to funerals and cremations?*

The executor appointed by a will is responsible for the funeral arrangements of the deceased. The will may contain directions as to the funeral arrangements. These are not legally binding, but such directions and the wishes of the deceased's family are normally complied with. Frequently, the funeral arrangements are made by the family rather than by the executor, and the family or friends will have to make the arrangements in any case where there is no executor.

Burial or cremation cannot normally take place until the death has been registered (see Q34). At the registration, the Registrar issues a 'certificate for disposal'; the undertaker will need this before the funeral. The paperwork required for both burials and cremations is in practice dealt with by the undertaker.

Burials commonly take place either at the burial grounds of parish churches or at the cemeteries of local authorities. Any person has a right to be buried in the churchyard or burial ground of the parish in which he or she lived, although not everyone is entitled to a funeral service at the parish church. Burial in churchyards of persons other than those living in the parish may be permitted in certain cases at the discretion of the church authorities. Everyone has the right to be buried at the cemeteries of their local authorities.

In the case of cremations, a certificate for cremation from an official called the medical referee is required. The medical referee is a doctor who works for the crematorium authority. He will need to see the appropriate certificates of the cause of death and of registration of death before issuing the certificate. An application for cremation signed by the executor or nearest relative of the deceased is also required. As stated above, the undertaker will handle the paperwork.

36 | *When is a post-mortem necessary?*

The Registrar of Births and Deaths is required to report certain deaths to the coroner, an official whose main function is to investigate any death if there's some doubt about the cause of it. (For examples of deaths that must be reported to the coroner, see HEALTH, Q25.) Once a death is reported to the coroner he will decide whether a post-mortem is necessary. A post-mortem is a medical examination of the body to establish the cause of death. The coroner has the legal power to insist on a post-mortem even if the deceased's family opposes it. If a post-mortem is held and proves the cause of death to have resulted from natural causes the coroner will usually decide not to hold an inquest (see HEALTH, Q26). If the coroner decides that no inquest is necessary (either with or without a post-mortem) he will inform the Registrar so that he can issue the certificate of registration; a funeral can then be held. When an inquest is held the coroner must issue a burial order (or certificate for cremation) after the inquest before the funeral can take place.

Administering the estate

37 | *I am the executor of my father's estate. What will my duties be?*

The duties imposed on a personal representative, which includes administrators as well as executors (see Q22), include: collecting the money, property and all the other assets of the deceased, paying his debts and liabilities, paying any inheritance tax on the estate (see Q50), paying funeral expenses, paying legacies, and finally handing over any remaining cash or other assets to the residuary beneficiary.

There are, therefore, really three stages involved in administering an estate: collecting, paying outsiders, and paying beneficiaries. However, these stages in the administration may overlap. For example, you may pay some of the debts before you have collected all the assets.

You must make any decisions required during the administration personally, but if you wish you can get other people to act for you in putting your decisions into effect. Many executors and administrators find it useful to have the assistance of a solicitor throughout the administration (he will of course charge for his services). Where the estate includes investments you may also need advice from an expert in investments such as a stockbroker.

38 | *I am the executor of my late uncle's estate. What do I have to do about income tax?*

As an executor you may have to pay out of the estate tax on income for two different periods of time.

First, the deceased may have owed income tax on income for the period before his death. This is a debt that you will have to pay out of the deceased's assets.

Second, you will be liable for tax on income such as dividends or interest received arising during the administration period, which is the period from the date of death until the day on which you are in a position to distribute the assets of the deceased. For that period you must pay the Inland Revenue income tax at the basic rate (currently 27 per cent) on all the income that you receive. To pay the Inland Revenue you can, as executor, use your late uncle's bank accounts and sell any assets; to do so you will need to show the bank manager, and any other appropriate person, the Grant of Representation before your signature is valid. If the estate is complex, you should probably seek the advice of a solicitor or tax consultant.

There are one or two exceptions that you should take into account in calculating income tax liability. You may, for example, deduct interest paid on certain loans used to pay inheritance tax (see Q52). And in many instances the income that you receive will already have had basic rate tax deducted, in which case you do not have to pay it again; this applies, for example, to dividends received on shares and to interest on building society and bank accounts.

When you pay the income that you have received over to the beneficiaries of the estate you must supply them with a certificate showing that you have deducted tax at the basic rate. Any beneficiary with a low income – a child whose income is lower than the single person's allowance of £2,425, for instance – may be able to claim back some of the tax from the Inland Revenue; on the other hand, beneficiaries with high incomes may find themselves with more tax to pay.

39 | *I am administering my late aunt's estate. What do I do about her debts? I've only just discovered she was buying a colour television on hire-purchase.*

The first thing to do is to find out what debts and other liabilities there are. You may be able to discover most of the debts by going through your aunt's papers. Other debts may come to light during the administration of the estate: you should make arrangements for all correspondence addressed to the deceased to be forwarded to you so that you can check on any bills like household bills, credit cards and personal accounts with department stores.

If there are any unpaid debts at the time when you come to distribute your aunt's assets to her beneficiaries, you will be personally liable to the people to whom the deceased owed the money *even if you did not know about the debts*. You can, however, protect yourself against this liability by putting advertisements in the government newspaper called the *London Gazette* and in other newspapers. The advertisements should say that you intend to distribute the estate and that anyone with a claim to it should contact you within two months. Unfortunately, the law is not very clear as to where you should advertise. In most cases an advertisement in one local newspaper (in the area where the deceased lived) and in the *London Gazette* is sufficient.

40 | *Where does the money come from to pay the debts of the deceased?*

You must pay the debts out of the deceased's estate. You can do this by using the deceased's cash and bank accounts and, if they provide inadequate funds, by selling some of his assets. Once you have paid the debts you will need to know *which part* of the estate the money comes out of – in other words, which beneficiary gets less because of the debt. The rules about this are very complicated. Normally, where there is a mortgage the beneficiary who is given the mortgaged property must pay off the mortgage or arrange to take it over. (If he will not or cannot then you will have to sell the property, pay off the mortgage and give him the balance.) In the case of debts other than mortgages the deceased's will usually specifies that certain gifts of specific assets or amounts of money are to be paid first, then the debts and then the balance of the estate is to go to a named person(s) – the residuary beneficiary. Where the will does lay down this or any other sequence, you must follow it. Where the will does not provide for the payment of debts, statutory Rules provide that property not given away by the terms of the will (if any) is to be used first, and then the residue of the estate, that is, property other than that specifically given to particular beneficiaries and other than property used to pay gifts of money.

If the debts and other liabilities are more than the

value of the assets, the estate is 'insolvent'. Special Rules exist as to who should be paid first where the estate is insolvent, and if you pay debts other than in this order you will incur *personal liability*. If there is *any* danger that the estate may be insolvent you should seek professional advice at once.

41 | *I am administering my mother's estate. In her will she left sums of money to a number of people. When should they be paid?*

You should not pay the legacies until you are sure that there will be enough money left in the estate to pay any debts, income tax (see Q38), inheritance tax (see Q49) and the funeral expenses. Once you are sure that there will be enough money available you can pay the legacies. As the legacies are cash gifts you may have to sell assets to raise the money if there isn't enough in bank and building society accounts and so on. For this purpose you can sell *any* assets of the estate, such as silver, china, the car, and so on, but should not sell any assets that have been specifically left to someone. When choosing which to sell you should always take into account the wishes of the residuary beneficiary who will inherit any unsold assets.

A legatee can legally force you to pay his or her legacy as soon as a year has elapsed from the date of the death. If you delay payment for longer than a year you may be called upon to explain the delay. Once a year has elapsed from the death, interest of 5 per cent per annum must be added to a legacy until payment is made. If the will specifies that a legacy must be paid at a certain date, any delay in handing over the legacy will involve paying interest between that date and the date of actual payment.

42 | *My mother has left people her personal property, like her glass and china, and shares in particular companies. How should I hand them over to the beneficiaries?*

Unfortunately there is no one simple answer to this question. The way that you transfer assets depends on what type of assets they are. Money and chattels – physical things like cars, furniture, books, and so on (but not land) – can be transferred simply by handing them over to the beneficiaries. You should ask for a receipt to avoid any arguments later on.

In the case of assets such as shares or national savings certificates, where institutions have received money from the deceased as an investment, various formalities for transfer are required. The particular formalities vary depending on the particular asset

involved. For example, in the case of shares you will have to fill in a document called a stock transfer form (you will also need the deceased's share certificate, the document issued by the company in which the deceased owned shares confirming her ownership). The institution concerned will be able to tell you what formalities are required in each case. Usually you will be required to produce evidence that you are the personal representative of the deceased, and you do this by producing an 'office' (official) copy provided by the Probate Registry of the Grant of Probate or Letters of Administration. Sometimes an unofficial copy like a photocopy of the original is sufficient.

Special formalities apply in the case of transfers of land where a written document called an assent is required. You should employ a solicitor about transferring the deceased's land to ensure that the formalities are complied with.

43 | *I'm my uncle's executor. In his will he left part of his property to a cousin who has lost touch with the rest of the family. What should I do?*

You should first try to trace the missing cousin. Other relatives and friends may be able to give you a hand or, if the amount of money involved is substantial, it may be worth hiring an enquiry agent; a solicitor will help you to appoint one. If, after you have made enquiries, you are still unable to find the beneficiary then you are faced with a problem because if you pay out all your uncle's assets to the other beneficiaries and then the missing beneficiary turns up you will be personally liable to pay him his legacy out of your own money.

There are two ways in which you can protect yourself against this. First, you can apply to the High

Court (see a solicitor about doing so) for what is called a 'Benjamin order', so called after a case concerning the estate of a person whose surname was Benjamin. This is an order that allows you to assume that the cousin died before your uncle and therefore lost his entitlement. If he later turns up he can claim his share of the estate from the beneficiaries but not from you. Second, you can ask the other beneficiaries to promise to compensate you if the cousin turns up and claims from you (this is called an 'indemnity'). The use of an indemnity saves the cost of going to court and so is in everyone's interest, but for your own protection you should accept an indemnity only when you are convinced that the beneficiaries will be able to pay you if necessary.

44 | *A friend of mine died last week leaving a will which appointed me executor. He left half his property to a charity and half to his brother, but the brother died before him. What happens to the half left to the brother?*

A gift in a will to a person who dies before the testator 'lapses' (see Q I I). Unless your friend made provision in the will giving the property to someone else in the event of his brother's death, there will be a 'partial intestacy'. This means that the part of his assets which would have gone to the brother will go instead to whoever is entitled on his intestacy (see Q31). As the executor, you will have to deal with the whole estate including the part in respect of which he died intestate.

45 | *I've just begun to administer my brother's estate. His widow needs money for the children. Can I pay anything to her now?*

If your sister-in-law is a beneficiary of the estate (as she will be if your brother died intestate – see Q27 – or if he left her anything in his will) you may consider making an immediate payment to her out of her share of the estate. In doing so you must be careful to ensure that you leave enough money to pay any debts and tax (see Q38) and the other beneficiaries.

If the deceased's children are beneficiaries you may make payments to them too (subject to the same qualification) provided that they are adults. If the children are still under 18 the position is more difficult. A will may provide for immediate payment of the child's legacy to the parent or guardian of the infant, in which case you can pay your sister-in-law. Otherwise, in most cases, payment must be made to trustees for the infant children. Quite often an infant child has only a 'contingent' interest in the estate –

an interest that depends on the happening of some future event. This is true, for example, of the interest of a child on his or her parent's intestacy (see Q30), where the interest is dependent on his or her reaching 18 or marrying first before his or her share of the estate is paid. Where there is a contingent interest you are generally allowed to use any income such as interest from the beneficiary's share of the estate for his 'maintenance, education or benefit'. You also have power to use half the capital for his benefit. The details of these rules are complicated and you should get professional advice whenever you are dealing with infant beneficiaries.

46 | *I'm my sister's executor. I want to deposit her cash to earn interest for the benefit of the estate. Can I do that?*

Yes. An executor or administrator has power of investment, which includes depositing money, such as at a bank or building society, to earn interest. Certain powers are granted automatically by Parliament. These give the personal representative the right to invest money from the estate in various types of investment. If you want to do anything with the money from the estate which is more speculative than depositing it to earn interest, such as investing on the Stock Exchange, you should seek professional advice.

47 | *I'm executor of my brother's estate. An accountant has told me that I must produce 'accounts'. What do I have to do?*

When you took out your Grant of Probate you swore that you would produce accounts to the High Court 'when required to do so'. In fact, the Court is very unlikely to ask you to produce accounts, but for your own protection it is essential that you should keep records of all the money and other assets that you deal with as executor. When you have finished dealing with the administration you should produce accounts for the residuary beneficiary (that is the person entitled to what is left over after the payments of debts, liabilities, expenses and legacies). You should ask the residuary beneficiary to sign the accounts to acknowledge that you have completed your work to his or her satisfaction.

There are no strict rules as to how the accounts should be presented. If the estate has been very simple to administer, a list of receipts and payments should be sufficient. Where you have received income during the administration – interest, dividends or rent – it is useful to show this separately (you should have paid income tax at 27 per cent on this; see Q38).

If the estate is complicated you may need professional help in drawing up your accounts. If you have used the services of a solicitor he will either prepare the accounts himself or arrange for their preparation.

48 | *I'm not satisfied with the way my father's estate has been dealt with by his executor. Is there anything I can do?*

This depends on the reason for your dissatisfaction, but you would certainly be well advised to see a solicitor to obtain advice on whether proceedings are necessary.

If you are dissatisfied with the personal representative's handling of the estate, as a beneficiary you may consider instituting 'administration proceedings'. These are proceedings in which you apply to the High Court (or get a solicitor to do so for you) to resolve any problems or disputes that have arisen – perhaps the executor has been unreasonably slow in winding up the estate, say. Like other court actions, administration proceedings are expensive and should be avoided if possible. The costs will normally come out of the estate, although the executor or you may be ordered to pay in some cases – the executor if he is found to be remiss in carrying out his duty or you if your claims are seen to be wildly exaggerated.

Where you consider that the executor has actually failed in his duty through fraud, negligence or otherwise you may, as a beneficiary, sue him personally at any stage in his administration. The object of this type of action is not so much to resolve a dispute or problem as to seek compensation out of the personal representative's own pocket for the wrong that has been done. If you are a creditor of the estate because your father owed you money when he died and you have not been paid, you can also sue the executor for the debt.

49 | *I'm the executor of my uncle's estate, and I understand I may have to pay inheritance tax. What is the tax payable on?*

When someone dies, inheritance tax (see page 371) is payable on 'the value of the deceased's estate immediately before his death', but generally only if the estate is worth more than £90,000. The deceased's estate includes all types of property – any houses owned by the deceased, his cars, furniture and other possessions, investments, and so on. While the property on which inheritance tax is payable is the property owned immediately before death, certain changes in value *resulting from the death* are taken into account. For example, if the deceased owned a life insurance policy on his own life the whole of the sum payable on his death to his estate is liable to tax (if it is payable direct to his wife or children, it belongs to them and so is not taxable); if the deceased owned a business his death may cause the value of the business to decline because the deceased was popular with the customers, say, and this decline is taken into account.

There are some comparatively rare types of property which are excluded from the tax (including foreign property in some circumstances), and certain interests in trusts (see page 378) are dealt with in special ways (the trustees may be able to advise on this).

Although the basic rule is that *all* property owned by the deceased immediately before death is taxed, there are very important exceptions to this rule. The main exemptions from inheritance tax are:

● all possessions, assets and property given to the deceased's spouse are exempt from tax; any property jointly owned by husband and wife passes automatically to the other partner without going through the estate and is similarly exempt;
● property given to charities;
● business property, in certain cases only half the value of which is taxable.

50 | *I am the executor of my late aunt's estate. How do I work out whether inheritance tax is payable and, if it is, how much is payable?*

The first thing to do is to work out what is liable to be taxed as part of your aunt's estate on death (see Q49). You must add to this the value of any gifts made by your aunt in the last seven years of her life (other than exempt gifts; see TAXES, Q38). The value of the estate and the gifts made in the last seven years is called the cumulative total. This is the figure on which tax is calculated. If the cumulative total is less than a certain figure, fixed by the Budget each year, then there is no tax to pay. If it exceeds that figure then tax is payable, but with reductions for gifts made more than three years before the death and for certain special types of gifts on which at least part of the tax has already been paid. The current rates of inheritance tax (for deaths on or after 17 March 1987 and up to about the same time in 1988) are as follows:

£	Rate %
0– 90,000	0
90,000–140,000	30
140,000–220,000	40
220,000–330,000	50
over 330,000	60

Let's say that your aunt gave £50,000 to her brother in April and died in September 1987 leaving property worth £100,000. The tax will be calculated as follows:

1 The estate is worth £100,000.
2 The cumulative total is £150,000 (estate and gifts within seven years before death).
3 The tax is therefore

On the first £90,000,	0% = nil	
On the next £50,000,	30% = £15,000	
On the top £10,000	40% = £4,000	
Total	£19,000	

51 | *I'm the sole executor of my father's estate. If inheritance tax is payable, am I the person who'll have to pay it and, if so, when?*

Inheritance tax on the estate is payable by the executor or administrator (except when the deceased was the beneficiary of a trust fund, when the trustees pay some). You will have to pay the tax before you receive the Grant of Probate (see QS 23 and 52). You will not normally have to pay tax on any lifetime gifts made in the last seven years before death. That tax is paid by the people to whom the gifts were made.

The tax is payable within six months of the end of the month in which the deceased died – if the deceased died on 23 November, for instance, the tax must be paid by 31 May. If the tax is paid late, interest is charged, currently at 6 per cent per annum. In the case of most types of land and business assets (but not personal property and assets), the tax can be paid over a 10-year period instead of all at once.

52 | *If inheritance tax is due to be paid by my father's estate, where will I get the money for it if it has to be paid before I can get a Grant of Probate? I obviously cannot raise the money from the estate until I obtain a Grant of Probate.*

As you say, your immediate problem is that you have to pay the tax on some of the estate *before* you can obtain a Grant of Probate (see QS 23 and 51). As you will find it very difficult or even impossible to deal with your father's assets until you have the Grant, you will find it necessary in most cases to borrow the money to pay the tax. The loan will often be outstanding for a fairly short time as you will be able to pay it off once you have the Grant of Probate. The most likely source for such a loan is either your own bank or your late father's bank. In some cases the beneficiaries of the deceased might be willing and able to lend too: it is in their interest that the estate should be wound up quickly to release their inheritances. Interest paid on a loan used to pay inheritance tax is deductible from the estate (and is deducted before any income tax is assessed), so you as executor will not be out of pocket.

Once you have paid the tax you will also need to decide how the payment affects the distribution of the estate of the deceased. Anyone who has been left a particular asset or sum of money by the deceased will usually have nothing deducted for inheritance tax because all the tax will be deducted from the residue of the estate – the amount left over once all the specific sums of money have been paid (the will itself can vary this rule, though).

53 | *My father owns a valuable painting. When he dies, will capital gains tax have to be paid from the estate?*

When someone dies owning an asset of this type worth more than £3,000, that asset is notionally revalued for capital gains tax purposes; the value should be shown in the executor's accounts. If such an asset is sold after the death, only the increase in value between the date of death and the date of the sale is liable to tax; any increase in value during the deceased's period of ownership is, in effect, tax free. See also TAXES, Q70.

The individual assets owned by a deceased person, in this case a painting, may either be sold by the executor or administrator – for example, to raise money to pay off debts – or they may be transferred to beneficiaries. When assets are sold by the executor or administrator the gain, that is, the difference between the market value at the date of death and the sale price, must be calculated and then deductions are made for the costs of the sale. This leaves the 'chargeable gain' on which capital gains tax is payable. However, in the tax year in which the death occurred and the following tax year the personal representative need not pay tax on the first £6,600 of gains.

Where an asset is transferred to a beneficiary there is no capital gains tax to pay until the beneficiary comes to sell the asset, and only then if the gain (together with other gains in the same tax year) is greater than £6,600.

Inheritance

54 | *If someone dies and his will specifies that his property is to be left to people other than his family and dependants, can anything be done about it?*

Yes, in certain cases. Some relations (children,

... AND I LEAVE MY ENTIRE ESTATE TO MISS DARE.

spouses and some former spouses) and other dependants, if any, can apply to a court (see Q55) for money or other property out of the estate under the Inheritance (Provision for Family and Dependants) Act 1975. Such claims are called 'family provision' applications. The rules about who may successfully claim are very complicated, but basically the applicant must show that the will (or intestacy Rules where there is no will) does not make 'reasonable provision' for the applicant. He or she must then persuade the court that an order should be made so as to make provision out of the estate for the applicant's maintenance. The effect of the order will be to deprive the beneficiaries of some or all of the deceased's property. The court must therefore balance the interests of the applicant against the interests of the people who inherited under the terms of the will. A strong case is required before the court will make an order, so applications should be made only if there are very good grounds for contesting the will. If possible, agreement should be reached with people who inherited the property so as to avoid the cost of going to court.

55 | *My grandfather, who was my closest relative, left me nothing. I would like to apply for some money out of his estate as a dependant. How do I go about it?*

You should first of all see what is the attitude of the people who were left property by the will. You would also do well to seek professional legal advice. Very

often the advice is that you should swallow your pride and forget about your claim. If you do feel that you have a strong case and your solicitor agrees, then you will have to make an application to the court. The court will be the High Court, or the county court if the value of all the deceased's property (not the amount of your claim) is £30,000 or less. The application must be made within six months of the making of the Grant of Representation. The court can extend this time-limit but will do so only in the most exceptional circumstances.

56 | *An uncle died recently. He left his collection of antique furniture to his next-door neighbour and made some other unexpected gifts. My husband and I think he was pressurised into making them. Can we do anything about it?*

A will or part of it is invalid and will be ignored if it was made as a result of fraud or undue influence or if the testator did not know and approve of the terms of the will.

Fraud occurs where the testator is deliberately misled about certain facts so as to make him give property to a particular person. Undue influence occurs where the testator is led but not driven into making a particular gift by pressure (usually over a period of time). Both fraud and undue influence are hard to prove.

A will is invalid to the extent that it includes terms about which the testator knew nothing. In a number of cases wills or parts of wills have been held to be invalid where they were drawn up by the person to whom most of the property was given. In such cases the person to whom the property was given must prove that the testator was aware of making the gift if the will is to be valid.

The procedure involved in contesting a will is complex and you should consult a solicitor about it.

57 | *My husband died recently and I inherited everything. What is my income tax position?*

Up to the date of your husband's death he will normally have been paying tax on both his own income and on your income. There may be some income tax outstanding in respect of this period; this will be met by your husband's estate. In certain circumstances you may be liable for the unpaid tax on your own income.

From the date of your husband's death you will be liable to tax on your own income. Income tax is assessed for tax years starting on 6 April each year and ending on the following 5 April. The first year you will be concerned with will cover the period from your husband's death until the following 5 April. For that period you are entitled to a single person's allowance of £2,425 and to a widow's bereavement allowance of £1,370. This means that income up to those combined amounts is tax free, so if your income is less than £3,795 for the period from your husband's death until the following 5 April you will have no tax to pay. The same allowances are available for the next full tax year after your husband's death. Thereafter you are entitled only to the single person's allowance and not to the widow's bereavement allowance.

If your husband owned investments or other income-producing assets which he has left to you, there will be an income tax liability on the income from these items from the date of your husband's death.

58 | My wife died recently. How does this affect my income tax position?

You are entitled to the married man's personal allowance for the whole of the tax year in which your wife died. This means that the first £3,795 of your income in that year will be tax free. You will also pay no tax on the amount of your wife's earned income relief of £2,425 up to the date of her death. In future tax years you will be a single person for tax purposes (unless you remarry) so you will be entitled only to the single person's allowance of £2,425.

Although you are normally liable to pay tax on your wife's income as well as on your own income (unless you have elected for separate taxation) any tax outstanding on your wife's income at the time of her death should be paid out of her estate.

59 | My late uncle has left me £2,000 in his will, but I'd really prefer to inherit his car instead. Would this be possible?

This is often possible, though you have no right to insist on having the car. An asset can be 'appropriated' to you instead of cash provided that:

● the asset (in this case the car) has not been left specifically to someone else, and
● the deceased's executor agrees to the appropriation.

If appropriation is agreed to, the car must be valued at the time of appropriation. This is necessary so as to be fair to you and to the other beneficiaries. If the car is worth £1,800, you will get the car and the £200 cash balance between its value and your legacy. If the car is valued at £2,200, then you will have to pay £200 to the estate before you can have the car. With an asset like a car which is relatively easy to value from published lists of second-hand values, the executor may be willing to rely on his own valuation, especially if the other beneficiaries agree. But with other assets the executor may get an expert valuation to protect himself from any possible disagreement between the beneficiaries.

60 | An aged uncle has left me some money in his will. We disliked each other so much that I'd feel guilty if I accepted it. Can I just refuse the inheritance?

Yes, you are entitled to 'disclaim' the gift if you want to. All you need to do is to write to the deceased's executor or administrator and say that you do not want the money. There are two restrictions on anyone's right to disclaim. First, you lose the right when you have actually received the property (or some benefit from it). Second, if you disclaim you must disclaim the whole gift; you cannot accept part and disclaim the rest. If, however, the deceased made two separate gifts to you in the will you can take one and disclaim the other.

Anything you choose to disclaim will go to the residuary beneficiary – the person who will get whatever is left over from the estate after all the other gifts have been dealt with. If you yourself are the residuary beneficiary the property will go to those who would be entitled to the property if your uncle had died intestate (see Q31). If *you* are entitled on intestacy you can disclaim your rights and the property will then go to the person who would have benefited if you had died before the deceased.

61 | *I've been left a lot of money by my grand-mother, but I think her will was unfair and I'd like to share it out among my cousins. What should I do?*

The simplest thing to do is to wait until you get the money and then pass it on to the people whom you want to benefit. However, if the amount is very large or if you have made large gifts out of your own money (or intend to do so in the future) this may not be a good idea from the inheritance tax point of view (see TAXES, Q38). Where inheritance tax is a problem, you can enter into an agreement with the people you want to benefit within two years of the death of your grandmother and give notice to the Inland Revenue in writing within six months after the agreement requiring them to treat the gifts you are making as if they had been made in your relative's will. This means that the only tax liability will be the liability of your grandmother's estate, not your own.

Discrimination

Sex and race

1 | *What types of discrimination does the law protect me against?*

The Sex Discrimination Act 1975 and the Equal Pay Act 1970 protect people against discrimination on the grounds of their sex. In the employment context the Sex Discrimination Act also protects people against discrimination on the grounds that they are married.

The Race Relations Act 1976 makes it unlawful to discriminate against people on the grounds of their colour, race, nationality or ethnic or national origins. The Sex Discrimination Act and The Race Relations Act have a very similar structure.

This legislation means that no one should be treated any worse than a person of the opposite sex – single or married – or of a different race is treated in similar circumstances.

2 | *Does the law protect me against discrimination wherever I may encounter it?*

No. The Sex Discrimination Act 1975 and the Race Relations Act 1976 apply only to employment, education, and the provision of goods, facilities, services and premises. Only in these contexts do you have a right not to be discriminated against on the grounds of race or sex. For example, all applicants for a job, and pupils at school and college, must receive equal consideration whatever their race or sex. In the same way, no provider of goods, facilities or services – like retailers, hotel proprietors and doctors – or premises – like landlords – can treat people less favourably on the grounds of race or sex.

3 | *What does the law mean by sex discrimination?*

The Sex Discrimination Act 1975 deals with two types of discrimination: direct discrimination and indirect discrimination. People are directly discriminated against if they are treated less favourably on the grounds of their sex than are people of the opposite sex in similar circumstances. The Act protects both women and men from sex discrimination; as Lord Denning, Master of the Rolls, said in one case: 'What is sauce for the goose is sauce for the gander.' So if you are refused a job, or a mortgage, or you are rejected for a university course, or whatever, and your sex is a substantial reason for the rejection, you have been directly discriminated against. Direct discrimination also covers cases of employers refusing women jobs because they assume that women cannot lift heavy objects or will leave to get married, and refusing men jobs because they assume that men cannot type. The Act prohibits people from acting on stereotyped assumptions about the abilities of both men and women, and entitles everyone to be considered on his or her individual merits irrespective of his or her sex and irrespective of characteristics associated with the sex. In one case the Court of Appeal held that a woman's employers were guilty of discrimination against her by dismissing her because of an assumption that she was not the family breadwinner (the reason for the dismissal being that she and her husband worked for rival organisations). In another case the Employment Appeal Tribunal found that a woman's employers had discriminated against her by acting on an assumption that women with young children did not make reliable employees. In each case the employers had acted unlawfully by failing to consider the women by reference to their individual abilities.

Indirect sex discrimination concerns practices that are fair in form – applying equally to men and to women – but which have an unfair impact on women or on men generally. If a practice hits disproportionately at women or at men and is unjustifiable, it will be unlawful. For example, in one case an employer decided to make part-time workers redundant prior to full-time workers. This hit disproportionately at women, as most of the part-time workers were women, and the practice was held to be unjustifiable. On another occasion it was held, for similar reasons, that the employer's refusal to provide a woman with part-time (as opposed to full-time) work was indirect sex discrimination. In another case the Civil Service was found to be indirectly discriminating against women by requiring all applicants for certain jobs to be under the age of 28. This hit disproportionately at women because in practice many women commence or recommence their careers after the age of 28 after having children; the age bar was not justifiable in all the circumstances.

4 | *What does the law mean by race discrimination?*

As in the case of sex discrimination (see Q3), unlawful race discrimination can be either direct or indirect. Direct discrimination occurs if people are treated less favourably on the grounds of colour, race, nationality or ethnic or national origins than other persons are treated. If someone rejects you for a job, say, or rejects your application to join a further education course or to take out a mortgage or to rent property, and race is a substantial factor in that decision, you have been directly discriminated against. Again, stereotyped assumptions are prohibited, and you are entitled to be considered on your individual merits, irrespective of race and irrespective of characteristics associated with that race.

Under the Race Relations Act 1976, indirect discrimination concerns a practice that is fair in form – applying to everyone irrespective of race – but which has an unfair impact on persons of a particular race and is therefore unjustifiable. The House of Lords found that a school acted unlawfully by refusing to admit pupils wearing turbans because the practice hit disproportionately at Sikhs and was unjustifiable. The Act also protects people who are unfavourably treated because of someone else's race; for example, someone who is dismissed from a job as a waiter or waitress because he or she disobeys his or her employers' instruction not to serve blacks.

5 | *What happens if I'm victimised for complaining about race discrimination?*

It is unlawful in the contexts covered – employment, education, and the provision of goods, facilities, services and premises – for a person to treat you less favourably than he or she treats other persons because you have complained or brought proceedings (see Q24) about discrimination, or that you have given evidence or information in connection with such proceedings brought by anyone else, or that you have alleged that anyone has discriminated against you (unless you made a false allegation in bad faith).

The Sex Discrimination Act 1975 prohibits the victimisation of complainants about sex discrimination in the same way that the Race Relations Act 1976 does about race discrimination. You can bring a case of victimisation to the attention of the Commission for Racial Equality or the Equal Opportunities Commission (see Q26).

Reverse discrimination

6 | *I've heard about 'reverse' discrimination, which favours certain minorities and gives priority to people in those minorities. Is this legal?*

Reverse or 'positive' discrimination, or 'affirmative action' as it is sometimes known, means the reservation for members of a group of society defined by reference to their sex, race, colour, and so on, of

certain benefits, or the taking into account of people's sex, race, colour, and so on, as one positive factor in deciding to whom to award those benefits. In general, such conduct is prohibited in the contexts covered by the Sex Discrimination Act 1975 and the Race Relations Act 1976. Both Acts are intended to protect from discrimination men as well as women and whites as well as blacks.

However, in very limited circumstances positive discrimination by employers and some other persons is permitted under the law. For example, employers are allowed to take affirmative action to five only women (or only men) access to facilities for training which would help to fit them for certain work, and are allowed to take affirmative action to give only to take advantage of opportunities to do such work where it appears that no persons, or very few, of the sex to be benefited have done the relevant work in the recent past. Similar provisions allow employers and training bodies (such as the Manpower Services Commission) to train and encourage workers from particular racial groups when no such people, or very few, have done that work in the recent past. The Sex Discrimination Act also provides that it is not sex discrimination against men to give women favourable treatment in connection with pregnancy and childbirth. The Race Relations Act states that it is not race discrimination to give persons of a particular racial group access to facilities and services to meet the special needs of people from that group in regard to their education, training or welfare, although the courts have yet to rule on how much positive discrimination this provision permits. The Race Relations Act also exempts anything done for the benefit of people who are not usually resident in Great Britain by affording them access to facilities for education or training where it appears that those people do not intend to remain in Great Britain after their period of education or training.

Finally, trade unions are allowed to take steps to ensure that a minimum number of people of one sex are elected to the managing bodies of unions.

Religion

7 | *Is it unlawful to discriminate against me because of my religion?*

Discrimination on the grounds of religion is not of itself unlawful under the Race Relations Act 1976. You would need to show that, directly or indirectly (see Q4), you have been treated less favourably than other people because of your race, colour, nationality or ethnic or national origins. The courts have accepted that Jews and Sikhs constitute racial groups for this purpose. But if a Roman Catholic, say, applied for a job and was turned down on the basis that his religion would antagonise his fellow workers, he would have little redress in the English courts.

Employment

8 | *Does the law regarding sex discrimination cover me if I'm dismissed from my job because I'm pregnant or if I'm forced to leave my job because of sexual harassment?*

The Employment Appeal Tribunal has held that to treat a woman unfavourably because she is pregnant may amount to sex discrimination. The law compares the treatment of a pregnant woman with the treatment given to a male worker suffering from a temporary incapacitating condition. If you are dismissed because of pregnancy you may also be able to make an unfair dismissal claim against your employers (see YOU AND YOUR JOB, Q64).

If you are refused a job or promotion, or dismissed or forced to leave a job because you will not succumb to your employer's sexual advances, or if your

working conditions are made intolerable by a sexually hostile atmosphere, you will have a legal remedy under the Act (see Q26).

9 | *What is the law regarding discrimination between the sexes in terms of pay?*

The basic position is that the Equal Pay Act 1970 covers any discrimination between the sexes in terms of pay. A woman is entitled to receive equal pay, and other contractual conditions, to a man doing 'like work', or 'work of equal value', or 'work rated as equivalent' (see Q10) under a job evaluation scheme, and in the same employment, unless the employers can prove that there is a good reason other than sex to treat the woman less favourably. Again, the law works both ways: a man is similarly entitled to pay equal to a woman's in these circumstances. The pay must be compared with that received by a person of the opposite sex 'in the same employment', which means the same establishment or another establishment of the same employers and with common terms and conditions.

Because of the impact of EEC law, people are entitled to compare their pay for this purpose not only with the pay of a person of the opposite sex who is contemporaneously working in the same employment, but they may also compare their pay with that received by their predecessor in the same job, if the predecessor were of the opposite sex. They can probably also compare their pay with that received by their successor if of the opposite sex. The courts have yet to decide whether an employee can win an equal pay claim if there is no person of the opposite sex doing the same work, but the employee who can prove that he or she would be paid more if of the opposite sex will probably find this sufficient to win a case.

10 | *I feel that I'm paid inequitably compared with a man doing a similar job to mine. Someone mentioned that I would have to prove that the two jobs are of 'like work'. What does this mean?*

The law defines 'like work' as work which is the same or of a broadly similar nature, so that any differences are not of practical importance in relation to the terms and conditions of employment of either a man or a woman. In one case, for instance, an Industrial Tribunal held that a woman employed in a restaurant entertainment to play the part of Nell Gwyn was doing 'like work' to men playing the part of court jesters and that she was entitled to receive pay equal to theirs.

Alternatively, you are entitled to pay equal to that of a man working in the same employment if your job has been rated as equivalent under a job evaluation scheme or if your job is 'work of equal value' to a man's. Whether work is of equal value is assessed by reference to the demands made on an employee under such headings as effort, skill and decision. The right to equal pay for work of equal value has been in operation since only 1 January 1984. It was introduced after the European Court of Justice held that the Equal Pay Act 1970 failed to comply with EEC law by providing only for equal pay for like work or for work rated as equivalent in a job evaluation scheme. The amendments to the Equal Pay Act regarding work of equal value were introduced to guarantee equal pay for men and women performing work of equal value. The amendments are extremely complicated and their full scope and effect will only be known after they have been interpreted by the courts.

11 | *If I'm doing work rated as equivalent under a job evaluation scheme to a man in the same employment, in what circumstances can my employers deny me equal pay?*

Your employers can pay you less, or more, than that other person if the difference in pay is genuinely due to a material difference other than sex between your case and the case of that other worker. For example, if the other worker has greater seniority, qualifications or skill than you, then one or all of these factors can account for a pay differential. It is not enough for the employers to show that the pay difference is because of market forces, for example that a man would not do the job for lower wages. The employers will not be able to establish that there is a genuine difference other than sex if the pay policy is indirectly discriminatory against one sex. In one case the Employment Appeal Tribunal held that the employers did not necessarily comply with the Equal Pay Act 1970 by paying part-time workers a lower rate of pay per hour than full-time workers, because the vast majority of part-time workers are women. Employers have to show that such a pay policy is designed to serve a legitimate purpose. You should note, however, that death and retirement benefits, such as pensions, are excluded from the scope of the Equal Pay Act just as they are excluded from the scope of the Sex Discrimination Act 1975 (see Q21). But again, EEC law may well give further rights to women (and to men) in this context.

12 | *How does the law regarding race discrimination actually relate to employment?*

It is unlawful for employers (however few employees there may be; see Q21) to discriminate against an employee or potential employee on racial grounds in deciding who to employ, in the treatment of employees and in deciding who to dismiss. If you are refused a job, or promotion, or dismissed, and this is directly or indirectly on racial grounds, the employers have treated you unlawfully. Discrimination on racial grounds is also unlawful if done by a partnership of six or more partners in their treatment of a partner or prospective partner, by trade unions or employers' organisations towards members or prospective members, by bodies that confer qualifications that help people to pursue a trade or profession, by training bodies, and by employment agencies. The Race Relations Act 1976 says that police officers are treated as employed for these purposes (in contrast to their position in bringing unfair dismissal claims).

'Employment' is broadly defined to mean working under a contract of service or apprenticeship or under a contract personally to execute any work or labour, so long as it is employment at an establishment in Great Britain.

As in sex discrimination law, so in the race discrimination context there are exceptions to the principle of no discrimination in employment (see Q21). The Race Relations Act allows race discrimination in employment at a private household (other than in a victimisation claim). Employers are also allowed to discriminate on racial grounds where being of a particular racial group is 'a genuine occupational qualification for the job', for example in a dramatic performance or in work as an artist's or photographic model, or in cases where a jobholder provides persons

of the same racial group with personal services to promote their welfare and those services can most effectively be provided by a person of that racial group.

13 | *Are employers responsible for sex and race discrimination carried out by their employees?*

Yes. Employers are responsible for what an employee does in the course of his or her employment, whether it was done with or without the employers' knowledge and approval. Employers have a defence if they prove that they took such steps as were reasonably practicable to prevent the employee from doing such acts. If a personnel officer rejects someone for a job because of his or her race or sex, say, that person will have a good claim against the employers unless they can show that they took necessary steps to prevent such discrimination.

Goods and services

14 | *When I was staying at a provincial hotel recently, I went into the bar for a drink and was told that the hotel couldn't serve 'unaccompanied ladies'. Was this lawful?*

No. The Sex Discrimination Act 1975 is concerned with discrimination in the supply of goods and services to the public, for example by banks, hotels, cinemas, transport operators, shops, estate agents or by any other person who offers goods, facilities, services or premises to people generally. The hotel was breaking the law by refusing to serve you. The Court of Appeal held that a London wine-bar, El Vino's, was acting unlawfully by requiring women customers to sit at a table but allowing men to drink at the bar. In another case the Court of Appeal held that a store acted unlawfully by allowing a woman customer to have credit facilities only if her husband signed the guarantee form, when it would have granted such credit facilities to a man without requiring the signature of his wife. The Court of Appeal has also found sex discrimination under this heading when a friendly society which admitted men and women to membership for mutual insurance allowed only the men members to be elected to the governing body of the society.

However, the Court of Appeal has rejected the argument that the Home Secretary provides 'facilities' under this part of the Sex Discrimination Act in granting immigrants leave to enter and to remain in the United Kingdom. Sex discrimination by the State in this area therefore is not contrary to the Act. In general, the goods, facilities, services and premises part of the Act covers sex discrimination by bodies that refuse or omit to provide any benefits on the same terms for both men and women.

15 | *I recently took out private health insurance, but I found from the actuarial tables that my premiums would be higher than those of a man of the same age and in the same health. Can the insurance company do this?*

Insurance companies often discriminate between men and women in these respects, and women are commonly charged higher premiums for health insurance, mainly as a result of the belief among insurance companies that they claim more than men. Because insurance companies offer services or facilities to the public or to a section of the public, they are within the scope of the Sex Discrimination Act 1975. But a special exception in the legislation excludes some sex discrimination in the insurance field: insurance companies can lawfully practise sex discrimination in relation to an annuity, or a life assurance or an accident insurance policy, or a similar matter involving risk, where the policy was assessed on the basis of 'reasonable' reference to actuarial (or other) data. Whether it is 'reasonable' for insurance companies to rely on actuarial data to treat men and women differently depends on the adequacy of the data relied on, in particular whether the actuarial data used by the insurance companies is so out of date that it tells us little or nothing about the claims of men and women today.

Accommodation

16 | *Some time ago my wife and I made an offer for a house we'd seen and liked. The offer was accepted by the vendor, but a few days later the estate agent rang up to say there was a mix-up and someone else's offer had already been accepted. The house is still on the market, and I'm sure the vendor didn't want us to have it because we're black. Is this unlawful discrimination?*

It could well be. The Race Relations Act 1976 covers discrimination (whether direct or indirect; see Q4) in the provision of premises to the public or to a section of the public. The Act protects you from someone who refuses or deliberately omits to provide you with the accommodation because of your race, and from someone who charges you a higher price because of your race.

The wide scope of the Act – which covers the provision of goods, facilities and services as well as accommodation – is illustrated by a Court of Appeal decision where the Inland Revenue was found to have discriminated unlawfully on the grounds of race in the way it provided the service of giving tax relief by asking a taxpayer originally from the Indian subcontinent who claimed tax relief for a child to produce the child's birth certificate and not asking other claimants to do the same.

17 | *I'm a 20-year-old student (male) and I recently applied to an ad. for a bedsit. I didn't get it, I'm sure because the landlady didn't want a man using her flat (it would have meant sharing her bathroom) even though the ad. didn't specify any preference for a man or woman. Is this unlawful discrimination?*

The Sex Discrimination Act 1975 contains many express exceptions, including the provision of accommodation in small dwellings where the 'supplier' (or a near relative) lives on the premises and shares some of the accommodation. As this applies to your situation, the landlady did not act unlawfully.

Other exceptions to the goods, facilities, services and premises part of the Act are:

- voluntary societies (those set up otherwise than for profit);
- political parties;
- hospitals or other establishments for men or women who require special care, supervision or attention;
- places occupied by or used for an organised religion whose doctrines or adherents frown on the admission of men or of women for religious reasons;
- places where the exclusion of one sex – at a sauna or a public lavatory, say – is necessary for privacy and decency.

Membership of clubs

18 | *Is it unlawful for a club to accept only men as members, or to accept both men and women as members but to allow only men certain benefits of membership?*

Such conduct is probably not unlawful under the Sex Discrimination Act 1975. Although such a club provides goods, facilities or services (see QS 2 and 14), the courts would probably conclude that such benefits are not being provided to the public or to a section of the public but to a private group of people selected according to their acceptability. The more objective the criteria for membership, and the greater the contact between the club and the public, the greater the chance of bringing the institution within the scope of the Act.

19 | *Are clubs allowed to practise race discrimination?*

The Race Relations Act 1976 makes race discrimination unlawful if it is carried out by any club or association of 25 or more members whose admission is regulated by the club's constitution. Such a club cannot discriminate on racial grounds in deciding who to admit to membership, in providing benefits to members or in depriving a person of membership. However, the Act recognises exceptions to this principle, allowing clubs to exist for particular racial groups. Where the main object of a club or association is to enable the benefits of membership to be enjoyed by persons of a particular racial group, the club may discriminate on the grounds of race, nationality or ethnic or national origins, but not on the grounds of colour. Thus, Indian shopkeepers' associations, Commonwealth war veterans' clubs and Jewish youth clubs, for instance, are all lawful.

Education

20 | *My son attends a co-educational school, and I particularly wanted him to do some cookery. The school has refused my request. Isn't this discrimination?*

Yes. The Sex Discrimination Act 1975 deals with sex discrimination by bodies in charge of educational establishments, such as local education authorities, managers and governors or (in the case of independent schools) proprietors of schools. These people are not allowed to practise sex discrimination in the way in which they treat pupils, by allowing woodwork classes for boys but not for girls, for example, and by allowing cookery classes for girls but not for boys. They are also forbidden to differentiate between pupils in terms of admission, for example by charging different fees for boys and girls, or in their reasons for refusing to admit pupils, or in their reasons for excluding pupils from the educational establishment.

Very similar provisions apply to prohibit race discrimination in education, and schools and colleges are not allowed to differentiate on racial grounds between students.

An exception to the sex discrimination provisions applies to single-sex educational establishments: they can discriminate by allowing entry only to males or only to females. Another exception is that the Act does not apply to sex discrimination in a further education course in physical training or a course designed for teachers of physical training.

Legal discrimination

21 | *Are there any cases in which discriminating against a person at work because of his or her sex can be lawful?*

Yes, there are. The Act does not apply to employers' discrimination in provisions for death or retirement, for example, pension schemes, though as a result of a European Court of Justice decision the law has been changed so as to prohibit sex discrimination in retirement ages in employment. Employers are allowed to discriminate on the grounds of sex where being a man or being a woman is 'a genuine occupational qualification for the job', for example in jobs where authenticity is important, such as acting, or where privacy and decency are involved, such as a lavatory attendant, or where the holder of the job provides individuals with personal services promoting their welfare or education, or similar personal services, and those services can most effectively be provided by a man or by a woman.

Although the Sex Discrimination Act 1975 applies

to service on behalf of the Crown, such as the Civil Service, it does not cover service in the naval, military or air forces or training corps administered by the Ministry of Defence. There are also special exceptions for ministers of religion and mineworkers. The Act also has a section exempting any sex discrimination that is necessary to comply with another Act of Parliament.

Some of these exceptions to the principle of no sex discrimination in employment, for instance in relation to pensions and other retirement benefits, may well be incompatible with EEC law, which applies throughout the United Kingdom. For example, EEC legislation guarantees that men and women in the same job are entitled to be treated and paid equally with no sex discrimination between them. The scope and effect of EEC law is a matter of considerable complexity which can be identified only on a case-by-case basis. EEC law has already helped some women to win their cases under the Sex Discrimination and the Equal Pay Acts by persuading English judges to give a broad interpretation to the Acts so that they do not conflict with EEC law.

22 | *Is it ever lawful to be discriminated against on the grounds of my race?*

Yes. Apart from membership of clubs (see Q19), as in sex discrimination law (see Q17) a person providing accommodation in 'small dwellings' when he or she – or a near relative – lives on the premises and shares part of the accommodation can practise discrimination by refusing to accept people of a particular race. Also excluded from the Race Relations Act 1976 are people who participate in arrangements whereby they (whether for reward or not) take into their own home, and treat like members of their own family, elderly people or persons, such as foster children, who require a special degree of care and attention. See also Q12.

23 | *Are there any other exceptions to the legislation banning race and sex discrimination?*

The Sex Discrimination Act 1975 does not cover the provisions for giving benefits to women only or to men only by charities. It also excludes from its scope competitors in single-sex events in sports, games or other competitive activities. This exception applies only to competitors: a woman who was refused the opportunity to referee men's judo competitions solely on the grounds of her sex won her sex discrimination claim. Apart from exemptions arising from the need to comply with other Acts of Parliament (see Q21),

and the exceptions for insurance purposes (see Q15), sex discrimination is also legal if practised for the purpose of safeguarding national security, though discrimination on these grounds has to be certified by the signature of a Secretary of State.

The Race Relations Act 1976 has very similar general exceptions. Charities can legally discriminate on racial grounds in providing benefits to people, so long as this is not done on the basis of a person's colour. Another special exemption allows a person's nationality or place of birth or length of residence in a particular place (but not colour) to be used as a basis for selection to participate in a sport or game: a Frenchman thus has no legal right to complain that he was refused the chance to play rugby for Wales because of his nationality or place of birth. Like the Sex Discrimination Act, the Race Relations Act exempts anything done to comply with other Acts of Parliament (see Q21). So, for example, one cannot challenge the provisions of the British Nationality Act 1981 as racially discriminatory and therefore unlawful under the Race Relations Act. Race discrimination is also lawful if it is done for the purpose of safeguarding national security (although it is difficult to think of cases when this provision would apply). See also Q12.

Making a claim

24 | What can I do if I think I've been discriminated against?

If you've been discriminated against on the grounds of either race or sex in the employment area, you can bring a claim to an Industrial Tribunal (see page 266). 'Employment' covers partnerships, trade unions, employers' organisations, qualifying bodies, training bodies and employment agencies as well as employers.

Cases of discrimination in education or in the provision of goods, facilities, services or premises must be taken to a county court. In education cases, you must first give notice to the Secretary of State for Education and Science (address on page 509) that you intend to bring such a claim. The Lord Chancellor has designated certain county courts as the ones in which race discrimination claims may be brought.

All cases of discrimination should be brought to the attention of the Commission for Racial Equality or the Equal Opportunities Commission (see Q26); the former will advise which county courts hear cases of race discrimination.

25 | If I want to bring an action for sex or race discrimination, how quickly after the act of discrimination must I make my claim?

In Industrial Tribunal claims for discrimination in employment (see Q24), you should bring your case within three months from the date of the act about which you are complaining. If there is a continuing act of discrimination, the time-limit does not begin to run until that discrimination ends. Thus, if your employers have a policy of not promoting women (or men) or persons of a particular race or colour, you can bring a claim before an Industrial Tribunal while you remain a victim of this policy or within three months of the policy ceasing to apply to you. There are special rules for equal pay cases. You must start your equal pay claim while you are working for the employers or within six months of leaving their employment.

In county court cases for discrimination in education and in the provision of goods, facilities, services and premises, the normal time-limit is six months from the date of the act of discrimination. This is extended to eight months in education cases.

The Sex Discrimination Act 1975 and the Race Relations Act 1976 allow courts and Tribunals to hear discrimination claims that are outside the time-limit when it is just and equitable for them to do so.

26 | What should I do first if I want to make a claim for discrimination?

You should first contact the Equal Opportunities Commission (EOC) in cases of sex discrimination, the Commission for Racial Equality (CRE) in cases of race discrimination (addresses on page 509). The former works towards eliminating sex discrimination and promoting equality of opportunity between men and women generally; the latter has the statutory duty to work towards eliminating race discrimination and promoting equality of opportunity and good relations between persons of different racial groups generally. They can conduct a Formal Investigation into the conduct of a person they suspect of discrimination. They can also take legal action against people who give instructions to others to discriminate, or who impose pressure on others to discriminate, or who publish discriminatory advertisements.

The EOC will give you free advice on the legal merits of your sex discrimination claim and how best to present it, and the CRE will give you similar advice about your race discrimination claim. The EOC and the CRE have the power to fund your claim, and will, in difficult cases or in test cases, pay for a solicitor (or sometimes a barrister) to act on your behalf. You should ask about this. You will, of course, also be able to obtain advice from Citizens Advice Bureaux, Law Centres and other similar institutions on whether you have a good claim under the Sex Discrimination Act 1975 or the Race Relations Act 1976 and how you should proceed in bringing that claim.

27 | *Are there any steps I should take before starting legal action in my race discrimination or sex discrimination case?*

Parliament has provided a special procedure to help people who think that they have suffered from sex or race discrimination. The Equal Opportunities Commission or Commission for Racial Equality (see Q26) will provide you with questionnaire forms (also available from Citizens Advice Bureaux and Law Centres) which you can serve on the person you think has unlawfully discriminated against you. On the questionnaire you can ask that person why he or she acted in a particular way, and ask any other relevant questions. The questions you ask, and any reply, will be admissible as evidence in any legal proceedings you may then bring if the answers to the questionnaire fail to satisfy you that you were fairly treated.

If the person you have questioned fails to answer your questions within a 'reasonable' period of time, then, if you do bring a claim, the court or Tribunal may draw any inference from that failure to reply, including the inference that there was an unlawful act of discrimination.

These special questionnaire procedures for race and sex discrimination claims cost nothing except the price of a stamp, and impose no obligation on complainants to start legal proceedings. The procedure is very valuable because complainants can get the other party to explain his or her behaviour. This may satisfy the complainant (and therefore avoid unnecessary cost and inconvenience to both sides) or, if he or she decides to go ahead with a legal claim, will make it very difficult for the other party to retract his or her explanation of events stated in the questionnaire.

The time-limits for bringing sex or race discrimination claims (see Q25) are not suspended because you have served a questionnaire. In addition to using the questionnaire procedure, it is very important in discrimination claims (often more so than in any other type of litigation) to keep a note or diary of relevant facts, incidents and conversations, etc. before sending the questionnaire. In this area of the law the facts tend to be hotly disputed. If you have a contemporaneous note of crucial events it makes it much more likely that the court or Tribunal will believe your version.

28 | *If I claim that I've been denied a job because of my sex or my race, whom does the burden of proof rest upon?*

In a direct discrimination case (see Qs 3 and 4) of this sort, the burden of proof is on you as complainant to show that you have been less favourably treated than another person and that this was on the grounds of your sex or race. Usually the case before an Industrial Tribunal will turn on whether you can show that your sex or your race was a substantial factor in the decision not to appoint you to the job but to appoint someone else. You do not need to show that your sex or your race was the *only* reason why you did not get the job (or whatever else may be at issue); you merely have to show that your sex or your race was a substantial or an important factor in the decision you are challenging.

Industrial Tribunals and courts have recognised that it is very rare for a claimant to have direct evidence to prove that employers, or other people, discriminate against women or blacks. Because of this, courts and Tribunals have said that they are willing, in appropriate cases, to draw an inference of sex or race discrimination from all the facts and circumstances. If the facts indicate that there could have been discrimination – for example, you have better qualifications for the job than the successful candidate who is of a different race or the opposite sex to you – then the employers or the other people accused of discrimination are obliged to give a clear and specific explanation of why they did not offer the job or the benefit in question to you. If the employers or other people accused of discrimination fail to give an explanation that satisfies the court or Tribunal, an inference of sex or race discrimination may be drawn.

In an equal pay case, say, the burden is on you to prove that you do like work, work rated as equivalent or of equal value to a person of the opposite sex who is earning more in the same employment (see Q9). To avoid being in breach of the Equal Pay Act 1970, the employers must then prove that there is a reason other than sex for paying the other person more than you.

In indirect discrimination cases – those in which a practice or policy is applied equally to men and women, or to all races, yet has a disparate impact on one sex or one race and is unjustifiable – the person accused of discrimination has the burden of showing that the practice or policy is justifiable irrespective of the sex or the race of the people to whom it is applied.

29 | *If I win my claim that my employers didn't promote me because they discriminated against me on the grounds of my sex or race, what remedies will I obtain?*

Where an Industrial Tribunal finds that a claim of race or sex discrimination is well founded, it has a discretion to give all or any of three remedies.

First, it can make an order declaring that you have been unlawfully discriminated against.

Second, it can order the employers who have discriminated against you to pay you compensation up to a maximum of £8,500. If the Tribunal decides that compensation is an appropriate remedy, the sum awarded will be assessed by reference to the loss and damage, including injury to your feelings, which you have suffered as a result of the discrimination. If you have been denied promotion because of your race or your sex, the Tribunal, if it considers compensation appropriate, will look at the difference between your salary and the salary you would have received had you been promoted.

The Tribunal has no power to award compensation in an indirect discrimination case – that is, a case where a policy or practice has a disparate impact on one sex or one race and is unjustifiable – where the discriminator shows that he or she did not apply the policy or practice with the *intention* of discriminating on the grounds of sex or race.

The third remedy that the Industrial Tribunal has the power to order if it finds that there has been discrimination is to make a recommendation that the discriminator, within a specified period, takes action that the Tribunal thinks is practicable for the purpose of obviating or reducing the effect on the victim of the unlawful discrimination. In your case this may involve promoting you. If the discriminator then refuses, without a reasonable justification, to comply with the recommendation made by the Tribunal, the Tribunal may award compensation to you as the victim, so long as the maximum compensation figure of £8,500 is not exceeded.

These remedies are different in equal pay cases. If you win an equal pay claim, proving that you do like work or work rated as equivalent or work of equal value (see Q10) to a person of the opposite sex in the same employment who earns more than you, then you will receive 'back pay' to cover the difference between that person's wages and yours back to a maximum of two years prior to the date when you started your claim. You will also be entitled to receive the same pay for the future as the person you have compared yourself with.

30 | *What remedies are available if I win my claim in a county court on the basis of discrimination against me in the provision of goods, facilities, services or premises?*

A county court has the power to give you a wide range of remedies, including damages, which will be assessed according to your loss, including injury to your feelings; there is no maximum, as there is in Industrial Tribunal cases (see Q29). It can also order a declaration that you have been discriminated against and issue an injunction to stop the discriminator from continuing to discriminate against you. You will receive no damages in an indirect discrimination case where the discriminator proves that he or she had no *intention of* discriminating on racial or sexual grounds; this is the same as in Industrial Tribunal cases (see Q29).

31 | *What general attitudes do Industrial Tribunals and county courts have to claims for race and sex discrimination brought before them?*

Few cases have been brought in this field, and lawyers, Tribunals and courts therefore still have surprisingly limited experience of handling the difficult issues that these cases can raise. The success rate is low in the cases that have been brought, and in those that are successful the remedies are often not strong enough to satisfy the complainants or to deter potential wrongdoers. On the other hand, the strongpoint of the legislation might be its educative value: as Lord Simon said of the Race Relations Act 1968, the hope is that 'the law might perform in this field one of its traditional functions – an educative one – namely, to raise moral standards by stigmatising as henceforward socially unacceptable certain hitherto generally condoned conduct.'

Defamation

1 | What is the difference between libel and slander? And what does defamation mean?

Defamation is the general term which includes both libel and slander. Broadly, the law of defamation protects individuals from untrue attacks on their moral or professional reputation and gives them the right to sue anyone who harms them in this way.

Libel and slander are the two main forms of defamation. The difference is that libel refers to a defamation which has some permanent visible form – in a newspaper, book or letter, for example. Slander is defamation by the spoken word, which doesn't leave a permanent record. A defamatory statement made on radio or television is treated as libel because a record of it can be preserved.

In practice, slander is the more difficult to prove, and it is usually less serious in its consequences because it reaches fewer people. Very few slander cases come to court.

2 | How do you tell if something said about you is defamatory and entitles you to sue? I'm involved with a local CND group, and the local newspaper, which is violently anti-CND, has made references to my past sex life.

It's not always easy to assess whether something is defamatory or not. Some false allegations are clearly defamatory, like saying someone is a crook when he isn't. But the line can be difficult to draw, and much depends on the particular circumstances and background. It might not normally be libellous to write that a particular man is fond of a drink, say, but it may become libellous if he's the president of the local temperance society.

Generally speaking, the question to ask is whether the statement made is untrue and whether it has the effect of lowering the reputation of the victim. If what's being said is factually true, then you won't be able to sue even if it has affected your reputation. So if you do have a lurid past life and the local newspaper finds out about it, there's little you can do if the newspaper gets it right. Similarly, even if what's said about you is false, you might not get anywhere unless you can show that it has made people think the worse of you.

If you feel you have been libelled or slandered, you should see a solicitor immediately. Defamation is a complicated subject and there are all sorts of pitfalls that the lay person might not discover.

3 | What are the difficulties in the way of successfully suing for defamation?

There is one main problem, and it's financial. You can sue for defamation only in the High Court, which is expensive and takes a long time. Also, you cannot get Legal Aid, as it's not available for defamation cases. You would be risking your own money and would have to be very sure that you've got a good case and that the person – or, more usually, the newspaper – you're suing can't take advantage of the various defences that are available. For instance, even if you *have* been libelled, the paper can say that the statement was a fair comment on a matter of public interest, or that it was 'privileged' – that is, that it was merely accurately reporting what was said in court or Parliament or in some other proceedings.

It is far better to try to negotiate an apology through your solicitor and to obtain a correction of the false allegation than it is to go to court.

4 | If I should win my case, how much can I expect in damages?

This depends totally on what view the judge (or sometimes the jury) takes of the harm that you have suffered. Damages would be high if, for instance, your professional reputation has suffered so much that you have lost part of your livelihood. On the other hand, damages are only nominal if you're thought to have not really suffered much at all, either financially or in your reputation. In very exceptional cases, the court can award 'exemplary' or 'punitive' damages against a newspaper or publisher who has behaved particularly repugnantly, for instance by repeating a libel.

Immigration and nationality

I | *Who qualifies as a British citizen?*

British citizenship law is complicated and can be confusing.

Before 1948, all those born in the UK or in any part of the British Empire and who 'owed allegiance to the Crown' were British subjects. The 1948 British Nationality Act subdivided this general-category 'British subject' into:

● citizens of the UK and Colonies (CUKCS) – those born, registered or naturalised in or connected by ancestral descent to the UK and its Colonies, and
● citizens of independent Commonwealth countries (Australia, New Zealand, Canada and India, for example, had their own citizenship laws).

The British Nationality Act 1981, which came into force on 1 January 1983, created further subdivisions. Those formerly CUKCS are now British citizens or British Dependent Territories Citizens (BDTCS) or British Overseas Citizens (BOCS). They automatically acquired their new citizenship on 1 January 1983. BDTCS are those born in or connected with the existing colonies (including Hong Kong, the Cayman Islands, Monserrat, Gibraltar). BOCS are mostly East African Asians or Chinese Malaysians who were CUKCS before 1983 but have no recognised connection with Britain or an existing colony.

British citizens are free to enter and remain in the UK and cannot be deported. BDTCS and BOCS must qualify for entry or qualify to remain here in accordance with the immigration Rules.

It is important to remember that the new Act does not affect anyone's rights under immigration law, and it does not mean that a person must now become a British citizen in order to remain living in the UK.

● *Immigration control*

The Immigration Act 1971 (which came into effect on 1 January 1973) and the associated Immigration Rules form the legal framework of UK immigration control. The Rules are rules of practice, setting down the conditions to be satisfied before visitors, students, business people, children and elderly parents are admitted to the UK or can extend or vary their stay here. The Rules have been amended several times since 1973. The current version (Statement of Changes in Immigration Rules HC 169) was approved from 16 February 1983.

British citizens and citizens of certain Commonwealth countries are 'free from immigration control'. They are free to come into, to stay and leave the UK without restriction and they cannot be deported. All other arrivals are subject to immigration control. Their passports are stamped by immigration officers on entry or departure; they can be admitted for short or for indefinite periods of time; prevented from working in the UK; prevented from changing jobs; and can be deported from the UK.

It is important to notice that the Immigration Act and Rules distinguish between different nationalities. British and certain Commonwealth citizens (for example, Commonwealth citizens with a parent born in the UK, and Commonwealth women married before 1983 to men born, registered or naturalised in the UK) are free from immigration control. EEC nationals and their families may benefit from the 'freedom of movement' provisions of EEC law, while Commonwealth citizens with close ancestral connection to the UK (a grandparent, say) also have favoured status in immigration law.

When passengers arrive at a port of entry in the UK, immigration officers look at their passports and assess whether the passengers are within the favoured nationality group who have rights of residence. The remaining passengers qualify for entry according to the purpose of their stay. The Rules distinguish between those students and visitors who are in a temporary category – given permission to enter for a limited time and prohibited or restricted from taking employment – and others who may be admitted for limited or defined time-periods but who have a work permit or permission to set up business in the UK. Under the Rules, work-permitholders, certain professionals, business people, or wealthy people of 'independent means' may in time qualify to settle here. In addition, the husbands, wives, children or elderly parents of British citizens or persons settled here, providing certain conditions are met, may be admitted to settle or admitted on a probationary period with a view to settle here. It is always important to be clear about the immigration categories: there are particular Rules for visitors, for students, business people or family members who may wish to enter, to extend their time here, who want permission to work or want to settle here. Under the Rules, it is extremely difficult to change from a temporary category (students and visitors, say) to a settled category from within the UK.

The Act simply brings nationality law and immigration law into line with one another. Those who were CUKCs on 31 December 1982 and who had a right of abode – that is, those who were free from immigration control – automatically became British citizens on 1 January 1983. CUKCs who did not have a right of abode on that date became BDTCs or BOCs.

2 | What is the significance of the 'right of abode'?

The term 'right of abode' should not be confused with 'settled' immigration status. A person is settled here if he or she is normally resident here without time-limits or restrictions on his or her stay. A settled resident is still subject to immigration control and in certain circumstances can be refused permission to enter the UK. Those residents with a right of abode are free from immigration control and cannot be deported. Persons acquire a 'right of abode' by their birth, adoption, registration or naturalisation in the UK or because their mother or father was born (or adopted, registered or naturalised) here. A female UK citizen may have acquired the right of abode by marriage. In addition, CUKCs (see Q1) who had lived here for five years and were settled here before 1 January 1983 have a right of abode.

3 | How would I acquire British citizenship?

The British Nationality Act 1981 has been criticised because of the complicated mechanisms for acquiring British citizenship after 1 January 1983. All those born in the UK before January 1983 (except those whose fathers were diplomats) were citizens of the UK and colonies with a right of abode and became British citizens under the Act. Those born in the UK after that date are British citizens only if one parent (or their mother if they are illegitimate) is a British citizen or is settled here. Children born in the UK whose parents are temporarily working or studying here or whose parents have overstayed their leave or entered the UK by deception (with false travel documents, say) may not be British citizens. They may have inherited their parents' citizenship or may even be stateless. The Act sets down criteria which will allow certain of these children to register as British citizens at a later date.

A person will be a British citizen if he or she:

- was born in the UK before 1 January 1983;
- was born in the UK after 1 January 1983 and either parent (or mother if the person is illegitimate) is a British citizen or lawfully settled here;
- was legally adopted in the UK and the parents are British citizens or would be if still alive (if the adoption was before 1 January 1983, and was a joint adoption, the father must be a British citizen);
- has been registered or naturalised in the UK before 1983 as a CUKC (see Q1) or registered or naturalised as a British citizen after that date;
- was a legitimate child born abroad before January 1983 to a father who was born (or adopted, naturalised or registered) in the UK;
- was born abroad after January 1983 and either parent (or mother if the person is illegitimate) is a British citizen, born or registered or naturalised in the UK at the time of the birth;
- was a CUKC born outside the UK, for example, in one of the remaining British colonies, and has lived in the UK for a continuous period of at least five years before January 1983 and had no time-limits on his or her stay at the end of the five-year period.

This list is simply a useful guideline; it is by no means exhaustive.

Prior to 1983, children derived citizenship from their mother only in exceptional circumstances – namely, when they would otherwise be stateless. Children can now take citizenship from either their mother or father. However, illegitimate children can derive British citizenship only from their mothers. If the parents of an illegitimate child born in the UK subsequently marry, their marriage can legitimise the child and the child can take citizenship from the father. If the child was born to unmarried parents, say a British father and a Swiss mother with limited leave to remain in the UK, the child would not be a British citizen at birth. If the parents subsequently marry, the child becomes legitimate and a British citizen.

Prior to 1983, children born outside the UK could acquire citizenship of the UK and colonies by legitimate descent from their father or grandfather. British citizenship is now passed on by a mother or father, but generally only for one generation. Thus, if a mother born in the UK has a daughter born in India, the daughter will be a British citizen, but that daughter cannot transmit her British citizenship to her daughter likewise born in India unless at the time of the birth the mother was working in Crown Service, the service of an EEC institution or other service designated as closely related to Crown Service (for example, the British Council).

4 | What advantages are there in becoming a British citizen?

The person gains the right of abode in the UK for the

rest of his or her life and keeps it however long he or she stays away from the UK. British citizens are exempt from deportation, have the right to seek and take up employment in the EEC, have the civil rights of voting, holding public office and working for the Civil Service (although Commonwealth citizens also have these civil rights).

5 | Do I have to lose my current nationality if I become British?

It depends. Britain and certain other countries, such as New Zealand, Pakistan, Jamaica and Barbados, allow dual nationality. A Jamaican citizen can therefore obtain British citizenship and retain his or her Jamaican citizenship. Other countries, for example India, Trinidad and Malaysia, do not allow their adult nationals to keep their citizenship if they become British citizens.

Children are often permitted dual nationality even by those countries that do not allow adults to be citizens of more than one country. When they become adults, though, they generally must elect to retain their citizenship of one or other country.

6 | How do I apply to become a British citizen?

Certain adults and children have the right to be given British citizenship if they apply for it. Others are eligible to apply for British citizenship but will be given it only at the discretion of the Home Secretary. To become a British citizen, a person applies either to register or to be naturalised a British citizen. There is little difference between the two processes. Adults who have a right to British citizenship apply for registration. Those who obtain citizenship at the discretion of the Home Secretary usually apply for naturalisation. Young people under the age of 18 are always registered. This is so even if they are asking for citizenship at the Home Secretary's discretion.

The Home Office produces a series of citizenship application forms and guides. These are available from the Home Office and most Law Centres. The guides clearly show how the forms are to be filled out, show what documents are required and explain the qualifications for citizenship. The completed form, the appropriate documents and fee are sent to the Fee Room of the Immigration and Nationality Department of the Home Office (address on page 510). (Applicants in the Channel Islands or the Isle of Man send their forms to the Lieutenant Governor; those living elsewhere send them to the nearest British Embassy, Consulate or High Commission.)

Acquiring British citizenship can be a slow and costly procedure. From May 1987 naturalisation fees

for a single person or married couple were £170, and £60 if the person applying for naturalisation was married to a British citizen. The Home Secretary cannot waive or reduce the fees in cases of hardship, and the DHSS will not give financial assistance to meet nationality fees. In May 1987 the average time taken to complete the processing of nationality applications was 10 to 24 months (6 months for registrations).

From 1 January 1983, most of those applying for British citizenship will be naturalised. Applicants for naturalisation must satisfy the following conditions:

- they have five years' residence in the UK with no more than 450 days' absence over the period, and during the last year they are free from immigration restrictions;
- they are aged 18 or over and of sound mind;
- they are of good character;
- they have sufficient knowledge of English (or Welsh or Scottish Gaelic) and intend to remain closely connected with the UK; these language requirements may be waived on grounds of age or physical or mental condition.

The wife or husband of a British citizen may apply for naturalisation after three years' legal residence in the UK with no more than 270 days' absence during the period. The language requirement is waived for husbands or wives, and they do not have to show that they intend to live in the UK once they are naturalised.

BDTCS or BOCS (see Q1) who have completed five years' residence here, including a year as a settled resident, are entitled to register as British citizens.

And during a transitional period of five years, commencing on 1 January 1983, certain Commonwealth citizens will likewise be entitled to register as British citizens. These will include those Commonwealth (and Irish) citizens settled in the UK since before 1 January 1973 and those Commonwealth citizens with a right of abode who are or have been normally resident here for five years. In addition, a woman who was married before 1 January 1983 and is still married to a man who was a CUKC and who became a British citizen on 1 January 1983 can apply to register as a British citizen before 1988. If the marriage has ended because of divorce or the death of her husband, the woman may apply for registration at the Home Secretary's discretion before January 1988.

7 | *How do children become British citizens?*

Children born here who are not British citizens, children born abroad to parents who are British citizens by descent (where the children have grandparents born here), and stateless children may be entitled to register as British citizens after they or their parents have been resident in the UK for certain periods of time. Children can also apply to register at the discretion of the Home Secretary, who will take account of their family connections here, and their character, in deciding whether to grant British citizenship. Parents should take legal advice not only to ascertain whether their children are entitled to register as British citizens but also to ensure that they choose for them the most appropriate registration procedure. In certain cases, children may acquire, through registration, British citizenship by descent which they cannot then transmit to their own children if those children are born abroad. Wherever possible they should choose registration which they can pass on to their overseas descendants.

8 | *I'm a Brazilian. I've lived here for four years, working for a computer company (I have a work permit), and I'd like to settle here. Will I get permission?*

Yes, you would probably be given 'indefinite leave to remain' in the UK.

'Settled' people are permanently resident here. They are still subject to immigration control – their passports are stamped to show their exits from and re-entry to the UK – but there are no time-limits on their stay and they are able to work in the UK without first seeking official permission.

Applications for settled status are made to the Home Office. It is unlikely that students and visitors will be permitted to settle unless they are accepted as refugees or qualify to remain on the basis of marriage. Anyone who is uncertain as to whether or not he or she qualifies for settlement should first take legal advice from a Law Centre or from the Joint Council for the Welfare of Immigrants (JCWI) (address on page 510). A premature or unwarranted settlement application can affect the person's short-term stay in the UK. If, for example, an overseas student were to apply for settlement, the Home Office would almost certainly refuse the settlement application and would probably refuse to let the person remain in the UK. Students are not entitled to settlement but must satisfy the Home Office that they will leave the UK at the end of their studies.

Those who can obtain settled status include:

● certain EEC nationals – those who have been working or self-employed in the UK continuously for four years;
● Commonwealth citizens who have a grandparent born in the UK;
● all Irish citizens;
● those who have completed four years here in permit-free or work-permit employment, as business people or persons of independent means. You would fall into this category;
● the unmarried children under 18, certain daughters between the ages of 18 and 21, elderly parents and grandparents of those settled here, or of those who are British citizens or Commonwealth citizens with rights of abode (see Q2);
● husbands and wives of British citizens or settled residents are generally admitted or permitted to remain for a probationary period of 12 months. At the end of that term they may be given settled status providing the marriage continues.

9 | *If I have to return to Brazil for a few years, will I have trouble getting back in to Britain?*

It depends on how long you've been away. Those with settled status qualify for admission under the immigration Rules as 'returning residents'. British overseas citizens – East African Asians, for example – previously settled here are re-admitted as returning residents even if they have been absent from the UK for considerable periods of time. Other residents are re-admitted for settlement as follows:

● Commonwealth citizens who were settled here at the coming into force of the Immigration Act on 1 January 1973 and were also settled here at any time during the two years preceding their return are admitted for settlement (unless there is a current deportation order against them);

● Others – Commonwealth or foreign (like yourself) – are re-admitted for settlement if they were settled here before they left, did not receive assistance from public funds towards the cost of leaving, and have been away for no longer than two years.

Residents who have been away from the UK for longer than two years may nevertheless be re-admitted at the discretion of the immigration authorities. This discretionary Rule is designed to avoid injustice that might arise where residents have otherwise lived here for most of their lives or where their lengthy absence was due to civil disturbance, accident or illness.

10 | *Is the law the same for husbands and wives?*

Since August 1985 the Rules for the admission and settlement of husbands and wives and fiancés and fiancées have been the same. The old Rules that admitted wives unconditionally now apply only to the wives of Commonwealth citizens settled in the UK on 1 January 1973.

All other spouses and fiancé(e)s now have to satisfy strict tests before they are granted entry clearance. These are:

● It is or was not the primary purpose of the marriage to obtain admission to the UK;
● The parties to the marriage intend living together permanently as husband and wife;
● The parties have met;
● There will be adequate accommodation for the parties and their dependants without recourse to public funds in accommodation of their own or which they occupy themselves;
● The parties will be able to maintain themselves and their dependants adequately without recourse to public funds.

Slightly different Rules apply where a person had been given permission to enter the UK, for example as a visitor or student, and had then married someone settled here. That person can apply for an extension of stay as a spouse, but such extension will not be granted unless the Home Secretary is satisfied that the conditions listed above are satisfied and, additionally, that:

● the applicant has not remained in the UK in breach of the immigration laws;

● the marriage is not taking place after a decision to deport has been made; and
● the marriage has not been terminated.

In all cases that comply with the Rules, the married applicant is given leave to enter or an extension of stay for a probationary period of 12 months and is permitted to settle here at the end of that term providing the Home Secretary is then satisfied that the marriage has not come to an end and that each of the parties still intends to live permanently with the other as his or her spouse.

11 | *I'm legally settled in the UK. My 15-year-old daughter stayed with my brother in India, but he has now died and I want to bring her here. Can I do so?*

The immigration Rules allow children to join their parents if they are settled in the UK, which means your daughter is entitled to join you. Yet the Rules are very restrictive; they are designed to limit the number of people joining parents or relatives here, and Home Office procedures for investigating, processing and delaying family claims cause considerable hardship and distress to separated families.

Under the Rules, unmarried children under 18 are admitted for settlement where both parents, or a widowed parent, are settled here (where the widowed parent has remarried, the natural and step-parent must be here). Children with a single, settled parent (this can include divorced or unmarried parents) are admitted for settlement only if the parent has had the sole responsibility for the child's upbringing or there are serious compelling family or other considerations which make the child's exclusion undesirable. Adopted children can join their single, adoptive parent or adoptive parents, but only if they show in addition that 'there has been a genuine transfer of parental responsibility' to their adoptive parent(s) because their natural parents were unable to care for them and that the adoption is not one of convenience arranged to facilitate their admission. Children aged 18 or over must qualify for settlement in their own right as students, visitors or workers, unless there are the most exceptional compassionate circumstances justifying their entry. However, special consideration is given to fully dependent, unmarried daughters over 18 and under 21 who formed part of the family unit overseas and have no other close relatives in their own country upon whom they can reasonably rely.

The sponsoring parent (who can be a stepfather or stepmother if the natural father or mother is dead, or the mother or father of an illegitimate child, or an adoptive parent) is required to show that he or she is 'able and willing to maintain and accommodate' the child without recourse to public funds. British citizens, Commonwealth citizens with a right of abode, and Commonwealth citizens settled in the UK on 1 January 1973 are not obliged to show that they can support or accommodate their applicant children.

12 | *My parents are getting a bit frail and I would like them to join me here too. Will they be allowed to?*

Under the Rules, widowed mothers of any age, widower fathers aged 65 and over, and parents travelling together, of whom at least one is aged 65 and over, can be sponsored for settlement by sons or daughters settled in the UK who have the means to maintain and accommodate them. Elderly parents must be wholly or mainly dependent upon their children here and must show that they have no other close relatives in their own country on whom they could reasonably rely or who are able and willing to provide them with some assistance (either a home or financial support). Parents and relatives *under* 65 years, other than widowed mothers, are not given entry except when they are living alone in the 'most exceptional compassionate circumstances'.

13 | *I would like a Canadian friend to come to stay with me for a few months. Will there be any problem?*

Visitors to the United Kingdom must show the immigration officer on arrival that they genuinely intend to stay for only the period of time that they request and that during their visit they will be maintained and accommodated here 'without recourse to public funds' and without taking employment. Visitors can be admitted in order to transact business here – to negotiate contracts or find buyers for their goods – and they can also enter for private medical treatment. They are normally given a time-limit of six months and can be allowed to remain for a maximum of twelve months.

Passengers from certain eastern bloc countries and certain countries in Africa and Asia, including selected Commonwealth or former Commonwealth countries, namely Bangladesh, India, Ghana, Nigeria, Pakistan and Sri Lanka, are termed 'Visa Nationals'; they must have a current visa before they can be given permission to enter or re-enter the United Kingdom. Other arrivals, like your friend, are not required to obtain prior entry clearance before coming here as visitors.

14 | *How do I go about sponsoring her visit?*

You can obtain a sponsorship form from most Law Centres and Citizens Advice Bureaux. This is a written declaration signed before a practising solicitor. Sponsors undertake to maintain and accommodate their visitors during their stay. Visitors need to show on arrival:

- a current passport;
- evidence of the purpose and length of the visit, which may include letters of invitation from friends or relatives;
- evidence that adequate funds and accommodation are available here – a bank statement, travellers' cheques, foreign exchange certificates or a sponsorship declaration form;
- evidence of their intention to return home – a return ticket, letter from a school or employer showing that they are here on temporary leave and have studies or employment to return to.

If the immigration officer is suspicious of the visitor's intentions on entry he or she may give the visitor temporary admission and allow him or her to stay here for a few days, with an instruction to report back for an interview at the port or airport. If this happens, the person should *immediately* seek assistance from the JCWI (address on page 510), a Citizens Advice Bureau or Law Centre, a solicitor or from their sponsor's MP. Those temporarily admitted have not been given 'leave to enter' and have no right of appeal here if the immigration officer decides to send them home.

15 | *What are the rules regarding foreigners coming to study in this country?*

Students should be able to satisfy an immigration officer on arrival:

- that they have been accepted for a course of study at a university, polytechnic, institution of further education, an independent school or a bona fide private educational institute; and
- that their proposed course of study will occupy the whole or a substantial part of their time (normally a minimum of 15 hours per week of organised daytime study, not a correspondence course, although this requirement is interpreted flexibly for higher-level students); and

• that they can meet the cost of their studies, their maintenance and accommodation, and that of any dependants arriving with them, without recourse to public funds; and

• that they are able and intend to leave the UK on completion of their studies.

The Home Office asks that overseas students obtain entry clearance prior to their arrival here. Their visa, entry certificate or letter of consent should be endorsed 'student'. However, the Home Office also recognises that many students have difficulty in making arrangements for their admission to their chosen course of study from abroad. Therefore, the Rules allow would-be students without prior clearance to be admitted for a short time so as to make arrangements for their studies (when those arrangements are complete and within the time of their leave, they can apply to remain here as students). Visitors and others temporarily admitted here can also apply to vary their status to that of student. Visitors intending to study here should disclose this to the immigration officer at the port of entry. The Home Office may be entitled to refuse to extend or vary their term of stay if they have deceived the immigration officer concerning the purpose of their entry. Students are usually given limited leave to remain to take account of the length of their course of study, and they can apply to extend their stay so as to continue or complete their education. Application must be made before their previous leave has expired, and it is always a good idea to apply several weeks before the expiry date. If students do not apply in time they will be what are called 'overstayers' and their application to remain can be refused. If their leave has expired and they have not yet applied for an extension, they should be sure to get legal advice before going to the Home Office.

16 | *What if I should fail an examination and to resit it will involve a longer stay than originally intended?*

In order to qualify for extensions, students must satisfy the Home Office that:

• they are enrolled for full-time courses of daytime study; and

• that they have been and continue to attend their studies regularly; and

• that they are able to maintain and accommodate themselves and their dependants without working or without the need for assistance from public funds (a wife's earnings can be taken into account when assessing the adequacy of a male student's main-

tenance arrangements, but there is no provision in the Rules for a woman student to have her husband here as her dependant); and

• that they intend to leave the UK at the end of their studies.

Students should be sure to attend their classes regularly, and if they are absent from college should inform the college authorities of the reasons for their non-attendance. The Rules specifically state that 'extensions of stay should not be granted to students who appear to be moving from one course to another without any intention of bringing their studies to a close'. Extensions of stay are normally refused if the student is spending more than four years on short courses of less than two years. The Home Office is also entitled to refuse extensions of stay to students who persistently fail their exams. This is not to say that students cannot change their courses or cannot fail exams. But the Home Office is suspicious of those who make little progress with their studies or who appear to be stretching out their time in the UK.

At the conclusion of their studies, students are expected to return home. However, students (mostly from developing countries) can apply to undertake practical training to gain work experience in their chosen field of study – experience which is not readily available to them at home. The training or work experience must be approved by the Department of Employment and must be of limited duration. The Rules make it clear that, in general, students have no claim to remain here in full-time, permanent employment or as self-employed or business people. Generally, only those students who qualify to remain here through marriage or as political refugees succeed in staying permanently in the UK.

Students with immigration problems can often get advice or representation from their students' union, the JCWI, United Kingdom Immigrants Advisory Service (UKIAS), and United Kingdom Council for Overseas Student Affairs (UKCOSA) (addresses on pages 510 and 512).

17 | *A Turkish uncle of mine wants to come to work in England. What is the position?*

When passengers subject to immigration control, as your uncle would be, arrive in the UK, their passports are stamped not only with the time-limit of their stay but also with their conditions of entry. The stamp indicates whether the person has permission to work.

Those settled here can work, follow professions or set up in business without the consent of the Home Office, and EEC nationals are generally free to enter and remain here to seek or take up employment or self-employment. Young Commonwealth nationals (aged 17 to 27) here on extended working holidays for two years can also work without first obtaining Home Office permission, but they can stay and work here only during the term of their permission.

The Rules also allow certain other passengers to enter to take work – au pairs, work-permitholders, business people, the self-employed and those in permit-free employment. Their passports usually carry the endorsement that they are 'not to enter or change employment paid or unpaid without the consent of the Secretary of State for Employment and not [to] engage in any business or profession without the consent of the Secretary of State for the Home Department'. They are permitted to work only in the specific job or profession approved for them by the Department of Employment or the Home Office.

Those coming here to visit or study are notified that they are 'not to enter employment paid or unpaid and not [to] engage in any business or profession'. These passport-holders cannot work here, although students with this endorsement can apply to the Home Office to vary their conditions of entry and permit them to take specific, part-time employment which will not interfere with their studies. The wives of overseas students (not husbands – the Rules are consistently sexist) can reside here for the duration of their husbands' studies, and they are free to take up employment to help maintain their husbands during their education.

As your uncle falls into none of these categories, he will need to obtain a work-permit before he will be allowed to work in the UK (see Q 18).

18 | *My uncle, a Hong Kong Chinese chef, wants to work in England. Does he need a work-permit?*

Yes. Work-permitholders must have the permit before they enter the UK to work. If they do not, they will be refused entry. The permit is given for specific posts with specific employers. It is up to employers to apply to the Department of Employment for permits for their foreign employees. If the permit is granted, the Home Office will then give the employee leave to enter to take up the post. This is generally restricted to 12 months, but can be renewed and extended.

Before granting a permit, the Department of Employment must first be satisfied that the applicant has the professional qualifications, skill or experience that are necessary for the job, that there are no suitable resident workers available to fill the post, and that the proposed wages and conditions of employ-

ment are similar to those given to local workers doing the same sort of work. Work-permitholders are expected to be between the age-limits of 23 and 54 years, although permits are also given to trainees between 18 and 30 years old who are coming here for a 12-month period of training on the job.

At the end of four years' work-permit employment, the employee will be eligible to apply to remain here indefinitely. If before this time the employee leaves his or her employment or is dismissed, he or she will require Department of Employment permission before taking another post. The Department usually gives permission only to change employers, not the type of job, so your uncle, as a Chinese chef, will have to find a post as chef in another Chinese restaurant should he be dismissed from his job.

19 | *I know a Swedish journalist whose newspaper wants him to be their UK representative. Will he need a work-permit?*

No. Some categories of entrants may come here to work without first obtaining a work-permit (although they will need to get entry clearance from their British Consulate, Embassy or High Commission). These are:

● ministers of religion, missionaries and members, including teaching members, of religious orders;
● representatives of overseas firms which have no branch, subsidiary or other representative in the UK;
● representatives of overseas newspapers, news agencies and broadcasting organisations on long-term assignments to the UK;

- doctors and dentists;
- private servants or staff members of diplomatic or consular missions or family members forming part of the households of such persons;
- persons coming for employment with an overseas government or those employed by the United Nations Organisation or another international organisation of which the UK is a member;
- teachers and language assistants under exchange schemes approved by the Department of Education and Science or administered by the Central Bureau for Educational Visits and Exchanges or the League for the Exchange of Commonwealth Teachers;
- seamen under contract to join a ship in British waters;
- operational staff of overseas-owned airlines;
- seasonal workers at agricultural camps under approved schemes.

Permit-free workers are generally admitted for an initial period of 12 months, although seasonal agricultural workers are limited to a summer season and exchange teachers to a two-year stay. Others may be granted extensions if they are still in their chosen occupation and their employers confirm that they will continue in their employment. If they quit their permit-free employment or are dismissed, they have no further claim to remain here unless they manage to find another job in the same permit-free category. After four years in permit-free employment, they can apply to remain here indefinitely.

20 | *A former business colleague of mine, who's American, wants to start his own business here. What does he have to show?*

Self-employed or business people must obtain entry clearance before coming to the UK. The Rules for their entry are very restrictive – only the wealthy can hope to qualify under this category.

The Rules state that those seeking to establish themselves here in business or self-employment, whether on their own account or in partnership, must:

- have at least £150,000 under their control and disposable in the UK to be invested in the business;
- have a level of financial investment proportional to their interest in the business; they must be able to bear their share of the liabilities;
- be occupied full-time in the running of the business; entry will be refused if it appears that the proposed partnership or directorship amounts to disguised employment or where it seems likely that applicants will have to supplement their business

activities by employment of any kind or by recourse to public funds;

- show that there is a genuine need for their services and investment – evidence has to be produced to prove that their services and investment will create new, paid and full-time employment in the business for persons already settled here.

Their business must be a worthwhile, viable concern. Self-employed or business people cannot take any additional employment. Again, they are generally admitted for an initial period of 12 months, which can be extended, and at the close of four years in self-employment or business they can apply for indefinite leave to remain here.

21 | *Is there any appeal for someone refused entry or permission to remain in the UK?*

Anyone applying for entry clearance at a British Consulate or Embassy abroad and who is refused an entry certificate or is refused leave to enter at a British port of entry, or is refused permission to remain living here or is about to be deported, will probably have a right to appeal against the decision. Such a person is notified of the decision at his or her last known address. There is a tiered immigration appeal system. Appeals are normally heard first by an immigration adjudicator in the UK, and in certain limited circumstances a case can be taken further on appeal to an Immigration Appeal Tribunal or even appealed again to the High Court. Notices of appeal should be returned promptly in the time-limits set.

As soon as you are informed of the refusal you should notify the appropriate officer that you intend appealing against the decision. The refusal notice shows you where to send the notice of appeal and the time-limit for appealing. Those outside the UK who are refused entry clearance have three months after their refusal date to submit a notice of appeal; those in the UK wishing to appeal against a Home Office refusal to extend or vary their leave or a Home Office decision to make a Deportation Order against them have fourteen days from the date of the decision to lodge an appeal.

When a person who does not have prior entry clearance is refused permission to enter on arrival in the UK, he or she may be sent back to his or her home country by return flight and will not normally be present in this country when the appeal against entry refusal is heard by an adjudicator. It is the same where people apply for entry clearance from British Embassies or Consulates abroad and are refused their entry certificates. They remain at home while the appeal is heard in this country. They can have legal representatives present to conduct their appeal and can submit documentary evidence from abroad or arrange for witnesses in the UK to attend and give evidence on their behalf. However, it is an unsatisfactory arrangement borne out by the high failure-rate in such appeals against immigration decisions.

22 | *What about those cases of people who are allowed in for 12 months, say, but who stay beyond that period?*

Those with limited leave to enter or remain in the UK are obliged to observe any restrictions on work conditions or time-limits endorsed on their passports. It is a criminal offence to 'fail to observe a condition of leave' or to remain here beyond the time-limit allowed, punishable by a fine of up to £200 or impri-

sonment for a maximum of six months; the court can also recommend the person's deportation. If the court does not recommend deportation, the Home Secretary can still decide to deport such a person, and at the very least the Home Secretary can refuse to extend the leave of those who have breached their immigration conditions. The Home Secretary's decision to deport an over-stayer can be challenged on appeal to an immigration adjudicator or to an Immigration Appeal Tribunal (see Q21).

Anyone refused entry or permission to remain, and those about to be deported or charged with an immigration offence, should seek expert legal advice. Legal Aid is not generally available for civil immigration appeals, but UKIAS and JCWI (addresses on pages 510 and 512) will advise and represent someone, and Citizens Advice Bureaux and Law Centres will also give advice and representation.

You and your home

Leasehold/freehold

1 | *I am thinking of moving from my flat to a house. I've noticed that some houses are freehold and others leasehold. What is the difference, and are there any disadvantages in buying a leasehold house?*

The basic difference between freehold ownership and leasehold ownership is that freehold is permanent and leasehold lasts for the period for which the lease was first granted. Commonly, that is 99 years. The lease not only defines the length of time for which you and anyone to whom you sell it can own the house, but it is a contract which binds the leaseholder for the time being. So while the house is yours you have to pay to the freeholder the rent which is specified in the lease (generally a small amount called a 'ground rent'), and comply with the detailed regulations about the use of the house which it lays down. Freehold properties can also be subject to restrictions, but they are generally less onerous.

2 | *I have a leasehold house, but would like to become a freeholder. Can I insist on buying out the landlord?*

Only certain leaseholders have the statutory right to buy their freehold, or 'enfranchise' their property as the process is known, and you must check that you qualify. First, examine your lease. It must originally have been granted for a period of more than 21 years, however little time there is still left to run. The ground rent which you pay must be less than two-thirds of the rateable value of the house on whichever of these three dates is the latest: 23 March 1965, when the house was first built, or the date the lease was granted. The current rateable value (see Q96) is also relevant. It must not be higher than the following limits, the figure in brackets applying to leases granted after 18 February 1966: house in Greater London, £1,500 (£1,000), house elsewhere, £750 (£500). Some houses with higher rateable values can qualify if the rateable value was pushed above the limit because of improvements paid for by you or by an earlier owner of the lease.

You can buy the freehold of a house only if you occupy it as your sole or main residence. You must have lived there as owner of the lease for at least three years, or for periods over the last 10 years which add up to three years. This does not mean you have to occupy the whole house yourself: you can enfranchise even if you have sublet part of the house, and even if it has been converted into flats.

You cannot buy the freehold when your landlord is a housing association and the freeholder is a charity.

3 | *How do I go about enfranchising?*

To start the process you serve notice on the landlord. The appropriate printed form is available from law stationers. The procedure is then similar to buying a house in the normal way, and you'd be well advised to see a solicitor. If the landlord does not accept that you qualify to enfranchise, you can apply to the county court to establish the point. If the terms of the purchase are not agreed, they are settled by a lease-hold valuation tribunal, which you can contact through the Rent Assessment Panel (listed in the telephone directory).

4 | *What will I have to pay to buy the freehold of my house from my landlord?*

There are two statutory formulae used to work out the price; which is used depends on the rateable value of the property. One is generally regarded as favourable to leaseholders of smaller houses, the other less favourable but still beneficial for larger ones. Both involve obtaining a surveyor's valuation of the house, and applying a discount to take into account the fact that the lease still has time to run so that the landlord would not be entitled to have the house back until the lease ended. The longer the lease has to run, the lower the price will be.

Once the price is fixed, you have a month during which you can back out if you cannot afford it. If you bought the leasehold house with the aid of a mortgage, you will generally be able to get a further loan to buy the freehold.

The Leasehold Reform Act 1967 makes clear that you have to pay the valuation and legal costs which the landlord incurs in selling you the freehold. These are in addition to the price.

189

5 | *My flat is leasehold. I should like to convert it to freehold. Can I do so?*

No. The statutory right to buy the landlord's freehold applies only to houses, not to flats. The reason for this is that a defect in the law means that there is no completely satisfactory way for the owner of a freehold flat to be sure that necessary repair work is done to the rest of the block.

For that reason, you should be wary about buying a freehold flat. Although they are common enough on the South Coast of England, they can be difficult to sell and to mortgage, which can make them worth less than the equivalent leasehold flat.

6 | *My flat is one of four converted from a large Victorian house. Each lease has 67 years to run. Can we, as leaseholders, collectively buy the freehold from the freeholder and, if so, what are the advantages?*

You cannot insist on buying the freeholder's interest in the house. However, he may well agree to sell. If he does, you can then arrange matters so that you no longer pay a ground rent, but that will not be a real advantage because you will have to pay the freeholder a lump sum to buy him out. The real advantage for you is the chance to control the management of the house, making sure that repairs are done, services provided and any improvements on which everyone agrees are carried through.

When only four flats are involved, the documentation and legal formalities when a flat changes hands can be more complicated than when the block is bigger. This is because it is usually not worth forming a company (see Q14) for fewer than 10 flats.

7 | *My lease is coming to an end. If I'm not in a position to buy the freehold, do I face the prospect of being turned out of my house?*

There are two possible forms of statutory protection to help you. The first applies only to houses, and the qualifications are the same as for leasehold enfranchisement (see Q2). You can claim a new 50-year lease. Under it, you have to pay a modern ground rent which will generally be more than you currently pay, and that rent can be revised again after the first 25 years of the new lease. This 'extended lease' must be claimed before your present lease expires.

The alternative protection is available in the case of both houses and flats, as long as they are within the limits to which the Rent Act 1977 can apply (see Q15). You become entitled to a 'statutory tenancy',

paying a fair rent and with full security of tenure, but without any interest which you can sell in the property. If you are relying on this, you do not have to take any action. A statutory tenancy arises automatically when your existing contractual lease comes to an end, for example by the landlord giving you the appropriate notice or where the term of years originally granted expires.

8 | *I have a freehold house, but I still have to pay a rent. How does this come about when there is no lease?*

There used to be a system for selling houses freehold under which the developer reserved the right to a rent in perpetuity in exchange for a reduction in the price. Those rents are generally called either 'rent charges' or 'chief rents', although they are occasionally known by other names. They are common only in the Manchester and Bristol areas. It is no longer possible to create that type of rent, except in very limited circumstances, such as to cover house owners' contributions to the upkeep of communal gardens.

These rent charges are being phased out. An Act passed in 1977 provided that they will all cease to be payable in the year 2037. Meanwhile, you have the choice of paying a lump sum to buy out the rent charge, unless it is one of those connected with maintenance payments. If you cannot agree with the owner of the rent charge what amount you should pay, the Secretary of State for the Environment will certify the amount. It is calculated on the basis of the length of time the rent charge has left to run and the current yield of Government Consolidated Stock.

Joint ownership

9 | *I am a joint owner of a house, and I want to sell it. We cannot agree between us. Can I insist on selling?*

The general rule is simple enough, and it applies if you buy a house jointly or inherit it jointly. Up to four people can be joint owners of any property with their names on the deeds, and the law always treats them as trustees with a duty to sell it. The people entitled to the proceeds of the sale, and to have the benefit of the house or flat until it is sold, who are the beneficiaries of that trust, are the joint owners themselves (and there may be other beneficiaries as well, with no limit on their number). The basic rule is that if any joint owner wishes to sell, he can insist on doing so because that is his duty under the trust. If the other joint owners will not co-operate, the court will usually order a sale unless the purpose for which the property was bought still exists, for example to provide a family home for the children. It makes no difference whether the beneficiaries are joint tenants, who automatically inherit each other's shares on death, or tenants in common, whose interests are separate (see LIVING TOGETHER, Q1).

There are two major departures from this general rule. First, there are special rules for husbands and wives who jointly own their matrimonial homes (see SEPARATION, Q6). Second, if joint owners agree in writing when they first buy that certain circumstances – one of them wanting to move out, for instance – will allow one of them to insist on selling, that agreement overrides the general rule.

Council tenancies

10 | *As a council house tenant, I believe I have a right to buy. How do I find out more, and what conditions do I have to satisfy?*

Yes, you have a statutory right to buy, and this applies not only to the tenants of councils, but also where a housing association is the landlord. Also, tenants of council flats qualify. To find out more you should contact the housing department or your landlord.

You have to have been a council tenant – although not necessarily in the same property, or even with the same local authority – for at least two years, and the house or flat in question must be your only or main home. Your length of time as a council tenant has a major impact on the price you have to pay. This is fixed by starting with the market value of the house or flat, which is assessed by the local authority, and then knocking a discount off it. The only case where that does not apply is to some modern properties, for which the price cannot be less than the properties cost the council to build. The discount starts at 32 per cent for those who have been council tenants for only two years, and rises by one per cent a year until it reaches 60 per cent for someone who has been a tenant for 30 years. A husband and wife can sometimes add together periods when each was separately a council tenant to bump up the total. Some or all of that discount has to be repaid to the council if you sell again quickly: on selling the house or flat within a year, you have to pay it all back; in the second year

you repay 80 per cent of it, and so on until after five years you can sell and keep all the proceeds.

Anyone who is entitled to exercise the right to buy also has a right to a mortgage. This comes from the council for their own tenants, and from the Housing Corporation (address on page 510) for housing association tenants. The mortgage can be large enough to cover the whole of the price, plus something for the costs involved. How much you can borrow depends on your income. Up to four members of the family can buy jointly, and this can increase your mortgage chances because all the buyers' incomes are taken into account.

The procedure for exercising the right to buy begins with your giving the council notice on a special form, which they supply free. Ask the housing department for one.

11 | *I started to investigate buying my council house, but I was told that my income was too low for me to receive a mortgage for 100 per cent of its discounted value. The housing department offered as an alternative a 'shared ownership lease'. What is this?*

This is a fairly new idea. As well as being an option open to council tenants who are buying (see Q10), some housing associations offer them. It puts you half way between buying and renting: you buy a proportion of your home, and you continue to rent the rest. If you decide to buy three-quarters, for example, you pay three-quarters of the full price, either from savings or with the help of a mortgage; the rent you then pay for the other quarter is 25 per cent of what the full rent would be.

When you exercise the right to buy, this option is open to you unless you qualify for a full hundred per cent mortgage. You have to buy at least a 50 per cent share, and you can increase that whenever you like in slices of $12\frac{1}{2}$ per cent. In each case, you have the appropriate discount (see Q10), calculated on the length of time you have then been a tenant.

This system does not stop you selling your home before you own a hundred per cent, but it does mean that you get only the appropriate proportion of the proceeds of sale. The remainder goes to the local authority or the housing association, which still owns the other part.

Housing associations

12 | What is a housing association?

Housing associations fall into two main groups. The first are charities set up to provide reasonably priced homes for renting, usually in town and city centres. They normally have waiting lists for tenancies, in much the same way as local authorities do.

The second type of association is sometimes called a housing society. A housing society is a self-help body which works by buying a number of homes – flats or houses – or even renting or building them, as a sort of co-operative. Every purchaser of those homes becomes a member of the society, and every member becomes a tenant of one of the properties. The society buys all the homes with the help of one mortgage, under which the repayments are usually over a longer period than an individual can negotiate, so the repayments are cheaper. The rent that a society member pays is simply the total of his or her share of the mortgage repayments, plus the society's other expenses such as repairs and management.

Financial help for housing associations is often provided by local authorities or by the Housing Corporation (address on page 510), which is the body that supervises housing associations.

13 | I have a lease on a flat from a housing society. I want to sell the flat but I'm told that I will not get the full market price. Why not?

You cannot yourself put the flat on the market but must hand the property back to the housing society. After you've lived in it for a minimum period, normally five years, the society will pay you for it (you receive nothing if you hand it back earlier). What the

society pays you for the flat is an amount that represents the share of the capital repaid on the mortgage while you were paying rent. Because no interest paid is taken into account, that sum is low and is generally less than the profit you would have made had you sold a normal lease.

14 | All the leaseholders of the flats in the block in which I live are shareholders of a company which owns the freehold. Does that make the company a housing society?

No. This is a different scheme which does not in any way restrict your ability to sell your flat. Because flats are best organised on a leasehold basis, with a landlord having overall responsibility for such things as structural repairs, decorating staircases, lift maintenance and gardens, a developer who does not want to keep any interest in the property after all the flats are sold creates a company to carry out those functions and makes the owners of the flats take shares in it, so that they are in effect their own landlords. This is generally a very satisfactory arrangement, because while the company can employ agents to manage the block if it wishes, the shareholders are able to ensure that matters are arranged exactly as they want.

There are a number of variations on this system. One gives the company a head lease, so that the flat owners still pay ground rent and service charges to the company, but the developer retains the freehold and receives a rent from the company.

In every case there has to be some machinery to ensure that when a flat changes hands the connected share in the company goes with it. This is necessary so that the membership of the company and the ownership of the flats is always in the same people. You will probably find provisions in your lease to cover that.

Rent Act tenancies

15 | I have been a tenant for 10 years and the landlord is now proposing to almost double the rent. Do I have any protection against paying an excessive amount?

If the Rent Act 1977 applies to your tenancy, then you certainly have protection. These are the basic rules for that Act to apply: what is let to you must be 'separate' in the sense that no living-room is shared, but it does not have to be self-contained, nor does it matter if you share a bathroom or WC. The rateable value of your home must not be over £1,500 in Greater London or £750 elsewhere. The rent you pay must be at least two-thirds of the rateable value on 23 March 1965.

The rents for some properties covered by the Rent Act have been fixed by the rent officer and registered by him; someone would need to have applied for this to happen. When a rent is registered, that is the maximum the landlord may charge. Check with the rent officer (listed under R in the telephone directory) if your rent is registered. If you pay more, you can recover the extra either by deducting it from future rent payments or by action in the county court within two years.

Tenants with full Rent Act protection are known as 'regulated tenants'.

16 | I agreed to pay £40 a week for my flat but it seems excessive. Can I have it reduced?

If the rent is not registered with the rent officer (see Q15), it is quite legal for the landlord to charge any rent he wants to. But you can apply for registration at any time, even just after you have started to pay a new rent to the landlord. Applying to register your rent would seem to be your best course of action. If the registered rent is lower than the one you agreed, you pay the lower registered rent. If you think that the rent fixed by the rent officer is too high, you can appeal to the rent assessment committee (in the telephone directory under 'rent').

17 | If a landlord wants to put up a registered rent, what increase will be allowed?

It is not possible to define a reasonable rent rise. Fair rents, fixed by rent officers, are normally assessed by comparison with other rents for similar properties in the area which have recently been registered. Once a rent has been registered, it can be reconsidered by the rent officer once every two years, unless something happens in the meantime to change the basis on which it was previously fixed, for example, the property is improved.

18 | I have just received notice to quit my rented flat. Do I have to leave on the date quoted?

Any notice to quit a house or flat must comply with some stringent requirements if it is to have any effect at all. It has to allow you at least four weeks between the date you receive it and the date it states you must go. That date must be one of the regular dates on which you pay the rent, or the day before in the case of a weekly, monthly or quarterly tenancy. If your

letting were for a fixed term, a notice to quit is not generally necessary. The notice does not have to be on a special form, but it does have to contain a notice with information addressed to you setting out your rights.

Even a valid notice to quit does not mean that you must actually leave on the date given. You have the right to test the matter in court, and the landlord cannot turn you out before there is a 'possession order' made by the court. To evict you earlier would be a criminal offence. Regulated tenants (see Q15) have security of tenure. That means that while the tenant continues to pay the rent and comply with the terms of his tenancy, there are only very few grounds on which the landlord can obtain possession. For instance, if your landlord has owned the property since 23 March 1965 (although in some cases this date may be different) and wants to occupy it or allow an adult member of his family to live there, that is a good ground. To be successful, the landlord also has to show that it is reasonable for the court to make a possession order against you, and that that would cause less hardship to either party than refusing it. You may be forced to move if you are offered suitable alternative accommodation. In assessing what is offered, you can take into account the rent, whether your needs for accommodation are taken into account, and whether the position is reasonable in relation to your place of work. Your own fads and fancies – about the style of decoration, for instance – will not carry much weight.

19 | When I die, can my daughter, who lives with me, take over my weekly tenancy?

Both the Rent Act 1977, which governs lettings by private landlords ('regulated tenancies'), and the rules about council lettings ('secure tenancies') give family takeover rights when a tenant dies. This can happen once in the case of a secure tenancy, and twice for a regulated tenancy. After that, the tenancy comes to an end and the property reverts to the landlord. If you are neither a regulated nor a secure tenant, there are no takeover rights. If there are takeover rights, the tenant's husband or wife always has a priority right to take over the tenancy. The only qualification is that the widow or widower was living in the property when the tenant died. Other members of the family can succeed to the tenancy only if no husband or wife is entitled. Their qualification is that they lived with the tenant for six months before the date of death in the case of a Rent Act tenancy, or 12 months if it is a secure tenancy. If more than one member of the family is entitled, they can settle between themselves who is to become the tenant, or ask the county court to decide, unless it is a secure tenancy when the local council (or housing association, where the same rule applies) can choose.

See also LIVING TOGETHER, Q10.

20 | *Security of tenure rights are obviously valuable for the tenant. What is to stop him selling his rights to someone else?*

The rights are intended to be a personal benefit to the tenant, not to give him a financial asset. There are two forms of restriction as a result. Once a tenancy granted by a private landlord comes to an end – either because the agreed period expires or because the landlord serves notice to quit – the tenant is allowed to stay in possession under what is called 'a statutory tenancy'. That is merely a personal right to occupation, so that if he leaves, even if he purports to transfer it to someone, his right comes to an end.

Council tenants cannot transfer their secure tenancies other than as outlined in Q19. Statute has made any other transfer totally ineffective, so there is nothing for anyone to pay for.

On top of all that, if someone does buy a statutory tenancy, he or she has a right to reclaim what was paid without handing the property back.

A tenancy from a private landlord can be transferred before it becomes a statutory tenancy if the terms of the tenancy allow it (and regulated tenancies give family takeover rights; see Q19). These terms are what the landlord and the tenant originally agreed. However, even if a transfer is permitted, the tenant still cannot *sell* the tenancy to someone else and a charge in such circumstances is illegal.

21 | *I have a cottage which goes with my job. Do I have to leave if I am made redundant, and what is my position about buying somewhere else for my retirement?*

The normal arrangement for tied accommodation – a cottage, a flat or whatever – is that when the job ends so does your right to live there. This applies where being in that accommodation is necessary for the job, like a caretaker who lives on the premises. It might not apply if you were given the chance to have the cottage merely as an inducement to take the job. Whether you pay rent is also an important factor. If you pay a full rent, then you may well have protection under the Rent Act 1977 (see Q15). If you do not, no special rules apply, unless a rent was fixed and then you agreed to a reduction in wages of the same amount. That counts as paying a rent.

People who have to live in tied accommodation are encouraged to buy somewhere else to retire to. You can normally claim the same income tax relief for mortgage interest payments as owner-occupiers (see Q109), and you can also sell with the benefit of relief from capital gains tax (see TAXES, Q71) as if you were living in the house. If you let the house pending your retirement, you can guarantee to get the tenants out if you serve an appropriate preliminary notice (see Q28).

There are special rules which apply to farmworkers in tied accommodation. Their right to stay there does not come to an end when their employment finishes. Sometimes, however, the farmer will have to house a replacement worker in that accommodation. He can ask the local authority to provide another home for his former worker, who then has the choice of moving to that alternative or simply to somewhere of his own choice and finding.

22 | *I moved into a furnished flat recently. The rent is fair (it's registered under the Rent Act), but the landlord charged me a high premium before I moved in. Was this fair?*

Not only was your landlord being unfair, he was also breaking the law. Because charging a lump sum over and above the rent is an obvious stratagem to get extra money from tenants, it has been expressly banned. In fact, not only is the landlord forbidden to charge what is often called a premium or key money, but a tenant cannot sell a Rent Act protected tenancy and collect a premium from the incoming tenant. The penalties are stringent. The money paid can be recovered by the person who paid it, even if he or she freely agreed to pay it, and there can be a criminal prosecution. You should go to a Citizens Advice Bureau or see a solicitor about what action you should take.

Another way in which landlords think they can

get round the rules is to charge an excessive amount for furnishings. This also is illegal, and any excess over the value is a premium. The proper procedure, although very often ignored, is for the person selling the furnishings to list them individually and price each item.

It may even be illegal for a landlord to charge his tenant with the legal and agents' fees which he has to pay in connection with letting a flat or house. There has been no final authoritative ruling about this, but certainly there has been one conviction in a magistrates' court.

23 | When I became tenant of a furnished flat, I had to pay a deposit which the landlord is holding. Does the ban on premiums mean that I can insist on having that money back?

Doubt surrounded this point for some time, but rules have now been laid down by statute. There is a maximum deposit which a landlord can require: one-sixth of the annual rent, that is, two months' rent. However, in addition to that calculation, the landlord has to be able to show that the amount is a reasonable one to cover the items which are to be covered by it.

If the deposit you have paid is above the limit, you are entitled immediately to demand the excess back. The simplest method of achieving repayment will probably be to deduct the excess from your next payment of rent.

You should receive the deposit – less any costs for breakages and so on – when your tenancy ends.

24 | Can I deduct anything my landlord owes me from future rent payments? Can I, for example, deduct the cost of repairs which should have been the landlord's responsibility or bills he agreed to pay, but which I have sorted out because I was fed up with waiting?

A tenant can set off money which the landlord owes, making a balancing reduction in the rent paid, as long as the landlord's debt arises from the same transaction. This means that you can deduct, for example, rates and electricity bills if the landlord has agreed to pay them; but, if your landlord also happened to be your employer and he was behind in repaying expenses to you, that would not be a proper deduction from the rent: the amount due did not arise under the tenancy agreement but for another reason, in this case as a result of your employment.

You have to be very careful about deducting the cost of repairs the landlord should have done from the rent you should pay. First, you have to be sure that the work was indeed something the landlord should have done. That involves two points. Not only must you be sure that the wording of the landlord's undertaking to repair is wide enough to include it, but he must also have been informed that the repair was needed. Second, you can claim only for the minimum cost of the repair, and you have to be able to show that what you paid was no more than the work should have cost. The best way to do this is to obtain competitive estimates for the work in advance. If you pay too much, you will not be able to reclaim the excess.

The danger involved in exercising this 'right of set-off' when it does not apply is that you will find you are still liable to pay the full rent. On top of that, being in arrears with the rent – which is the effect of it – is to brand yourself as a bad tenant and put your whole tenancy in jeopardy. Non-payment of rent which is due is a ground on which most tenancies can be forfeited.

25 | I am a student sharing a flat with a number of others. We have each signed agreements with the landlord, but between us we seem to be paying an exorbitant rent. Can we have it reduced?

Your landlord has attempted to give you sharing licences. If in fact all the licences cover the same period of time and between you you are entitled to

occupy the whole flat, the courts will interpret the arrangement as a tenancy. As tenants, you will be entitled to have a fair rent registered. You need pay only the fair rent or your contractual rent, whichever is lower.

Exceptionally, a landlord may be able to establish that he entered into individual arrangements at separate times with students who previously did not know each other and that they are not entitled either jointly or singly to have exclusive possession of the whole or part of the flat. In such a case each student will have to pay the rent as agreed. Once the agreement ends, the students will have no right to stay on, although the landlord may in some circumstances have to get a court order to evict them and they may be granted a few weeks' grace before they have to leave.

Letting

26 | *My house is now too big for me alone. I should like to let off the top floor. Can I do so without the tenants having security of tenure?*

If you let part of the house or flat you live in, which makes you 'a resident landlord', the tenancy comes into a separate part of the Rent Act 1977. The tenants' rights under this type of letting are effectively restricted to a three-month period to look round for other accommodation after you've served notice for them to quit. You have to take the tenants to court if they will not leave voluntarily when you want them to go, but you can be sure that you will get a possession order.

An elderly homeowner need not fear that bringing in a tenant will reduce the value of his house when he dies because his heirs will not get vacant possession. For two years after the landlord's death, his executors can force the tenant to leave so that they can sell the house.

There is a form of rent registration for lettings by resident landlords. It is the rent tribunal (the address is in the telephone directory under 'rent'), rather than the rent officer, which assesses the rent, though the amount is likely to be similar to a fair rent fixed by a rent officer. When a rent is registered, that is the most you can charge; otherwise you are free to charge whatever you like.

27 | *What difference does letting furnished accommodation make to any rules about tenancy agreements?*

The rules relating both to rents and to security of tenure apply equally to furnished and unfurnished lettings. Naturally, the landlord's provision of furniture is likely to put the rent up a little. Also, damaging the landlord's furniture has the same result as damaging the property as a ground on which the tenant may be evicted.

28 | *I am being sent abroad by my employers for two years. Can I let my house while I am away without fear that the tenants will insist on staying when I need the house back?*

There is a special procedure for this laid down by the Rent Act 1977, and if you follow the rules you are guaranteed to get the house back. You have to give the tenants a special written notice, available from law stationers, at the start of the tenancy or before it begins. If you have a series of tenants while you are away, you have to follow this procedure with all of them. The notice warns the tenants that you may require possession under the special arrangements.

As long as the notices have been given, you can make the tenants go provided the reason you want the house back is one of those the Act lays down. The most important reason is that you want the house back to live in. But if you should die while you are away, a member of the family who was then living with you can claim it, and so can someone to whom you leave the house in your will. There are two instances in which the tenants have to leave to allow the house to be sold empty. The first is if you come back to a job somewhere else and need to sell the house in order to buy another which is better placed for your employment. Second, your executors can obtain possession after you die in order to sell, so that your estate receives the full value from the house.

There are a few other similar special cases, where landlords who follow the procedure of giving this preliminary notice can be sure of getting their tenants out. One which is very similar to the person who goes away for business is for members of the forces who own a house. Another is lettings for a short period of between one and five years.

There are a number of points which you should note in thinking of letting a house on this basis. Although it guarantees that tenants cannot stay indefinitely, the amount of rent which you can charge is still limited because the tenants can apply to have the rent registered (see Q16). Even if you have slipped up in following the procedure about giving notices, you may still get a possession order, but the court will weigh up the relative merits of both the landlord and the tenant. If you let a house for a definite period, say three years, the special arrangements do not allow you to force the tenants out before the end of that period as long as they behave themselves. You merely have the guarantee that they will go at the end of that time. Finally, even though you can rely on getting a court order for the tenants to leave, it is still necessary to go to court if the tenants do not quit voluntarily.

29 | *I'm buying a large old house that has long-established tenants in the basement. What sort of notification do they get so that they know I've taken over and the rent must now be paid to me?*

One of the documents which the vendor's solicitor will hand over on completion will be a letter addressed to the tenant confirming that you are now the owner, and asking them to pay the rent to you (or however you may require it to be paid – to estate agents collecting the rent for you, for instance).

You should give the tenants that notification without delay. The technical position is that if they pay rent to the old landlord before they have been told that there has been a change, you cannot call on them to pay for a second time, and you may have trouble recovering what they paid.

On top of that there is a legal requirement that you give the tenants a written notice of the change of landlord within two months. You have to give your name and address, and failure to do so without reasonable excuse is an offence for which you can be prosecuted and fined.

30 | *Does the tenants' tenancy agreement simply continue, without my changing the landlord's name on it, once I've bought the house?*

The change of landlord does not vary the rights of the tenants or invalidate their agreement. If the tenants have a formal tenancy agreement or a lease, there should have been two copies in the first place, one signed by the landlord which they kept and one signed by the tenants for the landlord. That landlord's copy should have been among the deeds handed over on completion of your purchase. Even if it has been kept by the building society, you should have a copy of it for reference. There is no need to change the name of the landlord in the agreement itself.

All tenants who pay rent weekly, whether the letting is furnished or unfurnished, have a right to a rent book. This sets out the terms of their tenancy, gives them certain information and has spaces for recording payments of rent. For most residential tenancies, the form of the rent book is laid down under statutory authority.

Among the items of information which the rent book has to have written into it is the name and address of the landlord, so if your tenants have a rent book this needs bringing up to date. It may be convenient to start with a new book. They are available from stationers, but make sure that you buy an appropriate one – for furnished or unfurnished properties, for instance. You will also need to make sure that the printed terms of the tenancy are those that apply to your tenants. Although you have to supply all the information in the blanks in the book, you are entitled to change the tenancy terms as printed to make them comply with the actual agreement with the tenants.

A rent book has to include a leaflet of details of the local authority's rent allowance scheme. A rent allowance is a form of housing benefit available to tenants to help them pay their rent. The council housing department will give you the appropriate leaflet free.

31 | *I have four flats in a seaside resort which I let to visitors during the season. Surely I am not subject to rent control?*

No, holiday accommodation is outside the Rent Act 1977. There is no control on the amount of rent which you can charge, and tenants are not entitled to stay on for any longer period than is agreed. This applies when you are genuinely letting for holiday purposes. Some landlords have tried to pretend that ordinary lettings are for holidays in order to evade the controls, but the courts will look behind the wording of an agreement to the actual facts.

If you decide to let out of season, when the tenancy would not be for holiday purposes, you can generally guarantee getting the tenants out in time for the season if you serve them in advance with a notice similar to that used by a house owner who lets his house while living abroad (see Q28).

If the total rents you receive from holiday lettings in a year exceed the current minimum for VAT tax registration (see YOU AND YOUR BUSINESS, Q53), you will have to pay VAT on what you receive and will be entitled to charge VAT to the tenants.

Nuisance

32 | *Our neighbours are forever disturbing us with loud music from their stereo. What rights do we have to force them to turn it down?*

The law says that the occupiers of one property are not allowed to use it in such a way as to interfere with

is particularly sensitive to a particular form of interference cannot complain about behaviour that would not be nuisance to other people. To take an extreme example, if you suffer from hay fever, you could not say that your neighbour committed a nuisance simply because he grew plants in his garden to which you were particularly allergic.

34 | *A block of flats is being built next door to our block. The noise of the piledriving is intolerable. Is the noise a nuisance which the builders can be forced to stop?*

Obviously, buildings have to be demolished and new ones built, and some modern building techniques are noisy. An interference which is temporary may well escape being a nuisance on that ground. However, there always has to be reasonable give and take. The noise of piledriving night and day next door to flats in which people are living would seem to be unreasonable even if that were the most economic way to develop the new block. If it is necessary for the courts to intervene, they would impose a reasonable compromise, allowing piledriving some of the time but not continuously. If you have to resort to the courts, this is the type of case in which you would speedily be able to obtain an injunction (see SEPARATION, Q I 3).

You have no remedy in cases where the nuisance is very brief. That is the difference, for instance, between the work on a substantial new building and workmen digging a small hole in the road for a gas or water main repair. In the same way, the law does not offer protection against an interference which is only very occasional.

other people's reasonable enjoyment of their property. Your neighbour's loud music may well come into this category of 'nuisance', which the law uses as a technical term.

But merely because you find that something is a nuisance does not mean the law is being broken. In flats and semi-detached houses, some noises will inevitably penetrate from one to another. You have to put up with what is reasonable, and you yourself must behave reasonably. If you become so infuriated with a level of noise that people generally would consider reasonable that you deliberately make a lot of unnecessary noise in retaliation, it may be you who is guilty of nuisance and not your neighbour.

Anyone seriously disturbed by a noise nuisance can complain to a magistrates' court. If the complaint is upheld, the perpetrator of the noise will commit an offence if he repeats it. The local authority can also take action to help: contact the environmental health department.

Noise may come to disturb you from elsewhere, such as neighbouring factories. You have to take into account the type of neighbourhood in which you live. A noise which would be a nuisance on a quiet residential estate might not be on a busy high street.

33 | *When I'm working on night shifts I sleep during the day but find that my sleep is often interrupted by my neighbours. Does this come into the category of nuisance?*

There is probably nothing that you can do about this. The law long ago recognised that a homeowner who

35 | *I've bought a house on a new estate only to find that we can never hang out washing because of the smuts and grit from a factory chimney. Can the factory continue belching out smoke simply because it has done so for a long time?*

The smoke control laws now strictly limit what may be emitted by factory chimneys, and in the first place it may be worth contacting the environmental health department of your local council to see whether it can do anything.

Quite apart from official action, this may be a nuisance on which you can take action yourself. Smoke, smell and vibration are common causes of complaint which can constitute a nuisance from the legal point of view; you could seek the advice of a solicitor about what to do.

On the other hand, someone who commits a nuisance for long enough may achieve the right to do so. Once it has gone on for 20 years, no one can object, but it has to have existed as a nuisance for that time. So even if someone has been belching out noxious smoke for over 20 years across open fields where no one had been inconvenienced, a person who subsequently builds a house there can object in spite of the fact that he has brought the trouble on himself. It is no defence to a claim for monetary compensation that the person who is bringing the action 'came to the nuisance'. This will, however, be one of the things a court will take into account when deciding whether or not to make an order preventing the continuance of the activity.

36 | My neighbour objects to the smoke from my garden bonfires. Presumably, burning garden rubbish is a reasonable activity, and I cannot be held to blame if one particular family is generally downwind?

There are a number of hazards of which you may fall foul with your bonfire smoke. Certainly, like any other smoke, it could constitute a nuisance to your neighbours, but it comes within the principle of making reasonable use of land and of neighbours making allowances for one another. What you have to ask is: are you actually interfering with your neighbours' enjoyment of their property, for example, by stopping them from sitting in their garden when it would be reasonable for them to do so? And then, do you have bonfires more often than an ordinary person would consider reasonable? If the answer to both questions is yes, they could take action to stop the nuisance by reporting you to the environmental health department or going to law.

The local authority can also take action to stop or restrict the bonfires. It has the power to intervene if the smoke is a nuisance to the 'inhabitants of the neighbourhood', and if you do not comply with any restriction imposed the authority can take you to court.

One other thing must be remembered when making garden bonfires. It is an offence for which you can be prosecuted in the magistrates' court to light a fire within 50 feet of the centre of a road, if the result is that a user of the road is endangered or injured. Thick smoke obscuring the view of traffic on the road can be an offence under this provision.

37 | I am planning to keep a few hens in the garden simply to supply myself with eggs. Am I likely to run into problems?

There are some things you should check. Sometimes the deeds of houses contain restrictive covenants (see QS42 and 58) which forbid poultry-keeping because of the disturbance it can cause neighbours. Even without that, the people who live around you might complain that the noise – particularly if you also have a cockerel – was a nuisance. If you live in the country, where poultry-keeping would be much more common, there should be no difficulty on that score.

Apart from the possibility of creating a nuisance, keeping poultry means you have to allow inspectors of the Ministry of Agriculture to enter your property to see whether there is or has been any poultry disease there. Also, some water authorities make an extra charge for water if you keep poultry.

Smokeless zones

38 | I live in a smoke control area. What fuels am I allowed to burn?

In a smoke control area, which is designated by the local authority, open fires in a house or flat are usually banned. There are exceptions to this ban: wood and smokeless fuels can generally be burned, and specific types of grate have been specially approved, though these restrict you in the type and grade of fuel you can burn. Gas and oil appliances are both allowed.

If you are unsure whether you are in a smoke control area, ask the environmental health department of your local authority. This is one of the matters disclosed in reply to solicitors' searches (see Q140) when you buy a house or flat.

The smoke control legislation was introduced in 1956, and possibly no further control areas will be designated. However, if you do find yourself in a new one, and having to change your heating as a consequence, grants towards the cost are available from the local authority.

Boundaries

39 | Is there a general rule which I can apply to work out which of the fences around my back garden are mine and which belong to the neighbours?

The first and obvious rule about fences is that the person who puts up the fence owns it. But that does not help on a new housing estate, where the builder put up all of them. In that case, and in many others, the matter is settled by looking at the deeds of the property (the documents which prove ownership of it) or at the lease of it. Frequently, you will see on the plan that there is a small 'T' marked against the various boundaries. The convention is that the fence belongs to the owner of the property on the side on which the T is drawn. However, the T mark by itself has no meaning, and it is important to check in the body of the deed that its significance is stated.

If the question is not solved by the deeds, then it is necessary to see whether there is any record of who actually put up the fence, or whether anyone in the neighbourhood can recall it. If there is no such evidence there is a legal presumption on which you may be able to rely. This is only a fallback and is not a firm rule, and evidence to the contrary would overturn it.

This presumption is that a close-boarded fence, with supporting posts every so often, and a timber lap fence or chain link fence built similarly are assumed to belong to the owner whose side the supports are on. The reason for this is the presumption that anyone putting up a fence would erect it as near his boundary as he could, so that he fenced in the maximum amount of land. But if the fence line ran along the boundary, and the posts projected on the neighbour's side, the posts would be trespassing. The best the person putting up the fence can do is to run the fence along the boundary and have the projections on his side. The same general rule applies to a garden wall which has supporting pillars every so often.

40 | My neighbour's fence is in a disgraceful condition, and may well fall down on my herbaceous border. Can I insist that he repair it?

The fact that the fence belongs to your neighbour does not automatically mean that you can require him to do work on it. It is true that on many modern estates when the deeds allocate ownership of the fences the deeds also make the owner responsible for doing all the necessary work. But the reason why it does not necessarily follow is that the owner of the next door property may have voluntarily decided to put up a fence at some time in the past. If someone decides to erect a fence, it does not mean that he or she has to keep a well-repaired fence there for ever afterwards.

If the present fence does fall down and cause damage, you would be entitled to damages as compensation from your neighbour. Damages are normally limited to financial loss, and that could be difficult to prove in the case of garden flowers.

Even in a case where the deeds do not clearly lay down that one owner or the other is under a duty to repair a fence, long-established practice may settle the point. If you can show that over many years, certainly at least 20, your neighbour and the previous owners of his property have been in the habit of doing the repairs, you may be able to build up a case to oblige him to do so again; see a solicitor if this course of action is open to you.

41 | I am plagued by my next door neighbours' dog coming into my garden. If they can't keep it under proper control, can they be forced to fence their garden so that he can't get out?

The general rule is that pet owners do not have to fence to keep their animals in. If you want to keep out the dog you must do your own fencing. The same rule applies to cats, although in that case fencing is unlikely to be effective.

The position is different with farm animals. Unless the deeds of the property say something different, like putting the obligation to fence on to you, the farmer must prevent his beasts from trespassing. If they do stray and cause damage, he is responsible for paying for it.

42 | We have a toddler and want to fence the whole of both our front and back gardens to keep him safe. The front garden is part of an open-plan landscaped estate, and our neighbours have told us we cannot fence it. How can we get round this?

A fair number of post-war housing estates were planned on this basis, with no divisions between the front gardens. What, if anything, you can do about it depends on how the restrictions against fencing have been laid down.

Probably there is a restriction in the deeds under which the original purchaser of the house agreed with the developer that no fence would be built in front of the house. That is a 'restrictive covenant' which is probably enforceable both by the builder – who is probably no longer interested – and by other owners on the estate. You can find out if such a restriction exists by examining the deeds. If you have a mortgage and the building society holds the deeds, ask the society to look for you; it will probably send the deeds to your solicitor. Alternatively, you can enquire at the Land Registry if your property is registered; the addresses of the offices are on page 510. The Registry will for a fee supply you with an 'office' (official) copy of the register entries relating to your house.

The procedure for applying to modify a restrictive covenant, when it is shown to be obsolete, is outlined in Q 5 8 but it is unlikely to be successful in the case of a modern estate, and the expense would not be justified for this purpose. If your neighbours agree to your fencing the garden, you will probably be safe in ignoring the covenant.

There may well be another restriction. The original planning consent for building the estate may have been granted on condition that the front gardens were left open-plan. That condition is permanent, and it means that if you defy it the local authority can order you to remove the fence. Ask the planning department of your local authority if such a restriction exists; if it does you'll have to apply for planning permission to put up your fence. If it is granted, that cancels the original condition.

Even where there is no such condition in operation it is sometimes necessary to apply to the planning department of the local authority for planning consent to put up a fence. If it is on a road frontage and is more than one metre high you need consent, as you do for other fences over two metres high. The same rule applies to walls, but there is no planning restriction on the height of hedges.

43 | *I've consulted my deeds and it seems clear that one of my boundary fences is in the wrong place, giving me rather more land than I should have. Has that extra land become mine?*

If someone claims land to which he is not entitled,

and the true owner does nothing about it for a long period – usually 12 years – it becomes the claimant's property. During that period, you have to act as if the land is yours. The most obvious proof that you are acting as if you were the owner is the fact that it is fenced in so that only you can be the owner and the true owner is kept out. Your claim is not defeated by the fact that the fencing was done by a previous owner of your land. By becoming owner you get the benefit of the previous owner's annexation, and indeed you can add together his period of occupation of the extra land and yours so as to make up the 12 years.

Once the 12 years have gone by, the land becomes yours, and the fact that the deeds tell a different story does not alter that. It is not normally possible to change the deeds to agree with the facts, although that can be done in the case of registered land (of which the ownership details are registered by the Land Registry; see Q 1 70).

A word of caution is needed when consulting a registered land certificate to decide where boundaries run. Registrations are made with what are called 'general boundaries', which mean approximate boundaries. So, although the Land Registry has very good plans, their accuracy is not guaranteed from this point of view except to about the nearest foot or two.

44 | *I live in a terraced house, and I need to know who is responsible for repairs to the walls between our house and next door. It seems that on my neighbour's side there is rot in the wooden floor joists which go into that wall.*

The wall between one house and the next will normally be a party wall. That means that the law assumes that the boundary between the two houses runs exactly down the middle of the wall, and each neighbour owns half of it. You have the right to have your half of the wall supported by the other half, and your neighbour has the same right in reverse.

The traditional view was that this did not mean you could force your neighbour to do any work on his side of the wall, however desperately it was needed, but that you had the right to go into the property and do the work required at your own expense. But the courts now seem to be changing that. Certainly, where there is something harmful on the other side which is likely to spread and cause damage on your side, you are entitled to have your neighbour attend to it. Rot is likely to spread through the wall, and it comes into the category of a nuisance. If it harms

the neighbour can enter for specified purposes. This seems the sensible arrangement, but it is not always made. Alternatively, a property owner can obtain the right to go in for doing repairs by having done so for a long time, probably 20 to 30 years. It would be up to your neighbour to show that he and the former owners of the property had done that. For that habit to have become a right, it would have to have been exercised without the owner of your property actually giving consent.

Freeholders' responsibilities

46 | *A serious crack has appeared in the lintel above one of the windows in our flat. The lease says the freeholders must repair the structure of the building. The difficulty is actually getting the work done. What action can we take?*

There is a general rule about landlord's repairs: whatever the lease says, the landlord has no duty to do them unless and until he is notified that something needs doing. The reason for this is that the property is in the hands of the tenants, who can be expected to spot what goes wrong. This may not apply to common parts, like the staircase, if they are not included in any of the leases.

Once the landlord has been notified, tenants can take action on default either by applying for a court order that the work should be done, or by suing for damages.

47 | *If we very much disagree with the work the freeholder has done, do we have to pay our contributions towards it?*

Landlords of flats – and this does not apply in the case of a leasehold house – have a statutory obligation to consult leaseholders in advance of doing repairs when the likely cost of doing work to a block exceeds £500, or the number of flats in the block multiplied by £25 if that yields a higher figure. In that case, the freeholder has to obtain at least two estimates for the work, and one of them must be from someone completely independent of the freeholder. A notice describing what is to be done must be sent to each of the flat owners, or it must be displayed where it will come to the attention of all of them. The notice must give at least a month for tenants to state their views, and the landlord must take them into account before beginning the work. However, having taken them into account he is at liberty to ignore them. So the freeholder has the right to insist on repointing the entire building, say, and you as tenants will have to pay up.

your property you are entitled to damages, but if you have forewarning the courts will make an order obliging the neighbour to take the necessary action to eradicate the problem.

In dealing with party walls in Inner London, there is a special code of local laws. The basis is that not only repairs but also improvements can be done by either owner who reasonably requires them. One neighbour can add a floor to his house, for example, even though that increases the load on the party wall.

45 | *My neighbour has asked whether he can bring ladders into the side passage that runs between his house and mine to paint his gutters and repoint the brickwork. The side passage is clearly mine. Must I let him have access?*

Even where a house is built right up to the boundary of its plot, so that the only feasible way to do repairs and decorations to that side of it is to go on to the neighbouring property, there is no automatic right to do so. The basic rule is quite firm: going on to someone else's land without permission is a trespass. If an owner wants to refuse, he can do so whether other people think he is being reasonable or not. The courts cannot intervene.

However, a householder *can* have the right to go next door for repair purposes, and before barring the way you should check whether either of these two cases apply. The deeds can give this right, in which case the deeds of your house should make it clear that

A landlord who does not follow the procedure cannot recover any part of the cost over the £500 or £25 per flat limit, unless a court agrees that he should.

A discontented leaseholder should check the terms of the lease of the flat. Only those items mentioned in the lease have to be paid for as part of the service charge.

48 | *Does the tenant of a flat have to contribute towards whatever cost the landlord decides to pay for decorations and repairs?*

There is a statutory limit. A tenant need not pay more than what is reasonable. This seems to give protection in various ways.

First, the tenant can argue that the item in question was not one on which it was reasonable to spend anything at all. This could apply to repairing some out-of-date facility now likely to be of little use, like coal storage bunkers. Second, the tenant can say that the sum spent was unreasonably large. Third, the tenant can challenge the reasonableness of the price in relation to the standard of the work done. If, in any of those cases, it is established that the sum was unreasonably large, any excess over what would have been reasonable does not have to be paid by the tenant.

Even apart from those statutory rules, the courts will intervene to prevent a landlord taking advantage of his position. Even if the lease says that the choice of what is done and by whom is wholly the landlord's, that is not interpreted as a blank cheque. The landlord must justify the cost as reasonable.

49 | *I am proposing to let my house on a short-term basis, probably for a year. What is the position regarding any repairs that may be necessary? Are they my responsibility, or my tenant's?*

When a landlord lets a house or flat for less than seven years there are some repairs for which he is responsible. This is a compulsory obligation imposed by statute. His duty extends to the structure and the exterior of the premises, and also includes providing adequate heating provision.

Gas, water (including the means to heat the water) and electricity supplies come into his responsibilities, and they include sinks, basins, baths and sanitary conveniences, but not other fixtures or appliances for making use of water, gas or electricity. That means, for example, that the landlord is responsible for the electric wiring, but not generally for the light fittings or the lightbulbs.

The landlord is perfectly entitled to take this liability into account when he is deciding what rent to charge, but he cannot make the tenant pay directly for those items. Even in a short lease he can have a service charge for other items if the tenant agrees. This would normally apply in the case of a flat, and might cover the cost of porterage, lighting common parts and insurance.

Service charges

50 | *How do we find out what the landlord has been spending, and how the service charges have been fixed?*

Tenants of flats have statutory protection. They have the right to a written statement of the costs which are reflected by the service charge, and they can claim it for the preceding accounting year by writing to the landlord or his agent. Those accounts will normally have to be certified by a qualified accountant. Only if there are no more than four flats in the building, and the costs do not relate to any other building, can that certificate be dispensed with. A landlord who does not produce the information when he should may commit an offence and may be subject to a fine.

A tenant who wants to challenge a service charge demand, assuming he or she gets no co-operation from the landlord, can go to the county court to ask for a declaration that it is unreasonable and therefore not payable. Another way is simply to refuse to pay and to wait for the landlord to take the tenant to court for the amount outstanding.

51 | *I live in a house, but I have to contribute towards the maintenance of a communal garden and other facilities. Do I have the right to see how the service charge is fixed?*

The statutory rules specified in Q50 apply only to flats (except in the case of a few houses purchased by secure tenants exercising the right to buy; see Q10). That means that you have no statutory right to information, nor the right to consultation, nor the statutory right to challenge the sum as unreasonable. Also, a certificate of the amount of your contribution sent by the landlord can be final.

However, you should check the rights given by the lease or conveyance of the house which sets out the terms under which you pay. That may give you the right to accounts. Also, the general protection given by the courts against a landlord's having *carte blanche* to incur expenses which his tenants will have to pay still applies.

Damage by neighbours

52 | *Trees growing in my next door neighbour's garden are damaging my house because the roots are affecting the foundations. Does my neighbour have to pay the repair costs?*

Some trees are notorious for causing this trouble, poplars being one of them. It is not so much that they cause physical damage to the foundations, but rather that they take water from the soil, particularly clay, which then contracts and causes subsidence. The person on whose land the tree is growing is responsible for the damage, as long as it is proved that it was the cause.

You may well be covered for this damage by your house insurance policy. If you are, the simplest course is to make a claim under the policy, and let the insurers pursue the claim against your neighbour, or possibly his insurance company.

There have been cases in which this sort of damage was done by trees in the road in front of the house. In that case the local highway authority can be made to pay for the damage. This role is undertaken by the Department of Transport for trunk roads, sometimes subcontracted to county councils, and by local authorities.

53 | *My neighbour is threatening to lop branches off a large chestnut tree growing in my garden just because they are hanging over into his garden. Can I stop him damaging the tree?*

If one of your trees overhangs your boundary it is just as much a trespasser as if you trespassed yourself. Your neighbour is absolutely entitled to cut off branches at the point where they cross the boundary between your two gardens. The wood itself remains yours, so he should either throw it back or let you in to collect it.

54 | *Our next door neighbours have a very large tree in their garden. It is wholly on their side of the fence, but because it is on our south side it blocks out a lot of sunshine. Is there any way we can insist it is lopped or felled?*

A house has a very limited right to light, and you can complain only if some artificial structure, like another house, interferes with it. No complaint can be made when it is a tree that is in the way.

The right to light can arise in two ways. First, it can be expressly granted in the deeds of the house. This is unusual. Indeed, when rights to light are mentioned,

it is usually in the negative sense, saying that the owner of adjoining land is entitled to build on it even if that interferes with the access to light. Second, if light is enjoyed for 20 years, the right to it becomes a permanent one. It is not the house as a whole that benefits from this, but the particular windows in the places in which they are positioned. If they were altered or the house rebuilt with windows in different places, the long usage rights would be lost.

Even though bright light has come into a room for over 20 years, the house owner may be able to do nothing about a partial obstruction of it by something like a tree. If the room is still usable, although markedly less pleasant, he could probably take no action.

In a new development, a court decided that it might be possible to acquire a right to direct sunlight when that was essential, for a greenhouse, for example. Whether this can benefit people who want to protect the access of sunlight to solar heating panels has yet to be decided in the courts.

55 | *A building plot has been taken off the garden at the end of ours and a bungalow is to be built on it. What protection have I got for my privacy?*

The law does not recognise a right of privacy. Even though this is your objection in fact, your only chance of stopping the project is to frame your protest in some other way, like interference with a right of light.

Working from home

56 | *Is there anything to stop me starting up a business at home?*

There are a number of points you should look into. First, you may find that you are forbidden to do this by your deeds. If you have a lease, it is common to find that it allows you to use the premises only as a 'private dwelling-house', a term that covers flats as well as houses. If you defy that ban, you put your lease in jeopardy. If the freeholder learns what you are doing and objects, you could lose your lease if you did not stop. If you approach the landlord for permission, you may be charged a fee for it.

Starting a business at home can also be something that requires planning consent from the planning department of your local authority. A 'material' change of use is something for which you have to get planning permission, just as much as putting up a new building. If you turned over the whole of your home to business use, that would certainly be a material change of use. However, if what you do can truly be considered as ancillary to the residential use, no permission is needed. You should have no difficulty, for example, in doing journalism from home, using a room as a doctor's consulting room, or organising a mail order business as long as you do not have to store too much stock. On the other hand, something that could affect the neighbours, such as setting up a woodworking shop in the garage, is unlikely to be acceptable.

Some home businesses can involve other types of official intervention. If you organise a playgroup, both you and the premises will have to be approved by the social services department of the local authority, and setting up a catering service using your kitchen can subject it to the scrutiny of the health inspector, for example.

Finally, bear in mind that the rateable value of your home, and the amount of rates charged, could alter if you start to be charged on a business premises basis. Also you may be liable to pay capital gains tax when you sell your home if you've been using it as a business.

57 | *As I am a Rent Act tenant, with security of tenure, presumably I have nothing to fear from my landlord if I run a business from home?*

Business premises and residential premises are entirely different for the purposes of the Rent Act 1977. Business premises do not enjoy the Act's protection. That means that if you start a business at home you run the risk of losing your security of tenure.

Whether you do lose it depends on the amount of business use. If it is occasional and involves only one room it will probably make no difference. On the other hand, if it is a regular thing, and the business takes over a significant part of the house or flat, then you will no longer be a Rent Act tenant. The fact that you still live there does not help, because mixed business and residential use falls outside the Rent Act 1977.

Restrictive covenants

58 | *There is a 'restrictive covenant' in the deeds of my house, imposed when it was built in the last century, preventing me from using it for business. Many other houses round here have been wholly or partly converted to business use. Can I ignore the restriction?*

A restrictive covenant is a formal undertaking *not* to do a particular thing to or with a particular property, such as not to build on to it. Although the restriction may no longer be effective, it is risky simply to ignore it. If the restriction were imposed for the benefit of the other occupiers and they are inconvenienced by the business – a scrap metal merchant operating from his back garden, to give an extreme example – they may be able to impose the restriction and stop you carrying on the business.

You can apply to the Lands Tribunal (address on page 510) to have an obsolete restriction cancelled. This can be done on the grounds that changes in the character of the property or the neighbourhood make the restriction obsolete, or that it is impeding the reasonable use of the land. You would be helped with the former if you had the support of your neighbours; with the latter if you could show that you already have planning permission for the use which the restriction would forbid.

A practical alternative to a Lands Tribunal application is to insure. Many people do this because it is quicker and often cheaper. You insure for a sum which would be reasonable compensation if the restriction were enforced and you had to stop the business use.

Unmade roads

59 | *I live in an unmade road. The council now wishes to 'adopt' it, and says that it is going to* *charge us with the costs. I have never had to contribute to the repair of the road. Do I have to do so now?*

Although there are not many unadopted roads now, when a council decides to adopt one, which means making itself responsible for all future repairs, the expense of bringing it up to standard can be charged to the 'frontagers' – the people whose properties front the road. Once it has been brought up to standard, it is adopted by the council, which maintains it out of the rates. The making-up charges are normally divided between the properties according to the length of their frontages to the road. If you cannot pay immediately, you can claim to pay by instalments. The amount outstanding for the time being becomes a charge on the house, so that anyone to whom you sell it becomes liable to pay. The searches a solicitor makes for a purchaser on house purchase (see Q140) reveal whether there is anything of this nature outstanding.

The system is in theory the same on a new housing estate, although in practice the developer pays for the road to be made up to adoption standards. When the development starts, the builder enters into an agreement with the local authority. The builder agrees to make the road up to the council's requirements, and usually to maintain it for a year, and the council agrees to adopt it free of charge. This is reinforced in one of two ways. Either the developer deposits money with the council as a guarantee, or a bank or insurance company agrees to provide a bond under which the council can claim the cost if the road is not properly made.

Tree preservation orders

60 | *My solicitor tells me that a tree in my garden is subject to a tree preservation order. What is the significance of that?*

A tree preservation order, made by the local authority, can designate one tree, a group of trees, or even a hedgeline for protection. This means that you cannot fell a designated tree without consent. To do so without permission lays you open to prosecution and a fine. Obviously, there will be cases when felling is necessary in the interests of public safety, and then you would expect permission to be given. In other cases, for instance, because you want to build where the tree stands, or because you want more light to reach your windows, the prospect of getting permission is more doubtful.

Extensions and planning permission

61 | *I am proposing to build an extension at the back of my house, but the owners of the other half of our pair of semi-detacheds are objecting. Have they any right to interfere?*

Before any property owner takes a final decision about an extension, it is important to examine the deeds. You may find that there is a restrictive covenant (see Q58) under which you or a previous owner of the house agreed not to extend, or – and this is more likely – agreed to have plans approved by the original builder first or to limit an extension in size or position. The object of these restrictions will have been to ensure that the scale and siting of an extension is appropriate, and that you will not jeopardise the structural stability of the building. Whether the restrictions are still valid may be a complicated legal question. If they are, your neighbours could stop you building in contravention of them.

Even in the absence of restrictions in the deeds, you will probably have to take account of your neighbours' position. You share a party wall with the other semi-detached house, and you have to be sure that the result of your changes will not expose part of it so that rain on it can penetrate into next door. Your two houses also support each other. There is no automatic legal right to have your house supported by the next door property, but where houses are semi-detached or built in a terrace, that right is usually expressly granted at the time. Even if it is not, it will probably be implied and will certainly arise from long use. Your proposals therefore have to avoid removing any support from your neighbours' house.

62 | Do I have to obtain planning permission for a house extension?

Whether you have to obtain planning permission depends on the size of the extra building you have in mind, and on the history of the house. The general rule is that you always have to have permission for any building, but there are certain exceptions, so the question is whether you can bring yourself within them. You can enquire at the planning department of your local authority in any case.

Any house (except a listed building; see Q71) can be extended up to a certain limit. You can have more than one extension without permission provided the total size of the extensions does not go above this limit.

The limit for a house in the middle of a terrace is a maximum of 50 cubic metres or, if it gives a larger limit, 10 per cent of the size of the original house. End-of-terrace houses, semi-detached and detached houses have a limit of 70 cubic metres, or 15 per cent of the original size if that is greater. In both cases there is an overall limit of 115 cubic metres, however large the original house was.

If you need planning permission because you will be outside the size limits, you should apply to the planning department, which will give you the forms to fill in. You also have to supply a plan showing where the property is, and a detailed plan of the work you propose to do. Your architect or surveyor will draw these up. There is also a modest fee to pay.

63 | The extension I have in mind is building upwards to add a further top floor which will involve raising the roof. Presumably I can still take advantage of the percentage additions which are automatically allowed?

Any form of extension can be included within the 10 per cent or 15 per cent, as the case may be (see Q62). However, you will fall foul of other conditions that are laid down. Among these is a requirement that the height of any extension must not go above the highest point of the original roof. If you cannot comply, you will have to get planning permission.

Among the other conditions that extensions within the permitted category have to fulfil are that they do not extend nearer to the road than the part of the house which was nearest to the road. Generally,

this means that you cannot build anything on the road frontage side, but if the house has a projecting hip on that side you can add to the other part as long as you do not go further forward than that hip. There is a special exception for porches. They can be built nearer to the road than the original house – as of course they generally will be – if they come within these limits: the floor area does not exceed two square metres, they are not more than three metres high, and they are at least two metres from any road.

To avoid having to obtain planning permission, there are two other guidelines to observe. At any point where it comes within two metres of your boundary, an extension must be no more than four metres high. Anyone building an extension outwards, rather than upwards, is also limited by the rule that it must not cover more than half of the previously unbuilt-on part of the land.

64 | Do I have to apply for planning permission to put up a garage or a carport?

Any building needs permission, unless you can bring it within one of the exceptions given below, and this even includes a carport, which is no more than a roof supported by poles or pillars.

A garage can count as a house extension, which means that if you have not already used up your limit (see Q62) you do not need permission. For this purpose, a separate garage must be built within five metres of the house. A stable or a loose-box anywhere on your property can also count as a house extension. This means not only that you may not need permission for one of these buildings if that is what you now have in mind, but also that if you have used up your allowance by building one of them in the past you will need permission for any extension.

There are some outbuildings which you can put up without their coming into your extensions allowance, and without asking for consent, as long as you comply with the following conditions which have been laid down. These include a garage which is further from the house than five metres, and also dog kennels, poultry sheds and bee hives, as long as they are merely used for personal enjoyment and not for business. None of them must be nearer to the road than your house, if they have a flat roof they must be no more than three metres high, or four metres with a ridged roof, and they must not together cover more than half of the unbuilt-on part of the land.

65 | I asked for planning permission for a large extension, and I have been refused. Do I have a right to appeal?

You can always appeal against a local authority's refusal to give you planning permission by taking the matter up with the Secretary of State for the Environment. Details of the procedure will come to you with the notice refusing permission. You simply have to fill in a form giving the grounds on which you want to appeal. The authority's notice of refusal will state what its reasons were, so you will be able to marshal arguments against them.

The Secretary of State appoints an inspector to conduct the appeal, and in a house extension case the inspector will normally make the decision. The inspector decides on one of two alternative methods of conducting the appeal. Either he will invite you to submit a written statement, and ask the authority to do so also, and then make his decision on the basis of these written submissions, or he will conduct a public inquiry. This latter process is more suitable where other people want to have a say in the matter, but it means that the decision will take longer.

In just a few cases it is possible to take the matter further if the inspector also turns you down. You can appeal to the High Court if you believe that the inspector or the Secretary of State has made a legal mistake.

There is one other point to note about putting in an appeal. The local authority has only two months to consider your original application. It may ask you to agree to a longer period, but you do not have to agree. If you are not given a decision, either a consent or a refusal, within that two months or any extended period you agreed, you can assume that the authority has refused and appeal at once.

66 | *What happens if I don't bother to ask for planning permission when I should have done?*

The local authority has powers to enforce the planning rules and may serve an 'enforcement notice' on you. This will call on you to stop doing what you should not be doing without permission, or to take away buildings that you have put up without permission. The notice gives you a reasonable time-limit within which to comply.

You have the right to appeal to the Secretary of State for the Environment (forms are available from the Department of the Environment), and if you do so there will be a public inquiry. The two most common grounds for appeal are either that you did not need permission or that what you have done is something for which you should be granted permission. The argument may be about what counts towards your 10 or 15 per cent extension allowance (see Q62), and it could turn out that the authority has measured it

wrongly so that there was no need for you to apply for consent. The second ground for appeal gives you the chance, in effect, to apply for the permission that you should have asked for originally, and to argue the case in favour of your being permitted to do what you want to do.

If time goes by and the authority takes no action against you, it may lose the right to do so. But you have to draw a distinction between changes in the *use* to which you put property which needs consent and just the building work. However long goes by, an enforcement notice can always be served calling on you to stop an unauthorised use, but once four years have passed from your doing building work without consent, no enforcement action can be taken against you for the actual building.

67 | *Rather than building on to my house, I want to demolish an unsightly extension built by an earlier owner. Do I have to have planning permission?*

Demolition, by itself, is not something for which you have to have planning consent. When it is associated with a rebuilding operation, any permission you need for the rebuilding effectively covers both.

There is one case where you do need official permission before demolishing even part of a house, and that is when the house has been listed as being a building of special architectural or historic interest (see Q71).

Building Regulations

68 | *By building an extension for which I do not have to have planning permission, do I need to involve the local council at all?*

Yes. Most building operations at home will involve you not only in planning law, but also in the Building Regulations. These are detailed standards laid down to ensure that buildings now being built, including extensions, comply with modern standards. Most extensions mean that you must obtain a consent under these Regulations from the local council, and the planning department will need to see the plans drawn up by your architect, surveyor or builder. In your case the planning department is not exercising a judgement about the desirability of your proposal, and if your plans conform to the rules you will automatically receive consent.

The sort of matters that the Regulations cover are the adequacy of foundations, the need to have fume vents from foul drains, the insulation of walls, and having stair treads that are large enough to be safe. If you are adding an extension to an old house, you may well find that the house itself does not conform to these modern standards. That does not matter; you do not have to change what is existing, although the new extension will have to conform to the Regulations.

If you are adding a floor, or converting a loft into a living-room or bedroom, you may find that fire precaution Regulations require that you change the other doors in the house to increase their fire resistance, because you are changing the house from a two-storey one to a three-storey one, and different standards then apply throughout.

The Building Regulations not only require you to get consent in advance but also to allow the local authority's building inspector to look at the work as it progresses to ensure that the required standards are being observed. This can be a considerable protection to you. Not only do you have an independent expert checking the work, but if later it turns out that he overlooked some fault you may well be able to obtain damages from the local authority as a result of the inspector's negligence.

69 | *Do any of these rules about planning permission and Building Regulations apply to converting a large old house into flats but without altering the outside?*

You will certainly have to get planning permission. There is a special rule that when any 'dwelling-house', which means both a house and a flat, is converted into more than one dwelling-house, planning consent has to be obtained. The fact that there is no extension at all to the building is irrelevant, and does not remove the need for planning permission.

The Building Regulations also apply, and detailed plans of the work proposed will be required. Matters of particular concern in this type of case are often fire escapes, refuse disposal arrangements, and drainage.

A conversion of this type may also run up against the snag of a restrictive covenant (see Q58) in the deeds forbidding the use of the building as more than one dwelling-house. This is relatively common, as it is thought to maintain the value of property in the neighbourhood, and it can be a snag when planning a 'granny annexe'. There is a special procedure for varying restrictions in this case, and you would have to apply to the county court. You would need to show that changes in the character of the neighbourhood mean that the whole house cannot be readily let as a single unit, but that it could be let if converted.

70 | *I intend to modernise my kitchen. Are there any Building Regulations I need to comply with?*

Yes, you'll probably come up against a number of the detailed Building Regulation requirements. Take the cooker: the chimneys for oil and gas cookers that need them will normally have to be lined, or if a gas stove has a balanced flue, the flue will need to go through a wall to the outside. An electric cooker normally needs its own separate electricity circuit. A central heating boiler in the kitchen will have flue requirements, and will need an adequate air supply. In fact, if you plan an unusually large storage tank for an oil-fired boiler, you have to have planning permission for tanks holding more than 3,500 litres. If you have a cooker or boiler supplied from a tank of bottled gas you always need planning consent for installing the tank.

Kitchens have to have a minimum of ventilation, according to size. A kitchen of 12 feet by 10 feet must have openable windows of 3 feet by 2 feet; in some circumstances you can count a door opening straight to the outside. Larders also must comply with minimum ventilation standards, and they have to have durable fly screens over windows that open.

Other regulations include having a cold-water supply from the rising main, and not mixing that water with the hot supply through a mixer tap which does not keep the two streams separate, and not having a WC opening straight into the kitchen.

Listed buildings

71 | *I live in a Grade II listed building. What restrictions does this impose on me regarding any internal structural alterations and extensions I may want to make?*

Stringent controls apply to buildings listed by the Department of the Environment as being of special architectural or historic importance. (The list is transmitted by the DoE to local authorities; if you are not told a building is listed before you buy it, your solicitor's searches (see Q140) will reveal the fact before contracts are signed.)

Permission is needed for any alterations likely to affect the character of the building. As a general guide, this means something that will change the outside of a Grade II building, like adding a kitchen window. This would almost certainly apply to a Grade I building too. Grade II and Grade I buildings may well have particularly fine interiors, in which case permission would be needed for any changes,

like demolishing an internal wall to knock two rooms into one.

The permission needed is 'listed building consent'. You apply for it to the planning department of the local authority in the same way as for planning permission. It is quite possible that the same proposal will mean that you have to have both planning permission and listed building consent. If you are refused, you have a right to appeal to the Secretary of State for the Environment (see Q65).

Grants

72 | *Can I get a grant to help towards modernising my house?*

There are three main types of grant for which you can apply to the housing department of your local authority: intermediate grants, improvement grants and repair grants.

An intermediate grant is for the installation of a basic amenity where there is none at the moment. These amenities are: a fixed bath or shower, and a hot and cold water supply to it; a wash handbasin, and a hot and cold water supply to it; a sink and a hot and cold water supply to it; and a WC.

An improvement grant can be for any kind of improvement work, but it is given at the council's discretion. The council may withhold an improvement grant because of shortage of funds, because it considers that the work is really repair, not improvement, such as replacing a worn-out boiler with a more modern one, or because the improvement is of a kind it has decided not to encourage.

A repairs grant is available only for houses built before 1919. As the name implies, it is for repairs rather than improvements.

Other grants to which you may be entitled are something towards the cost of loft insulation, a contribution to sound insulation if you are particularly affected by aircraft noise near an airport, and for

converting fireplaces to take smokeless fuel in a smoke control area.

Not every house owner can claim these grants. For most of them, the rateable value of the house in question has to be below a certain amount.

73 | *How much grant can I expect?*

The amount of grant available depends on where your house is and what the work is going to cost you. The official limits are varied from time to time, and the grant is a percentage of the total cost of the work. You can enquire at the housing department of your local council. The ceiling on the cost to which the grant contributes is higher in Greater London than elsewhere, and is more in respect of homes which are listed buildings (see Q71). The percentage of the cost which you can claim is higher in the case of priority categories, like the disabled, and in areas of special housing need, where the authorities are specially trying to encourage improvements.

74 | *What strings are attached to improvement grants? In particular, do I have to pay anything back if I later sell the house?*

An owner-occupier is expected to continue to occupy the house for which he received an improvement grant for five years. However, if during that time you sell to someone who also intends to occupy it himself, then the council will not reclaim the money. This is something that needs to be expressly discussed with a potential purchaser, because some buyers are reluctant to take on the potential liability of having to repay and you will need to take that into account.

If you do move within the five-year period and have to repay, the amount for which you are liable is the whole grant plus interest. The fact that, say, three of the five years have gone by does not mean that you have to pay back only two-fifths of the grant.

Grants are also available to owners who want to let the premises once they have been improved. They have to keep them let or available for letting for the full five-year period to avoid having to repay. The tenancies have to be for use as residences, and cannot be for holiday purposes.

75 | *I recently finished converting into four flats a house I purchased for that purpose. I'm sure I could get at least a repairs grant for the work I did on the roof, but I never applied for one. Can I apply retrospectively?*

No. A grant application has to be approved before any work is started. If you are too quick off the mark, you lose the chance of receiving a grant. You can get an informal indication as to whether you will get a grant, and how much, before you buy a property, but you still have to await the final approval of the local authority before starting work.

76 | *I rent a small flat and would like to improve it by installing a handbasin in the bathroom. Can I get financial help from the council?*

Not only house owners but tenants are eligible for grants, and most tenancy agreements must now be read as if they conferred on the tenant a right to make improvements. The landlord should first give written consent, but that cannot be withheld unreasonably. This liberalisation was introduced by statute in 1980, and it applies whatever the terms of the tenancy agreement. Whether or not you'll get a grant to install a handbasin will be at the discretion of the council. If there is no handbasin at all in the flat you will definitely be entitled to an intermediate grant.

Builders

77 | *I employed a local builder to build my extension. The job is half finished and he seems to have deserted it. What can I do?*

It is important that arrangements with a builder who is going to do improvement work for you are definite and put in writing. This may not be possible when you have to call in a tradesman for an emergency repair, but there should be no reason for not having a contract for a job which is planned.

Very often the builder will suggest that you sign a formal contract, but an exchange of letters between you is just as binding. The important thing is to ensure that the terms of your agreement are accurately recorded, and that any contingencies such as the builder leaving off work are dealt with.

A well-drawn contract will not only define what the builder is to do and how much it will cost, but will say when he will start, state that he will proceed diligently, and give an estimated completion date. In that case, if he leaves the job without some reasonable excuse he will clearly be in breach of contract. The contract is broken by the builder abandoning the work even if nothing is said, but it becomes more difficult to say how long he must be away before you can assume that it has been abandoned.

Your remedy if the builder does not finish the job is to employ someone else to do the rest of the work and then deduct the second builder's fee from what you owe the first. Alternatively, you could sue the original builder. If in the end the fee is no higher than the original builder's estimate, you may very well have no claim against the original builder, because it does not really matter to whom you pay the agreed amount.

78 | *Can I insist that a building agreement quotes a fixed price for the job I am having done?*

Subject only to minor adjustments, your contract for improvement work should state exactly what the builder will charge. To make sure that you are not being overcharged you should obtain a couple of competitive estimates in advance. In contracts for some big jobs there is a clause that allows the price to be adjusted if wage rates vary while the work is under way. This would rarely be appropriate in a contract for a small job, because it is intended to cope with unforeseen changes.

One adjustment which you may have to agree is the provision of 'p c prices'. These 'prime cost' prices fix a provisional price for something on which you have not finally decided – light fittings or type of bath taps, for instance. If the arrangement is that you will choose them later, then the builder simply increases or decreases the amount in the contract for that item, depending on how the price of what you finally decide on compares with the provisional figure. The more definite decisions you can take in advance, the fewer of these adjustments you have to agree to.

The price you are quoted will say 'plus value added tax'. The rule is that VAT is charged on all building work to existing houses and flats.

The other important thing which the contract should specify about the fee is when it has to be paid. Payment in advance is highly unsatisfactory, and there should be no necessity to pay in advance for materials, as some small builders suggest, because they can normally obtain them on credit from builders' merchants.

Under contracts for big jobs, five or 10 per cent of the price is held back for six to 12 months after the work is finished to guarantee that the builder deals with any defects which may appear in that time. This is not so common in small contracts, but it is always worth trying for.

79 | *Apart from details of the work to be done, and the price I have to pay, are there other things I should look for in a building contract?*

The builder should make himself responsible for everything involved in the job. For example, the building inspector has to be informed when the work reaches various stages so that he can inspect for compliance with the Building Regulations (see Q68), and the builder should agree to notify him. Also there may be a lot of rubble and rubbish to dispose of. If this means hiring a skip, the builder should agree to arrange it as well as obtain the necessary permit from the local authority if it has to be left in the road.

The contract should specify too who is to be responsible for the various materials that are delivered to your house before they are actually built in to your alterations. Either you or the builder should insure them.

Finally, see whether you can settle definitely whether or to what extent the builder proposes to subcontract. He may need to have specialist work done by others, but this can often cause delay and difficulty because your builder does not have direct control over the subcontractors. If the contract makes clear who is going to do what work, the builder cannot subcontract at a later date more than originally agreed. Your contractual relationship is with the main builder, and he is responsible for the subcontractors; you yourself have no control over them.

80 | *I bought my house new from the builder. Nasty cracks have appeared in one of the side walls. Can I call upon the builder to deal with this under the guarantee?*

Almost all new houses and flats are now sold with the benefit of the National House Building Council (NHBC) guarantee. What this offers buyers is protection in two parts. For the first two years the builder is responsible for any defect that arises because the NHBC requirements have not been met. These requirements are a detailed set of building specifications, aimed at achieving the use of satisfactory materials with work of good standard. The guarantee during that first period should therefore cover most things that go wrong, except for very minor items and two categories that are expressly excluded: wear and tear and the result of neglect, and normal damp, condensation and shrinkage. The guarantee period for central heating boilers and electrical fittings with moving parts is only one year. This means the builder will put right your cracks if they result from a building fault, such as inadequate foundations or faulty bricks. But surface plaster cracks, which commonly appear when a new house dries out, are not his responsibility.

The second part of the guarantee, for the next eight years, is undertaken by the NHBC itself. This is limited to major damage, which means something that entails major repairs or complete or partial rebuilding. Defective foundations causing subsidence would be an example.

In either case, it is extremely important that you give written notice of any fault promptly, as you can lose the protection of the guarantee if you do not.

Drainage systems

81 | *Our block of four houses has drains that link up before joining the main drain in the road. There is a crack in our part of the drain. How do we share the expense of repair?*

The main drain is repaired at the public expense, but many houses share a length of private drain which is the owners' responsibility. Check with the local council or the water authority where the main drain begins, because it is possible that some of it may be laid under private land before it reaches the road.

When you share a private drain, the owners of all the houses connected to it must share the cost of repairs. Unfortunately, it is often not clear what the contributions should be. It is also often left in the air who is responsible for seeing that the work is done. The best thing to do, when it becomes clear that work is needed, is to contact all the owners who share the drain and agree on the procedure and contributions before the repairs are carried out.

82 | *My house has its own drainage system to a septic tank in my garden. I am told that if I build an extension, with a new bathroom and kitchen, the local authority may insist on my joining up to the main drain. Is that possible?*

When you build an extension, or a new house, the local authority can demand that it is drained into an existing sewer if certain requirements are met. These requirements are that: the sewer must be within 100 feet; the respective levels of the house and the sewer must make that drainage feasible; and you must have the right to construct a drain on the land that lies in between (if the land belongs to someone else who refuses to grant you the right to put a drain through it, then you do not have to connect up).

The main advantage of private drainage such as you have currently is that you are not liable to pay the drainage charge, which is levied with the water rate. But if you have a private system which has to be emptied periodically by the local authority, the authority is allowed to make a charge for that service and generally does so.

83 | *My house in the country drains to a septic tank on land belonging to the neighbour who sold me the house, and receives water through a pipe across his land. If he sells his property, do I risk having my pipes disconnected by the new owner?*

As a general rule, you acquire a right to use pipes or wires going through or over someone else's land in a form which entitles you to continue using them even if the ownership of the adjoining property changes hands (an 'easement'). The right is yours either by express agreement from the other property owner or from long use without challenge.

In your case, an easement arose immediately you bought, even if there was no express agreement. The law assumes that your neighbour who sold you the property gave you the right to carry on using the facility which the property already had laid on. Those rights automatically include the right to go on to his land to carry out any necessary repairs. You will have to pay for those repairs, and you are also responsible for making good any damage on his land which your work causes. These arrangements for repairs apply both if the easement is given by express agreement or if it comes from long use.

Some people in the country have a metered water supply, not direct from the mains but from perhaps a neighbouring farm. The arrangement then is normally that you have the right to the water so long as you pay the charges. The law enforces a conditional arrangement, which means that if you fail to pay you have no right to use the pipe through the other owner's property.

Rights of way

84 | *I have the right to go along a rear passage to the back of my garden. Each house in the road owns the section of it alongside the back garden. Some people's sections are in a very poor state, and others almost block it with parked cars. What can be done about the potholes and the cars?*

What you have is a private right of way along the passage-way. It is quite possible for a number of people to have separate private rights of way over the same land. As far as repairs are concerned, the rule is always the same for rights of way (unless a special agreement has been entered into): the owner of the land itself has no obligation to repair it, even if it gradually becomes impassable. The others who have the right to use the passage can do the repairs at their own expense if they want to.

On the other hand, the landowner is not entitled to obstruct the right of way. Even though it is his own property, the existence of the right of way means that what he is allowed to do with it is limited, and he cannot prevent those with the right of way from exercising their right of way. If the obstruction is serious, and persuasion is of no avail, the court will grant an injunction to stop the obstruction.

85 | *I am modernising an old cottage in the country. If services have to be brought across other people's land, can I insist they allow me to?*

Electricity boards have the power to compel landowners to let them run lines across their land. Generally, they try to reach agreement and to accommodate the wishes of landowners. But the threat of compulsion is always in the background. If poles are erected by agreement, the agreements generally say that the landowner can terminate the agreement. If he does so, the board can insist on keeping the poles there if necessary.

You cannot force the adjoining owner to have poles on his land, so you would have to work through the electricity board, persuading it to use its powers if it proves to be necessary.

Until recently, there have been no equivalent arrangements for telephone wires. Now, statute provides a principle that everyone should have a reasonable right to have telecommunications services, and landowners have to allow facilities to cross their land if they can reasonably do so.

Water authorities have power to insist on laying mains if a landowner's consent is unreasonably withheld. Laying gas mains for long distances in the country is impractical and uneconomic so this is unlikely to arise.

86 | Part of the land around my house consists of a field crossed by a public footpath. Am I entitled to stop people riding horses along it?

Yes. Public footpaths are for people exclusively on foot. Make sure, though, that the path is not a public bridleway, along which people are entitled to ride as well as walk. Apart from these two public rights of way, there is a third – public roads, which are open to all traffic.

Official maps are deposited with the local authorities' planning departments defining where public rights of way run, and which type each of them is. The information is also reproduced on 1:50,000 scale Ordnance Survey maps.

87 | The lease of my flat does not actually mention that I have the right to use the stairs and the lift to come and go. Presumably I have a right of way even though I have no agreement and have used it for only a short time?

It is more satisfactory if access arrangements are set out in the lease of a flat, but there is no need to worry if they are not. You have what is called an 'easement of necessity', which means that you have a right to use the means of access which there happens to be because without them your property would be useless. In a high block of flats, this covers both the stairs and the lift; in a lower block it could be that you would not be able to insist on using the lift because it is not then strictly a necessity.

The major benefit of having access arrangements expressly set out in the lease is that it is possible to impose restrictions for the benefit of all the flatowners, by keeping visitors' cars to certain areas and imposing one-way traffic schemes, for instance.

88 | Do I have to allow other flatowners into my flat to repair the electric wiring serving their flats?

This is the sort of thing which is usually dealt with expressly in the lease of a flat. The arrangement generally is that you have to give them access to your flat. Unless there is an emergency, they probably have to give you notice that they need to come in. They will be responsible for any damage which they may cause. The rights of access will no doubt be reciprocal, allowing you to go into other flats when that is needed for repair to your flat.

Even in the absence of arrangements in the lease, the general rule applies that where someone has the right to services through pipes and wires running through someone else's property – and it applies just as much to another flat as to someone's field – they have a right to enter that property to do repairs.

There will also be a right for other people to enter your flat to do more general repairs. Again, the lease probably says in so many words that whoever is responsible for the main structure of the building, which is probably the freeholder or a management company, can come in to do work if that proves necessary. Even if it does not say so, the very fact that in your lease they agree to do the work necessarily implies that they have that right.

Trespass

89 | I'm entitled, aren't I, to decide who comes into my property and to keep everyone else out?

Traditionally it was certainly true that anyone you did not want to come into your home, or on to your land, was a trespasser whom you were allowed to keep out or to evict. That is still the basic law, but there are a large number of exceptions. Most of the exceptions concern people whom you have agreed shall come in, even though you may not realise you have given them your permission.

Even a landlord has no automatic right to go into a property once it is let to a tenant unless the tenancy agreement reserves that right. Any well-drawn agreement will say that the landlord is entitled to go in for a number of reasons – to repair it, to see that the tenant is doing the repairs allocated to him or her, to show round prospective new tenants, to check on the furniture if it is a furnished letting, and so on. These are really examples of granting permission to someone to go in, not on a particular date but in general terms in advance.

More obvious invitations to enter are having friends in to tea, say. The law is that because you do not have any bargain with them, you can withdraw your invitation and ask them to leave at any time. When the permission to come in is part of a contract – which it is in the case of a tenancy agreement – you cannot withdraw it while that bargain is still in force.

90 | Can you give examples of cases of property owners giving consent for people to come on to their land, probably without realising it?

Obvious cases are those of people who come by arrangement with you to make deliveries – the milkman, the postman and the paper boy. They are entitled to come up your drive, but not into the house unless you particularly invite them.

A number of contracts which you enter into carry with them authority to enter your house. If you read the small print of a television hiring agreement, you will usually find that a company representative is allowed to come to check that you still have the set. By statute, gas and electricity board officers can come in. This is generally for safety reasons, but it is a condition of your having the supply.

Then there are the cases of people who are permitted to come in even though you may object. This class includes a policeman who is chasing a criminal or who has a search warrant or a warrant to arrest someone who is there. Similarly, a court bailiff who has a warrant to seize goods in settlement of a court judgment can enter. There are a number of other officials who can also come in under the right circumstances. The valuation officer can come in to look round to value the property for rating purposes, and the medical officer of health can come if someone there has had certain infectious diseases.

91 | I take it that a trespasser has no protection when he is on my property. Am I entitled to lay traps to deter any intruders?

As an occupier you owe a duty of care to all visitors to keep your property reasonably safe. Since 1984 this duty has been owed also to trespassers where the occupier knows of the danger. The occupier must take such care as is reasonable in all the circumstances to ensure that a trespasser does not suffer injury as a result of the danger.

You certainly must not lay traps to deter any intruders. If you make your property deliberately hazardous and someone, even a burglar, is hurt you will be liable to compensate him.

If you have some outbuildings on your premises which are in a dilapidated and dangerous condition, you can protect yourself against liability to adult trespassers by displaying a notice warning of the risks of entering.

92 | My next door neighbour habitually jumps over the fence separating the two gardens, then runs across our garden and into the street to avoid a longer journey through his own front door. Despite my requests, he keeps doing it. Can I get the police involved?

No. Your neighbour is trespassing on your property, and you are entitled to object, but it is not a criminal matter. You are allowed to bar your neighbour's way, and even physically throw him off your land. It is probably better, however, to take him to the county court to stop him trespassing. The primary remedy you have against any trespasser is a claim for damages, but as that is limited to the cost of damage done you might receive only a nominal sum. When faced with repeated trespasses, as you are, you should ask the court for an injunction – an order to your neighbour that he stops taking the short cut. Disobedience of an injunction is a contempt of court, which could have serious consequences for him.

93 | Can I call the police to deal with squatters who have moved in to a flat I've just bought?

Traditionally, simply trespassing without causing damage or intending to steal was not a police matter. However, the law was changed in order to cope with the rash of squatting in empty properties in the 1970s. In law, squatters are merely trespassers in someone else's property. The fact that they are homeless, or they wish to register some kind of protest, makes no difference to the legal position.

Squatters who go into property as trespassers and then refuse to leave if the person who previously lived there requests it are committing an offence. The same applies if someone who has just bought the house or flat in order to live there makes the request for the squatters to leave. The criminal law is therefore protecting someone who is temporarily absent from his or her home and returns to find squatters in occupation, and someone who buys a property which should be empty but discovers that squatters have taken it over.

The real help which this gives the property owner is not so much the fact that the squatters may incur a punishment but that both offences are ones for which a policeman in uniform can arrest the offenders. As soon as they are arrested, the home owner's major problem is solved. If squatters do damage while they are in occupation, you can sue them for damages to obtain compensation, but in practice it is rarely likely that this will be worth while.

94 | *A tenant who stays on after his tenancy has expired is a trespasser, isn't he? Can I evict him as one?*

Apart from the criminal offence that squatters commit, a landowner has always been able to throw a trespasser off his land physically, using the minimum force and using the shortest practicable route. This right still exists, *except* in the case of almost all tenants who overstay their time. So the answer to the question is no. Some tenants who stay on become statutory tenants and do not have to go at all. Most of the others are entitled to stay until a court order for possession is made against them, and then the court bailiffs will evict them if necessary. For the property-owner to exercise self-help against them is a criminal offence.

Liability

95 | *The girl who delivers our papers fell off her bicycle and hurt herself on our drive. Are we responsible?*

Every occupier of property has a duty to ensure that it is reasonably safe for the people who are there by permission or who have a right to be there. That does not mean that every time someone hurts him- or herself you must be liable; liability depends on why the accident happened. If the reason in this case is that you have neglected repairs which you know or should have known were needed to the drive, then it is your fault. If you had done all you could reasonably be expected to have done, then no blame attaches to you.

You are entitled to assume that people will take reasonable care. If you know that one of the steps up to your front door is broken and hazardous, it may be enough to put up a notice saying 'Mind the step', assuming that there is somewhere else that callers can tread. But if you know it is likely that children who have not yet learned to read will use the steps on their own, a written notice is obviously no protection for you.

Rates

96 | *How is the rateable value of my house fixed?*

The rateable value represents the rent which a landlord could have expected at the date the value was fixed had the property then been let on a yearly tenancy under which the landlord was responsible for repairs. That figure is reduced by an allowance for the cost of repairs. The allowance is on a fixed scale, and has no relation to the actual cost of the repairs which happen to have been required.

The last general valuation of property for rating purposes took place in 1973. Properties built since then, which have been rated when they were finished, are intended to be valued on the same basis, so that all homes are rated in a comparable way. It was originally the intention that there should be a general revaluation, to bring the rateable values up to date, once every five years. The statutory requirement for this has been repealed.

The amount of the general rate which you have to pay to the local authority is the result of applying the rate in the pound which the authority fixes each year to the rateable value of your house.

97 | *My house has a higher rateable value than the others in the road. How do I get mine reduced?*

You can appeal against the amount of your rateable value by making a proposal to the valuation officer (an Inland Revenue official) to change it. Valuation Offices are listed in telephone directories under Inland Revenue. You obviously have to have grounds to back up your appeal. These might be, for example, that strictly comparable properties in the locality have materially different values, that your home is now worth less than it was because recent development has reduced its amenities, or that major works like motorway construction are depressing its value. In that last sort of case, the possible reduction in rateable value would be only temporary and would last only as long as the effect of which you were complaining lasted.

98 | *The local authority charges far too much rate in the pound. How can I challenge it?*

There is no right of appeal against the amount of the rate in the pound (although you could try forming a pressure group and lobbying your local council). A few homes will have the benefit of the concessions made to charities for properties used for the purposes of the charity rather than merely as investments. This might apply, for example, to almshouses and to houses for staff on school premises. Charities are entitled as of right to a reduction of rates by a half, and local authorities are empowered to excuse them from paying the other half.

99 | If I cannot agree a change in my rateable value with the valuation officer, where can I appeal?

Although many changes are settled by negotiation with the valuation officer, you have a right to take the matter to the local valuation court. If that gets you nowhere, you can appeal in turn to the specialist land valuation court, the Lands Tribunal (address on page 510), and so also can the valuation officer if he is not satisfied with the result. Points of law can then be taken to the Court of Appeal and even to the House of Lords.

Rating law tends to be very technical. The local valuation court is informal, but it is still bound by the rules of this branch of the law. Some surveyors specialise in this type of valuation, and it is often advisable to obtain advice from one in advance.

If you are successful in having your rateable value reduced, the reduction will normally take effect from the beginning of the rating year (1 April) in which you made your proposal, and anything you have overpaid will be refunded by the council.

100 | Can my rateable value be put up if I improve my house?

In the same way as you can apply at any time to have your rateable value reduced, you may receive a proposal for its increase. If you carry out improvements, like building an extension, it is likely that you will receive one, both because a higher value will be justified and also because the council will have been notified of the work being done under the Building Regulations (see Q68).

There are certain concessions of which you may be able to take advantage, which are intended to prevent people being deterred from making small improvements from fear that an increase in rates will make them too costly. No increase results from installing central heating. Also, a structural alteration that would have resulted in the *gross* value – that is, the valuation before the notional deduction for repairs – going up by no more than £30 is ignored. These concessions may not be permanent. If there is a general revaluation for rating purposes of all properties, they will be valued as they then stand, including all improvements.

101 | My husband is disabled and we need to adapt our flat to make it easier for him to get

around in his wheelchair. Will we be penalised by an increase in rates?

There are special dispensations for the disabled. Under a special statute, amounts can be deducted from the rateable value of a home to counteract the effect of any improvements that have had to be made simply to accommodate the disabled. Deductions can be made for any extra bathroom, lavatory or other room provided to meet a disabled person's needs, floor space provided to accommodate a wheelchair, and for a garage, car port or parking area for a disabled person's vehicle. There can also be a discount for central heating or other facilities provided for the needs of a disabled person. It need not be the ratepayer in person (normally the head of the household) who is disabled, but the facilities must be specifically geared to the disabled person's requirements.

102 | Is there any settled rule as to who pays the rates if you let a house or flat? Is it the landlord or the tenant?

The landlord and the tenant should arrange this between them. When the tenant pays the rates, the rent is called 'exclusive'; when the landlord pays, the term is 'inclusive'. In practice, inclusive rents are fairly common on very short-term lettings and in the case of furnished tenancies. Most other tenancies are now let on exclusive rents.

When a rent officer registers a fair rent (see Q15), it is always on an exclusive basis. If a particular tenant happens to pay an inclusive rent, that bargain with the landlord is not overridden. The tenant simply has to pay the rates in addition to the registered rent. That means that whenever there is a change in the amount of rates, the inclusive rent changes with it, but there does not have to be any adjustment to the fair rent. To that extent, the fair rent is not the maximum payable to the landlord. If this applies, the register is noted to that effect.

As far as the rating authority is concerned, it is the person who is in possession who is primarily liable to pay the rates. That means that it is possible for a landlord who receives an inclusive rent to fail to pay the element representing the rates over to the council, and the tenant can be faced with a demand from them which represents an amount he has already paid to the landlord. That is not a defence to the council's claim, but the tenant has a statutory right to deduct from future rent payments any rates which he has to pay direct to the council. As an alternative, the council does have the right to proceed directly against a landlord who receives an inclusive rent.

217

The reason why some landlords opt to pay the rates in respect of properties which they let is that they can obtain discounts from the council. There are usually three possibilities. The greatest reduction is under an agreement to pay whether the property is empty or occupied, the next for payment only when it is occupied, and the smallest reduction simply for collecting rates on the council's behalf. There used to be standard amounts of discount, but councils are now empowered to fix the figures locally.

103 | What happens if I do not pay my rates?

Rating authorities have a statutory right to a special procedure for collecting unpaid rates, which is the one which they usually adopt if you ignore their final demand. They apply to the local magistrates' court for a warrant that authorises them to 'distrain'. That means that they send a bailiff round to seize your belongings which he finds in your home, and they are sold to raise the money which is due if you do not then pay. If you let matters get to that stage, but you pay to avoid goods being seized, you will find that the sum due has increased because the court and bailiffs' expenses are added to the rates due.

All councils have to offer householders the chance to pay their rates by 'monthly' instalments – normally they are spread over ten months of the year, nothing being payable in March or April when the following year's figures are being calculated.

104 | I am in the process of buying a house. How can I be sure that the former owner has paid all the rates he should have done, and that I shall not be faced with a bill for his share?

Although rates are a payment which is calculated by reference to the value of each individual property, and they are payable by whoever happens to be the owner of it, the liability for anything unpaid does not pass from one owner to the next. Statutory liability attaches to the person who is in occupation of the property for the length of time he or she is actually there.

In practice, arrangements for rates are normally made on the completion of the sale of the property, when it changes hands and the purchaser pays the vendor for it. The vendor will commonly have made an advance payment of rates. His solicitor notifies the local authority of the date of the changeover, and the authority calculates whatever refund is due and then pays it. If, on the other hand, something more is due from the vendor, the authority asks for payment direct.

The same procedure is not so common in the case of water charges (rates), mainly because the sums involved are smaller, so that it is uneconomic for the water authorities to become involved in the calculation and repayments. The solicitors for the vendor and the purchaser therefore agree a proper apportionment, and adjust the total sum payable for the house or flat to reflect this. If the vendor has paid in advance, he receives a little extra to cover the period he has paid for but during which he will not be the owner. If the water charges are overdue, the whole bill may be handed to the purchaser, who is given the appropriate allowance against the price to compensate him.

105 | If the occupier of property is the one who is liable to pay rates, does that mean that nothing is due for property which is empty?

Local authorities can decide what charge of rates is made on empty properties. Some do not charge any rates, anyhow on houses and flats, however long they are empty. Others charge half the normal amount of rates after the property has been empty for three months. The rating department of the local council will tell you what the position is in your area.

If you take over somewhere which has been empty for at least three months, then the free period has been used up and you have to start paying right away even though there is some delay before you move in. If, however, you do substantial work on the property, so that it is temporarily incapable of being occupied, then rates will not be payable while that work is being done.

Strangely, the position if you have squatters in a house has not been settled, and it is possible in some circumstances for an owner who has been excluded by the squatters to remain liable for rates.

106 | *What appeal procedure is there to reduce the amount of water charges which I have to pay?*

There is no independent appeal procedure in relation to water charges (rates). Water charges are based on the same rateable value of your house or flat as are general rates. If that rateable value is varied, it automatically also has the result of changing the amount of water charges for which you are liable. Some authorities do now offer you the alternative of paying for the amount of water which you consume, measured by a meter, rather than paying on the rating system. This would benefit a small family living in a large house with a high rateable value.

Although the arrangements vary from area to area, other charges are commonly collected along with the water charges. These are drainage charges, which are payments for being connected to the main drains. If you are not connected to the main drain, because you have a septic tank, for instance, there is no obligation to pay this. A charge payable by everyone, which may be a part of the drainage charge or may be noted separately, is an environmental charge which relates to river maintenance and major land drainage in the area.

Domestic consumers who use extra water, for example, a hosepipe or sprinkler, are charged more. It is an offence for which you can be prosecuted to use those facilities without declaring them and without paying the extra charge.

107 | *My house is deep in the country – so much so that my local authority will not collect my household rubbish. Shouldn't this service be available to all ratepayers?*

All local authorities have a basic duty to collect household waste in their area, and to do so free of charge to the householder (the service is paid for out of the rates). There is, however, an exception: they do not have to collect rubbish from you if they consider that your house is so isolated or inaccessible that the collection cost would be unreasonably high, and if they are satisfied that you have made or can be expected to make adequate disposal arrangements.

The authorities are also entitled to dictate what type of receptacle you put your rubbish into. For example, many councils nowadays require it to be put in plastic sacks; in blocks of flats there may be large bins that are specially adapted for use with lorries with a mechanism that picks them up to empty them. It is an offence for which you can be prosecuted and fined not to use the receptacles specified by the council.

Mortgages

108 | *There seem to be various types of mortgage available. Which is the best?*

It is impossible to recommend one type of mortgage rather than another as necessarily better. Everything depends upon your own circumstances. The choice also seems to increase as time goes on.

The traditional type of mortgage for home buyers is the 'annuity' or repayment mortage. Under this, you pay the lender a fixed amount monthly. That sum is a combination of interest and capital repayment. Its amount is worked out so that if the mortgage runs for the full period originally arranged, the whole loan will be repaid. Necessarily, at the beginning of the period only a very small part of each instalment is a capital repayment, and the bulk is interest. This gradually adjusts itself over the years. However, as a national average people move house every six or seven years, and as most mortgages are taken out for 20-year terms few of them reach the time when a lot of capital is being repaid. When the house or flat is sold the rest of the loan is repaid out of the proceeds of the sale.

The main alternative mortgage system is one supported by some form of endowment assurance. The simplest example of this is a 20-year mortgage under which interest only and no capital repayment is paid to the mortgagee. At the same time a 20-year endowment assurance policy is taken out, which pays to the mortgagee the whole of the sum borrowed at the end of 20 years or if the borrower dies earlier. The borrower assigns the right for the proceeds of the policy to go to the mortgagee at the end of the period. That is the way in which the loan is repaid.

There are variations on that endowment assurance system. Ingenious combinations of policies make it possible for borrowers to reduce their cost of a mortgage like that, which can otherwise be appreciably higher than an annuity mortgage, particularly if they choose a with-profits endowment policy.

Some local authorities and some building societies offer low-start mortgages specially designed for first-time buyers. Typically, this delays the need for any capital repayment for the first five years, so that during that time the borrower has to pay only the mortgage interest and no capital. There are even schemes which reduce the interest paid for that initial period. Clearly this is helpful in reducing the amount which has to be paid out, but the borrower should remember that the less that is paid at the beginning the more that has to be paid later. If nothing has been paid off the loan, there will be more to be deducted from the price received when the property is sold, leaving less for the next place purchased.

109 | What financial help can I expect when I take on a mortgage?

All mortgages up to a ceiling of £30,000 for each single person or married couple (and see LIVING TOGETHER, Q36) are paid under a system known as MIRAS (mortgage interest relief at source), provided you borrow from one of the usual lending institutions like a building society. This means that your interest payments – but not anything that you pay to reduce the outstanding amount of the loan – are reduced by the percentage of the basic rate of income tax. In effect, this gives income tax relief for the interest payments to everyone at the standard rate. If your circumstances are such that you pay less income tax than that relief amounts to, you have the benefit of the reduction all the same.

Anyone who pays income tax at the higher rates is able to set off their mortgage interest against those higher rates as well.

For first-time buyers, there is a subsidy scheme for those who think about it when they start saving. If you save regularly for two years with a bank or building society, you qualify for a cash bonus and a small interest-free loan for five years when you come to buy. One point to be watched is that there is a limit on the cost of the house or flat which you can buy under the scheme. The price limits depend on the area of the country, and they are adjusted from time to time to take account of changes in the general level of house prices.

110 | How does a building society decide how much it will lend on a mortgage?

This depends on two factors: the value of the house or flat and how much you earn. Statute obliges building societies to have a valuation of any property on which they lend money, so they always instruct a surveyor to inspect and report. He normally gives a brief summary of the condition of the property, and may well recommend repairs that need doing, but his main job is to assess what its value is. It is not uncommon for that valuation to be less than the amount which you have agreed to pay. The building society normally has a policy limiting the proportion of the value of a property which they are prepared to lend. Occasionally, this is as high as 95 or 100 per cent, but it is more commonly 90 per cent, falling to 80 per cent on property built before 1919. The society applies that percentage to the valuation given

by the surveyor, not to your agreed price, which explains why the amount you are offered is sometimes less than the amount you want.

Building societies also assess how much you will be able to afford to repay, and they have a rule-of-thumb formula for assessment. Commonly, building societies will lend two and a quarter or two and a half times your annual salary, before tax and other deductions. If two of you in the family are earning and you are buying jointly, at least part of the second salary is generally taken into account, but the practice of societies about that is less settled.

Where you have sufficient income to support repayments on the amount of mortgage loan that you want, but the valuation of the property does not justify your getting the full sum, there may be ways to bump it up. The society may agree to take out a special type of guarantee insurance policy. For a single-premium payment, the insurance company agrees that if you fail to pay what you should so that the society has to resort to the property to obtain repayment, and when sold the property does not fetch as much as necessary, the insurance company will bridge the gap. The policy is solely for the society's benefit, but you have to pay the premium on it. Another possibility is that if you have some other form of savings, such as an endowment policy which already has a surrender value, the building society will accept this as additional back-up security.

111 | What happens to my mortgage if I die before I have repaid the loan?

Death does not by itself cancel a mortgage loan. The money still has to be repaid to the building society or any other lender. If you have an endowment insurance mortgage, the policy will pay the amount needed to repay the loan, and as the payment is made to the lender the mortgage will be repaid. You can achieve the same effect by taking out a mortgage protection insurance policy when you obtain the loan, a policy which is linked to an annuity mortgage. Because, under that kind of mortgage, the amount which you owe to the lender gradually reduces, the amount secured by the policy goes down in the same way. This has two results: the policy is cheaper, because the amount of money which the premiums have to cover gets less; but, on the other hand, if the mortgage runs for the full term the amount secured by the policy goes down to nil and you never receive any return for the premiums you paid. This is a good way to provide security for dependants, because they have a house or flat free from a mortgage if you die, but it is not a form of saving.

The automatic security which someone who lends money on a mortgage has is that whenever the house or flat is sold the lender can demand repayment of what is owing. Because the lender holds the deeds of the property, it cannot be sold without the lender's co-operation. This applies just as much after the death of the borrower. For a single person without dependants this means that there is no need to make special arrangements to ensure that the mortgage is repaid on death. If you are in this position, you can merely assume that when you die the property will be sold, and any surplus will go to the beneficiaries of your estate.

112 | *I have two possible sources of finance to pay for the central heating I am proposing to install: I can either get a further mortgage from the building society who lent me the money to buy the house, or a second mortgage arranged through the installers. Is there any essential difference?*

There is a definite legal difference between a further mortgage and a second mortgage, and it has a practical effect which you should watch.

A further mortgage, sometimes called a further advance, is an extra loan by the company, such as a building society, that originally gave you a mortgage loan. It still has the house as security; all it is doing is topping up what you owe it. It may be possible to do that with little or no documentation if the original mortgage contemplated the possibility of later loans. If another document is needed, there does not have to be much formality, because the building society already has the deeds.

A second mortgage, on the other hand, is a loan made by someone quite new. The company has to make all the investigations about your ownership of the house from scratch. That is bound to make the formalities more expensive, and you as borrower will be expected to pay the lender's costs. More serious is the situation if the lender has to have recourse to your house because you fail to pay what is due. That is when the significance of your having a 'second' mortgage becomes apparent. The lender is second in the queue to be paid from the proceeds of any sale. The original lender is entitled to be paid in full, not only the balance of the loan, but also any outstanding interest, legal costs, and anything else that may be owing. If the price the house makes when sold is enough to cover all that and what you owe the second lender, there is no difficulty. If not, the second lender suffers the shortfall. Although you still owe the money, and no doubt the lender would press for

payment, it does not have the security of being paid from the house proceeds. For that reason the interest rate that lenders charge for second mortgages is considerably higher than it is for first mortgages.

113 | *I run my own business, and I need an overdraft in that connection. The bank is happy to give it to me by taking the deeds of my house, which is in my name only, as security. The bank has asked my wife to sign the mortgage as well, even though she is not named as an owner. Is this in order?*

It is quite possible for someone who contributes financially to the cost of a house to be in effect a part owner of it, even if this is not recorded on the deeds. This commonly occurs between husband and wife – when the contribution may be an indirect one arising from their contribution to the joint household – but there are other situations that occur often enough. Grandparents contribute to the costs of a house which provides them with accommodation, and a trust fund set up for a couple's children pays for some of the costs of housing the family. When someone who has made a contribution of that type is actually living in the house, the very fact that they are there safeguards their interest.

If a house belonging to a married couple is in the name of one of them – and it does not matter whether it is the husband or the wife – and he or she mortgages it without reference to the other, the lender takes into account that other partner's rights. If you default on the loan and the bank wants to sell the house, it could find itself stymied by your wife's claiming priority over them. For that reason, careful lenders now ask that anyone else who lives in the house should sign the mortgage, either agreeing that they do not have an interest in it or confirming that they agree that any interest they have should be subordinated to the lender's.

114 | *I am the owner of a long lease of my house, and I am proposing to buy the freehold. Am I entitled to a mortgage?*

You do not have a guaranteed right to any mortgage, but there will rarely be any difficulty in obtaining one. It is generally accepted that the cost of leasehold enfranchisement (see Q2) is favourable to the leaseholder, so a building society or other lender should accept the price. If you already have a mortgage for buying the lease, you will probably be able to borrow from the same source and combine the two interests and the two mortgages.

115 | *What exactly happens if I cannot keep up my mortgage payments?*

Lenders are generally reluctant to take enforcement action against their borrowers, and they normally respond to suggestions for reducing the size of payments and so lengthening the period of the mortgage, or even suspending payments for a time if that is likely to put things right.

Nevertheless, the lender's last resort is to 'realise his security', which means selling your house. To do so effectively, they have to sell it vacant, which means you have to leave; the lender will get a court order to evict you if necessary. You do not have to go unless they obtain a county court order. The court has wide powers to delay making a possession order, and will certainly do so if it looks likely that within a reasonable time what is due to the lender will be paid. Frequently, the lender's application for possession of the house is adjourned on condition that the borrower pays specified instalments.

Should the lender come to sell, it is not entitled to make a profit, and it has to make reasonable efforts to get a good price. After the lender has been fully repaid, and any second mortgage (see QI12) paid, any balance belongs to you, the borrower. On the other hand, if there is not enough to pay all the debts, you will have to pay from other resources.

116 | *Instead of selling a house which someone has failed to pay the mortgage on, can the lender simply take the house over for its own purposes?*

The process of a lender becoming owner of a mortgaged house when the borrower falls into arrears is called 'foreclosure'. It has always been hedged around with safeguards, and normally a court will first make only a preliminary order to the lender, giving the borrower six months to pay what is due in order to save his house before confirming the order. Foreclosure is only possible by court order.

On top of that, there is express statutory protection in the case of the mortgage of a house. As in the case of a lender who wants to sell, the county court has power to delay the case if by doing so it looks reasonably possible that the borrower will be able to retrieve the situation. This protection for house owners is not sacrificed merely because the borrower also uses his house for business purposes.

If a council tenant who bought by exercising his or her right to buy (see QI0), and who had a mortgage from the council, then defaults, there are special statutory powers for the council to take the house back. In effect this is a foreclosure, but the difference is that any surplus value goes to the borrower, as it would have done on a sale. The property is valued, and then not only is what the borrower owes deducted, but also any discount that was allowed on the original sale and which he would have to repay had he been selling then. Anything left over belongs to the borrower.

117 | *My mortgage application form says that I must arrange to insure the property through the building society, and not make my own arrangements. Can it validly impose such a condition?*

In theory, this is a matter of the bargain between you and the building society. In practice, you will find no way in which you can escape from this requirement, except in the case of a leasehold property where the freeholder insists on other arrangements.

The standard form of building society mortgage will contain a clause in which you agree to insure through the society. It is reasonable for any lender to require insurance, because if the house or flat is damaged or destroyed its security is lost, and it is quite likely that without insurance you would not be able to rebuild. If the building society arranges the insurance, and merely applies to you for the premium, it has the reassurance of knowing that the policy is in force, and knowing its terms. There is also a commercial reason for its insistence that it arranges the policy: building societies have commission arrangements with insurance companies, and make a good deal of money that way.

It used to be the case that you had no choice of insurer, because the building society merely dictated the company it had chosen. Now, by agreement with the Director General of Fair Trading, the societies have agreed to give borrowers a choice.

118 | *My building society demands that I do woodworm eradication work to the house I am buying before it will make its loan. Obviously I*

have no right to go in the property before I have bought it, and I cannot buy without the building society mortgage. How do I resolve this dilemma?

The first thing to do is to ask the present owner's permission to go in to do the work before you have completed the purchase. If the house is at present empty, and if the work you have in mind would be an improvement – which most building society demands would be – it is quite possible that the vendor will agree. You run the risk that you are pouring money into someone else's property, so you certainly should not do that before there is a binding contract, and sure that the house will become yours. If the vendor gives you permission, it will almost certainly be on condition that you do not move in and live there.

If the present owner is still living in the house, he may refuse your request just because he might not want workmen in the house. What you can then do is to approach the building society and ask that they hand over the loan in the usual way but hold back a reasonable amount until the work is done by you later. Many building society loans are made subject to a retention in this way.

Failing all else, you may have to arrange a bridging loan from a bank to stretch between completing the contract and when the work has been done.

Because you will have your building society mortgage offer before you exchange contracts, it should be possible to decide upon your course of action in advance. If you present the vendor with an ultimatum that he must agree to your having the work done before completion, or you cannot buy the house, he may well agree.

Insurance

119 | *How should I decide how much to insure my house for?*

When you first buy a house or flat, the building society will often suggest a figure based on the recommendation of their valuer. If you employ your own surveyor, you should ask him.

The principle is that you should insure for the full rebuilding cost. That may well be different from the market price, for two reasons. First, although a house can completely burn down, the land on which it is erected will never burn and will have some remaining value. Second, an old-fashioned house with high ceilings and complicated features from another era may cost much more to reproduce today than it is worth second-hand. All the same, that is the proper insurance figure.

Do not be tempted to insure for a great deal more than your property is worth as a gamble so that you would make a handsome profit if it was destroyed. That policy would count as a wager in law, and you would not be entitled to recover any surplus, because the contract would be void to that extent.

120 | *Is there any difference in principle between insuring a house and insuring a flat?*

If there is serious damage to a flat, it is more than likely that at least one other flat will also be affected. Because of the complications which are likely to be involved if negotiations have to be carried on with more than one insurer, leases of flats normally insist that all leaseholders insure with the same company. This is either done by the lease specifying with whom the leaseholder must insure, or by the freeholder effecting one policy on the whole block and requiring the leaseholders of flats to reimburse the cost. This latter is probably most satisfactory, because there can be a single policy covering not only the flats but also the common parts of the block. The manner in which the premiums are divided has to be considered carefully. Even if the flats are identical, there is clearly an argument for saying that the higher ones are more expensive to rebuild, but normally the division is on an equal basis.

Also, in the same way that a lender wants to make sure that the borrower has insured, because otherwise his security is undermined, so a leaseholder of a flat needs to be sure that all the other flats are insured. If your flat is insured, so that you have the resources to rebuild in case of a fire, it is small consolation if the flat below was not and therefore cannot be reinstated.

121 | *If a house which is mortgaged is destroyed by fire, what is to stop the building society taking what is owed to it from the insurance money, leaving insufficient for rebuilding?*

Many building society mortgages contain terms that appear to give the society this right, although it would probably be unlikely to exercise such terms against the borrower's will. Also, there is an eighteenth-century statute which may help. What it says is that if any property is damaged or destroyed by fire, any interested party can insist that the proceeds of any insurance policy on it are used for rebuilding rather than anything else. On the face of it, that appears to be what is wanted. The difficulties are: it relates only to fire and not to any other risk which may damage a building, and it does not cope with the position where the policy money is not in fact enough to cover the work that is needed. The owner might be better off selling the plot, repaying the mortgage, and buying another house by taking out a new mortgage on it in the normal way. This would also avoid the possibly considerable delay while the building work takes place.

122 | *My house was seriously damaged by fire, and insurance was arranged through a building society. The insurance company is refusing to pay out, using the excuse that many years ago I had a conviction for theft which it says it's only just discovered. The company never asked anything about this before, and anyhow I don't see its relevance. Can the insurance company refuse to pay?*

Insurance policies are a special kind of contract, and the rule is that anyone taking out insurance must voluntarily disclose to the insurance company anything he knows which might affect a prudent insurer in deciding whether to accept the proposal for a policy and what premium to charge. The connection between such things as convictions for theft and house insurance is hard to see, but the courts have in the past accepted that that sort of thing comes within the scope of this duty to disclose. The duty certainly applies even though the company never asked you expressly whether you had any convictions, and even where you were not even asked to fill in a proposal form.

It seems that your failure to disclose something which is considered to be relevant could deprive the building society of any money claimed under the insurance. On the face of it, it looks as if nothing will be paid out to anyone. But the courts have decided that it is possible to look at a policy as two different ones: the first protecting the borrower and the second protecting the lender, each for their respective stakes in the house. So the building society policy is not cancelled by your lack of frankness, but all the insurance company will pay out is the amount of the loan due to the building society.

123 | *Can you tell me what a 'flood' is? When snow melted, water covered our cellar floor not because of a river bursting its banks but because of a rise in the normal water table of the soil. Our insurance company says that that will not necessarily give us a claim for damage by flood, which the policy covers.*

The risks covered by insurance policies are construed very precisely. In the case of flood, water seeping in in the manner you've described – or from an underground stream – does not come within the term, and the company may well not pay under the clause that covers flood damage. 'Flood' seems to apply to a build-up of water on the surface outside the property – as happens when a river overflows – which then bursts in.

Another example of the very narrow meanings given to policies is damage by 'heave'. This is a risk now included in most policies, because it is separate from subsidence, the clause most people used to claim under. Heave has the reverse effect of subsidence. If trees are cut down before a house is built, the wetness absorbed by the trees' roots remains in the soil, and the soil expands. The house can then be damaged by an upward movement of the soil.

124 | *Two of us are going to buy a house and put it in both our names. Will it be enough if I'm the only one to insure?*

If you buy any property jointly with someone else, it is essential to ensure that the insurance policy is taken out in both (or all) your names. Because of insurance companies' insistence on disclosure, you should both complete the proposal form and supply any other information which could possibly be pertinent. If one joint owner withholds something it is possible that the whole policy will prove to be invalid.

Estate agents

125 | *I want to sell my house in a hurry. It seems to me that two, or even three, estate agents acting for me must give me a better chance of doing so, rather than my employing just one. Can I avoid paying more than one commission?*

What you pay an estate agent, and how many of them you have to pay, is completely a matter of bargain between you. You are quite entitled to employ more than one, although an estate agent is equally entitled to insist that it is the only one to be instructed if it is to take your house or flat on, and in some parts of the country agents do so. There are various ways to instruct agents, and you should be clear in advance which system you are adopting.

If you appoint one agent as the sole agent, there is in fact nothing to stop you instructing other agents as well. But if one of those other agents sells the property you will be liable to pay commission to both that agent and your sole agent. Alternatively, many people feel that a sole agent acting alone has more incentive to sell the property. And you may get the

best of both worlds by allowing your sole agent to instruct sub-agents to act with him. This means that the sole agent you choose allows other agents to handle your house as well. Although this is not apparent to enquirers from those other agents, the agents are acting on behalf of the sole agent on a commission-sharing basis. You pay only what you agreed to pay the sole agent. An estate agent is not entitled to put your property into the hands of other agents without your permission.

There are two other ways to have more than one estate agent handling your house or flat. You can approach two agents and ask them to act in co-operation. Joint agents usually charge between them half as much again as one would have charged, so this will cost you more. You can also separately put your property in the hands of as many agents as you choose, making it clear to each of them that this is what you are doing, and that you will pay commission only to the one who introduces the eventual purchaser.

The danger of instructing a number of agents is that it is often not clear which firm introduced the purchaser. It is quite possible that the purchaser first gets interested as a result of one agent's advertisement, but finally comes to negotiate through seeing another agent's board outside the house. That situation can result in your having to pay twice.

If you give an agent 'sole selling rights', that means you have to pay commission when the property is sold. Even if you sell privately, without any help from the agent, you still have to pay.

Many properties sell very quickly. If yours does not, you may want to think again about the way you are going about it. For this reason, it is common for vendors to appoint one agent as sole agent for a limited period, for example, six weeks, and then perhaps to appoint more. This is quite common, and you should suggest it at the outset if you are in any doubt.

126 | *I have not yet received the price of my house from the purchaser, but the estate agent has sent in his bill. At what point is commission due?*

When you are liable to pay an estate agent is a matter of agreement between the two of you. A reputable estate agent will send you a letter confirming the arrangements which he explained verbally to you. Alternatively, you may be asked to sign a form of contract. In either case, you should be quite sure before you agree that the terms are what you want.

There are two times at which commission can be payable, and their effects are very different. Most agents work on the basis that their commission is due on completion of the sale, that is, when the purchaser pays the vendor for the property. In other words, if there is no sale, you pay no fee. This is the most satisfactory arrangement from the vendor's point of view, because not only does it mean that you pay only for service received, but nothing has to be paid until you have the money in hand.

The alternative is that the agent is entitled to payment as soon as a purchaser who is ready, able and willing to buy has been introduced. On the face of it, that sounds fair enough: all you need is someone who wants to go ahead and is prepared to pay the right price. But at any time up to the date that the contract is signed and binding, you or the purchaser can withdraw. If you, the vendor, do this when you have this sort of contract with an estate agent, you incur no obligation to the prospective buyer, but you have to pay the estate agent's commission as if the sale had gone through.

127 | *How much should I reckon to pay an estate agent to sell my house?*

There used to be a standard scale of commission charged by estate agents for selling houses and flats. This has been abandoned, and agents are now forbidden to enter into that sort of price-fixing arrangement.

Most agents charge commission calculated on the agreed sale price with the successful purchaser. Outside major city centres, commission rates of one and a half per cent to two and a half per cent are normal. City-centre agents, and national ones that usually handle substantial properties, may charge as much as four per cent. Some agents, like property shops that advertise only on display cards in their own shops, charge a fixed fee irrespective of the price of the property.

Selling by auction costs more. The agent's basic commission should be the same, but there will be fairly substantial expenses on top. These include advertising costs, including printing posters, and the fee to hire the room where the auction is held.

In agreeing an agent's charges for selling in the ordinary way, make sure whether expenses are included, or whether they must be added. You can expect to have included within the basic commission the duplication of particulars of your property, circulating those particulars to people on the agent's books, and a notice displayed in the agent's shop window. The position about newspaper advertising varies. Some agents agree to insert details twice in the local paper without passing the cost on to you.

Value added tax has to be paid on an agent's fees, and this is normally charged on top of the percentages quoted.

128 | *What does a house buyer have to pay to the estate agent who sells the house?*

Nothing. Estate agents are appointed by the owner to sell his house or flat, and they are working entirely for the vendor. Even if a successful agent offers a service to the purchaser – such as help in obtaining a mortgage – that is merely a way to help to sell the property and it does not mean that he is representing the purchaser. Because the agent represents only the vendor, it is the vendor alone who has to pay the commission.

It is important for prospective purchasers to understand that the agent does not, and cannot, represent them. However friendly and co-operative an agent is, he cannot offer any potential purchaser a particular favour – such as a right of first refusal – without the direct approval and instructions of the vendor himself. Agents always act on behalf of the vendor.

It is common enough for someone who finds a house through a particular agent to put his own house in the same agent's hands to sell. Although an estate agent cannot properly represent both sides to the same transaction, this is a normal and proper arrangement. In the case of each house, the agent represents only the vendor. The fact that the vendor of one is the purchaser of the other does not alter that.

129 | *The estate agent gave a false description of my house by stating there was enough land at the side to build a garage on. In fact, the space is about six inches too narrow and now the purchaser is complaining to me. Have I any responsibility for the agent's error?*

Yes. What the agent does he does on your behalf, and in law it counts as if you did it yourself. That means that you will normally be responsible for his mistakes, although you may be able to pass responsibility back to him. He has a duty to you to act as a competent estate agent should, and if he fails to perform to that standard and the result costs you money, he has a liability to compensate you.

Because of your responsibility, you should ask to see the agent's drafts of his particulars before he finalises and duplicates them. Check them carefully: if you miss a very obvious error that may be a ground upon which the agent could later excuse himself. Be particularly careful about the fixtures, fittings and furniture which the agent says are included with the house or flat. If there is something obviously wrong with the description of the house – the size of a room, say – a purchaser may later have no complaint, because he either will have looked round for himself, or could have done so. However, he cannot know simply by looking round which of the light fittings, heaters, cupboards and so on you are planning to leave and which will be going with you.

If a mistake slips through, or you change your mind about something, tell your solicitor before the contract becomes binding so that he can make the position clear to the purchaser. Once the contract is binding, it is too late.

130 | *My estate agent actually says on the particulars it circulates that absolute accuracy is not guaranteed. Surely that avoids any comebacks from purchasers?*

Almost all estate agents' sheets of particulars have a disclaimer printed in small print at the foot. This says, roughly, that they do not guarantee the accuracy of the particulars that they are distributing. You might think that that completely protects you, as vendor, and them against criticism for any mistakes. But this sort of clause is now only valid if it is reasonable for them to excuse themselves in that way. Facts that a purchaser might be expected to check, such as which rooms have a southern aspect, perhaps, or matters his or her solicitor should find out, such as whether the council maintains the road, could reasonably be outside estate agents' responsibility.

Selling property

131 | *What fittings and furnishings will I have to leave behind in my house when I sell it?*

What you leave behind and what you take with you is completely a matter of agreement between you and the purchaser. If the matter is dealt with in the formal contract (see Q139) between you, you can decide what you like and there will be no difficulty. It is not really possible to deal with each and every item in that way, and therefore what is important is the general rule that applies when nothing is said.

What are properly called 'fixtures' automatically go with the property, and should therefore be left behind in the absence of a special arrangement. A fixture is something that is literally firmly attached to the building or the land and not simply put up for display purposes or so that it can conveniently be used. If you build a garage, that is obviously going to be a fixture. A decorative plaque which you screw to the wall is not a fixture for this purpose, even though it is firmly fixed. A light switch is a fixture, but many (although not all) light fittings are not.

There is often trouble about which items are included in a sale. The safe thing to do is to list all the items which the purchaser will have seen fixed when he came round to look at your property, but which you are not selling, and give the list to your solicitor promptly. The position can then be made clear in the course of the legal negotiations.

One legal oddity you may like to note is that the keys to all the locks in the doors, both outside and inside, count as fixtures even though they are not fixed in any way. They therefore are sold with the house.

If you are selling a leasehold flat or house, then obviously all the fixtures which belong to the landlord and were supplied to you with the property have to be passed on to the buyer.

132 | *Does the fact that I agree that some fittings and furniture are sold with the house mean that I cannot charge the purchaser for them?*

It is up to you to decide whether to ask a separate price for items you want to leave behind – curtains, carpets, cooker, for instance – or to include the cost in your selling price. The decision has to be made before the contract to sell the house becomes binding (see Q139). Once that is finalised, anything which it says you are including in the sale, without specifying a separate price, is included in the overall agreed price for the property. If you agree to sell other items, it is useful to list them in the contract and to state the agreed extra sum. Give your solicitor details.

This does not stop you and the buyer agreeing later that you will sell other items, but they must be ones that are not automatically included in the property sale.

133 | *I am paying for a central heating installa-*

tion by instalments. *Does the purchaser of the house take the agreement over?*

What you must do first is to look at the agreement between you and the installers (or their finance company). Does it allow you to pass on the liability to pay instalments to anyone else? If it does – though this would be unusual – then you can pass it on if the purchaser agrees. The position must be made clear to him before the contract is binding, and the contract should have a special clause dealing with the point.

In many cases, the instalment payment agreement which you entered into is a second mortgage (see Q112) even if you did not recognise it as one. The ordinary house sale contract is on the basis that the vendor is responsible for paying off all outstanding mortgage loans when the sale is completed.

Either way, you will end up paying yourself for the installation. If you tell the purchaser you want him to take over the responsibility of paying the instalments, he will probably expect a balancing reduction in the agreed purchase price of your house.

134 | *I'm not moving far, and, when I sell my current home, I'd like to retain ownership of the garage I put up at the end of the garden. Do I have to sell my present property in its entirety?*

Very occasionally, deeds (see Q172) contain restrictions that would force you to sell the property as a whole, although this would be most unusual, and if the property is leasehold the terms of the lease might forbid you to split the property. Assuming that neither of these applies, the decision on what you sell is a matter for you, although you would be well advised to consult an estate agent to tell you what effect on the price any retention might have. It is a perfectly simple legal matter to redraw the boundaries of a property, and you should consult your solicitor about it.

In your case, it might be easier to sell the house if you agreed to give the purchaser the right of first refusal over the garage. This means that if ever you decide to sell the garage, the owner of the house – whether the person to whom you sell it, or some other subsequent owner – has first claim to buy. That sale would be at the proper price for the garage at that time, and your agreement should include some arrangement for fixing that price if you cannot agree. A right of first refusal leaves the initiative in your hands, and no one can force you to sell at a particular time. On the other hand, you do not have a guaranteed buyer, merely a person who must be given a chance to buy.

135 | *I am advertising my house for sale privately, and hope to sell it without employing an estate agent. Once I find a buyer and agree the price, do I just write to confirm what we have agreed?*

Yes, but you must be very careful to say in your letter that the arrangements reached are 'subject to contract'. Use those very words. This is so important that you could even head your letter with that phrase.

The effect of saying that an agreement is subject to contract is that it is not legally binding. Neither of you could sue to enforce an agreement made on that basis, and therefore either of you can withdraw without incurring any liability.

The reason for this is that house selling is a technical business. When your solicitor comes to look at your deeds he may well find something that should be disclosed in advance to any purchaser so that the purchaser accepts liability for it and does not accuse you of misleading him. You will have been told about this when you bought, but may have forgotten.

There may also be things that have arisen since, of which you have not realised the significance in connection with selling your house. A second mortgage securing money being paid for an improvement is one example (see Q133); another is the protection given to a husband or wife when the matrimonial home is in the other partner's name (see SEPARATION Q6).

136 | *A company of property developers with a large local rebuilding scheme in mind has offered to pay me for an option to buy my house at a very tempting price. What is an option to buy?*

An option to buy gives the prospective purchaser the right to insist on buying the property within a certain length of time by giving the vendor a notice to exercise the option. The owner is therefore putting the timing of any sale completely in the purchaser's hands.

Where there is going to be redevelopment, a house may be worth more to the developers than its normal market price. They can therefore offer tempting terms. The reason they often need an option is that the decision to go ahead has to depend on buying all the properties in the area which is to become the development site. The developers make sure that they are not landed with only some of what they need by taking options on all the properties, and only exercising the options once they have bought all the options.

This is why developers find options worth paying for. As a property owner, there are a number of practical points you should watch. Every option should have a time-limit, and you must consider it carefully. While the option is running, you cannot sell your property elsewhere. No one else will want to buy it from you if he or she runs the risk of having it whisked away on the exercise of the option. What you are paid for the option goes towards compensating you for that inconvenience.

As you do not know when the option will be exercised, so you cannot make plans to move in advance, make sure that the agreement gives you enough time to make alternative plans after the option has been taken up. Finally, you need to be clear whether the price that you are paid for the option, which is yours whether or not the developer decides to exercise the option, is treated as part of the purchase price if the sale goes ahead, or whether the whole of the price is paid on top of it.

137 | *As a house owner, when should I think of using an auction as the way to sell it?*

There is one immense attraction of auctions from the vendor's point of view: once the hammer has fallen there is certainty about the sale. However, because the method is understandably unpopular with purchasers, there are only a few circumstances in which it is the best way to sell.

This is something on which you should seek the advice of the estate agent who is going to sell the house for you. On the whole, house auctions fall into two categories. At one end of the scale are small houses in poor condition, sometimes with tenants in them, which are unlikely to be bought by owner-occupiers. At the other extreme there are valuable

SOLD TO THE MAN IN THE BLACK CLOAK AT THE BACK

houses for which there is likely to be a lot of competition between people who are likely to bid each other up at the auction.

138 | *The risk for the vendor at an auction seems to be that because of a lack of buyers the house might not sell for a proper price. Can I guard against that?*

What you do is to place a 'reserve price' on the house. This is the price below which you are not prepared to sell. You are entitled to do this only if you tell bidders in advance, and almost every auction contract, the terms of which the bidders have in advance, states that the sale is subject to a reserve of this kind. You do not normally announce in advance what the reserve price actually is, although once the bidding has passed the reserve price the auctioneer often says so.

The other assumption might be that you and friends could do some bidding in order to push the price up. The vendor or one person – but no more – on his behalf is allowed to bid at auction provided that this is made clear in advance. The normal practice is for the vendor to delegate to the auctioneer his right to bid. By exercising the right, and appearing to accept bids from other people in the hall, the auctioneer will try to get the bids up above the reserve.

It is a criminal offence to contravene these auction rules about the reserve price and the limit on the vendor's bidding.

Buying property

139 | *My solicitor told me that I should make my offer for the house I want 'subject to contract' to ensure that nothing was binding at that stage. How long do I have to wait before being sure the deal is going through?*

Once you've made an offer for your house and your offer has been accepted, the agreement between you and the vendor is 'subject to contract'. This means that there's no legal commitment on either side until your solicitor has sorted out the details of the purchase with the vendor's solicitor (see Q135).

Once these details have been agreed, the contract to sell and buy the house is prepared in duplicate. The purchaser signs one copy and the vendor signs the other, and these two copies are exchanged. Thus, each party, or his solicitor, has the one copy signed by the other. This swap is known as 'exchange of contracts', and in this context exchange has become synonymous with making a contract legally binding.

Nowadays, because of the need to synchronise the exchanges of contracts throughout a whole chain of transactions so that everyone sells one house and buys another on the same day (Mr A sells his house to Mrs B and buys one from Miss C; Mrs B in turn sells to Mr D and buys from Mr A, and so on), solicitors have a procedure for 'exchanging' by telephone or telex. In fact, they are agreeing that the contracts shall be taken as binding at a certain moment, and undertaking to send on the document which they are holding in due course. This makes no difference to the effect of the sale.

It is unlikely that contracts will be ready for exchange much under four weeks after you originally agreed terms with the present owner of the house.

140 | *My solicitor keeps telling me that the delay to my signing the contract after making the offer to buy my flat is because he's waiting for the results of the searches he's making on my behalf. What are these searches?*

A lot of vital information about houses and flats is recorded in registers kept by local authorities. The registers say, for example, what properties may be bought by compulsory purchase in the future, what planning permissions have been granted, whether the building is in a smoke control zone, and whether a flat is in a listed building. There are also details about which roads and drains are repaired at public expense, where public rights of way run and even properties whose owners find themselves with special liabilities to maintain sea walls. Because these, and many other matters which are also recorded, are vital to the decision whether or not to buy a flat or a house, solicitors and local authorities have worked out a standard system for getting the information by submitting a standard form and paying a fee. Some authorities take longer than others to gather the information and return the form with the questions answered.

In special circumstances there are other enquiries your solicitor will find it prudent to make before you commit yourself to buying. If you are buying a country property, for instance, your solicitor should make sure that land which goes with the house is not part of a common (the county council has a register); if the garden of the house in which you are interested backs on to a railway line, British Rail will tell you whether you or they will be responsible for repairing the fence; if you are buying in a coal mining area, the National Coal Board will say whether you are likely to be troubled by subsidence.

141 | *Couldn't all these searches and enquiries, valuable though they obviously are, be carried out after contracts have been exchanged to save time?*

The whole point of the searches and enquiries is that they are early warning of trouble, allowing you to change your mind about the property you have agreed to buy before it is too late to retract.

It is in fact possible to make the searches and enquiries after the contract becomes binding at signature. So that you do not lose the object of them, giving you the chance to reconsider, you can have a special clause in the contract allowing you to opt out. The standard forms of contract used for house and flat purchase have this as an optional extra. This is usually called a 'subject to searches contract'.

The problem with this clause lies in the definition of the exact circumstances under which the purchaser should be allowed to withdraw. From the purchaser's point of view, the best thing is for him to have complete discretion. That would mean simply saying that if any enquiry revealed something he considered unsatisfactory, he would back out. But no vendor is likely to find that acceptable, because the uncertainty is too great. One formula, which still involves uncertainty although it narrows the field, is to permit withdrawal if there is anything that lowers the market value of the property below the figure the purchaser reasonably supposed it to be.

142 | *If a purchaser calls off a subject to searches contract, where does that leave the parties?*

If the purchaser backs out, there is no contract at all, and the vendor who thought that he had sold his property suddenly finds he has not. Both parties are then back where they started. This is the reason why subject to searches contracts are not popular.

Such a situation is obviously highly unsatisfactory in a chain of sale and purchase contracts (see Q139). In fact, it has to be regarded as unacceptable. No one can safely agree to enter such a chain when party to this type of contract, which can cause one of the links in the chain to spring apart.

143 | *What is the position about pre-contract searches in the case of an auction?*

At an auction, the contract for the sale of the house or flat is made and binding at the moment the auctioneer's hammer falls after the successful bid is made. The terms of the contract are set out in the conditions in the auction catalogue, and they cannot be modified.

That contract is not going to be in a subject to searches form, so if as purchaser you want the usual protection you must make the enquiries in advance. If you do not like what you find, you should simply not bid at the auction. This is one of the things that makes auctions an unsatisfactory way to buy a home. If you don't bid, or your bid is unsuccessful, all that you spend on your preliminary investigations will be wasted. Also, the uncertainty persists until the auction closes, so you cannot make any other arrangements with any certainty.

Finance is another practical difficulty of buying a property at auction. You do not know the price you are going to have to pay until you make the successful bid. It is therefore impossible to arrange a mortgage from any of the usual sources. If you have to borrow, that probably means making temporary arrangements with a bank.

144 | *Why does it take so long for the contract to buy a house to be made binding on exchange?*

You can put the reasons into two categories. There are the legal procedures for finalising the contract on the one hand, and on the other there is the time needed for doing everything else that needs to be tied up by that stage, such as the results of the searches mentioned in Q140.

In preparing a sale and purchase contract, both parties' solicitors have to ensure that the terms of the transaction are what the parties want. This goes much further than merely checking the price they agreed and the list of any furnishings that are to be included or paid for separately. The deeds of the property (see Q172) may contain restrictions, or requirements such as paying for the repairs of rights of way, which the purchaser must understand and find acceptable. A lot may be revealed by the searches and enquiries which the purchaser's solicitor makes.

In the meantime, the purchaser may want to instruct a surveyor to inspect the house, and it will take time for the report to come through. Almost certainly, he will need to apply for a mortgage, and he will have to wait for the building society offer. More everyday concerns, like booking removers after obtaining estimates, and looking at schools will occupy both the vendor and the purchaser.

Probably the greatest cause of delay is the effect of the sale and purchase chain (see Q139) so that everyone arranges to sell one house and to buy another on the same day. That way, no one in the chain has to pay for two houses at once, and all the parties always have a roof over their heads. Obviously, this means waiting until everyone in the chain is ready, and a good deal of time can be spent on liaison to find a universally acceptable moving day.

145 | Isn't there an alternative to having simultaneous purchases and sales, if that is such a source of delay?

This boils down to a question of money. Can a house owner who has not yet sold one house afford to buy another? The other way round, selling before you have had a chance to buy, involves obtaining temporary accommodation and storing furniture.

Some people do buy before they have sold, and they take out a bridging loan to finance their temporary ownership of the two properties. A bridging loan normally comes from your bank, although there are some employers who will help, particularly if your job is the reason for your move. A bank loan for this purpose can prove expensive. Naturally, the bank charges interest, and the rate will often be two or three per cent above the base rate. You should be able to obtain income tax relief on this interest, which will reduce its cost to you. The bank also usually charges a fixed fee for arranging the loan; this might be £100. Because of the short time for which the loan is likely to be outstanding, if you look at that payment as interest you will find that this is very costly borrowing. Worse, because the fee is not really interest you can expect no income tax relief on it.

Banks distinguish strictly between two sets of circumstances in which you may want a bridging loan. If the contracts for both your house sale and your house purchase have been exchanged and are therefore binding, the banks usually agree to a loan. But if you want to borrow to commit yourself to buy before anyone is legally bound to purchase your present house, they often do not agree. They call this an open-ended bridge because there is no guarantee of how and when they will be repaid. The risks are obvious both to you and to the bank if the prospective purchaser fails to sign the contract and withdraws at the last moment.

146 | As a purchaser, isn't it in my interest to have a binding contract immediately? A sale which is subject to contract may allow the vendor to gazump me.

A house purchaser who enters into a binding contract before carrying out the customary legal investigations runs a considerable risk. The normal form of house purchase contract makes the purchaser take the property subject, for instance, to any plans the local authority may have for the property. The auth-

ority may have announced an intention to acquire it compulsorily, it may want to widen the road outside, it may have given notice that an extension was built without planning consent when it was needed and must therefore be pulled down. These are among the many items that solicitors' usual searches and enquiries (see Q140) could reveal, and you should have the chance to consider them before finally committing yourself. That is the reason why it is best for the purchaser to make an agreement subject to contract.

It is true that the vendor can withdraw at any time, as indeed you can. He may seek to gazump you, which means turning round after he has agreed the price informally and saying that he is prepared to go ahead only at a higher price. Whatever you may think of that conduct, he is legally entitled to do so. You then have the option either of agreeing his new terms or saying that you will go ahead only as originally agreed or not at all.

If the agreement does fall through at that point, you cannot put in a claim for any of the expenses you will already have incurred.

There is a reverse situation to gazumping, to which no one seems to have yet applied a name. You may discover after having a survey of the property that it is not worth as much as you were told. You can turn to the vendor and say that you will go ahead only if the price is reduced. The vendor, in turn, has the alternatives of agreeing the price reduction or calling off the deal.

147 | *When making an offer for a house, should I make it subject to the other points that I still have to settle, like having a survey or getting a mortgage?*

People do make offers which they say are not only 'subject to contract' but also 'subject to survey' and 'subject to mortgage'. It is not really necessary to say anything more than 'subject to contract', because those words have now been universally accepted within the law as meaning that there is no binding commitment. They allow you to withdraw for whatever reason you like.

To say that an offer is 'subject to survey' can increase your liabilities. It commits you to commissioning a survey, although naturally you are not committed in advance to accepting the result of it. It does assume that if the result is satisfactory that impediment to the contract will be removed. The result of this is that if there is some other reason why you want to withdraw from the contract, so that having a survey would be a waste of time, you could find yourself still obliged to have one.

It may be, although the courts have not decided, that to say that an offer is 'subject to mortgage' means that you must at least apply for a mortgage – and, of course, you may not wish to if a survey shows the property to be worth less than the price you've offered.

148 | *Presumably, once a deposit is paid to the estate agent, that makes the contract legally binding?*

No, but this is a popular fallacy. Paying a preliminary deposit before the contract is signed and made binding makes no legal difference at all. Estate agents normally ask for a deposit – and it can be any amount up to around £250 – to show that the purchaser is serious; they sometimes imply that that settles the matter. As a matter of practice, it may well mean that the agent and the vendor are satisfied that the sale should go through, and therefore the agent makes no further efforts to try to sell the property. But the agent is not obliged to take the property off the market, and if a later offer is made the estate agent has a duty to pass it on to the vendor.

Similarly, because the deposit does not bind the purchaser, it does not stop him from withdrawing and demanding repayment of the money. A purchaser who feels that it is prudent to agree to pay a deposit is well advised to keep it to the lowest acceptable sum, because he will not earn interest on it.

149 | *I have withdrawn my offer on a flat I was going to buy, and the estate agent is taking its time in repaying me my preliminary deposit. If the agent does not pay, is the vendor liable to pay me instead?*

Until there is a contract, you can demand your money back at any time from the estate agent. This means that if the agent defaults, you must bear the loss. The only exception is where the agent is given express authority by the vendor to collect pre-contract deposits as the vendor's agent. This is not the usual arrangement, but where it does occur the vendor would be liable to repay you the money.

Once contracts are exchanged, you are not in a position to demand your money back. The deposit serves the dual function of being part-payment of the purchase price and also compensates the vendor if you back out of the contract without good reason; you will then not be entitled to reclaim your deposit. If the agent defaults with the deposit, the vendor has to bear the loss whether the agent holds it as stakeholder or as the vendor's agent. The reason for this is that the vendor has chosen the agent.

Where the agent holds the deposit as stakeholder, the agent must hold the money until he receives instructions from both parties about its disposal. Where the estate agent holds the money as agent for the vendor he can pass it on to the vendor before completion. The vendor is then able to use the deposit towards the purchase of another property. The purchaser therefore runs the risk that he may not be able to get the money back from the vendor.

The best arrangement for a purchaser seems to be to pay any deposit to an agent as stakeholder, provided he can be sure of the financial standing of the agent. A number of agents' professional organisations have bonding schemes, which guarantee the repayment of deposits held by their members. These include the Royal Institution of Chartered Surveyors, the Incorporated Society of Valuers and Auctioneers, and the National Association of Estate Agents; addresses on pages 511, 510 and 511.

The receipt that an agent gives you for the deposit should say expressly in what capacity it will be held.

150 | *I'm planning to bid for a house at auction. What do I do about insuring it, as I won't know in advance whether I'll become the purchaser?*

This is another inconvenience of buying at auction. What you have to do is to make professional arrangements in advance. Decide how much you will need to insure for: you should insure for the cost of rebuilding, not for the price you are likely to pay (see Q119). See a surveyor if necessary. You then complete a proposal form and lodge it with an insurance company on the basis that you can telephone the company to put the policy into force as soon as you know that you have made a successful bid.

151 | The house we are buying is empty and we are at present in a rented flat. The logical thing seems to be to move out of the flat and into the house. What reasonable objection can the present owner have once contracts have been exchanged?

House vendors are very reluctant to agree to purchasers moving in early. It may well seem logical, but long experience shows that for good reasons and bad once a purchaser actually takes over a house there is often delay in the purchase money being handed over.

All the same, there is no harm in asking, and the standard forms of house sale contracts do have clauses in them that regulate the terms on which a purchaser can move in. The clauses operate only if the vendor agrees that they should, and they give the purchaser no automatic right to occupy early.

In summary, the terms on which you would go into possession are these. You would not be a tenant, so there would be no chance of your having the benefit of Rent Act rights (see QS 15 and 18). Your permission to occupy could be ended by the vendor at any time, or at least at any time after you should have paid the purchase price but had not. You would have to take proper care of the property and not make any alterations to it. Finally, you would have to pay interest on the purchase price. The rate of interest will be stated in the contract, and the amount would normally be added to the purchase price to be paid on completion (see Q175).

152 | Are there any points about which I should brief my solicitor about the house I am buying?

The enquiries which your solicitor makes, both addressed to the local authority (and other authorities) (see Q140) and sent to the vendor's solicitor, normally concentrate on matters directly affecting the property you are buying. You should mention to him anything you feel should be queried with the vendor, particularly matters that could affect the price of the property or repairs the vendor should make before the flat is bought: the garden fence is falling down, for instance, or whether any open land opposite, say, is planned for development. If something about any neighbouring property particularly

interests you, you should say so. For example, if one of the things that attracts you to the house is a view in one direction, you would want to know if planning permission had been granted to build there. Unfortunately, no enquiries can guarantee what will happen in the future, although they may give some indication of the probabilities.

The other thing your solicitor cannot guess is any plans you may have for the house. It is well worth mentioning if you want to build an extension, say, or to let a floor to tenants.

153 | What will it cost me in legal fees and expenses to buy a house or flat?

There can be no definite answer to this question. In order to draw up a budget, however, the items you should take into account are: solicitors' fees, Land Registry fees (see Q170), solicitors' disbursements (incidental expenses paid on your behalf) such as fees paid to the local authority to answer queries about the drainage, for example, and stamp duty (see Q154). If you are having a mortgage, something must be paid to your solicitor for that.

There is no longer any fixed scale of solicitors' fees for this work, except for the work in connection with some building society mortgages. Solicitors charge on a basis which takes into account the amount of work they do and the amount of responsibility they accept. Many solicitors are prepared to give an estimate of their costs in advance, so you could telephone to get some quotations. As a guide, you may find that the final figure varies between one and a half and two and a half per cent of the price you pay for the house. The Land Registry fees are on a fixed official scale, varying with the price of the house. The 1987 fee for registering a house bought for £45,000 was £70. Solicitors' incidental expenditure on such items as search fees (see Q140) may be about £20. The basic stamp duty rate is £1 for every £100 of the price you pay above £30,000 (see Q154). You must add VAT to solicitors' fees, but not to stamp duty or Land Registry fees.

Bear in mind also that the building society charges a valuation fee – each society has its own scale of fees – and if you decide to have a survey of your own (see Q163) you will have a fee to pay to your surveyor as well.

Buying a flat is likely to cost more than buying a house at the same price. The reason is that a flat is likely to be leasehold, and, like leasehold houses, there is no standard form of lease for a flat. As well as being unique they are invariably long. Your solicitor has to assess the lease terms and explain them to you in some detail. When the flat is new, although not normally when it is second-hand, there may be the chance to negotiate improvements to the terms of the lease with the freeholder. Such assessment and negotiations will mean a higher solicitor's bill than would be incurred in buying a freehold property.

154 | What are the stamp duty rates?

Stamp duty – a form of tax payable to the Inland Revenue on buying a house or flat – is charged on the amount you pay for the property. Properties costing up to £30,000 are free of stamp duty.

While the transfer of a house for £30,000 bears no stamp duty, as soon as the price is over that limit stamp duty must be paid. So if the price is £30,100, the duty is £301 (one per cent). If anything moveable is sold, and is simply handed over and not recorded, its price does not bear stamp duty: if a carpet is included in the £30,100 sale, and the price of £100 is attributed to it and dealt with as a separate matter, the house transfer then bears a price of £30,000, and £301 has been legitimately saved.

155 | If I buy a long lease of a flat, do I have to pay stamp duty on it?

There is a charge of stamp duty on leases paid by the first leaseholder, and its total is calculated from two component parts: you may have to pay in relation both to the ground rent and to the lump sum you pay.

Stamp duty on a ground rent is calculated on the annual amount of the rent. On the most common 99-year lease, the stamp duty is £6 for every £50 per annum of the rent (12 per cent). The rate doubles if the lease is granted for a period of over 100 years, which is one reason why 99 years is the customary length. Some leases make the ground rent rise, perhaps taking a step up every 33 years. The duty in that sort of case is calculated on the average annual rent taken over the whole term of the lease.

The stamp duty charged on the capital payment ('premium') is at the same rate as applies to payments for a freehold (see Q154). The exemption for payments up to £30,000 applies only if the ground rent is not over £300 a year.

156 | The owner of the house I'm buying suggested that I should employ his solicitor to negotiate the purchase so that we should save time and fees because only one solicitor would be involved in the transaction instead of two. The solicitor said he could not do that. Is this an individual quirk, or an example of a restrictive practice?

Solicitors are extremely wary of putting themselves into a position where they have a conflict of interests. The obvious example of this is when they try to act for two separate clients, each of whom is trying to achieve something different and contradictory. This can easily happen when acting even in the most amicable house sale and purchase. How can one solicitor fairly advise both parties? If your survey shows up some unsuspected faults, the solicitor should try to force the agreed price down; the vendor would naturally want to keep the price up, which may be vital if he is to have enough money to pay for the house to which he is moving. The vendor may want to move out quickly so that the change of home takes place before the new school term or before Christmas or whenever; for similar reasons the purchaser may want to delay the moment when the house changes hands.

Because of these difficulties, there is a professional rule that prohibits solicitors from acting for both vendor and purchaser, except in specified circumstances. Among those exceptional cases are: where the two clients are relations, or where they are both established clients of the solicitor, or if there is no other solicitor in the vicinity whom either can be reasonably expected to consult. Even then, there are overriding prohibitions for the protection of the clients. A solicitor acting for a company of developers cannot also act for a person buying a house or flat from that company. Also, a solicitor must cease to act for both parties if a conflict of interest arises.

157 | If I buy a leasehold flat, what details am I entitled to receive about recent service charge payments?

Figures of the payments made by the vendor are part of the information which your solicitor collects from the vendor's solicitor. It is also important to enquire what work has recently been done to the block of flats, which may be charged to flat owners in the future. Say that the whole of the outside has recently been redecorated. When you inspect the property you would naturally be inclined to say that that was at least one worry out of the way: there should be no expenditure on that work for another five years or so. But the cost of the recent work may not have been charged to owners in the service charge, so once you have become owner you might find yourself paying. This is not something which you can avoid, but you can be forewarned. If the payment was substantial and unusual, you might even try to negotiate a reduction in the purchase price on the strength of it.

Once you become owner, you will be the one to

whom the landlord has to give information about the service charge (see Q50). You should note, however, that the landlord has to give details only once for each year. It is therefore important to ask whether the present owner has been given the details, and if so have them handed over to you.

158 | After I bought my flat, I discovered that the previous owner had fallen into arrears with his payments of the service charge. The landlord is now demanding the money from me. Do I have to pay any money due before I became owner?

All payments due from a tenant to a landlord in connection with the property can be collected from the person who for the time being is the owner of the lease. So you probably have to pay.

In fact, this is something that ought to have been settled when you bought the flat. Most contracts provide that all recurrent outgoings are apportioned between the old and the new owners, each paying the portion attributable to their period of ownership. This is something that your solicitor should have checked, and if there has been a slip up you may have a claim against the solicitor. The normal routine is to inspect the receipts for the latest payments.

The only difficulty about service charges is that effectively they are often a long way in arrears. By the time you take over, the landlord may not even have sent in a demand for expenses incurred some time before. There is no perfect way to deal with this. If the bargain between purchaser and vendor is that the vendor will pay when the demand eventually comes, you normally have to be content with his promise to do so. Sometimes some of the price you pay is kept on deposit by the solicitors involved as a guarantee of payment.

159 | If the vendor's solicitor gives my solicitor inaccurate information about the house I'm buying, can I get compensation from that other solicitor?

The replies to the enquiries which a vendor's solicitor gives are supposed to be his client's answers. The solicitor will ask the client to supply the necessary information. The normal questions on any house purchase have been standardised on to a printed form. It saves time if the vendor's solicitor gets the vendor to answer those questions in advance, but of course it is quite open to the purchaser's solicitor to add other queries to suit the circumstances.

Provided the vendor's solicitor has properly followed this procedure, and has not merely supplied the information from assumptions, it is the vendor and not his solicitor against whom your claim lies. If you are misled you may be able to call off the purchase. Once the sale has gone through, your remedy will generally be limited to damages which will give you money compensation.

160 | I am interested in buying a particular house because it's ideal for extending at the rear. What checks can I make on the likelihood of getting planning permission before I commit myself to buying?

Some local authority planning departments are prepared to have informal discussions with people interested in buying properties – and people already owner-occupiers – to give some idea of their prospects of building extensions. In default of that, the preliminary enquiries (see Q140) made by your solicitor should give some indication.

First, they should show whether any of the automatic allowance for small extensions (see Q62) has been used up, and if so how much of it.

In addition to that, the replies from the local authority to the standard enquiries to the solicitor should show whether the house is in any special area from a planning point of view. It is well known that green belts have been designated around London and major cities, and the intention is that building there should be severely restricted. Other areas have been declared to be areas of outstanding natural beauty and areas of great landscape value, the effects of which are similar from this point of view. Extending a house in such an area is more difficult than elsewhere.

161 | *Is that sort of planning difficulty restricted to rural areas?*

Different sorts of area designations for planning purposes are found in towns. Here you may find that your house is within a conservation area. This will generally be an older part of the town, where it is not so much an isolated property that needs to be saved but rather the general effect of the collection of buildings in the vicinity.

The effect of owning a building in a conservation area is much the same as if your house was a listed building (see Q 71), and even demolition is something for which you have to obtain permission. Any application for consent to an extension is bound to be critically scrutinised, and the design of the extension will have to be appropriate both to your own house and to the surrounding area.

162 | *I'm told that I'll have to contribute to the repair costs of a private road running up to the house I'm buying when I take over the house. How can I put a limit on the expenditure?*

The arrangement giving you the right to use the private road will have imposed the duty to pay towards its repair. Indeed, your right to use the road at all may be conditional on making payments. If the road is the only access to the house, paying for its maintenance is obviously vital.

This sort of obligation normally has no limit on it, but you can assess what the liability might cost you. The surveyor who does a survey of the house should be able to give you an idea of what work is now needed and of what it should cost. This you can contrast with information about the amount that the present owner of the house has paid in the past few years, which is part of the information which your solicitor should be collecting.

Buying property: surveys

163 | *If I apply for a mortgage, which involves paying the building society's surveyor's fee, do I have to have a survey of my own?*

There is never any obligation on you to arrange a survey – a report on the physical state of the property – of any house or flat you are buying, but it can sometimes be wise. There can be a duplication of effort between a building society surveyor and your own, but you should note the limitations of the building society inspection.

What the building society surveyor does is a valuation rather than a survey. His job is to assess the value of the property, to make sure that if it were sold because you defaulted in making your mortgage payments, the building society would not lose money. Naturally, he has to take into account the condition of the property in arriving at his valuation, but there are many minor defects which he can ignore because they make no real difference to the market price of the property. Nevertheless, they may be points of which you would like to be warned.

Many building societies will show you their surveyor's report, sometimes charging an extra fee. You might decide to delay a decision on whether to employ your own surveyor until you have seen that report. If you do want your own survey, you will probably find that there are two levels of service. Either you can have an inspection, which is not so detailed and gives you a brief report on a standard form, or, if you are prepared to pay more, you can ask for a full structural survey, which is translated into a very detailed report.

A survey is, in a way, a form of insurance. If it reveals major defects you will not want to go ahead and will be thankful to have been saved the headaches. If there is nothing alarming to report, you are paying for the reassurance. However, when the position is somewhere in the middle, with defects that need attention although they are not severe enough to put you off, a surveyor's report is a useful lever with which to negotiate a reduction in the price.

164 | *Is it ever necessary to have a survey of a house which is still covered by a National House Building Council 10-year guarantee?*

It is not normal nowadays to have a survey of a brand new property which is covered by the NHBC guarantee. There is, however, a good reason to have a survey of a second-hand house covered by the guarantee. The benefit of the guarantee passes to the purchaser, but there is an important exception to that. If any defect has occurred and shown itself during the time when the first owner had the house, so that it should then have been reported either to the builder or to the NHBC, the second owner can make a claim for work arising from that defect only if it was reported before the house changed hands.

That means that to avoid any doubt it is worth asking a surveyor to report to you anything that could need reporting under the guarantee terms. You can then be sure that the items are reported before you take over, so that the guarantee remains fully effective.

165 | I am buying a flat. Obviously the surveyor can conduct a survey of the flat itself, but what about the state of the entire building?

Buying a flat obviously poses a difficult problem when you are thinking about a survey. An inspection and report on the whole block would probably be prohibitively expensive, and it is impractical because you would be unlikely to be able to arrange for the surveyor to have access to all the flats. But the survey will certainly cover all the common parts, the structure of the building itself, the roof and so on. This is very important, because you are likely to have to pay a service charge which will include a proportion of the cost of major repairs not only on your flat but on anywhere in the whole block. To be warned in advance of any major trouble which seemed to be developing, and which might be reflected in inflated service charge demands at a later date, could be money well spent.

166 | I bought a house after having a full structural survey. Now I find that there is serious and costly trouble with the roof. Can I call upon the surveyor to pay for the repairs which have proved to be necessary?

A surveyor owes you a duty to carry out your survey in a professionally competent manner. Any falling below reasonable professional standards involves a liability for negligence. A surveyor is not expected to be perfect, but you are entitled to assume that no tell-tale signs, which would reveal trouble to an observant and knowledgeable surveyor, would be overlooked.

To tell whether you have a cause for complaint within the law, therefore, you will probably have to obtain a report from another surveyor, concentrating on what the first surveyor could have seen, and what he should have revealed.

Assuming that you are in a position to hold your surveyor responsible, the compensation you receive will not necessarily be enough to pay for the repairs. The test is *not*, 'how much will it cost to put matters right?' but rather, 'how much less should I have paid for the house had I known of the trouble?' Because some people are prepared to take risks, put up with faults and delay repair work, the market price of a property does not automatically go down by the whole of the cost of the work that needs to be done.

167 | I found settlement and damp problems shortly after I moved in to my house. I didn't have

a survey, but of course the building society did. Can I make a claim against their surveyor?

It is possible for you to claim against the building society surveyor in some circumstances. It does not matter that you did not pay a fee direct to the surveyor. It does not even matter that you did not see the survey report. What is important is that you were able to deduce the general sense of the report, and that in reliance on it you went ahead with the purchase and found you were misled.

You have to bear in mind that all the building society surveyor is doing is making a valuation (see Q163). But if a major defect is overlooked, that is bound to make the valuation unreliable. You may not see the valuation the surveyor makes, but you can often tell what it must have been. If you are borrowing as much as you can, the building society manager will have told you what the maximum percentage is. That makes it simple to calculate from the mortgage offer what the valuation must have been.

If in making that valuation, the building society surveyor has clearly overlooked something of importance, which should have been apparent, you can sue for compensation. The amount of any damages follows the same lines as a claim against a surveyor whom you instructed yourself (see Q166).

This sort of claim could be a good deal more difficult if you were borrowing a smaller percentage of the property's value. A surveyor could then argue that he knew that fairly substantial defects would not affect the building society, because its loan was small, so he saw no reason to report them. The exact limits of liability in this sort of case have yet to be decided.

168 | I did not have a survey of the house I bought, and at the time I did not realise that it suffered from subsidence. I feel that the vendor of the house should have told me. Can I claim compensation from him?

No. Houses are almost always sold on the basis that the onus is on the purchaser to make any inspection and enquiry that seems necessary, and then to take the property as it is. The only regular exception to that is new houses that are still being built at the time the purchaser signs the contract, so that there is no chance of seeing the defects at that stage. The standard forms of contract normally used for selling houses state specifically that the purchaser takes the property in the state and condition it is in.

This means that if you buy a leasehold property, and the repairing and decorating duties in the lease have not been fully complied with – and it is usually possible to find some fault – then it is the purchaser who has to put things right.

There is one case in which you might have some complaint against the vendor. No one is entitled to mislead you. If you ask a straight question about the state of repair, or whether something is in working order, the vendor must either give you a truthful answer or simply say that you may find out for yourself. If he or she does mislead you, and that causes you loss, you have a good claim for damages.

This means that if you are selling a house you must be careful to be scrupulously accurate. If a prospective buyer asks about something you do not know, do not guess, because if you are wrong you could be held responsible.

Buying property: guarantees

169 | *Is it possible to take over woodworm and similar guarantees when work was done for a previous owner?*

Almost invariably, guarantees for all types of specialist treatments to houses can be taken over by purchasers. This applies to timber treatment, specialist anti-damp treatments, roof sealing and special rendering and guttering. In every case you have to check the guarantee form. It may be necessary to inform the company concerned of the change of ownership, and possibly pay a small registration fee. It may also be necessary to have a formal written transfer.

Although many of these guarantees are for impressively long periods, some up to 30 years, experience shows that not every company that offers such a guarantee itself survives that long. When you are offered a house with the benefit of one of these warranties, you should check that the company is still in business.

Buying property: registration of ownership

170 | *I have read that there is official recording of the ownership of some houses, but not of others. What is the significance of this?*

Solicitors use one of two separate ways to prove ownership of a house, a flat or a piece of land. One is by reference to the records of the Land Registry – the 'official recording' you mention – which is a government department set up for the purpose of registering the ownership, or 'title', of land. Not all properties are

yet registered. The other is by the traditional method, which relies on tracing a chain of ownership by consulting the deeds (see Q172).

Registration is a good deal more simple than tracing a chain. The record for each individual property is divided into four parts. The first section is the 'property register', which describes the land very briefly, and if it is leasehold gives details of the lease. This is supplemented by a plan, based on a large-scale Ordnance Survey map. The third part is the 'proprietorship register', which gives the name and address of the owner, or owners, of the property. Finally, the 'charges register' states what interests any other people have in the land. This is where mortgages are recorded, and so are restrictions which other people can enforce and leases of the land which may have been granted to others.

The owner of the land is given an official copy of these entries, called a land certificate, and so is the leaseholder when a lease is registered. If the owner of either freehold or leasehold property has mortgaged the property, the certificate goes to the lender of the money, and it is then called a charge certificate. Even if the certificate is kept by the mortgagee, the owner can still get details of what is currently on the register ('office copies') by applying to the District Land Registry for that area (addresses on page 510); a fee is payable for this.

The availability of the details, the accuracy of the records, and the fact that the ownership carries the backing of a state guarantee – so that if you are registered as owner, and then find yourself dispossessed, you will probably get compensation – are all benefits of this system. Q153 gives an example of the sort of Land Registry fee purchasers can expect to pay.

171 | *The registration of title system sounds ideal. How can I make sure that the ownership of my house is dealt with in that way?*

You will probably have no option. The reason why registration is not universal is the enormous amount of work and expense involved. For that reason, the work has been phased, and because registration occurs only on the transfer of properties it's a long-term process.

Registration is compulsory in all the most populated parts of the country, but not everywhere. Even where it is compulsory, that does not mean that every property is registered. What happens is that when a house or flat is sold the registration of title becomes compulsory and the ownership is then registered.

This gradual approach takes a surprisingly long time. Compulsion was first introduced in London in 1899, but some properties are still not registered. The sort of reason might be that they belong to a charity which bought them before 1899 and still owns them.

In an area of compulsory registration, you can choose to have an unregistered property registered, but there is not usually anything to gain by it. Some properties in other areas are registered: new housing estates can be registered by the developers, and houses sold to council tenants under the right to buy scheme (see Q 1 0) are registered wherever they are.

172 | What is the alternative to the registration of title system?

The traditional system of proving home ownership is by consulting the deeds. A deed is a formal legal document, signed and sealed, which in this case is used to transfer property from one owner to another. Ownership is a matter of showing that you bought from someone who appeared to be the owner, because he or she in turn bought from someone else who seemed to be entitled to ownership, and so on. The chain of ownership can also include proof that an owner died and the property was then sold by his executors. Or it may deal with an owner going bankrupt, or a mortgagee having to sell the property.

The chain would extend back to the time the property was built. To prevent the inconvenience that that caused, Parliament stepped in. On the latest occasion it reduced the chain to a minimum length of 15 years. To prove ownership nowadays, you look back through the deeds until you come to the first deed which is older than 15 years. That is the 'root of title'. As time goes by, more recent deeds become the root of title. To establish ownership, you have to make sure that that chain back to the root of title is unbroken.

173 | Which system of proof of ownership applies to leasehold flats and houses?

A lease can be either registered or unregistered. If it is registered, the leaseholder needs both the lease and the land certificate (see Q 1 7 0) fully to establish his ownership. Leases are often such long and detailed documents that there is no scope on the register to record their full contents. So there is a reference to the lease to identify it, leaving people to consult the actual lease when necessary.

In the case of an unregistered lease, the ownership is established by referring to the original leaseholder who is named in the lease. Later owners prove their entitlement by producing both the lease and the assignments – the lease transfer documents – which transfer it when it is sold from one person to another. This chain can become too long, as it does for a freehold property (see Q 1 7 2). In that case, it can be truncated in the same way, except that the original lease is always required.

174 | Is buying and selling a house with a registered title cheaper than doing the same with one where proof of ownership depends on the deeds?

There should be some saving, but not very much. When solicitors had a scale of fees for buying and selling properties, there were always two figures, a lower one for registered properties and a higher one for unregistered. Since then, the difference has narrowed, because common to both are the searches and enquiries made before the contract is binding, and these are areas of work which have expanded.

When there is a sale of a property with a registered title, a registration fee (see Q 1 5 3) has to be paid to the Land Registry by the purchaser. This makes the land registration process self-financing, but also makes the cost nearer to the traditional methods of conveyancing by consulting the deeds. A buyer who is obliged to register for the first time gets the worst of both worlds. His solicitor's fees are on the basis of the work involved in a traditional purchase, but he also has to pay an official fee – albeit on a lower scale – for registration.

Buying property: completion

175 | I understand that the signed contracts to buy a property are legally binding when the contracts are exchanged. But what is meant by the 'completion' of the sale, and why does it occur later than exchange?

Completion is the stage at which the change of ownership of the property actually takes place and the purchase price is paid. This normally occurs about four weeks after the exchange of contracts, although certainly with co-operation from both parties solicitors can do the work more quickly (though sometimes they can take longer).

The reason for the delay is the number of pieces of legal work that takes place between exchange and completion. The vendor's solicitor has to show that the vendor is the true owner of the property and is entitled to sell it to the purchaser. This is called 'deducing title'. Technical defects in proving ownership are now comparatively rare, particularly in the case of registered titles (see Q170), but they are not unknown and, considering the cost of a house to the purchaser, the check is clearly important. It is just as important to the building society, whose security relies upon the purchaser acquiring the property.

There is also the documentation to be attended to. The transfer document which transfers ownership from the vendor to the purchaser – a 'conveyance' if the title to the property is unregistered, an 'assignment' if the property is leasehold and the title unregistered, or a 'transfer' for all registered properties – has to be prepared, approved and signed by the vendor. The mortgage document also has to be prepared and signed.

Finally there are the financial arrangements. The exact amount payable on completion must be calculated. This may change slightly because of the apportionments between the vendor and purchaser of the outgoings such as the rates. The vendor's solicitor has to find out how much must be paid to repay his client's building society, and arrange to hand over the money. The purchaser's solicitor has to give notice to get the new building society advance, and has to ask for any balance from the purchaser.

176 | What actually happens when a house purchase contract is completed?

Traditionally, the solicitors for the separate parties met and swapped the deeds and the money across a table. That was the moment when the ownership of the house changed hands. The money was in the form of a banker's draft, which looks like a cheque but is drawn by a bank rather than an individual, so that the person who supplied the money for it cannot stop it.

This has largely changed. It has become too costly and time consuming for solicitors to attend completion meetings of this sort, so the matter is largely done by post, with the money being transferred direct from one bank to another between the respective solicitors' accounts. The vendor's solicitor makes sure that all the documentation is complete and in his hands. The purchaser's solicitor then despatches the money, against the other solicitor's undertaking to send the documents. The moment when completion takes place, which is when the ownership changes hands, is in effect fixed by the vendor's solicitor when he deals with the documents in his office.

177 | If the change of ownership is all done in effect by remote control, how do I get hold of the keys of my new home?

Sometimes the vendor and the purchaser make informal arrangements between themselves. But the safe thing to do is for the vendor to leave the keys with the estate agent responsible for selling the property. The new owner then picks them up from there as soon as the sale has been completed. Confirmation of that comes to the estate agent by telephone from the vendor's solicitors.

178 | I shall be abroad on holiday on the date when I am due to complete the purchase of my new house. How can I be sure that all the documentation is signed on time?

There is nothing against your signing the documents abroad and sending them back. However, if there is some doubt whether they will reach your solicitor in time, you may be wiser to execute a 'power of attorney'. A power of attorney is a formal document under which you authorise someone else (your 'attorney') to do something on your behalf, including signing formal legal documents. The attorney has complete power to bind you, as if you had been doing the deed yourself. Obviously, therefore, you have to choose someone in whom you have complete faith. This can be your solicitor or a member of your family.

A power of attorney can be prepared so that it is for a single limited purpose, like signing one particular document. Alternatively, you can sign a general power, which gives your attorney authority to do practically anything on your behalf. The attraction of this latter type of power of attorney is that the standard form available for it is very short, so that the expense of preparing the power of attorney is kept to a minimum.

179 | *Who suffers the loss if a house is damaged by fire between the date of the exchange of contracts and the date when the contracts are completed?*

The general rule is that the risk of damage between exchange of contracts and completion lies on the purchaser. This may not seem entirely logical, because it is the vendor who is normally still enjoying the use of the property and the purchaser has no right of access to it. The reason lies in legal theory. The sale of a house is looked on as a sale of the land, plus whatever happens to be attached to it at the time. If the house burns down completely, the land still exists. That means that the vendor can still perform the contract by handing over the land. The vendor is therefore entitled to receive in exchange the price the purchaser agreed to pay.

In practical terms this means that as soon as contracts are exchanged the purchaser must immediately arrange to insure. At that stage, it is wise to fix the cover as a minimum at the full purchase price of the house.

180 | *How is insurance arranged on the sale of a flat, when it is the landlord's company which has taken out the policy?*

In this sort of case the same insurance policy remains in force even though the flat changes hands. In due course, the insurance company should be notified of the change in ownership, so that if there is a claim it knows that the purchaser is the leaseholder who is entitled to make the claim.

181 | *Presumably, once the document the vendor signs to pass the house over into my name is dated at completion it has to be stamped with the stamp duty which is payable. What is to stop me simply not paying?*

Not paying stamp duty (see Q154) is not a crime, but paying it is almost unavoidable. A deed (see Q172) cannot be used to prove title to a house if it has not been duly stamped. That means that when you come to sell your house, the deed would not be an acceptable proof of title for the purchaser. Moreover, if you stamp a document late, which is more than 30 days after it is dated, you have to pay a substantial penalty in addition to the stamp duty which would otherwise have been due.

If your house is registered (see Q170), you cannot show you are the owner until your name is entered on the register. It is an offence to register any document that should have been stamped but has not been. The result is that the Land Registry will not accept a transfer that has not been stamped.

Moreover, a building society will not let you get away without paying the stamp duty, because the validity of its mortgage depends in turn on the proof of your ownership.

Even a document which is free of stamp duty has to be shown to the stamping authorities. This is so that it can be checked against a form giving brief details of the transaction, which your solicitors have to supply. Those forms are sorted and sent to the government valuers for each district, so that they can have comprehensive information about property values in their areas.

182 | *Only two days before my house purchase was due to be completed, I heard that the vendor was not going to move out on time. The completion date was stated in the contract. Can it just be ignored?*

In a sense, the completion date stated in a normal sale and purchase agreement for a house or flat is not absolutely firm. If it were, both parties would have to complete on that actual day, or face the possibility that the other party to the contract would call it off completely. The tradition has been built up to fix a date which everyone expects to stick to for completion. That date is kept in the vast majority of cases, but there are so many minor difficulties that can prevent the sale going through for quite understandable reasons, such as sudden illness or accident, that it seems better not to impose a guillotine deadline.

It is perfectly possible to have an absolutely firm date, though. What the contract has to say, if that is what you want, is that as far as the completion date is concerned, 'time is of the essence of the contract'. If both the vendor and the purchaser agree to have that in their contract, there is no difficulty whatsoever. It does involve the risk that you cannot cope with the unexpected without running the danger of losing the sale or purchase of the property.

183 | *If the vendor simply refuses to complete the sale and move out of the house on the completion date fixed in the contract, there must surely be some way to have a firm date imposed?*

Once the contractual completion date has passed, the purchaser (or vendor if he is the one not causing the delay) can impose an immoveable date. If the vendor refuses to complete, you can serve on him a 'notice to complete'. This calls on him to complete the contract by a specified date, and it makes time of the essence of the contract (see Q182). If that new date were to pass without the vendor performing his obligations under the contract, therefore, you would be in a position to call off the purchase.

Most house and flat purchase contracts state how much extra time a notice to complete must give. Twenty-one days is now the most common period. If the contract says nothing, then you have to give a reasonable period, and that opens up arguments as to just how long is reasonable in your particular circumstances.

Once a notice to complete has been given, most overdue contracts are satisfactorily completed. It is not usual to wait until the end of the extended period. The delay is often only a few days, although clearly the sooner that a notice to complete is served, the earlier completion is likely to take place.

184 | *I'm selling my house, and because the purchaser did not complete on the due date my solicitor served a notice to complete. My circumstances have changed, and it would be inconvenient for me to complete the contract at the moment. Can I, in turn, wait to receive a notice to complete?*

Once a notice to complete is served, by whichever party to a contract, it makes time of the essence *of the contract* (see Q182). That is, it is not imposing a penalty on the party in default; rather, it is changing the terms of the contract so that the contract embodies a totally fixed completion date. Because that is now a term of the contract, it binds *both* parties. Although you served a notice to complete because the purchaser was at that time in default in complying with his obligations, you changed the contract terms, and these terms bind you as well. If, once the notice runs out, the contract has still not been completed, the purchaser has just as much right to call off the deal as you have.

185 | *Is there any real pressure on the purchaser who is buying my house actually to complete the deal if he has a change of heart?*

There is a major financial incentive. When contracts are exchanged and become binding, a purchaser is called upon to pay a deposit. This normally amounts to 10 per cent of the purchase price. If the purchaser has already paid a preliminary deposit (see Q148) to the estate agent selling the house, that is counted towards the 10 per cent. A purchaser who does not actually buy once a notice to complete has been

served and has expired faces the possibility that the vendor will keep that deposit.

It is not uncommon nowadays for a purchaser to ask the vendor to agree that the deposit he pays should be less than 10 per cent. The purchaser may have a good reason for doing so. He may be borrowing 95 per cent of the price from a building society, so that his own contribution is only five per cent. Or, in moving from one house to another, the bulk of the purchase price for the new property may be coming from what he receives from the old one, so that he does not have enough spare cash for the 10 per cent deposit.

This boils down to the relative bargaining powers of the vendor and the purchaser. If the demand for the house is strong, the vendor may well insist on having the full deposit. The complete 10 per cent could be needed to stop the vendor from suffering a loss if the deal falls through. If the house is more difficult to sell, the vendor may feel it right to be more accommodating.

186 | *If the vendor actually gets to the point of making his purchaser lose his deposit, can the vendor simply keep it?*

The normal property purchase contract simply provides that if the purchaser defaults, the vendor can 'forfeit' the deposit the purchaser paid, and the deposit then belongs to the vendor. There is, however, some statutory protection for a purchaser in those circumstances, although it is not often possible to invoke it. The court has power to order the return of a deposit to the purchaser, although the court is only likely to do so if it seems totally unjust that the normal consequences of failing to honour the bargain should apply.

Once the vendor has the deposit, he is totally free to decide what he wants to do next. He could change his mind about selling, and keep the house and the deposit money, or he can set about selling the house again. Even if that is successful, he does not have to repay any of the deposit.

187 | *I was going to buy a house, but had to let it go, and my deposit was forfeited. Luckily, it was only five per cent of the price. Is that the limit of my liability, so that I now have nothing further to worry about?*

Forfeiture of the deposit gives the vendor of a house or flat an instant weapon which generally forces a purchaser to complete the contract because otherwise he loses the deposit. However, that is not all that can be done. Although it depends on the exact wording of the contract, the position generally is that if the vendor suffers actual loss as a result of the purchaser's withdrawal there is a good claim for compensation.

What usually happens is that the vendor who has been let down still wants to sell the property. This is going to involve extra expense, both in terms of professional fees and also because money may have to be borrowed to bridge the gap. If the vendor was buying somewhere else at the same time as selling, the result of the sale falling through can be temporary ownership of two houses, the extra one financed by the vendor's bank (see Q145). That will involve the payment of interest which would not otherwise have been payable, and that goes to make up the vendor's loss which is a direct result of the first purchaser's default.

The second sale which the vendor manages to negotiate may not be for as much as the first purchaser agreed to pay. The vendor would not be able to resell at a ridiculous price, and the level of the market may have gone down. The first purchaser's offer may have been unrealistically high, which could account for the fact that the deal fell through. Any shortfall between the first and second contract prices represents a direct loss which the vendor suffers because the first purchaser did not complete the contract.

The vendor has the best of both worlds. If, once the property has been finally sold and all the financial consequences are totted up, there is still some of the original deposit in hand so that the vendor has made a profit, the vendor can keep that surplus. But if the result is a loss, then the extra over and above the deposit means the vendor has a good claim against the original purchaser.

188 | *Is serving a notice to complete necessarily a preliminary to calling a contract off? Won't the law help to ensure that I get the house I have a contract to buy?*

Cancelling a contract – 'rescission' is the legal name for it – is only one of the options open to the purchaser of a house who finds that the vendor is hanging back. You can in fact do exactly the opposite. You can ask the court for an order of 'specific performance', which is an order for the vendor to sell the house to you. Sometimes the reason why the vendor does not want to proceed is because there has been a sudden surge in market prices, bringing the prospect of a higher price on a sale to someone else. The only fair thing for you is to have the house at the price you originally agreed to pay.

If necessary, the court would force through a sale to you. If the vendor did not leave, there could be a possession order, which would force him out. If he did not then sign the necessary transfer order, the court could appoint someone to do it for him.

If the boot is on the other foot, and you are a vendor trying to force a contract through, you are also entitled to ask for specific performance. In the end, that might not be successful. If the purchaser does not have the money to buy, there is nothing a court can do about it. So, even with a specific performance order, you might find yourself having to fall back on cancelling the contract.

If you go for an order to force the contract through, you do not have to serve a notice to complete, and you certainly do not have to wait until it expires. All the same, it is usual to serve a notice when the completion date passes so that all your options remain open.

189 | *The completion of the sale of my house was a couple of days late. Does the short delay which took place give me a right to any compensation?*

The purchaser certainly has to compensate you for what you have lost. That compensation may take two forms. Either you can claim interest on what he should have paid you for that period of delay. Alternatively you may be entitled to compensation in the form of damages for breach of contract for the actual money losses you incurred (see Q190).

One thing you have to be careful about is that there may be a time-limit on your choosing which form of compensation you will claim.

The contract fixes an interest rate just in case something has to be paid. It should be enough to

243

repay you for any overdraft interest you may have had to pay a bank as a result of the delay. That interest is calculated not on the whole of the money that you should receive on completion, but on the amount that the purchaser has to pay, which is less than the total because of the deposit he has already paid. This seems unfair on you, because that deposit will be held by an estate agent or a solicitor, and you will not receive any interest which it earns. On the other hand, paying interest on the whole amount might seem unfair on the purchaser, who will have paid out the deposit some time beforehand.

190 | *My expenses arising from the delay caused by the purchaser in buying my house certainly go far beyond what interest would amount to. What sort of things can I claim for?*

The rule is that you can claim anything that the purchaser knew or should have known at the date of the contract would run you into expense if he went over the time-limit.

Some things must be perfectly obvious. If your contract was one of a chain of transactions, it is clear that without the money that should have come to you as a result of the purchaser paying when the money was due, you would have to borrow what you needed to complete your own purchase. That is likely to cost you more than the interest earned (see Q189), because it will be a bridging loan (see Q145) for which your bank will probably charge you a fee.

If the notification that the purchaser was going to be late did not come in time, you may yourself have been forced to call off the completion arrangements for the house you were buying. That lands you in trouble with the people selling the house. They may make a claim against you, and you can pass it on to your purchaser whose fault it really was.

There may be other things that are going to cause you expense which the purchaser could not have been expected to guess at the date that contracts were exchanged. Say, you had been going to emigrate, and needed his money to pay for your passage. If you did not pay in time you might incur some penalty. If, before the contract is made, you explain the circumstances which put you at risk, then the purchaser becomes responsible for any losses he causes.

191 | *If I am ready to buy the house, but the vendor will not complete and move out, can I claim interest?*

Interest is not appropriate for a purchaser whose vendor will not complete. Interest is compensation for not having money which should have been paid to you, and that applies only to the vendor of a property.

However, because of a strong feeling that both parties to this type of contract should have the same incentive to complete on time, and be subject to the same kinds of penalty for not doing so, one of the two widely used standard forms of contract does something which is in effect equivalent to your receiving interest (the other does nothing in this connection).

What the purchaser can claim is instant compensation of an amount which is equivalent to interest for the period of the delay on the money he was prepared to hand over. The important thing is that this provision makes available a remedy which can be put into effect when completion eventually takes place. You simply deduct the compensation due to you from what you would otherwise have paid. Establishing the precise amount of your actual additional expenditure would take time and trouble, and if the figure is small you may not want to bother.

There is a danger in that from your point of view. If the other party to your contract does not complete on the right date, the ripples of damage may go right down the contract chain. Normally, you would expect to pass on to the defaulter any claims that you receive. However, if you have agreed that his liability to you should be limited, you cannot pass on claims that exceed that limit. You could also find yourself having to pay out to other people in the chain. You cannot protect yourself from anyone with whom you do not have a contract. The position would really be safe only if all the contracts in a chain had the same terms in them.

192 | *When we arrived to move into our new house, we found that the vendor had not moved out and we had great difficulty in getting temporary accommodation and storing our furniture. My wife was very upset. Can we claim for the disturbance and dislocation, as well as our actual out-of-pocket expenses?*

There certainly should be no question of your being able to obtain from the vendor the cost of your extra accommodation – hotel or rent – and the cost of storing your furniture. Any other expenses that come directly from the situation you found yourselves in would also be proper damages – extra travelling expenses, perhaps. Additional legal fees would also be covered.

Compensation for the emotional disturbance is less certain, but really only because there is as yet no recorded case of such a claim having been made. That type of claim has been becoming more common in other areas of the law in recent years and has in most cases been accepted. It therefore seems likely that you would be able to ask for something – although the amount would probably not be very great – and it would be worth making a claim.

193 | *In a chain of house purchases and sales, the knock-on effect of one person's default might cause losses all the way down the line, all of which would eventually come back to the person responsible. Although I am not planning to default, can I guard against the possibility of a charge which sounds as if it could be enormous in the worst case?*

It is true that the bill could mount up very significantly, and it is something you could not control. If you feel that because of some sudden crisis you cannot move out on time, you will not know what the purchaser of your house will do. He may move out of his house as he should do, so that you have to pay for his extra expenses. On the other hand, he may feel that it is best to stay put, so that another family down the line is dispossessed. That family may be a much larger one, so that the expense of temporarily housing them, which will probably eventually come to you, will be greater.

There is nothing you can effectively do about this when the completion date is approaching or has passed. But if you think about it early enough there is a precaution. You could have a special clause in the contract limiting the amount of compensation which you can be called upon to pay. That kind of contract term is perfectly valid. If you suggest that the contract should contain a clause of that kind, you will inevitably have to agree that it applies to both parties under your contract. So not only will your liability be limited, but that if the person from whom you are buying or to whom you are selling defaults, their responsibility is limited as well.

194 | *If the purchaser does not complete and pay over his money when he should do, what happens about the expenses of the house?*

The contract will have a provision in it to cover this. The normal rule is that the purchaser takes over responsibility for the expenses from the date on which he should have completed, even if he actually completes late. The main expense will probably be rates, but if the house is empty after you move out, nothing may be payable. On the other hand, if the bargain is that you leave furniture and furnishings behind because the purchaser is buying them, rates will continue.

Even if rates are suspended, there could well be other expenses which will have to be apportioned between the two parties – water rates, and service charges for flats, for instance.

If you are selling a house with a tenant in part of it, the situation may be different. Here, the house is not only causing expense, it is also generating an income, the rent which the tenant pays. In this case you probably have a choice. Either you can receive the rent for the interim period, but be responsible for the outgoings, or you make the purchaser responsible for making the payments, but allow him the benefit of the income.

195 | *I have decided to keep the deposit paid by the purchaser of my house who has not completed. However, the estate agent holding that deposit claims that I am not entitled to do so. How can I get the deposit from the agent?*

If the circumstances are such that you are justified in forfeiting the deposit, and you have complied with any necessary formalities, then the estate agent is not entitled to withhold it from you. If it refuses to hand over the deposit then you will have to sue the agent to recover it.

Anyone holding a deposit may find himself in rather an unenviable position. The vendor of a property may claim that the deposit should be handed over by the agent because it has been forfeited. The purchaser may lay claim to it on the ground that it is the vendor who is in the wrong. The agent holding the deposit cannot be expected to sort out all the conflicting claims, and will certainly want to be sure that there is no question of paying out the deposit twice.

For these cases there is a special legal action called 'an interpleader'. The stakeholder, in this case the estate agent, can go to court and in effect say: 'I have this deposit which I know is not mine, but I do not know to which of the two claimants I should pay it. Please give me instructions.' The vendor and the purchaser then have to fight it out in court.

196 | *If my solicitor's investigations revealed that for some reason the present owner of the house was not the true owner and therefore was not entitled to sell it, where would that leave me?*

It seems nowadays to be extremely rare that there is any technical defect in a homeowner's title (see Q170), but it does very occasionally happen. This is an embarrassment for the vendor who is told that he is not entitled to sell, but it can be even worse for the purchaser. Because the investigation takes place after contracts have been exchanged and are binding, it is likely that you will already be committed to sell your present home.

Because of this strong pressure on you not to back out, you will sometimes feel that any risk is slight and you can ignore the technical defect in proving ownership. Obviously, this depends upon the nature of the snag, and your solicitor will give you full details. If you are raising a mortgage, the building society has to accept the position too.

Another possibility is to insure against the risk involved. Whether there is a chance of this again depends upon just what the difficulty is. When the matter can be resolved in that way, you would expect the vendor to foot the bill for the insurance premium, which generally is a single lump sum.

But if all else fails you have no alternative but to call off the deal. You may be able to get some compensation from the defaulting vendor, but that is far from certain. You can get back any deposit you paid. The worst thing is that you may be stuck with selling your own house, to which you are committed, so you have nowhere to go. This is one of the inevitable risks inherent in buying and selling simultaneously.

197 | *I feel that I have to call off my purchase because of the impossibility of proving that the vendor is the owner. How much compensation can I claim, bearing in mind that the vendor has not done what he agreed to do and sell me the house?*

Unfortunately, you may not be able to claim anything more than the legal fees that you have wasted. Your loss may be very much greater than that,

ARE YOU SUGGESTING I'M NOT THE OWNER GUV?

because you may have to pay for temporary accommodation for an appreciable period. That will not make any difference.

You are caught by an ancient legal rule which seems to be based on the assumption that the rules about land ownership are so complicated that no one can be blamed for making a mistake about them. This may well have been true in the past, but it is certainly not reasonable where the title to a house is registered (see Q170).

However, the rule still stands. There is a chance that you may be able to sue for damages. Because the old rule is so obviously dated, there have in recent years been a number of ingenious attempts to limit its scope. You may be able, for example, to base a claim on the suggestion that you were misled about the vendor's title, and statute now entitles you to damages for a misrepresentation which causes you loss, however innocent it was. It is worth taking legal advice to see whether you can obtain something more.

Joint ownership

198 | *My wife and I are buying a house in our joint names. Does this make any difference to the process by which we buy the house?*

As explained in LIVING TOGETHER Q1, there are two ways for any joint owners of a house to own it: as joint tenants or as tenants in common. This needs to be stated in the document that transfers the ownership to you, or in some other formal document drawn up at the same time, along with any other special terms about who may insist on selling when.

Apart from that, there is a technical difference between joint ownership and ownership by one person which has to be considered. Joint owners are always looked at in the eyes of the law as trustees, like the trustees of a family settlement or the trustees of a charity who hold the property on behalf of beneficiaries. Just because joint owners hold the house for themselves, making them their own beneficiaries, makes no difference to that technical position. In many ways that is convenient, but it can bring in the rules which govern proper trustees in situations to which they were not intended to apply.

For the protection of beneficiaries under trusts, trustees have only limited powers of leasing the trust property, and of mortgaging it; there is a limit on the length of the leases they can create; and mortgages can be entered into only for certain purposes. These restrictions are entirely inappropriate where the trustees are joint owners, and they will be cancelled by a declaration that the joint owners should have all the powers that an ordinary single owner would have. This is something your solicitor will deal with automatically for you, but it explains a clause in the transfer document which you will be asked to sign.

199 | My husband is going abroad on business just as we have settled on a house to buy. Can I act on his behalf if we buy jointly?

Unfortunately, this is the one case in which the power of attorney (see Q178) does not operate conveniently. The ordinary ability of anyone to delegate what they want to do to an attorney is fenced round with restrictions in the case of trustees, which is what you became by buying jointly (see Q198). For proper trusts, there is good reason for this: the person setting up the trust takes care to select his trustees, and does not want substitutes without safeguards.

Although a joint purchase is only nominally a trust, it does prevent the usual rules regarding power of attorney from applying. One of the prohibitions on trustees is appointing the only other trustee as his or her attorney. If husband and wife jointly own a house, they are the only two trustees and neither can make the other his or her attorney in connection with the house.

You may reasonably say that the trust arises only once you have bought the house and that surely there can be no reason against your operating the power of attorney and signing the purchase contract. You can. The real trouble is signing the mortgage. For a mortgage to be effective, it can come into operation only after you begin to own the house. It is dated the same day as the transfer of the property to you, but it is assumed to be signed and come into effect immediately afterwards. The result is that one partner cannot appoint the other attorney for signing the mortgage.

200 | I'm 19, but my fiancée is a few months short of her eighteenth birthday. Does that stop us jointly buying a house?

Yes. No one under the age of 18 can appear as the owner of a house on the deeds of the property. Also, a building society would not be prepared to lend money to a minor. Their loans have to be secured by mortgages, and someone who is under age cannot validly enter into a mortgage.

Short of waiting for the intervening months, if you are over 18 the solution may be for you to appear on the deeds as the buyer of the house, buying it on behalf of both of you. The building society may be persuaded to accept this, even if it is relying on your fiancée's income to support part of the repayments, by joining her into the mortgage as a guarantor.

Death of vendor

201 | I'm buying a bungalow from someone who is old and very sick and already in hospital, probably permanently. If the worst happens, and the vendor dies before I have completed the purchase, what happens then?

The death of one of the parties to a sale and purchase contract creates a hiatus. If the contract has not yet been signed, then it may be best simply to abandon the transaction, at least for the time being. But if there is already a legally binding contract, the fact that the vendor (or the purchaser) dies does not cancel the contract but means that temporarily there's no chance of making any progress.

When the owner of any property dies, the executors appointed under his will, or the administrators appointed by the court if he dies intestate, have the power and responsibility to deal with the property (see WILLS, DEATH AND INHERITANCE, Q22). If the person who died had entered into a binding contract, then the executors or administrators have to carry it out. The trouble is the time factor. It is not practicable, and sometimes not permissible, for anything to be done before there has been a grant of probate to executors or of letters of administration to administrators (see WILLS, DEATH AND INHERITANCE, Q22). It may not be convenient for you to wait.

All you can do is to take steps to cancel the contract by serving a notice to complete (see Q183) and calling the deal off when that notice has expired. Until you take those steps, the contract remains binding on you as well as on the owner's estate.

202 | Couldn't the possible difficulties which can arise if the ageing owner of a property dies before he has completed the sale be avoided by his appointing someone to act on his behalf?

It is always possible for a property owner to empower someone else to do on his behalf all that is necessary in connection with selling it. He merely grants a power of attorney (see Q178). The snag here is that as soon as the owner dies, the power of attorney is automatically cancelled. It may be possible for the attorney to continue to deal with the matter if he does not know that the person who granted it has died, but you can hardly rely on that being the case.

Not only is there no way round that, but there can be greater difficulties. A power of attorney is also made invalid if the person who grants it is no longer capable of managing his own affairs. That inability could be either physical or mental. It may well be extremely difficult to tell when that point arrives. In practice, if you are dealing with an attorney on someone else's behalf, you go on doing so unless he tells you that because of the owner's state of health he cannot continue.

The procedure then is for the owner's affairs to be put in the hands of the Court of Protection, but this tends to create considerable delays.

Vendors' responsibility after sale

203 | *What responsibility do I have for repairs to my house after I have agreed to sell it?*

While you would not be expected to do any major repairs to a house that you have agreed to sell, you cannot shuffle off all responsibility. Even if a lot needs to be done to the house, the purchaser buys the house in the state it is in and certainly cannot complain if you do not improve it.

What you have to do is to take reasonable steps to safeguard the property from extra harm. How far that extends depends on circumstances. It is well illustrated by moving out of a house in the winter. If freezing conditions are likely, you would be expected to take precautions against pipes freezing and causing damage. If you do not, and there is freezing and the pipes burst, you are responsible both for damage to the plumbing and for any consequential damage, such as ceilings brought down by flooding.

You must also take reasonable care of furniture and other moveables which you have agreed to sell as part of the bargain. What this involves again depends on circumstances. The care that a reasonable person could be expected to take of his own property is a good guide.

204 | *I am selling a leasehold flat. Are my responsibilities during the period between exchanging contracts and completing any different from those of the vendor of a freehold house?*

There is a difference, which stems not from the fact that you are selling a flat, but from the fact that what you are selling is leasehold. The comments apply equally to a leasehold house.

You have no right to do something before completion which puts the lease in jeopardy, and by the same token you must not omit to do something which the lease says you must do. This could involve you in doing repairs that you would not be called upon to do if the property were freehold – there is a tenant's agreement, say, obliging you to decorate the interior every five years. However, that does not mean that the purchaser of the flat has the free benefit of your efforts. If, just to maintain what he is to buy, you do some work to comply with the lease you will usually be able to claim the cost back from the purchaser.

The same principle applies to paying the ground rent. Say the rent is payable in advance on the usual quarter days – 25 March, 24 June, 29 September and 25 December. If you have agreed to complete on 20 July, you should pay the rent that falls due on 24 June even though you have already signed the contract to sell the flat. The fact that you have paid does not mean that in the end you shoulder responsibility for the whole quarter's rent. On completion, you reclaim from the purchaser an appropriate proportion relating to the period after completion – in this case from 20 July to 28 September.

Renaming/renumbering houses

205 | *I'd like to rename the detached house I've just bought. Is there any legal objection?*

As a matter of practice, you should check with the post office that the name you have in mind will not cause confusion with the name of any other house in the area to which they deliver mail. Write to the postmaster. Having done that, the procedure is to write to the local authority's legal department. It will probably send you standard instructions, which involve notifying the emergency services whose addresses are given on the instructions.

Local authorities are stricter about house numbering. You have to display the number of your house,

and if you are not doing so and the local authority gives you notice saying that you should, you are liable to be prosecuted and fined if you do not comply within a week. Sometimes, local authorities decide to renumber the houses in a road, usually because new houses have been built on previously empty plots in the middle and consecutive numbering is not possible. This renumbering is compulsory. The authority will give you a certificate of renumbering, and it is useful to keep this safely with the deeds of the house so that it is clear in the future how and when the number altered. Ask your building society to lodge the certificate if it holds the deeds, as it will if you have a mortgage.

Compulsory purchase

206 | What protection do I have against having my home seized by compulsory purchase?

Only an Act of Parliament can confer compulsory purchase powers, which are always carefully controlled. Normally only a public authority can exercise such a power, although occasionally a private company undertaking what is in effect a public project can do so, as in the case of a local authority contracting the building of a housing development, say.

Plenty of warning of compulsory purchase proposals is given, and this is publicly recorded. If you are in the process of buying a house, the early enquiries your solicitor addresses to the local authority (see Q140) should reveal any proposals pending, unless they are at a very early stage. That means that you should be able to change your mind and not buy the property if you find that it is threatened.

Owner-occupiers will see notices in local newspapers and receive letters warning them of future plans.

Compulsory purchase is normally undertaken only for schemes essential for the common good. They may be public works, such as new schools, hospitals or roads, or they may be comprehensive redevelopment schemes. Usually owner-occupiers will be offered the full market value of their homes in any compulsory purchase order.

207 | Can I protest against suggestions that my house will be taken by compulsory purchase?

Compulsory acquisition procedure varies depending on the type of project. Typically, there are two stages, at both of which you will have a chance to voice your protest at a public inquiry.

At the first stage, the project will be examined in principle. Take the example of a new road. The questions for the first inquiry would include: is a new road needed at all, and is the proposed route the best one? The exact area of land over which the road would stretch is not decided at that stage. Rather, the argument could be whether a town's bypass should run to the east or to the west of the town. Once all that has been decided, and the decision has been taken to proceed with the project, then orders may be made compulsorily to acquire the properties that are needed. Those orders can be contested. An inquiry then looks at whether it is necessary to take any particular property. The inquiry is not concerned with questions of compensation.

You can employ someone to represent you at a public inquiry. If you do not think that that is justified, but you do not fancy speaking in public to put your point of view, it is usually possible to submit a letter setting out your case.

208 | I have no wish to make a great fuss about my house being taken for a road widening project. In fact, I should prefer to get the whole thing over as quickly as possible and move now. Will the local authority agree to buy the house in the ordinary way before serving a compulsory purchase order?

In most of these public projects, quite a number of the properties and a lot of the land which are needed are purchased by agreement by whichever is the authority in charge of the project. It is not uncommon to find, by the time of the public inquiries, that the authority already owns a great deal of the property and land in question.

You should not be under any disadvantage as far as money is concerned if you sell in advance. The price you are paid should not be less than the compensation which is paid on compulsory purchase, and this should be the full market value.

209 | There have been long-term plans to include my house in the site of new council offices, but nothing has been done because of lack of money. I now need to sell for family reasons, and potential buyers are obviously put off by the uncertain threat hanging over the property. The council still says it hasn't the money to start the project. Am I stuck here?

The dilemma in which you find yourself has been given the name 'planning blight'. The threat that a published proposal of this sort hangs over a property virtually freezes it as far as selling it in the ordinary property market is concerned.

249

There is a procedure which gets you out of the difficulty. If you are an owner-occupier, you can serve a notice on the local authority, or on whoever has compulsory purchase powers for the particular scheme in question, which forces it to buy the property. This is generally called a 'blight notice'.

There are some rules limiting who can operate this procedure. You must have been occupying your house for at least six months at the date you serve the notice. You do not lose the right if you move out, provided you serve the notice within 12 months of going and also provided that in the meantime the property has been empty. If you have a lease of the house, it must have at least three years left to run.

If an owner-occupier of a house subject to planning blight dies, his or her personal representatives can serve the notice so long as the people entitled to benefit from the owner-occupier's estate are individuals and not a company.

There is a list of threats to a property to which this applies, and you have to be able to show that the proposed project comes on to the list. All the most common projects involving compulsory purchase do.

210 | Can the local authority contest a blight notice I serve on them, and if so on what grounds?

Naturally, the authority has to be satisfied that you are qualified to serve a blight notice before it accepts that it can be forced to buy your property. Therefore, the authority is entitled to be satisfied with the facts that you are an owner-occupier and that you come within the area affected by a relevant proposal.

There is also another thing that you have to be able to establish. You must show that the house really has been blighted. It is not enough simply to prove that there is public notice of the proposal in question, but the proposal actually has to affect your chances of selling as well. You have to establish that because of the blight you have not succeeded in selling, after making reasonable efforts to do so, at the sort of price the property should have fetched had the compulsory acquisition threat not been hanging over it.

This may mean that you have to go through the farce of having an estate agent offer it for sale, only to find that any deal which is negotiated falls through when the proposed purchaser finds out what is in store. Before even approaching an estate agent, take legal advice to see how this can best be managed.

If you cannot agree with the local authority whether or not it has to buy when you serve a blight notice, the question can be decided by the Lands Tribunal (address on page 510), which will supply you with the forms needed to start the process.

211 | How much compensation can I expect the local authority to pay if it buys my house compulsorily?

The basic principle is that you will be paid the market value of your house. Of course, that value in the actual market would be distorted by the existence of the compulsory purchase threat, so the price is calculated on the basis that the proposed project is not to take place.

Necessarily, this is an artificial assumption, and the price is in effect fixed by comparison with other comparable local properties which are not affected by the proposal. It is best to have a surveyor negotiate this for you with the local government valuer, as most people would find themselves out of their depth.

Generally, it is possible to agree a price, but if you cannot agree, you can take the matter to the Lands Tribunal for them to adjudicate upon it; the address is on page 510.

212 | My house is being compulsorily purchased. Although I do not relish negotiating with the local authority's expert valuer, I cannot afford to hire my own surveyor to value the property to make sure the authority's offer is fair. Is there any help I can get towards the fee?

There is a specific statutory right for those entitled to compensation when their properties are taken away by compulsory purchase to have a valuer's fees paid for by the acquiring authority. Your valuer will negotiate with the local authority's valuer on your behalf. The payment for your valuer's fees is over and above the price of the property. You can therefore instruct a valuer without it costing you anything.

Normally your legal fees for selling will be met too. After all, when there is a compulsory acquisition, you are pitchforked into moving against your will. Your entitlement to legal and valuer's fees is the same if you are put into the position of having to serve a blight notice (see Q209).

213 | My house is a listed building. Will the compensation I receive on compulsory purchase fully take that into account?

The fact that some people are prepared to pay more for a listed building is clearly reflected in the market price. You are entitled to receive compensation equal to the market price, so you will receive a higher amount than if the building were not listed.

Obviously, it can be much more difficult to reach a fair assessment of the market price of this type of

WE CAN OFFER £1500 FOR YOUR PROPERTY, SIR..AND THERE'S NO PRESSURE TO ACCEPT.

house because there will be fewer if any directly comparable buildings in the locality which have recently been sold. That, however, is a problem you can safely leave in the valuer's hands (see Q2 1 2).

There is one case in which the owner of a listed building is entitled to much less compensation. Because listed building consent is needed before a listed building can be demolished, it is not unknown for developers who own that type of building which is standing in the way of their plans deliberately to let it deteriorate. They feel that if they can show the local authority that it is in a ruinous state, the authority will not be able to refuse the necessary consent. For that reason, one of the weapons in the armoury of local authorities to protect listed buildings is to acquire them compulsorily where they feel that they are being neglected. The local authority can then make a 'direction for minimum compensation'. Compensation is assessed on the basis that no planning permision would be given to develop the site, and no listed building consent would be given to demolish or alter the existing building. The result is that the compensation is low, because it is the price for a neglected old building with which nothing else can be done.

214 | *You seem to imply that compensation for compulsory purchase is always satisfactory. What about those cases you read about where people have been offered ludicrously small sums?*

In slum clearance cases, it sometimes happens that the houses are so run down, as well as being out of date, that they really have no value in themselves. Naturally, the sites still have some worth, and the compensation then can be calculated on the site value. This is small compared with house compensation, not only because no sum is paid for the value of the house but also because in many such cases the site is very small.

The danger here for the houseowner is that he finds himself an exception to this because his house is not one which is run down. Local authorities in such cases are entitled to treat a whole area as worth site-only value, even though there may be one or two houses that have not been so neglected and where it is not fair to ignore their value as houses. If you have such a house you are entitled to claim full compensation. You have to show that yours is a well-maintained house. When the local authority sends you notification of the compulsory purchase order which they are making, you will receive a form which allows you to make the claim and you should return it without delay.

215 | *If, as a result of a compulsory purchase, I get turned out of the flat I've occupied as a tenant for many years, how can I expect compensation for the market value, as I don't own the property? Is there nothing I can claim?*

Everyone who is turned out of a home where he or she has lived for at least five years is entitled to a 'home loss payment'. It doesn't matter what your status was in the home. This is in effect compensation for the upset of losing your home.

The amount varies according to the rateable value of the property you have to vacate, and it is calculated as three times the rateable value, with a minimum payment of £1 50 and a maximum of £1,500.

You should receive your payment within six months of leaving. However, put in your claim as soon as possible, because an authority can take up to three months to pay you.

There is one case in which you are not entitled to a home loss payment. This is where you have forced the local authority to buy by serving a blight notice (see Q209). Presumably, the reason for this is that the payments were introduced to give people something for the upset of having to move from their homes when they do not want to. A blight notice is served by someone who wants to move, but finds he cannot.

216 | *Moving out of my house which is being taken by compulsory purchase and moving into somewhere else is obviously going to cost me more than just the value of the house. Can I make a claim for my expenses?*

If you are out of pocket simply because of being forced to move, and provided you disregard any profit you may make from having something better, you can claim compensation.

251

To give examples: your removal should be paid for, and you can claim for any alterations that need to be made to fitted carpets or to curtains so they fit into your new house.

On the other hand, you get no compensation if your new house is simply more expensive than the old one and involves you in greater mortgage payments; because you received the full market price for your old house, paying more for the new one must be because you bought something better. This remains so even if the fact is that nothing similar to your old house and at the same price was available.

217 | *I am being turned out of my home, which I own, by compulsory purchase, but at 68 I don't want the bother of trudging round to try to find a new home. Can't I claim that the local council must rehouse me?*

The local authority does have a duty to rehouse you and offer you a council flat. However, this does not apply in every case. The council does not have to rehouse you if other accommodation – such as suitable flats to buy, or even renting part of a relative's house – is available to you on reasonable terms.

The authority is entitled to assume that you will use your compensation to buy yourself somewhere to live. If in all the circumstances it is not enough to pay for somewhere else, and you cannot reasonably borrow the difference, you would have good grounds on which to claim to be rehoused. Your age does not change the rules, but it does mean that you need not consider housing which lacks any special facilities you need.

Road widening schemes

218 | *I've received notice from the council that part of my front garden is to be used to widen the road. This is going to have a devastating effect on the house. Not only will the road outside be busier and therefore noisier, but we shall be that much nearer to it. Can I insist that they take the whole house and compensate me?*

There is a procedure under which if you are threatened with compulsory purchase of only part of your property, you can challenge the authority to take all or nothing. If it agrees to take everything, then things go ahead as if this had been the intention in the first place. Should it decide to take nothing at all, then everything goes back to where it was in the first place.

However, if the council persists in its demand to take only part of the property, then you can take the dispute to the Lands Tribunal (address on page 510). If you will still be left with a relatively satisfactory front garden, the Tribunal is not likely to be very sympathetic, and will probably say you should simply rely on the compensation to which you are entitled.

That compensation will take two forms. First, you will get the usual payment for the land which is being taken away from you. That is not likely to be very much because the value of garden land on its own is not high. Part of the deal should be that the authority will put up an appropriate wall or fence for you along the new boundary, or pay you to do so.

The second form of compensation is for 'injurious affection'. This is the depressing effect on the value of your house which the widened road is likely to have. Say your house as a whole will go down in market price by five per cent, then you should claim that amount from the authority. The result ought to be that even if the authority refused to buy the house, but you still wanted to move, selling the house in the usual way should net you a price which added to the compensation would put you back in the same financial situation you were in originally.

219 | *When I bought my house, the local authority failed to point out that the road in front was due to be widened and the widening will reduce the value of my home. Can I claim the reduction in value from the authority?*

The standard enquiry about road widening, which local authorities answer, is one of a whole series of questions (see Q140) which they have agreed to answer, but they are not forced to. The local authorities' associations and the Law Society agree, and from time to time revise, this list of questions. The amount of responsibility local authorities are prepared to accept for the accuracy of this information is limited. If they are negligent, that is, if they or a member of their staff do not do their job properly, taking reasonable care, you can claim compensation. There is no claim for any other inaccuracy. In your case, claiming compensation may not be easy. Although you might have preferred to find another house, any money loss you may have suffered should be made up by the compensation paid as and when the work is done to make the road wider.

The list of agreed questions that local authorities are prepared to answer should be distinguished from the set of registers (see Q140) which local authorities

have to keep by statute, showing 'local land charges'. These are certain things affecting properties which purchasers need to be warned of. The list is rather miscellaneous and haphazard, ranging from payments still due for making a road up to the standard for adoption, for example (see Q59), to restrictions on the height of buildings because of interference with air traffic to a local airport. A purchaser's solicitor sends in an official request for any information on those registers affecting the property in question, and there is a statutory right to compensation if the authority gets it wrong.

220 | *The road outside my house is due to be widened, but none of my front garden has to be taken. Can I claim for the amount the new road will knock off the price of my house?*

Because compensation for injurious affection (see Q218) is separate from the compensation paid when local authorities acquire property, you can put in a claim for it when you are not due to lose any land. The basis of calculation will be just the same: the loss of value to your house made by the new road.

221 | *What about the appalling noise and interference that a major road scheme can cause while it is under way? Are neighbouring householders compensated for that?*

There is no statutory compensation scheme for the effect of construction works. It may be possible to make a claim based on the fact that it is a nuisance to you (see Q34), although the fact that the work is done on statutory authority may negate that. There may, too, be some possibility of obtaining a temporary reduction in rateable value.

Once a new road has opened, or a new airport, you can claim compensation for the physical effects it has on your property – things like noise, vibration, smell and smoke. The position is usually assessed a year after the new facility is open to the public. In some cases, of course, the value of your property will benefit from the new work – like a new road – even though affected by its unpleasant side. Compensation is reduced by any such benefit. Your compensation claim has to be put in during the two years following the first anniversary of the road or airport being opened to the public.

Being close to a new road may mean that only altering the house can make it reasonable to continue living there. When the noise level you suffer is likely to rise above a certain level, laid down by regulations, the highway authority is bound to do insulation work for you, or to give you a grant for that purpose. This would include providing double glazing and sound-resistant doors, and even air-conditioning where that is appropriate.

Mobile homes

222 | *I am proposing to buy a mobile home in which we'll live. Are there any special points I should bear in mind?*

The main thing you have to sort out in advance is where you are going to station your mobile home, because these large caravans are usually anything but mobile. If you have your own piece of land, you must get planning permission before using it for this purpose but you cannot assume that consent will automatically be given; you should apply to the planning department of the local authority.

There are many commercially run sites for mobile homes. Before arranging to have a space at one, you need to check that the planning department has granted a licence to it because some caravan sites are licensed only for holiday use. There is normally a condition in the licences for such sites saying that all the caravans must be vacated for a particular month every year.

223 | *I have parked my mobile home on a permanent site. When I asked the owner what the terms of the agreement with him would be he said he preferred to keep things informal and did not provide agreements. Should I insist on having something in writing?*

There is now considerable protection for mobile home owners whose homes are stationed on other people's sites. This applies where this is your only or main residence, and you are on a properly licensed site (see Q222).

The agreement between you and the site owner

can be made orally and informally, but within three months the owner has to give you a written statement which sets out the important terms. These include the owner's name and address, and yours, it identifies where you are entitled to station your home, sets out anything expressly agreed between you, and has to specify some terms which are compulsorily included. Among other things, these deal with how agreements can be brought to an end, and your rights if you sell your home.

If the owner does not volunteer this written statement, you should insist he gives it to you.

224 | *How can one of these mobile home agreements be terminated? Obviously, I want to be sure that I cannot be evicted summarily from the site.*

The terms that now automatically form part of the agreement between the site owner and the occupier of the mobile home are very favourable to the occupier. You have to give the owner four weeks' notice if you decide to move off the site.

The owner, on the other hand, has to allow the agreement to go on indefinitely unless the county court agrees that he may end it. If you do not comply with your obligations under the agreement, that would be a ground for the owner's ending it, although only if it was reasonable for him to do so. Again, if you ceased to qualify for protection, because your main residence was somewhere else, the owner would be allowed to end the agreement. The only other ground on which the owner can evict you is that the age and condition of your mobile home are such that it has a detrimental effect on the amenity of the site, or that it is likely to do so within the next five years.

The only exception to this rule which effectively gives you permanent rights while the condition of the mobile home remains reasonable is if the site owner himself has only limited rights there, say, a ten-year lease. He cannot give mobile home occupiers the right to stay beyond the end of his lease.

225 | *How often is a site owner entitled to put up the rent which a mobile home owner has to pay? I did not agree anything with the site owner when I first moved here with my mobile home.*

It is unusual for this not to be covered in the original agreement. As the rent is not specified in the agreement, within six months of your being given the written statement of the terms of your agreement (see Q223), either the site owner or you can apply to the county court to settle certain terms, and one of these

is the review of the payments at yearly intervals. If nothing was settled, the owner can ask for this to be put in.

It seems that if no application to court is made within the time-limit, nothing can be done about it, and all the owner could do would be to try to have your agreement terminated so that he could negotiate a new one with you.

226 | *I want to sell my mobile home, and have found a buyer. The site owner wants to vet the incoming purchaser. What right has he to interfere?*

He obviously does have some interest, because he wants to be sure that the new occupier will pay the fees and generally comply with the terms of the agreement. Statute gives him the right to approve anyone to whom you want to sell the home, although he cannot unreasonably withhold consent. That will normally mean that anyone producing good references has to be accepted.

Clearly the site owner has no say in the matter whatsoever if the purchaser of your mobile home is going to move it to another site.

When the home is going to stay where it is, the site owner is entitled to ask for commission on the purchase price which is changing hands. The rate is controlled by statute; the legal maximum is currently 10 per cent.

Cost of repairing parish church

227 | *I have heard that house owners have sometimes been confronted unexpectedly with large demands for payments towards the repair of the parish church. What on earth is all this about, and how can I guard against it?*

This can be regarded as an historical oddity, but it is certainly an alarming one and there's no sure way of guarding against it. Because of what happened in the past, the responsibility for paying for repairs to the chancel of the parish church became attached to certain land in the parish. Whoever now owns that land, or any part of it, can find themselves called upon by the church to pay for the repairs. The trouble is that many of the records of where the liability lies are obscure. The facts have generally been forgotten, but sometimes a diligent researcher manages to find the answer. It is possible, and occasionally happens, that a housing estate has been built on some of the land. That means any owner on that estate can be faced with the bill. That owner would be entitled to

I'M AFRAID YOU OWE 927 SOVEREIGNS FROM DECEMBER 1548

claim contributions from all the others, but that in itself is a daunting task.

What makes all this worse is that the usually careful process of transferring ownership which is geared to finding out in advance exactly what the house buyer is letting himself in for, has no machinery for finding out whether this risk exists. If it descends on you like a bolt from the blue, you are most unlikely to be able to blame the solicitor who acted for you when you bought the property, because there was no way in which he could have discovered the risk.

Moves are afoot for phasing all this out, but until the law is actually changed the position remains unsatisfactory.

Very occasionally, properties, mostly in the country, are subject to another unusual ecclesiastical charge, a corn rent. This is generally a small sum which varies slightly every year, theoretically at least in relation to the price of corn. Because this is a

regular payment, you should be given details of it by the person who sells you the property.

Gas and electricity bills

228 | *An elderly relative is worried about her gas bill. She thinks the meter gives the wrong reading, so that she receives excessive bills. What can I do about it, and can I prevent her supply being disconnected while any dispute is settled?*

You can ask the Gas Corporation to test the meter (don't attempt to do so yourself; tampering with gas meters is a criminal offence). If the meter is registering wrongly, the Corporation will assume that it has been giving that wrong result only from the last meter reading date. If the test shows that the meter is correct, you have to pay the cost of testing and replacing the meter. You should have no worry about the gas supply being cut off without warning. The Corporation has to allow 28 days after demanding that the charges be paid, plus another seven days' notice that it is intending to cut off the supply. Over and above that it has agreed to abide by a Code of Practice which rules out cutting off gas between 1 October and 31 March to households in which everyone is over retirement age, unless they clearly have adequate financial resources.

The position is much the same in the case of electricity, except that the Electricity Board has no statutory obligation to give notice before the supply is disconnected. However, electricity suppliers have also agreed to abide by a Code of Practice. You can ask the Board to send an independent examiner to test an electricity meter. The examiner's decision is binding both on the consumer and the supplier.

Those who let part of their house, and install coin meters for gas or electricity for the tenants, should note that there is a legal limit to the price that can be charged through such a meter. The local showroom will have details of the current amount. Anyone who is charged more has a right to claim back any excess.

You and your job

Contracts and conditions of employment

1 | *I've just landed my first job and the personnel manager has told me that he would prepare my contract of employment. What is that?*

The contract of employment sets out the terms on which you have agreed to work for your employers – pay, holidays, sick pay, pensions, and so on. The contract does not have to be in writing, but it obviously saves a lot of argument if the terms are written down and signed. Sometimes an employee is given a letter of appointment which he is asked to sign.

It is important to understand that the piece of paper headed 'contract of employment' may not necessarily cover all the terms of your contract. In the first place there may be a collective agreement between your employers and a union, and some of the terms of that agreement may legally form part of your contract. Second, there may be work rules (see Q4). Finally, some terms are said to be 'implied' by law – terms that will form part of your contract even though nothing is ever said at all. Your employers must, for example, take reasonable care for your personal safety, and you must not disclose their trade secrets or accept bribes from a competing firm.

2 | *Do all contracts of employment have to be in writing?*

No, a contract of employment can be oral or in writing, or partly oral and partly in writing (see Q1). You are probably thinking of what is called the 'written statement of terms'. When you start a job, your employers must give you a written statement within 13 weeks. This must contain a lot of information, including your job title, the date on which your employment began, your rates of pay, your normal hours of work, any arrangements as to sick pay, holidays and holiday pay, pensions, how much notice your employers have to give you (and how much notice you have to give them) to end the contract, how grievances are to be dealt with, and details of disciplinary rules and procedures. Sometimes the statement goes on to deal with other terms such as voluntary overtime and your employers' right to switch your place of work.

This statement of terms is a useful guide as to the terms of your contract, but it is not the contract. In one case the statement said that the employment had started on 19 November. But the employee had been working for an employment agency and he didn't start working for the employers until 30 November. The difference was vitally important because the employee was dismissed on 23 November in the following year and could qualify for an unfair dismissal claim only by showing that he had clocked up employment for one year to the date of his dismissal. The Employment Appeal Tribunal decided that he had only started his employment on 30 November. This meant that he hadn't clocked up the one year, and so he lost his case.

3 | *What can I do if my employers don't give me my statement of terms or if it's wrong?*

Very little. There was a time when employers could be brought before a court and fined for their default, but that didn't last very long. All that you can do is to bring a complaint to an Industrial Tribunal (see page 266). If the statement has not been given to you at all, the Tribunal can state what should have gone into the statement and you are then in the same position as if the statement had been given to you. If the statement has been given to you but it misses out some of the particulars, here again the Tribunal can decide what those missing particulars were. In one case, for example, the statement said nothing about wages during illness. The Employment Appeal Tribunal decided that it was a term of the contract that wages would be paid for a reasonable time, and that the written statement should have said this.

You may have a claim that the statement is wrong: it may, for example, state 'two weeks' holiday per year' when your employers have orally agreed to give you four weeks. Once again, the Tribunal can correct the statement by striking out the wrong term and putting in the right term. The only thing that the Tribunal cannot do is to create a term in a case where you and your employers have not come to any agreement at all.

It is, of course, much better to sort all this out with your employers, the Tribunal should be used only as a last resort.

4 | *My works manager keeps talking about work rules. What are they, and am I legally bound by them?*

Many companies have rules that set out what employees can and cannot do – such as take tea breaks, not smoke on the job, and so on – and the penalties if these rules are broken – such as loss of benefits, suspension, dismissal, and so on. The rules may also deal with other matters, such as safety,

RULES

sickness and holiday arrangements. Some of the rules are often vague, uncertain and out of date, and those won't be legally binding. You may, however, be bound by other rules if they form part of your contract. This will be so if you have signed a letter or any other document that confirms your agreement to be bound by them or if your employers have taken reasonable steps to bring the rules to your notice. In one case, for example, a notice about sick pay was posted on a factory noticeboard; the court held that the notice was legally binding even though the employers had not drawn it to the attention of the work-force. The written statement of terms (see Q3) should provide useful evidence if there is a dispute between you and your employers on this question.

One final point: the mere fact that your employers' right to dismiss employees is contained in the work rules does not necessarily make it reasonable for the employers to use that right in every particular case.

5 | *My union has just negotiated a new collective agreement. How does that affect my contract with my employers?*

Under English law the only persons who have rights under a contract are the parties to that contract. You yourself were not a party to the collective agreement, and so you don't have any direct rights under it. Nevertheless, your own contract may well be affected. As a practical matter any pay rise that has been negotiated will be reflected in your own pay packet. Also, you may have a clause in your contract which states that you are employed on terms set out in the collective agreement (as varied from time to time). Even if the contract does not spell this out, the result could well be the same. If, for example, the terms of the last collective agreement have been regularly observed by your employers and by yourself, this strongly suggests that they have been incorporated into your contract and that any changes will also have this effect – in other words they (or such parts of them as are appropriate) will form part of your contract.

6 | *I've had a letter from my employers telling me that my hours of work are being changed and that my overtime is being cut. Can they do that?*

The basic rule is that the terms of your contract cannot be changed without your consent unless the contract gives your employers the right to do so. In your case it certainly looks as if your employers are breaking the contract by altering your working hours, and the position is the same with regard to any overtime that your employers have agreed to let you work. You must therefore establish whether your contract gave you a legal right to a minimum period of overtime (which can't be changed) or whether you and your employers arranged it whenever it was convenient for both sides to do so.

If your employers try to change your contract you (and perhaps your union on your behalf) can object. If your employers insist on the changes you are faced with a difficult choice – you can stay or leave. If you stay and carry on working under protest you can still take your employers to court, although understandably not all employees are prepared to do so. In one recent case a local council told its school dinner ladies that it was cutting their pay. They stayed on and sued the council for not paying them at the old rate. They won their case.

If you decide to leave you can bring two claims against your former employers. You can take them to court because they have 'wrongfully dismissed' you by changing your contract without your consent (see Q 121). Second, you may be able to go to an Industrial Tribunal (see page 266) to claim compensation for unfair dismissal; however, there is no guarantee that you will win – your employers may be able to show that the dismissal was fair if the changes to your contract were essential for the business to survive (see Q 120).

7 | Are there any laws or rules relating to hours of work?

Yes. They vary from industry to industry, and in some cases the rules apply equally to men, women and young people. Thus, a lorry driver of either sex cannot lawfully drive more than eight hours per day or more than 48 hours per week.

A number of special rules regulate the employment of children and young people. Some of the most important of these are as follows:

● A child under 13 cannot be employed at all.
● A child of 13 or over but under 16 cannot be employed:
before the end of school hours, or
for more than two hours on any school day, or
before 7 am or after 7 pm on any school day, or
for more than two hours on a Sunday, or
for more than 44 hours per week in a factory.
● A 'young person' – someone of over 16 but under 18 – cannot be employed in a factory:
for more than nine hours per day (excluding meal and rest breaks), or
for more than 11 hours in any one day, or
for a period beginning before 7am or ending after 8pm (after 1pm on Saturdays), or
for more than 48 hours in any week.
● As a general rule a young person cannot be continuously employed in a factory for more than four and a half hours without an interval of at least half an hour for a meal or rest.

8 | I'm getting very bored at my job because my boss isn't giving me any work to do. Is he legally bound to give me work?

The basic rule is that there is no duty on your employers to provide you with work. In one case a judge said that if he paid his cook her wages she could not complain if he took all his meals out. From time to time the courts have suggested that the law may be changing (especially in cases where the work is available), but any such change is very gradual and the basic 'no duty' rule still exists. There are, however, a few fairly obvious exceptions. First of all employers may agree not only to pay wages but also to give the employee an opportunity to enhance his or her reputation; the employment of an actor or actress is an obvious example. Similarly, there will often be a duty to provide work if the employee is engaged on skilled work on the basis that his or her skills will disappear if the work is not provided. Third, it is obviously an essential implied term of the contract of employees who are on piece work or who are paid partly by commission that their employers will give them the opportunity to earn their wages or the commission by providing work. Finally, there have been cases in which the employee is in a position of authority and the employers proceed to undermine that authority by ignoring him completely and giving to other people the work that he has been doing. In all these examples the employers will be in breach of contract if they provide no work.

9 | We get four weeks' holiday every year, but last year I only took three weeks. Can I take an extra week this year or can I get holiday pay for the week I didn't take?

In most cases this will depend on the terms of your contract of employment. In many industries collective agreements negotiated by unions will deal with holidays and holiday pay as well as with wages; such provisions will often form part of your contract of employment (see Q5). Particulars of any terms in your contract relating to holiday matters should be set out in the written statement that your employers should give you (see Q2).

Many contracts give the employee a right to take a number of weeks' holiday either at any time during the year or during a specified period. On the whole the right to carry forward unused holiday is fairly rare, and similarly an employee who hasn't taken his or her full quota of holiday can't claim holiday pay instead unless his or her contract gives that right. The question of holiday pay usually comes up when an employee leaves (or is given notice) in the middle of a holiday year. He or she will usually be entitled to holiday pay for a proportion of unused holiday (as, for example, 'one week's holiday pay for each complete period of three months, less holidays already taken'). Everything will depend on your contract. However, in some industries in which unions have been particularly weak, including agriculture, laundering and catering, the government has set up Wages Councils (or, in agriculture, the Agricultural Wages Board). These Councils make orders on such matters as regulating pay, holidays and holiday pay. As the employee is usually in a poor bargaining position, the rules laid down in these orders cannot be changed by the contract.

If your employers go bust any accrued holiday pay will be a preferential debt (see YOU AND YOUR BUSINESS, Q47), and – most important – the government will pay it to you if your employers cannot. This is subject to a limit of six weeks' holiday pay to which you became entitled in the 12 months immediately preceding your employers' bankruptcy or the ending of your employment, whichever is the later.

10 | *My salary seems to vary month by month. How can I make sure that I'm getting the right amount?*

The Employment Protection (Consolidation) Act 1978 states that your employers must give you a written itemised pay statement whenever they make a payment of wages or salary to you. The statement must distinguish the gross amount, the net amount, and the amount of any fixed or variable deductions such as a variable pension contribution. In the case of a fixed deduction such as a union contribution, a single statement for a period of 12 months or less will be sufficient; your employers do not have to spell it out month after month even though the actual deduction takes place weekly or monthly. If you are not satisfied with the statement, or if your employers refuse to give you one, you can complain to an Industrial Tribunal. In such a case the Tribunal can order your employers to pay you any unnotified deductions for the whole or part of the 13 weeks before you made your complaint to the Tribunal. This can be done even where the deduction itself was completely lawful.

11 | *For the last few months before I left my last company my pay cheques were rather larger than usual and I spent the money on doing up my house. The company has now asked me to repay £1,000 (which I don't have) because it says that the computer made a mistake. Do I have to pay back the money?*

The basic rule is that if your employers pay you money by mistake they can ask you to pay it back and, if you refuse, they can take you to court. This rule is subject to an exception that may apply in your case; if the company led you to believe that the money was yours, and if you have altered your position as a result of this, a court may well decide that it would be unjust to order you to repay the money. So

in your case you should consider the circumstances in which the payments were made and the circumstances in which you spent the money. If the amount of the cheques was very different from all previous cheques, a court will probably say that the mistake must have been obvious and that you had no right to spend the money without checking whether the amount was correct. In that situation you would be ordered to repay the money. If, however, the mistake was not so obvious you may well be able to satisfy a court that you acted in good faith when you spent the money and that it would be unfair to order you to repay it.

12 | *I work for an engineering company, but I want to earn some money in my spare time as a consultant. Can I do that?*

There is nothing to stop your employers putting a clause into your contract that you must not work for anybody else (or run your own business) while you are employed by them. Such a clause is particularly common in the contracts of directors, managers and senior staff (many of whom have a contract for a fixed number of years). If such an employee breaks his or her contract the employers may be able to claim damages if they can prove loss. The employers can also get a court injunction to prevent the employee from doing the other work if the clause is properly worded, and they can dismiss the employee without notice if the breach of contract is a very serious one. Such a dismissal, apart from being lawful, will almost certainly be fair.

If there is nothing in your contract your employers can still prevent you from working in your spare time, or for a competitor, if your activities are likely to harm their business. In one case the Master of the Rolls said that it would be deplorable if it were laid down that an employee could, consistently with his duty to his employers, knowingly, deliberately and secretly set himself up to do in his spare time something that could inflict great harm on his employers' business. This would be so if, for example, you have access to confidential information; in that case the court can grant an injunction to stop you doing work that carries a real risk that the information could reach a competitor.

On the other hand, if your job does not involve access to confidential information then your employers cannot prevent you from working as a consultant unless your contract of employment gives them such a right.

13 | *I'm the manager of a firm of couriers. Our*

biggest customer has told me that he's not very happy with the service that he's getting and that if I set up on my own he'd transfer all his business to me. What is my legal position?

The strict legal answer is that you run the risk of being sued by your firm if you leave and take your biggest customer with you. The legal rule is that you owe your employers a duty of good faith. In 1967 a case on similar facts came before the courts; the employee in that case was a solicitor, employed by a firm of solicitors, who left to set up on his own and took a major client with him. The court decided that the employee had broken his duty of good faith to his employers. He should have tried to keep the client for the firm and he should have told the firm what was happening. As he had not done so he had allowed his personal interest to come into conflict with the duty that he owed to his employers. The court awarded damages of £500 to the employers based on the loss of any chance they now had to earn further fees from that client.

As a practical matter your employers will have a claim against you only if they can prove that the conversation between yourself and the customer took place. There is nothing to stop you from leaving and then circulating old customers after you have done so (see Q14). But you would not be able to even approach these customers if there is a valid restraint clause in your contract. If there is such a restraint, which may stop you from approaching, soliciting or servicing your former employers' customers, then clearly you cannot accept any business from those customers until the restraint has run out (see Q14).

14 | *The estate agent for whom I work has said that if I leave to set up on my own it will take out a court injunction to stop me from doing so. Can the company do that?*

The legal position depends upon whether or not your contract of employment contains a clause that restricts your business activities after leaving the company. You may, for example, have agreed that you would not engage in a similar business for a certain time and within a certain area. Such a clause is valid only if your employers can show that it is reasonable. They cannot use it to stop competition and can use it only to protect their know-how and trade connections. In a recent case a senior negotiator was employed by an estate agent. He had a great deal of influence over his employers' clients. His contract restrained him from being engaged in the business of auctioneer, valuer, surveyor, or estate agent within a

year of termination and within a mile of the employers' business premises. The judge struck out the words 'auctioneer' and 'surveyor' as being too wide (because the employee had never worked as an auctioneer or surveyor), but he held that the remainder of the clause was reasonable to protect the employers' clientele and he granted an injunction to stop the employee setting up in the prohibited period.

If the restriction is not valid, or if there is no restriction at all, then you are on much stronger ground and you can certainly set up on your own. The only thing you are not allowed to do is to use confidential information. You must not, for example, take advantage of any secret process and you cannot take away your employers' list of suppliers and customers. On the other hand you may commit to memory the customers' names, addresses and special requirements. If they have a contract to take supplies from your old employers you cannot induce them to break that contract, but you can contact them and tell them that you are now in business on your own. Similarly, if there is no valid restraint clause, there is nothing to stop you from offering employment to employees of your present employers. However, you must not do any of these things until after you have left.

15 | *I work for a plastics company and I've just designed a new type of flooring which should be an enormous commercial success. Will I be able to get a patent for it or will it belong to my employers?*

This matter is governed by the Patents Act 1977 which may well give you either the benefit of the patent or compensation.

To look first at the question of who owns the patent, the starting-point is that it belongs to you. There are, however, two cases in which it will belong to your employers. The first case is where

● the invention was made in the normal course of your duties, or
● the invention has been specifically designed for your employers, and
● in either case an invention might reasonably be expected to result from the carrying out of your duties. The second case is where the invention was made in the course of your duties and you had a special obligation to further the interests of your employers' undertaking. A great deal will therefore turn on the exact nature of your job and the circumstances in which the invention was made.

Even if the invention belongs to your employers,

you can apply to the Patent Office or to the Patents Court on the grounds that

• the invention has proved to be of outstanding benefit to your employers, or
• you have assigned the patent in return for benefits that are inadequate in relation to the benefits that your employers have obtained. If you prove either of these matters you may receive a 'fair share' of the actual or anticipated benefits derived from the patent.

16 | *My employers have said that they are going to suspend me on medical grounds. What does this mean and what are my rights?*

This is probably a case that involves a health risk at your place of work, and your employers are suspending you (which means taking you off your normal job) either because they are under a legal duty to do so or because suspension is recommended by a Code of Practice issued under the Health and Safety at Work etc. Act 1974. The regulations under which they are acting must be listed in Schedule 1 of the Employment Protection (Consolidation) Act 1978; the list includes regulations dealing with such materials as lead, india-rubber and radioactive substances.

If the suspension is lawful (and it has nothing at all to do with your own state of health) you can claim as a minimum one week's pay for each week of suspension subject to a maximum of 26. This will not cut down any rights that you may have under your contract, and the set-off rules are similar to those for statutory sick pay (see YOU AND YOUR BUSINESS, Q66).

To qualify for this suspension pay, you need to have been in continuous employment for one month before the suspension begins; there are special rules for short-term contracts. You will be disqualified from receiving statutory suspension pay for any period during which:

• you yourself are unable to work owing to disease or disablement, or
• you unreasonably fail to accept an offer of suitable alternative work, or
• you fail to comply with reasonable requirements imposed by your employers such as phoning in to let them know that you are available for work.

17 | *I work as a secretary at the Home Office. Do I have the same rights as my friends who work for private firms?*

There is a very wide gap here between theory and practice. We all know that civil servants very rarely get dismissed; nevertheless, under the common law your employers (the Crown) have the right to dismiss you at any time without notice. However, and this is an important point, most of the statutory employment protection rights – including unfair dismissal – do apply; your rights include the usual rights relating to maternity, equal pay, sex and race discrimination, guaranteed pay, time off, itemised pay statements and written statements as to the reasons for dismissal, as well as health and safety protection. You do not have the benefit of the redundancy payments scheme, but this is replaced in practice by your internal scheme (which is more generous).

18 | *My friends tell me that employees have lots of legal rights. Do these rights apply to part-time workers as well as full-time workers?*

There is no special rule which says that certain rights do not apply to part-time workers, but many of the rights that you have heard about do depend upon the number of hours you work. For many of the legal rights (maternity leave, redundancy pay, unfair dismissal, minimum notice, written statement of terms, and so on) you must have clocked up a period of continuous employment, which means adding together an unbroken number of weeks. A week counts if you are employed for 16 hours, or if for the whole or part of that week you have a contract that normally involves employment for 16 hours. Thus, if you get a job working four mornings per week you would probably clock up your 16 hours, but if you work only three mornings a week you would only qualify when you have worked for your employers for five years (because for those employees an eight-hour week is sufficient).

In the case of statutory sick pay (see Q24) there is a rather different rule. You will get this unless your normal weekly earnings are below the minimum figure above which you have to pay National Insurance contributions; at present this is £38.

Finally, some legal rights apply equally to all employees, full time and part time. These include equal pay for men and women, the right not to be discriminated against on the basis of sex or race, or to be victimised for trade union activities or for belonging to or not belonging to a trade union.

19 | *I'm paid only for the hours I actually work, and the company is in such a bad way that on some days I have no work at all. Can I get any money for those days?*

It is clear that under your contract you can't claim any pay for days on which you have no work to do.

You do, however, have a right to a limited amount of money under what is known as guarantee pay, which is payable under the Employment Protection (Consolidation) Act 1978 for what the Act calls workless days. To qualify you have to work a 16-hour week and have been continuously employed for at least a month before the workless day or work at least an eight-hour week and have been continuously employed for at least five years. In addition, the workless day must be a day on which you would normally have worked and the reason for the lack of work must be a cutback in the employers' business or some other event that affects the normal working of the business, such as a power failure, a natural disaster like flood, or the bankruptcy of a customer or supplier. There are also a number of exclusions. You won't be entitled to guarantee pay if the workless day was due to a strike or other trade dispute affecting your employers or associated employers, or if you unreasonably refuse a suitable offer of other work, or if you fail to comply with a reasonable condition imposed by your employers who may, for instance, ask you to telephone or turn up to see if any work is available.

20 | *If there's no work for the days I'm supposed to be employed, how much guarantee pay will I get?*

The payment will be geared to the number of days that you normally work in a week subject to a maximum of five. If, for example, you work a five-day week, you will be entitled to guarantee pay for a maximum of five workless days in any period of three months; if your working week is only a four-day week, the figure of five is reduced to four. The amount of pay for each working day is found by multiplying your normal working hours by your hourly rate of pay, and if you don't have normal working hours a 12-week average is taken. Thus, if your hourly rate of pay is £2 and your normal or average number of hours worked is seven, your guarantee pay should be £14 per day. However, it won't be as high as that because there is a maximum figure that changes every year but which is at present £10.90. So if you work a five-day week, the guarantee pay in a three-month period is £10.90 × 5 = £54.50.

There are two more snags. First, guarantee pay is subject to income tax in the same way as your pay. Second, any day on which you get guarantee pay will not be a day of unemployment, and this means that you cannot claim unemployment benefit for that day.

If your employers fail to give you guarantee pay, you can take them to the Industrial Tribunal (see page 266) and you can claim unemployment benefit while you are waiting for your money. The Tribunal can then order your employers to reimburse the DHSS for the unemployment benefit out of the guarantee pay which your employers will be instructed to pay to you.

Time off

21 | *I'm a governor of my local school and also a magistrate, but my boss refuses to let me have time off from work. How much time can I take off, and do my employers have to pay me for it?*

Under the Employment Protection (Consolidation) Act 1978 your employers must let you have a reasonable amount of time off to carry out your duties as a magistrate and also any duties that you may have as a member of the governing body of an educational establishment maintained by a local education authority. The position will therefore depend on whether the school is in the state system or private; in the latter case your employers do not have to give you any time off.

How much is a 'reasonable' amount of time off will depend on all the circumstances. The relevant facts will include

● how much time off is required for the performance of the particular duties;
● how much time off (if any) you have already been allowed as a trade union official or member (see Q148);
● the circumstances of the employers' business and the effect of the employee's absence on the running of the business.

It could well be that for a small staff-intensive business your employers might be justified in giving very little time off, and there may well be no duty on them to employ extra staff to cover for your absence.

In answer to your second question, the answer is no: your employers are not bound to pay you during your time off.

22 | What can I do if my employers consistently refuse to give me any time off to carry out my duties as a governor of a local LEA school?

You can make a complaint to an Industrial Tribunal. You must generally do so within three months of your employers' refusal. If, however, the Tribunal is satisfied that it was not reasonably practicable for you to make a complaint within this time, then it can allow a late claim. If you win your case the Tribunal must make a declaration in your favour. It can also award you compensation of such sum as it considers just and equitable, having regard both to your employers' default and to any loss you may have sustained. It is probably unlikely that you will have suffered any financial loss because taking time off in your capacity as a school governor is unpaid (see Q21). Nevertheless, the Tribunal can award you compensation if it feels that your employers should be penalized for their unreasonable behaviour.

In some cases the Tribunal has actually stated how much time off should be allowed in cases such as yours. This is obviously a useful guide, but it is not legally binding on employers.

23 | My company has given me notice because the branch where I work is being closed. I want to take time off to take a retraining course, but the managing director has said that I can't do this because there is too much work to do. What are my rights?

If you have been continuously employed for at least two years when your notice expires you have a legal right to a reasonable amount of time off during working hours in order to look for another job or to make arrangements for training for future employment. Like any other time off provisions the key word is 'reasonable', and it is once again necessary to balance your own needs as a redundant employee against the needs of the business. Your employers are probably acting unreasonably in refusing to give you any time off at all, but that apart there is obviously the question of the amount of time off they should allow you. If you can't make any progress then you could call in an ACAS Conciliation Officer (see page 298) to see whether a compromise can be found.

● *Industrial Tribunals*

These have been set up in most major towns and cities throughout England, Wales, Scotland and Northern Ireland. Each Tribunal has three members; one is from the employers' side of industry; one is from the employees' side and the chairman is a lawyer.

The Tribunals have been set up to provide an informal, quick and cheap way of deciding disputes between employers and employees and occasionally between an employee and his or her union.

Industrial Tribunals have a heavy caseload. In 1983, 37,526 cases were started in them. About 70 per cent of these cases were unfair dismissal claims; the balance covered many other areas including redundancy, maternity, equal pay, discrimination, time off and failure to provide written statements of terms of employment. Only about 30 per cent of cases go all the way to a hearing; most of the others are settled by agreement.

The procedure is straightforward and you do not need a solicitor. You can get a booklet from your local Job Centre or from the Tribunal telling you what to do. The address of the Central Office of Industrial Tribunals is given on page 510; the Office will tell you where your regional office is. See YOU AND YOUR JOB, Q104, for details of the procedure.

Sick pay

24 | Is it right that I'm paid my wages in full while I'm off sick?

No. The extent to which you can claim your wages during illness depends on the terms of your contract. Some contracts, for example, give you a right to full pay for three months and then half pay for the next three months. What you have the right to claim is 'statutory sick pay' (SSP) from your employers for any day during which you are unable to work because of illness or incapacity; this means you will receive the salary to which you are entitled, and your employers claim back from the DHSS the payment of SSP. SSP is payable for any day of incapacity provided it is a qualifying day (see Q27) and forms part of a 'period of incapacity' of at least four days and it is not a 'waiting day' – this means that you will not get any statutory sick pay for the first three qualifying days in any period of incapacity.

The amount of statutory sick pay is fixed by Parliament and it usually changes once a year. It is a flat-rate benefit (no increases for dependants) and it will be far lower than your actual pay. For the current year there are two rates of SSP and these are geared to your normal weekly earnings. The figures are:

Normal weekly earnings	Weekly rates of SSP
£76.50 and over	£47.20
less than £76.50	£32.85

No SSP is payable if your normal weekly earnings are below the lower earnings limit for National Insurance (£39 in 1987–8).

25 | How do I work out my normal weekly earnings?

This is normally done by your employers, and they will usually have accurate computerised records. The legal rules are to be found in the Social Security and Housing Benefits Act 1982 and in Regulations made under that Act. The rules vary according to how you are paid; the two most common cases are:

1. If you are paid weekly your normal weekly earnings are calculated by taking an average of your earnings in the eight weeks ending on the last pay-day before the start of your period of incapacity. If you have not yet worked for eight weeks, an average will be taken of the weeks you have actually worked.

Example

Week 1	£70
Week 2	£55
Week 3	£73
Week 4	£76
	———
	£274

Average = £68.50.

The lower rate of SSP is therefore payable.

2. If you are paid on a monthly basis the calculation of normal weekly earnings involves a three-stage calculation:

Stage 1. Calculate the total earnings for the last two months ending with the last pay-day before the period of incapacity

Stage 2. Multiply by six

Stage 3. Divide by 52.

26 | How do the sick pay rules tie up with my normal pay?

The sick pay will not cut down in any way your rights under your contract for the day in question, but any wages will be set off against any statutory sick pay that is payable to you for that day; you can't claim the sick pay on top of your normal pay. On the other hand, the sick pay rules can work to your advantage. They provide a minimum amount that *must* be paid to you, even in a case where you have used up all your rights to pay under the company's own scheme. There may even be a case where a non-working day can be a qualifying day (see Q27), in which case you can claim statutory sick pay for that day even though it is a day on which no money is payable to you under your contract.

SSP is paid for a maximum of 28 weeks in a period of entitlement. Periods of illness for which you receive SSP which are less than eight weeks apart are joined in the same period of entitlement. If a period of entitlement extends to more than three years, no more SSP is payable. If you change jobs, you can claim SSP in the usual way from your new employer.

27 | What is a qualifying day in terms of statutory sick pay?

The idea behind a qualifying day is that it should be a day on which the employee would normally be at work but for his or her incapacity. The legal rules do not, however, reflect this basic idea. Each week must have at least one qualifying date; apart from this basic rule it is up to your employers to agree with you which days shall be qualifying days in any week. The number doesn't matter – it can be any number from one to seven – and the actual days themselves must be agreed (for example, 'Tuesday and Wednesday in every week shall be qualifying days'). There is no need for all, or any, of the agreed qualifying days to be working days.

If for some reason there is no agreement the matter will be governed by Regulations made under the Social Security and Housing Benefits Act 1982. These Regulations provide that:

● all agreed normal working days in a week will be qualifying days;
● if you and your employers cannot agree which days are normal working days then all seven days are treated as qualifying days except those days (if any) on which it is agreed that *no* employees have to work;
● if it is agreed that there are no normal working days then Wednesday is treated as the only qualifying day.

28 | I developed flu last Saturday and I'll be off work for about a week. When can I start drawing sick pay?

As your illness is going to last for at least four days it will be a 'period of incapacity' and statutory sick pay will be payable. You should find out which days are 'qualifying days' (see Q27); remember that the first three qualifying days are 'waiting days' (see Q24) for which no SSP is payable. If, therefore, Tuesday to Friday are the qualifying days, Tuesday, Wednesday and Thursday will be waiting days and you will be paid SSP for the Friday only. The rate is found by taking the appropriate weekly rate (see Q24) and dividing it by the number of qualifying days, that is, four.

29 | *I have two jobs, one full time and one evenings-only. Can I claim two lots of statutory sick pay if I'm ill?*

You can claim SSP from each of your employers (or from your only employers if they employ you for both jobs) provided that you fulfil the necessary conditions in relation to each job. In particular you must consider the question of pay; you will qualify only if your normal weekly earnings (see Q25) from *each* job are above the statutory minimum – £39 per week in 1987–8.

Maternity

30 | *When I told my boss that I was pregnant he said that he would have to dismiss me. Can he do that?*

You can't stop your employers from dismissing you, but you may very well have a claim for unfair dismissal (see Q72) if you satisfy the necessary qualifying conditions. A dismissal for any reason connected with pregnancy is automatically unfair unless:

● the pregnancy will make you incapable of adequately doing your job, or

● your employers would be breaking the law by allowing you to carry on working. Many jobs involve health hazards for pregnant women, and employers who ignore these hazards would be criminally liable under the Health and Safety at Work etc. Act 1974.

Even in these two cases, however, you will still have a good case for unfair dismissal if your boss has some other job available which is suitable for you and if he doesn't offer you that other job before your dismissal.

If you win your unfair dismissal case, the Industrial Tribunal (see page 266) can order your employers to give you your job back, but this is fairly rare: what usually happens is that the Tribunal will order your employers to pay you compensation.

31 | *I joined the company eight months ago and my boss dismissed me when I told him that I was pregnant. Do I have a case against the company?*

The answer is almost certainly yes. You won't be able to bring an unfair dismissal claim because you haven't clocked up the necessary two years of continuous employment with the company. You can, however, claim that your employers were guilty of unlawful sex discrimination under the Sex Discrimination Act 1975 because you have been treated less favourably than a man would have been in similar circumstances. There was a strange case in 1980 where a Mrs Turley, who was dismissed for pregnancy, lost her case; the two male members of the Employment Appeal Tribunal decided that the Act did not apply because there was no such thing as a pregnant man and therefore no comparison was possible! Fortunately a 1985 case (again in the EAT) has restored some common sense to this area of the law, and the pregnant woman won her case. See also DISCRIMINATION, Q8.

32 | *When I was pregnant I had to visit the ante-natal clinic several times, but my employers wouldn't pay me for those days. Were they legally entitled to stop my pay?*

No. Your employers were under a legal duty to give you a reasonable amount of time off with pay for ante-natal care if the appointment to visit the clinic was made for you by a duly qualified doctor, midwife or health visitor. The question of what is reasonable will depend on such matters as the size of your employers' business, your personal role in it and whether another employee could cover for you while you were away. You should therefore write to your employers, draw their attention to your legal rights and ask for the pay they deducted. If they refuse you can bring a case to the Industrial Tribunal (see Q36); you should have no difficulty in winning the case, and the Tribunal can order your employers to pay you the money that you would have got if you had been paid for the days in question.

33 | *My baby is due in four months' time and my doctor tells me that I must stop working now. Can I still get any maternity pay?*

You are legally entitled to statutory maternity pay (SMP) from your employers if you satisfy the following conditions:

● You must have been employed by the same employers continuously for at least 26 weeks ending in the fifteenth week (the 'qualifying week') before the week in which the baby is due.
● You must give your employers details of the expected date of your birth and at least 21 days' notice of the date that you intend to stop work and start claiming SMP (or as soon after that as it is practicable for you to do so). It is up to your employers to decide whether notice is required in writing or not.
● Your average weekly earnings over the eight weeks up to the pay day before the end of the qualifying week must be £39 or more (the lower earnings limit for National Insurance contributions).
● You must not be doing any work for the employers while receiving SMP.

In your case, your absence will have to start before the fifteenth week, but that should not stop you from getting your SMP. In the fifteenth week you will still be *employed* even though you will not be *at work*.

It is of course possible that when you tell your employers they will react by dismissing you, but even this will not stop you from claiming maternity pay if you would otherwise be entitled to it either directly or as unfair dismissal compensation by bringing the matter before an Industrial Tribunal.

If you are not eligible for SMP, you may be able to claim maternity allowance from the DHSS (see BENE-FITS, Q8).

34 | *I recently took part in an unofficial strike. Will this affect my right to maternity money?*

You must have clocked up 26 weeks' continuous employment by the end of the fifteenth week before

the expected date of confinement. A week during which you take part in a strike does not count towards those 26 weeks, but at the same time your absence on strike won't break the continuity. If you worked for 10 weeks and then went on strike for three weeks, you will qualify for maternity pay only if you worked for at least 16 weeks after the strike came to an end. The rules here are the same for both official and unofficial strikes.

35 | *How much statutory maternity pay will I get and for how long will it be paid?*

You are entitled to up to 18 weeks' statutory maternity pay from your employers, but you have some choice over which 18 weeks you claim for. The earliest you can receive SMP is the eleventh week before the week in which the baby is due, but you can choose to stay at work for up to five weeks. The latest date at which you can start claiming SMP and get your full entitlement of 18 weeks is the sixth week before the week in which the baby is due. If you carry on working you will lose one week's SMP for each week or part of week in which you work.

There are two rates of SMP. The higher rate is nine-tenths of your average weekly pay. You are entitled to this for the first six weeks of your SMP claim if you have worked for your employers for at least 16 hours a week for at least two years or between 8 and 16 hours a week for at least five years. After the six weeks you will receive the lower rate of £32.85 a week for the remainder of your claim. You will be entitled to the lower rate for the whole of your claim if you have not worked for your employers for long enough to qualify for the higher rate.

SMP is paid in the same way as wages and is subject to tax and National Insurance contributions.

Employers often operate a more generous maternity pay scheme, possibly as a result of a deal negotiated by a union. You will not get SMP on top of any other agreement, but the SMP will be made up to the amount payable under the employers' maternity pay scheme.

36 | What happens if my employers don't pay me my statutory maternity pay?

If your employers refuse to pay SMP or you think you are getting the wrong amount, you are entitled to a written statement giving details of which weeks the employers regard as being weeks for which SMP is payable, how much SMP the employers regard as being payable for those weeks and why the employers think SMP is not payable for the other weeks. If you disagree with anything in the statement, an Adjudication Officer at the DHSS can make a decision on the question. Both the employers and the employee will be asked to put their observations in writing, and the Adjudication Officer will send a formal decision to both sides. If this does not resolve the dispute, either party can appeal to an independent tribunal (see BENEFITS, Q15).

37 | I have two part-time jobs. I'm expecting a baby in four months' time. Can I claim two lots of statutory maternity pay?

You are entitled to claim SMP from each of your employers provided that you fulfil the necessary conditions in each job (see Q33). In particular, you must consider the question of how much you are paid: you will qualify only if your average weekly earnings from each job are above the lower earnings limit for National Insurance contributions – £39 a week in 1987–8. If you are entitled to receive SMP from each job, you do not have to claim for exactly the same 18+-week period from each of the two employers.

38 | When I had my first baby a few years ago I received a state maternity grant. A friend has told me that I won't get one for the baby I'm expecting in a few months. Is this correct?

In the past, all mothers were entitled to a maternity grant of £25 for each baby. But since 6 April 1987 this has been abolished. Instead, some mothers are

entitled to claim a maternity payment of £80 from the social fund of the DHSS. You will be entitled to this payment if you (or your partner) are getting either Supplementary Benefit (see BENEFITS, Q1) or Family Income Supplement (see BENEFITS, Q6). If you have more than £500 in savings, the payment will be reduced by one pound for each pound of savings you have over £500. For more details see BENEFITS, Q8.

39 | I haven't decided whether I want to go back to work after I've had my baby. Can I leave my options open?

Yes, but you must fulfil certain conditions. Failure to do so may destroy your right to return. These conditions are:

1. You must comply with the three maternity pay conditions (see Q33).

2. At the same time as giving written notice you must inform your employers that you intend to return; this will not commit you if you later change your mind.

3. At any time after 49 days have expired since the start of the expected week of confinement your employers can send you a written request asking you to confirm in writing that you intend to return. You must then within 14 days confirm in writing that you intend to return; if this time-limit is not reasonably practicable then you must do so as soon as is reasonably practicable.

4. Your final decision to return to work must be notified to your employers in writing at least 21 days before the day on which you intend to do so. The right to return must be exercised within the period of 29 weeks beginning with your actual week of confinement.

These various time-limits are very important, and you should make a careful note of them if you want to preserve your right to return; if you don't comply with them you will lose your right to return. You can, of course, tell your employers at any time that you are not coming back.

40 | What happens if my employers don't let me return to work?

If you have complied with all the formalities described in Q39, the refusal to take you back will amount to a dismissal as at the date on which you were due to return. Depending on the circumstances, you may then have a claim for a redundancy payment and for compensation for unfair dismissal.

If your employers don't take you back because your job has disappeared or because they've cut back on staff, then you can claim a redundancy payment under the normal rules (see Q130). However, you won't get one if you were offered another job that was suitable for you and which you unreasonably refused.

The redundancy can also be an unfair dismissal if, for example, you were selected for redundancy while a much more junior employee was kept on. There is also a special rule about your employers finding you other work; if your employers (or one of their associated employers) have a suitable vacancy they *must* offer it to you and the dismissal will be automatically unfair if this is not done.

If there is no redundancy your employers' refusal to let you come back can still amount to an unfair dismissal. If you take them to an Industrial Tribunal they will have to justify their decision by showing one of the statutory grounds for dismissal (see Q71). The Tribunal must then decide whether they acted reasonably in treating that reason as justifying their decision. If, for example, your work was of a very poor standard and had not improved after several warnings the refusal to let you come back may well be fair.

A firm with five or fewer employees (including persons employed by associated employers) can escape any form of unfair dismissal liability by showing that it was not reasonably practicable to have you back in your old job or in any other suitable job. This doesn't affect any right that you may have to claim a redundancy payment.

Discrimination

41 | *I'm the only woman employed in the sales department. All the male salesmen have a company car, but I don't. Isn't this discrimination?*

Yes, it may well be. The Equal Pay Act 1970 (the name is misleading; the Act is not confined to pay and it applies to all terms and conditions of employment) states that if a man and a woman are engaged in 'like work' or in 'work of equal value' (see DISCRIMINATION, Q10) then they are entitled to the same terms and conditions of employment unless the employers can show that there is a genuine material difference (other than sex) between them. You must therefore start by comparing the work that you do with the work that your male colleagues do. You must be able to prove that the work 'is of the same or a broadly similar nature and the difference (if any) between your duties and theirs is not of practical importance in relation to the terms and conditions of employ-

ment'. If your male colleagues have to carry heavy goods to customers whereas you don't have to do so, this will indicate that you are not engaged in 'like work'. Similarly, if you work only in central London while your colleagues cover a much larger territory the difference may defeat your claim. Also, your employers may be able to show that there's a material difference between the male salesmen and yourself – age and length of service, experience and sales performance, and so on. Even if you were not engaged in 'like work', you could still win your case by showing that your work was of equal value to that of your male colleagues.

42 | *My company has several branches but I'm the only female branch manager. Can I compare my pay and bonuses with those of male managers at the other branches?*

Yes. A comparison can be made with men working at any other establishment of your employers at which similar terms and conditions are applied. If, for example, all branches are covered by the same collective agreement then you could compare yourself with a male employee performing like work or work of equal value (see Q41). But whether you would win your case would depend on all the circumstances – if, say, the cost of housing or travel is higher at the other branches – perhaps they are all located in central London – then this could justify a pay differential on the grounds of a material difference other than sex between their case and yours.

43 | *I'm paid less than my male colleagues at work, but management refuses to give me a salary increase to bring me in line. I'd like to take my case to a court or tribunal, but I also want to leave the company. Can I bring my case after I've left?*

Yes. A claim under the Equal Pay Act 1970 can be brought by an existing employee or by a former employee. There is a time-limit in the case of an ex-employee; you must bring the case within six months of the ending of your contract. If you win your case the court or Industrial Tribunal will rewrite your contract by including an 'equality clause' that will make up your pay to that of your colleagues. The clause will apply to the job in the future and it can be back-dated for two years. This means that if you have been underpaid by £10 per week compared with your male colleagues for five years before your contract ended, the court or Tribunal will award you only your arrears of pay over the two-year period – you would receive $104 \times £10 = £1,040$.

44 | *There are three male fitters (including myself) at the gas showroom where I work. The only woman worker is a demonstrator, and she's paid more than we are. How can I show that my job is of equal value to hers?*

The rules about equal value are new and haven't yet been tested in the Tribunals (see DISCRIMINATION, Q10).

If you cannot reach agreement with your employers you will have to bring a case to a county court or to an Industrial Tribunal. Although the main purpose of the Equal Pay Act 1970 was to stop the exploitation of women, the Act applies equally to women and to men. In an Industrial Tribunal case the Tribunal must first consider whether there are 'reasonable grounds' for allowing your case to go ahead. If it does so it will refer the matter to a member of an independent panel for investigation. The Tribunal can order you or your employers to give information and to produce documents to the investigator. When he has assessed these he will prepare a report and send it to the Tribunal and the case will

then go ahead on the basis of the report and any other relevant evidence. If you don't like the report you can call your own witnesses to show why the report is wrong. Bringing such an action can be very expensive and time-consuming.

45 | *I work part-time and so do the other five women in our department. The other four workers are men; they are full-time and their rates of pay are higher. Is this lawful?*

Basically, there is nothing wrong with a pay differential between full-time and part-time workers. However, it is obvious that this practice can be used by employers as a way of keeping women's wages down and the Tribunals have been very much alive to this situation. You must first establish whether you are engaged in 'like work' or 'work rated as equivalent' or 'work of equal value' with a man working full-time (see DISCRIMINATION, Q9). If you clear that hurdle then your employers will have to show that there is a 'genuine material difference' (other than sex) between your case as a female part-time worker and the men's case as full-time workers. A similar case went to the Employment Appeal Tribunal in 1981 and the Tribunal took a common-sense and realistic view. It said that the onus was on the employers to show that the difference in pay rates between full-timers and part-timers was reasonably necessary to achieve increased productivity. A mere statement by the employers was not enough. The EAT then sent the case back to the Industrial Tribunal so that it could decide whether the pay differential was necessary in order to enable the employers to reduce absenteeism and to obtain the maximum use of their plant.

46 | *I've just seen an advertisement for a very highly paid job as an interpreter. It says that the successful candidate must be under 30 and must have at least five years' practical experience. That rules me out because I only worked for three years before my baby was born. Isn't this a form of discrimination?*

The answer to your question may well be yes. The advertisement doesn't openly discriminate; it doesn't say that the job is open only to women or to men. Despite this, you may still have a claim under the Sex Discrimination Act 1975 if you can prove what is called 'indirect discrimination'. This will apply if:

● the proportion of women who can comply with the 'age and experience' condition is considerably

smaller than the proportion of men who can comply with it; and
- the condition is to a woman's detriment because she cannot comply with it; and
- the employers cannot show that the condition is justifiable irrespective of the sex of the person to whom it is applied. Thus, for example, a condition relating to physical strength may be 'justifiable' where the job involves heavy manual work even though this means that the job is likely to go to a man.

In your case you may well be able to bring a claim; after all, the proportion of women under 30 with five years' work experience is likely to be substantially less than the proportion of men because that period is obviously the time that many young women spend at home bringing up a family.

The Equal Opportunities Commission (address on page 509) will be able to advise you in the light of its extensive knowledge of similar cases.

47 | *I've been told that the company is paying for five of its female supervisors to go on a management training course but that any men who want to attend must pay themselves. Surely that must be unlawful?*

On the face of it you are right. The Sex Discrimination Act 1975 applies equally to discrimination against men and women, and quite a few cases have been brought by men. The Act makes it unlawful for an employer to offer access to promotion, transfer or training to members of one sex but not to the other. By paying for women but not men to attend the course, your employers seem to be acting unlawfully and if you fail to convince them of this you can make a complaint to an Industrial Tribunal.

There is, however, one possible exception that can be relevant. It may well be that your employers have very few women managers and that they are taking active steps to alter this; in other words they are adopting a policy of 'positive discrimination'. Employers can lawfully give the members of one sex access to training facilities that would help to fit them for particular work (in this case management) where at any time within the previous 12 months there were no persons of that sex doing that work or their number was comparatively small. If your employers can bring themselves within this rule, you won't have a claim under the Act.

48 | *My employers run a chain of betting shops and I've been working at the head office. They recently sent round an internal advertisement for the post of manager at a new betting shop in South London. I applied to be transferred there but I wasn't successful. They said that it's a rough area and that it needed a man to control the customers. Can I take them to court under the Sex Discrimination Act?*

The answer is almost certainly yes. Your employers have discriminated against you on the grounds of your sex by not giving you the transfer. In this sort of case the employers are not allowed to stereotype men and women. They are not allowed to say 'you cannot do the job because you are a woman'. They must look at the individual applicants on their merits. If they decide that a particular man is more suited to the job (perhaps because of his physique or because of his background as an ex-policeman) then they will be entitled to appoint him on that ground. The assessment must be made on the basis of individual characteristics and not on the basis of sex as such. In one equal pay case the Court of Appeal pointed out that the man may have been a smaller, nervous man who could not say boo to a goose while the woman may have been as fierce and formidable as a battle-axe.

49 | *I joined an agency 18 months ago and I always got on very well with the other 10 employees. Last week I told the manager that I was getting married and he reacted by dismissing me. What are my rights?*

It certainly looks as if your former employers have behaved very badly towards you, but you may have a problem in getting your job back or compensation. You won't be able to make a claim for unfair dismissal because you haven't been there long enough. If your employers have 20 or fewer employees you won't be able to bring an unfair dismissal claim unless you have been continuously employed by them for at least two years when you were dismissed.

You might have a better chance under the Sex Discrimination Act 1975. This Act forbids discrimination against a man or a woman on the grounds of sex and against a *married* person on the grounds of marital status. But in one of the first cases brought under the Act where the facts were similar to those in your case the woman lost her case. At the time of her dismissal she was not a married woman; the employers had discriminated against her because of her *future* marital status and that was not caught by the Act. There are just two possible ways in which you could take your case to an Industrial Tribunal and win. In the first place you might be able to prove *sex* discrimination by showing that a man about to get married would not have been dismissed. Second, you could, after getting married, ask for your job back. If they then refused you can take them to the Tribunal on the basis that they didn't re-employ you because of your marital status. If you win your case the Tribunal can award you compensation for your financial loss and injury to your feelings. It can also order your former employers to put the matter right by giving you the job; your employers can't be compelled to do this, but the Tribunal can increase the money payable to you if they refuse.

50 | *I'm separated from my husband and I have a small child. For the past two years I've been working for 15 hours a week as a waitress. When the company found out about the baby the manager gave me the sack and said that women with children are unreliable. What are my legal rights?*

The law that protects employees against unfair dismissal won't help because to bring such an action you have to work more than 16 hours a week. There is, however, a very good chance that you can bring, and win, a case against your former employers under the Sex Discrimination Act 1975. You could claim that they have discriminated against you on the grounds of sex on the basis that they don't dismiss men with children. Even if they do apply their 'no-children' rule equally to men and women you could still claim that this amounted to indirect discrimination against you as a married person because the number of married people who can comply with the 'no-children' rule is substantially smaller than the proportion of unmarried persons and that therefore the rule discriminates against married persons. Once again, a visit or telephone call to the Equal Opportunities Commission (address on page 509) should be helpful as a first step.

51 | *I am a Sikh and I work at a supermarket. About a year ago I gave evidence against my employers in a case under the Race Relations Act. Last week all my colleagues got a large bonus, but I didn't. If I prove that I've been discriminated against, can I get my bonus?*

Yes. If you can prove that your employers have vic-

timised you for giving evidence in the proceedings last year then they will be guilty of unlawful victimisation under the Race Relations Act 1976 – unless you made an allegation that you knew was untrue.

You may bring an Industrial Tribunal case against your employers, and the procedure is similar to that for unfair dismissal cases (see Q104). Your main problem will be to prove that the victimisation was linked to the evidence you gave. Under Section 65 of the Race Relations Act a questionnaire has been prepared to help employees in cases such as yours (see DISCRIMINATION, Q27). On this form you set out the facts on which you are basing your claim that your employers have discriminated against you. The replies given by your employers can be looked at by the tribunal; in particular any evasive reply (or any failure to reply) will strengthen your case.

The Commission for Racial Equality (address on page 509) will let you have copies of the form and will help you with your case.

If you win your case the Industrial Tribunal can order your employers to wipe out the discrimination by paying you the bonus.

52 | *I was recently interviewed for a new job and I met the other applicants while we were waiting for our interviews. I'm sure that I was the person best qualified for the job and that I didn't get it because I'm black. Can I get the company to disclose its personnel files and interview records?*

Under the Race Relations Act 1976 employers discriminate against a prospective employee if they refuse on racial grounds to offer that person employment. The words 'racial grounds' mean any grounds of colour, race, nationality or ethnic or national origins. You can bring a case under the Act and it will go to an Industrial Tribunal. If you can satisfy the Tribunal that you didn't get the job because you were black you will win your case. See DISCRIMINATION, QS 27 and 28.

Once again, the main problem is one of proof; you should approach the Commission for Racial Equality for help (address on page 509). The Commission will advise you to write to the employers asking them to produce the personnel files and records, or the Commission may write on your behalf.

The employers will almost certainly refuse on the grounds that the records are confidential. You can then start your Industrial Tribunal case and apply at an early stage for production (the legal term is 'discovery') of the personnel files. The Tribunal will look at the files to decide whether the documents are confidential and, if so, whether disclosure is essential for a fair hearing of your case. It may, for example, adopt a compromise by ordering disclosure of records that cover up the names of the other applicants or which include fictional names instead of the true ones.

53 | *I work for a company that makes furniture. The company employs quite a few Asians but they all work in the paintshop. Can employers segregate employees in this way?*

The segregation of employees on racial grounds is unlawful under the Race Relations Act 1976, but only if there is a *policy* of segregation by the employers. There was a case on similar facts in 1980 and the employee lost. In that case there was no positive discrimination policy because the Asians were a self-perpetuating group (when one left, another joined); there was no duty on the employers to desegregate the workforce. If the employee could have proved a policy of segregation he would have won.

54 | *A few years ago I got into trouble for stealing a car and I was given a conditional discharge. I'm afraid that the company to which I'm applying for a job may well discriminate against me if they know of it. Do I have to disclose it when I apply for a job?*

First of all, any duty of disclosure will arise only if you are asked about it. You may, for example, have to complete a form that asks you questions about any convictions and you must answer these questions truthfully. However, under the Rehabilitation of Offenders Act 1974 your conviction will be treated as 'spent' after one year or when the discharge becomes an absolute discharge (if that is later). Once you get to that point you can wipe the slate clean. If, after that, you are asked about any convictions you can ignore any spent conviction when answering the question; in other words, if the spent conviction was your only conviction the answer 'none' will be a true answer. Even if your prospective employers find out about it, they cannot refuse you a job on that ground. However, the Act doesn't specify what your rights are if your prospective employers do reject you on the basis of your spent conviction.

Leaving your job: notice

55 | *I've been offered another job and the new company wants me to start as soon as possible. How much notice do I have to give my present firm?*

If you are employed under a fixed-term contract of employment (see Q62) you cannot lawfully leave your job during the contract term unless your employers agree to release you. If you do leave without such agreement you will be in breach of your contract and this can affect such matters as your rights under the company's pension scheme. In theory, you could also be sued for damages for breach of contract, although employers only rarely resort to this. Your employers could also take out a court injunction against your new employers or sue them for their wrongful interference with your contract of employment.

If you are not on a fixed-term contract, your contract itself will probably specify what notice you have to give and if the contract says nothing about notice you can end it by giving reasonable notice (see Q62) subject to a minimum of one week. For example, if you have a responsible job as a senior cashier or as a foreman or manager then something between one month's and three months' notice might be considered reasonable. Hopefully you can come to an agreement with your employers.

56 | *Can my employers be legally compelled to give me a reference?*

No. Most employers give references for departing employees, but they are not legally bound to do so. A reference can be risky for employers. On the one hand, if it is too favourable (if, say, an employee dismissed for bad work is said to be satisfactory in every respect) the employers may be legally liable for negligence to the new employers who are relying on the reference and then suffer loss as a result. On the other hand, if the reference is unfavourable the employee may sue the employers for negligence (if the employers have failed to take reasonable care) or for defamation. As a result, if your employers say it's not company policy to give references then there's nothing that you can legally do.

57 | *I'm going for an interview for a new job, but I don't want my employers to know about it and*

I'm afraid that the new company will ask me for a reference. What can I do about it?

This is a common problem – you obviously don't want to risk losing your present job until you have clinched the new one. You should mention the matter at the interview if the question of references comes up, and you should offer the name of an earlier employer – if you have one – as a referee. If that doesn't do the trick you will have to persuade your new employers at the interview, and in your written application, that you are ideally suited to the job and are prepared to accept a probationary period to prove it.

58 | *Last week I landed a super new job but when I gave in my notice to my employers they immediately made me a better offer and I want to accept it. Can I do so?*

You will be breaking your contract by not going to work for the firm that offered you the job. The company can – at least in theory – sue you in the High Court or in a county court for the loss that it will suffer as a result of your non-arrival. It can also put pressure on your present employers by suing them for wrongfully interfering with your new contract. In one case a very senior employee had been head-hunted and a great deal of management time had been spent in making him familiar with the new company's activities. When he decided to break his contract by accepting a better offer from his current employers a High Court case was brought against both the employee and his current employers claiming all the wasted expenditure as damages. He soon decided that he had better join the new firm after all! This is obviously very rare, and in normal cases the new employers may well decide to drop the matter.

There is one further point – what does your new contract say about your giving notice? If you can give, say, a week's notice at any time in the first three months of the new job the damages that your new employers can claim will be limited to the loss of your services for that one week. In other words, they will be put in the same position as if you had given one week's notice to them on the first day of your new job (and even that loss may be reduced if they could have got someone else to fill the post without paying out any extra money).

59 | *How much money will I get during my notice period?*

As you are still employed during your notice period,

you are entitled to your wages and other benefits in exactly the same way as if you had not given notice. There is, however, a minimum pay rule during a minimum period of notice (see Q62), but this doesn't apply if the notice that your employers have to give you is one week longer than the minimum. If the minimum pay rule does apply you are given some minimum rights during the minimum notice period; your contract may give you more than this but it cannot give you less.

You will be paid not only for your normal working hours but also for the hours where you don't work because:

● no work is provided even though you are ready and willing to do it, or
● you are ill or injured, or
● you are on holiday under the terms of your contract.

For any of these non-working hours your employers must pay you at your hourly rate, which is worked out like this:

$$\frac{\text{a week's pay (see } \text{Q}60)}{\text{normal working hours}}$$

If you don't have normal working hours your employers must pay you a week's pay for each week in the notice period if:

● you are ready and willing to do work of a reasonable nature and amount to earn a week's pay, or
● you are ill or injured, or
● you are on holiday under the terms of your contract.

These rules apply only if you have been continuously employed for at least four weeks.

60 | *What is a week's pay?*

The phrase 'a week's pay' crops up again and again. The first point to make is that 'pay' means gross pay, that is, before any income tax or National Insurance contributions are deducted. Second, overtime does not count unless under your contract you were bound to work overtime and your employers were bound to provide it. Third, the term 'a week's pay' means cash. It does not include fringe benefits such as the benefit of a company car or luncheon vouchers. Fourth, your week's pay depends on your job and there are four possible situations:

● If you have normal and regular hours and are paid on a time basis your week's pay will be based on the pay that you get under your contract.

- If you have normal and regular working hours but are paid on a piecework basis your week's pay is normal working hours per week multiplied by the average hourly rate of pay over the previous 12 working weeks.
- If you have normal but irregular hours (rotating shift workers are an obvious example) a week's pay is your average hours worked over 12 weeks multiplied by your average hourly rate of pay.
- If you don't have normal working hours at all your week's pay is found by averaging your pay over 12 working weeks.

There is a ceiling for these 'minimum pay' rules. The amount is increased each year so as to keep pace with inflation. At present it is £158.

61 | Can I take my employers to court if they don't give me the notice to which I'm entitled? If so, how much will I get?

The short answer to your first question is yes, and the short answer to your second question is that you will get the money and benefits which you would have got if the notice had been given to you.

Your employers will be in breach of contract if they do not give you the notice to which you are entitled. In many cases employers who want to get rid of an employee will dismiss the employee straight away with money in lieu of notice without allowing the employee to work out his or her notice. The making of such a payment will not stop the employers from being in breach of contract, but it will usually mean that (for the reasons set out below) there will normally be no point in bringing court proceedings because the employee will already have received as much as the court will award, or more than that.

Turning to your second question, the court will award you a sum that will put you in the same position as if the contract had been performed; the sum will include any benefits that you would have got during the notice period. These damages will be based on your *net* pay, that is, after the deduction of tax and National Insurance contributions. The award will also be reduced by any unemployment benefit drawn by you or wages earned by you from a new job during the notice period, and by any payment in lieu of notice made by your former employers. They may also be reduced if you have unreasonably failed to look for other work during the notice period.

62 | How much notice do my employers have to give me if they want to dismiss me?

If you are employed for a defined period of time – a fixed term – your employers cannot dismiss you by notice before the end of that term unless your contract gives them such a right.

If you are not employed for a fixed term, a period of notice may be set out in your contract of employment, and this cannot be less than the minimum laid down by law. If your period of continuous employment is less than two years the legal minimum is one week; after that the minimum is a week for each complete year of service but subject to a maximum of 12. You may be entitled to more than this notice period under your contract, but it cannot be less.

If you are not working for a fixed term and there is no notice period in your contract, your employers can dismiss you by giving you 'reasonable notice', subject again to the legal minimum. The question of what is reasonable will depend on many factors – how you are paid, what is normal in your trade and, perhaps most important, the status of your job. Thus, a week may be reasonable for a shop assistant, a month for a monthly paid clerical worker, three months for a supervisor, and six to 12 months for a managing director.

If you are guilty of a serious breach of contract – stealing the company's property, sending in false time-sheets, accepting bribes, for example – your employers may be able to dismiss you summarily without giving any notice at all.

63 | My company has just dismissed me with money in lieu of notice. Do I have to pay income tax on it?

No. Such a payment is not salary; it is to compensate you for your employers' breach of contract in not giving you your correct notice (see Q62). It is tax-free up to £25,000 in the same way as a payment made to a departing employee without any legal obligation at all (sometimes called a 'golden handshake').

By getting money in lieu of notice you are better off in two ways than if you had been allowed to work out your notice. In the first place, you get a tax-free payment instead of taxable pay. Second, you have the chance of finding other work during the notice period. If you are lucky enough to start another job fairly soon, then your financial position (notice money plus wages from the new job) will be better than getting just net wages from the old job.

Leaving your job: dismissal

64 | *I think I've been unfairly sacked. What can I do about it?*

Every employee has a legal right not to be unfairly dismissed. There are some exceptions however, and you should first check to see whether or not any of these exceptions apply to you. They include:

- members of the armed forces
- the police
- dockers
- employees ordinarily working outside Great Britain (see Q69)
- employees with less than two years' continuous employment (see Qs 65 and 67).
- employees who have reached the normal retiring age in their job (being the same age for men and women) or – if there isn't a normal retiring age – the age of 65. (This rule applies to employees who are dismissed on or after 7 November 1987; the position is slightly different for anyone dismissed before then.)

If you qualify, then you should write to your employers asking for written reasons for their dismissal (see Q70). When you have their reasons (or if you don't get them within 14 days) you can write to tell them that you propose to bring an unfair dismissal case. You can also get in touch with ACAS (see page 298); the Service will try to get the matter settled straight away by persuading your former employers to give you your job back or to find you another suitable job or to pay you compensation.

If no immediate settlement can be reached, then you must make your application to an Industrial Tribunal (see page 266). The time-limit for these claims is very short – three months from the dismissal. For the procedure for bringing a claim, see Q104.

65 | *I've worked for a company for nearly two years and my contract gives me the right to four weeks' notice. Yesterday I was given a letter saying that I was dismissed because I was too old for the job and enclosing four weeks' pay in lieu of notice. What are my legal rights?*

Your employers have done what many employers do when they want to get rid of an employee. The payment of money in lieu of notice is technically a breach of contract (see Qs 61 and 63), but legal proceedings will usually be pointless because you won't get any more money than you've got already (although see below).

Your main problem is in deciding whether you qualify for unfair dismissal. An employee can bring an unfair dismissal claim only if he or she has been continuously employed for two years.

If an employee is dismissed with money in lieu of notice the contract terminates there and then – you can't add on the four weeks' notice period. Therefore it looks as if you haven't clocked up your two years' service. But there are two rays of hope. The first is that an employee who is dismissed without notice can add on the minimum *statutory* notice to which he or she was entitled (see Q62), which in your case is one week. This week might just bring you over the two-year hurdle, and it would then be for an Industrial Tribunal to decide whether the dismissal was fair (see Q71). If you still haven't clocked up the two years you won't be able to go to a Tribunal for unfair dismissal. You can, however, bring a case for wrongful dismissal in a county court (see Q101) and you could argue that your employers dismissed you in breach of contract, that their breach destroyed your chance of bringing an unfair dismissal claim and that the court should award you damages for the loss of that chance.

66 | *Last week my firm dismissed me and gave me a month's notice. I've just found another job. Will I lose my unfair dismissal rights if I don't work out my notice?*

This is a very common problem and there are two ways for you to cut down the notice period. The first possibility is to talk to your employers and ask them to agree to your leaving early. If they agree, then you can start your new job straight away without losing your unfair dismissal rights. If you think that the dismissal was unfair you can apply to an Industrial Tribunal (see page 266) within three months of the date on which your contract ended. Second, you can yourself give notice to your employers and then leave when that notice has run out. Here again, your rights to claim compensation for unfair dismissal are not cut down in any way even though the notice you gave was shorter than the notice which you should have given. The one thing that you must not do is just walk out during your employers' notice period. If you do that you will have lost your right to claim unfair dismissal compensation. A Tribunal would say that you have resigned from your job by walking out and that you have not been dismissed at all.

67 | *I've worked for a number of different firms for the past five years but I think that they were all run by the same man. Can I add all those five years together if I want to bring a claim for unfair dismissal?*

It depends on whether the firms were 'associated employers'. The Employment Protection (Consolidation) Act 1978 tells us that two employers are 'associated' if (i) one employer is a company and is 'controlled' by the other or (ii) both are companies and they are controlled by a third person. The word 'control' means that the one employer has the power to decide what happens by exercising a majority of the votes. It is clear from the decided cases that a pair of employers can be associated only if at least one of them is a company. You will, therefore, have to look closely at the various firms or companies for which you have worked to see whether they are associated. If they are, you can add all the periods together and treat yourself as having worked for one employer for five years. But you have to be careful: in one case, a man who ran two companies owned 99 per cent of the voting shares in company A but only 46 per cent in company B. On these facts the Employment Appeal Tribunal held that the employers were not 'associated'. There is, of course, one further possibility: if they same individual owned all the businesses but not through companies then he will have been your employer throughout the five-year period.

68 | *I'm 60 years old and very fit, but my employers have said that it's time I made way for a younger man and they will dismiss me if I don't go now. Can I go for unfair dismissal if they carry out their threat?*

The unfair dismissal rules in the Employment Protec-

tion (Consolidation) Act 1978 contain an age bar; you can't bring a claim if at the date of dismissal you have attained the normal retiring age for employees of your description (being the same age for men and women) or, if there is no such age, then the age of 65.

In your case your right to bring an unfair dismissal case will depend on whether or not there is a normal retiring age. If there is a retiring date in your contract this will be strong evidence of a normal retiring age, but even this is not conclusive. According to a 1983 case in the House of Lords, you have to consider 'the reasonable expectation or understanding of the employees holding that position at the relevant time'. For example, if you sign a standard form of contract which says that the company can retire you at 60, but then if you can go on to show that most other employees doing your type of work in your company are kept on until, say, 63, then 63 will become the normal retiring age and, as you haven't reached it, your claim can go ahead. If the evidence shows that your colleagues retire at all sorts of different ages – some at 60, some at 61, and so on – that will indicate that there is no normal retiring age at all. In that case, we come back to the '65' bar, and as you are under 65 your claim can go ahead.

There is, of course, no guarantee that you would automatically win your unfair dismissal case; you may well lose if your employers can show, say, that the quality of your work has deteriorated as you've got older.

69 | *For the last three years I've been working for a construction company and much of my time has been spent in Saudi Arabia. While I was there I received a letter of dismissal. Do I have a claim for unfair dismissal?*

You will not be able to bring an unfair dismissal claim if under your contract of employment you ordinarily work outside Great Britain. You should have a look at your contract to see if it states where you have to work. If it states that you are employed as the manager of the plant at Riyadh then that may well take you outside the unfair dismissal legislation even though you perhaps occasionally visit England to attend meetings. If there is no such provision in the contract, it will be necessary to look at all the surrounding circumstances to see whether it was an *implied* term of your contract that you should be based outside Great Britain. In one recent case, for example, an employee of a Pakistani bank was 'posted' to England although he could be recalled to Dacca at any time. The Court of Appeal confirmed the Tribunal decision that he ordinarily worked outside Great Britain even though the greater part of his time was spent here.

70 | *The managing director of my company has just handed me a letter of dismissal. When I asked why I was being dismissed he said he wasn't obliged to give me a reason and told me to clear off. Can he do that?*

There is no rule that says employers have to give any reasons for dismissal at the time when the dismissal takes place. Nevertheless, there are many cases in which the manner of the dismissal can make it unfair, and it is difficult to imagine anything more unfair than the conduct of your managing director in this case. If you have been continuously employed for six months you can ask your employers to let you have a written statement of the reasons for the dismissal. If they then unreasonably refuse to do so within 14 days (and delay of itself is not a refusal) you can make a complaint to an Industrial Tribunal and the Tribunal will award you two weeks' pay (see Q60). The procedure is similar to that for unfair dismissal (see Q104) and the two claims – unfair dismissal and refusal to give reasons for it – are often brought together. If you do go for unfair dismissal the

written statement of reasons can be part of the evidence in the case. The Tribunal will look closely at the reasons to see whether they are genuine and they will ask your employers why they didn't give them at the time of dismissal.

71 | *If I go for unfair dismissal what do I have to show?*

The case can be divided up into three parts. In the first place you must prove that you were dismissed. In many cases this will be obvious and it will not be denied. Sometimes, however, the matter is in dispute – you may claim that you were dismissed and your employers may claim that you resigned. In this sort of case it will be up to you to prove that you were dismissed; if you can't do that you will lose.

The next stage is up to your former employers. They must prove that the dismissal fell within four grounds or that there was some other substantial reason which would justify the dismissal.

The four grounds are:

● capability – either that you were no good at your job or that you couldn't do it because you were injured or ill;
● conduct – this can include such things as bad timekeeping, upsetting customers, suppliers or staff, stealing company property or breaking company rules;
● redundancy – even if you are made redundant because your employers are cutting down on staff, your dismissal can still be unfair if, for example, your employers unreasonably chose you for redundancy and kept on another employee who had been employed for a much shorter time;
● illegality – the obvious example here is the continued employment of a driver who has been banned from driving after being convicted of a motoring offence or an overseas worker whose work permit has expired. In both of these cases the continued employment of the employee in his or her job would be illegal and therefore the dismissal of that employee is likely to be fair.

Apart from these four grounds there is a fifth, namely some other substantial reason for the dismissal. These words are interpreted widely, and they are most commonly relied on by employers who reorganise their business in a way involving the alteration of individual contracts of employment. Other examples could be a serious personality clash between an employee and his or her colleagues which is harmful to the business, or where an employee gets married to or starts living with someone who is actively involved in a competing business.

The third stage is for the Tribunal to decide whether, in the light of the grounds shown by your former employers, they acted reasonably in dismissing you. This will depend on all the relevant circumstances, including your length of service, the seriousness of the matter, the size and administrative resources of your former employers and the way in which they handled the dismissal.

72 | Are there any exceptions to the rules about an employee showing that he was unfairly dismissed?

The only exceptions relate to the third stage described in Q71 – the question of whether the employers acted reasonably. There are several cases in which a dismissal will be automatically unfair, but it will be up to the employee to bring himself within these exceptions. The dismissal will be automatically unfair in the following cases:

● where the pregnancy rules apply (see Qs 30 and 33);
● where the employers, without any special reason, select the employee for redundancy in breach of an agreed or customary arrangement (see Q88);
● where the employee is selected for redundancy because of his trade union activities;
● where the employee is dismissed for trade union membership or activities, or for not belonging to a union or a particular union (see also Q152 for unfair closed shop dismissals).

On the other hand, a dismissal is automatically *fair* if the case comes within the very limited class of fair closed shop dismissals (see Q152) or if it is on the grounds of national security.

73 | My boss has told me that the company cannot keep me on and that he wants me to resign. What is my legal position if I do resign?

If you want to go for unfair dismissal or for a redundancy payment you will have to show that you were dismissed. You should have no trouble in proving this if your employers try to dispute it. Although you may have written the letter of resignation, the driving force behind it was your boss's ultimatum for you to resign or be sacked. Many employees react to this by resigning, but in reality they have been dismissed. There have been many cases before Industrial Tribunals in which the facts have been similar to those in your case, and in all of them the Tribunals have

decided that the employee was dismissed. If you do decide to bring an unfair dismissal claim you will have cleared the first hurdle of proving dismissal (see Q71).

74 | I left work after a row with my boss and went home, actually saying to him: 'I'm going home.' When I turned up for work the following day he told me that I'd resigned and he gave me my cards. Where do I stand?

An Industrial Tribunal would look at the words used in the circumstances of your case and ask itself whether the words were unambiguous in order to establish what precisely you meant. If it decides that your only possible meaning was 'I am resigning', then you will lose your case. This result is unlikely, however, because the words can mean either 'I am resigning' or, more probably, 'I'm going home for the rest of the day'. If the Tribunal finds that the words were ambiguous then it will have to ask a further question: how would the words be likely to be understood by a reasonable employer? If, on that basis, the Tribunal finds that the reasonable interpretation was 'I'm resigning', then you will lose; if it makes the opposite finding, then you will win; if it cannot decide one way or the other then you will have failed to prove that you were dismissed (see Q71) and you will lose.

75 | When my company gave me a month's unpaid leave to visit my sick mother in Jamaica I had to sign a form which said that if I stayed away for longer than a month my contract would automatically come to an end. There was a strike at the airport and I returned three days late. The company now says that it won't take me back. Can it do that?

Yes, but your employers' conduct may amount to unfair dismissal. If you bring an unfair dismissal case to an Industrial Tribunal you will have to show that you have been dismissed (see Q71). There was one case in 1978 when a Mr Ashraf, an employee of British Leyland, lost his claim in a case not unlike yours. The Employment Appeal Tribunal held that the contract had come to an end by mutual consent – that was the legal effect of the form the employee had signed. This meant that the employee had not been 'dismissed' at all. Fortunately, this case is no longer good law because in 1985 the Court of Appeal said that it was wrong. The form, said the Court, was an attempt to take away the employee's unfair dismissal rights and this cannot be done. By not letting you come back to work, your employers have dismissed you. If you bring an unfair dismissal claim the normal rules will apply (see Q 7 1). Your chances look good.

76 | *My contract runs for five years, but the company can give me six months' notice at any time during those five years. Do I have any protection against unfair dismissal?*

Yes. If the company gives you notice you will have the same protection as any other employee; the unfair dismissal rules will apply to you unless you happen to belong to one of the excluded classes (see Q64). If the company does not give you notice your contract will expire at the end of the five-year term. If the contract is not renewed the expiry of itself will be a 'dismissal' for the purposes of the unfair dismissal and redundancy laws. You will therefore be able to bring a claim unless you have agreed in writing (either in the contract or in any other document at any time before the five-year term expires) that the expiry of the term will not give rise to a claim.

77 | *Fifteen months ago I joined a company to supervise the rebuilding of the factory. The company has now told me that the work will be finished at the end of next month and that my job will finish with it. Will I have any claim for unfair dismissal?*

No. You can bring a claim only if you can show that you have been dismissed, which doesn't apply in your case.

Your contract has not been terminated by your employers; it has merely come to an end because the work for which you were employed has been completed. If you had been employed for a fixed term, the expiry and non-renewal of that term would have been a dismissal (see Q76). It has, however, been held that a fixed term must have a defined beginning and a defined end. In your case, nobody knew at the beginning how long the job would take and it was not therefore a contract for a fixed term. In legal language your contract has come to an end by 'performance' and not by dismissal, and for that reason you will not have a claim.

78 | *I work in a textile factory and recently left one of the machines on overnight. When I came in the next morning the manager called me in and told me that I was being demoted. Can he do that?*

Under the general law your employers cannot demote you, because doing so would amount to an alteration of your contract of employment without your consent. There may, however, be a right to demote you under your company's work rules, and you should study them to see what they say. The matter must be looked at by asking three questions: first, do the rules give your employers the right to demote you? Second, were the rules brought to your notice? Third, has the company acted reasonably? The statement that must be issued at the start of your employment (see QS 1 and 2) should spell out any disciplinary rules or it should refer you to a document where you can find them. Even if your employers have done this, that is not necessarily the end of the case because, in the interests of fairness, the punishment must fit the crime. In one recent case involving the BBC, a long-serving employee was demoted following an isolated breach of the Corporation's rules. The disciplinary rules of the Corporation gave it the right to demote the employee. The employee then left and brought an unfair dismissal claim; he won. The Employment Appeal Tribunal decided that it was an implied term of his contract that the disciplinary rules would be operated in a reasonable manner. The punishment was far too severe for a single offence by a long-serving employee, and accordingly he could regard himself as dismissed.

79 | *Can I be dismissed just because I'm ill?*

You must start by looking at your contract of employment. If your employers have an express right to retire you on health grounds then they will not be in breach of contract if they exercise that right. Similarly, if your contract gives them the right to end your contract by notice then they can lawfully do so.

Even if your employers are acting lawfully under the terms of your contract, the dismissal may be unfair. A dismissal can be fair if the reason relates to the capability of the employee for performing his duties; clearly your illness can undermine that capability, and the fairness of the dismissal will depend upon whether your employers have acted reasonably in dismissing you for that reason. The cases decided by the Employment Appeal Tribunal draw a sharp distinction between continuing illness and intermittent illness. If the illness is a continuing illness your employers should discuss the matter with you and should arrange for a medical report to be obtained from your own or an independent doctor or from the company's doctor. They must then make a judgement, and if this results in a decision to dismiss you the dismissal may well be fair. On the other hand, if the illness is intermittent your employers can give you a warning; they can tell you that you must improve your attendance record and that they will dismiss you if it does not improve. If your absences then continue a dismissal may well be fair.

Finally, your contract may give you the right to sick pay for certain periods – perhaps full pay for the first three months, half pay for the next three months, and so on. It will be difficult, though not impossible, for your employers to show that a dismissal during that period was fair.

80 | *I recently had to go to hospital with back trouble and my doctor told me to tell the company that I wouldn't be able to return to work for at least four weeks. When it got the doctor's letter the company dismissed me. Can I claim that I was unfairly dismissed?*

The first thing to do is to check what your contract says about sickness and sick pay; if, for example, it gives you a right to full or partial wages for a period longer than four weeks, the company may be dismissing you unfairly during this sick-pay period (see Q79). Second, if you have had any previous illnesses, it is important to know what kind of discussions, if any, took place between you and your employers on those occasions. It is also important to know whether your employers are a large firm or a small firm. A company with a large staff may find it easier to cover for someone who is ill. A Tribunal would have to decide whether your employer acted reasonably (see Q71), and this means striking the right balance between fairness to you and fairness to the company. In one case a small company had a sudden rush of work. An employee became ill and his doctor told the company that he wouldn't be back for six weeks. The

I'VE STILL GOT THE PAIN DOCTOR
.... AND A NEW ONE IN MY
BACK POCKET.

company decided that it couldn't wait that long and dismissed the employee. On the particular facts of that case the Employment Appeal Tribunal decided that the dismissal was fair.

81 | *I'm the manageress of a dry-cleaning shop and I have been dismissed because the company thinks I've stolen some money from the till even though I'm innocent. I've just heard that a friend of mine has won a case which is very similar to mine. Does that mean that I'm sure to win?*

No. In the first place each case turns on its own facts, and an unfair dismissal decision reached by one Industrial Tribunal is not legally binding on another Tribunal. Second, the unfair dismissal rules give the Tribunal a wide area of discretion. Two of the three members of the Tribunal are persons with industrial experience, and opinions may well differ as to whether employers have acted reasonably (see Q71) in any particular case. In the past few years the Employment Appeal Tribunal has said many times that employers have a range of reasonable responses to the conduct or capacity of employees. This range runs from summary dismissal at one end to an informal warning at the other. The task of the Tribunal is somewhat limited: it must look at the decision that the employers took and ask whether it was within the 'band of reasonableness'. If the answer is yes, then the dismissal will be fair. In other words there may well be cases where a decision not to dismiss would have been equally fair. The Tribunal is not allowed to consider what it would have done if it had been in the employers' shoes.

82 | *I worked my way up without any formal training and now my company wants to dismiss me so that it can bring in a man with a degree in engineering. Can the company do that?*

In theory the answer is yes, but in practice the company may well be liable to you for unfair dismissal if it goes ahead. One of the grounds for fair dismissal relates to the qualifications of the employee for performing work of the kind that he was employed to do. If the nature of the job is going to change dramatically (perhaps through computerisation), then the employers may well be able to argue that they need a different kind of person for that job; they will say that your job will, in effect, disappear and that you will be dismissed on the grounds of redundancy. If these are the facts then the dismissal could well be fair – provided that there is sufficient consultation and attempts to find you another job in the company.

If the job itself is not going to change dramatically then your employers will have considerable difficulty in justifying their dismissal. If you have been doing the job without any complaints from customers for many years, and if the company has never suggested to you that you should study for a degree, then your chances look good of bringing a successful unfair dismissal claim.

83 | I've just had my first driving accident after driving for the company for three years. When I reported it to the company I was told that I was incompetent and I was dismissed. Surely that's unfair?

It certainly looks like it. The competence of an employee is one of the grounds that employers can put forward to support their claim that the dismissal was fair, but the employers will win only if a Tribunal is satisfied that they acted reasonably in treating the lack of competence as sufficient to justify dismissal (see Q71). A dismissal for one error after three years of accident-free driving will almost certainly be an unfair dismissal unless the facts are very, very special – a first offence dismissal might be fair in the case of the driver of an express train, an airline pilot or the driver of a heavy lorry carrying a load of sulphuric acid, for example, but these cases are exceptional and your claim for unfair dismissal looks very strong indeed.

84 | I've been charged with stealing some cans of paraffin from the company's warehouse and my solicitor has told me not to say anything about it to my employers or to anyone else until the trial has taken place. Will I lose my job?

It is clear from many cases that your employers do not necessarily have to wait until the case has been heard before dismissing you. One of the grounds for a fair dismissal is the conduct of an employee. In the case of suspected theft, a dismissal can be fair if the employers believe on reasonable grounds that you are guilty and that this belief was formed after a reasonable investigation and that dismissal is within the band of reasonableness (see Q81). In this case your employers may well look into the matter straight away. If the evidence points strongly to your guilty conduct, then they may decide to dismiss you, and if they can clear the three other hurdles set out in Q71 then the dismissal may well be fair. Any decision on your part not to make any kind of statement could be counterproductive.

85 | If I'm dismissed because of a suspicion of theft, how will the outcome of the trial affect my dismissal?

If you are acquitted by the Criminal Court, your acquittal will not affect the fairness or unfairness of your dismissal because your employers must make their judgement at the time of dismissal. If at that time your employers had a reasonable belief in your guilt, and carried out a reasonable investigation and acted reasonably (see Q71) the dismissal will be fair and your acquittal will not make it unfair.

If you bring an unfair dismissal claim and you are convicted before the case is heard, your chances of success are obviously very slight. Even if the dismissal was technically unfair because, say, your employers carried out no investigation at all, the chances of your getting your job back or compensation are so slight that you would be well advised to drop the case.

Finally, what happens if a Tribunal makes a finding of unfair dismissal before the trial takes place and subsequently you are tried and convicted? This happened in one case where the employee had been awarded compensation for unfair dismissal. When he was convicted the employers went back to the Industrial Tribunal and got the compensation reduced to nil.

86 | My employers have dismissed me for sleeping on the job during the night shift, but other workers have got away with a fine. Isn't that unfair?

If you bring an unfair dismissal case your employers will argue that they dismissed you because of your conduct in sleeping on the job. It will then be for a Tribunal to decide whether your employers acted unreasonably in dismissing you, having regard to 'equity' – in accordance with generally accepted ideas of fairness and justice – and the merits of the case. Obviously, the question of treating other employees differently can be highly relevant in appropriate cases, and it may well be inequitable and unfair for the employers to do so. The Employment Appeal Tribunal has recently said, however, that such arguments must be looked at with some care; it is most important for employers to have flexibility in their treatment of particular offences. The Tribunal went on to say that an employee's argument based on the employers' inconsistency was relevant in only three cases, namely:

● if the employers have lulled the employee into a sense of false security (so that the employee thought

WHEN YOU WAKE UP YOU CAN COLLECT YOUR CARDS
Signed The Boss

that he could get away with it because his colleagues had not been punished in the past); or

● if the decision made in other cases indicates that the reason for dismissal given by the employers was not the true reason; or

● if the decision made in relation to other employees in truly parallel situations supports an argument that dismissal was inappropriate.

In the light of these guidelines, a Tribunal will consider facts such as the relative seniority of yourself and the non-dismissed employees and whether you had been caught sleeping in the past.

87 | *I've recently had two criminal convictions, one for drunken driving and the other for assault. Neither of them has anything to do with my job. If my employers find out about them, can they dismiss me?*

A lot depends on the nature of your job and the effect that these convictions can have on your capacity to do that job and on your relationship with your fellow employees and with customers. In one case the dismissal of a labourer found guilty of incest was found to be unfair: his conviction for incest did not affect his job in any way. Obviously, each case will be examined on its merits, but the following passage in the Advisory, Conciliation and Arbitration Service Code on Disciplinary Practice and Procedures is highly relevant: 'Criminal offences outside employment. These should not be treated as automatic reasons for dismissal regardless of whether the offence has any relevance to the duties of the individual as an employee. The main consideration should be whether the offence is one that makes the individual

unsuitable for his or her type of work or unacceptable to other employees. Employees should not be dismissed solely because a charge against them is pending or because they are absent through having been remanded in custody.'

88 | *I'm a technician working for a photographic equipment company and I've just been made redundant. The company has a long-standing last-in-first-out agreement with the union. I'm the most junior technician at my branch, but two other technicians at our other branch are junior to me and have not been made redundant. Does that give me a claim for unfair dismissal?*

A redundancy dismissal may be unfair if the employers have not acted reasonably (see Q71), and there are two cases where it is automatically unfair. This will be so where persons with similar jobs to yours in the same undertaking were faced with the same redundancy situation and either

● the company selected you because of your trade union activities (see Q72), or

● the company selected you without good reason in breach of a customary or agreed procedure.

In your case you would have to show that your branch and the other branch were a single undertaking; if each of them is completely self-contained this might be difficult. If you can clear that particular hurdle you would have to show that the three of you were all faced with redundancy and that the company had no good reason for departing from the union agreement. For example, if the other two are much better at their jobs than you are, the company may have acted fairly in keeping them rather than you.

Finally, even if the dismissal was not automatically unfair it may still be unfair if the company did not give you adequate warning of the impending redundancy or if it didn't try to find you another job in the company.

89 | *The building company I work for employs workers on several different sites. When the work on my site was finished we were all made redundant. Do I have a claim for unfair dismissal?*

On the facts you've given there is no evidence of victimising you or of departure from an agreed procedure, so your chances of success would depend on whether your employers have acted reasonably. The mere fact that the site-by-site selection may have been agreed by your employers with a trade union doesn't let them off the hook because you may be able to satisfy an Industrial Tribunal that the selection procedure was not a reasonable one. In a case in 1982 the Employment Appeal Tribunal laid down guidelines for employers in redundancy cases. The key factors are:

• adequate warning to the employee:
• consultation with the union, if there is one, not only to agree the basis of selection – to minimise hardship to employees – but also to check that the actual selection is in line with the agreed formula;
• a basis of selection which can be checked against such matters as attendance records, efficiency, experience or length of service;
• attempts to find the employee another job within the company.

In practice, the most important of these is the third one – the manner of selection. In the case of the others the employers may win if they can show that their failure to warn or consult or try to relocate would have made no difference to the decision to make the employee redundant.

On the question of selection, the Industrial Tribunal will look carefully at the system operated by the employers and the employers will win the case if the system and its operation fall within the 'band of reasonableness' (see Q8 1). Since opinions as to what is reasonable can differ, the Tribunal must not substitute its own method of selection for that of the employers.

On the facts of your case your employers seem to have totally ignored the skill, experience, length of service, and so on, of the employees. This must be outside the band of reasonableness and your chance of success looks very strong indeed.

90 | *I've read somewhere that every employee is entitled to at least three warnings before he is dismissed. Is that right?*

No. An employee is not 'entitled' to any warnings at all. His or her only legal right is for his or her employers to act reasonably in all the circumstances in deciding whether or not to dismiss the employee. In 1977 ACAS (see page 298) drew up a Code of Practice on Disciplinary Procedures, and the advice given in that Code can be taken into account by an Industrial Tribunal when deciding whether or not a dismissal was fair.

There are five main grounds for a fair dismissal (see Q7 1) and for three of them – redundancy, illegality and any other substantial reason – a system of warnings is not really appropriate. The Code deals only with warnings for misconduct, but the courts, the Employment Appeal Tribunal and Industrial Tribunals have said that warnings are also important in the case of bad work (see Q8 3) and even in the case of intermittent illness (see Q79).

The advice given by the Code is that employers should adopt the following procedure:

• for minor offences an oral warning should be given;
• for more serious offences a written warning should be given;
• further misconduct might warrant a final written warning;
• the final step is dismissal or some other penalty;
• employees should be told what offences carry the penalty of summary dismissal.

When one looks at the decided cases the following points come through very strongly:
• the guidelines set out in the Code are not law;
• the key factors are the size of the business, the seriousness of the offence or bad work, and the personality of the employee;
• in bad work cases a dismissal without warning for a first offence will be unfair, unless the facts are very special (see Q8 3), and the employee must be given the chance to improve;
• in misconduct cases there should usually be at least one warning, but this will not be so where the conduct is very serious – as, for example, accepting bribes, stealing company property or sending in false time-sheets – or where the employee knows that discovery of his behaviour will lead to dismissal or where it is quite clear that a warning would not have affected the employee's conduct in any way.

91 | *My boss has told me that a large number of customers have complained about my rudeness and that this has left the company with no alternative but to dismiss me. Do I have a claim for unfair dismissal?*

Your employers can certainly prove one of the grounds for a fair dismissal – either your conduct or some other substantial reason (see Q71). If you cannot settle the dispute with your employers you could bring an unfair dismissal claim before an Industrial Tribunal and the result of the case will depend on how your employers handle the matter. A great deal will depend on the following factors:

• Have there been previous incidents?
• Did the company discuss them with you?

YES, IT DOES SUIT YOU, MADAM
... especially with the veil !

● Did the company talk to the customers to find out what was happening?
● Did the company give you a chance to explain?

If there have been previous incidents that have been discussed with you the dismissal will almost certainly be fair. But if this was a first offence you might be able to argue that the dismissal was too drastic a remedy. Even if you do win your case – and there is no guarantee that you will – your compensation would be substantially reduced if your rudeness to the customers has played a part in making the company decide to dismiss you.

92 | *When I got my present job as a secretary the company told me that it was a temporary job to cover the work of a secretary who was going to have a baby. Does this mean that the company can dismiss me as soon as she comes back?*

The unfair dismissal rules apply only where an employee has been employed for a continuous period of two years. As you were only covering for a secretary who was on maternity leave, you will almost certainly have worked for less than this when the time comes for you to leave. If that is so, the company can dismiss you in accordance with the terms of your contract and there is nothing that you can do about it. If, however, you have worked for two years (perhaps because you previously worked for an associated employer; see Q67), then you might have a case for unfair dismissal. The company will show one of the grounds for a fair dismissal, namely 'some other substantial reason' (see Q71): a special rule applies this ground to the dismissal of a pregnant

woman's replacement. Once again, the result of the case would depend on whether the company acts reasonably when the time arrives for dismissing you. If, for example, at the time the company has plenty of vacancies, you can argue strongly that it will have acted unreasonably, and will therefore be dismissing you unfairly in not offering any of those vacancies to you.

93 | *Last month, 10 of us in the paintshop went on strike and the firm told us that we would all be dismissed unless we went back to work. Two men went back and the rest of us were dismissed. What are our chances if we claim we were unfairly dismissed?*

Not very high, and on the facts given you may well have no claim at all. If *all* the strikers were dismissed, an Industrial Tribunal would be unable to hear your unfair dismissal claim. The idea is that the Tribunals should not have to get involved in deciding whether a strike is justified or not. On the other hand, employers are not allowed to victimise some strikers by sacking them and keeping on the rest. The fact that two men went back to work won't help your case; the vital time is the time of *your* dismissal, and you must disregard anyone who was *not* on strike at that time. In other words, if your employers dismissed every employee who was on strike at the moment of your dismissal, then none of you will have a claim.

There is only one ray of hope. If any of your fellow strikers are taken back in his or her old job or some other reasonably suitable job within three months of his or her dismissal, then you can bring an unfair dismissal claim on the basis that no such offer has been made to you. In deciding whether your dismissal was fair or unfair the Tribunal will consider the reason why you were not offered re-engagement.

The strike rules set out above apply equally to official and to unofficial strikes (see Q166).

94 | *If my employers dismiss all the employees who take part in a go-slow or a work-to-rule, can we bring an action for unfair dismissal?*

No. The rules described in Q93 apply where employers conduct or institute a lock-out or where the employees take part in a strike or other industrial action. A number of cases have made it clear that a go-slow or a work-to-rule or a refusal to work new machinery come within the definition 'other industrial action'. Such action can also include an overtime ban – even where the overtime was voluntary.

The words 'taking part' have also been given a wide meaning: in one case, someone who stayed at home during a strike because he was afraid of abuse from his colleagues if he crossed the picket line was held to be taking part in the strike – with the result that the rules described in Q93 applied to him too.

95 | If I win an unfair dismissal case, how much will I get?

There are two elements, a basic award and a compensatory award.

The basic award is worked out in the same way as a redundancy payment and is based on:

- your age at dismissal;
- your final week's pay (see Q60);
- your length of service, with a maximum of 20 years.

The calculation is:
- one and a half week's pay for every year of service over the age of 41;
- one week's pay for every year of service between 22 and 40;
- half a week's pay for the year under 22.

If you are unfairly dismissed at, say, 63 after 25 years' service and are earning £200 per week, you will have qualified for the maximum basic award, which is:

$1\frac{1}{2} \times 20$ years (maximum) $\times$ £158 (maximum) = £4,740

The compensatory award is a sum that the Tribunal considers just and reasonable to compensate you for the loss caused by the unfair dismissal. It includes:

- lost pay;
- lost benefits – luncheon vouchers, pension rights, a company car, and so on;
- likely future unemployment;
- the cost of looking for other work.

The compensatory award can never exceed £8,500 even if your loss is greater than this. In practice, the average compensatory award is around £900; it has been getting higher year by year as the period that people find themselves out of work gets longer and longer. The award can also be reduced if your own conduct has brought about your dismissal or if you have failed to look for other jobs.

96 | My company has dismissed me without giving me my three months' notice money. I was lucky to get a job with another firm at the same

● Employment Appeal Tribunal

This body hears appeals from Industrial Tribunal cases. It has a central office in London but it can sit anywhere in Great Britain. Like an Industrial Tribunal, it usually has three members – an employer representative, a union representative and a judge of the High Court. It has the same powers as the High Court, including the power to send someone to prison for disobeying an Order.

In most cases you can bring an appeal to the EAT only on a question of law. You must show that the Industrial Tribunal has made a mistake in applying the legal rules or has reached a result which is obviously wrong. The fact that you are unhappy with the Tribunal's decision doesn't give you the right to take it to appeal.

You can conduct your own case without a solicitor, but as the appeal will involve legal argument you may well find yourself at a disadvantage if you don't have a solicitor to argue your case.

---

pay two weeks after my dismissal. If I take my former employers to an Industrial Tribunal and claim that I was unfairly dismissed, can the Tribunal order them to pay me the notice money?

Yes. In one sense you've lost only two weeks' pay, and if you had sued for your notice money in a county court you wouldn't have got it. The court would say that the damages payable by your former employers should be limited to any *loss* that you suffered as a result of their breach of contract and that for most of the three-month period you haven't suffered any loss because you got an income from the new firm.

The Industrial Tribunal, however, takes a broader view – not what you would have got if your employers had performed their side of the contract but what you would have got if your employers had followed good industrial relations practice. The argument goes like this:

- Good employers would have paid you three months' money in lieu of notice.
- You would then have had the right to earn more money from a new job during those three months.
- As a result, a Tribunal will put you in the same position as if your employers had behaved as good employers.

97 | When I was made redundant my employers

gave me a cheque for £3,000 as a farewell present. How would this affect any unfair dismissal claim I may make?

The redundancy 'gift' would be taken into account in measuring your loss, and if the payment is greater than what you would have got under your compensatory award (see Q95) the excess would be set against the basic award. If your lost earnings and benefits came to £5,000, the farewell payment would reduce your loss to £2,000, and that's what you'd get apart from the basic award. If, however, your lost earnings came to, say, £12,000, the payment would reduce your loss to £9,000 – but you'd still get your maximum compensatory award of £8,500. In other words, you get exactly the same from a Tribunal as if the £3,000 had never been paid at all. That's why some employers make these farewell payments only if they form part of a settlement involving ACAS (see page 298).

98 | My official wages were £90 per week, but my employers used to put an extra £10 in my wage packet. I've now been dismissed. Will my compensation be based on £90 or £100?

It may well be neither. Your arrangement sounds very much like an agreement to defraud the Inland Revenue. If this is so, a Tribunal will award you no compensation at all, the reason being that courts and Tribunals will not enforce a contract which is illegal. In one case the Employment Appeal Tribunal quoted the words of A.P.Herbert that 'the dirty dog gets no dinner here'. In another case it was pointed out that in common language such an arrangement was a fiddle, and both parties knew and intended it to be so. An employee has sometimes tried to argue that he or she was unaware of the unlawful purpose, but that doesn't seem to apply in your case. If the matter does come before a Tribunal, the Tribunal is quite likely to order the papers to be sent to the Inland Revenue.

99 | I've been drawing unemployment benefit since I was dismissed. How will this affect my unfair dismissal compensation?

If your case goes all the way to an Industrial Tribunal and you win, the amount awarded as the compensatory award (see Q95) by the Tribunal is divided into two parts. The first part, known as the 'prescribed element', is frozen in the hands of your former employers. The Tribunal will send a copy of the order to the DHSS, which will ask your former employers to pay them, out of the prescribed element,

a sum equal to what the DHSS has paid you. The rest of the prescribed element and the second part of the compensatory award will go to you in the normal way.

If you reach an 'out-of-tribunal' settlement with your former employers you will be able to keep whatever sum you have agreed, and it won't be clawed back by the DHSS. The rules about the prescribed element apply only where the money is paid under a Tribunal order.

100 | I'll probably get a tax rebate because I've been out of work. Will that be taken into account by the Tribunal if I make a claim for unfair dismissal?

Probably not. In calculating compensation for unfair dismissal, one message has been handed down time and again by the Employment Appeal Tribunal – keep it simple. In a case decided in 1983 the President of that Tribunal said: 'Where the sums are of the order normally coming before Industrial Tribunals it does not seems to us that it is "just and equitable" to take into account rebates without also taking into account possible tax repercussions as to the future. In our judgment it is just and equitable in the ordinary case for the Tribunal to ignore the tax repercussions on both sides balancing the one against the other.'

101 | If I take my employers to court or to a Tribunal for my dismissal, what are the chances of my getting my job back?

Not very high. If you are going to sue your employers in the High Court or a county court on the basis of a wrongful dismissal (see Q121), the court can give you compensation but it will not order your employers to take you back. If you go to an Industrial Tribunal for unfair dismissal and you win your case, the Tribunal will explain to you its powers of making orders for re-instatement (old job back) or re-engagement (different job). The Tribunal will then ask you if you want it to make one of these orders, and if you want it to do so the Tribunal will consider what to do. It will first decide whether or not to order your employers to give you your old job back, having regard to your wishes, whether it is practicable for the employers to comply with such an order, and (in a case where you were partly to blame) whether it would be just to give you your job back. If it decides against a re-instatement order it will then consider whether to make an order for re-engagement and the terms on which it is to take place. The factors that the Tribunal must take into account are similar to those that apply to re-instatement. If it decides against both re-instatement and re-engagement it must make an award of compensation. In practice, the number of re-instatement and re-engagement orders is very small. Figures published by the Department of Employment show that:

● at present about 36,000 unfair dismissal cases are started every year;
● about 70 per cent are withdrawn or settled before the hearing;
● of the remaining 30 per cent (10,800) the employers usually win about two out of every three;
● in the cases won by employees, re-instatement or re-engagement is ordered in only about one per cent of cases.

If you start proceedings quickly (and you can do this while your notice is still running) you may be able to get re-instatement or re-engagement as part of an ACAS settlement.

102 | How is a re-instatement or a re-engagement order enforced?

The Tribunal will not send one of its staff along to supervise your re-instatement and it has no power to fine or imprison employers if they ignore the order. The only thing that it can do is to punish your employers by ordering them to pay you extra money known as an 'additional award' – unless the employers can satisfy the Tribunal that it was not practicable for them to comply with the order. This could be so if, for example, they have abolished your job, or if the other employees make it clear that they will leave if you are taken back. The Tribunal can make an additional award of between 13 and 26 weeks' pay or, in cases of sex or race discrimination or unfair trade union dismissals (see Q72), between 26 and 52 weeks' pay. The term 'week's pay' is at present subject to a ceiling of £158 (see Q60). This additional award is in no way geared to any financial loss that you may have suffered; it is designed to punish your employers for disobeying the court order. In addition, the Tribunal will make the usual basic and compensatory awards (see Q95).

If your employers refuse to follow the order for re-instatement or re-engagement because of your trade union membership or activities, the additional award will not apply; instead, the employers may have to pay a very large sum known as a 'special award' (see Q150).

103 | If the Tribunal makes an order for re-instatement, can it make a money order at the same time?

Yes. By the time of the hearing you will usually have been away from your old job for at least 10 weeks and possibly much longer. The Tribunal's order will therefore set out (among other things) 'any amount payable by the employer in respect of any benefit which (you) might reasonably be expected to have had but for the dismissal, including arrears of pay, for the period between the date of termination of employment and the date of re-instatement'. This can include any pay rise or other improvement which has been introduced since your dismissal. Any such sum will be reduced by wages in lieu of notice or ex gratia payments made by your employers, wages from another job, and any other benefits that the Tribunal thinks appropriate.

If the company then takes you back but doesn't pay you the money, you can make a fresh complaint to the Tribunal and it can award you a sum to reflect the loss that you have suffered as a result of the company's default.

104 | I want to bring an unfair dismissal claim against my former employers. How do I start?

You start the case yourself, without having to use a solicitor, either by filling in a form called IT1 or by writing to an Industrial Tribunal (see below) to say that you are making an unfair dismissal claim. It is probably better to use the form; you can get one from your local Job Centre or from the Department of Employment, and you should complete at least two copies and keep one of them.

In the form or in the letter you should give your name and address, the name and address of your employers, the job you were doing, the dates when your job started and finished, details of your basic wages, bonuses, overtime, pension arrangements and any other benefits such as luncheon vouchers or a company car, your average take-home pay, what you are claiming (unfair dismissal), the remedy that you want (your job back, another job or compensation) and a short statement of the facts of the case – in particular, how, when and why you were dismissed.

When you have done this you should sign the form or letter and send it to the Central Office of Industrial Tribunals (address on page 510) or to your regional office; the Central Office will tell you which regional office applies.

105 | What happens after I've sent off the letter or form?

You will receive an acknowledgement from the Tribunal which will have on it the number that the Tribunal has given to the case; you should quote that number if you have to telephone or write to the Tribunal for any reason. Within a few weeks you should receive from the Tribunal form IT3, or Notice of Appearance, in which your former employers give their answer to your case. You should also get a telephone call from a conciliation officer because a copy of your claim will have been sent to ACAS (see page 298). ACAS should try to achieve a settlement of the case before it reaches the Tribunal, and its success rate is very high. You may also get a letter from your former employers (or their solicitors) asking you to send them copies of any letters or papers that are relevant to your case and also to let them have further details of your case: if, for example, you make a general statement that you were constructively dismissed (see Q116) because your employers treated you differently from your fellow employees, they can ask you to give some examples. If you don't give them the documents or details, the employers can ask the Tribunal to make an order that your case will be dismissed unless you give them the details by a certain date. It is not all one-way traffic – you can do the same to your employers.

You may get a notice from the Tribunal telling you the month during which the case is likely to be heard. The Tribunal will also ask you to let it know what dates are not convenient and to inform it if you think that the hearing of the case will last for more than one day. A similar notice will be sent to your former employers (who will be known as the respondent; you will be the applicant). The Tribunal will then fix a date for the hearing of the case and will write to you and your former employers to tell you and them what it is. As a rough guide you can expect the hearing to take place 10 to 12 weeks after your claim has been sent in to the Tribunal.

106 | Can I instruct a solicitor to take my case to an Industrial Tribunal, and will it be expensive?

You can certainly use a solicitor and you should ask him whether you qualify for legal assistance under the Green Form Scheme (see page 490). If you qualify, your solicitor will be able to do a lot of the preliminary work for you under the Scheme, including writing letters, drafting the application, interviewing witnesses, preparing statements for you and your witnesses, and negotiating a settlement with your former employers. The Green Form Scheme does not cover the hearing itself, and you should ask the solicitor when you first see him how much he will charge for this. You may well have to pay a sum in the region of £300 plus VAT for a solicitor to spend a

day at the Tribunal conducting your case; it can, of course, be more than this, as it certainly will if the hearing lasts for more than a day. If you can't afford this then you will have to conduct your own case at the Tribunal (although your solicitor can come along and tell you what to say).

If you do not qualify for help under the Green Form Scheme you should discuss the question of legal costs with your solicitor during your first appointment with him. Even if you win your case it is very unlikely that the Tribunal will order your former employers to pay any part of your costs. The average Tribunal award is around £900, and your solicitor's charges, including VAT, could easily eat up the whole or a very large part of that award. On the other hand, your solicitor might be able to bring about a settlement of the case by writing the right kind of letter; in that situation the costs will not be very high.

You may also be able to get help from your trade union or from a Citizens Advice Bureau or Law Centre. There is also a booklet published by the Department of Employment and available from the Department's offices to guide you through the procedure.

107 | I've brought an unfair dismissal case against my former employers and the Tribunal has sent me a form called a pre-hearing assessment. What is this all about?

This procedure was introduced in 1980 to weed out cases that look weak on paper. The pre-hearing assessment is a preliminary hearing at which the Tribunal will decide whether or not a 'costs warning' should be given to you. The assessment may have been asked for by your former employers or by the Tribunal itself. There are a large number of legally qualified chairmen of Industrial Tribunals throughout England, Scotland and Wales, and the staff of the Tribunal may have sent the papers to one of those chairmen and he or she may have decided, after reading the papers, that a pre-hearing assessment is necessary. The form will tell you where and when the assessment will take place. At the assessment the Tribunal will consider your originating application – that is, the form or letter (see Q104) – the Notice of Appearance (see Q105), and any written representations by you or your employers about the strength or weakness of your case and any oral argument on this question. The average length of a pre-hearing assessment is about 15 minutes.

After looking at the papers and hearing the arguments, the Tribunal may feel that the whole or part of your case has little or no chance of success. In that case it will tell you that you may run the risk of being ordered to pay legal costs if you persist in your claim and lose – this is on the basis that legal costs can be awarded by the Tribunal where a party has acted vexatiously, frivolously or otherwise unreasonably. You then have a three-way choice. You can carry on with your case, drop it altogether, or carry on and at the same time try to negotiate a settlement. If the case goes to a full Tribunal hearing it must be heard by an entirely different panel; none of the pre-hearing assessment members can be involved. The pre-hearing decision will have been placed in an envelope and the chairman will not consider it until the case has been decided one way or the other and the only remaining issue is that of costs.

108 | *Six months ago I was dismissed for suspected theft, even though I was innocent. I went to a Law Centre and was told to get the criminal case over first and, if proved innocent, to sue my employers for unfair dismissal. I've just had the criminal case and I was acquitted. What do I do now?*

You have a problem. An unfair dismissal claim must be presented within three months of the dismissal. If you are outside this time-limit the Industrial Tribunal will hear the case only if it is satisfied that you could not reasonably have brought your claim within the three-month period. There have been many cases in which employees have asked the Tribunal to allow late claims, but the employee must be able to show that he has very good grounds for such a request. In your case your chances are almost nil. Since you took legal advice (which seems to have been bad advice) it was obviously reasonably practicable for you to present your claim within the three-month period and you should not have waited until the result of the case was known. Even if the Tribunal were to allow you to put in a late claim (and the chances are very slight) you would not necessarily win your case (see Q85).

109 | *When will a Tribunal allow a claim outside the normal three-month time-limit?*

A number of guidelines have been clearly established by decided cases, some of which have gone to the Court of Appeal. The main guideline is obvious: as each day goes by it gets more and more difficult for an employee to satisfy a Tribunal that he or she was unaware of the unfair dismissal rules. As Lord Denning said in a 1978 case: 'Had the man just cause or excuse for not presenting his complaint within the prescribed time? Ignorance of his rights – or ignorance of the time-limit – is not just cause or excuse unless it appears that he or his advisers could not reasonably be expected to have been aware of them. If he or his advisers could reasonably have been so expected, it was his fault and he must take the consequences.'

Thus, it will be refused if the employee has taken advice from his union or solicitor or Law Centre or Citizens Advice Bureau or if he or she should have made further enquiries during the three-month period. On the other hand, an extension was allowed where a former employee thought that a National Insurance Tribunal – which was considering his claim for unemployment benefit – was also dealing with his unfair dismissal. It was also allowed where the employee discovered on the last day of the three-month period that the reason for his dismissal given to him by his employers at the time of the dismissal was not true.

110 | *What happens if the last day of the three-month period is a Sunday?*

This point has been considered on several occasions by the Employment Appeal Tribunal and by its predecessor, the National Industrial Relations Court. The essential point to grasp is that the claim must be *presented* within three months. Thus, the act of *posting* the application on the last day is not enough. Now what about Sundays? The application can be presented at the Central Office of Industrial Tribunals in London or at one of the regional offices. They are all

closed on Sundays, but that does not answer your question because you may still be able to present your claim on that day. In the most recent case the public had access to a door containing a letterbox. The Employment Appeal Tribunal held that (i) the regional office had held out a postbox as the means by which it would receive communications; (ii) accordingly, a letter that was put through that box was 'presented' to the office; (iii) since this could have been done on the Sunday a claim presented on the Monday was out of time.

111 | *My employers have just dismissed me and given me three months' notice. I want to make a complaint for unfair dismissal. How soon can I present my case to an Industrial Tribunal?*

You can do so straight away. As a matter of strict law you are not 'dismissed' until the notice expires, but it is obviously in everyone's interest that the matter should be dealt with as quickly as possible before attitudes harden. In particular, it is desirable to bring in ACAS (see page 298) to try to achieve a settlement (including a possible re-instatement) at the earliest opportunity. It is therefore possible to start your case and for the Tribunal to hear the case while your notice period is still running.

112 | *What can the Tribunal do to penalise my employers if they don't pay me the money which the Tribunal has awarded to me?*

If you have to take steps to enforce payment of a money order you must do it through a county court, usually the county court for the district in which your employers reside or carry on their business. The Tribunal's order will have been entered in the Register at the Central Office of Industrial Tribunals. When this has been done you can swear an affidavit as to the amount owing and file it at the county court together with a copy of the order itself (this will have been sent to you by the Tribunal at the end of the case). The county court Registrar will then make an order that the award can be enforced as though it were a judgment of the county court itself.

There are various ways of enforcing the order, perhaps the most effective being to 'garnishee' your employers' bank account (assuming that it is in credit) or any debts owing to them. This involves getting a court order requiring the bank or debtor to pay the amount of the order direct to you and not to your former employers. Other possibilities include sending in the bailiffs, getting a charge on property owned by your employers (which means the amount of the order will be passed on to you when the property is sold) and enforcing that charge by an order for the sale of the property, or taking proceedings to have your employers made bankrupt (winding-up proceedings if the employers are a company).

113 | *Under my company rules I can appeal against my dismissal to an appeals board consisting of the company secretary, the personnel officer and a director. How does that tie up with the general rules about unfair dismissal?*

The two rights exist side by side and you should certainly take advantage of the appeals procedure. After all, it may result in your being able to keep your job; if you go for unfair dismissal the chances of your getting anything other than money are very slight (see Q101). Also, the availability of the internal appeals procedure is relevant when the Tribunal has to decide in the unfair dismissal case whether your employers acted reasonably (see Q71); the employers may say 'He had a chance to appeal against the dismissal but he didn't take it' and the Tribunal may well ask you to explain why you made that decision. The terms of your contract may also say that you can carry on drawing your pay until the appeal has been decided.

There is just one word of warning: don't forget the time-limit of three months for an unfair dismissal case. If your dismissal is confirmed by the appeals board, the decision will usually mean that you will be treated as having been dismissed on the original dismissal date and the three-month period will run from that date. If there is any danger of your being late you should make a complaint to the Tribunal even while the appeal to the appeals board is still pending.

114 | *I recently took a few days off without telling the company and then I received a letter enclosing my P45 and saying that I had dismissed myself. What does that mean?*

The words 'self-dismissal' or, to use the lawyer's words, 'constructive resignation', have been used from time to time in cases in which an employee has committed a serious breach of his duties. Obvious examples include not turning up for work or leaving the workplace without permission. This can be of considerable practical importance in relation to certain dismissals because some cases have held that an employee's breach of itself brings his or her contract to an end; the result is that the employee cannot claim unfair dismissal because he or she has ended the contract and therefore has not been dismissed at all. In one case an employee left work complaining of pain; his employers tried many times to get in touch with him, finally discovering that he had gone on holiday! They then wrote him a letter stating that he had ended his own employment, and in the unfair dismissal proceedings brought by the employee the employers' argument was upheld. It may be, however, that this case might now be decided differently; it is clear from later cases that the idea of self-dismissal is not particularly popular with Industrial Tribunals because it would greatly weaken the protection against unfair dismissal that Parliament has given to employees. In most cases a breach of contract by the employee will not end the contract – unless the Tribunal finds that the employee has resigned.

In your case you should claim that the letter from your employers was a letter of dismissal and your chances of success on this point are good.

115 | *While I was in hospital recovering from a serious illness I got a letter from my firm telling me that my contract of employment had been frustrated. What does this mean?*

A contract is frustrated if, without the fault of either party, an event happens which destroys the entire basis of the contract or changes its terms into something quite different. An example would be a contract for the export of goods to another country which becomes impossible to perform because of a government embargo on selling to that country or because of the outbreak of war. In the case of a contract of employment, there have been situations like yours in which employers have tried to argue that the illness of an employee has frustrated the contract. If this argument is successful, the employee cannot bring an unfair dismissal claim; the contract has been frustrated and the employee has not been dismissed at all. Industrial Tribunals are not very keen on this argument, however, because it weakens employees' protection. If you do bring an unfair dismissal case, the Tribunal will look at all the relevant factors, including the nature of your job, the nature of your illness, how long your job was likely to continue, the likely length of your illness and your period of past employment. In one recent case an employee had been away from work with heart trouble for 12 months and a doctor indicated that he would never be able to work again. The House of Lords decided that the notice given by the employers could be disregarded because,

IT'S NOT THE ONLY THING THAT'S FRUSTRATED.

when they gave it, the contract had already been ended by frustration.

116 | *I've heard of something called constructive dismissal. What is it?*

The words 'constructive dismissal' do not appear in the Employment Protection (Consolidation) Act 1978, but they have been used by the courts and by Industrial Tribunals in unfair dismissal and redundancy cases for many years. A constructive dismissal occurs when employers commit a serious breach of the contract of employment and the employee reacts by terminating the contract – either with or without notice – as a result of that breach. The idea behind it is similar to 'resign or be sacked' cases (see Q73). In other words the physical act of ending the contract is the employee's, but the real reason for his or her doing so is the employers' conduct and therefore the employee can treat him or herself as having been dismissed. The obvious problem is in deciding whether in any particular case the employer's conduct was such that the employee can regard him or herself as having been dismissed. In many cases (and especially in borderline cases) the employee should complain to his or her employers before making the decision to leave: if he or she has overreacted the Tribunal may decide the case against him or her.

No special formalities are required, although the employee should tell the employers why he or she is leaving.

Constructive dismissal is not the same as an unfair dismissal. It merely means that the employee has cleared the first hurdle of proving dismissal (see Q71) in an unfair dismissal case. A constructive dismissal, like any other dismissal, can be fair, and there have been many cases where this result has been reached.

Employers will not be guilty of a constructive dismissal if they are merely exercising their contractual rights. You should therefore read your contract carefully to see whether your employers have the right to alter your place of work, for example, or the nature of your job. Subject to this warning, the following examples of employers' behaviour can be given of situations in which you could claim constructive dismissal:

● reduction in pay;
● the abolition of compulsory overtime;
● fundamental changes in job duties (in one case an employee had numerous sales responsibilities reduced by his employers until he was left with the keeping of VAT returns and other humdrum clerical duties; his claim based on constructive dismissal was upheld);
● a major change in the place of work;
● suspension without pay;
● disciplinary action which is out of all proportion to the seriousness of the offence;
● failure to provide a safe system of working;
● conduct that undermines the trust and confidence between employers and employee (see QS 117 and 118).

117 | *I'm a supervisor at a food processing plant. The girls who work under me are rude and don't follow my instructions, and when I complain to the manager he just laughs and sometimes says, 'Well, that's because you're no bloody good'. I've just about had enough. Can I go for unfair dismissal?*

Your statement of terms of employment (see QS 1 and 2) should give details of how and by whom complaints by employees will be dealt with. This is known as a grievance procedure, and if there is one then you should use it. It may, of course, merely tell you to make all your complaints to your manager, and that won't be very helpful in your case. Nevertheless, if you are thinking of leaving you should follow the grievance procedure or at least write to someone more senior. Subject to this, the conduct of the manager could well come within the area of constructive dismissal (see Q116) known as undermining trust and confidence. Managers must give support to their supervisory staff, and yours has certainly not done so. The swearing may also be highly relevant. In one case, for example, an employee complained of constructive dismissal when his immediate supervisor told him he couldn't do his 'bloody job' anyway. This was wrong and the supervisor knew it was wrong; the words had been spoken in order to needle the employee into resigning. The employee won his case; the employers had, without reasonable and proper cause, conducted themselves in a manner intended or likely to destroy or seriously damage the relationship of confidence and trust between the parties. There have also been other cases in which the use of foul language by employers has led to a finding of constructive dismissal. On the facts of your case your chances of success are good.

118 | *The man I work for keeps trying to make sexual advances. I always complain bitterly and it's getting very embarrassing. What are my legal rights if I leave?*

Your contract of employment will not have any express terms about this harassment, but it is a fundamental implied term of your contract that your employers will do nothing to undermine the trust and confidence between you. In a leading case in 1977 Lord Justice Lawton decided that persistent and unwanted amorous advances to a female employee were an obvious example of a constructive dismissal situation (see Q116). Three other points should be mentioned. The first is one of timing; you must make up your mind to leave within a reasonable time after the last of the advances; if you continue to work there for any length of time you may well lose your rights. Second, you should tell your employers that you are leaving because of the advances. Third, if you do bring an unfair dismissal claim the circumstances could well attract a lot of publicity. This can work both ways: on the one hand, the publicity may be embarrassing for you; on the other, it may be even more embarrassing for your boss, and this could result in your employers making a good settlement to stop the case reaching the Tribunal.

119 | *If I bring an unfair dismissal claim based on constructive dismissal, can I carry on working as usual until the case is heard by the Tribunal?*

No. The basis of a constructive dismissal claim is that your employer has undermined your contract of employment and that you have reacted to that by leaving. If you then turn up for work in the usual way you will be acting in a manner inconsistent with your claim. You are not allowed to go on behaving as if you are still employed when the basis of your claim is that your contract has come to an end. You cannot have your cake and eat it, and if you do carry on working you will certainly lose your case. Your employers may well ask the Tribunal to throw the case out on that ground and to order you to pay costs on the grounds that you have acted unreasonably. You could, of course, take a different job with your employers but this would affect your compensation.

120 | *A friend who had good grounds for making a claim for a constructive dismissal was found by a*

Tribunal to have been fairly dismissed. How can this be?

The question of whether there has been a constructive dismissal is relevant only in deciding whether there has been a dismissal at all. If the employee satisfies the Industrial Tribunal that he or she has been dismissed it will be up to the employers to prove the reasons for it. If they do so the Tribunal must decide whether, in all the circumstances, the dismissal was fair. Obviously, the fact that the employers have repudiated the contract is a relevant factor, but it is not conclusive.

In practice, the most common types of fair constructive dismissal are those involving business reorganisation. Employers may find it necessary to alter the employees' places of work, hours of work, wage structures, or job content. The problem then is to find the balance between the employers' rights to make the business more efficient (and also perhaps to ensure its survival) and the employees' rights not to have their contracts changed without their consent. If the employees refuse to accept the changes and leave, they can bring a claim based on constructive dismissal. Whether they will win is another matter. The employers will argue that the dismissal was for some other substantial reason justifying the dismissal (see Q71). They must, of course, discuss the matter with the employees and with any recognized union, and they must consider the objections of the employees to the proposed changes. Nevertheless, there have been many cases in which a constructive dismissal resulting from a reorganisation has been held to be fair.

121 | *If I get some money in an unfair dismissal claim how will that affect my claim for wrongful dismissal?*

Wrongful dismissal – a dismissal in breach of the contract of employment – is not the same thing as unfair dismissal, but they do overlap. The short answer to your question is that you cannot get paid twice over for the same items of loss. If a Tribunal awards you unfair dismissal compensation for money and benefits which you would have got for the rest of your contract term, this will reduce or wipe out any claims which you can bring for the same items in a wrongful dismissal claim in the High Court or a county court. On the other hand, any unfair dismissal compensation for the period after your contract would have ended – compensation for future unemployment – will not reduce your wrongful dismissal claim at all because the wrongful dismissal case is

concerned only with losses suffered during the contract term. If you were earning a very high salary or if you had benefits under your contract or if your contract still had several years to run, in the wrongful dismissal case you should get a much higher award than the maximum compensatory award of £8,500 which you can get in the unfair dismissal proceedings (see Q95).

A wrongful dismissal award will only be reduced by unfair dismissal compensation which is payable to you. It will not be reduced by any part of the award which goes to the DHSS (see Q99).

122 | *I used to get a pay rise at the start of every year. Will this be taken into account in working out my damages for wrongful dismissal?*

If your contract gave you a legal right to the pay rise then the answer to your question is yes; you have lost that benefit by being wrongfully dismissed and the High Court or a county court would award you what you would have got if your contract had run its full course. On the other hand, if your contract said nothing about pay rises then the decision could go either way. Your employers will argue that the pay rise was discretionary, and since they weren't legally bound to give you one the court should not treat this as part of the loss resulting from your dismissal. You would argue that the pay rise was given like clockwork every year and that everyone knew it was coming – if only to keep salaries in line with inflation.

Most wrongful dismissal cases are settled out of court, and the loss of the pay rise is obviously something on which you will have to negotiate – and perhaps compromise – as part of the settlement.

123 | *My company gave me free life cover, membership of a private medical scheme and the use of a car. If I claim that I was wrongly dismissed, can I get compensation for the loss of these items and how would it be worked out?*

Yes, these items will be included in working out what you have lost. On the life insurance and private medical cover the loss to you will be the money that you will have to pay out of your own pocket to buy the benefits that you will have lost. You should find out what the premiums are.

With regard to the car you can get substantial compensation if the car was available for your private use. If you mainly used the car to travel to and from work, then these are journeys that you will no longer have to make and the compensation will reflect this. A court would also consider whether the company

£10,000 O.N.O.
REDUNDANCY
CHEQUES ACCEPTED

provided free petrol and servicing. In one recent case a managing director was summarily dismissed when his contract still had 30 months to run. Damages for the loss of a year-old Daimler car were assessed at £10,000.

124 | *I've read somewhere that some special tax rules apply in cases of wrongful dismissal. What are these?*

The compensation payment is tax-free up to £25,000; on the next £25,000 the tax bill is reduced by half and on the next £25,000 the tax bill is reduced by one quarter. After that the normal tax rates apply.

The other tax consideration is how tax will affect the calculation of the award (this is important not only if the case is heard in court but also if you are negotiating an out-of-court settlement). The basic idea is that the damages for wrongful dismissal should compensate you for your loss, which means that they will be based on your net pay and not on your gross pay – in other words, on your lost pay packet. If your lost earnings come to £25,000 or less then, as explained above, the payment itself is tax-free and a court would give you compensation based on your lost net pay. If, however, the lost earnings come to more than £25,000 then the matter becomes a bit more complicated; a court would give you a sum which, after the deduction of tax, will leave you with your pre-dismissal net loss. You should ask an accountant or solicitor to make these calculations and try to get them agreed with your former employers or their solicitors.

125 | *I went into a deep depression when I lost my job and I can't face anyone – least of all pro-spective employers. Can I include this in any claim?*

No. A claim for wrongful dismissal covers only financial loss, and the House of Lords decided as long ago as 1909 that a dismissed employee couldn't recover compensation for injured feelings nor for the fact that

the dismissal had made it harder for him or her to find another job. There is only one possible exception to this rule – if your employers have committed some other breach of contract as well as the dismissal you can sometimes get damages for mental distress caused by that other breach. In one case a man became depressed and ill when he was wrongly demoted; later, he was wrongfully dismissed as well. A High Court judge awarded him £500 for the distress after the demotion as well as the usual wrongful dismissal compensation (see Q61). If, however, the employers' only breach is the dismissal itself you won't get compensation for your depression.

Leaving your job: redundancy

126 | *I was made redundant two months ago and my company paid me my redundancy money and £12,000. I remember signing a form but I can't remember what it said. My contract had three years to run and I was earning £20,000 a year. Can I get any more money and, if so, how long will it take?*

You have probably signed a form accepting the £12,000 in full and final settlement of all claims against the company. If that is so then your right to claim compensation for wrongful dismissal (in other words your dismissal three years too soon) has been signed away. This compensation, based on your net salary for the three lost years, could well have come to very much more than £12,000. You also have a right to bring a claim of unfair dismissal, and this cannot be excluded by agreement unless an ACAS conciliation officer has become involved. If ACAS has not become involved a form by which you sign away your unfair dismissal rights is not legally valid and you could still bring an unfair dismissal claim. Unfortunately, even if you prove that the dismissal was unfair you won't get much money because the basic award is wiped out by the redundancy payment, the £12,000 will have reduced your overall loss in any case, and the maximum sum a Tribunal can award is £8,500 as the compensatory award even where your loss is much greater (see Q95). You should also bear in mind that any unfair dismissal case must be presented within three months of the dismissal.

If for some reason you haven't signed away your rights to go for wrongful dismissal then you will have a large claim against your former employers. Since the claim is going to be for more than £5,000 you will have to bring it in the High Court.

127 | *Will my redundancy payment reduce the damages that I could claim for wrongful dismissal?*

No. A redundancy payment is paid to you in respect of your past service. It is not a payment to compensate you for future loss of employment, and therefore it cannot reduce any loss that you might be able to claim as resulting from wrongful dismissal. If, say, two employees are made redundant and if both of them are on a month's notice, one of them may be allowed to work out his or her notice while the other one is dismissed straight away without any notice; each of them gets his or her redundancy money when his or her contract comes to an end. Thus, the redundancy payment is payable whether or not the employers have broken their contract by not giving notice, and therefore it is not a payment that reduces the loss following the employers' breach.

128 | *The works manager says that business is very bad and that he can't guarantee that the company can carry on for more than a few months. Will I be better off finding another job and leaving now, or staying put?*

This is a very difficult problem because if you find another job now you may lose your rights to a redundancy payment and/or compensation for unfair dismissal. Both of these rights are available only if you are dismissed and not if you resign. The gloomy words of the manager are a long way short of dismissal. To give an example: in one particular company the staff were told that the factory would close on 31 December and that they should all try to find other jobs. A number of them did so, then, when the factory did close, they claimed redundancy payments but lost. The Employment Appeal Tribunal ruled that they had not been dismissed because they had not been given a definite date on which their contracts would come to an end. The giving of a date for the closure of the factory was not enough. So although it is obviously sensible for you to find another job as soon as possible, you will get a redundancy payment and/or compensation for unfair dismissal only by hanging on until you are dismissed.

129 | *I read somewhere that you can only be made redundant if the work falls off. Is that right?*

No, the definition of redundancy is much wider than that. A dismissal is treated as being by reason of redundancy if the employers cease or intend to cease to carry on business (either temporarily or permanently) at the place where the employee is

Advisory, Conciliation and Arbitration Service (ACAS)

This body was set up under the Employment Protection Act 1975 with the objects of improving industrial relations and encouraging the extension, development and reform of free collective bargaining.

As its name implies, it can offer advice to industry (including the preparation and publication of Codes of Practice), conciliate in industrial disputes, and provide voluntary arbitration where this is required. One of ACAS's main functions relates to individual claims brought by an employee against his or her employers. The ACAS conciliation officers must try to promote a settlement of these claims; their success rate is very high.

In an unfair dismissal case the Industrial Tribunal (see page 266) sends a copy of the claim to ACAS, and the conciliation officer will then approach the parties to see whether they can reach a settlement – either by giving the employee his job back, or another job, or by a payment of money. Such a settlement reached through ACAS is legally binding. You can also reach a binding settlement through ACAS without going to the Tribunal at all. Everything said to ACAS is confidential and cannot be disclosed at a Tribunal hearing.

employed, or the requirements of the business for employees to carry on work of a particular kind at that place have ceased or diminished or are expected to cease or diminish. A drop in the volume of work is obviously one example of redundancy, but it is not the only one. For example, if the business is computerised there may be a need for fewer employees and a dismissal in such a case is likely to be by reason of redundancy. A second example is where the employers carry out a reorganisation as a result of which the overall size of the workforce is reduced. A third example is where the employers decide that they will cut down on their staff and have the work done by self-employed people.

130 | *I joined the company as a welder on my twenty-fourth birthday and I've been working here for twenty-five and a half years. My gross pay is £200 per week. We've had a bad year and four of us (including me) are being made redundant. What redundancy money will I get?*

It depends on whether or not your company runs its

own redundancy scheme. The government brought in a legal right to redundancy payments in 1965, and the rules are now set out in the Employment Protection (Consolidation) Act 1978. Many employers have their own schemes that top up what employees can claim under the Act. The rules of the scheme will tell you how much you can get.

Under the Act a redundancy payment can be claimed by an employee who

- has been continuously employed for two years, and
- is under the age of 65 (male) or 60 (female), and
- is dismissed by reason of redundancy or is laid off or put on short-time work (see Q140).

The amount of a redundancy payment is based on
- your age at dismissal, and
- your final week's pay (see Q60), subject to a maximum at present of £158, and
- your length of service, subject to a maximum of 20 years.

The formula is one and a half weeks' pay for each complete year over the age of 41, one week's pay for each complete year between 22 and 40, and half a week's pay for each complete year between 18 and 21.

Your 20 years' service will be worked back from the date of your dismissal, so you would get:

for the years over 41 (8 years) $1\frac{1}{2} \times 8 \times £158$
$$= £1,896$$
for the years between 28 and 40 (12 years)
$1 \times 12 \times £158$ $$= £1,896$$

Total £3,792

131 | I've heard of something called a bumped redundancy. What on earth does that mean?

The practice of 'bumping' arises from the legal definition of redundancy. A dismissal will be by reason of redundancy if the employers cease or intend to cease to carry on the business at the place where the employee was employed, or if there is a drop in the need for employees to do work of *a* particular kind at that place. The definition does not say *the* particular kind of work that the dismissed employee was employed to do. Suppose that a company carries on the business of selling and servicing cars. The sales side is hit by a recession and the company decides to close it down. The sales manager is such a good worker that the company wants to keep him and he's moved sideways to become the service manager of the servicing department. The company dismisses the former service manager who is not as good at his job. Since there has been an overall drop in the number of employees required by the company, the former services manager will have been dismissed by reason of redundancy. He was 'bumped' out of the way in order to make room for the worker the company wished to retain.

132 | I live 30 miles from the office and my employers have always provided a bus free of charge to take us to work. Last week they said that they are losing so much money that they can't run the bus any more and that we'll have to make our own way to work. That's going to cost me a lot of money. Can I claim a redundancy payment if I leave?

Your rights to a redundancy payment will depend on two factors – were you dismissed and was the dismissal because of redundancy? The rules about dismissal are the same as for unfair dismissal (see Q71). In particular, you may be able to show that you have been constructively dismissed (see Q116) by your employers' breach of contract in withdrawing the free bus service. If you can show that the provision of the bus was a term of your contract (and you should be able to do this) you can leave the company and claim that you have been constructively dismissed.

The second question of whether it was a dismissal by reason of redundancy is more difficult to answer. There is a presumption in your favour that it was, but your employers can bring evidence to show that it wasn't and they may well be able to do so. Redundancy means a drop in the need for employees to do work of a particular kind. If the company can show that it needs the same number of employees as before then there is no redundancy even though the company is cutting back the benefits that it has provided for the workforce.

You may have a stronger case if you can show that the conduct of your employers is not only a constructive dismissal but an unfair dismissal. Although they will argue that the need for the business to survive by cutting expenses was 'some other substantial reason' (see Q71), the dismissal may still be unfair if they didn't discuss the matter fully with you before deciding to withdraw the bus service.

133 | I've been employed for the last three years as a chief accountant. The company has reorganised and I've been dismissed because my job has disappeared. Can I claim redundancy money?

The definition of redundancy includes a case where the requirements of that business for employees to carry out work of a particular kind have ceased or diminished. If, as a result of the re-organisation, the need for a chief accountant has disappeared, then this looks like a clear case of redundancy; you would qualify for a redundancy payment and the question of unfair dismissal will also have to be considered (see Q71). There is, however, one additional point: you should examine your contract of employment to see how it defines your duties. A quite common clause in contracts gives employers the right to ask employees to perform any and all duties that reasonably fall within the scope of their capabilities. In one case an employee claimed unfair dismissal on the basis that he was *not* redundant, relying on the wording of such a clause to support his case. In the end he lost, but only because the Court of Appeal held that the wide, general duties specified were ancillary and subsidiary to the main position that had disappeared; therefore, the Court of Appeal decided that he *was* redundant and the Court then went on to decide that the redundancy dismissal was fair. In your case you should see whether you can be required to perform other duties and, if so, you will have to consider how far, if at all, your claim will be affected.

134 | *I work as an engineer at a garage which has just been sold. The new boss is going to make a lot of changes, and I've got to take over some of the selling and the paperwork that goes with it. Do I have to take on all this or can I leave and claim redundancy money?*

You can claim a redundancy payment only if you are dismissed by reason of redundancy. Your chances of claiming a redundancy payment are very slight and this is so for two reasons. First, you haven't been dismissed; the only possibility is to claim that you have been constructively dismissed (see Q116), but this means showing a serious breach of contract by your employers. You have no right to expect that your job will remain unchanged, so the change from engineer to engineer plus salesman will not give you the right to treat yourself as dismissed.

Even if there was a dismissal your second problem would be to show that it was by reason of redundancy. A mere reorganisation of duties does not itself amount to redundancy. If, however, you could show that the new boss was going to cut down on the total number of employees, then that would be a redundancy situation.

As your employers haven't broken their contract

you will either have to adapt to the new set-up or, if you don't like it, you can give notice and leave.

135 | *I worked as a polisher until the department closed down six weeks ago. The company told me that I could work in the trimming department and I said I'd try it out. I now find that I can't do the work. Is it too late for me to claim a redundancy payment?*

No. When your department was closed you were redundant. Redundant employees offered a different job have a four-week trial period under the Employment Protection (Consolidation) Act 1978. This means that you won't lose your right to a redundancy payment just because you try out the new job, although you will lose your rights if you stay in the new job for more than four weeks. The Employment Appeal Tribunal has construed this rule in a way that is very favourable for employees. Where employers break the contract of employment – and they may well have done so in your case by stopping your employment as a polisher – you have a reasonable time in which to make up your mind whether or not they are going to treat that breach as ending the contract. This 'reasonable time' can be longer than the four-week trial period, and the trial period won't start to run at all if you leave your new job within a reasonable time of your employer's breach. It very much looks as if your six weeks in the new job will not stop you claiming a redundancy payment.

136 | *I work as a feature writer for a magazine, but I'm not very happy at my job. Will I get a redundancy payment if I volunteer for redundancy?*

Yes, if there is a genuine redundancy. If you and your employers end your contract by mutual agreement there is no dismissal and therefore no right to a

redundancy payment. But if you merely ask to be dismissed, and your employer agrees, there is a dismissal even though you part company as the best of friends. If the dismissal is by reason of redundancy (cutting back on staff) then you can claim a redundancy payment.

137 | I work as a buyer and from time to time I've accepted gifts from suppliers. The company has just found out and said it's making me redundant. Can I claim redundancy pay?

If you are dismissed by your employers it will be presumed in your favour that the dismissal was by reason of redundancy; this gives you the right to a redundancy payment if you have clocked up the necessary two years of continuous employment. If they don't make a redundancy payment your employers will have to show that the dismissal is not for redundancy but for misconduct. Even if you were dismissed for redundancy you won't get a redundancy payment if your employers can show that they had the legal right to dismiss you without notice which they clearly did because of your serious breach of your duty of good faith, and that they dismissed you

● without notice, or
● with short notice, or
● with your normal notice and a statement in writing that they could have sacked you without notice.
　Your chances of a successful claim are not good.

138 | Last week my boss gave me a month's notice because he was making me redundant. The union has now called a strike. Will I lose my redundancy money if I join it?

The rules are complicated and a lot depends on the length of notice to which you are legally entitled. If you are entitled to a month's notice under your contract or under the general law (see Q62), a strike during that month will not destroy your right to redundancy pay even if your employers dismiss you for striking. If, however, you are entitled to, say, only a week's notice you may lose your right to a redundancy payment if your employers dismiss you for striking at any time before your final week.

　There is another special rule dealing with strikes by employees who are already under notice. The employers can serve what is called a 'notice of extension', which will extend the notice by the number of working days lost by the strike. If you refuse to turn up for work during the extension you will lose your right to your redundancy money unless you bring a claim before an Industrial Tribunal and can satisfy the Tribunal either that you were unable to comply with your employers' request (perhaps because you were ill) or that it was unreasonable for your employers to serve the extension notice. If you can satisfy the Tribunal in this way it can order your employers to pay you your redundancy money in whole or in part.

139 | My boss is moving his plastics factory 50 miles out of London and he says that I've got to work at the new site. Can I claim redundancy pay if I refuse?

Not necessarily. The first question is to decide where you were employed, and this will depend on the terms of your contract – if a clause in the contract gives your employers the right to ask you to work anywhere in the UK then they can ask you to do so; if you refuse they may decide to dismiss you for not performing your contract.

　If, however, the contract does not give your employers the right to move you elsewhere (the clause is sometimes called a 'mobility clause'), you could claim that you have been constructively dismissed by the alteration in your place of work (see Q116) and that the dismissal is by reason of redundancy because your employers are no longer carrying on business at the place where you were employed.

　That, however, is not the end of the story because you will lose your right to a redundancy payment if you unreasonably refuse a suitable offer of fresh employment. If you can show that you have a good personal or family reason for refusing the move – the effect of the move on your children's education, say – your refusal will not destroy your right to a redundancy payment.

140 | I'm employed as a machinist by a small factory. I work from home and the foreman brings me my work every morning. If I get no work for a week, can I expect any redundancy pay?

In general, you can claim a redundancy payment only if you are dismissed, but there is an exception where your pay depends on the amount of work that you do (piecework is the obvious example). In such a case special rules enable you to claim a redundancy payment if you are laid off or put on short time.

　For this purpose you are treated as laid off for a week if no work is provided for you at all during that week; you are treated as being on short time if your remuneration for that week is less than half a week's pay. The rules are rather complex, but broadly work as follows:

- you must give your employers a written notice of your intention to claim a redundancy payment;
- at the time of that notice you must have had *either* a continuous period of four weeks of layoff or short time ending within four weeks of the notice or a total of six weeks (with no more than three of them consecutive) in a 13-week period with the last of such weeks ending within four weeks of the notice;
- within seven days your employers can serve a counter-notice saying, in effect, that the layoff or short time is purely temporary;
- you also have to give notice of termination of one week (or such longer period as may be required by your contract). You must do this within three weeks of giving your notice of intention to claim redundancy payment unless your employer serves a counter-notice and you then take the case to an Industrial Tribunal. In that case your notice of termination must be served within three weeks from the date on which the decision of the Tribunal is notified to you.

141 | What happens if my employers serve this counter-notice?

The counter-notice will state that your employers will dispute your right to a redundancy payment; if such a notice is given and not withdrawn you cannot get a redundancy payment without an order of an Industrial Tribunal. The procedure for claiming a redundancy payment is similar to the unfair dismissal procedure (see Qs 104 and 105).

Your employers will have to satisfy the Tribunal that it was reasonably to be expected that within four weeks of your own notice you will have a period of at least 13 weeks without being laid off or put on short time for any of those weeks. If, however, you carry on working for at least four weeks after your notice, and if you are laid off or put on short time for each of those weeks, then your employers' defence will collapse and you will get your redundancy payment in the usual way. If the matter does go before the Tribunal as a result of the counter-notice, you do not have to give your notice of termination until three weeks after the Tribunal's decision has been notified to you.

142 | I'm a single woman of 59 and I'm about to be made redundant. I was hoping to carry on working for another two years and then to draw my

pension. Will I get my redundancy payment or am I too old?

If you have been continuously employed for two years and you are dismissed by reason of redundancy you can claim a redundancy payment. However, your age will lead to a reduction in the amount of the payment. In general, a woman can claim a redundancy payment if she is dismissed for redundancy at any time before attaining the age of 60. If she is dismissed in her sixtieth year the payment is reduced by the number of months after her fifty-ninth birthday divided by 12.

If you are dismissed three and a half months after your fifty-ninth birthday your redundancy payment will be reduced by three-twelfths. There is a similar rule for men who are dismissed in their sixty-fifth year.

There are also detailed regulations under which your redundancy payment will be reduced if your employers have to pay you a pension starting within 90 weeks of your dismissal.

143 | I worked overtime for years, but when I got my redundancy money I found that my company had ignored my overtime altogether. Can it do that?

The answer to this question may well be yes. The redundancy payment represents a number of weeks' pay (see Qs 60 and 130), and a week's pay is based in many cases on normal working hours. Your contract may state that you are entitled to overtime pay if you work for more than 40 hours in any week. In that situation the 40 hours will be your normal working hours and for the purposes of redundancy pay any overtime will be ignored. If the contract states that your working week is, say, 45 hours, with overtime pay starting after 40 hours, you can treat 45 as the number of normal working hours. Overtime comes into the redundancy pay calculation only if it is compulsory on both sides, as it is in this latter case: there must be an obligation on the employers to provide it and an obligation on the employee to work it.

144 | You said that a redundancy dismissal can also be an unfair dismissal. Does that mean that I'll get two lots of compensation?

No. Any redundancy payment is deducted from the unfair dismissal basic award and any balance is deducted from the compensatory award. In most cases the statutory redundancy payment will be the same amount as the basic award (see Qs 95 and

130). If you get more than the statutory payment under your employers' own redundancy scheme, the same rules will apply. In other words the entire redundancy payment will be set against the basic award and any balance will reduce the compensatory award.

145 | How do I claim a redundancy payment and is there a time-limit?

No special formalities are needed. You should write to your employers telling them that you are claiming a redundancy payment and asking them to pay it to you. When they make the payment your employers must give you a written statement showing how it has been calculated; your employers can be prosecuted if they fail without reasonable excuse to give it to you. If your employers are in default you can make a written request for such a statement and they then commit another offence if they fail without reasonable excuse to let you have it within seven days.

There is a six-month time-limit. You will lose your right to a redundancy payment unless within six months of your dismissal:

● the redundancy payment has been agreed and paid, or
● you have made a claim by notice in writing to your employers, or
● a question as to your entitlement, or as to the amount of the payment, has been referred to an Industrial Tribunal, or
● you have presented an unfair dismissal claim to a Tribunal.

If there has been a trial period (see Q135), the six months will run from the termination of the 'trial' contract and not the original contract.

If you miss the six-month time-limit an Industrial Tribunal can extend the time if within the following six months you take one of the last three steps set out above. In any such case the Tribunal will consider whether, in all the circumstances (including the reason for the delay), it is just and equitable to give you any extra time. You will note that this extension of time is wider than that under the rule which applies to unfair dismissal claims (see Q109). In particular, there is no need for you to show that it was not reasonably practicable to bring your claim within the original period.

146 | The company made 10 of its machine-minders redundant but it hasn't paid us our redundancy money. I think that it has a lot of cash problems. How can we get the money?

The Employment Protection (Consolidation) Act 1978 gives very valuable rights to a redundant employee who isn't paid redundancy money by the employers. He or she can claim the money from the Department of Employment, which operates a fund called the redundancy fund, if:

● the employer is insolvent, or
● the employee has taken reasonable steps to enforce payment.

On the question of insolvency, it is not enough to show that the company has cash problems. The company is insolvent only if a winding-up order has been made or if a winding-up resolution has been passed or if a receiver has been appointed (see YOU AND YOUR BUSINESS, QS 47 and 49).

Leaving aside insolvency, you will normally be expected to take the case to an Industrial Tribunal (see Q104) and get a decision from the Tribunal that you are entitled to a redundancy payment from your employers. You don't have to go as far as trying to enforce the Industrial Tribunal award and you don't have to take your former employers to court.

Go along to your local Department of Employment office and ask for the claim forms.

Trade unions

147 | My boss says that if I join the union he'll never give me any time off and that I'll never be promoted. Can he lawfully do that?

No, he can't. Every employee has a legal right not to have action (short of dismissal) taken against him as an individual by his employers for the purpose of preventing or deterring him from being, or seeking to become, a member of an independent trade union, or prejudicing him for doing so. Your boss's conduct is clearly an infringement of this right. If, as seems likely, he is not prepared to alter his position you can bring a complaint to an Industrial Tribunal, and your union may well give you any necessary financial support. If you win your case the Tribunal will make a declaration in your favour, and it can also make an award of compensation. There is no ceiling to the amount of the award, and it is not limited to any financial loss you may suffer, although on the whole the awards tend to be fairly low.

148 | Can my employers stop me from attending a union meeting?

Your employers are not allowed to dismiss or victimise you for taking part in union activities at an 'appropriate time' which means at a time either outside your working hours or during your working hours if your employers have given consent for the meeting to take place. Even if nothing has been said, it may be possible to infer such a consent from the general relationship between employers and union. It is also clear that employers cannot dismiss or victimise you for going to a meeting during your lunch or tea-break (as this is not normally a time during which your contract requires you to be at work).

There are also two other rights that are important in this connection, but only if the union is independent (this means independent of your employers) and is *recognised* for bargaining purposes by your employers (see Q149).

If you are a *member* of such a union you are entitled to a reasonable amount of time off, though without pay, to take part in the activities of that union. The question of what is reasonable should if possible be negotiated between your employers and the union, but a Code of Practice published by ACAS in 1978 makes it clear that regard must be made to the needs of the business, including disruption of production, services and safety.

If you are an *official* of an independent, recognised union you are entitled to a reasonable amount of time off *with pay* to enable you to carry out your industrial relations duties or to undergo training which is relevant to those duties and is approved by the union or by the TUC.

149 | When is a union recognised?

The Employment Protection Act 1975 states that a union is to be treated as 'recognised' if it has been recognised by the employers to any extent for the purposes of collective bargaining. The cases (and there have been quite a few of them) show that the evidence of recognition must be absolutely clear. In a leading case that went to the Court of Appeal, the employers had had a limited amount of correspondence with the National Union of Goldsmiths, Silversmiths and Allied Trades and one meeting had taken place between them. The Court of Appeal held on these facts that the stage of recognition had not yet been reached. The opposite result was found in a case decided shortly before this and involving the Union of Shop, Distributive and Allied Workers. The employers in that case had allowed the union to put up a notice publicising wage increases and negotiations, and consultations on such matters as security, discipline and allocation of duties had taken place for some two years. On these facts there was clear evidence of recognition.

150 | When I joined a union I was dismissed. What are my rights?

If you can prove that this was the principal reason for dismissal, or the principal reason why you were selected for redundancy, it will be automatically unfair and in addition the qualifying period (see Q65) and the age-limit rules (see Q68) will not apply. In addition, the compensation that you can get in 'trade union unfair dismissals' is far higher than in any other case. In the first place the basic award (which is based on age, length of service and final week's pay) is subject to a *minimum* amount of £2,300 – although this can be reduced by reason of your pre-dismissal conduct and by your unreasonable refusal of an offer of re-instatement. If you are not re-instated or re-engaged, you will get your usual compensatory award (see Q95) and if you have asked the Industrial Tribunal for a re-instatement or re-engagement order you will *also* get what is known as a 'special award'. This appears to be entirely penal – that is, it is in no way geared to your actual loss – and it is worked out in one of two ways:

● If the Tribunal does not make an order for re-instatement or re-engagement, the special award will be the greater of £11,500 or 104 weeks' pay subject to a maximum of £23,000.
● If the Tribunal does make an order for re-instatement or re-engagement which is not complied with, the special award is increased to the greater of £17,250 or 156 weeks' pay (with no top limit) unless

the employers can satisfy the Tribunal that it was not practicable to comply with the order.

In working out the special award the normal ceiling on a week's pay (see Q60) does not apply.

151 | *My company dismissed me when I joined a union and I've taken the matter to an Industrial Tribunal. Can the Tribunal give me my job back before the case comes up for hearing?*

The answer is generally no, but there is one special rule that applies in trade union cases. If you claim that you have been unfairly dismissed because of your union membership or activities or your refusal to join a closed shop union (see Q152), you can make a special application to an Industrial Tribunal for what is called 'interim relief'. You must do this not later than seven days from the dismissal date, and you must also send in a certificate in writing signed by an authorised official of the union; this will state that you were, or proposed to become, a member of the union and that there are reasonable grounds for believing that the principal reason for dismissal was the one that you have alleged. Any such case will be heard as soon as possible, but the Tribunal must give your employers at least seven days' notice of the hearing. If the Tribunal decides before then that you are likely to win your case, it will explain what it can do; it will then ask your employers if they are willing to give you your job back, or to give you another job on no less favourable terms, until the case has been heard. If they agree to either of these suggestions the Tribunal will make an order to that effect. If they do not agree, or if they do not turn up, the Tribunal will make an order for the continuation of your contract of employment.

152 | *What is a closed shop and how does it work?*

A closed shop is a union membership agreement under which employees of a particular class have to belong to a specified union, or to one of several specified unions. Any employee who refuses to join, or who does not remain a member of that union or unions, can be lawfully dismissed by his or her employers, and any such dismissal is fair. The union membership agreement must be approved by ballot within five years of such a dismissal.

A closed shop dismissal is unfair if:

● the employee objects on grounds of conscience or deeply held personal conviction to being a member of any trade union or of a particular union, or

● the employee was already a member of the class of employees covered by the agreement when the agreement was made and has at no time since then been a member, or

● the employee was entitled to vote in the closed shop ballot and has not been a member at any time since the ballot was held, or

● the employee has obtained, or is claiming, a declaration that he or she was unreasonably excluded from the membership of a union and has not been a member (or failed through his or her own fault to become a member) since the making of the complaint to a Tribunal.

If the dismissal is found to be unfair, all the special rules set out in Q150 will apply. The Tribunal does not have to consider whether or not the employers acted reasonably.

153 | *Are there any special rules for closed shop ballots?*

Yes. The three conditions covering closed shop ballots are as follows:

● All those entitled to vote in the ballot must so far as practicable do so *in secret.*

● All employees of the class covered by the ballot can *vote* on the voting day; if there are several voting days the agreement can specify a 'qualifying day' but it must not be an unreasonable time before the last voting day.

● The *majority* required is a very large one (some people would say an impossibly large one) – 80 per cent of all employees entitled to vote. If the employees are voting to renew an existing agreement which has already been approved by ballot then a slightly less Draconian majority – 85 per cent of those actually voting – will be sufficient.

154 | *I thought that all closed shops had been declared unlawful. Isn't this the case?*

Not quite. In 1981 three employees of British Rail – Mr Young, Mr James and Mr Webster – sued the British government in the European Court of Human Rights, claiming that the closed shop rules *as they stood in 1976* were in breach of Article 11 of the European Convention of Human Rights. The case received a lot of publicity, especially when a majority of the judges upheld the claim. This majority said that Article 11 gives a right to join a union; this brings with it a right *not* to join, and therefore the closed shop rule (as a result of which the employees were dismissed) was unlawful.

The practical result of this case is rather limited

because the European Convention of Human Rights does not form part of English law and the closed shop rules as they stood when the three employees were dismissed have since been changed. In particular, a non-union employee who was already employed at the time of the closed shop ballot cannot be fairly dismissed if he refuses to join (see Q152).

155 | *My employers have told me that I was dismissed because the union was threatening an overtime ban if I wasn't sacked for not joining the union. Does this give my employers a good defence if I go for unfair dismissal?*

No. Any pressure on employers by the taking or threatening of industrial action must be disregarded in deciding the reason for any dismissal and whether the employers acted reasonably in treating that reason as sufficient for dismissal. The matter must be looked at as if no such pressure had been exercised. This may well result in a finding of unfair dismissal – especially if it is a case of 'automatic' unfairness (see Q150) – but your own pre-dismissal conduct may in appropriate cases lead to a reduction in the award: in one case in 1979 the reduction was assessed at 100 per cent.

If the reason for the pressure was the fact that you were not a union member, either you or your employers can apply to have the union 'joined' in the proceedings, and the Industrial Tribunal must grant the application if it is made before the hearing of the complaint. If the unfair dismissal claim is upheld, the Tribunal can make the whole or part of the award against the union.

156 | *I've read somewhere that employers have to consult recognised unions about redundancies even though some of the staff who are going to lose their jobs aren't members of a union at all. Is that right?*

Yes. The redundancy consultation rules were introduced in 1975 in response to an EEC Directive. They require employers to consult representatives of a trade union if they propose to dismiss as redundant 'an employee of a description in respect of which an independent trade union is recognised' (see Q149). Thus, the employee must belong to the description but he need not belong to the union. The usual redundancy qualifying period (two years' continuous employment) does not apply in this case. The result is that an employee may be entitled to the benefit of a 'protective award' (see Q159) even though he is not entitled to a redundancy payment.

157 | *I'm a union official and the management has told me it's considering making some employees redundant. When do the consultations have to start between the union and our employers?*

Under the Employment Protection Act 1975 the consultations must start 'at the earliest opportunity', and this provision is amplified by the following two rules:

● Where the employers propose within 90 days to dismiss as redundant 100 or more employees at one establishment, the consultations must begin at least 90 days before the first of the dismissals is to take effect.
● Where the employers propose within 30 days to dismiss as redundant 10 or more employees at one establishment, they must start the consultation process at least 30 days before the first of the dismissals is to take effect.

The Act does not say how the start of consultations is to tie up with the actual giving of dismissal notices, but the Employment Appeal Tribunal has said that the consultation process must start *before* the dismissal notices are given. Also, if the gap is a very short one (perhaps as little as a day) it may well be possible to argue that there has never been any meaningful consultation at all.

If a complaint is made to an Industrial Tribunal based on a failure to observe these rules, the employers can avoid liability by showing that:

● it was not reasonably practicable for them to comply, and
● this was due to 'special circumstances', and
● they took all such steps as were reasonably practicable in the circumstances.

An attempt to save the business through top-secret takeover or loan negotiations will be a 'special circumstance', but not advice given by an official at the Department of Employment. A very sudden and unexpected insolvency will be a 'special circumstance', but the position is different if insolvency has been on the cards for a long time.

158 | *What form do these redundancy consultations have to take?*

The object of the legislation is set out in the EEC Directive on which the rules are based. The Directive states that where the employers are contemplating collective redundancies they must enter into consultations with the workers' representatives with a view to reaching an agreement and that these consultations must at least cover ways and means of avoiding collective redundancies or reducing the number of workers affected and mitigating the consequences.

No special formalities are required, but the employers must, personally or by post, give the following information to the union representatives:

- the reason for their proposals;
- the numbers and descriptions of the employees the company proposes dismissing as redundant;
- the total number of employees of that description employed at that establishment;
- the proposed manner of selecting the employees who may be dismissed;
- how the dismissals are to be carried out (having regard to any agreed procedures) and the period over which the dismissals are to take effect.

The employers must then 'consider' any representations made by the trade union representatives. They must also reply to them, and if they reject any of them they must state their reasons.

Ultimately, of course, it will be for the employers to make the dismissal decisions.

159 | *My company has just announced 20 redundancies without informing the union beforehand. What can the union do on our behalf?*

A recognised union (see Q149) can make a complaint to an Industrial Tribunal that the employers have failed to comply with the consultation requirements (see Qs 156 to 158). If the complaint is successful, the Tribunal can make an award requiring the employers to pay remuneration – known as a 'protective award' – in respect of such descriptions of employees as may be specified in the award, being employees in respect of whom the employers were in default. The remuneration has to be paid for what is described in the Employment Protection Act 1975 as the 'protected period'. This starts at the date of the award or at the date when the first dismissal takes effect (whichever is the earlier) and runs for such time as the Industrial Tribunal thinks just, having regard to the seriousness of the employers' default. There is, however, a maximum period; this is 90 days in 90-day cases, 30 days in 30-day cases, and 28 days in any other case (see Q157). There is also a financial limit. The employee will receive a week's pay for each week covered by the protective award; the amount of a week's pay is subject (at present) to a ceiling of £158.

160 | *I was given a month's pay in lieu of notice when I was made redundant and I've now got* another job. Can I claim a protective award from my last employer?

Only a union can ask for a protective award. You yourself as an employee come into the picture only if you are within the description of employees covered by the award (see Q156) and your former employers have failed to pay you any money due to you under the award. The following points must be considered:

- Has a protective award been made?
- If so, were you within the description of the employees to which the award related?
- When did the protected period (see Q159) start and how long was it?
- Have your employers failed to pay any part of the award to you?

If the protected period is 28 or 30 days, the money that your employers have paid you in lieu of notice will be treated as satisfying their liability under the protective award – unless the protected period started later than your own dismissal. The mere fact that you have another job doesn't stop you being included in the protected class of employees; the words 'having regard to the seriousness of the employers' default' show that the rules are designed to punish your employers as well as to compensate the employees. It follows that you may have a claim for non-payment even though you have suffered no loss of any kind.

161 | *The union has turned down my application for membership and that means that I won't be able to get a job. Can the union do that?*

If your prospective employers operate a closed shop (see Q152), the Employment Protection (Consolidation) Act 1978 gives you a right not to be unreasonably refused membership of the relevant union. In deciding whether or not the refusal was a reasonable one, you must consider some guidelines laid down in the ACAS Code of Practice of Closed Shop Agreements and Arrangements. A refusal of your application may be fair if, for example:

- you do not have the necessary qualifications, or
- there are too many workers chasing too few jobs, so that the union must restrict numbers in order to preserve a reasonable level of pay and conditions, or
- acceptance of your application would put the union in breach of the Bridlington Agreement, an agreement that regulates the poaching of members as between unions.

162 | *What can I do if the union refuses to accept me as a member?*

There is a conciliation service operated by the Independent Review Committee of the Trades Union Congress, but this body can deal with the matter only if the union is a member of the TUC and you have actually been dismissed from your employment as a result of the union's refusal to let you become a member. Apart from this you can present a complaint to an Industrial Tribunal, and you must do this within six months of the refusal (although an extension of time will sometimes be allowed). If you win your case the Tribunal will give you a declaration that you have been unreasonably excluded. If the union lets you in you can go back to the Tribunal to claim compensation for your losses – subject to the same ceiling as the compensatory award in unfair dismissal cases (see Q95). If, however, the union still refuses to let you in you can take the case on to the Employment Appeal Tribunal, which can award you whatever sum is just and equitable having regard to, among other things, your past and future losses. The ceiling is high – 30 times a week's pay (see Q60) plus 52 times a week's pay plus a maximum unfair dismissal compensatory award. You must take reasonable steps to mitigate your loss and your own conduct can lead to a reduction in the award. One final point: the rights and remedies described are also available if you are unreasonably *expelled* from a union.

163 | My union has fired me for some remarks I made about the president. I think I've been treated very unfairly. Can I appeal to the courts?

There have been some cases like yours where the courts have granted a declaration and an injunction to stop the union acting on the decision that has been made. The courts may interfere if the union rules do not permit the punishment that has been inflicted, or the evidence before the union hearing did not support a finding that the offence had taken place, or the union hearing did not observe the rules of natural justice. These rules require that you must have been given a fair hearing; this will not be so if you were not made fully aware of the charges brought against you, or you were not given a right to be heard, or the person who decided the case was so obviously biased that he could not possibly have heard the case with an open mind. An extreme example occurred in 1977 when a Mr Roebuck was disciplined for allegedly misleading the solicitor of the National Union of Mineworkers in a case involving the then president of the Yorkshire Area, Mr Arthur Scargill. Mr Scargill condemned the parties, and he then presided at the tribunal that punished Mr Roebuck and at the Area

Council that confirmed the punishment. This case clearly infringed the fundamental rule that 'justice must be seen to be done', and the High Court set aside the tribunal's decision.

164 | The company wants to make some of the fitters redundant and I want to organise a sit-in to make the management change its mind. What is the legal position?

There are two main risks to bear in mind here. The first is that if employees remain on the premises after the employers have asked them to leave they will be trespassers. Trespassing is not a crime, but a special form of procedure is available which will enable the employers to get a court order very quickly, and the employers can send in the bailiffs to evict the employees as soon as they have the order. Second, the sit-in will involve a breach of the contract of employment, and workers involved can face criminal liability under an old Act, the Conspiracy and Protection of Property Act 1875. This Act was passed at a time when trade unions were engaged in a running battle with Parliament and with the courts to uphold their right to organise industrial action. A criminal offence is committed under this Act where a person 'wilfully and maliciously breaks a contract of service or hiring knowing or having reasonable cause to believe that the probable consequences of his so doing . . . will be to endanger human life or cause serious bodily injury or to expose valuable property . . . to destruction or serious injury'. Apart from this criminal penalty, an injunction to stop the sit-in taking place can be brought by the Attorney-General or by a private individual whose private rights will be infringed and who is likely to suffer substantial damage if the sit-in goes ahead. The organisers (including yourself) would also risk claims for conspiracy and for interference with contacts.

165 | When can the court grant an injunction to stop a strike taking place?

The right to apply for what is known as an 'interlocutory injunction' is a powerful weapon for employers. The term 'interlocutory injunction' is used to describe an injunction granted on a temporary basis before the case has been fully argued out at a trial. That is the theory; in practice, most of these cases never come to trial at all because the interlocutory injunction to stop the strike taking place is what the employers really want. An injunction can even be granted to the employer 'ex-parte' – without hearing the other side's case at all – but this will usually be for a few days only and the union will then have the chance to argue why the injunction should not be continued. In order to get an injunction, the employers must satisfy the judge on affidavit evidence that the proposed strike may be unlawful and not protected by the 'golden formula' (see Q168). Note that they do not have to prove that it is unlawful, only that it might be. If they clear that hurdle, the court must decide whether the 'balance of convenience' lies in favour of granting or refusing the injunction. Often the balance will tilt to the employers, who can show that the proposed strike (which may be unlawful) will cause them irreparable losses.

166 | Is there any difference between official and unofficial strikes?

There are two points here. The union can be sued if the act in question (such as calling a strike) is 'authorised or endorsed by a responsible person'. The term 'responsible person' covers any of the following:
- the principal executive committee;
- any other person who is authorised by the rules to authorise or endorse acts of the kind in question;
- the president or general secretary;
- any other official who is an employed official;
- any other committee of the union to whom an employed official regularly reports.

This means that the union funds can be put at risk by a fairly junior official. To prevent this, the union can avoid liability for an act within the last two points above if the act is repudiated by the principal executive committee or by the president or general secretary and this is done as soon as practicable after the authority or endorsement has come to the knowledge of the person who repudiates it, and the person who has authorised or endorsed the act is informed of the repudiation in writing and without delay.

The second point relates to ballots. In the case of an 'official' strike, as defined above, both the union and the official who called the strike will lose various legal defences if the union failed to comply with the following balloting provisions of the Trade Union Act 1984: that a) a ballot of those entitled to vote must have been held *before* the strike, b) a majority must have answered 'yes' to the appropriate question (for example, 'Are you prepared to join the strike even if it means breaking your contract of employment?'), and c) the first authorisation (see above) took place within four weeks after the ballot date. In the case of an 'unofficial' strike the ballot rules do not apply; this means the 'golden formula' (see Q168) can give protection to the persons who called the strike even though no ballot were held.

167 | My union is in dispute with my employers, Mean Ltd, about wage rates. Can I legally ask the union members at other firms to strike in support?

You must be very careful because you and your union could face heavy financial penalties. If you call out the men at the other firms you are bringing about breaches of the contracts of employment between those men and their employers; those employers may well react by claiming an injunction and/or damages on the grounds that the employees are not in dispute with their employers. You could avoid legal liability only by showing that the other firms are suppliers to customers of Mean Ltd and that you are calling on the employees in order to apply pressure on Mean Ltd. Even then you would still have to show that this pressure ('secondary action') was likely to achieve its purpose.

168 | We union members are strongly opposed to the government's policy of privatisation. What happens if we organise a go-slow?

If a union, or the officials of a union, induce a breach of contract there can be legal liability for damages and/or for an injunction unless there is protection under what has been described as the 'golden formula'. This formula, which confers legal protection for acts done 'in contemplation or furtherance of a trade dispute', has been somewhat tarnished by recent legislation. The law makes it clear that there must be an actual or imminent dispute between workers and their employers which relates wholly or mainly to one or more of the following matters:

- terms and conditions of employment;
- engagement, non-engagement, duties, suspension or dismissal of one or more workers;
- allocation of work as between workers or groups of workers ('demarcation disputes');
- discipline;
- membership or non-membership of a union;
- facilities for trade union officials;
- machinery for negotiation or consultation.

The key factor to bear in mind here is there must be a dispute about one of these matters between the employers and the employees. The law does not give protection to political strikes – even though the consequences of the government policies could have an adverse effect on the employment, or the terms of employment, of the union members. It may well be that the 'go-slow' you have described will be outside the protected area and legal liability can result.

It is, however, necessary to distinguish between official and unofficial strikes. If the strike is 'authorised or endorsed by a responsible person' (see Q166), the golden formula will not be available if the ballot provisions have not been complied with.

169 | We're out on strike. Can we picket our company's premises to stop the lorries getting in?

No. There is no crime called picketing, but there are various crimes which can be committed by pickets. They include assault, intimidation, obstruction of the highway, and obstructing the police in the performance of their duties – especially in cases where the police consider that a breach of the peace is likely to occur. There is a narrow protection for pickets against such liability under the Trade Union and Labour Relations Act 1974, but this applies only to cases – as in yours – where a person attends at or near his own place of work or, if he is a trade union official, at or near the place of work of a member of that union whom he is accompanying or whom he represents. Further, the immunity is available only if the act is done in contemplation or furtherance of a trade dispute and for the purposes only of peacefully obtaining or communicating information or peacefully persuading any person to work or abstain from work. It may well be that the lorry drivers will tell you what you can do with your information, and you have no legal right to enforce your 'peaceful persuasion' by preventing them from entering the premises.

170 | What about flying pickets and secondary pickets? Are they lawful?

Certain types of 'peaceful' picketing can take place in circumstances that would otherwise be criminal,

such as obstruction of the highway and obstruction of the police (see Q169). The Employment Act 1980 made the immunities for picketing much narrower than they had previously been. In particular, the immunity is available only where employees picket their own place of work. It follows that if flying pickets – non-employees who are brought in from elsewhere – are guilty of obstruction then the defence of 'peaceful' picketing will not be available to them. Similarly, if employees of a company with whom those employees are in dispute picket the premises of a customer or supplier of that company – 'secondary picketing' – they run the risk of normal criminal liability without the 'peaceful' picketing defence. This is of course a very live political issue; some union leaders and members are obviously determined to organise flying pickets in support of their claims even though the practice has been unlawful since 1980.

171 | What about mass picketing? Is that lawful?

This is almost certain to lead to criminal liability under the rules described in Qs 169 and 170. No court is going to accept an argument that the pickets have massed outside a factory or wherever just to pass on information or to 'peacefully persuade' a person not to work. In the words of a famous Scottish judge, Lord Reid, 'it would not be difficult to infer as matter of fact that pickets who assemble in unreasonably large numbers do have the purpose of preventing free passage.' This raises the further question as to how many pickets can be sent along without falling foul of the criminal law. The law itself does not lay down any maximum, but the ACAS Code of Practice on picketing offers the suggestion that 'pickets and their organisers should ensure that in general the number of pickets does not exceed six at any entrance to a workplace; frequently, a smaller number will be appropriate'. Although this is not law in itself, the provisions of the Code can be considered in court proceedings and the Code will obviously be highly relevant if, for example, a question arises as to whether a picket is 'peaceful'.

172 | If legal action is taken against a union for calling out its members on strike and the union loses its case, how much will the union have to pay out?

Apart from legal costs – and those can be substantial – there is a ceiling on the amount of damages which can be awarded against a union which unlawfully calls a strike or other industrial action. The ceiling is linked to the number of members of the union, so that the larger unions have to pay more than the smaller ones. The ceilings are as follows:

Number of members	Ceiling on damages
fewer than 5,000	£10,000
5,000 to 25,000	£50,000
25,000 to 100,000	£125,000
100,000 or more	£250,000

Even if such an award is made, it cannot be enforced against certain types of property, known as 'protected property', and the union political fund is one example of this.

173 | Are there any cases where these ceilings do not apply?

Yes. There are a number of special cases:

● The ceiling applies only to *damages* and not to legal costs.
● There is no ceiling in the case of damages for personal injury resulting from negligence, nuisance or breach of duty. An injury caused by a union official to a policeman or other person during a picketing scuffle is an obvious example of this.
● There is no ceiling where damages are awarded for breach of duty in connection with the ownership, occupation, possession, control or use of any property. Examples can include the collapse of a building owned by the union or damage caused by a person while driving a car on union business.
● There is no limit on the union's liability for contempt of court if an injunction is not obeyed or if damages are not paid.
● Quite apart from all this, a union may find itself involved in claims for unfair dismissal or unfair victimisation. Very large sums can be awarded in closed shop cases, and these can obviously involve a heavy drain on union funds if a large number of employees are involved (see Q150).

174 | I'm a trade union official and I find that the company will never let me have any information. Isn't there a duty on management to let me have it?

Yes, there is. Under the Employment Protection Act 1975 employers must disclose to the representatives of an independent trade union any information in the employers' (or associated employers') possession without which the union would be impeded to a material extent in its conduct of collective bargaining and which would be in accordance with good industrial relations practice for them to disclose.

Obviously, the type and the amount of disclosable information will vary from case to case, but the ACAS Code of Practice on Disclosure suggests that all or any of the following matters should be disclosed in appropriate cases:

● pay and benefits;
● policies on recruitment, training, redundancies, health, safety and welfare;
● manpower and manning standards, labour turnover, absenteeism, overtime, short time and investment plans;
● sales, productivity and the state of the order book;
● financial matters, including cost structures, gross and net profits, assets and liabilities.

There are, however, certain types of information which the employer is not bound to disclose. Perhaps the three most important are:
● information that the employers have received in confidence;
● information relating specifically to an individual (unless he consents to disclosure);
● information the disclosure of which would cause substantial injury to the employers' undertaking for reasons other than its effect on collective bargaining (leaks to competitors being the obvious example).

175 | If my company persistently refuses to disclose information to me as a union official, how can I make it comply with the rules?

There is an elaborate two-stage procedure involving the employers, the union, ACAS and a statutory body known as the Central Arbitration Committee (CAC), which was set up under the Employment Protection Act 1975.

Stage 1. The union makes a complaint to CAC, which will examine the case to see whether it can usefully be referred to ACAS. If ACAS manages to persuade the employers to provide the information, then that's that. If the case is not referred to ACAS or if the efforts of ACAS are unsuccessful, the complaint will be heard by CAC. If the complaint is upheld, CAC will make a declaration to that effect and will give the employers a further opportunity to provide the information within a stated period of not less than seven days.

Stage 2. If the employers default again, the union can make a further complaint to CAC and this time it can put forward terms and conditions which it wants to have included in the employees' contracts. There will then be a further CAC hearing, and if the further complaint is upheld CAC can require the employers to observe those terms and conditions and such other terms and conditions as CAC considers appropriate. The only way for the employers to avoid this result is by giving the necessary information at any time before the new terms are awarded.

Health and safety

176 | *Four of us work in a tiny office, the temperature in winter often seems to be below freezing, and the lavatories haven't been cleaned for weeks. What can we do to get things done?*

The Health and Safety at Work etc. Act 1974 provides that it is the duty of employers to look after, so far as is reasonably practicable, the health, safety and welfare at work of all their employees: this includes the provision and maintenance of a working environment which satisfies these requirements. From what you say it certainly sounds as if your employers are in breach of their duties under the Act. There is also another Act – the Offices Shops and Railway Premises Act 1963 – which spells out some of the duties in greater detail.

The question of what to do depends to a large extent on whether you have a safety representative (see YOU AND YOUR BUSINESS, Q72); he or she has a number of important functions. Your employers are required to consult the representative in order to set up and maintain adequate health and safety precautions in co-operation with the employees. He or she also has the right to investigate complaints and to take them up with your employers.

177 | *What happens if our employers just ignore our complaints about the poor standards of our working environment?*

If this happens your safety representative (or any of the employees if you don't have one) should get in touch with the Health and Safety Inspector, who has been appointed by the Health and Safety Executive or by your local authority (which is the 'enforcement authority' under the 1974 Act). The Inspector can arrange to visit your office at any reasonable time – and he can bring a policeman with him if he thinks that your employers may refuse to let him in. Once he has arrived, the Inspector can, as his name implies, inspect the premises; he can take photographs and measurements and make recordings; he can require your employers to answer questions and he can call for the production of any relevant documents. If he feels that action is called for he can issue an 'improvement notice' or a 'prohibition notice' (the latter perhaps prohibiting the employers from using any unsafe part of any premises). As a last resort a criminal prosecution can be brought.

178 | *We have a colleague who normally likes playing practical jokes, and last week he threw a sharp piece of wood at my assistant and nearly blinded her. What happens if he does cause someone physical damage?*

If your employers don't know what has been happening you must tell them straight away. As a matter of law your employers would not be liable for any negligence on the part of your colleague unless he was acting in the course of his employment, and that seems pretty unlikely on the facts of this case. Your employers will, however, be liable for their own negligence in failing to take reasonable care for your safety. It is obvious that your colleague will either have to be very closely controlled or (more probably) dismissed. If your employers fail to take any action after the facts have been reported to them, that failure would raise an overwhelming case of negligence against them. As a practical matter you may not want to wait to be injured; you could therefore tell your employers that you will leave and regard yourself as constructively dismissed (see Q116) unless they take adequate steps to protect your safety. Alternatively, you might take the less extreme step of saying you will not come in to work until something has been done.

Pensions

179 | *I'm about to join my employers' pension scheme. How does such a scheme work?*

There are various types of scheme around but the most common works as follows. You and your employers both make regular contributions to the scheme, yours being five or six per cent of your salary and theirs rather more than that. Both of you get tax

relief on the payments. These contributions are paid to the trustees of the pension scheme, who normally include senior officers of the company, and it is their duty to invest the contributions and to pay out the benefits in due course.

In practice, the trustees hand over the contributions and the day-to-day duty of administering the fund to an insurance company specialising in pension schemes; the insurers will deal with the investments and enter into a contract to make the payments to members and their dependants when the time comes. Some of the contributions go to buy life insurance to provide lump sums in the event of death before retirement. Most of the large insurance companies offer employers 'off-the-peg' schemes approved by the Inland Revenue, and of course the security of the insurance company provides the guarantee of payment whatever may happen to the employers.

You can ask to see a copy of the trust deed setting up the scheme, though it is probably difficult to understand because of the legal terms it uses. Most companies provide a simple guide to their scheme in the form of a booklet written in layperson's language. See also Q187.

180 | *I'm just going to join my company pension scheme. Will I get any tax benefits?*

Yes. If the scheme is an 'exempt approved scheme' under rules laid down by the Inland Revenue you will get full tax relief on your contributions to the scheme and you will not have to pay tax on your employers' contributions. If the scheme provides for employees to pay a contribution equal to, say, five per cent of salary, you can top this up with voluntary contributions if the rules of the scheme allow you to do so – but there is an overall limit of 15 per cent of your remuneration (see Q182). Thus, if you earn £10,000 a year your maximum overall contribution to the pension scheme is £1,500 per year.

When the time comes for you to draw your pension tax will have to be paid – but the rate of tax is likely to be lower than the top rate of tax which you had to pay while you were working. Also, and this is another tax bonus, the scheme will usually give you the right to commute (that is, surrender) part of your pension for a tax-free lump sum; the maximum is one and a half times your final remuneration after 20 years' service.

181 | *What sort of pension will I get?*

The rules of the scheme will usually deal with this

matter, and they obviously have to keep in line with the guidelines issued from time to time by the Inland Revenue. Some schemes allow you to draw a pension equal to two-thirds of your final remuneration (see Q182) after 10 years' service, the maximum the Inland Revenue allows. The following scale is sometimes found in pension schemes and has Revenue approval:

Years of service	Proportion of final remuneration
1–5	$\frac{1}{60}$ for each year
6	$\frac{8}{60}$
7	$\frac{16}{60}$
8	$\frac{24}{60}$
9	$\frac{32}{60}$
10 or more	$\frac{40}{60}$

If, say, you reach your normal retirement age after eight years' service with a final salary of £18,000, your pension would be:
$$£18,000 \times \tfrac{24}{60} = £7,200 \text{ per year}$$
If you had retired after eight and a half years' service this figure would be increased by a further $\frac{4}{60}$, that is £1,200.

182 | *How is my final remuneration worked out?*

The Revenue allows firms to use one of two alternative methods. The first is to take the salary for any one of the five years before your normal retirement date; you can choose the best year of the five. You then add to it a three-year average of fluctuating items such as loans and commission. The total will be your final remuneration for pension purposes.

The second alternative is to take the annual average of total earnings over a three-year period ending not less than 10 years before your normal retirement date; you can choose the three-year period most favourable to you. An example will show how this works:

Year	Salary (£)
1977	8,000
1978	8,500
1979	10,800
1980	9,900
1981	9,400
1982	9,400
1983	9,000
1984	9,000

If you retire at the end of 1984 your best three-year period is 1979–81 and this produces an average of £9,700. There is, however, one year in the last five which is better than this (£9,900 in 1980) and under the first option already mentioned you can choose this as your final remuneration.

An exception relates to a 20-per-cent director – where more than 20 per cent of the voting rights in a company are owned by a director, his or her spouse, his or her minor children and the trustees of a settlement created by the director or by his or her spouse. In any such case the single-year option is not available and the three-year average must be used.

183 | *Apart from a pension payable to me when I retire, does a pension scheme provide any other benefits?*

Yes. Most schemes provide that on your death after retirement a pension will become payable to your widow and/or dependants. The only limits are that no pension payable after your death can exceed two-thirds of your own maximum, and the total of all the pensions payable after your death cannot come to more than your own maximum.

You can also elect to surrender part of your pension so that your widow or dependants will get one; this is in addition to any pension that they may get under the rules just described.

Another common and valuable benefit relates to death in service. If you die before retirement many pension schemes provide for a lump-sum payment equal to a return of your contributions (with or without interest) plus four times your final salary (or £5,000 if this is greater). In nearly all cases the lump sum is payable at the discretion of the trustees; it will not be an asset of your estate and therefore it will not be caught for Capital Transfer Tax as part of your estate.

184 | *I'm joining my employers' pension scheme and I'm told it is 'contracted-in' to the state pension scheme. What does this mean?*

Since 1978 the law has provided for an employed (as opposed to self-employed) person to receive an extra pension over and above the normal basic state retirement pension, that extra amount being earnings-related to the wage or salary of the person concerned. This extra amount can come from one of two sources – either the state, where the cost is financed by a person's increased National Insurance contributions, or from the employers' own scheme.

If the latter applies, the employers' scheme is said to be 'contracted-out' of the state scheme, and it must provide a 'guaranteed minimum pension' which must be at least as much as an employee would receive from the state.

In your case, your firm's scheme is 'contracted-in' to the state scheme, which means that when you come to retire you will get the basic state pension and whatever you are entitled to from your employers, and on top of these the state will also pay you an 'additional pension'.

The amount of that additional pension will depend on your level of earnings in each year since 1978 adjusted in line with the general rise in earnings in the meantime. This is fed into a rather complicated formula to find the final amount. As the scheme has only been in operation since 1978, the sums payable are quite small at present, but as years go by people who retire will do so on progressively larger pensions.

185 | *I'm 28 and about to change jobs. I'd like to cash in my contributions to my present company's pension scheme. Can I do so?*

The answer depends on whether you have been a member of that scheme for five years at the time you leave.

If you have been a member for less than five years you will probably be able to get a refund of most of your contributions. There will be a deduction of 10 per cent for income tax and if you are leaving contracted-out employment (see Q184) your employers may also have to deduct a further amount to cover the guaranteed minimum pension under that scheme. In any case, you can cash in only your *own* contributions; your employers' contributions cannot be cashed and must stay in the fund, so you lose the benefit of them.

If you have been a member of the scheme for more than five years, you will not be entitled to cash in your contributions. You will, however, have the right to use what is known as the 'cash equivalent' of your pension rights either by transferring it into the pension scheme of a new employer (if the trustees or managers are able and willing to accept you) or using it to buy a so-called 'Section 32 transfer bond' from an insurance company. If you don't do either of these, your accrued rights will be deferred until you reach retirement age, when a pension will start to be paid. The Social Security Act 1985 provides for an annual upward revaluation, designed to make sure that the value of your 'frozen' pension does not disappear by reason of inflation.

186 | *Do I have the right to retire early from my company and take a reduced pension?*

On the face of it you do not have a right as such to retire, although you can leave your job at any time. If you leave, your pension entitlement depends on the terms of your particular pension scheme, but the

Inland Revenue rules (which have to be observed for tax relief to be available on contributions) mean that certain limits have to exist. In particular, retirement on a pension is not generally allowed under the age of 50 other than for health reasons.

If the fund rules allow you to retire and draw a pension early, it is likely to be much smaller than if you stayed on. It would be based on fewer years' contributions and a lower final remuneration (see Q182), and in addition most schemes provide for a reduction in the amount payable because it is likely to be paid for longer. A reduction of half a per cent per month of early retirement is common. Widow's and dependants' benefits may be affected too.

Early retirement on health grounds is treated more generously by most schemes. Some have permanent health benefits attached to them to provide a higher income than the bare pension, and many do not impose the reduction that would otherwise apply for early retirement.

187 | *I understand that there are going to be a lot of changes to pensions law. What's it all about?*

This is a highly complex field, but the government is committed to widening 'choice' in this, as in other fields. There are four major changes in the pipeline;
1 As from 1 October 1987, members of occupational pension schemes will have the right to set up what are called 'free-standing AVC plans'. AVC stands for Additional Voluntary Contributions, and these top-up arrangements will exist side by side with the main scheme.
2 As from 4 January 1988, employees who are not in company schemes will be allowed to take out personal pensions (with various tax benefits). It is estimated that this could apply to some 10 million employees.
3 As from 6 April 1988, option 2 will become available to employed people as an alternative to their employers' contracted-out scheme.
4 As from 6 April 1988, the five-year period referred to in Q185 will be reduced to two years.

188 | *I'm not retiring at the normal retirement age, which I've reached, but hope to carry on for another two years. What happens to my pension? I'm a member of the company pension scheme.*

This really depends on the rules of your particular scheme, but the chances are that you will be able to defer drawing your pension until you actually stop work, and the benefits you receive can be based on your final remuneration (see Q182) at that time rather than what it is now. That will be an advantage to you if your salary rises because your pension will be bigger. The only exception is that if you elect to take a lump sum by commuting part of your pension, it can only be based on your earnings up to now.

You could also probably choose to draw your pension and carry on working (although a disincentive to this would be paying income tax on two salaries).

You should check up on whether your own scheme allows you to postpone your pension. Some state very clearly that this cannot be done.

189 | *I joined my present company five years ago when I was 49. While I am a member of its pension scheme, I also have a frozen deferred pension from my previous company. That company has now gone into liquidation. Does that mean I lose my deferred pension?*

Almost certainly the answer is no and your deferred pension is safe. This is assuming that it was part of a scheme managed by an insurance company (see Q179); your pension is as safe as that insurance company and most pensions are dealt with in that way.

But in a very few cases pensions could be at risk. This could happen where the obligation to pay the pension rests simply on an agreement by the employers, who intended to pay out of future profits. Such schemes are rare, but if yours should be such a one you will have to make a claim against the liquidator of the company, and your chances of getting anything depend on the assets and liabilities of the company.

Another possible risk is that the pension scheme was 'self-administered', which means broadly that the investment, or part of it, was handled directly by the trustees of the fund. Because of the existence of the trust, the pension fund itself is not an asset that the liquidator can seize, but if some of the fund were invested in shares of the company that employed you, then the fund may now be worth less and your pension could suffer.

190 | *If I bring an action against my employers for unfair dismissal, how will the Industrial Tribunal work out my loss of pension rights?*

It will be up to you to prove what that loss is – even though the papers will be in the hands of your employers. You will have to ask them to let you have these papers and if they refuse you can ask the Tribunal to order the employers to produce them. It is a very complicated matter and there are several ways of working out your loss. You can, if you like, get an actuary or a pension broker to give evidence on your behalf (in which case your employers may do likewise), but obviously this will be expensive and it will make the case much longer. Tribunals prefer a broad, common-sense approach, and you should try to get your loss agreed with your former employers before your case is heard. The guideline specially prepared by the government actuary may provide the right answer (ask your local Department of Employment office to let you have a copy).

The calculation will be based on

● the difference between the pension that you've already built up and the value that pension would have if you hadn't been unfairly dismissed;
● loss of pension rights while you are looking for another job;
● how long it will take you to catch up – in other words, how long it will take you in your new job to get pension benefits as good as those in your last job. Many schemes allow employees to join only after they have been employed for a year.

It is likely that the law on this may change, because the government has made proposals that will give every employee the right to take his pension with him when he leaves his job.

191 | *How are these various pension losses worked out?*

The first item is past loss. This is found by taking the value of the past contributions if you hadn't been dismissed and deducting the 'dismissal' value of these contributions. In many cases the contributions will go towards a pension based on your salary at 60 or 65; on dismissal the pension is frozen and is based on your salary at the time of dismissal – obviously far smaller. Accordingly, the past contributions have lost a great deal of their value. This calculation can be made using the tables provided by the government actuary. If, for example, a man who is to retire at 65 is dismissed at age 40 with a deferred pension of £1,500 per year, the tables produce the following figures:

Capital value of the 'no-dismissal'
pension = £9,900
Capital value of the frozen pension = £3,600
Total of past loss = £6,300

The second head of loss is loss during the period of unemployment. This can be measured by the loss of your former employers' contribution during this period.

The third head of loss is the loss in a new job. This can occur because the new job has no pension scheme or there is a waiting period before a new employee can join and/or the salary (and therefore the salary-based pension) is lower. The loss calculation can be based on the difference between the old employers' contributions and the new employers' contributions from the start of the new job until you have caught up.

The final stage in the calculation is to make a percentage reduction (again set out in the government tables) for the possibility of withdrawal before the normal retirement age. If, for example, you are dismissed at the age of 40 and would have drawn your pension at 65 you can't automatically claim pension loss for the remaining 25 years because during that time you might have died, or left, or retired on health grounds, or been fairly dismissed. Some reduction must be made to cover these possibilities.

It will be seen from these figures that the claim for pension loss can be the largest part of an unfair dismissal claim and can often use up the full compensatory award of £7,500.

Self-employment

192 | *I work as fashion editor on a women's magazine and my friends tell me that I'd be much better off if I was self-employed. Is that right?*

From an income tax point of view the answer may well be yes, but there are many disadvantages in other areas. If you are an employee you are taxed under Schedule E, and income tax is deducted from your pay under the PAYE system (see TAX, Q3). If, on the other hand, you are self-employed you are taxed under Schedule D, usually on a preceding year basis (see YOU AND YOUR BUSINESS, Q38), on the profit shown by the accounts that you send in to the Inland Revenue. The main advantage of Schedule D lies in the time for payment of the tax. There can often be a gap of 18 months or more between earning the money and having to pay income tax on it. Also, you can claim some allowance for business expenses.

The rules for National Insurance contributions also favour the self-employed; the total which they have to pay (Classes 2 and 4) is nearly always less than the Class I contribution suffered by an employee.

The great disadvantage of being self-employed is that you do not enjoy many benefits that are available to an employee, including:

● employment protection benefits such as maternity pay, minimum notice periods, redundancy pay and the right not to be unfairly dismissed;
● many social security benefits including unemployment benefit and statutory sick pay;
● many of the detailed legal rules intended to protect you from accidents at work.

193 | *If I pay my own income tax and National Insurance contributions, does that always mean that I am self-employed?*

No, these are only two of the many factors (although they are obviously very important). There have been quite a few cases in which a worker has chosen to be self-employed for tax reasons but later on has successfully argued that his legal status was one of an employee so that, for example, he could claim a redundancy payment or compensation for unfair dismissal. A court or tribunal must consider not only tax and National Insurance but also many other factors, including whether your employers can tell you how to do your job, whether you belong to your company pension scheme, whether you provide your own tools, how you are paid, whether your employers are bound to give you work, and whether you or your employers can end the arrangement without notice.

When all these factors have been weighed up, the final question will often be: are you in business on your own account or, as the Employment Appeal Tribunal put it in one case, 'are you your own boss?'

If you are accountable only to yourself and not to anyone else then you will definitely be self-employed.

194 | *I work at home for a company that makes trousers and jackets. I can choose my own hours, and on some days I just don't take any work at all. Do I have the same rights as my friends who work at the company's factory?*

The answer depends on whether you are an employee or whether you are self-employed. There have been quite a few cases about homeworkers (or 'outworkers') and they show that there must be a duty on the employers to provide work and a duty on the worker to accept it. The mere fact that you keep your own hours doesn't stop you being an employee. In your case you sometimes decide not to take on any work at all. This would make it difficult for you to claim that you are an employee, although a recent case in the Court of Appeal says that it's not impossible to do so. You could have what they called an 'umbrella contract' under which your employers are bound to provide work and pay for it while you are bound to continue to accept the work and to do it. The facts of this recent case were similar to yours, and the Court of Appeal decided that the homeworker was an employee. A lot depends on the exact terms of the arrangement between yourself and the company and how it has been working out.

If you *are* an employee you will have many of the same rights as your friends in the factory. The only possible snag is the number of hours that you work, because many rights of employees (maternity, unfair dismissal, redundancy, and so on) are only available after a period of 'continuous employment' and this usually involves employment for 16 hours per week (or eight hours per week after five years). If you work fewer hours than that, then many of the employees' rights will not be available to you.

You and your business

Starting a business

1 | *I've been told that nearly all businesses are run as companies. Is that correct?*

No. A lot depends on the nature and size of the business and on the risks involved. A great many businesses, especially in the non-manufacturing sector, are run by sole traders or as partnerships.

A sole trader, as its name implies, is a business run by a person who is totally and solely responsible for the business: he or she takes all the profits but is also personally liable for any debts he or she may incur in running the business.

While a sole trader need not necessarily work alone, a partnership is an association of two or more people working together as one business and sharing the profits. Tax is assessed singly for the partnership, not for its individual partners, and the partnership is liable for its debts (if one of the partners cannot pay for any reason, the others will have to absorb his or her share).

A survey has shown that 20.3 per cent of non-manufacturing businesses – which include smaller businesses like cafés, restaurants and retail outlets – are partnerships and 45.8 per cent sole traders.

2 | *What is a company?*

A company is a body that is formed by complying with a number of rules and formalities laid down by the Companies Act 1985 and which is widely used by businessmen to carry on a business. There are basically three ways in which you can run a business: as a sole trader, or as a partnership with one or more other persons (see Q1), or as a company.

The special feature of a company is the 'legal personality' of the company itself – the company is a separate legal entity quite distinct from the people who actually run the business. It may seem strange, but if a husband and wife, for example, carry on a business using a company, there are *three* legal persons involved – the husband, the wife and the company. This can be very important indeed; in particular the company is often a barrier that stands between the people who run the business, in this case a man and his wife, and the creditors of the business.

3 | *I've read about a company being limited by shares. What does this mean?*

In most cases the persons who start up a company will take 'shares' in the company – this is their stake in it. The size of that stake – the number of shares which they take – is a matter for agreement, and they will obviously have to consider how much money the business needs and where it is to come from. Each share has a face value, called the 'nominal value', and this is usually what the person taking the share, the shareholder, must pay the company.

The company must have at least two shareholders and each of them must agree to take at least one share. This means that you may find a company issuing one £1 share to Mr A and one £1 share to Mr B. The number of shares that each takes, and the proportion as between the various shareholders, is a matter for agreement. Someone may, for example, go into business with two colleagues and a share capital of £100 split 40–40–20, or he may decide that since the business is really his, he will take 99 of the 100 shares and the other shareholder will take just one share: it is all a question of agreement.

In the case of a company which is 'limited by shares' (and nearly all companies are of this kind) the legal liability of the shareholders to the creditors of the company is limited to the amount, if any, unpaid on their shares; the creditors have no claims against the shareholders. This limit is what is meant by a 'limited company'.

4 | *What is an unlimited company?*

The difference between a limited and an unlimited company lies in what happens if the company goes bust. If that happens, in the case of a limited company the shareholders have no personal liability to the creditors. In the case of an unlimited company, however, the creditors can still look to the company for payment of their debts but – and this is the important point – they can also look to the shareholders (or to the members of the company if there are no shareholders) for any debts that they cannot recover from the company. Not surprisingly, the number of unlimited companies is small.

5 | *What is a public company?*

Under the Companies Act 1985 there are two main types of company – public and private. A company is a public company if it satisfies four conditions, namely:

● The Memorandum (see page 322) says that the company is to be a public company.

● The name of the company must end with the words 'Public Limited Company' or a suitable abbreviation, the most common being PLC.

● The company must have issued shares having a nominal value (see Q3) of at least £50,000.

● At least a quarter of the nominal value of those

shares must have been paid to the company. There can also be cases where the price payable by the shareholders is greater than the nominal value of the shares. This excess is called a 'premium', and in the case of a public company the whole of that premium must have been paid to the company.

Public companies are generally large, and most of them have a very great number of shareholders. One of the special features of shares of a public company is that they can generally be bought and sold by the general public on the Stock Exchange or the Unlisted Securities market. The vast majority of shareholders of public companies take no part at all in the running of those companies. They merely hold the shares as an investment, hoping to receive income from them and also the chance to sell the shares at a good price if the company is doing well.

In contrast, private companies are any companies that are not public companies; the names of such companies end with 'Limited' or 'Ltd'. A private company is not allowed to offer its shares to the public. This means that if you own shares in a private company it may be very difficult to find a buyer of those shares if you want to sell them, unless, of course, it's a family-run company and you sell your shares to a member of your family. The rules of some private companies contain what is called a 'pre-emption clause'; this means that a shareholder who wants to sell his shares must first offer them to the other shareholders.

6 | Do the shareholders run a company?

Not necessarily. In both a private and a public company there are two groups of people who may or may not be the same. One group consists of the shareholders, or members, and the other group are the directors.

The shareholders are the people who own the shares in the company and sometimes (but not always) they are also the people who put up the money to enable the company to run its business. To give a simple example, Mr A buys one £1 share and thus puts £1 into the company; Mr B buys one £1 share and thus also puts £1 into the company. The company then gets its working capital by bank borrowing. Under the Companies Acts such shareholders are the people who make the major decisions about the company. They can, for example, vote at general meetings to alter the company's constitution, approve the accounts, declare a dividend, and increase or reduce the company's capital.

The directors are the people who are responsible for the day-to-day management of the business either

How would we set about forming a limited company?

These matters are complex and are usually handled by a solicitor or accountant, and there are also specialist firms of company formation agents who do a great deal of this work. The first thing to do is to get the agents to search the index of names at Companies House (address on page 509) to see whether the name that you want to give your company is available. If another company already has that name you will have to find another one.

After that, two important documents have to be prepared – the Memorandum and the Articles of Association. The Memorandum is the company's basic constitution; it must contain five basic clauses and it must be signed by at least two persons, each of whom must agree to take at least one share in the company. The five basic clauses are:

1. The name of the company.
2. A statement that the registered office of the company is situated in England and Wales or in Scotland (the actual address is not given in this clause).
3. The purposes for which the company is formed. This is nearly always a very long clause indeed, because the persons running the company obviously want the widest possible powers to undertake any new activities that they consider to be commercially desirable. Any contract that falls outside this 'objects clause', as it is known,

by actually working in it, when they are known as executive directors, or by attending board meetings to make comments and suggestions, when they are known as non-executive directors. Directors may or may not own shares in the company.

While the directors are in office, the shareholders cannot tell them what to do, but shareholders always have the right to use their votes at general meetings to dismiss all or any of the directors. If the shareholders are not in agreement with each other, the majority will get their way.

7 | I've read a lot about shareholders receiving dividends but I don't really understand what's involved. What are dividends?

A person who invests money in a company by buying shares in it hopes to get an income from it in exactly the same way as if he or she were to invest the money cannot be enforced by the company.

4. The 'capital clause', for example, 'The capital of the company is £100 divided into 100 £1 shares'.

5. A statement that the liability of the members is limited (see Q 1 2).

The Articles of Association, which are usually bound up with the Memorandum, deal with how the company is run. They cover such matters as the issue of shares by the company to shareholders, the rights of shareholders to transfer their shares to someone else, meetings of shareholders, the appointment, meetings and responsibilities of directors, and their borrowing powers.

These documents must be sent to the Registrar of Companies together with:

● Form 1, which contains the address of the registered office and the names and addresses of the first directors and the company secretary;

● Form PUC 1, which sets out the capital of the company and the number of shares that the persons signing the Memorandum have agreed to take;

● Form 47a, which must be signed by a director (or by a solicitor or other agent engaged in the formation of the company) confirming that the requirements of the Companies Acts have been complied with;

● The Registrar's fee (currently £50).

The forms are available from any firm of law stationers or from the Companies Registration Office (address on page 509).

---

in a building society or in a deposit account at a bank. If the company makes a profit the directors may recommend to the shareholders that the whole or part of that profit shall be paid to the shareholders. Such a payment to shareholders is known as a dividend. The dividend is expressed as a proportion of the nominal value of the shares, or sometimes a proportion of the amount actually paid for the shares by the shareholder; as the value of a company increases, so does the cost of the shares changing hands.

If you own shares on which a dividend is declared, you will usually receive from the company a 'dividend warrant'. This consists of two parts, the first a statement of the dividend payable and the other in the form of a cheque which you pay into your bank in the same way as any other cheque.

The Companies Act 1985 contains detailed rules as to the money which a company can use to pay a dividend. If, for example, a company makes a profit after several years of losses it can use only the amount, if any, by which that profit exceeds the total of all the previous years' losses. Then again, if the company makes a profit on paper because one of its buildings has increased in value, it cannot use this to pay a dividend until this profit has been turned into cash.

8 | If I'm a director of a company, how do I get paid?

In many cases directors have a formal written contract called a 'service agreement'. This will provide for a salary payable in the same way as for people who are not directors. There may also be a right to a bonus or commission depending on the company's results, and the written agreement will set out all the details. Finally, the written agreement will nearly always provide for some fringe benefits such as a company car and membership of a pension scheme.

The amount of remuneration for directors who have no written contract will be decided by the shareholders. In many small family businesses, the shareholders and the directors are the same people and in that situation they (wearing their shareholders' hats) will vote themselves what is known as 'directors' remuneration' at the end of the financial year. They will usually draw out a sum monthly or weekly on account of the remuneration which they are going to vote themselves at the end of the year.

9 | How many people are needed to set up a company?

As regards shareholders, the answer is two. A company must have at least two shareholders, and each of them must agree to take at least one share. There is no maximum number, and in the case of public companies there will be a very large number of shareholders.

A company also has to have at least one director and a company secretary. If there are two or more directors, one of them can be the company secretary, but a sole director cannot also be a company secretary. Once again, there is no maximum to the number of directors a company can have.

To summarise, two people can form a company on the basis that they are both shareholders and directors with one of them the company secretary, or they are both shareholders with one of them director and the other company secretary.

10 | What sort of risks are involved in running your own business?

Every business carries an element of risk and some businesses, depending on their nature, carry greater risks than others. The main risks are:

● You will often have to undertake financial commitments to banks, landlords, and so on, before you know whether or not your product or service is going to be successful.

● There is always the danger that the arrival of a competing product, or a government policy, or a change in the economic climate may destroy the market for your product.

● You may be let down by one or more of your suppliers, and this can cause havoc to your business and can lead to large claims by your customers through your failure to meet delivery dates.

● Conversely, your customers may be bad payers (or may go out of business) and this can cause havoc to your cash flow because you will still have to meet your suppliers' bills.

● If you supply goods that turn out to be defective or dangerous you may find yourself legally liable for very large sums (even though you yourself may not have been at fault) and it may be that such claims are not covered, or not fully covered, by insurance.

11 | I've heard of a company described as a 'separate legal person'. What does this mean?

A company becomes a separate legal person as soon as it is formed (see page 322). This means that:

● the property of the company belongs to the company and not to the shareholders,

● business contracts are made by the company,

● the company continues to exist even if all the shareholders are dead (or insane), and

● the debts of the business are the debts of the company and not those of the shareholders.

12 | What is meant by the 'limited liability' of a company?

You may sometimes see after the name of a company the words 'a private company limited by shares'. This is misleading, because what is limited is the liability of the shareholders.

Say two people form a company and each takes 50 shares in it. The shares are issued to them at the face value of £1 per share, as is usually the case. Should the business collapse the company will be wound up. If it owes £20,000 to its creditors and only owns assets worth £5,000, the liability of the two shareholders to contribute to those debts is limited to the amount (if any) which is unpaid on their shares . This is what is mean by 'limited liability'. If they have not paid for their shares the liquidator can look to each of them for £50 – that is all. With regard to the remaining debts of £14,900 (which may be owing to suppliers, employees, the bank, the Inland Revenue, etc) this is money that the creditors have lost; they cannot go behind the bankrupt company and try to get money from the shareholders.

Limited liability is vitally important because it protects the shareholders from any personal liability to their creditors if the company goes out of business. Conversely, limited liability also poses a risk to suppliers who provide goods and services on credit to a limited company.

13 | My brother and I have formed a limited company. Does this mean that should the company go bust we are not liable for anything except the amount unpaid on our shares?

Despite limited liability (see Q12), in practice the shareholders will often be liable for some debts if their company goes out of business. First of all there is the landlord. If a company takes a lease of its business premises, almost inevitably the landlord will demand a personal guarantee from one or more of the directors. This means that the director who gave the guarantee – often backed by a mortgage on his house – will be personally liable down to his last penny for the company's failure to pay the rent and to perform any other obligations under the lease. To make matters worse, such a guarantee may well continue for the whole term of the lease even after the company has sold the lease to a new occupier.

The directors may also be personally responsible to pay the amount outstanding on any bank loans. Most, if not all, new companies are financed by bank overdrafts and, here again, personal guarantees perhaps backed up by house mortgages will usually be required. This means that if the company goes bust the bank can call on the directors under their guarantee to pay the amount of the company's debt to the bank. If they cannot do this the bank may in the last resort sell the guarantor's house and make him bankrupt.

Despite all this, however, the principle of limited liability is still of great value, especially in recessionary times when a business can collapse without any fault on the part of its owners.

For a further example of directors' liability, see Q48.

14 | I've just been made redundant and I'm thinking of using my redundancy money to start a small business specialising in the sale of sports equipment. Should I form myself into a company?

In weighing up the pros and cons of having a company you should consider both the risks involved (see Q10) and the enormous advantages of limited liability (see Q12). If you do form a company (see page 322) you will have to prepare a number of documents (both at the time of formation and subsequently every year) and send these to the Companies Registry at Companies House (address on page 509). The formalities take time and money, and you may well instruct a solicitor or accountant to deal with this matter on your behalf.

Another feature of running your business through a company is the publicity involved. A large number of documents (including your business accounts) have to be filed at Companies House, and this means that they can be seen by your creditors and competitors and by members of the public.

From a tax point of view there is one possible disadvantage of having a company. Any business losses made by the company are locked into the company and cannot be set against your own income for tax purposes. If, on the other hand, you run the business as a sole trader (see Q1) you can deduct any business losses from your other income for tax purposes. Apart from this, there is not a great deal to choose from a tax point of view between a sole trader and a company.

In a recent survey, only about a third of small retail businesses, such as the one you are considering setting up, were run as companies. Whether or not you do so is a question of balancing the advantages of limited liability against the extra formalities and publicity, and then deciding where the balance of advantage lies.

15 | I've been unemployed for several months. I'd like to try my hand at starting my own business, but I need a lot of advice and I obviously need to know where my income will come from in the early days. Any ideas?

Yes. In 1983 the government introduced an experimental 'enterprise allowance scheme'. It offers financial and other help to persons who have been unemployed for at least 13 weeks. You will be eligible to join the scheme if you are between 18 and state retirement age, you have at least £1,000 available to invest in the business, and you can show that the business is new, independent and suitable for public funding.

If you apply to join the scheme you will be asked to attend a preliminary briefing session which is run jointly by the Manpower Services Commission and the Small Firms' Service run by the Department of Trade and Industry. The discussions with them will help you to decide whether or not to go ahead. If you do go ahead, you can get further help and advice from the Small Firms' Service, Local Enterprise Agencies, and perhaps also from your local Chamber of Commerce.

You will be paid a weekly sum (at present £40) for a year as compensation for losing your Unemployment or Supplementary Benefit.

16 | Can I get any help towards the cost of setting up a new business?

Yes. You may qualify for a government or an EEC grant. There are many different schemes, and each of them has its own rules and qualifying conditions. The Department of Trade and Industry has a great deal of information about what is available, and you should get in touch for further details and leaflets. For example, if you have lots of ideas or new products that you want to exploit commercially, a grant may well be available if you can satisfy the authorities that you have the technical know-how to carry the project through and that the grant will help you to achieve that result.

Grants may also be available if you set up a business in areas that have been designated as assisted areas because of very high rates of unemployment; once again the Department of Trade and Industry will be able to give you the necessary information.

Formerly, a trader who bought machinery or plant for use in his business could get tax relief for the full cost in the first year. That relief has been abolished, but you can still get an annual 'writing-down allowance' of 25 per cent of the unrelieved expenditure. This will enable you to get tax relief for the full cost over the working life of the asset.

There are somewhat similar rules for industrial buildings where the basic relief is four per cent of the cost every year for 25 years.

17 | *I'd like to start a new business and I'm considering ways of raising the capital. Apart from the bank, are there any other sources that I could try?*

Yes. The government has introduced a number of schemes designed to help small businesses to raise money. Three of these are as follows:

1. The Loan Guarantee Scheme: if your bank (or other lender) considers that your scheme is viable it can lend up to £75,000 repayable over an agreed period ranging from two to seven years and the government will guarantee payment of 70 per cent of the loan if you should go out of business and default in repaying the loan.

2. An individual may be encouraged to invest in your company by a special tax concession conferred by the Finance Act 1980. There are a large number of conditions to be fulfilled (the object being to stop the rules being used purely to save tax) but the basic principle is clear: if an individual takes shares in a trading company whose shares are not quoted on the Stock Exchange (see Q5) any loss which the individual makes on those shares can be set against his income for tax purposes. This could be relevant if, for example, an individual paying income tax at a high rate took 10,000 £1 shares in your company only to see all his money disappear if the company went into liquidation with large debts and no assets.

3. An individual is given a further tax incentive to invest in small businesses under the Business Expansion Scheme, although again a number of detailed conditions have to be satisfied. If these conditions are satisfied an investment of up to £40,000 in any one tax year can be set against the investor's income at his highest rate of tax; this rule is not limited to cases where the money is lost. The relief may be withdrawn in whole or in part if the shares are sold within five years. Someone who pays tax at 60 per cent on £10,000 of his income can thus invest that sum in your business and claim the full amount as a tax deduction. Looked at another way, the true cost to

him of a £10,000 investment is £4,000; the Inland Revenue takes care of the rest.

You should first get in touch with your bank to see if it is willing to lend you the money. If not, the bank may know of customers it could put in touch with you who may be interested in making an investment, especially with the incentives outlined above; your solicitor or accountant may have clients willing to make an investment too. You could also contact Industrial and Commercial Finance Corporation Ltd (ICFC), a subsidiary of Invest in Industry PLC (a public company owned by the English and Scottish clearing banks and the Bank of England); ICFC has branches in at least 18 towns and cities in England, Scotland and Wales. Finally, the Department of Trade and Industry may be able to help (see QS 15 and 16).

18 | *How does a company raise the money it needs to run the business?*

Apart from government aids (see Q16) and apart from ploughing back profits into the business, a company can raise money either by the issue of shares ('share capital') or by borrowing ('loan capital'). The shareholders hope to reap the benefit of their investment by the receipt of dividends and/or by an increase in the value of the shares themselves. If the shareholders want to cash in on their investment, they can sell their shares to outsiders or, in appropriate cases, to the company itself. It is also possible, if the Articles of Association (see page 322) contain the necessary powers, for a company to raise money by creating a special class of shares, known as 'redeemable' shares, under which the company will be given the right to pay off the shareholder, get back the shares and then cancel them.

Loans can be made by the shareholders, by directors, by a bank or by other persons, or by financial institutions. They will receive interest (which will normally be a tax deductible business expense to the company). Lending money to a company can be risky (see Q12) and therefore the lenders may often insist on getting a personal guarantee from the directors and a 'charge' over the assets of the company (including a mortgage over the company's business premises). From a tax point of view dividends and loan interest are investment income to lenders and, until the passing of the Finance Act 1984, were subject to a special 15 per cent tax charge known as the Investment Income Surcharge (IIS). The removal of the IIS should encourage more people to lend to companies and to buy companies' shares.

19 | I've been told that it takes several weeks to form a company. I want to start my own business immediately because I want to tender for an important contract. What can I do?

You can go along to a firm of company formation agents and buy a company 'off the peg'. The agents should have stocks of ready-made companies for most types of business. Thus, if you want to trade as a builder or as a hotelier or as a dealer in household appliances you should be able to get a company with an objects clause (see page 322) that is suitable to your needs.

These companies have been formed by the agents for the purpose of being sold to businessmen who want a company quickly and, to comply with the formalities, employees of the agents have been formally appointed as the first director and as the company secretary. These employees have also agreed at the end of the Memorandum (see page 322) to take at least one share each. When you get the company from the agents, they will give you a form recording the resignation of the first director and of the company secretary so that you can appoint yourself and some other person to those positions (as stated in Q9, a company needs to have only one director, but a sole director cannot also be the company secretary). The agents will also give you a form that will allow you to change the registered office to an address of your own choice (in practice, this is often the business address of your accountant), and forms whereby the original shareholders can be replaced by persons of your own choosing.

There are, however, some further points that you must bear in mind if you buy an off-the-peg company. In the first place you must decide whether you want to change the name of the company (for which a fee of £40 is required). Second, in many cases you will also find it necessary to change the Articles of Association (see page 322) in order to tailor them to your particular needs. These matters should not prevent you from starting to trade straight away as long as you ensure that the stationery contains the company's correct registered name (see Q21).

20 | I'm considering forming my own company. Can I choose the company's name and are there any restrictions?

The answer to both questions is yes. In general you can choose any name you like, but you will not get it if it is identical to the name of an existing registered company (see page 322). Also, certain words such as 'royal', 'British' or 'worldwide' will not be allowed as part of the name unless evidence can be produced to justify its use. The name must end in Limited (or some abbreviation of it such as Ltd), unless the company is formed for certain specified purposes such as a professional association or a company formed for charitable purposes and ploughs back all its profits for the purposes of its activities and does not distribute those profits to the members by way of dividend.

It is important to appreciate that the registered name of a company is not necessarily its trading name. If, for example, you have been running a restaurant under the name The Gourmet's Table which has become very well known to the public, you can carry on trading under that name even after you have formed yourself into a company that has a different name registered at Companies House. It is, however, essential that the correct registered name of the company (including the word Limited or its abbreviation) appears on the company's invoices and other stationery, although this is often done in very small print.

21 | My husband and I have a shop which we've recently made a limited company. We've been using our old stationery without stating that we are now a company. Does that cause any problems?

Yes, it does. The stationery of a company must contain the company's name and number, the place of incorporation (England and Wales or Scotland) and its registered office. An example is:

Shoppers' Delight Limited
Incorporated in England No 1234567
Registered Office 12 High Street, Anytown.

It is particularly important for you to make sure that all cheques and orders for goods contain the company's correct name. The Companies Act 1985 provides that any director or other officer of a company who signs an order form or a cheque on which the company's name (including the word Limited) does not appear in legible characters is liable to a fine and, more important, he or she is personally liable to the supplier of the goods or to the holder of the cheque if the company fails to pay. There have been quite a few cases in which directors have been made personally liable under this rule, so check your stationery carefully; even an error in the spelling of the company name can make you personally liable on the cheque or order.

22 | I've just noticed that the name written on the sides of a van is the same name as my company's. Is there anything I can do? I'm afraid that people will confuse the two companies.

There are three facts you need to establish before you can take any action. In the first place you should arrange for a search to be made at Companies House by a firm of company formation agents (see page 322) to find out whether the offending name is the registered name of the other company or merely a trading name (see Q20). Second, if it is the registered name of the other company the agents must find out which of you registered first. Third, you need to ascertain whether the other company is in the same line of business as your own and in actual or prospective competition with you.

If the other company's name was registered before yours, then obviously the Registrar of Companies should not have allowed your company to be registered with the same name. In these circumstances there is nothing that you can do to get the name of the other company changed or to stop the company using it.

On the other hand, if the other company's name was registered after yours, you can ask the Registrar of Companies to direct the other company to change its name on the grounds that it is too similar to that of your company. He can direct such a change within 12 months of the registration of the name complained of, and he may well do so if you can satisfy him that the two companies are in the same line of business. If the 12 months have gone by, he cannot order this and your only rights will be if you can prove that the company is passing off (see below). Finally, if the name gives so misleading an indication of the nature of the company's activities as to be likely to cause harm to the public, under the Companies Act 1985 the Department of Trade can direct a change of the registered name.

The Registrar of Companies has no power to control trading names, but there may be a claim for what is known as passing off if a trader uses the name of a rival trader, or gets up his goods or business in such a way as to indicate that they are the goods or business of a rival trader. In one case, for example, a firm of wine merchants called Short's Ltd brought a court injunction against a Mr Short who set up a similar business and called it Short's. In another case the well-known furniture manufacturers Parker-Knoll got an injunction to stop another company using that name. In a third case a trader sold sweets bearing a red wrapping that the public had come to associate with sweets marketed by a rival firm. Once again, a court injunction was granted.

It is not necessary in these cases to show evidence of an *intention* to deceive the public, but there must be some evidence that the public was *likely* to be deceived. If you feel that your business has suffered, or is likely to suffer, you should immediately get in touch with the other trader (if you can trace him), preferably appointing a solicitor to do so. If the company is uncooperative then you may well be able to take court proceedings for an injunction to stop the company using your company's name and for compensation for your business losses, if any.

23 | The company my friend and I have formed has issued 100 shares, with 50 going to me and 50 to him. Should I give any of my shares to my wife?

It sounds as if the arrangement you have made with your friend is for the company to be run on the basis of complete equality, with the equal split of the shares reflecting this. Nevertheless, there can be some advantages in a husband or wife putting at least one share into his or her spouse's name. The husband or wife can, of course, agree – preferably in writing – to hold the share as the spouse's nominee so that he or she will have to vote in accordance with the spouse's wishes.

There are three possible advantages in making your wife a shareholder:

• If you and your friend were to disagree and if, as sometimes happens, he were to refuse to attend any meetings, you could call a meeting yourself. At that meeting you and your wife would almost certainly be a quorum and could take decisions that would be legally binding on the company.

• In the case of a two-man company there could be serious problems if either or both of you were to die. If you died, for example, there could be a delay of several months before your own shares could be put into the name of the person due to inherit them under your will; your wife could look after your interests until this is done. Another possibility is that you and your friend might both die together in a car accident or plane crash. The company, as a separate legal person (see Q11), would continue its ghostly existence even with no shareholders! The existence of a third shareholder would overcome many practical problems in that situation, even though it might be necessary to get a court order to enable a meeting to be held with a quorum of one.

• There can be tax advantages in giving your wife some of the shares. If the shares are valuable, a spread of the value between your estate and hers could lead to a substantial saving in tax when you die. In addition, it would allow each of you to take advantage of the various rules that allow transfers of shares to be made free of capital transfer tax.

24 | My brother-in-law and I are going to run our company together, with my brother-in-law as chairman and myself the managing director. Is this a good idea?

While it sounds a good arrangement, there is one important point to bear in mind. If you want to work with your brother-in-law on the basis of complete equality, you must make sure that the Articles of Association (which contain the rules about how the company is run; see page 322) do not give the chairman a casting vote. This point is often overlooked and not fully understood by businessmen. Many companies adopt the Specimen Articles set out in Table A of the Companies (Table A to F) Regulations 1985. These Specimen Articles give the chairman a casting vote, with the result that the person who is chairman controls the company. You must make sure that this does not apply in your case unless, of course, you are happy with that situation.

If you go along to a firm of company formation agents when you form a company you will often find that they will give you a form of Articles of Association which merely says that Table A is to apply as the Articles of the company subject to some particular changes which are then set out. If you want to see what Table A says, you should ask the agents to give you a print of the Articles which set out Table A in full and ensure that the agents amend the Articles as necessary.

One final point: it is perfectly possible for the shareholders (in this case your brother-in-law and yourself) to enter into what is called a shareholders' agreement whereby they agree with each other how they will use their votes in particular situations. Such an agreement is perfectly valid, and as it is a private document it does not have to be sent to the Companies Registry and is therefore not open to public inspection.

25 | My uncle is the majority shareholder in a private company. He wants to retire and has offered to sell the shares to me. I'd like to buy them, but I haven't got the money. Can the company itself lend me the money?

Under various rules (set out in the Companies Act 1985) it is unlawful for a company to give financial assistance for the purchase of its shares.

However, the Companies Act 1985 contains a number of exceptions to this prohibition. In the case of a private company, a loan can lawfully be made to you if three conditions are satisfied:

• the directors prepare a formal legal document called a 'statutory declaration' setting out the nature of the loan and their opinion that the company is able to pay its debts and will remain in that position for at least 12 months;
• the directors' opinion is supported by a report of the auditors of the company (and that report must be annexed to the statutory declaration);
• within one week of the declaration the loan is approved by a special resolution, that is, by a three-quarter majority of the shareholders who actually vote for or against the resolution.

26 | My co-director and I have started to have violent arguments over the running of the business, and as a result the company is grinding to a halt. We each own 40 per cent of the shares, so if I bought him out I'd get control. The only problem is

that I don't have the money. Is there any way in which I can get control of the company without borrowing?

One possible solution, made available by the Companies Act 1985, is that if certain conditions are satisfied the company itself can buy the shares of your fellow director. Any such shares bought by the company would be cancelled, and the shares still owned by you would then be sufficient to give you control. The conditions to be satisfied are broadly similar to those stated in Q25 (special resolution, directors' statutory declaration and auditors' report); the underlying idea is that the capital of the company is a fund available to creditors and it should not be returned to the shareholders. In addition, the Articles of Association (see page 322) must contain a power for the company to buy its own shares; if the Articles do not contain such a power, they must first be altered so as to include one although this should present no problem. In deciding whether a special resolution has been passed, the votes of the shareholder owning the shares which are to be bought must be ignored.

If you discuss the matter with your fellow shareholder, he will obviously want to know how he will be taxed on the money he gets from the company. As a result of the Finance Act 1982, the position depends on whether or not the company buys the shares wholly or mainly for the benefit of a trade carried on by it (or by some other company controlled by it). In view of your violent arguments, your business would probably benefit if one of you dropped out, and it may well be that this test will be satisfied in your case. If so, your fellow shareholder will have to pay only capital gains tax at 30 per cent (but no income tax) on any gain that he makes on the disposal of his shares to the company.

27 | *I think that the overseas market for my products is much stronger than the UK market. How would I go about selling abroad and are there any legal considerations I should take into account?*

There are three main options available to you.

The first is to set up a branch of your business abroad. This will involve many legal problems, including the best structure of the business (whether just to set up a branch of your own company or to form an entirely new company in the foreign country), taxation, employment and business contracts. Second, you may appoint an overseas agent to obtain contracts which you will then carry out by exporting direct to the overseas buyers. Third, you may enter into a distributorship agreement with a local trader: you sell your goods to him, perhaps requiring him to take a minimum quantity, you give him sole selling rights, and he agrees to use his best endeavours to promote your products and not those of your competitors.

All these options involve questions of English law (including EEC law) and also local law, and it is vitally important that you get comprehensive advice on all these issues from a lawyer practising in the foreign country. The Law Society (address on page 510) may be able to give you names and addresses of foreign lawyers.

You could start by discussing your plans with the British Overseas Trade Board (address on page 509), a government body that advises exporters. The Board may be able to offer advice as to the best markets for your products, the best ways of operating in those markets, and whether your goods will have to be modified to meet local technical standards. It will also tell you about various schemes that may help you, including the Market Entry Guarantee Scheme, which provides 50 per cent towards the cost of setting up foreign sales outlets, and the facilities of the Export Credits Guarantee Department (address on page 509), which insures exporters against default by their customers.

28 | *My company employs only four people and the turnover is quite modest. Do I have to send my profit and loss account to the Registrar of Companies?*

No, probably not. The rules relating to accounts are set out in great detail in the Companies Act 1985, and they are modified in the case of small and medium-sized companies. A small company is exempt from the duty to file a profit and loss account; it is a small company if it has fulfilled any two of the following conditions for the previous two financial years:

- turnover is £1,400,000 or less,
- assets are £700,000 or less,
- the weekly average number of employees is 50 or fewer.

Even if your business is not small, it may still be medium-sized. This will be so if the company has fulfilled any two of the following conditions for the previous two financial years:

- turnover is £5,750,000 or less,
- assets are £2,800,000 or less,
- the weekly average number of employees is 250 or fewer.

If the company is a medium-sized company the accounts will not have to give particulars of the turnover, and the profit and loss account need not be as detailed as in the case of large companies.

Partnerships

29 | I feel that I can no longer run my business on my own and I'm thinking of taking in a partner. What sort of matters should the partnership agreement deal with?

There is no legal rule stating that every partnership must have a formal written partnership agreement, and in many cases the agreement is purely oral. It is often a good idea, however, to have an agreement in writing because this can help to avoid disputes as to what has been agreed. The Partnership Act 1890 lays down certain rules to govern the relationship between partners, but these rules can be changed by an agreement and they will apply only if the partners themselves have not agreed on the particular matter.

Since a partnership agreement involves consideration of many rules of law, it should be drawn up by a solicitor and it should deal with the following points:
1. The firm's name.
2. The principal place of business.
3. The duration of the partnership (if any): perhaps it should continue for a fixed term or until it is brought

to an end by, say, six months' notice given by either partner.
4. Whether the premises and other assets used by the firm are to be treated as partnership property or whether they will remain the personal property of the person who has brought the asset in.
5. How much money each of the partners is going to put in. The stake of a partner in the firm is known as his capital just as in the case of a company a shareholder's stake is reflected by his share capital (see Q3).
6. The proportion in which profits are to be shared and whether either partner or both is to be entitled to a salary or to interest on capital.
7. Drawings and repayments of capital, if any, bearing in mind the crippling effect that a sudden withdrawal of capital can have on the continued existence of the firm.
8. What provision each partner should make for his or her retirement. The agreement may, for example, require each of you to invest a proportion of your profits in a suitable retirement annuity scheme created by insurance companies.
9. The authority of particular partners to be responsible for particular acts and, in particular, the arrangements for the drawing of cheques.
10. What is to happen to the share of a partner who dies. It is common to find that the share shall accrue to the surviving partners. Such a provision makes a lot of commercial sense because it keeps the business alive and avoids any need to have it sold. It can also save capital transfer tax because passing the share to the surviving partner is not a gift but results from a mutual commercial bargain ('I'll have your share if you die and you can have mine if I die').

30 | In a partnership, are the salaries always based on the amount of capital the partners have put in?

No. The proportion in which profits are shared between the partners is a matter for agreement between them, and it is not usually or necessarily linked to the proportion in which they have provided capital. Let's suppose that you, having put £20,000 into your own business, decide to take your manager into partnership and that he is not in a position to put in any money at all. You can agree that the profits shall be split equally (or in any other agreed proportion); if you agree nothing at all the Partnership Act 1890 will apply and the profits will be split equally in any case. But you may feel that you want some tangible recognition for the fact that the firm has the benefit of your money (which, if it were not invested in the firm, would be earning interest elsewhere). You may therefore agree with your fellow partner that in splitting the profits you will first be entitled either to a proportion of the interest payable on your capital or to a salary of a specified amount, and that the balance of any profit shall be split between you, equally or in some other way. From a commercial point of view the amount of the interest or salary must obviously bear some relation to the money that the business would have to pay to a bank or other lender to borrow the capital.

31 | *I'm thinking of taking my eldest son into partnership, but I'm a bit worried that he may negotiate contracts that we won't be able to carry out. What can I do to restrain him?*

You can have a clause in the partnership agreement itself or in some other agreement, made between yourself and your son, forbidding him from negotiating contracts without your consent. You could also agree with him that he is to be legally liable to indemnify you against any losses that you may suffer if he breaks his agreement and does negotiate a contract with a third party on his own.

Even with such a clause, there is one risk: the Partnership Act 1890 states that any contract made by a partner will be legally binding on all the partners if it is 'an act for carrying on in the usual way of business of the kind carried on by the firm of which he is a member'. Therefore, if your son does make a contract with a third party the mere fact that you have forbidden your son to do so will not stop you from being legally liable to the third party unless (and this is highly unlikely) that party knows of the restriction or does not know or believe that your son is a partner.

32 | *When I was considering taking on a partner, my solicitor mentioned the Partnership Act. How will this impinge on the partnership?*

The Partnership Act 1890 contains two sets of rules. In the first place there are the rules governing the relationship of the partners between themselves as regards voting, management, profit shares, and so on. In these cases the rules laid down in the Act will apply only if the partners themselves have not made their own partnership agreement on the matter (see Q30).

The second set of rules are those governing the relationship between the partners and outsiders. These are rules of law and cannot be altered by any partnership agreement. To put the matter in another way – if you allow your partner to occupy a position where to the outside world he appears to have authority to make contracts and so on (see Q31), then an outsider can rely on this and can treat the contract as legally binding on the partnership as a whole.

33 | *What would happen to the business if my partner were to have a serious accident or illness?*

His illness or accident could have very serious consequences for the business, especially if he or she is very active in it. It is therefore vitally important that you and your partner should discuss the consequences of such an eventuality, preferably when the partnership is formed. One possibility is for each partner to take out disability insurance for the benefit of his fellow partner or partners; the premiums on such policies will usually be paid by the firm. The moneys payable under such a policy would be paid to the partnership and would enable it to engage an outsider to do the work that the sick partner was doing in the hope that the profits would thereby be maintained. The sick partner would in such a case continue to draw his profit-share in the usual way in accordance with the terms of the partnership agreement. Such an arrangement can also be linked to an agreement for compulsory retirement if the illness lasts beyond a specified time; the remaining partner or partners will then have sufficient cash to buy the share of the sick partner without having to sell up the assets of the business. It may be, of course, that on retirement the retiring partner may become entitled to some form of retirement pension, but it is usual to require each partner to make his own retirement arrangements (see Q34).

If you have failed to cover the matter by express agreement, then you have no right to be paid more for the extra work that you may have to do during your partner's illness. Provisions in the Partnership Act 1890 allow a court to order a dissolution of the partnership in such circumstances, which you could consider if your partner is ill for a long period. Bear in mind, though, that an application to the court costs time and money and should be used only as a last resort.

34 | *I want to start planning for my retirement, though I haven't yet discussed this with my partners. What should I do?*

You should plan now, in a tax-efficient manner, to secure a reasonable income for yourself and for your family after your retirement. There are substantial tax advantages for a self-employed person, which includes a partner, who contributes to a retirement benefit scheme which is approved by the Inland Revenue (under the Income and Corporation Taxes Act 1970). Under such a scheme you can pay up to $17\frac{1}{2}$ per cent per annum of your 'net relevant earnings' – your share of the firm's profits less losses and capital allowances. If your net relevant earnings this year are £16,000, say, you can pay £2,800 into the scheme and such payments are fully tax deductible at the highest rate of income tax you pay. If, therefore, you're paying tax at 60 per cent on £4,000 of your income the whole of that £2,800 can come out of that slice, leaving only £1,200 taxable at 60 per cent. In other words, the true cost to you of a premium of £2,800 is only 40 per cent of that amount – £1,120. In return for this you will receive an annuity when you retire. In addition, up to 5 per cent of your net relevant earnings can be used to provide benefits for your spouse or dependants, though this is part of, and not additional to, the $17\frac{1}{2}$ per cent ceiling. Many firms make it compulsory for partners to plan for their retirement in this way.

An alternative is for you to suggest to the firm that when you reach a specified age, perhaps 50, you change your status from partner to consultant. The firm may then be able to set up an approved retirement scheme for an employee (that is, yourself); the firm would then get full tax relief on its contributions to provide the maximum benefits for you which the Inland Revenue will allow. As a general rule, the Inland Revenue allows an employee to draw a pension equal to two-thirds of his final salary after 10 years of employment.

35 | *I'm a partner in a construction firm and am about to retire. Is there anything I should do before I actually retire?*

When you retire you remain legally liable for any debts or obligations that were incurred before you retired. You should go through the books with your accountant and work out any amount involved and negotiate any necessary arrangements about this with the remaining partners. You may also be liable for prospective claims made by clients or customers. These should also be investigated and discussed. If, for example, a building falls down owing to negligent work done while you were a partner, a customer can bring a claim within six years from the date of the damage (in personal injury cases it is three years). Your fellow partners will probably have insured against such claims, but you yourself may wish to take out insurance to cover yourself personally (bearing in mind that the amounts involved can be enormous) for the six-year period.

There is also the question of future debts. Here you can safeguard yourself in one of two ways:

● You must give actual notice of your retirement to all the customers and suppliers who have dealt with the firm while you were a partner and who knew that you were a partner.
● You should also insert a notice of your retirement in the *London Gazette*. The notice will protect you from claims brought by persons who have not dealt with the firm before your retirement but who knew that you were a partner in the firm.

One final point: make sure that the continuing partners don't carry on using stationery on which your name appears as a partner.

36 | *My partners and I have decided that our small engineering business isn't working out and we are going to go our separate ways. I own the workshop that we have been using; its value has doubled since we started. Does it still belong to me?*

You must look carefully at the arrangements you made with your partners because the answer to your question will depend on whether you originally brought in the workshop as part of the firm's assets. One important factor is the way in which the workshop has been treated in the books of the firm. Your 'capital account' will show your contribution to the business (as well as any profit that has increased your stake and any loss that has reduced it). If the workshop appears in that account as part of your capital contribution it suggests that it was intended to be part of the firm's assets. If this is so, the workshop will be 'partnership property' and any increase in value must be split between your partners and yourself according to your profit-sharing rights. If, however, you merely allowed the firm to use the workshop, it may have always remained your property and in that case the increase in value does not have to be shared with your partners.

Tax

37 | How does the Inland Revenue work out the profits of my business for tax purposes?

As a general rule profits are worked out on what is called the 'earnings basis'. This means that you must include all money that you have earned even though you may not have received the income, perhaps because invoices you have sent out have not yet been paid. You can deduct from your income expenses that you are legally liable to pay, again even though you may not yet have paid them. Subject to this, the calculation is worked out as follows:

1. All your earnings are added up and there will then be added to them the value of any closing stock or work-in-progress, which is assessed at cost or market value, whichever is the lower.

2. Deducted from the earnings are business expenses such as wages, rent, rates, normal bank interest, stationery and other office equipment, advertising and the cost of business travel (but not the cost of travelling from home to your place of work). Added to the business expenses is the value of opening stock or work-in-progress, again assessed at cost or market value, whichever is the lower.

3. The total of the expenses is deducted from the total of the receipts. Work out how much, if any, your Class 4 National Insurance contributions will be. Deduct half this figure from the receipts figure. The result will be either a profit or a loss. However, certain tax allowances in respect of capital expenditure (known as capital allowances) can be deducted from the profit or loss figure.

4. If, after making all these deductions, there is a profit, then this will be the profit of your business for the tax year in question. Conversely, if there is a loss you will have no tax to pay in respect of your business activities for this year and, in addition, there are various rules giving you tax relief in respect of that loss.

This is only a very general survey and omits a number of detailed rules – for example, you will get no tax relief for sums spent on business entertainment unless you happen to entertain an overseas customer. An accountant will provide more information, and it is generally vital to appoint one to prepare your business accounts and submit them to the Inland Revenue. See above for a sample of accounts submitted to the Inland Revenue.

38 | My accountant mentioned the preceding year basis for the assessment of income tax. What is this?

● Accounts submitted to the Inland Revenue for William Brickman & Co. (Building Contractors)

Tax computation for year to 31.12.86

	£
Work-in-progress as at 1.1.86	5,000.00
Receipts	100,000.00
	105,000.00
Trade expenses	60,000.00
	45,000.00
Work-in-progress as at 31.12.86	20,000.00
	25,000.00
Capital allowances	15,000.00
	10,000.00
Deduct half Class 4 NI contributions	184.00
Profit liable to tax	9,816.00

The income tax year runs from 6 April to the following 5 April and tax on the profits of a sole trader or partnership is charged on the profits made in the accounting year ending in the tax year *before* the one in question, that is, the preceding year. This rule can have dramatic cash flow advantages. Say your accounting year ends on 7 April 1987 and shows a profit of £10,000. This accounting year ends in tax year 1987–8 (that is, between 6 April 1987 and 5 April 1988); the profit will be taxed in tax year 1988–9 and tax is payable by two equal instalments on 1 January 1989 and 1 July 1989. So you have between 21 and 27 months' use of the money before tax has to be paid.

The position is different, and less favourable, in the case of the tax payable by a company; this is known as corporation tax. The preceding year basis does not apply and tax is payable nine months after the end of the accounting period. If the profit referred to above for the accounting year ending 7 April 1987 had been made by a company, all the tax would have to be paid within nine months from that date, that is, by 7 January 1988.

In the case of a sole trader and a partnership there are even more favourable tax rules about starting a business (although once again these do not apply in the case of companies). For the tax year in which the business starts, tax is payable on a proportion of the first year's profits. For the second tax year, tax is payable on the first year's profits. For the third and subsequent years the preceding year basis applies, although the taxpayer can elect for years two and three (both or neither) to be taxed on an actual basis. As an example of these 'opening year rules', suppose that a business starts on 6 January 1988 and that the first year's profit is only £1,000. The tax assessments for the first three years will be as follows:

1987–8 three-twelfths × £1,000	£250
1988–9	£1,000
1989–90	£1,000

The calculation for 1987–8 is arrived at because three of the first 12 months were before 5 April 1988 and were therefore in tax year 1987–8.

These figures should show that there is plenty of incentive to keep profits low in the first year, because the first year's profit will be reflected in the tax assessment for the first three tax years.

39 | I've just lost a highly paid job and I'm thinking of starting a small business on my own. What's my tax position if the business makes a loss?

Many new businesses make a loss at the beginning, and a number of tax reliefs are available to you if this should happen. If you run the business as a sole trader or in partnership you can deal with the loss (or with your share of the loss) in any of the following ways:

● You can set it against any of your taxable income (at your top rate of tax) for the loss year or for the following year if the business is still being carried on in that year.
● You can carry it forward against future profits of the same business without any time-limit.
● Perhaps the most valuable option of all is that a business loss arising in the first four years of the business can be carried back and set against your taxable income arising in the three preceding years – even income arising before the business started. As a result, if you paid a lot of tax on your salary (or perhaps on a compensation payment) you may well get that tax back as a result of any business loss.

Your taxable income includes the income of your wife if your incomes are (or were) jointly assessed.

40 | Are the tax rules very different for companies and partnerships?

In some respects they are similar. Thus:
1. The rules for working out business profits are very similar.
2. If you run a company and draw out all the profits as directors' remuneration, your personal tax bill will often be the same as if you ran the business as a sole trader or in partnership, although the rules governing the time for payment of tax are different.

There are some important differences, however, as follows:
1. A partner pays income tax on his income and capital gains tax on capital gains, a company pays corporation tax on all its profits (including capital gains).
2. A shareholder cannot get tax relief for losses made by the company.
3. The preceding year basis of assessment, when coupled with the rules governing the time for payment of tax, gives a sole trader or partnership substantial cash flow advantages and scope for tax planning (see Q38).
4. If the company pays dividends (although this is unusual in the case of small family companies) the company has to pay 'advance corporation tax' at the rate of three-sevenths of the dividend; this tax has to be paid to the Inland Revenue even where the company has no profits liable for corporation tax. If, however, the company does have to pay corporation tax then the advance corporation tax can be deducted and only the balance has to be paid to the Inland Revenue.
5. If the company has investment income this must usually be paid out to the shareholders by way of dividend, and there will be a tax charge if this is not done unless the retention can be commercially justified; the tax in question can be recovered from the shareholder if the company fails to pay.

41 | Which is better from a tax point of view, a company or a partnership?

It is difficult to give a direct answer because so many different factors must be considered. In the early years of trading a partnership is probably better, especially if there may be losses, because partners can set their losses against their other income – and this includes a right to set losses against pre-partnership income (see Q39). Company losses are locked into the company and cannot be used in this way. Then again, a partnership can have major cash flow advantages through the operation of the preceding year basis of assessment (see Q38). A third advantage is that the partners may draw out money without having to pay tax on it; this will be so if, for example, previous losses and capital allowances (see Q37) reduce the tax bill to nil. In contrast, the owners of a company will always have to pay tax on money that they pay themselves (as directors' remuneration or as dividends on their shares) even though the company has no taxable profits.

As the profits expand there will come a point at which profits kept in the company will be taxed at a lower rate than partnership profits; for a partnership there is no tax difference between money drawn out and money kept in the partnership. This reduction in the tax bill will be particularly strong in the case of companies where the shareholders have other taxable income and where they can afford to keep the profits in the company. The personal tax rate of a partner can rise above 27 per cent on income in excess of £21,555 (and sometimes this figure is lower); in contrast, the 27 per cent 'small company rate' of corporation tax applies to all company profits – including capital gains – up to £100,000. This advantage to companies will of course have to be offset against an eventual liability to capital gains tax because the retained profits may well increase the gain which the shareholders will make when they dispose of their shares.

42 | How would our choice of company or partnership be affected if we brought our wives in?

If you run your business as a company and employ your wife as a director or in some other capacity there are two tax advantages. In the first place money paid by the company to your wife as an employee or director would be tax deductible in computing the company's profits. Second, your wife's income can be separated from your own income for income tax purposes if you elect for separate taxation (see TAXES Q32). There is, however, one major snag. The Inland Revenue will want to be satisfied that the payments were made wholly and exclusively for the purposes of the business, and large payments to your wife may well be non-deductible if her duties are fairly light.

Let us now take the case where you make your wife an equal partner in your business so that the money which you yourself were earning in that business is now split equally between your wife and yourself and an election is made for separate taxation of your wife's earnings. If the Inland Revenue were to query this, you would have to satisfy it that your wife was actively involved in the partnership; if you could not do this the overall tax saving would disappear because her share would not be earned income and consequently no election for separate taxation could be made. If, however, this hurdle can be overcome, the tax effect can be quite dramatic. If we assume that you, a colleague and each of your wives are equal sharing partners in the partnership, and if we also assume that none of you has any other income, the rate of tax will not rise above 27 per cent until the profits of the firm are in excess of £71,600 (for tax year 1987–8) plus reliefs plus allowances. Accordingly, it is only when the profit exceeds that figure that the use of a company is likely to lead to a saving in tax.

43 | A woman I know who runs a highly successful boutique has offered to take me into partnership. What will my tax position be?

Where a sole trader takes in a partner, the general rule is that the new partnership is taxed under the new business rules described in Q38. There is, however, an alternative: the two of you can sign a written 'continuation' election that the profits will continue to be assessed on the preceding year basis as though no change had occurred. It is important to remember that while you will be taxed on the preceding year basis, the profit will be split between you and your partner according to your profit-sharing rights in the actual year in question.

Suppose that in the accounting year to 31 December 1985 the boutique produced a profit of £15,000 and in the following year produced a profit of £20,000. You became a 50 per cent partner on 1 January 1987 and a continuation election was signed by you and your partner. For tax year 1986–7, on the preceding year basis the firm's profit is £15,000. Three-twelfths of this is treated as arising in the three months from 1 January to 5 April 1987 during which you were a partner; therefore you will suffer tax on 50 per cent of three-twelfths of £15,000, that is, tax on £1,875, even though you never saw a penny of it! For the tax year 1987–8 your profit share is 50 per cent; you will therefore have to pay tax on 50 per cent of the firm's profit for that year, and that profit, calculated on the preceding year basis, is £20,000. Accordingly, your share for tax purposes will be £10,000 – even though, once again, you will never have received a penny of it.

All this is obviously a matter for negotiation when the terms of the partnership are discussed. You will have to look at the accounts and then decide whether or not it is in your interest to sign the continuation election. At first sight it looks rather frightening that you should have to pay tax on money which you never earned. Nevertheless, it may be a blessing in disguise; after all, if the profits are rising, it is better to be taxed on last year's low profits than on this year's high profits.

While your case deals with a continuation election where a sole trader takes in a partner for the first time, the same rules apply whenever there is a change in a partnership – for example, if an existing firm takes in a new partner or if a partner retires from his firm.

44 | How does capital gains tax apply to businesses?

If a sole trader disposes of a capital asset used by the business – for example, a building, a machine or a car – he may have to pay capital gains tax at 30 per cent on any resulting gain. The gain is usually calculated by taking the proceeds of the sale (less the cost of the sale) and deducting from it the cost of acquisition and the cost of any capital improvements. This gain must be added to any other gains made by the trader in the year in question. No tax is charged on the first £6,600 of gains accruing to an individual in any year; there is also a special relief for inflation introduced by the Finance Act 1982.

There are also two other important reliefs from capital gains tax.

First, an immediate tax charge can be avoided where certain types of business assets, including land, buildings, fixed plant and machinery, and goodwill, are disposed of and the proceeds are then used within three years to acquire other assets within that same general class which are then used in the business. Any gain is deducted from the purchase price of the new asset (so that the eventual gain on that new asset will be that much greater). For example, Mr Merchant buys a factory for £60,000 in 1984 and sells it in 1985 for £80,000; a year later he buys a shop for £45,000, which he sells in 1987 for £55,000 without replacing it. The effect of the tax relief is to wipe out the gain made on the factory in 1985 while at the same time reducing the purchase price on the shop to £25,000. Accordingly, the sale in 1987 produces a gain for capital gains tax purposes of £55,000–£25,000 = £30,000.

Second, an individual who has attained the age of 60 or who has been compelled to retire on health grounds below that age can claim what is called 'retirement relief' if he disposes of the whole or part of his business. The amount of relief depends on the time during which he has owned the business; the maximum relief is £125,000 if it has been owned for 10 years.

These rules relating to sole traders apply also to partnerships, and any gains made by the firm must be split between the partners according to the proportions in which they share profits. There can also be tax problems where there is a change in profit-sharing rights – for example when a new partner comes in and is given a share in the firm.

The basic rules apply also to capital gains made by companies – and the special rules about disposals by people over 60 can be used by a shareholder who disposes of shares in a company which has been his family company and in which he has been a full-time working director.

The rate of tax is the appropriate rate of corporation tax (27 per cent on profits to £100,000) and not the 30 per cent payable by individuals.

Getting money out

45 | I've put a lot of money into the business and now I need to draw some of it out. Can I do so?

If you are a sole trader there are no legal restrictions; the only restrictions are financial ones in that the withdrawal may make it difficult for the business to carry on, and you would have to consider how this could affect such matters as your liability under a bank guarantee (see Q13). The same is true in the case of a partnership, although your right to withdraw capital may well be governed by an agreement between your partners and yourself (see Q29).

In the case of a company, however, the legal position is very different. The general rule is that invested share capital cannot be returned by the company to the shareholders until the company is wound up. The only two exceptions are: a reduction of share capital with the consent of the Companies Court, and the purchase of your shares by the company itself (see Q26). This latter involves a complicated procedure and must be approved by a three-quarter majority resolution, excluding in this calculation the shares that you want to sell. The reason for these rules is that the share capital is regarded as a fund for the creditors which should not be handed back to the shareholders.

The normal way of getting your money out is to sell your shares to an outside person – if you can find one, and in the case of a private company this may be difficult. You should also examine the Articles of Association (see page 322) because they may contain what are called 'pre-empted clauses' under which any shareholder who wants to sell must first offer the shares to the other shareholders at a price fixed by agreement or (if you cannot agree) by an auditor's valuation. This is very common in small family companies; occasionally, the Articles go further and compel the other shareholders to buy the shares of any shareholder who wishes to sell.

Finally, if you have merely made loans to the company, these legal restrictions will not apply and you can demand the return of any money repayable to you under the terms of the loan agreement.

46 | Is there no other way of getting any money out of the company?

There are at least four possibilities other than those mentioned in Q45:

1. The company can pay a dividend to its shareholders (see Q7). It is most unlikely, however, that this will equal the total amount of your investment. Also, the company gets no tax relief for any dividend that it pays, and it must pay advance corporation tax on the dividend (see Q40). There are also restrictions on the value of property which can be used by the company to pay the dividends (see Q7).

2. If you are a director the company can pay you a sum by way of a director's remuneration (see Q8) but the company will get tax relief only for a payment which is made to you wholly and exclusively for the purposes of the trade. One possibility is for you to resign as a director and then for the company to make you a payment as compensation for loss of office. Up to £25,000 would be tax free in your hands and the company could also get substantial tax relief; the amount of the compensation would depend on your age, your salary and your length of service.

3. The company could make a loan to you. However, there are major snags here. In the first place the loan must be authorised under the terms of the objects clause of the company (see page 322). Second, if you are a director the effect of the Companies Act 1985 is that loans to directors are allowed only in very limited circumstances (for example, where the loan is necessary to enable you to perform your duties and is approved by the shareholders under detailed rules set out in the Act). Third, even if you are not a director, a loan to you in your capacity as a shareholder could substantially increase the company's tax bill – and your own tax bill could be substantially increased if the loan was written off.

4. A final possibility is to wind the company up. This will involve the appointment of a liquidator (see Q49), although if the company is able to pay all its debts (and interest on those debts) the shareholders

can choose the liquidator; he must, however, be a 'licensed insolvency practitioner' under the Insolvency Act 1986. The liquidator must get in the assets, pay off the creditors (and this would include his own fees) and then distribute any balance among the shareholders. From a tax point of view this option is very inefficient; tax will be charged on any capital gains that the company makes on disposing of its assets, and a further slice of capital gains tax will be payable by you on any gains that you make in disposing of your shares. If, for example, at the end of the liquidation the liquidator pays you the sum of £5 for every share, and if you originally paid only £1 per share, you will have made a capital gain of £4 on each of those shares.

If you have invested money in the company by way of a loan the company does not suffer any tax penalty if it merely repays the loan to you, and you will have to pay income tax only on sums that represent interest on the loan (including arrears of interest which have accrued from the past).

The above summary should make it clear that for a shareholder to get his money back from the company can be both difficult and expensive.

Insolvency

47 | My company has defaulted on a bank loan and the bank is threatening to call in a receiver. What does this mean?

When the company borrowed the money from the bank it will almost certainly have signed a written document called a debenture. This deals with such matters as the terms for repayment of the loan and the rights that the bank has if the company goes into default. The debenture will also usually give the bank a mortgage over the company's business assets. One of the rights that the bank nearly always has under the terms of a debenture is the right to appoint a receiver. This is a person selected by the bank (usually an accountant) to take charge when it looks as though the bank is in danger of losing its money. The job of the receiver is to collect all the assets covered by the bank's mortgage, dispose of them in the best possible way, and then distribute the money in accordance with rules laid down in the Insolvency Act 1986. Under these rules, certain creditors have special rights and must be paid first. These include the Inland Revenue (which can claim one year's unpaid PAYE tax), the DHSS (one year's unpaid National Insurance contributions), the Customs and Excise (six months' unpaid VAT) and employees (arrears of pay for four months with a maximum of £800). When these preferential debts have been paid off, the balance is paid to the bank.

It sometimes happens that the receiver decides that at least part of the business can be saved. In that case he will look for a buyer and then transfer that part of the business as a going concern to the buyer. This operation is known as 'hive-down', and it can some-times help to save jobs as well as to raise money for preferential creditors and for the bank.

48 | *I am a part-time director of a company which I think is losing money fast. Am I perso-nally liable to the creditors if the company folds up?*

In general a director (full time or part time) is not personally liable for the debts of his company. Nevertheless, there are exceptions to this rule, and one of them relates to what is called 'wrongful trading'. A director must realise that he is handling other people's money, and he must not carry on when it is obvious that the company is going to fail. Under the Insolvency Act 1986, where a company goes into 'insolvent liquidation' at any time on or after 28 April 1986, the liquidator can ask the Court to make an order requiring a director to make a contribution to the company's debts. An order can be made if at some time during his directorship the director 'knew or ought to have concluded', that there was no reasonable prospect of survival. The director 'knew or ought to have concluded' that he 'took every step with a view to minimising the potential loss to the company's creditors as . . . he

ought to have taken'. The standard is that which can be reasonably expected of a director holding that particular position and any higher standard which that director actually has. So if you just do nothing you could be in trouble. You must insist on seeing up-to-date accounts as a matter of urgency; you may also have to insist on:

- calling in an accountant to advise on the com-pany's chances of survival, or
- working out a rescue plan, or
- asking the bank to put in a receiver.

If your fellow directors don't agree, you may have to consider resigning and having your views clearly minuted.

49 | *How is a company wound up and is that the same as liquidation?*

Yes, the two terms have the same meaning.

A company is wound up, or put into liquidation, normally after a court procedure. The basic idea of a winding up is to close down the company. A person or body will file a formal document in the High Court (in certain cases in a county court) asking for a court order that the company should be wound up. The document in question is a petition, and the person who sends the petition to the court is nearly always a creditor (although in some cases it can be a share-holder). The grounds for a winding-up order are set out in the Insolvency Act 1986, and by far the most important of these grounds is the fact that the company is unable to pay its debts.

A winding-up petition is usually the beginning of the end. What happens is as follows:

1. A copy of the petition is sent to the company.

2. If the petition has been sent in to the court by a creditor it must be advertised in a government news-paper known as the *London Gazette* (for England and Wales), the *Edinburgh Gazette* (for Scotland) or the *Belfast Gazette* (for Northern Ireland); it must also be advertised in a national or local newspaper. In this way the petition will come to the notice of other creditors who may get in touch with the petitioning creditor to indicate whether or not they support the request to have the company wound up.

3. There is a court hearing at which a judge con-siders the views of the petitioning creditor, any other creditors, and the company itself; the judge will decide whether or not a winding-up order should be made. In nearly all cases he will make such an order, but he may well refuse to do so if the company can show that it does not owe the money.

4. While all this is going on the assets of the com-

pany are in effect frozen although the court does have the power to allow payments to be made in the ordinary course of business.

5. Once a winding-up order is made the company's papers are sent to a government official called the Official Receiver. He will look into the matter and will decide within 12 weeks whether or not meetings of creditors and shareholders should be called so that they can decide whether another person (being a 'licensed insolvency practitioner') should take over as liquidator from the Official Receiver. The creditors and shareholders can also decide whether or not to appoint a group of persons (known as a 'liquidation committee') to supervise the winding up. If the company is unable to pay its debts, then the views of the creditors will obviously have priority over the views of the shareholders. If the Official Receiver decides not to call meetings, he will remain the liquidator.

The liquidator will get in the company assets, pay the debts in the order laid down by the Insolvency Act 1986 (see Q47), pay interest that has accrued since the start of the winding up and distribute any surplus to shareholders. He will then inform the Registrar of Companies that the winding up has been completed, and three months later the company is dissolved (in other words, it no longer exists). The Official Receiver can also apply for an early dissolution (after informing the creditors and shareholders of his intention to do so) if he is satisfied that the assets of the company are not large enough to cover the expenses of the winding up and that no further investigation is necessary.

The other type of liquidation or winding up does not involve court proceedings. This is known as 'voluntary liquidation' and it takes place if the shareholders pass, by a 75% majority, a resolution for the company to be wound up.

If the directors make a 'declaration of solvency' stating that the company can pay all its debts (and interest) within 12 months, the liquidation can be under the control of the shareholders but if, as is more usually the case, the company cannot pay its debts the directors must call separate meetings of shareholders and creditors and, not surprisingly, the creditors' choice of liquidator will prevail. The creditors can also choose up to five persons as a 'liquidation committee' to supervise the liquidator; the shareholders can then appoint up to five of their own nominees – but the creditors can veto all or any of them.

The rules governing the powers and duties of the liquidator and the dissolution of the company are broadly similar to those that apply where the company is being wound up by the Court.

50 | *The company of which I am a director has run into some financial problems. Should I arrange for it to pay off the bank overdraft which I guaranteed?*

You can do this (and it is often done), but you will not be in the clear for two years.

Under the Insolvency Act 1986, if a company goes into liquidation, or if an administration order is made, within two years of the payment, the liquidator or administrator may be able to set aside the payment as a 'preference'. To do this, he must show (and he clearly can) that the payment into the bank account reduces your personal liability on the guarantee and accordingly, if the company were to fail, your position will be better than it would have been if the payment had not been made.

Normally, the liquidator or administrator would also have to show that the company was influenced in deciding to make the payment by a desire to achieve that result. However, you, as a director, are 'connected' with the company, and this means that the burden is reversed; in other words it will be for you to show that the company was not influenced by a desire to benefit you. Obviously you would have great difficulty in proving this unless you had some kind of independent evidence that the bank was threatening to withdraw facilities unless the payment was made. You can, however, stop the payment being set aside if you can show that when it was made, the remaining assets of the company were sufficient to cover its liabilities.

If the payment is set aside under the rules mentioned above, the bank will have to return the money to the liquidator or administrator and your liability under the guarantee will revive.

VAT

51 | *I don't know the first thing about* VAT. *How does it work?*

Value Added Tax (VAT) is charged, currently at 15 per cent, on the supply of goods and services by a person carrying on business in the United Kingdom. All suppliers are covered, whether they are individuals, partners, companies or any other organisation. The tax applies equally to people who supply goods (manufacturers, wholesalers, retailers, etc.) and to people who provide services (solicitors, accountants, authors, hotels, travel agents, etc.). There are, however, two classes of exemption:

- traders whose volume of business is below £21,300 per annum (or £7,250 in any quarter), and
- certain types of suppliers, including those supplying insurance, postal services, medical services, education, burial and cremation, and interests in land.

If the exemptions referred to above do not apply, the supplier, who is known as a 'taxable person', must charge the VAT to his customers ('output tax'). He must account for this tax quarterly to the Commissioners of Customs and Excise, but he is allowed to set off against his output tax any VAT which he himself has had to pay to his own suppliers in the same quarter ('input tax'). In effect, therefore, it is a tax on the 'mark-up' at each stage of distribution and, apart from the administrative chore of having to keep VAT records, traders usually end up in the same financial position as if VAT did not exist because the ultimate burden falls on the end user who cannot pass it on.

To give an example of how VAT operates:

1. M (Manufacturer) produces an article for £100 and sells it to W (Wholesaler). The invoice shows:

Goods	£100
VAT	£15
Total	£115

W pays M £115 and M pays £15 (output tax) to the Customs and Excise.

2. W sells the article to R (Retailer) for £140 plus VAT. The invoice shows:

Goods	£140
VAT	£21
Total	£161

W will deduct his £15 input tax from his £21 output tax and will pay £6 to Customs and Excise.

3. R sells the article to C (Consumer) for £180 plus VAT. The invoice shows:

Goods	£180
VAT	£27
Total	£207

R will deduct his £21 input tax from his £27 output tax and will pay £6 to Customs and Excise.

4. Thus, M, W and R have each had to pay tax on the value added by them, but they have been able to pass it on. C cannot do so, and the ultimate burden of VAT therefore falls on the consumer.

52 | *I recently sent a customer a quotation of £1,000 for redecorating his flat. But I forgot to add on VAT and the customer refuses to pay me more than £1,000. What happens now?*

If your quotation form uses the words 'All prices are exclusive of VAT' either on the front or as part of your conditions on the back, the customer should pay your fee plus VAT, that is, £1,000 plus £150. If the quotation does not do so then you should alter it to make sure that it does in the future.

In the absence of such a provision, all prices charged by a trader are VAT-inclusive. To find the VAT element which you are treated as having charged the customer, you will have to apply the following formula, where P is the VAT-inclusive price and VAT is at 15 per cent:

$$P - \left(P \times \frac{100}{115} \right)$$

In your case, this calculation produces a VAT element of £130.43, which is your output tax on the transaction.

53 | *Do I have to register the business for VAT?*

VAT registration is compulsory if

- your turnover exceeds £21,300 a year or £7,250 in any quarter, or
- at any time there are reasonable grounds for believing that your taxable supplies will exceed £21,300 in a one-year period.

In the former case, you must notify the Commissioners of Customs and Excise (listed in the telephone directory under Customs and Excise Department) within 10 days of the quarter concerned, and the Department will then register you as from the twenty-first day of the next quarter or such earlier date as may be agreed between you. Even if registration is not compulsory, you can apply to be registered and the Commissioners have a discretion to do so.

Customs and Excise have published a booklet for new traders explaining the machinery for registration.

54 | *I have a small business dealing in gem-stones, but I don't think that I'm going to reach*

the £21,300 turnover. Should I still register for VAT?

The principal advantage of registering a business for VAT, even if turnover is below £21,300, is that you will be able to deduct your VAT inputs (see Q51) which you would otherwise have to bear yourself. It is not, however, as simple as that because you also have to consider the sort of persons to whom you will be supplying the gemstones. If they are VAT-registered dealers, they will often be willing to pay a higher price if part of that price takes the form of a deductible VAT input. On the other hand, if your customers are themselves not VAT-registered they will not be concerned with input relief and they will be attracted by the lower prices that you may be able to offer if you do not have to charge VAT.

To illustrate this, say you buy an item for £230 (including £30 VAT) and that you want to make a profit of £50 on the transaction. If you are not registered for VAT you will put the £50 on to the £230 and charge your customers £280. On the other hand, if you are registered for VAT you would charge £250 (the original purchase price, less VAT plus the £50 profit element) plus VAT of £37.50, making a total price of £287.50. You would hand to Customs and Excise the sum of £7.50 (being the difference between your VAT output of £37.50 and your VAT input of £30), leaving you as before with your desired surplus of £50.

A customer who is registered for VAT would prefer to pay the higher price of £287.50 because £37.50 of this is a deductible VAT input. On the other hand, a customer who is not registered for VAT would find your price of £280 very competitive compared to your VAT-registered competitors.

The choice is not an easy one, and if the difference in price is small then you may decide that you don't want to be bothered with the chore of keeping VAT records and accounts when this is not in fact necessary.

55 | *I've been told that VAT can create nasty cash flow problems. Why is this?*

The problem arises because the 'tax point' – the date that the supplier's liability for VAT falls due – can and very often does arise before he has received payment from his customer. The time of supply of goods is when they are delivered or made available to the buyer or when an invoice is issued or a payment is made (whichever is the earliest). In the case of services, the tax point is the issue of an invoice or the receipt of payment (whichever is the earlier) even if

this is later than the performance of the service. Thus, suppliers can find themselves liable to pay VAT before they have received any payment for their goods or services.

It is sometimes possible for suppliers of services to render a 'fee note' containing the words 'This is not a tax invoice'. If this procedure is correctly followed, the VAT tax point arises only when payment is received and any cash flow problems will be avoided. You may, for example, receive an invitation to attend a seminar or conference where the form invites you to send off your cheque to the organisers and states that 'A VAT invoice will be supplied'. This invoice has to be supplied to the recipient of the service so that he can claim relief for the relevant input tax.

The government has announced new proposals to ease some of the cash flow problems mentioned at the beginning of this answer. It proposes that as from October 1987 a trader with a turnover of £250,000 who is approved by the Commissioners of Customs and Excise will have the option of not having to pay VAT on a particular supply until payment is actually received.

56 | *What about customers who just don't pay their bills? Will I still have to pay VAT on the goods and services I supply them?*

The law here is tough on suppliers and many people would say that it is most unfair. The mere fact that you write off a debt does not reduce your VAT liability. If your debtor is an individual, you will get VAT bad debt relief only if he is made bankrupt or if his creditors approve a voluntary arrangement under the Insolvency Act 1986. If the debtor is a company, the making of a voluntary arrangement will not give you VAT bad debt relief, but such relief is available if an administration order is made or if a certificate of insolvency is issued by an administrative receiver or if the company goes into liquidation. In all these cases you can recover from Customs and Excise VAT that you have paid to them on the debt in question.

Sometimes a suitably worded solicitor's letter to the debtor, perhaps linked to the threat of winding-up proceedings (see Q49), might induce him to pay you something, although you'd probably get nothing from companies in the hands of a receiver.

57 | *I'd invoiced a customer before he complained about the quality of the goods. I'm now thinking of giving him a price reduction. What happens to the VAT?*

The original invoice was the tax point (see Q55) for

the supply and you are therefore accountable for the VAT. But if you make a genuine price adjustment you can issue a credit note followed by a fresh invoice for the altered amount. The effect of the credit note is to alter your VAT liability so that you will debit your output tax account with the amount of the VAT shown on the credit note, and the customer will credit his input tax account by the same amount.

This principle is not confined to faulty goods or services; it also applies if the customer complains that he has been overcharged and you agree to reduce the price.

58 | *Do I have to pay VAT on goods that I import from abroad?*

All Customs duties must be paid before imported goods can be released, and the Value Added Tax Act 1983 provides that VAT is charged as if it were a Customs duty on any importation of goods into the UK. Accordingly, if you are not registered for VAT you will have to pay VAT as well as other Customs duties before the goods will be released to you. If, however, you are registered for VAT, the position is different because you will have an immediate right to deduct the VAT as an input. As a result you will merely make two entries in your VAT records – one showing money due to the Customs and Excise and the other showing money due from them. It is purely a bookkeeping exercise, and no money will change hands.

Relationship with customers

59 | *I recently sent a customer a quotation for plastic mouldings. One of our conditions of trading, which are printed on the back of the quotation, gives me the right to increase the price of the goods if my overheads go up. The customer has sent me an official printed order, but his terms are different and there is nothing about a price increase. Can I put up the price if I need to?*

This difficult area is often known as the 'battle of the forms'. Is the contract between you governed by your terms or by his terms, or is there no contract at all? In answering this question, the normal legal rules must apply that one party must make an offer and the other party must accept that offer without making any changes. In many cases a quotation is an offer that can be turned into a legally binding contract by the customer's order; whether this is so or not will depend to a large extent on how the quotation is worded. However, this has no relevance to the facts of

your case because since your customer sent you a form with different terms he has not accepted any offer that you have made. His order is known legally as a 'counter-offer' and the legal position depends on what happened next. Have you, for example, sent the customer an acknowledgement of his order on a form which again incorporates your terms? Have the goods been delivered? It is a difficult area, but the strict legal position appears to be that if you have re-introduced your terms by acknowledging the customer's order on your quotation form and if the customer has accepted delivery of the goods, then your own terms (including the right to increase the price) will govern the contract. But if you have merely delivered the goods in response to the customer's order, then it may well be that you have agreed to the customer's terms; in that case the price cannot be increased. If nothing at all has happened since you received the customer's order, then you may be at a point where there is no contract at all and you should send the buyer an acknowledgement incorporating your terms as soon as possible. Perhaps your covering letter might expressly draw his attention to the relevant clause. This is of course a commercial decision, and if he objects you may have to negotiate or risk losing the order altogether.

60 | *A regular customer gave me an order for some timber and I passed it on to my supplier. Unfortunately, he's had a labour dispute and his deliveries to me are likely to be delayed. I don't want to offend my customer by not delivering the timber, and at the same time I don't want to offend my usual supplier by going to another one. Can the customer cancel his order or will I have to obtain the timber from another supplier?*

To deal first with the question of cancellation: the position depends on the terms of your contract with the customer. In very many cases the terms of business give a supplier such as yourself protection where, for example, delivery is delayed owing to circumstances beyond his control. Such a clause is valid if you can prove that it is reasonable, and in many cases this will be so. If you do not have such a clause, then you should consider whether you or one of your employees made a firm promise that the timber would be delivered by a certain date. You should also consider whether the customer made it clear to you that it had to be delivered by a certain date. If he made this clear to you, it may well be that the time of delivery will be a vital term of the contract and a breach of such a term could well give the customer a right to cancel. Even if no delivery date had been agreed, there may well be an implied term that delivery would take place within a reasonable time; once again, the customer might have a right to cancel if this reasonable time has expired without his having received the goods. A further possibility is that he might send you an ultimatum threatening to cancel unless the timber is delivered by a specified date.

Perhaps the best course of action in all the circumstances is to speak frankly to your usual supplier and explain to him that to avoid offending your regular customers you will have to buy your timber from another supplier until the labour dispute is settled.

61 | *I've just received a contract to modernise a factory. What happens if I sub-contract some of the work and the sub-contractors then make a mess of it?*

The short answer is that you may very well find yourself having to pay compensation to your customer for any poor work done by the sub-contractors.

The first thing you should establish is whether you are legally entitled to sub-contract at all. This depends very much on the nature of the business. If, for example, the customer is relying on your personal expertise in carrying, storing or repairing his goods, you may be in breach of contract if you sub-contract. You may then find yourself legally liable for loss or damage sustained by the customer even in cases where the loss or damage was completely accidental. The practical solution is to make it clear to the customer – either orally or in your written terms of business – that you have the right to sub-contract.

Even if sub-contracting is lawful, the customer can still look to you to carry out the terms of the contract. If, for example, you agreed to carry out the work with reasonable care the customer can hold you legally liable if that promise is not carried out; the mere fact that you were let down by your sub-contractors is irrelevant. If the sub-contractors fail to take reasonable care, you will be in exactly the same legal position as if you yourself had failed to take reasonable care.

Finally, if you have to pay compensation to the customer because of the sub-contractors' poor workmanship, you will have a legal right to claim that money from the sub-contractors, although this may well be worthless if they have gone out of business or if the claim is so big that they can't pay it. If, however, they have insured against their legal liability then you may very well have a claim under their insurance policy.

62 | *I'm about to start a company supplying expensive computer hardware to businesses. What happens if one of my customers goes out of business before he's paid for the goods I supply?*

By and large, ordinary trade creditors such as yourself get a very raw deal. Apart from insurance and adequate credit control systems, there are only two safeguards that you can take. First of all, if you are supplying goods to a limited company you can tell the company that you will supply the hardware only if one of the directors signs a personal guarantee. This is dealt with in Q13 in relation to guarantees to landlords and the bank, but there is no reason why other creditors should not insist on a personal guarantee to cut down some of the risks of dealing with a limited company.

Second, your conditions of trading may contain a 'retention of title' clause which says that the ownership of the goods will remain yours until the price is paid. The condition can also give you a right to enter the premises of your customer in order to recover your goods if the customer defaults.

63 | *My retaining ownership of the equipment I sell my customers until they've paid me sounds very useful. Are there any snags?*

First, to invoke a retention of title clause (see Q62) you must be able to identify the goods. If, for example, a customer has bought timber from lots of different suppliers, including some from you, you may have difficulty in pointing to a particular consignment and saying 'That one is mine'. Even if all the timber has been supplied by you, it is almost certain that some of it will have been paid for and it may well be very difficult for you to point to any particular consignment and say 'This is the timber I supplied last week and which has not yet been paid for'. Second, your right to recover the goods will not be available if they have been incorporated into some other product (as, for example, furniture). In one case a supplier of resin found that it had been used for the manufacture of chipboard; the Court of Appeal held that the resin had lost its separate identity and therefore the supplier's rights in respect of the resin had disappeared even though he had not been paid for it. Third, the right of the supplier to recover his goods will be lost if the supply is something (as, for example, central heating) which becomes fixed to land. Fourth, the right of recovery is lost if the goods have been sold and delivered to somebody else.

A situation that sometimes happens is that a customer owes a supplier money on a general balance of account but the only goods the supplier can find are goods that have actually been paid for. The supplier may try to cover this by using a very wide clause in the contract, such as: 'The ownership of the goods supplied under this agreement shall remain with the seller until all sums owing by the buyer to the seller shall have been paid.' As a result of a recent case it seems clear that such a clause is legally valid.

64 | What are my legal rights if my customers don't pay on time?

You can protect yourself in a number of different ways, and these should be spelt out in your printed conditions of trading. You must take reasonable steps to bring these conditions of trading to the notice of your customers before they agree to buy your goods. The best way to do this is to have them printed on the back of your quotation form and to have some suitable words on the front of the quotation form such as 'For conditions see back'.

First of all you can have a retention of title clause (see Q62) linked to a right to repossess those goods if the buyer defaults in payment. Second, your conditions can give you the right to bring the contract to an end if the buyer defaults; if, for example, you agree to supply goods to the customer by instalments, such a clause may release you from any duty of making any further supplies. Third, you can provide that all work-in-progress on other contracts for that customer shall be ended or suspended if the customer defaults. Fourth, you can include a clause that the price will be payable by specified instalments but add a clause that the entire balance shall become due if, for example, the customer fails to pay an instalment on the agreed date. Finally, you can provide that any sum in arrears shall carry interest at a specified rate. The only problem here is that such a clause must be linked to the loss that you yourself are likely to suffer in the event of late payment by your customer. Thus, for example, if the extra interest payable by the customer is far higher than any interest that you are likely to have to pay to your own bank, the courts would not allow you to recover that sum from the defaulting customer.

These are the standard default provisions. In practice, of course, most traders provide a carrot as well as a stick by giving a price discount if payment is made within a specified time.

65 | I have a small printing business and, apart

from my other employees, I've taken on two salesmen. Is there anything I should bring to their attention, as they'll obviously be representing the company in their dealings with potential clients?

You should make sure that the salesmen understand your conditions of business and why they are important. The salesmen should make sure that the conditions are brought to the customers' notice before any orders are accepted. You should explain to them that it is legally possible for a contract to be made face-to-face or over the telephone and that your conditions of business will not be of any help to you if the contract was made by customers before they knew anything about the conditions. You should therefore make sure that the salesmen refer to the conditions in some way when they get an enquiry over the telephone or when they negotiate with a prospective customer whether at your premises, at the customers' premises or elsewhere.

You must also try to restrain the salesforce from trying to clinch a deal by making rash promises. A promise as to delivery or performance or as to the time for payment could easily override a clause in

..... AND SHE'LL CRUISE ALL DAY AT 75 M.P.H. ON 60 M.P.G.

your conditions of business. If the promise is not kept, the customer may be able to cancel the contract and claim damages from you; such damages can be very high indeed. You should also tell the salesmen not to agree to any variation of the standard terms without referring the matter to a director or manager. Finally, you should underline the seriousness of the matters by telling the salesforce that a breach of these rules is a disciplinary offence which can lead to dismissal.

Employees

66 | Do I have to pay my employees if they are ill?

There are two separate aspects to this question,

namely your duty to pay wages during illness and your duty to pay statutory sick pay (SSP).

Dealing first with wages, you are legally bound to pay wages during illness only if it is a term of the contract of employment that wages are payable. The matter is often covered by an expressed term in the contract – full pay for three months' sick leave or half pay for three months, and so on. The contract may also state that wages during illness (usually called sick pay) are conditional on the employee's being examined by the employers' doctor, and there may also be a clause giving the employers a right to dismiss the employee if the illness continues beyond a certain time. Such a clause does not necessarily stop a dismissed employee bringing an unfair dismissal claim, but it will be taken into account by an Industrial Tribunal in deciding whether the dismissal was fair.

If the contract specifies nothing your legal duty to pay sick pay will depend on what terms a court would imply into the contract. The court would consider such matters as the nature of the job, past practice, and the custom of the trade. If, for example, you can show that in practice your employees have never claimed wages while off sick, this can be strong evidence that wages are not payable. On the other hand, in one recent case the Employment Appeal Tribunal heard evidence of a national working rule agreement in the building trade and decided that an employee was entitled to sick pay for a reasonable period.

Statutory sick pay is a state benefit payable by employers to their sick employees. It doesn't cost employers a great deal, because when they have paid the benefit they can recover it in full by deducting it from the Class 1 National Insurance contributions they make to the government at the end of each month; if these are insufficient they can deduct it from their PAYE liabilities. The only snag is that employers have to pay the National Insurance contribution which is payable on the SSP itself.

67 | Do I have to pay both wages and the statutory sick pay to staff who are ill?

There are four possible permutations:

- you may have to pay wages but no SSP. This will be so where the employee's contract of employment gives him or her a right to sick pay but his or her right to SSP has been used up or he or she is an employee to whom SSP does not apply (see Q68);
- you may have to pay SSP but no wages. This will be so if no sick pay is payable under the employee's contract of employment but the employee qualifies for SSP;

- you may have to pay both wages and SSP in a case where sick pay is payable under the contract and the employee qualifies for SSP. In that situation you can set SSP against the wages. If, for example, the wages are £60 a week and SSP is £32.85 per week, you pay the full amount of SSP (recoverable as described in Q66) and then pay only a further £27.15 as the balance of wages due;
- you may have to pay neither wages nor SSP. This will be so where the employee is not entitled to sick pay under his or her contract of employment and he or she is not covered by the SSP rules or has used up his or her entitlement (see Q68).

68 | Do all employees receive statutory sick pay when they are absent from work as the result of illness?

In general, SSP is payable to all employees whether full time or part time and regardless of how long they have been employed. However, there are ten special cases when no SSP is payable, and these are as follows:

- if the employee is employed under a fixed-term contract of less than three months;
- if the employee's average weekly earnings are below the National Insurance minimum (at present £39);
- if the employee is taken ill in a country outside the EEC – whether he or she is visiting that country on holiday or on business or for some other purpose;
- if the employee is in prison or police custody;
- if a female employee is within the pregnancy disqualification period. This begins with the week beginning 11 weeks before the expected date of confinement and ends 18 weeks later. Statutory maternity pay, but not SSP, can be claimed by the employee during this period;
- if the employee is taking part in, or has a direct interest in, a stoppage of work at his or her place of employment;
- if the employee has reached the age of 65 (man) or 60 (woman) unless he or she was receiving benefit immediately before that time;
- if the employee has used up his or her SSP rights. The maximum payable by one employer to one employee is 28 times the weekly rate during a single spell of sickness;
- if the employee has done no work under his contract – by signing a contract to start a new job and falling ill before he starts, for example;
- if the employee has received certain other state benefits, such as invalidity pension, during the

previous 57 days. These state benefits include state sickness benefit, a benefit payable by the DHSS to a sick employee if he or she is not covered by the SSP scheme or has used up his or her SSP rights *and* if a sufficient number of National Insurance contributions have been paid.

69 | *I'm the managing director of a small company. What alternatives are open to me about paying my staff when they can't work due to illness? I'd like to add a clause to their contracts of employment.*

A common situation is for employers to agree that the employees will be entitled only to the difference between their wages and any state sickness benefit (see Q68) which may be due to them. This can be highly relevant in those cases where SSP is not available or where it has been used up. You could also agree that the employees are entitled to full wages for three months, half wages for the next three months, and so on. They will then be entitled to claim both their wages and sickness benefit and the sickness benefit will not affect you in any way.

Finally, if you have agreed nothing at all a court or Tribunal would have to decide what terms are to be implied into the contract. It seems from a recent case in the Court of Appeal that the courts or Tribunals will now be quite prepared to find a term that the only sum payable to an employee is a sum sufficient to bring his state sickness benefit up to his wages. This seems fair enough; after all, state sickness benefit is designed to protect an employee who loses income through illness and it should not be a bonus for an employee who does not lose any income.

70 | *What are my legal duties relating to the health and safety of my employees?*

Under the general law you must take reasonable care for the safety of each employee; this means that you must provide proper and safe plant, premises and machinery, competent fellow employees, a safe system of work, and adequate supervision and instruction. If you break this duty an employee who is injured by your breach may sue you. You are also under a legal duty to insure against such liability.

Accident prevention is one of the main features of the Health and Safety at Work etc. Act 1974, by far the most important Act in this field. There are a number of other important Acts, such as the Factories Act 1961 and the Offices, Shops and Railway Premises Act 1963, but these are gradually being replaced by the 1974 Act. The main provisions of this Act can be summarised as follows:

● It lays down broad general duties which apply to all workplaces. These duties are filled out by Regulations, Codes of Practice and Guidance Notes.
● It imposes criminal liability for employers' breach of the duties set out in the Regulations, and in most cases injured employees will also have a civil claim against the employers for damages.
● It set up the Health and Safety Commission to promote health and safety standards and the Health and Safety Executive to enforce them.
● It provides for unions to appoint employees as safety representatives (see Q72) and it gives those representatives a major role in promoting high health and safety standards.

71 | *Do I have to provide first aid facilities for my staff?*

Yes, you must, and you must also inform your staff about the arrangements that you have made. The Health and Safety at Work etc. Act 1974, as well as a number of earlier Acts, make health and safety very important aspects of the duties that employers owe to their employees. The Act allows Regulations to be made to fill out the detail, and in 1981 the government made a set of Regulations dealing with first aid. These Regulations themselves are backed up by a Code of Practice which has been drawn up by a government-appointed body called the Health and Safety Commission. The provisions of that Code are not law, but they can be taken into account by a court if a case is brought against you for not carrying out your legal duties regarding health and safety.

The Regulations say that you must provide:

- such equipment and facilities as are adequate and appropriate for enabling first aid to be rendered to employees who are injured or become ill at work, and
- such number of suitably trained persons as is adequate in the circumstances for the provision of such first aid.

The duty to appoint a qualified first aider will not apply in every case; if you have only a small business with a low health and safety hazard it will be sufficient for you to appoint someone to be responsible for first aid even though he or she has not had the necessary training. The Code of Practice recommends that a qualified first aider should be necessary only if you have more than 150 employees in a low-risk business or more than 50 in a higher-risk business (as for example factories, dockyards and farms).

72 | *One of my employees has sent me a memo to say that he is a safety representative. What does he do and how does it affect my position?*

A safety representative is an employee appointed by an 'independent' trade union which is recognised by the employers for the purposes of collective bargaining about terms of employment. An independent union is one *not* controlled by the employers; for example, the employers' own staff association would not be an independent trade union. In some but not in all cases, the union appoints a shop steward as a safety representative.

A safety representative has a number of rights and functions under the Health and Safety at Work etc. Act 1974 but no duties that can be legally enforced by you against him. Thus:

- You will have to consult him with regard to the making and maintenance of arrangements to bring about effective co-operation between the employees and yourself on health and safety matters.
- He can investigate any health and safety complaints made by any employee that he represents.
- He can make representations to you about such complaints or about health and safety generally.
- He can investigate potential hazards whether he has been asked to do so or not.
- He is entitled to disclosure from you of information which is necessary to enable him to perform his duties – accident reports, for example, or technical information about machinery which is relevant in assessing health and safety risks and future changes affecting health and safety matters. You need not,

however, disclose information which would (for reasons other than health and safety) cause substantial injury to your business. Also, you do not have to disclose information which is 'privileged' from disclosure – where you have obtained an expert's report to prepare your defence against a legal claim brought by an injured employee, for example.

- He is entitled to paid time off to carry out his health and safety duties or to undergo suitable training for that purpose.

73 | *What penalties will I suffer if I don't carry out my duties regarding health and safety?*

If you fail to carry out these duties, an employee who is injured by a breach of one of your duties may be able to sue you. In order to succeed in such a claim the employee must prove that:

- he belongs to a class of person for whose protection the Regulations (see Q71) were made,
- he suffered the kind of damage that the Regulations were passed to prevent,
- you were in breach of your duty, and
- that breach caused or materially contributed to the injury which the employee sustained.

You may also find yourself criminally liable, with a criminal prosecution in a magistrates' court and a fine not exceeding £1,000. However, this is unlikely to happen straight away because the inspectors who are appointed under the relevant legislation will try to get you to carry out your obligations by advice and persuasion rather than compulsion. A prosecution is generally brought only in cases of persistent default where persuasion has failed to produce the desired results. Alternatively, you may receive what the Act calls an Improvement Notice requiring you to remedy the defect within a specified period of time.

Very few of the Regulations carry a sanction of imprisonment for any breach of them – although you could be sent to prison if you didn't pay the fine.

74 | *My manager has a lot of influence over our customers and I've heard rumours that he is going to leave and set up business in competition. Can I stop him from doing so?*

The question of what an ex-employee can or cannot do after leaving his or her employment depends to a large extent on what his or her contract says. Contracts may contain a clause which states that an employee will not, after leaving the employment, carry on, or work for, a similar business. Such a clause is legally enforceable only if it is reasonable in the interests of the employer, the employee and the public. If, for example, the customers of an employment agency or of a transport company or of a security business always deal with the manager, a clause which protects the employers against loss of those customers to the manager may be legally valid – provided that it goes no further than is necessary. Such a 'restraint clause' (which should always be drafted by a solicitor) is invariably limited in time (for example, 'one year') and in space (for example, 'five miles'). Sometimes the clause merely stops the employee dealing with or approaching any person, firm or company who was a customer during the year preceding the end of his or her employment.

If there is no such restraint, then the employee can compete freely. The only restriction is that he or she must not use any confidential information. The former employee must not, for example, use for his or her own benefit any secret processes of the ex-employers, nor can he or she take away a list of the employers' customers. But there is nothing to stop the employee from making a mental list of customers and then approaching those whom he or she remembers. In a recent case an ex-employee of a company that sold frozen chickens knew that certain customers had special terms of business; he was therefore in a very favourable position to offer more attractive terms to those customers. His employers tried to stop him from using that knowledge, but they lost. It is a very grey area and, in the absence of a restraint clause, employers have very little protection. See also YOU AND YOUR JOB, QS 13 and 14.

75 | *I'm a director of a small engineering company. Do I have all the rights of an employee?*

The answer depends on whether you are what is known as an executive or a non-executive director. If you are non-executive, which means that you attend board meetings and collect your fees and expenses but take no part in the day-to-day running of the company, the answer is no. If you fall out with your fellow directors, the Articles of Association of the company (see page 322) may give them the right to vote you off the board. There is also a legal right for shareholders to remove a director by a majority vote at a shareholders' meeting. Certain formalities have to be followed, but in the end the majority of the shareholders will always get its way.

If you are an executive director, which means that you are a working director, the position is different because legally you will be wearing two hats – you will be both a director and an employee. In that case

you will enjoy all the various employment protection rights and many social security rights as well. The employment protection rights include such matters as a right to redundancy payment, the right not to be wrongfully or unfairly dismissed, the right to a minimum period of notice, the right to time off for public duties, and the right to treat eight weeks' arrears of pay (with a maximum of £800) as a preferential debt if the company goes bust.

There may be exceptional cases where even a working director is not an employee. This may be so if, for example, you are the controlling shareholder of the company or if the company is a partnership between yourself and one or more other shareholders.

76 | *I'm thinking of buying a hotel from the proprietor, who wants to retire. Do I have to take on all the employees?*

In 1981 the government brought in some Regulations based on an EEC directive to protect the rights of employees when the ownership of the business for which they are working is transferred. The effect of the Regulations is that all employees who are employed by the vendor immediately before the sale are automatically transferred with the business to the purchaser. Thus, in buying the business you 'buy' the employees as well. This can be a most important and expensive matter which you must bear in mind in your negotiations with the vendor.

The Regulations go further. The employees' contracts of employment will still be in force, and any claims that they may have against the vendor for unpaid wages, sick pay, compensation for injuries, and so on, can be enforced against you. There can also be problems of integration of these employees with your own staff, if any. The vendor's employees may, for example, earn more money than your employees, or may have better fringe benefits. If you alter the employees' terms of employment they may be able to resign and claim that you have unfairly dismissed them.

All this applies only to employees who were employed by the vendor *immediately* before the transfer, and the vendor can, of course, dismiss the employees before the sale takes place. In one recent case, employees were dismissed by the vendor's receiver just an hour before the business was sold, and the Court of Appeal held that the purchaser incurred no obligations in respect of them because they were not employed by the vendor 'immediately' before the transfer. Such employees may, of course, have a claim against the vendor for unfair dismissal and/or a redundancy payment. As regards unfair dismissal, the Regulations provide that it is automatically unfair unless it is due to an organisational, technical or economic reason involving changes in the workforce (in which case it may be fair if the employer acts reasonably.) Accordingly you can choose which employees you want to take and then insist that the vendor dismisses those whom you do not want before the sale takes place. It may well be, of course, that the vendor will insert a clause into the sale agreement requiring you to indemnify him against any legal liability which he may incur as a result of such dismissals.

TAKE A MEMO, MISS PICKLES. YOU'RE FIRED.

77 | Do I have to give an employee a written warning of any misconduct before I can dismiss him?

No, there is no such rule, and your only legal duty is to act reasonably towards any particular employee if you are considering dismissing him. The degree of formality may be much greater in the case of a large public company or corporation than in a small business, but the underlying principles are the same.

ACAS has issued a Code of Practice relating to disciplinary matters; you can obtain a copy of the Code by writing to the address given on page 509. As a matter of good industrial relations and common sense, you should observe the following rules regarding disciplinary measures and dismissal:

● Make sure that every employee knows the disciplinary rules and procedures.
● Try to get the disciplinary rules agreed with representatives of the employees like union officials.
● If an employee's work is not satisfactory try to locate the cause, provide training if this is appropriate and give the employee a sufficient opportunity to improve before you dismiss him or her.

● You should not dismiss an employee for a first offence unless it is an extremely serious matter. You should give an oral warning, followed by a final written warning and then proceed with dismissal.
● Before you give a warning, or before you dismiss the employee, you should discuss the matter with the employee and hear what he or she has to say. It must be a genuine hearing and not merely a formality in a case where your mind is already made up.
● When considering whether dismissal is appropriate you must look at each case on its merits and in particular the seriousness of the matter, the needs of the business and the employee's length of service and previous record.
● You must be seen to act fairly between different employees. If, for example, several employees are guilty of an identical act of misconduct and only one is dimissed, that dismissal may very well be unfair.

78 | I'm the owner of a small company and I've been told I can't sack anyone these days without the employee taking me to an Industrial Tribunal? Is this correct?

Most definitely not. The Employment Protection (Consolidation) Act 1978 does give employees the right not to be *unfairly* dismissed, but there are many employees who do not have this right. By far the most important excluded group relates to employees who have been with you for only a short time. An employee will qualify for an unfair dismissal claim only if he has been continuously employed by the same employer for two years or more. Secondly, the unfair dismissal rules do not protect people who work for you for less than 16 hours per week (although when they have been working for you for five years this period is cut down to eight hours for both past and future periods of employment). Thirdly, you will have no unfair dismissal problems if you dismiss someone who has attained the normal retirement age for his or her job (being the same age for men and women) or, if there is no such age, who has attained the age of 65. Formerly, there were different rules for men and women, but these were abolished for dismissals on or after 7 November 1987 by the Sex Discrimination Act 1986.

Even employees who have the legal right not to be unfairly dismissed can be fairly sacked if you can show that you had a good reason for doing so. Reasons for dismissal include a poor attendance record, bad work, dishonesty or redundancy, and in these cases the dismissal will be fair if you acted reasonably (see Q79).

79 | *A former employee has threatened to take me to an Industrial Tribunal claiming that he was unfairly dismissed. Should I fight the case or should I just pay him some money to avoid any bother?*

This question is often asked by employers and it can only be answered by considering four matters:

● What are your prospects of winning the case?
● What would it cost you if you win?
● What would it cost you if you lose?
● Are there any sound commercial reasons for fighting the case?

The employee must prove that he or she is covered by the unfair dismissal rules (see Q78) and that he or she has been dismissed. It is then up to you to show grounds for dismissal, such as a poor attendance record, bad work, dishonesty, redundancy, or the need to re-organise your business. Once you have done this, the Tribunal will have to decide whether, in all the circumstances, you acted reasonably in treating those grounds as sufficient for dismissal. If you can prove the grounds and if you can also show that you went about it the right way (and this means in particular that you gave the employee warnings and a chance to improve) then you should win.

This is the strict legal position. From a commercial point of view you must face the fact that Industrial Tribunal cases are expensive not only in legal costs (if you decide to use a solicitor) but, more important, in terms of management time. In practice, therefore, many employers will settle a case rather than fight it even if their case is a good one. They are unlikely to get an order for costs against the employee even if they win. The powers of the Tribunal to award costs are very limited and can be exercised only if the employee has acted vexatiously, frivolously or unreasonably. Even in these cases, the actual amount of costs which the Tribunal orders to be paid to the employers is usually very small – far less than the true cost to the employers of fighting the case.

Quite apart from these costs, there is always the possibility that the case might be decided against you – in which case the payment to the employee of compensation must also be considered.

These factors (and particularly business disruption and irrecoverable costs) often lead employers to the conclusion that it is commercially more sensible to settle a claim rather than to fight it. There may of course be cases where your attitude will be closely watched by the other employees, and in these cases there may be overriding commercial considerations requiring the case to be fought.

80 | *I've received a letter from solicitors acting for one of my senior employees whom I recently dismissed. They say that they are going to claim compensation for wrongful and unfair dismissal. What is the difference between these claims?*

A claim for wrongful dismissal can be brought only if the employee can prove that you have broken his or her contract of employment by dismissing him or her before the expiry of the term of employment or without giving the notice period that was legally due. The first of these cases could apply if, for example, the employee had a contract of employment lasting for three years and you dismissed him or her before the three-year term had expired. An example of the second case would be where the employee's contract specified a six-month notice period and you dismissed the employee without giving that notice. In either of these cases the dismissal would not be wrongful if the employee had committed a serious breach of his or her own duties – for example, by accepting bribes or by completing false expenses sheets.

Claims for wrongful dismissal go to the High Court or to a county court; the employee can get Legal Aid.

On the other hand, unfair dismissal is any dismissal which is found to be unfair under the rules laid down in the Employment Protection (Consolidation) Act 1978. Claims go to an Industrial Tribunal and Legal Aid is not available. The legal rules of unfair dismissal are not based on the idea that the employers have broken the contract of employment. If, for example, the employee is entitled under the contract to six months' notice, the dismissal can still be unfair (even though not wrongful) where the full six months' notice was given.

There is considerable overlap between wrongful and unfair dismissal, and a dismissal may be wrongful only, unfair only, both, or neither. In a case decided some years ago, a female employee used to antagonise her colleagues by boasting about her sexual exploits and adventures. The complaints by her colleagues led to her dismissal without notice and she went to an Industrial Tribunal with an unfair dismissal claim. The Employment Appeal Tribunal decided that her dismissal was fair even though the employers were in breach of contract in not giving her the two weeks' notice to which she was entitled under her contract. In other words, she had a claim for wrongful dismissal. The Tribunal had no power to deal with this matter so that, if she wanted her notice money, she would have to start fresh proceedings in the High Court or a county court.

81 | Can I get my employees to agree that they won't take me to the Tribunal at all?

The unfair dismissal rules are designed to give employees security of employment, certainly far more security than was previously the case. The starting-point is that every employee who is covered by the rules (see Q78) has the right not to be unfairly dismissed. This valuable rule would of course be greatly weakened if it were possible for the employee to agree in every case that he or she would not bring a Tribunal claim; the individual employee is in a much weaker bargaining position than employers, and if the employers insisted on such a clause the employee would usually have no choice but to agree. Accordingly, the general rule is that an agreement by an employee not to bring an unfair dismissal claim has no legal effect; in legal terms it is 'void'.

Looked at from the employers' side, unfair dismissal proceedings can be expensive and time consuming even if their case is a good one (see Q79). To avoid being taken to an Industrial Tribunal there are two things that employers can do. First of all, they may consider taking on staff for a fixed period of time – one year, two years, or whatever. If that term runs out and is not renewed, this will be a dismissal but, if the term is for at least one year, the employee can agree in writing that the expiry of the term will not give rise to a claim for unfair dismissal (there is a similar rule relating to redundancy payments in which the period is two years). Second, employers can do a deal with an individual employee at the time of the dismissal (or resignation). They can offer to pay him or her a sum of money in full and final settlement of any claims that he or she may have against the employers (including unfair dismissal). If the employee agrees to the offer, it will become legally binding – but only if it is done through an ACAS conciliation officer. The ACAS conciliation officers are attached to the Department of Employment and their task is to promote settlements. The vast majority of settlements are achieved after proceedings have started, but conciliation officers can also become involved at an earlier stage so as to prevent proceedings being started at all. They will usually make sure that the employers and the employee understand the legal consequences of their agreement, but they will not consider (and indeed they must not consider) whether the agreement that the employers and the employee may have reached is a fair one.

Licences, planning, regulations and insurance

82 | Someone mentioned that I might need a licence to start my business. Is this true?

Not every businessman needs a licence, but there are rules governing particular types of business. Thus, for example, a licence is required for:

- market traders,
- the sale of alcoholic liquor,
- the use of premises for a casino or for other gambling purposes,
- road hauliers,
- dealers in company stocks and shares,
- a deposit-taking business, where money received by way of deposit is lent to others or where any other activity of the business is financed wholly or to any material extent out of the capital of or interest on money received by way of deposit.

Apart from these special cases (and there are others as well) the Consumer Credit Act 1974 lays down a licensing system for seven different types of business. At present more than 90,000 traders are licensed under the Act, and anyone who wants to start one of these businesses must have a licence (see YOU AS CONSUMER, Q120). The types of business are:

- consumer credit – money lending, the sale of goods on credit terms, hire purchase, etc.,
- consumer hire – the hiring out of television sets, computers or business machinery, for instance,
- credit brokerage – introducing customers to people who will lend them money,
- debt collection,
- debt adjusting,
- debt counselling, that is, advice,
- credit reference agencies.

It is important to understand that the word 'consumer' is misleading; the licence rules will apply to you even where you do business only with other businesses – although they will not apply if you deal only with companies.

83 | I want to start a business hiring out office equipment. How do I set about getting a licence?

In your case you will need a Class B licence (Consumer Hire) unless you do business only with companies, in which case no licence is required (see Q82. You must get forms cc1/75 and cc2/75 from the Consumer Credit Licensing Branch of the Office of Fair Trading (address on page 511) or from your local

Trading Standards Department (the address is in the telephone directory as a department of your local authority). The licence should be applied for in your name, or in the firm's name if your business is run as a partnership. If you run your business as a company, it is the company that needs the licence. The fee for a Class B licence is currently £45; it normally remains in force for 10 years.

In deciding whether to grant you a licence, the Office of Fair Trading will have to consider whether you are fit to have one. For instance, if you or one of your employees, agents or associates has practised sex or race discrimination or has been guilty of undesirable business practices (even though they may not be unlawful) a licence can be refused. You will be allowed to make representations if there is a possibility of such a refusal and you can appeal against refusal to the Secretary of State.

If you need any further information about business licences, the Office of Fair Trading has a large number of pamphlets that explain the procedures.

84 | I'm in the television rental business and have a Consumer Hire licence. Can my licence be taken away?

Yes. The Office of Fair Trading can at any time revoke your licence if you or one of your employees, agents or business associates are guilty of conduct making you unfit to hold a licence (see Q83). However, the licence will not be revoked immediately. The Office of Fair Trading will send you a notice which states that it is considering revoking the licence and which asks for your comments. You can then make both written and oral representations; once again, you have a right of appeal. This ability to revoke licences (and thereby driving unsatisfactory traders out of business) is a very powerful weapon in the hands of the Office of Fair Trading for keeping up and improving business standards.

85 | I've just seen some business premises at an ideal site but I'll have to make substantial alterations. Will I need planning permission?

Planning permission is required for building, engineering, mining or other operations in, over or under land. Works of maintenance, improvement or alteration are exempt from this rule if they:

● do not materially affect the exterior, or
● do not alter the building by providing additional space below the ground.

You should discuss the matter with an architect or surveyor. He will tell you whether your plans go beyond alteration and amount to 'rebuilding', because in that case planning permission will be required. He will also advise you about the need to comply with Building Regulations on such matters as fire precautions, stairways, toilets, sewers and drains.

You will also need planning permission if the use to which you want to put the premises differs materially from their existing use. However, there is a government Order called the Use Classes Order (and this is changed from time to time). If the old use and the new use are in the same Use Class, then the change does not need planning permission. For example, you will not normally need planning permission if you change from one type of shop to another. Then again, the use of premises for either offices or research and development of products or indeed for any industrial process which can be carried out in a residential area without detriment to the area by reason of noise, vibration, smell, fumes and the like is permitted without planning permission.

Finally, permission for a main use will cover other uses that are incidental to it. Thus, the running of a café or snack bar is incidental to hotel use so that no separate planning permission is required. On the other hand, the installation of petrol pumps is not incidental to a car repair business and will therefore need planning permission.

86 | How do I get planning permission?

You or your surveyor or architect should get the appropriate forms from the planning department of your local authority. Once completed, you should lodge them with the local authority together with the building or alteration plans as drawn up by your architect or surveyor. The planning officer will make a recommendation to the appropriate committee of the council, which will decide whether or not to approve the application. The authority will then notify you of its decision.

If you are dissatisfied with any refusal to allow you planning permission, you can lodge an appeal within one month and an inspector appointed by the Department of the Environment will decide the matter either in correspondence or at a local public inquiry. His decision is final (although you may be able to appeal to the High Court on a point of law).

There may be cases where you merely want a planning decision in principle. An obvious example is when you want to buy a piece of land if, and only if, you can get permission to build on it. In that case you can lodge an application for what is called 'outline' planning permission before you buy the land, and you must notify the owner of the land that you have made the application. The local authority will usually notify neighbouring owners of pending outline planning applications together with the address of the place at which the building plans can be inspected and the person to whom and the date by which any objection should be sent. The application will be considered by the Development Control Committee of the local council. The Committee can refuse or grant the application or grant it subject to conditions such as the time within which the work must be completed or even the size of the name board to be erected outside the premises.

87 | I've just taken on the lease of a shop. I don't need planning permission because I don't propose making any alterations. Is there anything else that I have to do?

Yes. The first thing to do is to register with your local authority. Ask for registration form OSR 1 (O, office; S, shop; R, railway premises). The form is free.

You will also need a fire certificate from your local fire authority (this is usually the County Council or the County District Council). Such a certificate will be required if you have more than 20 people employed at any one time, or if more than 10 persons are employed at any time elsewhere than on the ground floor. Ask your local fire authority for form FP 1(REV); the authority will inspect the premises and may require changes to be made before it gives you a certificate.

Apart from this, you must comply with numerous statutory obligations on such matters as cleanliness, temperature, overcrowding, safety, and notification of accidents. To get more detail contact your local branch of the Health and Safety Executive Information and Advisory Services, which will provide the appropriate literature; your local Chamber of Commerce will tell you how to contact the Services. The object of these provisions is to protect employees. They will not apply where there are no employees, or the only employees are the immediate relatives of the owner, or no employees work on the premises for more than 21 hours per week.

88 | Are there any rules about how long I can keep my shop open?

Yes. You have to consider the detailed provisions of the Shops Act 1950. Subject to numerous exceptions, including the sale of meals and car accessories, the Act seeks to protect employees by controlling closing hours. The general rule is that a shop must not serve new customers after 8pm but that it can have one particular day of the week as a 'late day' on which new customers can be served until 9pm. In the case of a shop selling tobacco, sweets, chocolates, ice-cream or confectionery, the above rules are relaxed and in these cases customers can be served until 9.30pm on a normal day and until 10pm on a late day.

Second, the shop must close for the serving of customers not later than 1pm on one day in every week. However, it is possible for your local authority to make a 'six-day trading order' in which case early closing will not apply; get in touch to find out if an order has been made.

Finally, there is a general ban on Sunday trading, but once again there are numerous exceptions including newsagents, greengrocers and sweetshops. The legal consequences of Sunday trading will depend largely on the attitude of the local authority which is responsible for bringing prosecutions.

89 | What sort of insurance do I need for my business?

As an employer you must take out insurance against your legal liability to your employees (see Q70). You will commit a criminal offence if you don't do this. Second, if a motor vehicle is used on a road for the purposes of the business, you will have to insure against the legal liability of the business for causing death or bodily injury to a third party. There is no difference here between a businessman and other motorists, but the premium for business use will almost certainly be higher than a premium for private use. You must of course tell your broker or the insurance company that the vehicle is required for business purposes. Incidentally, the policy has only to cover the 'user' of the vehicle (that is, yourself) and it need not cover the driver, although it will often do so.

Apart from these cases of compulsory insurance, many other types of insurance must be considered. They include loss or damage to stock and premises (especially in cases of fire and theft), legal liability if goods supplied to your customers prove defective, fidelity insurance against dishonest employees, and insurance against bad debts. You should in all cases read the small print carefully, and it may also be worth while taking advice from an insurance broker or from your solicitors. For example, if you are insured against the legal liability for claims brought by customers, your solicitor will want to see how this policy ties up with the conditions of trading which you supply to your customers (see QS 59 and 64). You may also find that a fire policy on your premises will be limited to the cost of reinstatement and will not cover your loss of profits while the building is out of use. An additional premium to cover this can usually be arranged. The important thing to do is to make the necessary arrangements in good time.

The premiums, despite being tax deductible, will make quite a dent in your cash flow – but a saving on insurance would be a false economy in the long term.

Relationship with landlords

90 | *I want to carry out a lot of building work to my workshop. Can I get my landlord to pay me for it?*

The Landlord and Tenant Act 1927 has some rules that may help you here, but you have to follow very carefully the procedure and the time-limits laid down. You must start by serving a notice on the landlord giving details of the improvements that you want to make. The landlord can then do one of three things, namely:

● he can offer to do the work himself in return for an increased rent; you can then decide whether or not to accept his offer;
● he can agree to let you do the work;
● he can serve a notice of objection, in which case you will have to take the matter to court to get a certificate that the proposed work is a proper improvement. Such a case is brought in a county court if the rateable value of the premises is £5,000 or less; above that value the case will have to be brought in the High Court unless the parties agree that a county court should deal with it.

If you have followed the procedure correctly you will be entitled to claim compensation from the landlord when you leave the premises at the end of your lease. The compensation will reflect the increase in the value of the premises resulting from the improvements, and if you cannot agree the amount with the landlord you will once again have to go to court (the choice of court is the same as for the certificate proceedings explained above). Once again there are detailed procedures and time-limits which must be strictly followed.

There is one major snag about which you should seek advice from a surveyor or from the solicitor who acted for you when you took the lease. Nearly every business lease has a 'rent review clause'. This gives the landlord the right to adjust the rent (usually upwards!) at specified times during the lease – every five years or every seven years are quite common.

The clause will often state that if you and your landlord cannot agree on the new rent it will be fixed by a surveyor appointed by the President of the Royal Institution of Chartered Surveyors. In fixing the new rent, the surveyor will take into account the sort of rents that are being paid for similar properties and, unless the wording of the lease excludes this, he will also take into account the improvements that you have made. In other words, the value of the premises has been increased by your work and you may well be penalised for it by having to pay higher rent.

91 | *The freeholders of the building in which I have my photographic studio let it to a construction company, and that company has sub-let the ground floor to me. The construction company is now in liquidation. Where does that leave me?*

The freeholders of the building (the 'head landlord') may go to court to bring the construction company's lease to an end. If that happens, your sub-lease will also come to an end. You can, however, ask the court to give you what is called 'relief against forfeiture' on the basis that you should be allowed to stay on. You should see a solicitor about this. If the court thinks that your case is a good one it can order the head landlord to give you a lease for the rest of the term of the lease held by the company in liquidation. You can even ask for a lease of the whole building, although there is no certainty that you will get it. The court will normally order you to pay off the arrears of rent owing to the head landlord – or at least a proportion corresponding to the proportion of the building which you occupy – plus the head landlord's costs.

Another possibility is that the liquidator will 'disclaim' the lease. This means that the company in liquidation will drop out of its responsibilities under the terms of the lease. Once again, you can protect your own position by going to court; the court can make a 'vesting order' giving the head lease to you. You must obviously take legal advice to find out what you can do with the building before you decide to ask for such a vesting order.

If you don't get a vesting order the legal position is rather strange. The disclaimer won't stop you occupying the ground floor for your photographic business and the construction company won't collect your rent! But the head landlord has a right of 'distress' if rent is owing to him. This right of distress is a right to seize *any* goods which he finds on the premises – whether or not they belong to the tenant. There is a real risk that the head landlord may seize *your* goods to satisfy rent owing to him from the construction company, his tenant. These goods can be sold if the arrears are not paid off within five days. You may be able to save your goods if you act quickly enough – but you will have to undertake to pay future rent to the head landlord until the arrears covered by the distress have been paid off. It is a difficult area and you should seek legal advice immediately.

92 | My lease will end in about nine months' time. What happens when that date arrives? Will I just have to pack up and go?

The short answers to your questions are nothing and no. The Landlord and Tenant Act 1954 gives security of tenure to tenants of business premises. The effect of the Act is that your lease will not expire on its normal expiry date; it will just run on until your landlord serves on you a notice of termination. When the landlord serves you with such a notice you may be able to apply to the court for a new lease, or you yourself can serve the landlord with notice requesting a new lease.

The landlord's notice will have in it a date when the lease is to end. That date cannot be earlier than the date on which the lease runs out, and the notice itself cannot be for less than six months. If, therefore, your lease is due to end on 31 December and the landlord's notice is given on only 30 September, the notice cannot give an earlier termination date than 31 March – that is, six months. Two matters are vitally important. In the first place the notice will require you to tell the landlord in writing within two months whether or not you are willing to give up the premises when the lease ends. If you fail to do this, you will lose your right to have the lease renewed. Second, the notice will tell you whether the landlord would oppose the granting of a new lease and, if so, on what grounds.

If you want to take the initiative, you can send the landlord a written request for a new tenancy and this must include your proposals as to the rent and other terms. The landlord can then, within two months, send you a counter-notice stating that he objects to the granting of a new lease.

93 | When the lease runs out on my business premises, will I get a new one?

The first thing to do is to find out whether the landlord is prepared to grant you a new lease; the terms of his notice or counter-notice (see Q92) should make this clear to you. If there is a possibility that there will

be no agreement then you can apply to the court, but only within very strict time-limits: you must apply not less than two nor more than four months from the date of the landlord's notice or counter-notice. You apply to a county court where the rateable value is £5,000 or less or to the High Court in other cases; this choice of court can be varied by an agreement between your landlord and yourself.

If you comply with these rules then you will get a new lease. You will not get a new lease if your landlord proves one or more of the grounds of objection as set out in Section 30 of the Landlord and Tenant Act 1954. The grounds are:

- default in carrying out your repair and maintenance obligations;
- persistent delay in the payment of your rent;
- substantial breaches of obligation or other reasons connected with your use or management of the premises;
- the provision by the landlord of alternative accommodation which is suitable to your needs;
- the fact that your tenancy has been created by sub-letting and the landlord now needs possession in order to deal with the property as a whole as sub-division is uneconomic;
- an intention by the landlord to demolish or reconstruct the premises, or to carry out substantial work of construction, in a case where he cannot reasonably do this without obtaining possession;
- an intention by the landlord to occupy the premises for the purposes of his own business or as his residence. This last ground is not available if he acquired his interest less than five years before the expiry date of your tenancy.

94 | Will the terms of a new lease of my business premises be the same as before?

No, probably not. For a start, the new lease will usually cover only premises previously occupied by you for business purposes; it will not cover any parts which you have sub-let. This can be varied by agreement between the landlord and yourself, and Section 32 of the Landlord and Tenant Act 1954 allows the landlord to insist that the new lease will cover all the premises (including sub-let parts) which were included in the old lease, but it is obviously financially advantageous to the landlord to negotiate a separate lease with the tenant of the sub-leased part.

Then there is the rent. This can of course be fixed by agreement. If it is not fixed in this way, the court will fix it. It will be based on a market rent that is arrived at by looking at the rents of other premises and the terms of the new lease other than the rent. By Section 34 of the Act, certain matters must be disregarded – for example, improvements carried out by you, any goodwill built up by you (or by previous owners of your business), and any deterioration in the premises arising from your failure to repair.

The length of the lease is again a matter for agreement. If you cannot agree, the court will fix a term which cannot be longer than 14 years.

Finally, any other terms will be fixed by the court if they have not been agreed. The starting-point will be the terms of the old lease, and it will be up to the party proposing any changes to show what the reasons are for those changes.

95 | Can I get compensation if I have to leave my business premises when the lease expires?

Apart from compensation for improvements (see Q90), you will be entitled to compensation (unless you have signed away your rights) if the court refuses to grant you a lease on any of the last three points specified in Q93, but not for any other reason. The amount of compensation is normally the annual rateable value of the premises multiplied by a figure which is laid down by Parliament, at present two and a quarter. If the same business has been carried on for a continuous period of 14 years (and that includes previous owners of the business as well as yourself) then the compensation is doubled. The compensation is based on the value of the part of the premises actually used for your business; it would not include the value of any part which you have sub-let.

Relationship with debtors

96 | I run a printing business and some of my customers each owe me between £100 and £600. I'm thinking of taking them to court but I don't know how to go about it. How do I start?

The first thing to do is to write to each debtor what is called a 'letter before action'. The letter should claim the amount due and it should tell the debtor that you will sue him unless he pays within seven days. A formal demand from a solicitor may have a more immediate effect on the debtors than just a letter from you. If this doesn't produce the money then you will have to sue the debtors in the county court. The procedure is straightforward, and you can bring the case yourself without using a solicitor; in fact, the rules of the court actively discourage the use of solicitors in 'small claims' cases. This is because in claims for £500 or less you will not get back your legal costs

from your opponent even if you win the case and would therefore yourself have to pay your solicitor's fee. If, despite this rule, you do decide to use a solicitor, you may well find that the whole of the money which you recover from your debtor will be used up in paying his charges.

The Lord Chancellor's Department has issued a booklet, *Small claims in the county court*, for people who want to run their own cases; copies can be obtained free of charge from the court itself.

The procedure is as follows:

1. You must choose the right court. In debt cases, your own local county court can be used.

2. You then write to the court, or telephone or go along in person, to ask it to send you copies of form N201, 'Request for the issue of a default summons'. You fill in this form and send it to the court together with:

- the particulars of claim – a short statement of your case supported by the unpaid invoice,
- a copy of the particulars of claim for the debtor (or more than one if you are suing more than one debtor for the same debt),
- the court fee – including £5 for service of the summons by the court bailiff if that is what you want (see Q97). The fee itself depends on the amount of the debt; the court will tell you how much the fee is for each of the summonses that you want to issue,
- a stamped addressed envelope if the post is to be used.

It may be possible to prepare a combined document for all the debtors rather than a separate document for each of them.

97 | What happens after I've requested the court to prepare a summons for the payment of the debt?

The court will prepare the summons and will serve it (or attempt to serve it) on the debtor. If you know the debtor's address, you can ask the court to serve the summons by post. The court will then post it first class (there is no need for registered post or recorded delivery) and someone from the court will prepare a certificate of posting which states that the summons was properly addressed, pre-paid and posted. The court will normally accept this as sufficient proof of service. If the envelope is returned marked 'Gone away' you will have to find some other form of service – either by the court bailiff, or through a private firm of process servers, or by asking the court to make what is called an order for 'substituted service'.

If the debtor happens to be a limited company, the summons must be served at the registered office of the company. To do so, you will need to carefully examine the debtor's stationery because the company may well be using a trading name and address different from its registered name and address; the latter may appear in small print at the bottom of the note-

paper. You may also have to make a company search to find the current address of the registered office; a firm of company formation agents can do this for you (see page 322).

The next step will depend on what the debtor does or does not do within 14 days from receiving the summons. There are four main possibilities:

● The debtor does nothing. In this case you can complete and send to the court form N14 which is a form of request for judgment. The court will then enter judgment for the debt and the costs of the summons.

● The debtor may send the court an admission and an offer to pay by stated instalments. If you decide to accept this proposal you can write to the court and it will enter judgment on that basis; if you do not accept it the court will fix a date to hear the case and then, after hearing evidence from you and from the debtor, the court registrar will make an order fixing the time for payment.

● The debtor may offer to pay a smaller sum. You must again decide whether or not to accept this offer. If you refuse it, the registrar will fix a date for a preliminary hearing called a 'pre-trial review'. At that hearing the registrar will see whether or not the matter can be settled by agreement and, if not, he will arrange the full hearing of the case at a later date.

● The debtor may put in a defence – that he never received the goods, for example – or a counterclaim – that the goods were faulty, say. There will then be a pre-trial review and this will lead to a full hearing at a later date, unless the claim is for £500 or more and you can satisfy the registrar by affidavit evidence that the defence is obviously bogus.

A defended claim of £500 or less is heard by the registrar as a small claims arbitrator. The hearing is informal and some of the technical court rules will not apply: in a normal court case there are strict rules about how you can prove your case, and you cannot usually build up your case by describing a conversation you overheard between two other people; in the case of a small claims arbitration, however, the registrar will normally allow each side to tell his own story in his own way.

98 | How does the court enforce its judgment?

It doesn't. Enforcement of the judgment is entirely a matter for you to do. As soon as you have a judgement (see Q97), you can apply to have the debtor attend the court in order that he can be orally examined as to his means; he will then have to produce his books and records so you can see how much money he can repay.

The main ways of enforcing the judgment ('execution') are as follows:

● Sending in the court bailiff to seize the debtor's goods. There may be cases where the mere appearance of the bailiff (especially at the debtor's business premises) can produce some money. In many cases, however, he comes back empty-handed after being told by the debtor that all the goods are on hire-purchase or belong to his wife.

● If the debtor is owed money by a third party – if he has some money at a building society or at his bank, say – it may be possible to get a special form of court order known as 'garnishee'. The legal effect of this is that the bank or building society will pay the money direct to you and not to the debtor.

● If the debtor is an employee it may be possible to get an 'attachment of earnings' order under which a proportion of his wages or salary will be paid by the employer direct to you.

If the debtor owns a house you can ask the court to make a 'charging order' on the house. This is rather like a second mortgage, and it will make it very difficult for the debtor to sell the house without your agreement. If the charging order doesn't produce the money the court can order the house to be sold.

You and your money

Taxes

Income tax

1 | *How is my earned income from my employment taxed?*

You are liable to pay tax on your total income from your employment – salary or wages, overtime, bonuses, tips and holiday pay – and you may also be liable to tax on fringe benefits from your employment, such as a company car (see Q8). You may be allowed to deduct from your income certain expenses incurred in your employment (such as the cost of necessary overalls and protective clothing; see QS 14 and 15) and the balance is the income liable to tax.

You then deduct your personal allowance and other reliefs from this amount, and tax is calculated on the rest. Tax itself will generally be deducted under the Pay as You Earn system (PAYE), which means that your employer takes it from your pay before you receive it.

2 | *Do my employers have to operate a PAYE system? Can't I sort out my tax with the inspector of taxes each year?*

Your employers are required by law to deduct tax under the PAYE system unless your earnings are less than one fifty-second of the single person's annual allowance (£46.63) if you are paid weekly or one twelfth (£202.08) if you are paid monthly. This threshold is reduced to £1 per week or £4 per month if you have other employment or if you refuse to sign the Inland Revenue form P46 which requests details of your other income. If your employers fail to deduct the right amount of tax, they may find that they are liable to pay it themselves.

3 | *How does the PAYE system work?*

Each year you are entitled to a number of reliefs and allowances (see Q25), which effectively means that on part of your income you pay no tax. These allowances are given to you under the PAYE system evenly throughout the year – one twelfth per month if you are paid monthly, or one fifty-second per week if you are paid weekly. The amount is calculated by your employer from the code number given him by the Inland Revenue, and he then uses tax tables to see how much tax you should pay on the balance of your pay.

You can check your tax-free pay quite simply if you know your code number, and if it ends with either 'L'

or 'H' or 'T' (see Q4). First, replace the letter at the end of the code number with the digit 9, so that code 245H, for example, becomes 2459. Then divide this figure by 12 if you are a monthly paid employee or by 52 if you are weekly paid. One twelfth of 2459 is £209.71, and that is the monthly tax-free pay for that code.

To work out your taxable pay, subtract any contributions you make to a pension fund from your monthly or weekly pay, and then deduct your tax-free pay. If you are not liable to the higher rates of tax (see Q9), your tax bill is 27 per cent of your taxable pay and this gives you, within a pound or so, the tax that should be deducted each month or week. However, this formula will not work if your code number has recently been changed or if you are liable to a higher rate of tax.

4 | *What do the letters 'L', 'H' and 'T' mean in my notice of coding?*

'L' is added to your notice of coding if you are entitled to the single person's allowance of £2,425 or to wife's earned income relief. 'H' applies if you are entitled to the married man's relief of £3,795, or to additional personal allowances. 'T' is used in special circumstances – for example, if you are entitled to age allowance, or if you do not want your employer to know what personal allowances you are getting (if, say, you are not legally married, and therefore not entitled to the married man's allowance, but do not want this known by your employer or the people at work who handle your pay).

An 'emergency code' is used where an employee is unable to present a form P45 to his new employer, except in the case of a school-leaver or someone returning to employment after a period of full-time education. This is a temporary code operated on a week-to-week basis (or month-to-month basis if monthly paid), and is always equal to the single person's allowance.

5 | *I have an income from some investments; how does the PAYE system deal with this?*

If the Inland Revenue know that you are getting a small amount of investment income which is not taxed at source, such as rent, it will estimate what that income will be for the tax year, and your personal reliefs set out in your notice of coding will be reduced by an amount equal to it. This has the effect of increasing the tax on your earnings to a level where the total amount paid is sufficient to cover the tax on both your earnings and the investment income. In most cases, although not always, an adjustment is necessary at the end of the year when the exact amount of the income is known.

It may well be better to ask the Revenue to assess you directly on your investment income so that your PAYE position is kept as straightforward as possible and you do not have to pay tax in advance. Although this involves paying any tax due on your investment income direct to the collector of taxes in one lump sum, rather than spreading it throughout the tax year, nevertheless the tax will be paid later than it would have been under PAYE.

6 | *I think my code number is wrong. What should I do?*

Write to the inspector of taxes at the tax office shown on the notice of coding, quoting the reference number shown, and tell him that you think an error has been made, or ask him to explain any matter you do not understand. The tax officer responsible for your tax will deal with any points you raise, and he will, of course, adjust your code number if there has been a mistake or if any estimate made by him initially is subsequently agreed to be excessive.

You have a further check at the end of the tax year when your employer should give you a certificate on form P60, 'statement of pay and tax deducted for the income tax year'. You can do your own calculations from this. If you then think that you have paid too much, you should write to your inspector enclosing form P60 and asking him to issue a formal notice of assessment for the relevant year. He will almost certainly send you a tax return form for completion before he replies to you in detail, as he will need the information it gives. In due course an assessment will be sent to you and a refund made if one is due.

Incidentally, make sure that you keep photocopies of any documents you send to your inspector in case they are lost in the post.

7 | *I am a working married woman. How does this affect my tax position?*

You are given a separate code number from your husband which will take into account your entitlement to wife's earned income relief (see Q25) – this, incidentally, is always the same as the single person's allowance. For methods of paying your tax, see QS 32, 33 and 34.

8 | *What are fringe benefits, and how are they taxed?*

These are benefits that you get from your employment, or as a result of being in your employment, and which are not normally included in your salary cheque. They are often known as 'perks' and they include private use of cars, rent-free or low-rent accommodation, interest-free loans, luncheon vouchers, pension and life assurance benefits, season tickets, cash travel allowances, relocation expenses, subsidised canteens, staff discounts, vouchers and credit tokens, use of holiday accommodation, and membership of private medical insurance schemes.

You are not liable to tax on all these; for example, staff discounts are tax-free for the employee, and how the others are taxed depends on whether you are a 'higher-paid employee'.

9 | *How are 'higher-paid employees' defined?*

Broadly speaking, these are people whose annual remuneration amounts to £8,500 or more. Allowable expenses, except for contributions made to pension schemes, are added to the salary in calculating this figure, so the level of their perks will in itself help determine whether someone is a higher-paid employee or not.

Company directors are treated as higher-paid employees even if their earnings are below £8,500 per annum, unless, together with their relatives, they also own no more than 5 per cent of the shares of the company for which they work. They cannot get round this limit by having several different employments with different associated companies because all employments with associated companies are regarded as one for this purpose.

The employers of higher-paid employees and directors have to make a special tax return for them each year, giving details of their expenses payments, fringe benefits and income. As the form used is called a

PIID, such employees are often referred to as PIID employees.

10 | *As a higher-paid employee, how will I be taxed on my fringe benefits?*

This depends on the type of benefit you get. Luncheon vouchers of up to 15p per working day, meals in staff canteens, and pension scheme contributions, provided the scheme is approved by the Inland Revenue, are not liable to tax. However, you will be taxed on most other benefits, such as private medical insurance, interest-free loans, and rent-free or low-rent accommodation.

You will be taxed for your employer's costs in providing you with private medical insurance as if the premiums are part of your income. However, despite the tax this is often an attractive fringe benefit because your employer can usually obtain much cheaper premiums than you could yourself.

The benefit of any cheap loan made to you by your employer is taxed by taking the interest actually charged and comparing this with what is known as the 'official rate of interest'. This rate is determined by the Government, and is periodically revised. If you pay less than the official rate of interest you will pay tax on the difference, and if the loan is interest-free, you are taxed on the full official rate. But if the difference between the official rate and the actual interest paid is £199 per annum or less, then no tax is levied. Tax on differences of £200 or more is charged as if it were income. When you borrow from your employer and use the proceeds for a purpose where the loan would qualify for tax relief (for example to buy your principal private residence; see Q28) no tax is charged.

If your employer provides free or cheap accommodation, you will pay tax on an amount equal to the rateable value of the property each year or part of the year in which you live there. If your employer rents the property instead of owning it, then you will be assessed on the rent paid by your employer to the landlord if it is greater than the rateable value. Moreover, if your employer meets any of the costs of the upkeep of the property such as rates, redecoration or repairs, these will also be assessed on you as if they were part of your income. The assessed value of the benefit is reduced by the amount of any rent that you pay your employer, and no tax at all is levied if your living there is an essential part of your job, such as a flat provided for you in an office block where you are caretaker. An additional tax bill is levied on higher-paid employees who live in rent-free homes costing more than £75,000.

You are also taxed if your employer provides you with assets such as a television set, stereo equipment and the like. These are assessed on a 'deemed' annual value which is calculated at a rate of 20 per cent of the cost of the asset, or 20 per cent of its market value at the time it is first provided if your employer owned the asset for some time before that. Therefore, if you use the asset for, say, eight years, you will be taxed altogether on 160 per cent of the original cost and it may have been better for your employer simply to have given it to you.

If your employer does give you the asset, you will be assessed on its market value at the time, unless it was already in your possession. In that case you will be taxed on its value when it was first provided, less any amount already assessed on you for its use.

11 | *How is my company car assessed for income tax purposes?*

If you have the free use of a company car you will pay tax on the annual value of the car as registered in the table below. These figures are revised annually, the ones here being for 1988–9 with 1987–8 in parentheses:

Engine capacity	Car under 4 years old	Car over 4 years old
1400 cc or less	£580 (525)	£380 (350)
1401 cc to 2000 cc	£770 (700)	£520 (470)
over 2000 cc	£1,210 (1,100)	£800 (725)

The above amounts are deemed income for tax purposes and are added to your earnings. If your business mileage is less than 2,500 per annum, the amounts are increased by 50 per cent and if your business mileage exceeds 18,000 miles they are reduced by 50 per cent.

If your car costs more than £19,250, a different set of rules applies, as follows:

Market value when registered	Car under 4 years old	Car over 4 years old
(i) 1988–9		
£19,250 to £29,000	£1,595	£1,070
over £29,000	£2,530	£1,685
(ii) 1987–8		
£19,250 to £29,000	£1,450	£970
over £29,000	£2,300	£1,530

If you are also provided with any petrol for your private use – however much or little – you will be taxed in accordance with a fixed scale in addition to the value of the car, as follows (the figures for 1988–9 and 1987–8 are the same):

Engine capacity	Value
1400 cc or less	£480
1401 cc to 2000 cc	£600
over 2000 cc	£900

These figures are reduced by 50 per cent where the business mileage exceeds 18,000 per annum.

As an example, the benefit on a 1600 cc car for 1987–8 which has business mileage in excess of 18,000 and which is less than four years old is assessed as follows:

scale benefit	£700
less 50 per cent reduction	£350
Private petrol benefit	£600
less 50 per cent reduction	£300
Total	£650

A company car is not regarded as a fringe benefit if it is a 'pool' car, in other words it is used regularly by two or more employees, is not normally kept overnight at (or near to) your home, and your private use of it is just incidental to the main reason for your being provided with it.

12 | *My expenses are only things like travel and entertaining where my employer reimburses me in full. As a higher-paid employee do I have to pay tax on them?*

Not necessarily. While all expenses payments received by you will be disclosed to the Inland Revenue by your employer, you can make a claim to show that the expenditure was incurred 'wholly, exclusively and necessarily' in the performance of your duties or, in the case of travelling expenses, incurred 'necessarily' in the performance of your duties.

In practice, many employers negotiate special arrangements (known as 'PIID dispensations') whereby the employer may be able to avoid disclosing items which do not give rise to an income tax liability.

13 | *I earn £5,500 and have been told that I am not a higher-paid employee, so how am I taxed on my fringe benefits?*

You are very much better off when it comes to the taxation of fringe benefits than a higher-paid employee or director. Normally you are only taxed on a benefit if it can be converted into money, or in other words can be sold, in which case you are taxed on the sale value of the benefit. Most of your fringe benefits will therefore not be taxable, including the use of a company car for private purposes, free hairdressing on your employer's premises, private medical insurance, reasonable removal expenses incurred with relocation, contributions to approved pension schemes, use of a staff canteen, luncheon vouchers to the value of 15p per working day, and free social and sports club membership.

The most common benefits on which you will be taxed are assets given to you by your employer, travel vouchers and rent-free or low-rent accommodation.

Tax is charged on assets given to you which become your property and which you will keep if you leave the job, such as a car or clothing. The tax is assessed on their second-hand value immediately after you acquire them, even if they are brand new. This can often be very low.

Travel vouchers are liable to tax as if the cost to your employer was part of your income.

Rent-free or low-rent accommodation is taxed in the same way as if you were a higher-paid employee (see Q10) including the special rules that apply if the original purchase cost to your employer exceeded £75,000.

14 | *Can I claim tax relief against earnings for my fares to and from work?*

No, although you can claim relief for some expenses which are not reimbursed by your employer. You can claim relief for the cost of travelling that is 'necessarily' incurred in the performance of your duties as an employee, and you can claim relief for other expenses provided that they are incurred 'wholly, exclusively and necessarily' in the performance of your duties as an employee.

The cost of travelling to and from your place of employment is not incurred in the performance of your duties as an employee, but in order to put you into a position to carry out your duties, and this is why you get no tax relief for it.

The Inland Revenue has in recent years tightened up on what expenses are deductible, but there is still considerable uncertainty in many areas. However, it can be safely said that, in addition to travel costs to work, you will not get relief for expenditure on studying for and taking examinations, even if you are required to do so by your employer, on entertaining fellow members of staff, on books and magazines that you feel necessary to read to keep you up to date, on ordinary clothing worn to work, or on parking outside your employer's premises, even if the car you use is a company car.

15 | *I sometimes use my own car for business trips and only the cost of petrol is reimbursed. Can I claim relief for depreciation and other running costs?*

Yes, provided that you can show that the car has to be used for business purposes. You can claim a capital allowance calculated at the rate of 25 per cent, broadly, of the purchase cost of the car. But this allowance is reduced by the amount you use the car for private purposes. So, if only half your mileage is in business use, then only half of the 25 per cent allowance will be given.

In the year following your first claim, and in each subsequent year, the allowances you have been given to date are deducted from the cost of the car before calculating your new allowance. In other words in the second year you get 25 per cent of the cost of the car after 25 per cent has been deducted, and in the third year 25 per cent of the cost of the car after deduction of the allowances for the previous two years.

As far as road tax, insurance, servicing and repairs are concerned, you can claim a proportion of these, but again how much depends on the extent to which the car is used for business and private purposes. If it is used, say, half the time for private purposes and half the time for business purposes, the expenses will be apportioned 50: 50. It is sensible to keep detailed records of your expenses and of your business mileage, although you should still claim even if you do not have all the necessary documentation.

16 | *My employer does not need my services any more, and he is prepared to pay me a lump sum in redundancy money when I go. Is it taxable?*

Statutory redundancy payments, paid under the Employment Protection (Consolidation) Act 1978, are specifically exempt from income tax. In addition, payments made without legal obligation when you leave your employment will not normally be taxable. If, however, such payments are added to your statutory redundancy pay and the total exceeds £25,000 they can become taxable.

On the other hand, if it is a condition of your employment that a redundancy or other payment will be made to you when you leave your employment, it may well be that the whole amount is taxable as an emolument from your employment. For example, if your contract of employment states that in the event of redundancy three years' salary will be paid, this lump sum payment may well be liable in full to income tax. By concession the Inland Revenue will

not seek to tax a genuine redundancy package where the payments are not excessively large in relation to earnings, length of service and the like, and provided that all employees with over two years' service qualify for the package.

17 | *I work part-time at the Jolly Tax Man public house as a barman. No other part-time employee there seems to pay tax. What is the tax liability on part-time earnings?*

The general rule is that if you are resident in this country, you are liable to income tax on all your income, not just that from your main employer. You must therefore disclose your part-time earnings on your tax return or, if a return is not sent to you, you must tell the Revenue within twelve months of the end of the tax year in which the income first arises. The inspector of taxes responsible will then work out what tax liability you have, taking into account any other income, and he will issue a code number to your part-time employer, unless the sums are small, in which case it may be possible to adjust your main employer's code to collect the tax on both employments. It is better that you tell the inspector as soon as possible of your second job, or you may find yourself faced with a large bill later!

The landlord of the pub should consider his position too. He should either ask all new employees to supply a form P45, which is given to everyone on leaving employment (and which tells him all he needs to know how to calculate their tax), or obtain their signature on a form P46. A P46 gives the tax office the details for it to issue a correct code number, and one must be completed for each employee who cannot produce a P45.

It is possible, of course, that the other part-time employees in the pub do not also have full-time jobs, and do not earn enough to have to pay tax.

Don't forget National Insurance. This is due on your part-time earnings as well as on your income from you main employment if you are earning £39 a week or more. However, if your total earnings from both employments take your income to over £295 a week, you may well be entitled to a refund of some of the National Insurance paid by your part-time employer on your behalf, as you are not required to pay National Insurance on income over a maximum level of £295 per week. In fact, if you are already paying the maximum National Insurance contributions on your main employment, you can arrange with the Department of Health and Social Security that your part-time employer should not deduct

National Insurance contributions from your income. This would not exempt your employer from the employer's share of the Class I National Insurance contributions.

18 | *How much tax will I pay on any part-time work?*

All your allowances and reliefs (see Q25) are set off against your income from your main employment, and because of this the tax bill on your part-time employment will normally be 27 per cent (unless you find yourself in the higher rate tax bands; see Q24). You are therefore no better or worse off in tax terms by earning money from a part-time employment than you would be by getting a pay rise in your main employment. Exactly the same amount of tax will be deducted, and exactly the same amount of National Insurance (if you earn more than £39 per week).

19 | *My casual income is only really a hobby which helps pay for my summer holidays and for the children's clothes. What happens if I just keep quiet about it for tax purposes?*

If you are in any form of casual employment, or even if you are self-employed during the evenings or at weekends, you should disclose your income from it to the Inland Revenue. If you fail to do so you are acting illegally. If you are found out later, not only will the inspector of taxes seek interest on the outstanding tax, but you may also be liable to penalties.

The Revenue is vigilant in seeking out undisclosed employment and businesses, for example, by following up advertisements in local newspapers. If you get caught 'moonlighting' you will definitely regret not having disclosed your extra job!

20 | *I don't want my main employer to know about my part-time employment. Will the tax inspector inform him?*

Your inspector should not impart any information about your affairs to your employer, other than your code number. As this indicates only allowances (see Q3), it will not reveal that you have part-time or other employment. Just to make the matter clear beyond doubt, however, you should make a point of informing your inspector that the information you give him about your part-time employer is to be treated in the strictest confidence. This should be done in writing, though you may prefer to see the inspector first to explain your concern. You do not have to tell him why you insist on confidentiality.

21 | *I know I should declare both my own and my wife's earned income. Is there any other source of income I must declare?*

You should declare all income from whatever source. Apart from your earned income and your wife's earned income, the most common of these are:

● pensions, including the state retirement pension
● interest not taxed at source, such as National Savings Bank investment account interest and certain income from government securities
● building society and bank interest received net of basic rate tax (as the basic rate tax is paid at source by the society you will not have to pay twice)
● overseas income
● dividends (see Q22)
● rents, such as lettings from holiday cottages
● income from the estate of someone who has died, or trust income. These will also be received after tax has been deducted
● Unemployment and Supplementary Benefit.

22 | *How is my tax liability calculated on the income I get other than from my employers?*

This depends upon the source of the income.

Pensions are taxable in the year of receipt. Most employers deduct tax from them at source under PAYE. State pensions are paid without deduction of tax but you have to declare your pension on your tax return. War Widow's Pension is, however, tax free, as are certain disability pensions.

Special rules apply to the taxation of interest received gross, such as National Savings Bank 'special investment' accounts. Normally the interest is taxed according to the income of the previous tax year if you had a source then. For example, if the interest received on a long-established account is

£100 in tax year 1984–5, £120 in 1985–6 and £110 in 1986–7, the 1985–6 assessment will be £100 (that is, the amount received in 1984–5), the 1986–7 assessment £120, and the 1987–8 assessment £110. There are special rules for new sources of income and for sources which cease, for which you should consult an accountant. However, the first £70 of interest on 'ordinary' National Savings Bank accounts is tax-free, and this applies separately to both husband and wife even if they are assessed together.

You have no further basic rate tax liability on bank or building society interest, but equally you cannot recover the tax paid if you are not liable to basic rate tax. However, if you are liable to the higher rates of tax, then the gross amount of your interest (what you receive plus the tax on it paid on your behalf) will be taxed at these higher rates, with a basic rate tax credit.

The rules for overseas income are complicated and you should seek professional advice from an accountant, taxation consultant or other tax advisor.

Dividends received from shares are also deemed to have been received after deduction of basic rate tax, so for every 73p received you are deemed to have received £1 with a basic rate tax credit of 27p. As with building society interest, if you are liable to higher rate tax, the gross income from the dividends will be assessed at this rate with a basic rate tax credit. However, unlike building society interest, if you are not liable in full to the basic rate of tax, you may be able to recover the tax credit.

If you have any rental income, this will be received without deduction of tax and you will be liable to tax on it, after deduction of your allowable expenses such as repairs and agent's commissions. There are special rules for furnished holiday lettings, treating them like any other trade.

Income and interest received from the estates of those who have died will usually be received after deduction of basic rate tax, and will, therefore, be treated in the same way as dividend income. In some cases settlement income will be received after deduction of 45 per cent tax, and if the beneficiary is only liable at 27 per cent (or below) a refund may be claimed.

Finally, Unemployment Benefit and Supplementary Benefit are in the main taxable and should be entered into your tax return. The Inland Revenue publish a leaflet which deals especially with unemployment benefits: 'IR41 Income Tax and the Unemployed.' It is available from all tax offices.

23 | I work part-time in a restaurant and my wife works in a hairdresser's. We both receive tips. Do we have to declare them?

Yes, you should. You are probably liable to tax on any tips or gratuities you receive during the course of your work and these must be disclosed.

24 | I have been earning quite a lot of money this year from different sources and I expect to go over the limit for the basic rate of tax, even after deducting my various reliefs. What are the higher rates of tax?

Over the basic rate, tax is assessed according to different rate bands which increase every year according to inflation. The following table gives the rates up to 6 April 1988 (showing in the third column the tax on the full earnings in each band):

Taxable income	Rate	Tax on band	Cumulative tax
£	%	£	£
1–17,900	27	4,833	4,833
17,901–20,400	40	1,000	5,833
20,401–25,400	45	2,250	8,083
25,401–33,300	50	3,950	12,033
33,301–41,200	55	4,344	16,377
over 41,200	60		

25 | What are personal tax reliefs and how much are they worth?

All tax reliefs are sums deducted from your income before tax is calculated. There are various personal reliefs, some of which vary year by year. Everybody who pays income tax qualifies for some relief, the exact amount depending on your status – whether you are single or married – and on such dependants as you may have. The rates for 1987–8 are set out in the table below.

26 | *Does my dependent mother have to live with me for me to qualify for the dependent relative relief?*

No, but if she does live apart, then you have to show that you have made a financial contribution to her upkeep. If these contributions come to less than the allowance available, then the relief is reduced to equal the amount that you have spent. So if you only spent £75 on her in the tax year, then you would only get relief on £75.

Moreover, whether she lives with you or apart, if she has an income in excess of the basic state retirement pension, then your relief is reduced by the amount of the excess. So, with the state pension at

£2,012, if she has an income totalling £2,061, your allowance for her will be reduced by £49, and you will get relief of £51.

27 | *I am over 65, but I am still working and I earn a good salary. Am I still entitled to the age relief?*

You are not entitled to the full age relief if your income is over £9,800. For any amount earned over that sum your allowance is reduced by two thirds of the difference between your income and the £9,800. However, the allowance stops reducing when it has reached the ordinary person's relief. This means that if you are a married man you qualify for only the normal married man's allowance of £3,795 when your income exceeds £11,120, and if you are single you qualify for only the single person's allowance when it passes £10,603.

28 | *What other tax reliefs are there?*

In addition to the personal reliefs, you may be able to get relief on pension contributions, interest on loans, and life assurance contributions.

Life assurance relief applies only to policies taken out before 14 March 1984. It is a deduction of 15 per cent of the premiums, on condition that the policy is on your own life or that of your spouse and that the total premiums you pay in a tax year are less than one sixth of your total income, or £1,500, whichever is the greater.

The relief on pension scheme contributions depends on whether you are an employee and contribute to an approved pension scheme set up by your employer, or whether you have an individual pension plan. If the former you can generally deduct the amount of your contributions from your salary before calculating tax. If you are in non-pensionable employment or you are self-employed, and you pay premiums to a pension plan, you can deduct the amount of premiums you pay from your income up to a maximum of $17\frac{1}{2}$ per cent of your net relevant earnings (broadly your earnings from non-pensionable employment or self-employment). However, if your employer provides you with a pension scheme, you cannot also claim tax relief for premiums on individual pension plans. Higher rates of contribution can be made by people born before 1934.

You may claim relief on interest on the following types of loan:

● loans up to £30,000 made to you to enable you to buy or improve your principal private residence. (This figure applies to a single person and is the same for a married couple.) Such interest may, however, be

Personal relief	
Single person's relief	£2,425
Married man's relief	£3,795
Wife's earned income allowance equal to the amount of the wife's earned income up to a maximum of	£2,425
Additional personal allowance	£1,370
Dependent relative relief for your relative or a relative of your spouse who is incapacitated by old age (over 65) or infirmity	£100 (per relative)
Increased for single, divorced or separated women to	£145
Housekeeper relief, available in certain circumstances to widows or widowers who have a housekeeper living with them	£100
Blind person's relief	£540
Age relief for persons over 65	
Single	£2,960
Married	£4,675
Age relief for persons over 80	
Single	£3,070
Married	£4,845
Widow's bereavement relief. In the tax year of death of your husband and in the following tax year only	£1,370
Daughter's (son's) service. A relief for individuals who by reason of old age or infirmity depend on the services of their own son or daughter resident with or maintained by them	£55

paid under the MIRAS scheme (see Q29)
● loans which enable you to buy shares in your family company or lend money to it
● loans to enable you to buy shares in or provide working capital for a partnership
● loans to finance the purchase of shares as part of an employee buy-out of the shares in the company which employs them.

Strict conditions have to be fulfilled in all interest relief circumstances to enable relief to be given, and, except for loans to buy or improve your home, you should take professional advice.

29 | *What is MIRAS?*

MIRAS stands for mortgage interest relief at source and is a system whereby you automatically claim your tax relief at 27p in the pound by deducting it from the interest you pay on your mortgage. In many cases no further relief is due and no adjustment is made to your PAYE code number.

Before the introduction of MIRAS, if you took out a repayment mortgage on your name your repayments were mainly of interest. But as the years went by a greater proportion of each repayment went to pay off capital and thus the interest element gradually diminished over the years. As you get tax relief on only the interest payments, not on payments made to refund the capital sum, under the pre-MIRAS system your tax relief on the mortgage started high, but went down each year. Under MIRAS the total interest payment for the whole length of repayment of the mortgage is calculated, and then averaged out so that an equal amount is deemed to be paid each year. This means that the income tax relief remains constant, subject only to changes in the tax and overall interest rates.

MIRAS does not apply to all mortgages. It can only be used for mortgages on your principal private residence. (If you are temporarily absent from your home for reasons of business so that it ceases to be your main residence the MIRAS scheme may still apply, however.)

30 | *What effect do my personal reliefs have on my tax bill?*

Effectively every £1 of relief gives you £1 of income that you can enjoy tax free. So if you are entitled to the married man's relief of £3,795 your income in the tax year will have to exceed £3,795 before you pay any tax at all. In weekly terms this means that a married man has to earn over £12.98 before tax becomes payable, and then it is only payable on the excess. The same rule applies to all the other reliefs except life assurance relief and mortgage interest paid under the MIRAS scheme (see Q29).

31 | *I want to cash in a regular premium life assurance policy. Will there be tax to pay?*

If a policy is cashed in or paid up (that is, no further premiums are to be paid in and the benefits are revised accordingly) within four years of its being taken out, the Revenue will claim back the relief that you have been given. After 13 March 1988 this will not apply, as tax relief is not available on policies taken out after 18 March 1984. If you cash them before then, the Revenue will claim back 5 per cent, with an upper limit of 5 per cent of the surrender value. The life assurance company should make the necessary adjustments by deducting these amounts before reimbursing you, but in the event of dispute you should take the matter up with the Inland Revenue.

There is also a tax liability if the proceeds derived from the surrender of an endowment policy exceed the original premium, but the profit is only liable if you pay higher rate tax. If your taxable income plus the profit on the assurance policy is insufficient to make you liable to the higher rates of taxation (see Q24) then no tax on the profit element of the proceeds is levied. You are not liable to tax at all if the policy has been maintained for 10 years or more, or for three quarters of the full term, whichever is the lesser.

32 | *My tax return asks me for details of my wife's income. The tax inspector's wife might well tell him what her income is, but mine doesn't want to! What should I do?*

The law that a married man has to declare and is taxed on his wife's income is under review at the moment, but for the time being you have to declare your wife's income, whether or not you know what it is.

You or she could make a 'separate assessment' election (see Q33) – not the same as separate taxation of wife's earnings (Q34) – by which you get separate tax returns. Such an election must be made within the six months preceding 6 July in the relevant tax year, so if you wish to make the election for 1988–9, you must do so no earlier than 6 January 1988 and no later than 5 July 1988. Once the election is made, it remains in force until revoked. It also cannot be revoked for a tax year unless the inspector is notified before 6 July in the relevant year.

If you have missed the notification date and your wife still does not want to give you details of her income, you should write and tell your inspector, who may be sympathetic. He may be able to bend the rules a little, for example, by using his discretion and accepting a late election for separate assessments, although this would be very unusual.

33 | What is the effect of making an election for separate assessments?

For a start, you don't save any tax. All a separate assessment election means is that your wife will receive a tax return as well as you. She will have to fill it in, and you will not be required to give details of her income on your tax return. The tax bill will then be split between you so that you each pay a share of the total tax based on your income and reliefs. In practice it does little to preserve secrecy because the reliefs available are shared in proportion to income, and you can therefore work out each other's income.

34 | I gather that an election for separate taxation of wife's earnings can be made which reduces the overall amount of tax payable, but which can result in the husband having to pay more tax. Just what is the position?

You and your wife can elect for separate taxation of your wife's earnings, so that she is taxed on her earned income as if she were a single person, receiving a single person's allowance. You are taxed on your total income together with your wife's unearned income as if you were a single person. You get a single person's relief only and, of course, do not receive wife's earned income relief. As a result your reliefs are reduced, but the election may have the effect of reducing the rate of tax at which you are assessed (see Q24) as your wife's earnings no longer form part of your income. The election becomes worthwhile when the amount saved on your tax is greater than that lost on replacing the married man's allowance and the wife's earned income allowance with two single person's allowances. It may, therefore, be worthwhile in the tax year 1987–8 if the joint income is at least £26,869 before deduction of married man's relief and wife's earned income relief, but after deduction of all other reliefs and allowances such as dependent relative reliefs, providing that the wife's earnings are in excess of £6,544. The example at the bottom of the page demonstrates the position.

The election must be made by husband and wife jointly (on form 14) not earlier than six months before the beginning of the relevant tax year and not later than 12 months after the end of it. In other words, you have 30 months in which to make the election. Once made, the election continues in force until a joint notice of withdrawal is made on form 14-1.

Even though an election is made, the husband still has to return details of his wife's income on his tax return, unless an election for separate assessment is also made (see Qs 32 and 33).

The effects of a husband's and wife's election for separate taxation	Joint income (no election) £	Separate income (with election) Husband £	Wife £
Husband's salary	30,000	30,000	
Wife's salary	7,000		7,000
Less married man's allowance	3,795		
Less wife's earned income allowance	2,425		
Less single person's allowance		2,425	2,425
charged to tax	30,780	27,575	4,575
first 17,900 at 27%	4,833	4,833	1,235
next 2,500 at 40%	1,000	1,000	
next 5,000 at 45%	2,250	2,250	
next 5,380 (2,175) at 50%	2,690	1,087	
Total tax	10,773	9,170	1,235
plus wife's tax		1,235	
total tax		10,405	

An election would therefore save £368

Advice should invariably be sought from an accountant before making an election because beyond 12 months after the tax year you cannot withdraw the election. Once made, the election should be reviewed annually shortly after the end of each tax year concerned.

35 | *Do I have to fill in a tax return?*

There is strictly no legal obligation to complete the simplified return form (form P1) but, if you persist in failing to complete this, a more complicated return is likely to be issued (form 11 or 11P) which you have to fill in. It is almost certain to be in your interest to complete a tax return as soon as you can, to ensure that the Revenue have up-to-date information on you, for example, to calculate your allowances. Anyway, you may have income from other sources and you have to tell the inspector about this.

If you fail to submit your tax return once you have been sent it, a notice of coding may be issued for you with limited allowances, and that could cause you to pay more tax than you should, at any rate initially. Longer delays could result in interest charges and penalties, although penalties rarely have to be levied for failure to submit a tax return because the threat of them is normally sufficient to elicit the return.

Where income is not declared on the form, the maximum penalty is £100 plus double the tax involved, and in the case of fraud the maximum penalty is £100 plus triple the tax involved.

Your tax return should be completed within 30 days but the Revenue accepts that, if everybody filled in their return within the 30-day limit, they would be inundated with work which they could not hope to handle without delay.

36 | *I have received a 1987–8 tax return to complete but the year is not yet over so how can I state my income?*

The tax return is always in two main parts. The first part asks for details of income and certain outgoings (interest paid) for the preceding year (the 1987–8 tax return asks for details of the 1986–7 income). The second part is where you claim your personal relief (see Q25) for the year of the return. (For example, your claim for married man's allowance for 1987–8 should be made on the 1987–8 tax return.)

37 | *If I do not get a tax return, what should I do?*

The Revenue do not always issue returns each year. In fact, most employees receive them only every three years. However, because you have to inform the inspector of any new source of income, you must write and give details if you have such a change in your circumstances. You will then almost certainly be sent a return form to complete.

You can also request a tax return if you wish to claim a relief to which you feel you have become entitled for the first time.

Your employer will be able to tell you the name and address of the tax office dealing with your affairs and your file reference number. If not, write to your local tax office – the address can be found in the telephone directory – stating your employer's name and address.

Inheritance tax

38 | *Do I have to pay inheritance tax on gifts I make during my lifetime?*

Inheritance tax took over from capital transfer tax on 18 March 1986. Capital transfer tax was a tax on lifetime gifts and gifts on death which was levied on all types of assets including, for example, cash, property and shares. Inheritance tax is based on capital transfer tax and follows the same principles, but the most important change is that there is no inheritance tax at all if you make outright gifts or gifts into 'accumulation and maintenance trusts' (see Q60) and then survive for seven years (without reservation of benefit). These types of gift are called potentially exempt transfers (PET) and give a very important opportunity to save inheritance tax.

Another important exemption is for gifts to a spouse who is domiciled in this country, and there is no inheritance tax to pay if you make gifts to your spouse whether during your lifetime or on death.

HALF-SCALE RATES

IHT: scale of tax for lifetime chargeable transfers (from 17 March 1987)

Chargeable transfers £	Rate %	Tax on slice £	Cumulative tax £
0–90,000	nil	nil	nil
90,001–140,000	15	7,500	7,500
140,001–220,000	20	16,000	23,500
220,001–330,000	25	27,500	51,000
over 330,000	30		

39 | *If I make potentially exempt transfers and then die within seven years, how is inheritance tax calculated?*

What happens is that tax (at the scale in force at the date of death) is levied retrospectively on the gift as if it had been chargeable at the date when it was made. Tax is payable at the full scale and is calculated on a cumulative basis. This means that chargeable gifts (those that are not exempt) made in the seven years before the date when the potentially exempt transfer (PET) was made must be taken into account in calculating the inheritance tax payable on the PET. Chargeable gifts include gifts made during the capital transfer tax era.

For example, assume that you die having previously made a PET the value of which (after exemptions and reliefs) was £50,000, and that the total of the chargeable gifts you made within the seven years before the PET was £100,000. To calculate tax on the PET, it is cumulated with the £100,000 chargeable gifts. So tax will be levied on £50,000 as a top slice starting at £100,000. Using the table on page 373, tax will be:

Rate band £	Amount in band £	Rate %	Tax £
100,000–140,000	40,000	30	12,000
140,000–150,000	10,000	40	4,000
	50,000		16,000

So the inheritance tax on the £50,000 is £16,000.

Bear in mind that even if the PET is caught because you die within seven years, the taxable value is the value at the date of the gift, not the value at your death, and so the gift 'freezes' the value of what you have given away.

Another relief is that if the PET were made more than three years before your death, only a percentage of the tax is charged. The relief is called 'tapering relief', and is:

Years before death	Percentage of tax leviable
3–4	80
4–5	60
5–6	40
6–7	20

Of course, if when taking into account previous lifetime chargeable transfers the PET is within the nil-rate band (currently £90,000), then there is no inheritance tax to pay on it.

40 | *How can I cover myself against an inheritance tax liability on a PET in case I die within seven years?*

The first thing to bear in mind is that if the PET does become chargeable, the inheritance tax bill is payable by the donee. However, the Inland Revenue can seek to recover the inheritance tax from your personal representatives if the donee fails to pay within 12 months after you die.

The best way to ensure that there are no problems is to take out a life policy payable if you die within the next seven years. The policy should be taken out in the name of the beneficiary (or in the name of the trustees of the relevant trust) so that the policy proceeds themselves are not treated as a taxable part of your estate on death. There are policies that have reducing cover after three years to take into account tapering relief. However, so long as the amount of the policy adequately covers the inheritance tax likely to be payable, it is not essential to make accurate calculations of what inheritance tax is due. If the proceeds exceed the inheritance tax payable, the donee can keep the balance inheritance tax-free! See also Q51.

41 | *My main asset is my residence. I want to make a PET to give my adult children interests in*

FULL-SCALE RATES

IHT: scale of tax for transfers on death or within seven years before death (from 17 March 1987)

Chargeable transfers £	Rate %	Tax on slice £	Cumulative tax £
0–90,000	nil	nil	nil
90,001–140,000	30	15,000	15,000
140,001–220,000	40	32,000	47,000
220,001–330,000	50	55,000	102,000
over 330,000	60		

it, but I intend to continue to live there. Does this cause a problem?

An outright gift of your home to your children will be a PET, but to start the seven-year period running you must be excluded from all benefit from the gifted property. If you have any benefit from the gift, the residence will be treated as remaining part of your estate for inheritance tax, and if that benefit lasts until you die the residence will be part of your estate on death. If you release the benefit, you will be treated as making a PET at the date of release. These reservation-of-benefit rules mean that you cannot make a gift with strings attached, and they apply if you stay in occupation of a residence which you have given away. So if you want to make an effective PET of your residence, you will have to move out when you make the gift.

However, there are three important exceptions to the rule. The first is that your continuing occupation can be ignored if you pay a full market rent. This is unlikely to be something worth contemplating except in the case of the gift of a holiday home that you occupy for a few weeks in a year. The second exception is for the impecunious donor who goes back into occupation after making a gift, but only if there is a change in circumstances after the date of the gift and the donor is unable to maintain himself or herself through old age, infirmity or otherwise. The third exception is more important. It is the common case where someone gives away a net share in a house which is then occupied by all the joint owners, including the donor. For example, elderly parents make unconditional gifts of shares in their house to their children, and the parents and the children occupy the house as their family home, each owner paying his or her share of the running costs. In these circumstances, the parents' occupation or enjoyment of the part of the house that they have given away is in return for the similar enjoyment by the children of

the other part, and the reservation-of-benefit rules do not apply.

42 | *What about lifetime gifts which are not PETs?*

PETS are absolute gifts and gifts into accumulation and maintenance trusts. Other lifetime gifts include gifts into discretionary trusts and gifts into fixed-interest trusts (see Q60). These other gifts are not PETS and may be liable to tax at the time they are made, whether or not the donor dies within seven years. Subject to exemptions and reliefs, tax is calculated at one half of the scale at the time when the gift is made, but will be payable retrospectively at the full scale if the donor dies within seven years (subject to tapering relief; see Q39). Credit is given for any lifetime tax paid when calculating the tax due on death.

As for PETS (see Q39), tax is calculated on a cumulative basis. However, when the lifetime chargeable transfer is actually made, only chargeable gifts made in the last seven years (including those made during the capital transfer tax regime) have to be cumulated, and PETS are ignored. If the donor then dies within seven years, PETS made within the seven years before death then become chargeable and the retrospective charge or the lifetime chargeable transfer must take these into account. Tapering relief (see Q39) is available.

For example, say that a donor makes a PET of £50,000 in 1987 and then makes a chargeable gift of £100,000 in 1988. When calculating tax on the 1988 gift, the PET is ignored and, using the half-scale rates on page 372, tax on £100,000 is £1,500. However, if the donor then dies in 1989, tax is recalculated at the full-scale rates. The 1987 PET becomes chargeable and is within the nil-rate band. To calculate tax at the full scale retrospectively on the

1988 gift, it now has to be cumulated with the 1987 gift and tax on the 1988 gift is;

Rate band £	Amount in band £	Rate %	Tax £
50,000–90,000	40,000	nil	nil
90,000–140,000	50,000	30	15,000
140,000–150,000	10,000	40	4,000
	100,000		19,000

Credit is given for the £1,500 already paid, so the tax bill on the 1988 gift is £17,500.

The lifetime tax on a lifetime chargeable transfer is payable by the donor (and grossing up may be necessary) unless the donee actually bears the tax. The extra tax payable retrospectively on a death within seven years is payable by the donee, and, as for PETS (see Q40), insurance can be taken out to protect against this possible charge.

43 | *When is this tax payable?*

Inheritance tax on a lifetime chargeable transfer (not a PET) is due six months from the end of the month in which the gift is made, although if the gift is made after 5 April and before 1 October in a tax year the tax is due on the following 30 April. If tax is not paid then, it becomes subject to interest at eight per cent per annum.

The extra inheritance tax on lifetime chargeable transfers and the inheritance tax on PETS, when death occurs within seven years, is due from the donee six months from the end of the month in which the death occurs.

If the donee pays inheritance tax, tax will be payable by 10 annual instalments, the first instalment being due when tax would otherwise be payable in accordance with the rules stated above. However, only certain types of property qualify the recipient to pay tax by instalments. These are:

● land;
● shares and securities which give the donor control of the company immediately before the gift;
● other unquoted shares and securities if the Inland Revenue is satisfied that inheritance tax cannot be paid at once without hardship;
● other shares if not quoted and worth over £20,000, if they form not less than a 10 per cent holding;
● businesses and interests in businesses;
● in certain cases, timber – in other words, trees and underwood.

There is no interest in general on outstanding instalments, unless an instalment is not paid on time, in which case interest is charged from the date on which that instalment was due. On land, other than agricultural land, however, interest at eight per cent is payable on all outstanding instalments.

44 | *When I made a gift in 1985, I paid capital transfer tax of £5,000 at the lifetime scale and I expected to be charged retrospectively at the full scale only if I died within three years. Now there is inheritance tax, does this mean that my gift will be caught if I die in seven years instead?*

No. There are transitional provisions under which no gift will involve more tax under the inheritance tax legislation than it would have under the capital transfer tax legislation.

45 | *Apart from gifts to my spouse, are there any other exemptions from inheritance tax?*

Yes. Gifts to charity, to qualifying political parties, to certain national institutions, such as the National Gallery and the National Trust, gifts of certain types of works of art (if the Treasury agrees) and gifts to qualifying employee trusts are all exempt, whether made in your lifetime or on death. There are other gifts that are exempt only if made in your lifetime, most notably the £3,000 and £250 annual exemptions (see Q46), wedding gifts (see Q52) and the 'normal expenditure out of income' exemption (see Q51).

'Qualifying political parties' are those that had two or more MPs elected at the last general election, or had only one MP but won over 150,000 votes overall. If the gift is made on death or within a year of death, there is an upper limit of £100,000 to the exemption.

46 | *What are the £3,000 and £250 annual exemptions?*

Taking the £3,000 annual exemption first, the first £3,000 of non-exempt gifts in a tax year (6 April to following 5 April) is ignored for inheritance tax, which means it is tax free and does not have to be taken into account when calculating the inheritance tax bills on subsequent gifts. A PET qualifies for this exemption only if it becomes chargeable because of a death within seven years, and then the PET is treated as being made at the end of the relevant tax year (for this exemption only) so that lifetime chargeable gifts in the same tax year – whether made before or after the PET – qualify for the exemption in priority.

If transfers fall short of £3,000 in a tax year, the

balance may be carried forward, but only for one year. The effect of this carry-forward can be illustrated by the following example:

Tax year	Exemption available	Gift made	Carry forward
First	£3,000	nil	£3,000
Second	£6,000	£2,900	£100
Third	£3,100	£3,000	nil

The second annual exemption is that outright gifts to any number of people in a tax year are exempt if they do not exceed £250 each. Gifts of more than £250 lose the exemption completely, so that a gift of £250 is exempt but not one of £251.

47 | Am I entitled to any relief for business interests or farm land?

Yes. Business interests and farm land qualify for relief from inheritance tax which is given by reducing the value of the site. The reliefs apply to lifetime gifts and gifts on death, but in the case of lifetime gifts (including PETs) relief in each case is given only on a retrospective charge on death within seven years if the donee then owns the gifted property or a qualifying replacement. This is an important point for those making lifetime gifts of qualifying property, and donees must be told that if they sell up or give away the property their potential tax bill can be very substantially increased.

Business property relief is a reduction on value of 50 per cent for businesses or partnership interests and for shareholdings of over 25 per cent in trading companies. The reduction is 30 per cent for shareholdings of 25 per cent or less and for land and buildings, fixed plant and machinery owned by the donor but occupied by a company controlled by the donor. In each case the asset must generally have been owned for at least two years. The same applies to agricultural relief, and the reduction is 50 per cent for agricultural land you own and 30 per cent for land which is let for a term exceeding a year. Agricultural relief is given to the 'agricultural value' only, which excludes any value attributable to development potential. Development potential may, however, qualify for business property relief.

Both reliefs apply to lifetime gifts and gifts on death. They are given to lifetime gifts *before* applying the lifetime £3,000 exemption. So if you give away £20,000-worth of farm land, the value for inheritance tax is:

	£
Land	20,000
Less 50 per cent relief	10,000
	10,000
Less annual exemption (this tax year and last)	6,000
Potentially chargeable	4,000

and *not*:

	£
Land	20,000
Less annual exemption	6,000
	14,000
Less 50 per cent relief	7,000
Potentially chargeable	7,000

48 | How is inheritance tax on death calculated?

As with lifetime chargeable gifts, to calculate the inheritance tax on death, exemptions and reliefs must first be deducted. The main exemptions that apply on death are the spouse exemption and gifts to charity (see Qs 38 and 45) and business reliefs (see Q47). The resulting chargeable estate is then added to the deceased's previous chargeable gifts made within the last seven years. Chargeable gifts include PETs. The chargeable estate of the deceased also includes gifted property where the deceased had reserved a benefit (see Q41).

To take a simple example, if you die leaving the whole of your estate, worth £60,000, to your children, having made chargeable gifts of £100,000, including PETs, within the preceding seven years, the inheritance tax is calculated by adding the £60,000 to the £100,000 and treating it as a top slice. So, applying the full-scale rates on page 373, tax is:

Rate band £	Amount in band £	Rate %	Tax £
100,000–140,000	40,000	30	12,000
140,001–160,000	20,000	40	8,000
	60,000		20,000

The tax is due six months from the end of the month in which the death occurs.

Bear in mind that tax on lifetime gifts will have to be reassessed (see Qs 39 and 42).

49 | Is the situation altered if I leave only some but not all of my property to my spouse when I die?

If you leave some of your property to non-exempt beneficiaries, such as your children or grandchildren, then unless the amount passing to them is covered by your nil-rate band at the date of your death (taking into account gifts made within the preceding years) inheritance tax will be payable. And the way it is calculated is horribly complicated if you also leave property to your spouse or to charity: it can involve double grossing-up unless non-exempt gifts are stated to pay their own tax.

Normally, recipients of non-exempt gifts of money or property ('legacies') do not pay their own inheritance tax because inheritance tax is normally payable out of the remaining estate ('residue'). So if you give your child a legacy of £1,000, the tax on that will not come out of the legacy (assuming the nil-rate band is inapplicable) but will be paid out of the rest of the estate.

However, this can work in a more undesirable way. Assume you have an estate of £100,000 and you have left a legacy of £40,000 to your children and the residue of your estate to your wife. Assume also that you have made lifetime chargeable gifts in the preceding seven years of £330,000, so that the relevant inheritance tax band applicable to your chargeable estate is 60 per cent. The £40,000 legacy is treated as a net sum after tax at 60 per cent has been deducted. The gross is therefore £100,000, tax is £60,000, and since this tax is paid out of the residue there is nothing left to go to your surviving spouse. Very great care must therefore be taken in these circumstances, and the problem can be avoided by stating in your will that the recipients of chargeable gifts must pay their own inheritance tax.

50 | *If gifts to my wife are exempt, surely the best idea is to give everything to her on my death by will?*

It is certainly the case that if you leave everything to your surviving spouse, no inheritance tax is payable when you die. However, if she takes no further steps, this may not be the best course of action if you are only interested in saving tax. Your estate will now be added on to that of your wife, if she has any. When she dies and it passes on to children or grandchildren, or to other chargeable beneficiaries, it will then be fully chargeable. This can aggravate the inheritance tax bill because the escalating rate bands of tax mean that the burden increases as the estate grows and you will have lost the use of your lower-rate bands, including the nil-rate band.

However, to leave everything to your wife by will

can be the most sensible course of action, especially if she is aware of what opportunities there are available after your death. She could enter into a written variation of your estate within two years so as to redirect benefits to chargeable beneficiaries if she wishes, perhaps to use up your nil-rate band (see Q58). She could also use up all or part of your estate by making PETS herself (see Q33). And if she wishes she can keep all or part of the estate for her own use.

The same principles apply if your wife dies first and leaves everything to you. So each of you should own sufficient to give the other the opportunity to re-arrange your dispositions or to make PETS, if he or she wishes to do so, whoever dies first.

51 | *Apart from the amounts allowed as tax-exempt gifts, is there any other foolproof way of passing money on to my children when I die without paying inheritance tax?*

Yes. One of the most tax-efficient ways is by taking out a life assurance policy. Usually the parent takes out a policy on his or her own life, making the sum payable on death to a child but paying the premiums him- or herself. When the policy moneys become payable to the child, there is no inheritance tax (or capital gains tax). In the meantime the premium payments should be exempt from inheritance tax on the basis of the 'normal expenditure out of income' exemption, under which any gift is exempt if it is shown that:

● it was part of the normal expenditure of the donor,
● (taking one year with another) it was made out of income, and
● after allowing for all gifts forming part of the donor's normal expenditure, the payer was left with sufficient income to maintain the usual standard of living.

If the normal expenditure of income exemption does not apply, the payment of the premiums should be within one of the annual exemptions (see Q45).

Policies taken out before 14 March 1984 also qualify for life assurance relief for income tax. Despite the withdrawal of this relief on 14 March 1984, life assurance policies can still be a very tax-efficient way of passing money from one generation to another, and, if you can afford to do so and have not done so already, you might take out a policy in the name of your child or grandchild.

52 | *Our elder daughter is about to marry and we would like to give her and her husband a*

fairly substantial gift. What is the inheritance tax position on wedding gifts?

There is a special exemption for them. If the donor is a parent of either party to the marriage, any gift up to £5,000 is exempt from tax. If the donor is a grandparent or is actually one of the parties, the exempt amount is £2,500. For anyone else it is £1,000.

Every donor has one exemption each per marriage, rather than per party to the marriage, so, if your child is about to marry, you and your spouse can each give the couple £5,000 without inheritance tax, making a total gift of £10,000.

If the couple want to give each other gifts, rather than using the £2,500 exemption they can wait until they have actually married, when gifts between them are completely exempt.

To qualify, the gift must be 'in consideration of the marriage', which means that the gift must be made on the occasion of the marriage, it must be made on the condition that it takes effect only if the marriage takes place, and it must be made to encourage or facilitate the marriage.

Weddings can therefore be quite a tax bonanza. With four parents and eight grandparents, a total of £40,000 can be given without inheritance tax liability, and before any other people add their exempt £1,000.

53 | *I recently inherited from my grandmother a house worth £50,000 which I'm leaving to my children in my will. If I die, would the fact that inheritance tax was paid on the house I inherited have any effect on the tax payable on my death?*

Yes. 'Quick succession' relief may be given if your estate was increased by a chargeable gift less than five years before your death. Any inheritance tax payable on your death is reduced by a percentage of the tax paid on your inheritance. The amount varies according to how long before your death the gift was received: it is 100 per cent if the gift to you were made within one year before your death, 80 per cent if within two years, 60 per cent if within three years, 40 per cent if within four years and 20 per cent if within five years. This relief applies whoever inherits your estate and whether or not the house is still part of your estate when you die. If, however, no inheritance tax is payable, for example because you leave everything to your surviving spouse, your estate loses the benefit of the relief although your spouse's will qualify on the basis outlined above if he or she

also dies within five years of your grandmother.

So, if for the sake of argument the inheritance tax payable on your grandmother's death on 1 June 1986 was £10,000 and the amount attributable to the increase in your estate as a result of the gift was £3,000, and you were to die on 10 October 1990 (more than four years but less than five years after your grandmother's death), the inheritance tax (if any) payable on your death would be reduced by 20 per cent of the £3,000, which is £600.

54 | *My will contains a clause which says: 'If any beneficiary fails to survive me by a period of 28 days such beneficiary shall be treated as predeceasing me for the purposes of this my will.' Does this clause create any inheritance tax problems?*

No. It is very common to leave property by will to your spouse on condition that he or she survives you by a period of 28 days, failing which the property is to go to your children or grandchildren. If your spouse survives you but dies within the 28-day period, your children or grandchildren will inherit, and for inheritance tax they are treated as inheriting directly from you and not from your spouse. If, however, the period stated in the will is over six months the children or grandchildren will be regarded as inheriting from your spouse, and not from you if he or she dies within the period.

55 | *I don't really want to make outright gifts in my will to some of my beneficiaries since I would rather give them trust interests. What effect does this have on the tax bill on my death?*

None. If you give a trust interest to your surviving spouse, the gift is exempt like any other gift to a spouse. If you give trust interests to your children or other chargeable beneficiaries, the gift is still chargeable, but the tax consequences subsequently may well be different. For this, see Qs 59 to 64.

It is quite normal to make substantial gifts to young beneficiaries for when they reach a specified age. This is usually stipulated as 25, although it can be any age and there are no adverse tax implications whatever age it is.

56 | *I am about to make my will. Are there any other points regarding inheritance tax I should bear in mind?*

Yes. It is worth considering skipping a generation by giving to grandchildren rather than to children – this saves the inheritance tax which may be payable when your children pass on your property when they die to their own children. But only do this if your children are already well provided for, either because they can look after themselves or because you have already given them sufficient in your lifetime.

57 | *Under the terms of my employers' pension plan, if I die before retirement my next of kin receives a lump sum of four times my annual salary. Is this liable to inheritance tax?*

No. Inheritance tax on death is levied on the value of your chargeable estate, but, if assets do not form part of your estate, they will not be liable to inheritance tax. Your estate includes all the property you own outright and also any property in a trust in which you are entitled to the income. So your bank accounts, savings, building society accounts, the matrimonial home, stocks and shares are all included. However, a lump sum benefit payable on your death from your pension fund does not form part of your estate. This is because it is paid at the discretion of the pension fund trustees (although they will respect any wishes you may have expressed). A policy on your life payable to your children on your death is likewise free of inheritance tax: your children own the policy and not you, so that when you die the money is paid to them, or to a trust for them.

58 | *My father died recently and left me the whole of his estate. I don't really need the money and I'd like to put it into a trust for my children. What are the tax implications of doing this?*

What a testator puts into a will can often be redirected by the beneficiaries after death without adverse inheritance tax consequences. You are quite at liberty to redirect your father's estate into a children's trust and, provided you do so in accordance with certain rules, there will be no extra inheritance tax bill. The same applies if you want to give it outright to your children or any other person.

The rules are that you make a voluntary variation in writing of the dispositions of your father's estate within two years of the date of his death, and that you give written notice to the Inland Revenue less than six months after you make the variation. Then the variation itself is ignored for inheritance tax and the estate is treated as if your father had willed it direct to the children's trust.

The same principle applies if you disclaim an interest under your father's will. The disclaimer must be made within two years of the date of the death, but

there is no need to notify the Revenue within six months.

However, there is a big income tax pitfall in passing the estate on in this way. Such an arrangement is treated as a settlement by you on your children, and if they are minors and unmarried you and not they could be liable to income tax on the income produced from the estate property. This is a serious problem and you must take professional advice if you think such a situation is likely.

Trusts

59 | *I'm middle-aged and expect to live for a good many years longer. I want to give a large sum of money now to my eight-year-old daughter and possibly make further gifts to her later. However, she is far too young to control the money. Is there a way to give her the money now for use when she is grown up?*

Yes. You can create a trust. This means you give the money or assets to trustees to hold for her benefit. The trustees will receive the interest or income from the money or assets ('capital') and either keep it (accumulate it) or pay it over to her, depending on the type of trust. The terms of the trust deed will set out what is to be done with the income or interest, when, if at all, a beneficiary is to be given the capital, and what administrative powers (such as investment) the trustees are to have. You specify in the terms of the trust when she is entitled to the capital, such as on reaching the age of 25.

Although there are three types of trust (see Q60), the trust for your daughter should be an accumulation and maintenance trust because any gift into it is a PET and thus not liable to inheritance tax if you survive seven years without reservation of benefit (see Qs38 and 61).

You can also create a trust in your will so as to specify at what age your daughter will become entitled to the property you are leaving her on your death.

A trust does not have to have a single beneficiary, and you can, for example, nominate all your children in the one trust.

60 | *What are the different types of trust?*

There are three main types: 'accumulation and maintenance' trusts, 'fixed-interest' trusts and 'discretionary' trusts. Each has a different tax effect.

Accumulation and maintenance trusts are trusts where the trustees are directed to hold the capital for beneficiaries up to a specified age, not exceeding 25, and to use the income for the maintenance, education or benefit of one or more of the beneficiaries, at their own discretion. Income not so applied must be held by the trustees, in other words, accumulated. The accumulation and maintenance trust ends when the beneficiary reaches the specified age, whereupon he or she will either take a fixed interest in the trust or take the property outright.

In fixed-interest trusts, the trustees hold the money or assets ('capital') and pay the interest or income only to a named beneficiary or beneficiaries usually for the life of the beneficiary. The trustees may also have power to hand over capital to that beneficiary, or to a beneficiary who is to take the capital after the current beneficiary dies. This sort of trust is sometimes used to make a gift by will to a surviving spouse so that the capital can be kept intact for the next generation, and is generally used for adults.

Finally, discretionary trusts are trusts where the trustees have a discretion over income, and they can decide whether they should accumulate the income or distribute it, and it is up to them which of the beneficiaries they pay it to if they do distribute it. No one has a right to the income. The discretion is usually extended to capital, too. Such trusts can be extremely flexible.

61 | *If I give assets to trustees to hold on an accumulation and maintenance trust for my children until they reach the age of 25, what is the tax effect?*

A lifetime gift into accumulation and maintenance trusts is a PET (see Q59) and once it has been created there is no inheritance tax. A gift by will into such trusts is, however, liable to inheritance tax. Once it has been created, there is no inheritance tax. So there is no inheritance tax when your children get the capital at age 25, nor is there any inheritance tax payable by the estate should one of your children die before reaching 25. For income tax, the trustees will pay the basic rate of tax (currently 27 per cent) and

the investment income surcharge (18 per cent), a total of 45 per cent, whether the income is accumulated or distributed. If it is distributed, the general rule is that the child is taxed on the gross amount of the income received inclusive of the tax paid, but receives a 45 per cent credit. If your child is an unmarried minor, because you, as parent, created the settlement, while you are alive you and not your child will be taxed on the gross amount of all income distribution.

Finally, on any gift of assets into a trust, capital gains tax hold-over relief is available (see Q80) if the donor so elects.

To summarise: an accumulation and maintenance trust can be a very tax-efficient method of passing cash or assets on to those under the age of 25 during your lifetime, and will be the method to choose for gifts on death.

62 | *I want to form a fixed-interest trust to pay the income from the trust capital to my wife for life. What are the inheritance tax consequences?*

For inheritance tax, your wife is treated as owning the trust capital, so that when she dies the property is treated as forming part of her estate and will be liable to inheritance tax at the relevant rates calculated by adding the rest of her estate and trust property together (see Q48). The trustees are liable to pay the inheritance tax out of the trust capital, but the effect of adding estate and trust capital together is to increase the overall inheritance tax liability on your wife's other estate as well. This may seem unfair, particularly as when your wife dies the distribution of the trust property will almost certainly be determined not by her will but by the terms of the trust.

If the trust property is handed over early, but during your wife's lifetime, to someone entitled to the fund when she dies, this too is treated as a gift by your wife to the person who receives the money or assets. However, in this case the £3,000 annual exemption and the exemption for wedding gifts may be claimable (see Qs 46 and 52) by an election by your wife to the trustees within six months.

When you form the trust, the spouse exemption will apply, whether it is formed during your lifetime or by will, and no tax will be payable. In the (unlikely) event of your forming a fixed interest trust for someone else, tax may well be payable.

63 | *What is the income tax situation of a trust created in favour of my wife?*

The trustees are taxed on the trust income at the basic rate (currently 27 per cent). The beneficiary is taxed on the gross income of the trustees but then receives a basic-rate tax credit on that income. So if the trustees receive income of £100, they must pay £27 basic-rate tax. The beneficiary will be taxed on £100-worth of investment income and will suffer tax at his or her normal rates, with a recoverable tax credit for the £27. If the trustees receive the income net of basic-rate tax (for example, dividends and building society interest), the same principles apply except that the trustees do not actually have to hand over the 27 per cent already deducted at source.

There are some thoroughly complex income tax anti-avoidance rules that can impose an income tax liability on those who create lifetime trusts, and professional advice is essential.

64 | *What is the inheritance tax effect of giving money or assets to trustees on discretionary trusts for the benefit of my children or any other beneficiaries?*

The person (or persons) creating the trust is treated for inheritance tax as making a chargeable gift (see Q42). Thereafter, every 10 years the trust property is charged to inheritance tax at 30 per cent of the life-time rates that would have applied if the person creating the trust had made a gift of the value of the trust property then, taking into account chargeable gifts made by that person before the trust started. When the capital is distributed, a proportionate charge is made depending on the length of time since the last 10-year charge or, if none, since the start of the trust.

What this means is that small discretionary trusts can be very tax-efficient, particularly if they are within the nil-rate band of the person creating the settlement at the time they were started. No inheritance tax is payable then, and provided the trust property does not grow faster than the rate of inflation, none will be payable in future despite the 10-year charges. Consequently, discretionary trusts can be a useful way of making a gift to get property out of your estate without having to decide immediately who is to get capital, but lifetime gifts into discretionary trusts are not so tax efficient as ac-cumulation and maintenance trusts (see Q61).

The same adverse income tax implications apply as which govern accumulation and maintenance trusts, including those for payments to a minor child of the person creating the settlement.

Covenants

65 | *I have heard that a deed of covenant is a tax-efficient way of making gifts. How does a deed of covenant work?*

A deed of covenant is a legally binding agreement for one person (the 'covenantor') to make regular pay-ments to another. The covenantor normally saves income tax on the payments because he or she may deduct and keep tax at the basic rate on the gross amount when making the payments and the reci-pient receives a credit for the amount of the basic rate tax reduced. So if a grandparent, say, agrees to pay £100 a year to a grandchild, he or she deducts tax at the basic rate (£27) and hands over £73; the grandchild then has a tax credit of £27, and if his or her income is low enough for no tax to be paid, claims back the £27 from the Inland Revenue. A 'certificate of deduction' (Form R185 (AP), available from any tax office) has to be submitted to the Revenue; it is completed by the grandparent first and then handed over to the grandchild.

The payments are made to the recipient direct, year by year, but if the recipient is under age it is usual to make the payments to his or her parents for them to use the money for his or her benefit.

66 | *Does every deed of covenant qualify for income tax relief?*

No. For a start, no relief is allowed if the payments under the covenant cannot go on for more than six years (hence seven-year covenants), or three years if the recipient is a charity. The covenants do not have to go on this long; it is just that it must be a condition that they can (see Q68). Covenants are ignored (and therefore paid without deducting tax) if they are in favour of the covenantor's infant unmarried children. Covenants are also ignored if the person making the payments, or his or her spouse, receives any benefit in any way from the payments.

67 | *I want to donate a regular amount each year to charity. Is a deed of covenant a good method of doing so?*

Yes, because special rules apply to covenanted payments to charities. If the covenant can continue for more than three years, it is fully tax-deductible for the covenantor – in other words the covenantor gets full tax relief for the payments. The payments should still be made under deduction of basic rate tax, but since charities are not liable to income tax on covenanted donations (and if the money is applicable and applied to charitable purposes only) they may recover the basic rate.

What this means is that if your income is such that you pay income tax at one of the higher rates, that part of your income that you covenant to charity is only taxed at the basic rate. You therefore benefit further by paying less tax. If, for example, your top rate of tax was 60 per cent, and you covenanted £1,000 per annum to a charity, £1,000 of your income would be taxed at the basic 27 per cent, or £270 instead of £600. Given that you deduct basic rate first from the sum, the covenant would effectively cost you only £400.

68 | *If I covenant to pay my 18-year-old student son the amount of my parental contribution, will it affect his grant?*

No, not as he is an adult. If he were under 18, unless he were married, you could not deduct tax when paying the money (see Q66), although the grant itself would not be affected. If he were a mature student (over 25), or classified as independent, then the grant would be assessed on his income, and your covenant would be taken into account in the assessment.

Since the covenant only has to be capable of continuing for more than six years, the term of the covenant (as in the example on this page) can be the shorter of either seven years or until the son ceases to undergo full-time education (which can be, but hopefully will not be, more than six years).

69 | *What form should a covenant take?*

A deed of covenant must be a deed, which means it must be signed, sealed and delivered by the covenantor. Charities usually provide their own forms of

covenant. The Inland Revenue has its own form for covenants in favour of students (see below). The covenantor should sign the deed and get someone other than the recipient to witness it. The deed should also be sealed and delivered, but no special formalities are necessary provided the deed states that it is 'signed, sealed and delivered'.

Form IR 47

To be completed by a covenantor (parent)
resident in England, Wales
or Northern Ireland

Deed of Covenant

I

name of person making covenant

of

address of person making covenant

covenant to pay my son/daughter

full name of child

of

address of child

the sum of £   (gross) on   in each year
state date or dates

for the period of seven years, or for the period of our joint lives, or until he/she ceases to be receiving full-time education at any university, college, school or other educational establishment (whichever is the shortest period), the first payment to be made on

Dated

Signed, sealed and delivered by (name)

signature of person making covenant

in the presence of
witness's signature and address

Person making the Covenant

Please state below the Tax District (and reference number) which deals with your tax affairs
District
Reference

Capital gains tax

70 | *I'm about to sell an antique I bought several years ago, but I'm told there might be tax to pay on any profit I make. Is this correct?*

You could be eligible for capital gains tax, which is a tax charged on the gain made on the disposal of an asset. It is subject to a variety of exemptions and reliefs, and is levied if you are resident in the United Kingdom or usually resident here.

A 'disposal' is normally defined as being when you sell or give away an asset, but it can also occur when you receive money in respect of an asset – for example, when an asset is damaged or destroyed and you receive insurance money for it. Thus, if you had bought the antique for £5,000 but, instead of being sold, it was accidentally destroyed and your insurance company paid you £7,000, the receipt of this money would be treated as a disposal and you would have made a gain of £2,000. If you dispose of only part of an asset, for example, if you sell off part of a plot of land you have bought, that is also a disposal, and your acquisition cost will be apportioned appropriately in working out your gain.

71 | *Are there any exemptions from capital gains tax?*

Yes, there are several. Those that affect most people are for your main residence – and a second home 'occupied' rent-free by a dependent relative – for transfers of assets between spouses living together, private cars, and assets held at death.

There is also no capital gains tax on the disposal of chattels, that is, tangible movable property, if the disposal does not exceed £3,000 per item. If the consideration is just over £3,000 marginal relief is given. Chattels that are 'wasting assets' are completely exempt from capital gains tax – that is those which have a predictable useful life of less than 50 years at the date of acquisition. Boats and racehorses are included in these.

Gains made on the disposal of life assurance policies are exempt, including the proceeds paid at maturity – for example, on the death of the life assured. But capital gains tax is payable if the person receiving the money is not the original owner of the policy but bought it from someone else.

No tax is levied on the first £6,600 of all chargeable gains made by an individual in a tax year. This relief is applied after all other reliefs, and therefore applies only if you are left with what would otherwise be a chargeable gain. The only exception to this is

trustees, who only qualify for a maximum annual exemption of £3,300. The exemption is index-linked.

Finally, if you dispose of business assets or shares in your family trading company and you are over 60 or in ill-health, the gains you make can be exempt up to a maximum of £125,000.

72 | *I recently sold some shares at less than I paid for them. Is there any provision in capital gains tax for losses?*

Yes. If you make a loss on a disposal you may offset it against chargeable gains in the same tax year. So, if you lost £1,000, but later in the year make chargeable gains of £2,500, you will be liable to tax on only £1,500. If, on the other hand, your losses mean that your gains do not reach a chargeable limit – say, they do not amount to £6,600 – the extent to which the allowance is not used can be carried forward and offset against future gains without time-limit.

73 | *I bought a holiday home for £20,000 and spent £5,000 on improving it. I'm now about to sell it for £35,000. How do I calculate my gain for the purposes of capital gains tax?*

You take your 'disposal consideration', which is the amount you get when you sell the house, and subtract the cost of acquisition and your expenditure on improvements. So your gain is £10,000. This is so regardless of any mortgage you might have.

Your improvements are defined as being what has created a permanent increase in the value of your property, such as installing central heating or adding an extension. Short-term expenditure such as re-decoration and carpeting does not qualify.

74 | *If, instead of selling my holiday home for £25,000, I let my daughter have it for £10,000, partially as a gift, does that mean that I will not have to pay capital gains tax?*

No. Your disposal consideration is either the price you get on a normal commercial sale, or what you would get on goods you dispose of if they were sold commercially. If the disposal is a gift to someone, or if it is made to a 'connected person' – broadly a member of your close family or certain trustees and business associates – it does not matter what price you get, if any, and you will be treated as having made the disposal at the market value of the asset. Thus, if the house cost you £20,000, including improvements, you will still be treated as receiving the £25,000 as your disposal consideration, even though you only receive £10,000, and you will still be taxed on £5,000, subject to exemptions and hold-over relief (see Q80).

75 | *I acquired a country cottage in 1969 for £10,000, which I sold for £40,000 in May 1983. But most of my 'profit' arises from inflation. Is there any provision for this?*

Yes, capital gains tax is now index-linked, as from April 1982. But there is no index-linking for any part of a gain attributable to the period before April 1982.

The relief for index linking is given by deducting an indexation allowance for the gain. This indexation allowance is calculated by multiplying your acquisition cost by the Retail Price Index for the month in which the disposal takes place less the Retail Price Index for the month of acquisition or March 1982, whichever is later, divided by this latter figure. The Retail Price Index for March 1982 was 313.4 and the monthly figures are published regularly. If you acquired the asset before 31 March 1982, you can choose to use the market value on that date instead of the acquisition cost. Do this if the market value is higher.

If you bought a new cottage in 1969 and sold it in May 1986 when the Retail Price Index was 386.0 your taxable gain would be as follows:

Sale price	£40,000
Less cost of acquisition	£10,000
Gross gain	£30,000
Less indexation allowance	
$386.0 - 313.4 \div 313.4 \times £30,000 =$	£6,949
Net gain	£23,051

76 | *I want to sell £20,000 worth of shares to raise some capital to buy a cottage we will eventually retire to. Will I be liable to capital gains tax?*

Yes. If you dispose of shares, that will be a normal disposal for capital gains tax and generally the gain will be calculated in the same way as any other assets as will the indexation allowance.

77 | *I want to sell some shares which are all ordinary shares in the same company, but I bought them at different times. For capital gains tax purposes, which shares should I sell?*

If you have shares of the same type in the same company bought at different times, or sell them at different times, the calculation for indexing becomes more complex than if you were selling an entire holding all acquired at the same time. The different prices at which you bought and sold the shares will have to be identified in calculating the indexation allowance and the gain.

If you acquired all your shares before 6 April 1982, they are all lumped together and the combined cost is treated as your acquisition cost of the whole holding. If you sell only some of them the gain is calculated by apportioning the appropriate percentage of the acquisition cost to that part of the holding. The indexation allowance is calculated from March 1982 on the acquisition cost on that part sold. (Special rules apply where some of the holding was acquired after 5 April 1981.) If you also acquired some shares in that class on or after 6 April 1982, you are assumed to have sold shares in a sort of last-in, first-out order:

Pool 1: any shares of that class you buy on the day you also sell some

Pool 2: any shares of that class you acquired in the 10 days before you sell some

Pool 3: any shares of that class you acquired on or after 6 April 1982 which are not included in Pool 1 or Pool 2

Pool 4: any shares of that class you acquired on or after 6 April 1965 and before 6 April 1982. This pool would also include any shares which you got before 6 April 1965 but which you have chosen to value for CGT purposes on their market value on 6 April 1965

Pool 5: the final Pool is for shares of that class, other than in Pool 4, which you bought before 6 April 1965. These shares will be identified as separate purchases if there are more than one. You are assumed to have sold them on a last-in, first-out order.

Note there is no indexation allowance on Pools 1 and 2.

The following example should illustrate what happens. Let us assume the following purchases of shares in the same company:

Date of purchase	Number of shares	Cost	Cost per share
1. 6 March 1965	2,000	£2,000	£1
2. 12 December 1975	3,000	£6,000	£2
3. 15 May 1980	1,000	£2,500	£2.50
4. 10 July 1983	2,000	£6,000	£3
5. 19 June 1987	1,000	£6,000	£6

Now let us assume that on 26 June 1987 you sold 5,000 shares. Which ones have you sold? As far as your Tax Inspector is concerned, you have sold the shares you bought on 19 June 1987 (on which there is no indexation allowance) and also the shares you bought on 10 July 1983. This accounts for 3,000 out of the 5,000 shares you have sold. The shares you bought on 12 December 1975 and 15 May 1980 are put together in one Pool; this gives 4,000 shares in the Pool that you bought at an average cost of £2,500 plus £6,000 divided by 4,000, that is £2.13 per share. Your Tax Inspector will assume that on 26 June 1987 you have sold 2,000 shares from this Pool.

78 | *We want to sell our home, but we've not lived in it all the time we've owned it. Does this mean that we'll have to pay capital gains tax?*

It depends on the reasons for your absence.

Normally your dwelling-house, together with land up to one acre occupied with the house, is exempt from capital gains tax provided that it was your only or main residence throughout your period of ownership. If you did not live there continuously you will have to pay capital gains tax on your profit on the basis of the time of your absence relative to the length of your ownership.

However, you are exempt from the tax if you were away for a total period of not more than three years for any reason, or for a total of not more than four years if your absence was necessitated by your work or your spouse's work, or for any period during which you or your spouse were employed abroad. You have to have lived in the house before and after these periods. However, any absence in the last 24 months of ownership is exempt, whether you occupied the house before and after or not.

You are also exempt if you were absent because you were in job-related accommodation and you intended to occupy your dwelling-house as your only or main residence at some time thereafter.

Where part of your house is let you are exempt without time limit, but the relief is only given to that part of your gain attributable to the part let, up to a maximum of £20,000.

79 | *What happens if I have two houses?*

If you live in two or more houses you may elect which of them is to be treated as your main residence. This election operates retrospectively for up to two years, and you may change it every two years. If you fail to elect, the Inland Revenue can do so for you, so if there is any doubt you should confirm the position with your tax inspector. It is usually better to elect to treat

as your main residence the house which is going to make the greatest profit when you sell.

If, on the other hand, your second house is occupied rent-free by a dependent relative, it is exempt. A dependent relative is defined as either a relative of yours or your spouse's who is incapacitated by old age or infirmity from maintaining himself or herself, or your, or your spouse's, mother who, whether or not incapacitated, is either widowed, or living apart from her husband, or a single woman in consequence of dissolution or annulment of marriage. If the relative who occupies your second house qualifies as a dependent relative, the gain you make when you dispose of the house is exempt for the period during which the relative has occupied it.

80 | *I've been told that if I give my daughter my country cottage there's some way in which we can avoid capital gains tax. Is this true, and what's involved?*

You will not have to pay capital gains tax if 'hold-over relief' applies. This applies where you make a disposal, otherwise than at full market value, to another individual. The relief, introduced in 1980, has taken the bite out of capital gains tax, and together with indexation has made capital gains tax less of a terror than it used to be.

If both you and the recipient so elect, the chargeable gain which would otherwise arise to you is exempt, and the amount of the recipient's acquisition cost will be reduced by an amount equal to that gain.

If, say, you bought your country cottage for

£20,000 and then gave it to your daughter, providing she was not a minor, when it was worth £30,000, the nominal gain you made is £10,000. Normally you would pay capital gains tax (subject to the annual exemption of £6,600; see Q71) on the £10,000 at 30 per cent, and the tax bill would be £3,000. But if you and your daughter both elect for hold-over relief, you will have no capital gains tax liability and your child will acquire the asset for the £30,000 less the held-over gain of £10,000, in other words for £20,000. When your daughter disposes of it, her gain at the time of the sale will include that held-over gain and capital gains tax will be payable then on that held-over gain as well as on any gain your daughter makes, unless hold-over relief applies on that later disposal or it then qualifies for some other exemption or relief.

Furthermore, if your daughter paid you more than it cost you to buy the cottage, your held-over gain would be reduced by the difference.

81 | *I know that capital gains tax was introduced in April 1965. What if I acquired my asset before then?*

Capital gains tax was introduced to take effect as from 6 April 1965, and, since it was not designed to be retroactive, any gain which arose before that time is not liable to capital gains tax. When you dispose of an asset acquired before 6 April 1965, you have to work out what part of your gain can be attributed to the period before capital gains tax was introduced.

Two main sets of rules exist to do this. The first applies only to quoted shares and securities; the second applies to all other assets. There is a special rule for land with development value.

For quoted shares and securities, you are usually treated as acquiring your stocks and shares at market value on 6 April 1965. It is easy to find out what that is, because Stock Exchange lists exist for that date. However, you should calculate from the original cost of the shares if this makes a smaller gain or a smaller loss (for loss relief see Q72). If one way of calculating produces a gain and the other a loss, neither gain nor loss is deemed to arise.

For other assets it may not be easy to establish their market value on 6 April 1965. Thus, when computing the chargeable gain or loss, the original cost of acquisition is taken as the basis of calculation, and any gain or loss resulting is deemed to accrue at a uniform rate over the period of ownership. Only that part of the gain or loss apportioned to the period after 6 April 1965 is then chargeable. You may, instead, elect to be treated as having acquired the asset at market value on 6 April 1965, but not so as to increase a loss. But if the 6 April 1965 valuation would create a loss and the normal rule produce a gain, then neither gain nor loss is deemed to arise. You can imagine that it could be quite difficult to prove to the satisfaction of the Inland Revenue what was the market value of some assets on 6 April 1965.

To take an example, assume that you bought a second home on 6 April 1964 for £2,000 and you sold it on 6 April 1984 for £22,000. Of your 20 years' ownership only 19 years arise after 6 April 1965 so nineteen-twentieths of your gain of £20,000 is chargeable – £19,000. However, if you could establish that the market value of the house was £3,250 on 6 April 1965 your gain would be £18,750 and you would elect to be taxed on this.

82 | *Does capital gains tax apply to trusts?*

Yes. There are special capital gains tax rules applying to trusts, numbering four basic ones in all. First, if you put property into a trust, that is a straightforward disposal (see Q70) and capital gains tax applies; hold-over relief is usually available. Second, if the trustees sell trust property, that is also a disposal, and their capital gains are calculated in the normal way, although they only get half the individual's annual exemption (see Q71). Third, if trust property is handed over to a beneficiary, that, too, is treated as a disposal, with capital gains tax payable. Hold-over relief is available if both the trustees and the beneficiaries agree. Four, on the death of the beneficiary entitled to a fixed interest, the trust assets are exempt from capital gains tax and the trustees are treated as acquiring the trust assets at market value at the date of the death, unless hold-over relief was used on the creation of the trust.

Tax and divorce

Income tax

When a marriage has broken down and one party is paying maintenance, it is usually possible to 'spread' the income among the members of the family so as to reduce the income tax burden. When there is a sole earner – in most cases the husband and father – what he pays to each recipient can cease to be regarded as his income for tax purposes and instead becomes the income of the payee. His taxable income is therefore reduced. In addition, each person, even a very young child, has a personal tax relief, which makes the first slice of his or her income free of tax. The combined total of these individual tax reliefs will be higher than the married man's allowance, so a large part of the family income will not be subject to tax at all. This saving can be taken into account in deciding the correct level of maintenance.

Before looking at how this spreading operates, we have to establish some basic principles of income tax:

● income for tax purposes includes earnings and maintenance receivable under a court order or enforceable agreement, but not most state benefits
● income tax is calculated on yearly figures (6 April–5 April)
● the basic rate of income tax (for tax year 1987–8) is 27 per cent, charged on taxable income up to £17,900, with higher rates above that (see page 367)
● taxable income is a person's gross annual income (statutory income) less 'charges on income', which includes maintenance payable under a court order or enforceable agreement, and personal reliefs.

The relevant personal reliefs (for 1987–8) are:

● £2,425 for an individual, including usually a single or separated adult, or a child – known as the 'single person's relief'
● £3,795 for a married man living with his wife, or 'wholly and voluntarily' maintaining her if separated – known as the 'married man's relief'
● £3,795 for a person otherwise entitled to the single person's relief, but who has the care of a minor child still in education or training; this category includes widowed, separated or divorced parents and unmarried parents. Though single or separated, such people have an extra £1,370 added to the single person's relief, known as the 'lone parent's relief'. This gives them the equivalent of a married man's allowance.

As an example of how spreading the income can work, let us assume that Alan earns £19,150 per annum, and that his wife, Betty, does not work and has no income, neither do their two children. For the tax year before separation Alan claims the married man's relief. This gives him:

	£
Earnings	19,150
less married man's relief	3,795
Taxable income	15,355
Tax payable at 27 per cent on £15,355	=4,145
Total tax	=4,145

After separation, Alan is ordered by a court to pay £5,000 per annum to Betty, and £2,000 to each of the children. He is no longer entitled to the married man's relief, only the single person's relief, but Betty becomes entitled to the lone parent's relief. Both children have single person's reliefs. The £9,000 maintenance is deducted from Alan's earnings in calculating his taxable income, making his position now:

		£
Earnings		19,150
less single person's relief	£2,425	
Maintenance payable	£9,000	11,425
Taxable income		7,725

Tax at 27 per cent on £7,725 = £2,086

Betty now has an income for tax purposes, and is assessed as follows:

	£
Income (maintenance)	5,000
less lone parent's relief	3,795
Taxable income	1,205

Tax payable at 27 per cent = £325

Each child has an income of £2,000, but, as this is less than the single person's relief, they pay no tax on it. They would only be eligible for tax if they also had other income which, combined with the maintenance, took their earnings above the single person's relief.

The total tax bill for the family has fallen from £4,145 to £2,411 a year, a reduction of £1,734, or about £33 a week. This saving will help meet the extra costs of running two households instead of one.

However, the tax position on divorce is not always as in this example, as it varies according to the type of maintenance agreement reached. The important factor with Alan and Betty is that they had a court order, and that the order was worded to make the child maintenance payable to each child, making it the child's own income. Such an order is not only made after a contested hearing, but can also be made as a consent order, with both parties agreeing.

There are two other ways in which a couple might arrange for maintenance to be paid, by voluntary maintenance and by an enforceable agreement. In voluntary maintenance the husband pays amounts which have been informally agreed without any court order or enforceable maintenance agreement. This is common in the early days of a separation. An enforceable agreement is an agreement, usually drawn up formally by solicitors, which requires the husband to pay specified amounts of spouse or child maintenance.

Each of these three ways of paying maintenance affects the amount of tax payable and the machinery by which the tax due reaches the Inland Revenue, as the following examples show.

Let us assume that Colin earns £11,000 per annum. His wife Diana has no income. There are two children of whom she has custody. Colin is to pay a total of £4,500 per annum by way of maintenance, with £2,000 for Diana and £1,250 for each of the two children.

VOLUNTARY MAINTENANCE

This will have no real tax effect. The position is just as it was when the couple were still together, with Colin claiming the married man's allowance (the couple are not yet divorced).

	£
Earnings	11,000
less married man's relief	3,795
Taxable income	7,205

Tax payable at 27 per cent = £1,945

After paying tax and maintenance Colin has £4,555 left.

Neither Diana nor the children has an income for tax purposes, so, no tax being payable, she has £4,500.

ENFORCEABLE AGREEMENT

Enforceable agreements are effective in transferring income from one spouse or ex-spouse to the other, but the child maintenance is not regarded as the child's income; it is seen as the income of one or other parent. The benefit of the child's own personal relief therefore, does not apply.

If you try to get round this by wording the agreement so that the child maintenance is payable to the child, a complex anti-avoidance rule comes into play, and the maintenance is treated for tax purposes as the father's income. As a result this form is not used. However, you can word the agreement so that the child maintenance is payable 'to the mother for its benefit'. Then the child maintenance becomes the mother's income for tax purposes. It is added to her other income and taxed accordingly.

If Colin and Diana entered into such an agreement, with £2,600 payable to her for her own benefit, and £950 to her for the benefit of each child, the result would be as follows.

For Colin:

		£
Earnings		11,000
less single person's relief	£2,425	
maintenance	£4,500	6,925
Taxable income		4,075

Tax payable at 27 per cent = £1,100

After paying maintenance and tax he has £5,400 left.

For Diana and the children:

	£
Income (maintenance)	4,500
less lone parent's relief	3,795
Taxable income	705

Tax payable at 27 per cent = £190

After paying tax on the maintenance she has £4,310. The total tax payable by Colin and Diana is £1,290.

COURT ORDER FOR MAINTENANCE

These are also effective to transfer income from one spouse or ex-spouse to the other.

Child maintenance can be expressed either as payable 'to the child' or 'to the mother for the child's benefit', but with different effects from those under an enforceable maintenance agreement. If the order is worded 'pay to the child', the amount of the maintenance will become the *child's* income for tax purposes, and will not be that of either parent. If the order is for payments 'to the mother for the child's benefit' the income will be the mother's, as it was in the case of an enforceable agreement.

So, if there is a court order requiring Colin to pay £2,600 to Diana for her own benefit and £950 to her for the benefit of each child, the positions will be just the same as they were under an enforceable agreement. But if the order was for Colin to pay £2,600 to Diana, and £950 to each child, there is a bigger tax saving.

Colin's position will be the same as in the previous example, because all the maintenance is still deductible from his income for tax purposes. He pays £1,100 tax.

Because Diana now has an income of only £2,600. and therefore less than her lone parent's personal relief, she pays no tax. Also, because each child's income of £950 is less than its single person's relief, no tax is payable on the child maintenance either. Therefore, with no tax to pay, she has £4,500.

To summarise the tax consequences of the various methods of arranging maintenance for the family:

Tax payable where voluntary maintenance is paid during marriage	£1,945
Tax payable under an enforceable maintenance agreement	£1,290
Tax payable under an order giving child maintenance to the mother for the child's benefit	£1,290
Tax payable under an order giving child maintenance to the child	£1,100

This is assuming that neither Diana nor the children have any income apart from the maintenance. But if any of them does, it will be added to the maintenance and tax, or more tax, may be paid accordingly.

Suppose that Colin is again ordered to pay £2,600 to Diana and £950 to each of the children, but that now she earns £2,600 from part-time work. Colin's position is not affected, nor is that of the children, but Diana's tax is calculated as follows:

	£
Earnings	2,600
add maintenance	2,600
	5,200
less lone parent's relief	3,795
Taxable income	1,405

Tax payable at 27 per cent = £379

Children do not usually have any income apart from maintenance, but if one of them here, for example, received interest on a legacy or accident damages invested for him, it would be added to his maintenance and the tax calculated accordingly. Colin will not be affected in either case.

It is obvious from what we have seen that the best way to save income tax is to have a court order which is worded to make the child maintenance payable to the child. This takes best advantage of the child's own personal tax relief and keeps the mother's taxable income down.

Collection of tax

The ways in which tax is paid to the Inland Revenue depends on whether maintenance is being paid by an enforceable agreement or a court order. As voluntary maintenance has no real tax effects, it will just be paid over by one party to the other without any tax formality at all.

PAYMENTS UNDER DEDUCTION OF TAX

Where one person is obliged to make payments of income to another person who provides nothing in return, the law requires the payer to deduct tax at the basic rate of 27 per cent from each payment. The payee gets only the net amount, and the tax deducted is added to the payer's own tax bill and paid to the Revenue with the rest of his or her tax. This is not confined to maintenance on marriage breakdown, but applies to all such payments, such as covenants to charities and to student children. This rule always applies to payments made under an enforceable maintenance agreement and, depending upon the amount of the payments, can also apply to those made under court orders.

If the payee has paid too much tax by having basic rate tax deducted from the whole of the maintenance, the excess can be reclaimed from the Revenue at the end of the tax year, or sometimes earlier if the inspector of taxes agrees.

We can illustrate this by looking at Colin and Diana's position on page 387. There we were only concerned to work out the total tax bills for the family, and found that Colin should bear tax of £1,100 on his taxable income of £4,075 and that, after paying tax and maintenance, he was left with £6,400. On her income Diana should pay £190 tax and be left with £4,310. These are the net result figures. For Colin to have arrived in this position, the following calculations apply:

		£
Earnings		11,000
less single person's relief	£2,425	
maintenance	£4,500	6,925
Taxable income		4,075

Tax payable at 27 per cent	=£1,100
Add back 27 per cent of £4,500	=£1,215
Colin pays to the Revenue	£2,315

Since he is paying basic rate tax on Diana's income – the maintenance – he recoups it by deducting the £1,215 from the payments he makes to her, and pays her the net amount of £3,285. Therefore, after paying £2,315 to the Revenue and £3,285 to Diana, he has £5,400 left, as before.

For Diana and the children:

	£
Income (maintenance – gross)	4,500
less lone parent's relief	3,795
Taxable income	705

Tax payable at 27 per cent=£190

But Colin has already deducted £1,215 in tax, which is more than she should have paid. She therefore reclaims the excess of £1,025 from the Revenue. She then receives £3,285 from Colin and £1,025 from the Revenue, so she has a total of £4,310, as before.

Diana may, however, have 'cash flow' problems by not getting all her maintenance when she should. She has a lower income through the tax year and something of a bonanza at the end when her refund comes in. As a result, the inspector of taxes may agree to give her some or all of her refund early, or Colin could 'lend' her some of the tax he would otherwise deduct if she agrees to repay him out of the refund when she gets it.

To enable her to claim the refund, Colin will give Diana a tax deduction certificate with each payment of maintenance, showing the amount of tax deducted.

SMALL MAINTENANCE PAYMENTS

Maintenance payable *under a court order* can sometimes be paid gross, without the payer deducting tax. This does not affect the total amount of tax payable, only the method of tax collection. It never applies to enforceable maintenance agreements.

Small maintenance payments are governed by certain financial limits:

● £48 per week/£208 per month/£2,496 per annum spouse maintenance
● £48 per week/£208 per month/£2,496 per annum child maintenance if expressed payable to the child
● £28 per week/£108 per month/£1,296 per annum child maintenance if expressed payable to the mother for the child's benefit.

To illustrate this, let us assume that Eric earns £8,000 per annum and is ordered to pay £1,500 to his ex-wife Frances and £750 to each of their two children. These amounts are all within small maintenance payments limits, so he will pay gross. For Eric:

		£
Earnings		8,000
less single person's relief	£2,425	
maintenance	£3,000	5,425
Taxable income		2,575

Tax payable at 27 per cent=£695

There is no deduction of tax from the maintenance and therefore nothing to add to this tax figure.

If the amounts of maintenance are below the amounts for their personal reliefs, Frances and the children have no tax to pay, and as none has been deducted by Eric there is no refund of tax to claim. But if Frances has an income herself, say of £2,500 from part-time earnings, she would be liable to pay tax because her income would now be £4,000, and the excess of this over her lone parent's personal relief would attract tax. The fact that a small maintenance payment is made gross does not stop it being income of the payee on which tax may be payable.

A single order may contain items some of which are small maintenance payments and some of which are not. Each must be treated as appropriate. In the example of Colin and Diana, the £2,600 payable to her is not a small maintenance payment because it is too large, but the £950 payable to each child falls within the limits. This is a common situation in middle-income cases.

Therefore, the full calculation for Colin's payments on a court maintenance order is as follows:

		£
Earnings		11,000
less single person's relief	£2,425	
maintenance	£4,500	6,925
Taxable income		4,075
Tax payable at 27 per cent	=£1,100	
Add back 27 per cent of £2,600		
(Diana's maintenance)	=£702	
Total tax	£1,802	

Colin therefore pays:

	£
to the Revenue	1,802
Diana's maintenance net	1,898
the children's maintenance gross	1,900
	5,600

After paying these, he has £5,400 left, just as before.

Diana's and the children's personal reliefs exceed the amounts of maintenance, and so they will not pay any tax. The child maintenance will be received gross. Her maintenance will be received net, but, because she is not liable to tax, the £702 deducted by Colin will be reclaimed in full. She will therefore have:

	£
from Colin, child maintenance gross	1,900
from Colin, her maintenance net	1,898
from the Revenue, her refund	702
	4,500

Again the inspector might agree to give her a refund before the end of the tax year, or Colin might lend her the amount of tax deducted until the refund is received.

Small maintenance payments help the payee with domestic cash flow arrangements, and they save both parties the irritation of having to operate the usual deduction scheme.

Income tax and maintenance

1 | *Is a court order always better than an agreement from a tax point of view?*

At best an agreement will only be as good as an order, and in the average case an order will be better because the child maintenance can be made the child's income for tax purposes. This will usually save tax for the payer and produce a maintenance amount that is quite tax-free.

Also, an order for small enough amounts will create small maintenance payments which are paid without deduction of tax. This helps cash flow for the recipient, and both parties avoid the irritation of dealing with deduction of tax. Where, however, there are no children, and the spouse maintenance paid exceeds the small maintenance payment limit, an agreement will be just as tax-efficient.

2 | *My wife and I are separating. We would like to save tax by having a court order now, but we do not intend to get a divorce for two years when we will get one by consent. What can we do?*

The simplest course is to apply to the magistrates' court for a consent order. That court has power to make an order for spouse or child maintenance at any stage during the marriage, the amount being whatever the parties have agreed. The procedure is straightforward.

3 | *Can I save tax on school fees if we have a court order for maintenance?*

Yes. Curiously enough, the parties to a broken marriage have a tax advantage in paying school fees out of current income which they did not have before the breakdown.

Most parents who are paying school fees are likely to be in the higher-rate tax brackets, and before their marriage broke up would have been paying the fees out of taxed income. If you are a higher-rate taxpayer, you will save on tax if an order is made shifting income from you to a child who will pay no tax on some of the maintenance and only basic rate on the rest. So if you include the amount of the school fees in the child maintenance and let the child pay the fees, notionally at any rate, you get tax relief at your highest rate on the fees.

There is, however, a complication. As the parent pays the money over to the school the Inland Revenue insists that the school must receive the fees as the child's agent, and that these fees are the child's responsibility which the parent is discharging, rather than the parent's own responsibility. Consequently, a special form of order has been agreed between the courts and the Revenue. Schools have contracts which provide accordingly for such cases.

4 | *My wife is staying in the house. Should I pay the mortgage or give her more maintenance so she can pay it?*

Usually it is best for the husband to pay the wife enough maintenance to enable her to pay the mortgage. He will get tax relief on the maintenance, provided that it is paid under a court order or enforceable agreement, and she will get tax relief on the mortgage interest which she pays, so long as she owns or co-owns the house.

Although you could get tax relief if you pay the interest (provided that you own or co-own the property), the amount of the mortgage debt would reduce the size of loan on which you could get tax relief were you to buy another house. You can only get tax relief on loans not exceeding £30,000 in all, or the first £30,000 of a larger total. So if the present mortgage is for £20,000 and you pay the mortgage interest, you can only get relief on another £10,000 if you buy another house. If your wife pays the interest on the old home out of increased maintenance, you can get relief on a loan of up to the full £30,000 on a new one.

5 | *What is the best way for my wife and me to arrange for rent, rates and other outgoings to be paid?*

No tax relief is available for paying these, unlike mortgage interest. The normal practice on divorce is for the wife to pay them out of maintenance provided by the husband and calculated to enable her to do so.

You will get tax relief on the maintenance in the normal way, which will save tax at your highest rates if your wife or ex-wife is paying tax at a lower rate than you, or none at all. In addition, if she is paying these outgoings out of a modest income, she may well be able to claim Housing Benefit which will cover all or part of the rent and rates, and that will make it cheaper for both of you.

Other taxes

6 | *When is capital gains tax likely to be payable on marriage breakdown?*

There are two common situations which may give rise to a capital gains tax liability. The first is the sale of an asset to a third party, which may happen where some property is being sold and the proceeds divided, or where one spouse is selling property to raise a lump sum to pay to the other. The second is the transfer of property by one party to the marriage to the other, including a part share in property.

Both these will be 'disposals' for capital gains tax purposes. The normal exemption for disposals between spouses applies only until the tax year of separation, but the home is subject to special rules (see QS2 and 3).

For a tax liability to arise in the first place the asset being disposed of must have risen in value since it was acquired. If it is co-owned, each party is liable in respect of his or her part of the gain only. The first £6,600 of gains made in a tax year are exempt, and the element of gains made since March 1982 due to inflation is taken out of charge by the indexation allowance.

In short, capital gains tax is only likely to become payable where an asset other than the home has risen in value since it was acquired and it is now transferred or sold, with a gain in excess of £6,600. Assets which are particularly likely to attract this tax are second homes, stocks and shares and business assets, but it is prudent to take advice if in any doubt. Property worth £50,000 will not raise a £50,000 lump sum or buy a £50,000 house if tax has to be paid on the sale.

7 | *We are selling the house and splitting the proceeds. Is there any capital gains tax to pay?*

It would be unusual to find any payable. Gains on the disposal of your 'only or main residence' are exempt, provided that you have lived there throughout your period of ownership. You are treated as having lived there during your last two years of ownership whether you did or not. Therefore, provided that the sale takes place within two years of separation, neither party will have a chargeable gain.

If either of you left the home more than two years before the sale, he or she may have a tax liability, but only in respect of that part of the gain made between his or her departure and the date two years before the sale. If it is less than £6,600 (after allowing for the indexation allowance) the gain will be covered by the annual exemption; if it is more, only the balance is taxed. A party who was in occupation throughout the period of ownership, or all but the last two years, will have no chargeable gain.

8 | *I am transferring my half of the house to my wife. Will I be liable to capital gains tax?*

It is most unlikely. If the transfer takes place in the tax year in which you separate there will be none, because of the spouse exemption. If the transfer takes place within two years of your leaving the house, there will again be none because of the 'only or main residence' exemption. If it takes place later, you should still be all right, because the Inland Revenue will still treat you as having occupied the house, provided that it has been occupied by your wife and that you have not elected to treat some other property as your only or main residence in the meantime.

Should none of those apply, the gain attributable to the time you were in occupation and the last two years of ownership is exempt, and the annual exemp-

tion for the first £6,600 of gains in a tax year, together with the indexation allowance for the period after March 1982, will help with the rest, if they do not cover it all.

9 | *Is there any likelihood of inheritance tax being payable as a result of the property and financial settlement on divorce?*

No, not really. Although property or money may well pass from one party to the other as part of the settlement, it is most unlikely to attract inheritance tax. Transfers between spouses are exempt without limit, so any transfer made before the decree absolute will not be taxed. For transfers after the decree absolute, other provisions except those made for family maintenance and what are known as arm's length transfers 'not intended to confer a gratuitous benefit'. Since the parties may well be at daggers drawn, in addition to being at arm's length, the Inland Revenue not surprisingly accepts that a *bona fide* settlement is covered by the exemption.

Benefits

Supplementary Benefit

1 | *My husband left home two months ago. Although he sent some maintenance for the first four weeks, I've not had anything since either for myself or our two children. Apart from £800 in a building society, I have no other money. What help can I get?*

First, you should claim Supplementary Benefit (SB) as quickly as possible; it is payable from the date of claim and is not normally backdated. SB is a means-tested

BENEFIT RATES

Benefit	Rate
	£
Unemployment	31.45
Sickness	30.05
Retirement pension (single person)	39.50
Invalidity benefit (payable after sickness benefit elapsed)	39.50
Severe disablement allowance	23.75
Attendance allowance (higher)	31.60
(lower)	21.10
Mobility allowance	22.10
Invalid care allowance	23.75
Maternity allowance	30.05
Widow's allowance	55.35
Widowed mother's allowance	39.50
Widow's pension	39.50
Child benefit (each child)	7.25
(one parent addition)	4·70
Supplementary benefit	page 395
Family income supplement maximum where one child in family aged under 11	25.85*
increase for each child after first under 11	2.60*
prescribed level (one child under 11)	100.70*
increase in prescribed level for extra child under 11	11.90*
Disablement benefit	page 402

* higher if child aged over 11

benefit – whether you get it and, if so, how much depends on your circumstances and how much income you have. It is available to anyone over 16 lawfully residing in Great Britain who is not in full-time work. In general, you have to be available for work in order to claim SB, but there are exceptions – one of them being single parents, that is those who have sole care of dependent children under 16.

You will also have to satisfy the DHSS that your separation from your husband is genuine. If it is clear that the separation is not due to breakdown of your marriage – for example, if your husband has gone away for a few months on business – the benefit will not generallly be payable unless there is an emergency and you are destitute; such payments, known as urgent needs payments, may have to be repaid later when your husband can be contacted.

In calculating the amount of SB you will get, the DHSS first works out your resources, both capital and income. If those resources fall short of your needs then you receive as SB the amount of the shortfall.

If your *capital* is more than £3,000 you will not be entitled to SB. The home and its contents are not treated as a capital resource and neither is the first £1,500 of the surrender value of life assurance policies.

Most *income* resources, whether from part-time work, maintenance received, other benefits and so on will be taken into account. If you take a part-time job (up to 30 hours a week) the DHSS will disregard up to £12 a week of your *net* earnings (it disregards £4 in all cases, plus, for single parents only, half of any earnings beween £4 and £20, giving a maximum of £12). Travelling, work and child-minding expenses can be deducted from earnings. Any maintenance you receive from your husband will be taken into account, but if you refuse to apply for maintenance the DHSS should accept your decision and not pressurise you to do so.

Assuming that you have no income other than £14.50 Child Benefit (£7.25 per week per child, to which anyone looking after a child living in the same household is entitled) and that your only capital is £800, which can be disregarded, you will get a basic SB (assuming both your children are under 11):

single householder rate	£30.40
2 × £10.40 for each child	£20.80
	£51.20
less Child Benefit	£14.50
	£ 36.70 per week

Certain of your housing costs will also be met by SB. Mortgage interest you pay is included when calculating your SB – though only half is taken into account for the first 16 weeks after you claim. You will also get a sum (currently £1.95) each week towards the costs of house repairs and insurance and a further sum to cover your water rates.

There are a number of additional weekly payments that can be regularly met by SB, depending on individual circumstances. For example, a regular addition is paid if you have a child under five. There are also single lump sum payments to meet special needs (see Q4).

In April 1988 SB will be replaced by *income support*. It will be means tested in the same way as SB, though the capital cut-off will be increased to £6,000. However, the distinction between householders and non-householders, and the long-term rate, will be abolished, and there will be no more additional weekly payments. Instead, *premiums* will increase the weekly requirements for families, single parents, pensioners and the disabled.

In addition to Supplementary Benefit you will also get Housing Benefit from the local authority to cover your rates (and rent if you are a tenant; see Q6).

As a single parent you will be entitled to One-Parent Benefit. £4.70 per week is payable irrespective of the number of children you have. It will be payable 90 days after the beginning of the separation (unless a court order is obtained before this, in which case One-Parent Benefit is payable from the date of the court order). This benefit can be backdated for up to a year. However, it does count as income for SB purposes, so you will not receive arrears for any period during which you were receiving SB.

Finally, you will be entitled to other benefits automatically once you receive SB – free prescriptions, dental treatment, glasses vouchers and free school meals for the children.

2 | *When I was declared redundant I received a redundancy payment of £7,000. While I was receiving Unemployment Benefit we spent some of the money and I now have £5,500 left. Soon my entitlement to Unemployment Benefit will end and I have no other income. Will I have to spend this money before I am entitled to Supplementary Benefit? I'd like to give a nice reception for my daughter, who is getting married soon.*

You cannot claim Supplementary Benefit if your capital is more than £3,000. On the face of it, therefore, once you have spent £2,500 of your £5,500 you

will be entitled to Supplementary Benefit. But if the DHSS considers that you have spent the money deliberately or given it away in order to claim SB then it will treat you as though you still had it and refuse to pay the benefit; it will regard you as having 'notional' resources of £5,500. If you use your money for yourself in a reasonable way, the DHSS will not be able to prove that you deliberately spent it to claim benefit. According to the guidance issued by the DHSS, you can take a reasonable holiday, pay for home improvements, buy reasonable personal possessions such as a cooker or a washing machine; but if you buy luxury items like jewellery, the Adjudication Officer will take their value into account when calculating your capital. However, it would be thought reasonable to buy a modest wedding present for a son or daughter, say. Providing a lavish wedding reception might well be construed as deliberately spending money in order to obtain benefit, although a reasonably modest one will be disregarded. The important factor is your motive: if you spend the money deliberately in order to get benefit then the money you spend will be treated as notional resources and the benefit will be denied or reduced.

3 | *I'm 20, living at home and unemployed. I want to get some A-levels by studying at a college of further education. Will this effect my Supplementary Benefit?*

The general rule is that if you are under 19 and at school or college you will not be able to get Supplementary Benefit at all (there are some very limited exceptions to this rule, such as students who are orphaned, or estranged from their parents). If you are 19 and over, you will also not be able to get SB if you are in full-time education at least during term-time. The reason is that one condition for getting SB is that you must be available for work and if you are a student at college doing a course you will not be available. It does not matter that you are prepared to give up the course if an offer of a job arises; nor does it matter if, although the course is defined as being full-time, it in fact requires attendance at college for only a few hours a week. People *not* required to be available for work – single parents, the disabled, the sick, and the blind – will be able to do a course of full-time education without its affecting their Benefit. However, it is arguable that the rules apply only to higher education courses, and as A-levels are not, provided you are available for work you should be eligible for benefit.

If your course is not full-time but part-time you will

SUPPLEMENTARY BENEFIT

Normal requirements	ordinary rate £	long-term rate £
Couple (whether married or not)	49.35	61.85
Single householder	30.40	38.65
Any other person* aged:		
18 years and over	24.35	30.95
16–17 years	18.75	23.70
11–15 years	15.60	15.60
under 11 years	10.40	10.40
Personal allowance for boarders		
Couple (whether married or not)	20.00	22.30
Single boarder	10.00	11.15
Dependant aged:		
over 18	10.00	
16–17	6.00	
11–15	5.15	
under 11	3.35	
Standard additional requirements		
– if sick or disabled	2.20	
– if housebound or suffer from serious illness	5.55	
– if home difficult to heat	2.20	
– if home exceptionally difficult to heat	5.55	
Age addition if aged 80 or over	0.25	
Blindness addition	1.25	
Resources disregarded		
Capital resources disregarded	3,000	
The surrender value of life policies		
– the first	1,500	

* This includes non-householders

hours a week. This provision has caused much difficulty. Should you count only the hours you have to attend classes or also include the hours spent on homework or in meal-breaks at college? The rule now is that in calculating the 21 hours you include supervised hours in the classroom or laboratory but *not* meal-breaks or unsupervised private study, even if done in the college library.

If, later on, you decide you want to go on and do higher education such as a degree or diploma of some kind, then you will not be entitled to SB during term-time. If you have an educational grant of some kind (the amount is generally related to your parents' income unless you are 26 and over), then this will normally be expected to last for the Christmas and Easter vacations also, so you will not get Benefit for these periods. However, you could be entitled to SB for the summer vacation provided you are available for work. This is a complex area of law and you should contact your students' union welfare officer for more details.

If you have been told by the DHSS that as a student you are not entitled to Benefit because you are automatically regarded as being unavailable for work, get in touch with the Child Poverty Action Group (address on page 509) for help in making an appeal.

Single payments

4 | *I've been receiving Supplementary Benefit for several years but find it difficult to manage. The house badly needs work doing on it and my five-year-old son needs a new pair of shoes. Can I get any extra help?*

be regarded as being available for work provided the following conditions are satisfied:

● you will give up the course as soon as a suitable job is offered, *and*

● *either* for the three months immediately before the course you were getting SB, Unemployment Benefit or Sickness Benefit or were on a Youth Training Scheme *or* you got these Benefits or were on schemes for at least three months in the past six months even though in between those spells you were working full-time.

A part-time course is one of not more than 21

One-off grants, known as single payments, are available to help people on Supplementary Benefit with items that they cannot afford to buy out of their weekly Benefit. To qualify for a single payment you must genuinely need the item (and not already possess it or a suitable alternative), and you must not have unreasonably disposed of an item you wish to replace or refused to accept an offer of a suitable alternative. You will qualify for single payments even if you have savings, but if they are more than £500 your single payment will be reduced by the amount by which they exceed £500.

Single payments are available for essential redecoration only if you or one of your family is a pensioner, chronically sick or physically or mentally disabled and you have lived in your home for at least a year and are an owner-occupier or, if you rent your home, are responsible under your agreement for decorating it. The redecoration must not be caused by any major repairs, renovations or alterations to your home. The single payment will cover the cost of the materials. If there is a non-dependant in the household who uses the part that you are decorating, you will be paid less and the non-dependant will be expected to pay a proportion of the cost. However, if he or she receives SB or cannot afford to pay you will get the full cost.

If more substantial work is needed you may qualify for a single payment for repairs 'essential to preserve the home in a habitable condition'. However, you must have no other way of paying for the repairs, such as a council grant or a loan from a building society (the interest on which would be paid by the DHSS). The cost of the repairs and consequential decoration necessary to keep the home habitable must be too high to be met from the maintenance and insurance addition (see Q1) but less than £325. You will receive the 'reasonable' cost up to £325. Where repairs would cost in total more than £325, a single payment will be made only if the repairs which cost less than £325 would alone make the home habitable.

Single payments are not normally available to cover the cost of repairing and replacing clothing and shoes unless the need arose 'otherwise than by normal wear and tear' such as rapid weight gain or loss. However, a single payment will be made if it is the only means by which serious damage or serious risk to the health and safety of any member of the family may be prevented. You could argue, for instance, that your son's shoes are too small and that permanent damage could be caused by ill-fitting shoes and that a single payment is the only way to prevent a serious risk to his health. This type of single pay-

ment is made only as a last resort and it will not be made if you have any savings or are a member of a clothing club to which you could turn.

For further advice see *National Welfare Benefits Handbook* published by the Child Poverty Action Group and available from the address on page 509.

In April 1988 single payments will be replaced by social fund loans and payments. Except in the case of maternity and funeral payments, whether or not help is given is at the discretion of the DHSS and there will be no right of appeal if you are unhappy about a decision. Most payments will be in the form of loans repayable out of weekly benefit.

Unemployment Benefit

5 | *I've worked as a teacher for several years but I'm thinking of leaving to take a part-time teaching job or perhaps to work in a voluntary organisation. If I leave my job before having anything to go to, will I be entitled to Unemployment Benefit?*

If you leave your job voluntarily you will be disqualified from Unemployment Benefit for up to 13 weeks unless you had 'just cause' for leaving. Feeling like a change is unlikely to be a just cause, but starting a job and finding soon after that you are not suited to it might be. Other grounds that disqualify people from Unemployment Benefit for up to 13 weeks are:

- losing a job through misconduct
- refusing, without good cause, an offer of suitable employment.

Further disqualifications relate to failure to take up training or offers of help to find a job.

While you are disqualified from Unemployment Benefit, you receive less Supplementary Benefit than you would normally get; it is reduced by 40 per cent of the householder rate (see Q1), that is, £12.15. However, if you, or a member of your family, were pregnant or seriously ill and you had capital of less than £100, your Supplementary Benefit would be reduced by 20 per cent of the householder rate, that is, £6.08.

Unemployment Benefit is a contributory benefit (paid for by National Insurance contributions) payable for 52 weeks, or 312 days (Sundays not included), during a 'period of interruption of employment' for a 'day of unemployment'. A 'day of unemployment' is a day on which you are capable of and available for work; a 'period of interruption of employment' consists of at least two days of unemployment within six consecutive days. Also, if there are two or more such periods of interruption of employment separated by eight weeks or less, they are treated as one period of interruption of employment (this is called the 'linking rule'). Unemployment Benefit is not paid for the first three days of a period of interruption of employment (called 'waiting days'). Thus, if you left your job, were unemployed for six months and then found another job only to lose it seven weeks later, you would not have to serve the waiting days again because it would be treated as one period of interruption of employment.

You must be available for work, which means that you must not put unreasonable restrictions on the jobs you would be prepared to accept or the place where you would work. If you said you were prepared to accept only teaching jobs this would not prevent you from claiming Unemployment Benefit, but if after some weeks or months you still had not found a job then it might be considered reasonable that you should be prepared to accept some other job, such as clerical work.

If you found a part-time job you would not be entitled to Unemployment Benefit on the days that you were working if you earned more than £2.00 a day *or* were working in your normal occupation (unless it was working for a charity) *or* if it prevented you from being available to take a full-time job. However, you would be entitled to benefit on the other days if you were available for work and they formed part of a period of interruption of employment. You would have to show that there was a reasonable prospect of obtaining a part-time job on the days you were not already working or that you were prepared to take a full-time job if offered one. If you do a part-time job for more than about a year, the 'full extent normal' rule comes into play, which means that where you have an established pattern of part-time work you will not be able to receive Unemployment Benefit for the days you do not work. You might be able to claim Supplementary Benefit provided that you work for no more than 30 hours a week, but, again, you would have to show that you were available for work. Once you have received 312 days' Unemployment Benefit, you will not be entitled to any more until you have found a job and worked for at least 16 hours a week for a total of 13 weeks or more.

You should claim Unemployment Benefit as soon as possible as it can be paid for a day before you make a claim only if you had good cause for the delay.

Family Income Supplement

6 | *I work full-time but my wages are low – only £80 per week gross. I have two children, aged three and six. My wife helps out at a pub, for which she gets about £15 a session. Am I entitled to any state help?*

The benefit available to people in full-time work is Family Income Supplement (FIS). To get FIS you must satisfy two conditions:

● you must be in normal full-time work, defined as a minimum of 30 hours a week (24 hours in the case of single parents);
● you must have one or more dependent children living at home with you.

To calculate how much FIS you will receive, find out the normal *gross* income of both yourself and your wife over the past five weeks and add the two together. If either of your incomes fluctuates considerably, it may be averaged out over a longer period. Do *not* deduct either tax or National Insurance contributions.

Second, add any other income you may have – interest on savings, occasional freelance jobs, and so on. Do *not* include Child Benefit or Housing Benefit; these benefits are disregarded (although the amount of Housing Benefit you get will be affected by the amount of FIS you receive). Capital such as savings in a building society is also disregarded; only the *income* from capital is taken into account.

Now compare your gross income with the 'prescribed level' of income. If your income is less than the prescribed level, you will be entitled to half the amount by which it falls short. Assuming your wife's average weekly earnings are £15 and you have no other income, the calculations will be:

gross earnings self	£80	prescribed amount	£100.70
wife	£15	addition for each child after first	£11.90
total	£95	total	£112.60

£112.60 − £95 = £17.60
FIS = half of £17.60 = £8.80

You will receive this sum for 52 weeks before any reassessment is made. It will not change even if your income increases or decreases or if you have another child. FIS cannot normally be backdated.

In addition to FIS you can claim Housing Benefit (see Q7) from your local authority to help with rent and rates (*not* for help with paying a mortgage).

Finally, you should not forget some of the other benefits to which you may be entitled: free prescriptions, vouchers for glasses, dental treatment, milk-tokens for expectant mothers and pre-school children, free school meals for children at school, and refunds of fares for trips to hospital for treatment.

In April 1988 FIS will be replaced by *family credit*, and anyone working at least 24 hours a week will be able to claim. You will not be automatically entitled to milk tokens, vitamins or free school meals.

Housing Benefit

7 | *I'm a pensioner living on my own in a privately rented flat for which I pay £20 rent, £10 rates and £1 water rates a week. I have a retirement pension of £39.50, an occupational pension of £4 and a disablement pension of £5. I've fallen behind with my rent and I'm worried that my landlord may try to evict me. Can I get any help with my housing costs?*

Your local authority is responsible for paying Housing Benefit, which consists of a rent allowance (or a rebate for council tenants) and a rate rebate. For those receiving Supplementary Benefit, the DHSS pays other housing costs such as water rates, maintenance and insurance, and mortgage interest.

'Standard' Housing Benefit is payable to people who do not receive Supplementary Benefit. It is paid from the rent day before the date of your claim. You may also be able to get help with your arrears, because the local authority has the power to back-date your benefit for up to 12 months before the date of your claim if there are exceptional circumstances. You should argue that the circumstances are exceptional because you have accrued arrears during a time when you would have been entitled to Housing Benefit.

To work out how much Housing Benefit you are entitled to, you must calculate your weekly income, the 'needs allowance', and your eligible rent and rates.

First work out your gross *weekly income* before deductions (certain income is not counted, for example the first £4 of a war or industrial disablement pension, the first £17.30 of earnings, or attendance and mobility allowances). Your income is thus:

retirement pension   £39.50
occupational pension   £4

HOUSING BENEFIT

Rent rebates and allowances and rate rebates

The needs allowance	£
Married couple or single parent	72.15
Single person	48.90
Addition for each dependent child	14.75
Single handicapped person	54.50
Married couple, one of whom is handicapped	77.75
Married couple both of whom are handicapped	80.45
Single person who is handicapped and has dependent child(ren)	77.75
Addition where person claiming housing benefit where partner of pensionable age	0.85

Earnings disregard	
Occupier	17.30
Partner	5.00

Deductions for non-dependants living in household		
Non-dependant	Rent	Rates
18 or over to pensionable age, unless covered below	8.05	2.70
over pensionable age	2.90	1.15
25 or over on supplementary benefit	2.90	1.15
sole income consists of unemployment benefit, sickness benefit, maternity allowance, child benefit or one parent benefit	2.90	1.15
aged 16 or 17 and not on SB or YTS	2.90	1.15
aged 16 to 24 on supplementary benefit	Nil	Nil
On YTS training allowance	Nil	Nil
giving domestic help	Nil	Nil
student wholly or partly maintained by the claimant	Nil	Nil

---

disablement benefit	£1	(the other £4 is ignored)
total	£44.50	

The *needs allowance* (fixed by the DHSS) for a single person without dependent children is £48.90 (higher for families); 85p is added for pensioners. Your needs allowance is thus £49.75. The difference between your income and the needs allowance is £5.25.

To assess your *eligible rent and rates*, include only your general rates, not water rates. If your rent includes heating, hot water, lighting or cooking, deduct the amount paid for each of these from the rent. Assuming that these items are not included in your rent, your eligible rent will be £20 and your eligible rates £10.

The *calculation* depends on whether your income is more or less than the needs allowance. As your income is less than the needs allowance, your Housing Benefit is worked out as follows:

Rent 60 per cent of rent plus 50 per cent (25 per cent for non-pensioners) of the difference between your income and the needs allowance:

£12 + £2.62 = £14.62

Rates 60 per cent of rates plus 20 per cent (8 per cent for non-pensioners) of the difference between your income and the needs allowance:

£6 + £1.05 = £7.05

Total Housing Benefit = £14.62 + £7.05 = £21.67

You will also be eligible for Housing Benefit Supplement because your income, including Housing Benefit, is less than the amount you would receive if you were on Supplementary Benefit. It is worth claiming even just a small amount of Housing Benefit Supplement because it is treated as a payment of Supplementary Benefit which then entitles you to single payments, and to free prescriptions, for instance. You will not qualify for the Supplement if your capital is more than £3,000. Although it will be paid by the local authority you should claim it from your local DHSS office. The DHSS will work out whether you are entitled to normal Supplementary Benefit. If you are not entitled because your income is too high, you will be given a form to claim Housing Benefit Supplement. You should send this form to the Housing Benefit office of your local authority. Housing Benefit Supplement can be backdated only if you have good cause for delaying your claim.

To calculate Housing Benefit Supplement, you must work out the 'excess income' and your net housing costs.

Excess income is the amount by which your income exceeds your normal and additional requirements for Supplementary Benefit.

income		£44.50
SB requirements		
normal	£38.65	
water rates	£1.00	
heating addition	£1.20	£40.85
difference		£3.65

Net housing costs are worked out as follows:

rent	£20.00	
rates	£10.00	£30.00
less Housing Benefit		£21.67
		£8.33

Calculation Your net housing costs exceed the 'excess income' figure by £4.68. This is the amount of Housing Benefit Supplement payable.

For further information on Housing Benefit see the Child Poverty Action Group's *National Welfare Benefits Handbook*, available from the address on page 509.

After April 1988 the housing benefit scheme will be broadly the same but the most important change is that if you have more than £6,000 in savings (capital) you will not be able to claim. The needs allowances will be the same as the rates used for income support and the actual calculations will change significantly.

Maternity Benefits

8 | *I'm expecting a baby in six months' time. I've not yet decided when to give up work. What help will I be entitled to from the state?*

Lump-sum maternity payments from the social fund are available if you or your partner are getting FIS or SB. The amount of the payment is £80. But if you have more than £500 in savings the payment is reduced by one pound for each pound of savings over £500. You may claim no more than 11 weeks before the week in which the baby is due but no later than three months after the birth (or adoption) unless you can show 'good cause' for the delay – for example, that you were suffering from nervous strain after the birth. There is an absolute time-limit of 12 months after the birth. If your claim is turned down you can appeal to an independent tribunal (see Q15).

If you have worked for your employers continuously for at least six months ending in the fifteenth week before the baby is due (the 'qualifying week') and your average earnings over the eight weeks ending with the qualifying week are at least £39 a week you are entitled to Statutory Maternity Pay (SMP) paid by your employers (see YOU AND YOUR JOB, Q35).

If you have not been with your employers long enough to get SMP but were working elsewhere you may be able to get maternity allowance instead. Self-employed women can also claim this. To get maternity allowance you must have paid National Insurance contributions for at least 26 out of the 52 weeks ending with the qualifying week. If you are entitled you will get £30.05 for up to 18 weeks. You may also be entitled to an increase of £18.60 a week for an adult dependant such as your husband or someone who is looking after your child as long as he or she earns less than the increase. The period in which you can claim is the same as that for SMP (see YOU AND YOUR JOB, Q35). You will not get benefit for any week earlier than three weeks before you claim unless you can show that you had a good cause for a late claim.

If you are entitled to maternity allowance you may be able to claim Supplementary Benefit (see Q1) once you have given up work, but if you are living with your husband or with a man as his wife your resources will be added together. If you qualify you will also be able to claim a maternity payment from the social fund (see above) to help with the cost of equipping a new baby. You may also be able to claim a single payment (see Q4) to buy equipment such as a pushchair or cot. You are also entitled to the cost of replacement clothing which you need because of the pregnancy or birth. Remember that if you have capital over £500 the amount of any single payment will be reduced pound for pound for the amount over £500.

Widow's Benefits

9 | *My husband died suddenly a few weeks ago. I'm in my mid-40s and haven't worked for some years. I have two children. Am I entitled to any help from the state?*

If you are receiving Supplementary Benefit, Family Income Supplement or Housing Benefit and you take responsibility for a funeral which takes place in the UK you can claim a funeral expenses grant from the social fund administered by the DHSS. You must claim within three months, in writing on a form from the DHSS. If you claim late, but within a year of the funeral, you will still be entitled if you can show you had a good cause. The grant will be based on the cost of a simple funeral including a plain coffin, transport for the coffin and bearers and one extra car, reasonable flowers, undertaker's, chaplain's and organist's fees and cemetery or cremation fees. Any money left by the person who died is deducted from the grant, as is any money paid out from an insurance policy or charity, as it is expected that this should be used to pay for the funeral. If you are unhappy about any

decision you can appeal to an independent tribunal (see Q15).

Widow's Benefits consist of three allowances, all of which cease if either you remarry or cohabit with a man as his wife. All depend on the National Insurance contributions paid by your husband, all except the increases for dependants are taxable, and all will be paid even if you decide to get a job.

Widow's allowance is paid for the first 26 weeks after your husband's death, but you must claim it within three months of his death because it will not be paid for any time more than three months before the date of claim unless you had 'good cause' for the delay. You will also be entitled to an increase on the basic rate for each of your children.

After 26 weeks you will be entitled to a widowed mother's allowance, including an increase in the pension for each child. This is paid until your youngest child is 19 or, if over 16, leaves home permanently. You may also be entitled to an additional pension which is earnings-related – the calculation will be different according to whether your husband's employers' occupational pension scheme was contracted out of the state scheme or not (see YOU AND YOUR JOB, Q184).

You need not make a claim, as the DHSS will transfer you automatically from widow's allowance at the end of 26 weeks.

When you cease to be entitled to a widowed mother's allowance because your children have reached 19 or left home, you will be entitled to a widow's pension provided that you are under 65 when your widowed mother's allowance stops (you must be over 40 either when your widowed mother's allowance starts or when your husband died). Like the widowed mother's allowance, there is also an earnings-related additional pension payable, calculated in the same way. If you are under 50 when your husband died or your widowed mother's allowance stopped, the basic pension and the additional pension are reduced by seven per cent for each year under 50 at the time of your husband's death or when the widowed mother's allowance ended. There are no dependants' additions payable with widow's pension. Again, you need not claim, as the DHSS should notify you of your entitlement when your widowed mother's allowance stops (or, if you have not been receiving it, when your widow's allowance ceases).

There will be changes in the benefits paid to women widowed from 6 April 1988. It is planned that widow's allowance will be replaced by a lump-sum payment of £1,000. Widowed mother's allowance and widow's pension will be paid from the beginning of widowhood in addition to the lump sum.

For further details of these benefits, contact the National Association of Widows (address on page 511).

Care Allowances

10 | *I'm a woman of 45 and I recently left my job in order to stay at home and look after my mother, who has severe arthritis, a heart condition and is incontinent. What social security benefits can I claim?*

First, you might be entitled to a benefit that is specifically designed to help those who are looking after a disabled person. This is the Invalid Care Allowance. It is non-contributory and entitlement depends on presence in Great Britain. It is taxable. You may apply for this if your mother is in receipt of an Attendance or Constant Attendance Allowance (see QS 12 and 13). In addition, you must satisfy the following conditions:

● You must give regular and substantial care to your mother every day of the week for at least 35 hours a week (you are entitled to four weeks' holiday a year without losing your entitlement).

● You must not be in employment or over pensionable age. You will not be regarded as being in employment if you do some paid work and your earnings (less certain deductions such as free meals) are *under* £12 a week.

You should claim the allowance promptly, as generally the allowance will be backdated for only three months. For the amount payable, see page 393. This benefit is not means tested.

Second, you may be entitled to Supplementary Benefit (see Q1). If you are getting the Invalid Care Allowance this will be taken into account in full in calculating any SB to which you may be entitled. You will be treated independently of your mother when SB is calculated. Whether or not you get the householder or non-householder rate (see page 395) will depend on who owns or rents the house you live in, and who is responsible for household bills. You might be considered joint householders, especially if you and your mother are liable jointly to pay the rent or mortgage and rates. In this case, you will receive

the non-householder rate plus half the difference between that and the householder rate. However, it is unusual for relatives to be considered as joint householders. Usually, the householder will be the person who is legally liable for the housing costs and other household bills like gas and electricity. As with all other claimants for Supplementary Benefits you will not be entitled to it if you have capital over £3,000.

Third, either you or your mother (depending on who is liable for housing costs) may be entitled to Housing Benefit from the local authority (see Q7).

Finally, you will be able to satisfy the contribution conditions for long-term benefits such as a retirement pension even though you are no longer working. The years in which you have 'home responsibilities', that is, looking after your invalid mother, will count towards the number of years in which you would otherwise have had to make National Insurance contributions. However, you must have actually contributed for at least 20 years. In order to benefit from these provisions you have to be actually receiving the Invalid Care Allowance.

11 | *What is my position if I fall ill and can't go to work?*

If your illness was not caused by industrial injury or disease (if it was, see Q12), you may be entitled to the following:

● statutory sick pay (SSP) from your employers for the first 28 weeks of sickness. You are entitled to this whatever your position relating to National Insurance contributions. It is taxable. You will not be entitled to SSP if you earn less than £39 per week or if your contract of employment is for less than three months. See also YOU AND YOUR JOB, Q24.

● Invalidity Benefit. After your entitlement to SSP ceases you will be entitled to Invalidity Benefit if you are still sick. Again, entitlement depends on sufficient National Insurance contributions.

● Severe Disablement Allowance. If you do *not* have sufficient National Insurance contributions to qualify for Sickness or Invalidity Benefit you may be entitled to a Severe Disablement Allowance. The conditions for this are that you are 80 per cent disabled and are incapable of work (and have been so incapable for 196 days before you claim).

Industrial injury

12 | *I'm a physical education teacher. I've been off work since I damaged my back after slipping on some food in the school canteen during the lunch break. My doctor has told me that the injury may be permanent, in which case I would probably not be able to return to my job. I currently receive statutory sick pay, but I've not made enough contributions for Sickness Benefit. What benefits will I be entitled to after my statutory sick pay runs out?*

You will be entitled to benefits under the industrial injuries scheme as they do not depend on National Insurance contributions. To qualify under the scheme, you must be an 'employed earner' who has suffered personal injury 'by accident arising out of and in the course of' your employment. This means that generally you will be covered if the accident happens at your workplace and the accident is linked in some way with your work. Having lunch at your employers' premises will not normally take you out of

DISABLEMENT BENEFIT RATES from 6 April 1987	claimant £ pw
disablement pension, 100%	64.50
reduced earnings allowance (maximum)	25.80
constant attendance allowance (higher)	51.60
(lower)	25.80
exceptionally severe disablement allowance	25.80

the course of employment. You should report the accident to your employers as soon as possible after it, otherwise you may not be entitled to industrial injuries benefit.

Two types of benefit are available: one is payable while you are incapable of work and the other compensates you for disablement caused by the accident.

If you are still incapable of work when your entitlement to statutory sick pay is exhausted (see YOU AND YOUR JOB, Q24), you will transfer to Invalidity Benefit for as long as you remain incapable of work; you do not need to have made any National Insurance contributions if you are off work due to an industrial accident or disease. An additional amount called Invalidity Allowance is also paid to people who become unfit for work more than five years before pension age, the amount depending on the date you became ill.

If you have suffered disablement from 'loss of physical or mental faculty' and it is assessed as being 14 per cent or more, you will be entitled to Disablement Benefit whether or not you are capable of work. 'Loss of faculty' means impairment of the functioning of part of the body or mind. It is payable from 15 weeks after the accident. The amount you receive depends on the assessment by the Adjudicating Medical practitioners of your disablement. The maximum weekly disablement pension is £64.50, with the amount depending on the severity of the disablement. An assessment may be for life or, if your condition might change, for a provisional period.

There are several allowances available in addition to Disablement Benefit:

● *Reduced Earnings Allowance* compensates for reduced earning capacity if your injury or prescribed industrial disease prevents your returning to your regular occupation or work of an equivalent standard. The allowance will make up the difference between your current earnings and the amount you would be earning in your regular occupation but for the accident. You must *either* have been incapable continuously since the end of the 15 weeks following the accident *or* be likely to remain permanently incapable. It is paid up to a maximum of £25.80 a week. You may apply to have a gratuity converted into a pension while you are receiving Special Hardship Allowance. The Allowance is usually calculated for a year at a time.

● *Constant Attendance Allowance* is payable if your disablement is 100 per cent and you need care and attention because of the injury. It is payable at two main rates, but the lower rate may be reduced or increased.

● *Exceptionally Severe Disablement Allowance* is payable if you are entitled to Constant Attendance Allowance at more than the maximum lower rate.

You should claim Disablement Benefit and the increases as soon as possible since a weekly disablement pension, including pension in lieu of a gratuity, can be backdated for only three months unless you have good cause for not claiming. There is no time-limit for claiming a disablement gratuity. The Adjudication Officer will decide whether there has been an industrial accident. The 'disablement' questions will be referred to the Adjudicating Medical Practitioners. The Adjudication Officer will then decide the amount payable.

Finally, you may be able to sue your employers for the accident and you should seek advice from your union, from a Citizens Advice Bureau or a solicitor. For a fuller account of the industrial injuries scheme see *The Industrial Injuries Benefits Scheme*, published by the Legal Action Group (address on page 510).

Disability

13 | *I suffer from a heart ailment. I can't get out of bed unaided, or dress and undress without help, and as I can't stand for long it is difficult to cook. I am receiving Supplementary Benefit. Am I entitled to any other benefits?*

You may be entitled to Attendance Allowance and Mobility Allowance. Both are non-contributory and tax free. Neither counts as a resource for Supplementary Benefit purposes. To qualify for either allowance you must be ordinarily resident in Great Britain and have been present for at least 26 weeks in the last year (Attendance Allowance) and 52 weeks in the last 18 months (Mobility Allowance).

Attendance Allowance is paid if you are, and have been during the six months before your claim, so severely disabled, physically or mentally, that you need help from someone else during the day and/or night. If you need help during the day *and* the night, you will qualify for the higher rate; otherwise you will receive the lower rate (see page 402). To satisfy the *day* condition, you must need *either* frequent attention throughout the day in connection with your bodily functions, such as dressing, going to the lavatory, washing, eating (but not cooking), *or* continual supervision throughout the day in order to avoid substantial danger to yourself or others. The night condition requires you to need prolonged or repeated attention during the night in connection

with your bodily functions *or* continual supervision throughout the night in order to avoid substantial danger to yourself or others. 'Continual supervision' means regular or frequent but not necessarily non-stop supervision.

You may put in your claim for Attendance Allowance before you have satisfied these conditions for six months. A claim cannot normally be backdated before the time you claimed it, but if you claimed Supplementary Benefit after 29 August 1977 it can be treated as a claim for Attendance Allowance if you made it clear that you needed help because of your disability but did not actually ask for the Allowance. The attendance questions will be decided by the DHSS Attendance Allowance Board who will send a doctor to your home to examine you. You should give the doctor as much information as possible about your condition and the things that you are unable to do as a result of it. If the Board refuses your claim, you may apply for a review within three months of the decision. An appeal can be made to the Social Security Commissioner (see Q15).

As you are receiving Supplementary Benefit you should make sure that you claim any additional requirement additions that you might be entitled to. While you are waiting for your claim for Attendance Allowance to be decided, or if you have not satisfied the conditions for Attendance Allowance for six months, you may be able to receive an additional requirement for attendance needs. The conditions are similar to those for Attendance Allowance. It stops after six months if you have not claimed Attendance Allowance. You will receive the actual cost of attendance up to a maximum of £21.10 a week (the lower rate of Attendance Allowance).

If you have to pay someone to help you with essential domestic tasks such as cooking or cleaning you may be eligible for an additional requirement for 'reasonable' costs. You will not be entitled if you have a local authority home help or if the tasks are performed by a close relative who has only 'minimal' expenses; however, if that relative gave up a job to help you, you will be eligible.

You may qualify for Mobility Allowance (see page 393); this is available for people who are unable or virtually unable to walk because of physical disablement and are likely to remain so for at least a year. You are treated as virtually unable to walk if your 'ability to walk out of doors is so limited, as regards the distance over which, or the speed at which or the length of time for which or the manner in which [you] can make progress on foot without severe discomfort ... or the exertion required to walk would constitute a danger to [your] life or is likely to lead to a serious deterioration in [your] health'.

If your heart ailment would be aggravated by walking you are likely to fulfil these conditions. When making your claim, the Adjudication Officer will decide on the medical questions after obtaining a medical report from a doctor or referring them to an Adjudicating Medical Practitioner. You should take evidence from your own doctor to give to the doctor or Adjudicating Medical Practitioner. If your claim is turned down, you can appeal within 28 days of the decision.

You must claim Mobility Allowance before your sixty-fifth (or, exceptionally, your sixty-sixth) birthday, but once granted it continues until you are 75 provided that you satisfy the conditions.

You should claim as soon as possible, as the allowance is payable only from the date of your claim. Backdating of the claim is possible only if your claim has been lost in the post or you are making a renewal claim, and then only for a maximum of three months.

Finally, if you are awarded Mobility or Attendance Allowance you will be entitled automatically to an additional requirement for heating at the higher rate (see page 395).

For more information on these and other topics relating to the disabled, see the *Disability Rights Handbook* available from the Disability Alliance Educational and Research Association (address on page 509).

14 | *An elderly friend of mine, who is disabled, has just been told by her doctor that she could apply for a number of benefits such as Supplementary Benefit and Attendance Allowance. She didn't know about them before and didn't make enquiries because she always said she didn't want any charity. Can she get her benefits backdated?*

The answer is that in general benefits are not backdated unless there was 'good cause' for failing to claim in time. But there is provision for backdating some claims even if there is no good cause. For example, Sickness Benefit can be backdated for one month in some cases; Invalid Care Allowance for three months, and Retirement Pension for three months.

Attendance Allowance cannot be backdated at all even if good cause is shown.

However, if your friend claimed SB when she should have claimed Attendance Allowance (see Q13) then the payment of this allowance can be backdated to the date of the claim for SB.

Your friend will thus get her late claim for SB

backdated only if she can show good cause. This will be difficult, as simple failure to try to find out about entitlement to benefit is not enough to establish good cause. It is considered that people should take reasonable steps to find out what they might get. If she took advice from a reasonably informed source such as a DHSS office or a Citizens Advice Bureau (but not a friend or doctor) and was misinformed or misunderstood what she was told, then this might amount to good cause. Similarly, failure to claim because of illness or disability might be good cause, as would failure to understand because of illiteracy or mental illness.

Appeals

15 | *I was recently refused Sickness Benefit because the Adjudication Officer found that I am no longer incapable of work. I disagree with this decision and would like to challenge it. How should I go about appealing?*

There are two ways that the decisions of DHSS Adjudication Officers can be challenged – by asking the Adjudication Officer to review his or her decision or by appealing direct to the Social Security Appeal Tribunal. The procedure that applies to the main social security benefits is similar, but not identical, to the procedure for challenging decisions on Supplementary Benefit and Family Income Supplement.

The decision of the Adjudication Officer can be reviewed on one of two grounds: first, that it was based on ignorance of, or a mistake about, some material fact or, second, that since the decision was made there has been a relevant change in the circumstances on which the decision was based, for example if the Officer had not seen a medical certificate. You should apply in writing to the office which made the decision. Although there is no time-limit for an Adjudication Officer's review, you should apply as soon as possible because payment of arrears is normally limited to a short period (10 days for Invalidity Benefit) before the date of application unless you can show continuous good cause for delaying the application and then, generally, arrears will not be paid for a period more than 12 months before the application. The Adjudication Officer must make a decision on the review within 14 days. If you are dissatisfied with this decision, you may appeal to a Social Security Appeal Tribunal.

An appeal to the Social Security Appeal Tribunal must be made within three months of the original decision or, where you applied for a review, within three months of the review decision. A later appeal may be allowed if there is a 'special reason'. You should explain your reasons in writing. Your letter or form (available from DHSS offices) should state the reason for appeal; this may prompt the Adjudication Officer to reconsider the decision. You will receive a letter acknowledging your appeal. A few weeks later you will be sent copies of all the papers relating to the appeal. You must be given at least 10 days' notice of the hearing. You should ensure that you take any evidence that will back up your case to the hearing, such as a letter from your doctor. The public may attend the hearing, unless intimate personal or financial details are involved, although in practice there is hardly ever anyone there. You will get the decision there and then or you may be notified of the Tribunal's decision within a few days.

If your appeal to the Tribunal is unsuccessful, the next stage is appeal to the Social Security Commissioners. The appeal can be on a point of law only – if the Tribunal made a decision based on a mistake in the law, for example, or failed to give adequate reasons for the decision, or made a decision that no reasonable Tribunal could have come to. You must apply for leave to appeal from the chairperson of the Tribunal either orally at the end of the hearing or in writing within 42 days of the Tribunal's decision. If the chairperson refuses, you may apply to a Commissioner for leave within 42 days of the chairperson's refusal. The application for leave to appeal will usually be decided on the papers alone, so you should be sure that your grounds for appeal are set out as fully as possible. Once you have received leave, you have 42 days in which to actually submit your appeal. The appeal before the Commissioners may be made on the basis of the papers alone unless you request a hearing. If a hearing is held, it will normally be in public.

If you lose before the Social Security Commissioner, you may appeal to the Court of Appeal provided that leave has been obtained from the Commissioner or, if refused, from the Court of Appeal. An application for leave to appeal must be made in writing within three months of being notified of the Commissioner's decision. Again, the appeal can be on a point of law only. Provided you meet the financial conditions, you will be eligible for Legal Aid (see page 490) for the Court of Appeal hearing but not for appeals before then.

If you are unsure about appealing, you should consult a Citizens Advice Bureau, Law Centre or a solicitor. For further information about appealing, see two publications produced by Child Poverty Action Group (address on page 509): *Rights Guide to Non-Means-Tested Social Security Benefits* and *National Welfare Benefits Handbook*.

Gambling

1 | *I recently had a £100 bet with an acquaintance on the result of the Cup Final. We put it in writing and it was witnessed by a mutual friend. I won, but the acquaintance refused to honour the bet. I would have paid up had I lost. How can I get my money?*

You can't. Under the law, gambling debts are binding in honour only; they are not enforceable in the courts. The reason for this has to do with 'public policy'. Betting and gambling, even though legal, are still officially regarded as not completely respectable, and the legal system doesn't want to sully its hands by allowing people to use it to resolve gambling disputes. Whether the money is won at cards, betting on horses, in a casino, or on the pools, the winner cannot go to court if the loser doesn't pay. Of course, betting shops or casinos would probably lose their licences if they didn't honour their commitments. But that's of small comfort to the gambler done out of his winnings after a private bet.

2 | *I do the pools regularly and give my coupon to a collector. I was delighted recently when I thought I'd won a couple of hundred pounds, but the collector then told me he'd been ill and hadn't sent my coupon to the pools company. Can I sue him for the winnings I didn't get?*

No. In general, the law usually allows a person to sue an agent for negligence in carrying out his duties. But once again (as in Q1) we come up against the principle that obligations that arise from gaming are not enforceable in the courts. But if, for instance, someone actually collects winnings on your behalf and refuses to hand them over, you may be able to sue him because he will have committed fraud or theft, both of which are criminal offences. In each of those cases the fact that the origin of the money is gambling becomes secondary.

3 | *I'm in a regular poker club that always plays at my house. Each player puts in a couple of quid to compensate me for my trouble in arranging the game and holding it at home. A new member of the school has now told me that this is illegal. Is that true?*

Yes, what you're doing is illegal. All forms of gambling are strictly controlled by the law, mainly the Gaming Act 1968. A Gaming Board grants licences to casinos, betting shops and other gaming establishments, but without such a licence anyone who tries to run or organise gaming may be committing an offence. For instance, in your case the players are charged something other than their stakes (their contributions to you), which is not allowed; nor would you be allowed to take a small cut of the winnings. Of course, it's highly unlikely that the authorities would be interested in house games of poker, so in practice there is not too much to worry about.

The same principles apply if, for instance, you want to organise a roulette wheel, even if the proceeds go to charity.

4 | *I'm just filling in my income tax returns. During the year I had a lucky win on the pools of nearly £1,000. Is this taxable, and do I have to declare it?*

No. Ordinary gambling winnings are not regarded as taxable income. This applies to all forms of gambling – wins from cards, pools, bingo, horses, dogs, casino games, newspaper competitions, lotteries, raffles or sweepstakes (Premium Bonds too). Only if you're a professional gambler – if you do it for a living – are you in danger of being taxed on your income. Many people would regard playing the Stock Market just as much gambling as betting on the horses, but the Inland Revenue doesn't treat speculation in shares as gambling and all profits are considered part of your taxable income.

You as consumer

Shopping: retailers and private buyers

1 | *I bought a pair of sandals to take on my summer holidays, but after wearing them only twice one of the straps became unstitched. Is the shop responsible?*

Yes. Where goods are bought from a trader, the sale includes an implied term that they will be of *merchantable quality*, which means that the goods must be reasonably fit for the normal or common purpose for which such goods are used and that they must be safe and work properly. Clearly a sandal with a faulty strap cannot be used as footwear, so the shop is responsible to you for the fault. (See also Q5.)

The merchantable quality provision is arguably the most important piece of consumer protection legislation ever passed by Parliament. It appears in Section 14(2) of the Sale of Goods Act 1979. If you have to mention it specifically to the person in charge of the shop to back up your argument, it should come as no surprise.

2 | *Recently I bought a three-year-old car from a local garage for £2,600. It broke down on the first long journey within a month of buying it, and it now needs a new gearbox. The garage has rejected my complaint with a few choice monosyllables. Is the garage responsible?*

You have a good case against the garage. It may believe that it can sell used cars with impunity, but even second-hand goods must be of merchantable quality (see Q1) and the garage is responsible if it sells goods that aren't. This does not mean that the goods have to be perfect, but they must work and be safe to use. You should get 'value for money' in view of the price paid. As your car can't be driven due to a serious defect, which will be expensive to repair, the sellers are in breach of contract. It would be a different matter if the car had only minor defects that could be cheaply repaired – a faulty heater, for example.

3 | *I saw an electric lawnmower advertised in the small ads of my local newspaper. I paid £30 for it, but when I got it home it wouldn't work because the motor clapped out. Will the seller have to pay for the repair?*

Not if he was selling privately. The merchantable quality term (see Q1) does not apply unless the sale is made by a business. You have probably heard of the maxim 'caveat emptor' – 'let the buyer beware' – and

it is a principle that must be borne in mind when buying goods from someone selling privately. You will have redress for defects only if the seller was unwise enough to make *express* statements about the lawnmower prior to your clinching the deal, perhaps by saying that it was in good working order or in excellent condition. The more he says, the stronger your position.

Next time you buy from a private householder, make sure that you ask him the sort of questions that will give you the advantage of such specific replies, remembering that there are no such *implied* obligations working in your favour under the Sale of Goods Act 1979. If he stands quietly by and keeps his mouth shut, the private seller has no responsibility for defects.

4 | *When I took a newly bought toaster back to the shop because it was faulty, I received the argument that the shop was not to blame as they did not realise that the toaster was defective. Is that argument correct?*

No. Many traders do not seem to realise that they may be responsible even though they are not to blame in a moral sense. The Sale of Goods Act 1979 imposes *strict liability* on sellers. This means that they must satisfy each of various implied terms, including the merchantable quality condition (see Q1), to avoid being liable for breach of contract. It is no defence for the seller to show that he was not negligent, did not realise that the goods were faulty, and could not reasonably be expected to have discovered the fault. In other words, the customer does not have to show that the seller was negligent or careless in supplying goods with defects in them.

So although the fault in the toaster may have been caused by the wiring, say, or in a computer or television set by a defective microchip which the shopkeeper could not possibly have noticed, the shopkeeper is still fully responsible by virtue of the contract with his customer.

5 | *The carpet in our bedroom is wearing badly and has bald patches after less than two years. We paid a good price in the expectation that it would last for many years. The furniture store rejected our claim for compensation on the grounds that the carpet was not faulty when delivered to us and 'you can't expect carpets to last forever'. Have we any legal rights against the store?*

Yes. Although the Sale of Goods Act 1979 does not specifically refer to durability, it is clear that this is covered by the implied term of merchantable quality (see Q1). In 1981 the House of Lords pointed out, in a case about a towing hitch that broke more than a year after it was fitted to a vehicle, that the obligation relating to merchantable quality is a continuing warranty. It is not enough for the supplier to deliver goods that function at the stage of purchase; they must continue to be fit for their normal purpose for a reasonable time. No particular time-limits are laid down, as obviously they will vary from one type of goods to another and will depend also on the price and the related quality of the goods.

Although your carpet may have appeared to be of the proper quality when it was delivered, the mere fact that it has worn out so quickly would indicate that there *must have* been a defect in it initially, although that defect was a latent or hidden one. This is sometimes called the 'must have' argument, because when the faults later reveal themselves they are themselves evidence of the fact that the goods must have been faulty to start with.

Probably the store will suggest that you have misused the carpet in some way, although that is more usually argued in the case of cars and other mechanical goods where careless servicing and maintenance are blamed by unhelpful suppliers. But it is difficult to envisage any activity that the carpet should not have survived, and you can pursue the furniture store with some confidence.

6 | *I bought a new car some months ago. While I'm happy with its performance, some faults have developed: the seats squeak badly, the radio doesn't work properly, the paintwork is imperfect with patches of matt appearing, and the chrome is flaking off the window winders. The garage where I bought the car shows no interest in my complaints. Is there anything I can do?*

This is one of the occasions when a manufacturer's guarantee proves to be very useful. If you have one, which is likely, and it has not yet expired, you can look to the manufacturer to pay for the repairs (see Q49).

Until recently it was thought that there was no form of redress against the garage if the car is running properly and so is fulfilling its main function of safely carrying passengers from one place to another. One of the major problems with the implied term of merchantable quality (see Q1) is that it emphasises function rather than appearance. However, in 1986 the Court of Appeal decided (*Rogers* v. *Parrish Motors*) that a Range-Rover which, though drivable and roadworthy, had faults in the gearbox, engine, oil seals and interior and exterior finish was not merchantable. The buyer was able to return the car and recover the price in full from the garage.

The Law Commission has since recommended in May 1987 that the 1979 Act should be amended to make it clear that minor defects and the appearance and finish of goods also fall within the definition of merchantable quality.

7 | *I saw a table in a furniture shop with its original marked price of £300 reduced to £180. I only had a quick look at it before deciding to buy it. When it was delivered, it wobbled badly because the joints on one of the legs had come loose. The shop tells me that it was like that when I saw it, propped up against the wall, and it's my fault if I didn't notice. Do I have to keep it as it is?*

The answer is probably yes. Unfortunately, where a buyer examines the goods before he agrees to buy them, he cannot afterwards complain about obvious

YES, MADAM, TABLES OF THIS PERIOD ARE MEANT TO WOBBLE

Sale of Goods Act 1979

This Act means that any contract of sale implies the following terms for the benefit of buyers:

- the seller is the owner, and the **title** to the goods will be transferred to the buyer (Section 12)
- where the goods are sold by **description**, the goods supplied correspond with the description (Section 13)
- where goods are sold by a business seller, the goods are of **merchantable quality** – reasonably fit for their common or usual purpose (Section 14(2))
- where goods are sold by a business seller and the buyer makes known to the seller any **particular purpose** for which the goods are being bought, the goods are reasonably fit for that particular purpose (Section 14(3))

---

defects which he either saw or should have seen had his examination of them been less cursory. This is one of the two exceptions to Section 14(2) of the Sale of Goods Act 1979, the section that implies the merchantable quality term (see Q1). Your only hope is that as the table was leaning against the wall, even a more thorough visual examination by you might not have discovered the strained joints, and that's the only argument you can use. The moral for the future is that when you buy goods on display, check them thoroughly.

8 | *I bought a leather coat the other day at a very reasonable price. I saw pinned to the sleeve a note stating 'tear on right shoulder'. I bought it thinking I'd be able to repair the tear easily. I've now changed my mind, as the repair will look obvious and spoil the look of the coat. Will the shop let me change it?*

Whether the shop changes the coat is up to the shop, but there is no obligation for it to do so. There is a second exception to the merchantable quality condition (the first was mentioned in Q7). This exception operates where – again before a contract is made – the seller *specifically* points out a defect to the buyer. Since you entered into the contract aware of the tear, you are stuck with the deal you made. However, if some other fault were to be discovered, such as the stitching on the seams coming undone, you would be able to claim compensation for that.

9 | *My son suffers from asthma. The bed I bought for him recently is stuffed with material that brings on wheezing attacks during the night. The shop refuses to take back the bed. Have I any rights against the shop?*

This depends on whether or not you drew your son's medical condition to the attention of the sales staff or sought their advice before placing your order. If you did not do so, and had already made up your own mind, the shop will not be liable. It seems that there is nothing wrong with the bed and that it could be used safely by the vast majority of the population. In other words, it is of merchantable quality (see Q1).

But if you informed the shop of your son's asthma, you will have brought into play another provision of the Sale of Goods Act 1979. The Act provides that where a buyer has a *particular* purpose which is made known to the seller before the agreement is made, then the goods supplied must be suitable for that particular purpose. It will not be enough that the goods are of merchantable quality and fit for their usual purpose. That will be of no assistance to the particular buyer with special and unusual requirements.

The practical point to bear in mind is that if you propose to put goods to some exceptional use, or there are some exceptional circumstances like your son's asthma, ensure you make them clear to the seller before placing an order. The seller will then be responsible if the goods prove to be unsuitable.

10 | *Recently I bought a blouse to go with one of my skirts. When I reached home, I found that the colours didn't match. What can I do about it?*

Nothing. If the blouse is of the right quality and perfectly wearable, you cannot blame the shop because you made a mistake in choosing the wrong colour. The practical solution in future is to arrange with the shop when you buy any clothes that if they are unsuitable you will be able to return them and change them for something else, or be given a credit note or even your money back. If the shop is prepared to agree to some such arrangement to start with, then your purchase will be made on those *express* conditions. But if the shop refuses and you still go ahead with your purchase, you will take the risk yourself.

11 | *What if clothes I buy don't fit me?*

Nothing could be done about it if you selected the clothes yourself and made up your own mind about the size. It would be a different matter if the blouse mentioned in Q10 had been incorrectly labelled, so that you bought what appeared to be a size 16 and it turned out to be a size 12.

Of course, some shops have no fitting rooms, and as part of their terms of business allow customers to return or exchange goods provided that they have not been worn. It is this fairly common practice that misleads consumers into thinking that they have a right to return goods whether they are faulty or not.

12 | *What if I asked the advice of a shop assistant and, perhaps after being measured, bought a garment that turned out to be too small?*

As you had relied on the shop, the goods would have to be suitable for your particular requirements. Nothing could be more clearly special to a particular customer than his or her size, and you would have a right to your money back if the clothes did not fit.

13 | *I'm always being told that when I buy things in a sale I have no comeback if they are faulty. Is this true?*

No. Your informants are wrong. You have just the same rights as you do when buying goods and there's no sale – the goods must be of merchantable quality (see Q1).

14 | *I bought some garden furniture from a cash-and-carry store because the price was substantially lower than the recommended price. The store is now refusing to accept my complaints about faults in the chairs on the grounds that the price was reduced. Is the store liable?*

Yes. The store's responsibility is not reduced merely because it chooses to compete with other retailers by selling its goods at a discount. The goods should be of the same merchantable quality (see Q1) as goods of the same type sold at the full price. You may experience poorer service by going to cash-and-carry retailers, but you do not have to put up with lower quality.

15 | *Frequently in sales, goods are sold more cheaply than usual because they are marked as 'imperfect', 'sub-standard' or 'seconds'. How does this affect the customer's position?*

Descriptions of this sort will affect the *standard* of quality that you may expect, although they do not allow the seller to supply useless rubbish. The combination of the two factors – the description indicat-

ing they are of lower quality coupled with a lower price – will reduce the quality that the consumer is reasonably entitled to expect. For example, the pattern in the weave or printing of a sweater, socks or curtain material may be imperfect and you could not complain about that. But if a pair of shoes fell to pieces very quickly or the sweater or socks unravelled, you would have grounds for redress.

16 | *While looking at a nest of coffee tables in a furniture showroom I was told by the sales assistant that they were teak. I placed an order but the tables the store delivered are not solid teak, as I had expected, but teak-veneered chipboard. The store has rejected my complaint on the grounds that the tables on display were also veneered. Can I force the store to take the tables back?*

Yes. It seems clear that the word 'teak' was part of the description of the goods that you ordered. It follows that the goods delivered to you should have been made entirely of teak. If the sales assistant meant 'teak veneer', he should have said so explicitly.

The Sale of Goods Act 1979 is helpful, as it implies a condition that where goods are sold by description they should correspond to that description. You should return the tables and ask for your money back.

Problems relating to the materials used in the construction of furniture are so common that they are specially covered by the Code of Practice for Furniture drawn up by the five big furniture trade associations in consultation with the Office of Fair Trading. Under this Code, members of the trade associations should provide information of this sort by labelling the furniture, unless leaflets or catalogues are available. This information should explain whether the furniture is solid wood, wood veneer or plastic laminate. A free leaflet, *Furniture*, explaining the Code is published by the Office of Fair Trading and available from your local Citizens Advice Bureau, Trading Standards Department of the local authority, or Consumer Advice Centre, if there's one in your area.

17 | *A car dealer sold me a second-hand car with a recorded mileage of 42,000. I subsequently met the previous owner, who told me that the milometer must have been tampered with and that the true mileage was 78,000 when the car was traded in to the dealer. What should I do?*

Two courses are open to you. First, you may pursue your rights in civil law under the Sale of Goods Act 1979. The dealer broke his contract when he delivered a car which did not match its description – the milometer reading was part of the description. You may either return the car, assuming you haven't kept it for too long (see Q 34), or keep it and claim damages for the reduction in value bearing in mind its true mileage.

Second, you can ask the Trading Standards Department of your local authority to look into the matter. The dealer has almost certainly committed an offence under the Trade Descriptions Act 1968 by supplying a car with a false trade description. If a trading standards officer decides to prosecute and the dealer is convicted, you may ask the court for compensation under the Powers of Criminal Courts Act 1973. This second course of action is easier and cheaper for you, as the prosecution is undertaken at its own expense by the local authority. In practice, the intervention by the local authority may at least persuade the dealer to give you your money back for the car or compensate you, even if he is let off with a warning.

18 | *Last year I bought a used car privately. It now transpires that the car had been stolen (though the person I bought it from was unaware of this) and the original owner is claiming it back. Must I hand it over?*

Yes. Your seller had no right to sell the car, as he was not the owner himself and was not in a position to transfer the ownership to you. The original owner remained the owner throughout. If you refuse to return the car, he will be able to bring a civil action in the courts for what lawyers call 'conversion'. He will be awarded the value of the car at the date when you bought it, presumably the price you paid, or the court may order you to return it.

Even if this happens, all is not lost, because you may recover the full price from your seller. The reason is that under the Sale of Goods Act 1979 he has impliedly promised that he owns the car and that under the agreement with you the ownership will pass to you. As he has broken this contractual obligation, you are entitled to a full refund. It is irrelevant that the seller was completely innocent and had no knowledge or suspicion that the car was stolen. Like many other obligations under the Act, this one imposes strict liability on the seller. It is equally irrelevant that your seller was a private seller, as this provision applies to private and trade sales alike.

There is one odd statutory provision which may help you keep the car. This is called 'market overt'. It applies where goods were sold in a market or fair established by charter or custom, and means you would be able to keep the car. For example, in a 1949 case the Court of Appeal decided that the sale of a car in Maidstone Market was within the exception to the rules of ownership because the Market had been running since 1747 (although the sale of cars was obviously more recent). This exception is full of complicated points – for instance, that the sale must take place between sunrise and sunset. If by chance you discover that the car was sold by auction or in some market either by the thief himself or by somebody who handled the goods before they reached your seller, it will be worth taking legal advice on this technical provision.

19 | *What if I spent money on repairing or improving a car that I did not know was stolen before the true owner turned up out of the blue?*

You are entitled to receive compensation for the repairs and improvements. The problem is covered by the Torts (Interference with Goods) Act 1977. To take advantage of this Act you should refuse to hand over the car and hope that the true owner does not arrive and drive off in it. If he goes to court to recover damages from you, the court in assessing damages will make an allowance for the increase in the value of the car attributable to the repairs and improvements you made. Your position will be much weaker if you let the true owner retake the car, as the Act does not give you a right in that case to sue for the value of the improvements – a quirky but important point.

Apart from payment from the true owner for the cost of the repairs and improvements, you will also be entitled to recover the full purchase price from the person who sold you the car. As a result, you should not be out of pocket at all.

20 | *I bought a second-hand car but, unknown to me, it was still on hire-purchase. The finance company is now reclaiming the car. Should I let the company take it?*

No. It is true that your seller had no right to sell the goods to you until he had paid all that was due under the hire-purchase agreement. Until then he has nothing more than a right to possession of the car and is no more entitled to sell it than if he had hired it for a week. However, the problem of people with cars on hire-purchase selling them to innocent buyers has been prevalent for so long that in 1964 a special provision was introduced by the Hire-Purchase Act. It applies only to *motor vehicles* and it assists only private purchasers. (Trade purchasers can check to see whether vehicles are still on hire-purchase by making a search with Hire-Purchase Information Limited. Indeed, private purchasers can do the same through the AA or the RAC if they are members.)

The provision works in this way. Provided the private purchaser did not know about the existence of the hire-purchase agreement, or was even told about it but was informed that it had been paid off, he will obtain a good title to the vehicle and be able to resist the claims of the finance company. Not surprisingly, this provision does not help the dishonest seller, who is left to fight out the matter with the finance company.

21 | *My aunt gave me an electric toaster as a wedding present, but it doesn't work properly. I returned it to the shop where it was bought, but the shop refused to deal with my complaint. Is there anything I can do?*

No. The shop is acting quite reasonably. As *you* did not buy the toaster, you have no contract with the shop and the Sale of Goods Act 1979 cannot help you. But your aunt as the original buyer should take the toaster back and ask for her money back or the cost of having it repaired.

Of course, there may have been a guarantee (see Q49) with the toaster. Often guarantees operate in favour of not merely the original purchaser but later owners. Check its wording: it may entitle you to a free repair.

● *Codes of Practice*

One of the duties of the Office of Fair Trading is to encourage trade associations to prepare Codes of Practice. To date, 22 Codes have been published covering these areas: cars, direct selling, double glazing, electrical goods, funerals, furniture, holidays, launderers and dry cleaners, mail order, photography, postal and telecommunications services, shoes, motor cycles and caravans.

The Codes of Practice are intended to raise business standards by recommending trade practices to members of the relevant associations. The recommendations in the Codes have no legal force, however, and no action can be taken in the courts if they are not followed by a member.

A common feature of the Codes is the provision of free conciliation by the trade association in the case of a dispute between a member and a customer. Many Codes also provide a system of cheap arbitration to which an aggrieved consumer may resort instead of suing in the courts.

The Office of Fair Trading publishes leaflets on almost all the Codes; the leaflets may be obtained from the OFT, public libraries, Citizens Advice Bureaux and Consumer Advice Centres. The Codes on direct selling and postal services are published by the Direct Selling Association and the Post Office respectively and should be available from the same sources.

22 | *I bought a television set from a large retail chain, choosing a particular make because included in the price was a 'free' radio cassette recorder. The television works perfectly but the tuner of the radio has broken. The shop says that, as it was a free gift, there is nothing I can do about it.*

The retailer has misunderstood the position. The attitude of some shops is: 'You get what you pay for. As you paid nothing for the free gift, you can hardly complain if it is useless rubbish!' But the legal position is that the shop has supplied the recorder as part of a contract with you, and the shop is responsible if the recorder is not of merchantable quality (see Q1) and will not function. The retailer will have to pay for the repair. This is the effect of the Supply of Goods and Services Act 1982.

23 | *As retailers are strictly liable for defects in goods sold, why have patients who have suffered serious side effects from drugs and medicines sup-*

plied under the NHS *taken on the daunting task of suing the pharmaceutical companies for negligence? Would it not have been easier for them to sue the pharmacist?*

At first sight suing the pharmacist seems a good idea. Unfortunately, the position is anomalous because the patient does not pay the full price of the drugs, but only the prescription charge the pharmacist collects as agent for the NHS. The point was discussed by the House of Lords in a 1965 case in which the House of Lords reached the conclusion that there is no contract at all between the patient and the pharmacist, although there is a contract between the chemist and the NHS Family Practitioner Committee which obliges the chemist to supply the drugs on the presentation of a prescription.

That is why in the absence of a contract the patient has to resort to proving negligence under the head of what is generally called 'product liability' (see Q46). Of course, if the doctor had been careless in prescribing the drug or the pharmacist had been careless in making up the prescription, the patient would have a claim against them for negligence.

One final comment. If the patient is receiving private medical treatment from a hospital or GP, he will pay the full price of the drug and so will have the benefit of the Sale of Goods Act 1979 in his dealings with the pharmacist or hospital and should be able to make a claim against them.

24 | *I recently bought a new gas cooker and received a cash allowance for trading in my old one in part-exchange. What is the legal position if there are faults in the new gas cooker?*

You are in exactly the same position as if you had paid in full for the new cooker. You have entered into a contract for the sale and purchase of goods with the trader and have the complete protection of the Sale of Goods Act 1979 including the right to receive goods of the proper quality. Over the years, some misleading advice and information has been given on the terms of trading in in part-exchange. But it is immaterial in part-exchange transactions – and they're now common in the case of cars, cookers, washing machines, vacuum cleaners and cameras – that the buyer pays part of the price with goods instead of money.

25 | *Am I responsible if traded-in goods don't work properly?*

No, unless you expressly stated that they were in good order. The implied duty to provide goods of proper quality operates only against business sellers, not private sellers like yourself. So make sure that you play it carefully when trading in the goods, and don't, in a moment of optimistic salesmanship, state that they are in good working order or whatever (see Q3).

One word of warning, though: remember that if you describe the goods, even as a private seller you are obliged to deliver goods which satisfy the description. Describing a car as 'Immaculate 1979' when it is a 1978 model in poor condition, for instance, will lead you into trouble. Even newspaper advertisements need to be carefully worded for this reason.

26 | *I broke a teapot in a chinashop when my coat dragged it off the shelf as I was walking through. The assistant then pointed out a notice which read: 'All goods damaged or broken by customers must be paid for.' I hadn't seen the notice. Will I have to pay?*

The answer will depend on whether or not the shop can prove that you were negligent or careless. Certainly the notice does not affect your position and it is irrelevant whether or not you saw it.

Much will turn on the layout of the shop. If the display cabinets were close together, so that it would be difficult for the ordinary shopper to walk along the aisles without being in danger of knocking off a piece of china, then you can argue that the accident occurred in spite of your being careful. Or it may be that the spout of the teapot was projecting. If, on the other hand, you were rushing through the shop with your coat tails flying, the responsibility would be yours. It may be a bit of each. Perhaps you were partly to blame, but a contributory factor was the layout of the shelving in the shop; if so, you would have to pay part of the price, taking into account the contributory negligence of the shop.

27 | *My son of eight knocked a piece of china off a shelf in a shop. What is my position?*

Shop assistants frequently try to persuade parents to pay for damage caused by their children. In law, parents have no such responsibility. The children may themselves be liable, but their age would have to be taken into account in deciding what standard of care should be expected from them. And it is unlikely that a shop would wish to sue a child, if only because the chances of recovery of the money due would be slim.

There may be circumstances where a parent

I DEMAND
THE £275
NOW

would be responsible because of the parent's own negligence in allowing children to rampage round a shop with valuables in easy reach. But that would be a question of proving that the parent was negligent. The same test would apply if you were to take your dog into a shop.

28 | *While shopping in a supermarket I slipped over on the spillage from a broken jar of salad cream. I broke my wrist and tore my coat as I fell. The supermarket manageress has said that as the jar was dropped by a customer, the supermarket is not responsible. Is that correct?*

Maybe. You must prove that the supermarket had been negligent. The Occupiers' Liability Act 1957 imposes on 'occupiers' – people in control of premises – a duty of care towards people coming on to their premises. But if the jar had just been dropped by a customer and the supermarket staff had not yet had time to cordon off the area or clear up the mess, then you would not be able to prove that the supermarket had been negligent. On the other hand, if the staff had seen the breakage or been told of it by a customer and had not very quickly tried to clear it up, bearing in mind the obvious danger that it posed to customers, then you would succeed. Your compensation would cover both your personal injury, for which the damages would be substantial, and the cost of repairing your coat. The difficulty in your case will be proving negligence.

29 | *What if I tore my coat on a jagged piece of metal on one of the trolleys at the supermarket?*

It would be a matter of proving negligence. Here your

task would be easier than the situation in Q 2 8 as it is quite likely that the dangerous trolley was in that state at the opening of business in the morning and so should have been repaired before being put into use. Again the supermarket would have to pay for the cost of repairing the coat if repair were possible. If the garment were so badly damaged that any repair would be so obvious as to make it virtually worthless, you would be right in claiming the cost of a replacement garment. But bear in mind that if the coat was not brand new, you can claim only the cost of replacing it with a second-hand one. In other words, depreciation would need to be taken into account.

30 | *I ordered a hair-dryer by mail order, choosing it from a catalogue. It was delivered in a battered box. When I opened it, the plastic casing of the dryer had been smashed. The delivery man told me that the van carrying it had been in a collision on its way from the warehouse. Do I have to pay for the hair-dryer?*

Surprisingly, this is an area about which the law is unclear. The general rule is that if goods are damaged in transit, whoever is the owner of them at the time of the accident has to bear the loss. So to discover who was at risk, you have to discover who was the owner while the goods were on their way to you. The rules relating to this are set out in the Sale of Goods Act 1979 and are quite complicated. One view of the law is that once the goods have been handed over by the seller to the carrier for delivery to the buyer, the ownership in the goods passes to the buyer and with it the risk of accidental loss or damage en route. That seems a tough rule, as the buyer will not even have seen the goods at that stage and will not have insured them anyway. Fortunately, as the seller is likely to have covered them by insurance, he is usually willing to replace the item without arguing the legal niceties. (If the accident is caused by the carrier's negligence, the carrier will be responsible to the owner and will no doubt have covered that liability by insurance.)

In any case, one important point to remember is that a Code of Practice has been adopted by members of the Mail Order Traders' Association (MOTA) (address on page 510) after discussions with the Office of Fair Trading. All the larger mail order businesses are members of the Association. The Code contains the following provision:

Where goods are found to have been damaged in transit, they may be returned and a replacement, if available, shall be despatched immediately. If a replacement is not available, the member will immediately offer a full refund of any monies paid, including carriage costs if applicable.

You should therefore get a replacement or your money back.

There are other similar schemes. For example, books and records bought through the post are likely to be covered by the Code of Practice of the Association of Mail Order Publishers (address on page 510). A leaflet briefly explaining the Codes and related matters, *Buying by Post*, is published by the Office of Fair Trading and available free from the OFT, many public libraries, Citizens Advice Bureaux and Trading Standards Departments. (On Codes of Practice generally, see page 414.)

31 | *When goods are faulty, can I insist on having my money back or do I have to accept a credit note or allow the supplier to repair the goods?*

You are entitled to a full refund because the seller has broken a condition of the Sale of Goods Act 1979 by not supplying goods of merchantable quality (see Q1). The commonplace remedy for a buyer in these circumstances is to treat the contract as at an end because of the seller's breach. This has a dual effect – the buyer is entitled to reject the goods and as a corollary to recover the price in full. As a result, you can insist on a full cash refund and should not be fobbed off with a credit note.

The usual way to reject the goods is to return them to the shop and make it clear that you want an immediate refund. This may be difficult or impossible in the case of some larger products like fridges, particularly if the seller physically prevents your returning them. In this case, if a verbal statement gets no results you should give written notice to the seller making it clear in your letter that you are rejecting the goods and seeking complete repayment. If that has no effect, in the last resort you will have to sue the retailer.

32 | *I bought a number of items at a department store a few days ago. When I came to pay, the cashier charged for the price of five pairs of socks instead of the four pairs I had in the pile. He refused to give me a cash refund but instead offered me a credit note. A credit note for such a small amount is ridiculous, especially as I don't normally shop at the store. Could I have insisted on a cash refund?*

Yes. You had offered to buy only four pairs of socks and the store should have charged you for those only. The cashier had no right to retain the amount of the overcharge, and you were legally entitled to a cash refund.

33 | *I recently bought a new fridge, which the store delivered. The motor failed as soon as I switched it on. I'm naturally reluctant to take the fridge back. Is the store obliged to repair it free of charge?*

In effect, yes. Whenever someone breaks a contract, the innocent party is entitled to recover damages and thus to be compensated for any loss. You may claim compensation under the Sale of Goods Act 1979 instead of exercising your right to reject the fridge. You cannot insist on the seller repairing the goods himself, though you will obviously discuss this with the store. If the store cannot or will not carry out the repair, you may have the job done by somebody else and claim the cost from the store. This will include not only the cost of replacing the motor and any other faulty components but also the labour charges, which are often the more expensive item.

34 | *Eighteen months ago I bought a new freezer. Although it's kept in a well-aired cellar, the door is beginning to rust badly. The shop refuses to acknowledge that I have any cause for complaint. What is my legal position?*

It seems clear that the freezer has not proved to be durable enough, so the seller has broken the condition of merchantable quality (see Q1). The main question concerns what remedy you have. First, can you reject the freezer? Your problem illustrates a particularly difficult area, in which defects are not discoverable initially but show up only during the life of the goods (see Q5). Your right to reject the freezer has

● *Refunds*

The Sale of Goods Act 1979 takes away the buyer's right to reject goods and obtain a cash refund (though leaving the buyer with a claim for compensation) where:

● the goods have been delivered to the buyer **and**
● the buyer has had an opportunity to examine them **and**
● the buyer accepts them – for example, by retaining the goods for more than a reasonable time without informing the seller that he or she has rejected them.

been lost with the passage of time, because of a special provision of the Sale of Goods Act 1979 which removes the right to reject when the buyer has accepted the goods. One example of acceptance is where the buyer retains the goods for a reasonable time before rejecting them. This provision, which is very prejudicial to consumers, may well start to operate after only a week or so. For example, in a well-publicised 1986 case (*Bernstein* v. *Pamson Motors*) it was too late to reject a new Datsun car after only three weeks and 142 miles, even though the defect – a blockage in the lubrication channel to the crankcase – could not have been discovered earlier and caused £700 damage. Even so, the buyer was fully compensated, including £150 for a spoilt day – the day of the breakdown. Many suppliers would think that this is not unfair, as the consumer will often have had the use of the goods for a considerable time and, if he or she were entitled to a full refund, that use would have been free of charge in spite of the depreciation.

However, even though it may be too late to reject the freezer, you still have the other remedy – the right to compensation. The shop ought to pay the full cost of supplying and fitting a new door.

35 | *When a furniture store delivered a dining-room suite to my home, I was asked to sign a delivery note. The note stated: 'I acknowledge that the goods have been delivered in good order.' When*

ONE TABLE IN GOOD ORDER, MADAM.

I unpacked the furniture I found it badly scratched. Should I have signed the note?

It is better not to sign a delivery note such as this one with simply your signature, because by doing so you could lose your right to reject the furniture later. Adding your signature is an example of accepting the goods. It would be safer to add some formula to your signature such as 'goods unexamined', which merely acknowledges the receipt of the package without admitting that you have checked the contents and found them to be perfect. It is also a sensible course of action even where the goods are visible and not delivered in their factory packaging, as you may be unable or unwilling to delay the delivery truck while you make a careful inspection of your purchase.

36 | *A few days ago I bought a self-assembly wardrobe from a local store. I tried to put it together, but it has been incorrectly manufactured and the components don't fit. The store has offered me my money back, but has refused to order a replacement as it does not stock this particular range any longer. I want the same type of wardrobe because it matches the rest of my bedroom furniture. Am I right in thinking that I am entitled to an exchange?*

No. The remedy of exchange is not known in English law. You will have to be content with a full refund, and any extra cost of buying the item elsewhere at a higher price.

Your misunderstanding probably arises from the fact that because some shops are prepared to exchange goods, purchasers think that this is one of their rights rather than an option on the part of the store. If an exchange is offered, the consumer may accept or refuse it as he or she wishes. He or she can insist on an exchange only if he or she has entered into the contract on the basis that that is part of the shop's terms of business.

37 | *A fortnight ago I bought a spade from a garden centre. The handle broke in half the first time I used it. The garden centre exchanged it for another one, but that was no better and it broke in half in a few days. When I took it back the garden centre refused to exchange it, saying that the second spade was a gift. Is this correct?*

You are not the first consumer to meet this nonsensical argument. The same contractual obligation applies to the replacement spade as to the original, namely, that it should be of the proper quality. You are entitled to a full refund, as very little time had elapsed from when you made your purchase and so you had not yet accepted the goods (see Q 3 4). (If the second spade had lasted for some weeks or months, you would have been entitled only to recover the cost of fitting a new handle as compensation.)

38 | *I bought a freezer just over a year ago. While I was away on holiday, the motor failed and when I opened the lid on my return I was met with a nauseating mess. The discount store where I bought the freezer is prepared to repair it free of charge but refuses to compensate me for the wasted food. Is the store's refusal valid?*

No. The store should reimburse you the full cost of the contents of the freezer as well as doing the repair, as it has broken the original contract of sale by supplying you with a defective freezer. The store is responsible for all losses which, in lawyer's language, are not too 'remote'. This means that it must compensate you for consequential losses that the parties could have contemplated or foreseen at the contract date as being likely to result from the defect in the goods. An electrical supplier should obviously expect you to keep frozen food in your freezer, and should have anticipated that if the motor broke down the almost inevitable consequence would be that the contents would be ruined.

It should be added that the store's position is no different even if you had chosen to insure the contents of the freezer, except that in that case you may choose to claim on your policy instead of chasing the supplier. (If you do make an insurance claim, the insurers may decide to claim against the supplier.)

If your dispute is not resolved by the shop, check whether it is a member of the Radio, Electrical and Television Retailers' Association (RETRA); members usually have RETRA labels attached to their display items. If it is, you can take advantage of the Code of Practice for the Selling and Servicing of Electrical and Electronic Appliances. The Association operates a free conciliation service under which it tries to resolve disputes promptly and informally. Complaints should be notified in writing to the Secretary of RETRA (address on page 5 1 1). If that fails, you will have to go to court, as there is no arbitration procedure under the Code.

39 | *Occasionally I go shopping to a town about 20 miles away to buy clothes. I bought a pair of shoes there and, the first time I wore them, a nail*

came through the sole and laddered my tights. The shop readily agreed to repair the shoes for nothing – I didn't want my money back – but refused to pay for another pair of tights or reimburse me my travelling expenses. Can the shop get away with that?

The tights are an example of consequential loss for which the seller is responsible, as the fault in the shoes caused the ladder in the tights and that sort of damage could easily have been foreseen. The shop is therefore liable to pay for another pair of tights.

The travelling expenses are more of a problem. The shop might reasonably assume that most of its customers come from the immediate neighbourhood and that, if any goods are faulty, the customer could bring them in while doing other shopping. Even if the shop is aware that many customers come from further afield, it might assume that the return visit to complain about the shoes would coincide with a trip made for another reason. Because of this, your case is a weak one, unless at the time of purchase you mentioned that you had travelled some distance and seldom came to the town.

40 | *A few days ago a salesman called at my house representing a double-glazing company. I signed an order form there and then, tempted by a substantial discount for paying in cash. On reflection I cannot afford it. Can I get out of the agreement?*

The answer from a strictly legal point of view is no. Assuming the company has accepted your order already, you have entered into a legally binding contract. You have no grounds for having the contract set aside, as there is no suggestion of any misrepresentation by the supplier and there is no question of any breach of contract yet.

Under some circumstances the law gives a cooling-off period to consumers who have entered into contracts at home as a result of door-to-door selling, but this applies only where credit facilities are involved (see Q 1 0 6). (But legislation will be introduced soon to extend this cancellation right to certain non-credit situations – this must be done by 1 9 8 8 to comply with an EEC Directive.)

Nevertheless, if your supplier is a member of the Glass and Glazing Federation you can take advantage of the Federation's Code of Practice. This provides that where contracts are negotiated away from business premises, whether for cash or credit, the customer has the right to cancel the agreement. You must act quickly, as cancellation must be notified in writing within five days from the date on which the contract was signed. The written contract ought to state the address to which your cancellation notice must be sent.

41 | *Four months ago I bought a low-mileage, two-year-old car from a local garage. The garage gave me a three-month guarantee covering parts and labour. A number of small faults developed during the first three months which the garage put right free of charge without argument. But now there's something seriously wrong with the transmission which will cost hundreds of pounds to repair. As the guarantee has expired, the garage has washed its hands of the matter. Will I have to pay for the repair?*

In spite of giving a guarantee of a limited period, the garage continues to be responsible for the car under its initial obligation to supply goods of merchantable quality (see Q1). It follows that any express guarantee given by a trader to a private buyer is a bonus and cannot reduce the rights that the buyer would have in any case. But because many consumers imagine that the guarantee replaces their statutory rights, the trader is under an obligation to state in the guarantee that the statutory rights are unaffected. Failure to include such a statement in the document is a criminal offence.

In the event, tell the garage that although the guarantee has run out it must repair the vehicle free of charge as the car has not proved to be of merchantable quality or fit for its purpose, bearing in mind the age and price of the vehicle (see Q5).

42 | *I've noticed signs in shops which say things like 'No refunds – credit note only' and 'Sale goods may not be returned'. What legal effect do such signs have?*

None. Notices like these are attempts by suppliers to rob purchasers of their rights to reject goods and obtain a full refund when the suppliers have sold goods that are not of merchantable quality (see Q1) or which have been misdescribed. These so-called 'inalienable rights' are unaffected by the sort of exclusion clause written on such signs because they have been invalidated by statute (the Unfair Contract Terms Act 1977). You can ignore such signs.

Apart from being void as far as the civil law is concerned, the use of such clauses or notices is a criminal offence. The reason for the intervention of the criminal law is that traders were continuing to use such clauses in the confident expectation that most of the public had no idea that they were void and therefore were misled into thinking that their rights had been taken away. So Parliament has made the use of these signs a criminal offence. If you see one, report the trader to your local authority's Trading Standards Department, which doubtless will ensure that the notice disappears by threatening criminal prosecution.

43 | *Frequently in furniture sales goods are labelled 'Sold as seen'. What does this mean?*

Nothing. Retailers use these signs to protect themselves from any complaints resulting from their selling defective goods, but such signs are like those mentioned in Q42: they have no legal effect and their display is a criminal offence. If a trader wishes to legally prevent himself being liable for particular known defects in the goods, he must point out the defects *specifically* (see Q8); a broad, general disclaimer is illegal.

44 | *What's the legality of notices that say 'No exchange' or 'Sale goods may not be exchanged'?*

These notices are perfectly legal. This is unfortunate in some ways because most customers will see little difference between notices of this type and a notice saying something like 'No refunds' (see Q42). However, notices of this sort are not controlled by the legislation relating to unfair terms because they do not attempt to remove a remedy but accurately explain the legal position, which is that a consumer has no right to an exchange (see Q36).

45 | *Even reputable shops are in the habit of putting up notices such as 'No refunds without a receipt'. How do they affect me?*

One can sympathise with the trader's reasons for requiring this sort of evidence to prove that a particular purchaser bought the goods from his shop when there is a possibility that they were shoplifted or bought elsewhere. But this again is an exclusion clause attempting to take away the buyer's right to reject goods unless he can produce the required receipt, so it is void and illegal.

There is nothing to stop the shopkeeper exhibiting a notice such as 'Please keep your receipt as proof of purchase.' And when you try to get your money back he is entitled to ask you to prove that you bought the

goods from him. Clearly the best evidence of this is a receipt issued by the trader in question. But other evidence may suffice, for example a witness who was with you when you bought goods, or even your own word. If it came to a fight in court, the registrar or judge would have to decide who was telling the truth.

As traders generally know what the law is on this point and broadly try to comply with the law, disclaimers are gradually disappearing. But as it is a criminal offence to exhibit or use only *written* exemption clauses, the practice is growing up of shop assistants stating *orally* to customers that they must keep their receipts to obtain a refund or even that refunds will not be made on sale goods. Such statements have no legal effect, but no doubt produce the practical result required by the trader – they deter customers from going back to complain.

Shopping: manufacturers

46 | *My son broke his right arm when he fell off a stepladder at home as a result of one of the steps collapsing under him. Apparently it had been badly riveted. He had to take sick leave until the fracture mended. Can he claim any compensation?*

Presumably the stepladder was bought by you or your spouse, not by your son. Because of this he will be unable to recover compensation for his injuries from the shop, as he had not made a contract with them. This is what lawyers call the 'privity of contract' rule – only the *parties to a contract* can claim the benefits of it or be burdened by its obligations.

However, your son might be able to make a claim against the manufacturer. 'Product liability' is the jargon phrase normally used to describe the liability of manufacturers and producers to users of their products. The liability arises whether or not there is a contract between the user and the manufacturer and so is relevant when considering your son's rights against the stepladder manufacturer. As there is widespread misunderstanding of the limits of the liability of a manufacturer to consumers, it may be helpful to set out the crucial part of the judgment in the memorable House of Lords case about a snail in a bottle of ginger beer (*Donoghue* v. *Stevenson*) which introduced the principle of product liability just over 50 years ago:

A manufacturer of products, which he sells in such a form as to show that he intends them to reach the ultimate consumer in the form in which they left him with no reasonable possibility of intermediate examination, and with the knowledge that the absence of reasonable care in the preparation or putting up of the products will result in an injury to the consumer's life or property, owes a duty to the consumer to take that reasonable care.

The consumer has to prove that

- the goods were defective
- the defect was likely to cause injury, death or damage to some property other than the product itself – in other words, the goods were unsafe or dangerous
- the defect was not so obvious that a retailer or some other intermediate distributor should have noticed it before the product was put into circulation
- the manufacturer was negligent.

Your son should recover damages from the manufacturer because the stepladder was clearly unsafe and likely to cause injury, as in fact it did, and presumably the poor riveting was not obvious. The damages would cover loss of pay and compensation for pain and suffering. It need hardly be added that in a case like this where substantial damages are being sought, you should obtain expert legal advice.

47 | *Two years ago I bought a new car. I've now read in the newspapers that the manufacturer is recalling all models because of a defect in the braking system which has already caused a number of accidents. Who will have to pay for the repair?*

You have a choice. The garage that sold you the car is strictly liable for the defect, since clearly the car is not safe to drive and has not proved to be as durable as it should be. Obviously, you do not expect the braking system of a car ever to prove defective if properly serviced. The garage will be responsible for the full cost of the job including parts and labour (see Q33).

You may prefer to exercise your rights directly against the manufacturer under its product liability (see Q46). The required elements of the claim seem to be present: the defect makes the vehicle dangerous and is not one that was discoverable by the distributor when it sold you the car. The only possible difficulty is in proving that the manufacturer was negligent. But where a defect appears in the entire range, usually you will be trying to allege a negligent design. The problem in these cases is that often you will have to take on a very large company with more resources than yourself. Nevertheless, it is clear that in your case the manufacturer will be anxious to complete the repair, no doubt free of charge, to prevent accidents with the inevitable expense of paying very substantial damages for personal injuries and even death.

Other examples of this sort of problem are electrically unsafe goods such as Christmas tree lights and lamps, contaminated tinned foods such as salmon, and cosmetics or clothing (in one celebrated case a pair of sulphurous underpants) containing harmful chemicals.

● Consumer Protection Act 1987

This Act will be in force by July 1988 at the latest. It imposes *strict liability* (see Q4) on these businesses:

- manufacturers of end products and components;
- importers of goods from outside the EEC;
- suppliers of 'own-label' goods;
- suppliers of anonymous goods.

The goods must be 'defective', i.e. unsafe, not merely shoddy (see Q48). It will not take away the existing liability of suppliers, e.g. for negligence or under the Sale of Goods Act 1979.

---

48 | *The motor on my fairly new lawnmower has broken. The manufacturer is refusing to repair it or to replace it without charge. Surely it is the manufacturer's responsibility?*

No. Product liability does not help a consumer when goods are merely shoddy or cease to function. You have to show that the fault was likely to cause injury or damage (see Q46), and a lawnmower that does not work is unlikely to harm anybody. You should go back to the shop and exercise your rights as a buyer under the Sale of Goods Act 1979.

But check to see whether you received a manufac-

turer's guarantee when you bought the lawnmower. If the guarantee has not expired, the manufacturer will then be responsible too (see Q49).

49 | *Often a guarantee card is included with electrical goods and other products. How does that affect the buyer's position?*

If the goods are guaranteed by the manufacturer, the buyer can take advantage of the guarantee, if he or she wishes, instead of using his or her rights against the retailer.

The effect of the guarantee is to create a contract between the manufacturer and the buyer in addition to the contract of sale between the retailer and the buyer. Strangely, there is not a single court case on the legal validity of such guarantees. Most lawyers take the view that they give rise to contractual liability if only because in many cases the consumer must go to the trouble and expense of completing certain particulars, affixing a stamp and returning the card.

As manufacturers are under no legal obligation to give a guarantee they may make it as limited in scope as they wish. For example, the length of the guarantee period is a matter for the manufacturer, although generally the period of one year has become almost traditional and gives the impression that this is the only period of durability which the consumer is entitled to expect. A producer may also provide that the guarantee will not operate unless the buyer returns the guarantee card. The one thing that he may not do, as this is prohibited by legislation, is to exclude his own liability for negligence.

For many years consumers were advised to throw away guarantee cards. That advice is certainly incorrect today. A manufacturer's guarantee cannot reduce the consumer's rights against the retailer and is likely to add to them by giving him rights against the manufacturer. To make this clear, there is now a legal obligation for the manufacturer to explain the fact, which is generally done with some such formula as 'This does not affect your statutory rights'.

50 | *The switch on my coffee grinder broke within a few weeks of purchase. The guarantee with it says that the manufacturer will replace defective parts free of charge but that I must pay labour costs and the costs of return postage. Are manufacturers allowed to do that?*

Indeed they are. If you use the guarantee, you will have to pay for those items. But remember that the guarantee cannot reduce or affect the retailer's liability to you. So you can either ask the retailer to repair the grinder himself, or to replace it (although you cannot insist on a replacement; see Q36).

Work and materials

51 | *Is it correct that when an agreement is made by word of mouth I can do nothing about it if the supplier does not carry out what he promised to do?*

No. This is probably the greatest misunderstanding of the law of contract. Every day most of us make many contracts without putting them in writing: we buy food in shops and supermarkets, we travel by bus or taxi, a hotel room may be booked by phone, or a plumber called out to do a repair. All these involve perfectly valid contracts.

In many cases receipts for goods are given and it is useful to keep these in case you need to prove later where they were purchased. And in cases where a dispute may arise as to precisely what work is to be carried out by a supplier, it will be sensible to have a written record of the agreed terms (for example, building work like a new bathroom or extension, or repairs to the bodywork of a car). A written quotation will often fulfil this function.

There are a couple of exceptional cases where written contracts are necessary. Contracts for the sale or leasing of land should always be evidenced in writing. Also, many hire-purchase agreements and similar credit and hire transactions must be in writing. (See QS101 and 62.)

52 | *My car broke down when the starter motor failed. A local garage fitted a new motor but now, only a few weeks later, it's faulty and will itself need replacing. The manager of the garage says that I will have to pay for the new work as he had no reason to believe that the replacement was faulty – the mechanic checked it carefully – and cannot be held responsible for manufacturing defects. Is he correct?*

No. The garage should have supplied a starter motor in good working order. It is no defence for the garage to say that the staff were careful and had no reason to suspect that the motor was defective. No charge should be made for putting it right. The manager is wrong and the garage should do the entire job free of charge – the labour costs as well as another new starter motor.

Contracts of this type, where the supplier provides not merely goods, spare parts or materials but also the labour element, are classified in law as contracts for 'work and materials'. The classic judicial definition of such contracts is 'half [of the cost of the job] is the rendering of service and, in a sense, half the supply of goods'. In fact there is no need for the job to be precisely split 50:50 between materials and labour; it is enough if the labour element is a substantial factor in the contract. Contracts of this type are governed by the Supply of Goods and Services Act 1982, which imposes on the supplier an obligation to supply goods or materials which are of merchantable quality. This has the same meaning as under the Sale of Goods Act 1979 (see Q1).

53 | *What difference would it have made if the new starter motor had not been faulty but the reason for a later breakdown was that it had been fitted incorrectly by an incompetent mechanic?*

In this case too the garage would have to put it right free of charge. But the reasons are different from those given in Q52. It is not enough for the supplier to provide sound spare parts. The other element – the labour element – of a contract for work and materials must also be borne in mind. The Supply of Goods and Services Act 1982 implies a term in favour of the customer that the supplier will carry out the work with reasonable care and skill. As the garage was under a duty to carry out the repair carefully, it is responsible for the incompetent and careless work of the mechanic.

But there is one danger. If you were asked to sign an order form when you authorised the repair, you may have signed away your rights because the form may well have contained a clause excluding the garage's liability for negligence, which will protect the garage if the clause is reasonable.

If the garage is a member of the Motor Agents' Association (MAA) (address on page 511), the repair should have been 'guaranteed against failure due to workmanship for a specific mileage or time-period which should be stated in the invoice' to comply with the Code of Practice for the Motor Industry. The Code also provides for a free conciliation service and a low-cost arbitration scheme, both operated by the Motor Agents' Association.

54 | *I live by a noisy main road. I explained the problem to a double-glazing company which visited my home and advised me on the type and positioning of secondary glazing to alleviate the problem. The company has now finished the work but the*

423

noise is almost as bad. A friend tells me that the workmen should have left a larger gap between the window glass and the secondary glazing or used special glass with a double skin to cut down the noise efficiently. Am I right in refusing to pay the bill until they have done the job correctly?

It may be necessary to consult an independent expert to see whether your friend's comments are correct. But on the assumption that the double-glazing company left an insufficient gap or used the wrong glazing, it is the responsibility of the company to return to your house to put the job right and to make good any damage to your window-frames or walls caused by the incorrect fitting.

I SAID, "THIS DOUBLE GLAZING DOESN'T STOP TRAFFIC NOISE."

Your problem is another one covered by the Supply of Goods and Services Act 1982. As you made known your particular requirements to the supplier before the agreement was made, the supplier is under an implied obligation to provide secondary glazing suitable for your particular requirements. The fact that the secondary glazing is of the proper quality and not defective is irrelevant. It must also satisfy your special needs. You should refuse to pay until the company has complied with the terms of the agreement.

Remember too that there is a Code of Practice prepared by the Glass and Glazing Federation (address on page 510) in consultation with the Office of Fair Trading. You could ask the Federation to conciliate in your dispute if your supplier is a member.

55 | *I've had a small extension built on to my*

house. The agreement with the builder included detailed specifications, but the structural timbers are thinner than agreed (although the builder says that the extension is still safe), and much of the paint undercoating was missed out. The quality of the work, particularly the joinery, is appalling. The builder says that the joiner was a subcontractor and so he is not responsible. What is my legal position?

There are a number of legal issues here. First, the extension should have been built precisely in accordance with the specifications, as the Supply of Goods and Services Act 1982 implies a condition that the supplier shall supply goods that correspond with the contractual description. The builder has broken that contractual condition by using timber of the wrong size and by not completing the decoration correctly. Second, the work should have been carried out reasonably skilfully, which does not appear to be true of the joinery. The argument that the builder is not responsible for subcontractors is incorrect. He has undertaken to do the work and it is immaterial whether he does it personally or by using employees or by subcontracting. If the job is not done properly, the main contractor bears the responsibility.

If the builder will not put right the defects, you are entitled to call in another builder to finish the job off properly and deduct the cost from the first builder's account.

Although there are no 'official' Codes of Practice covering building work of this sort, there are two schemes operated by the major trade associations. Both the Federation of Master Builders and the National Federation of Building Trade Employers (addresses on pages 509 and 511) have introduced schemes to cover work undertaken by their members. Telephone to see whether your builder is a member of either of these associations. If so, contact the association to see whether it can help. For example, it may be able to resolve the dispute by conciliation or even by independent arbitration if you wish.

56 | *When my washing machine broke down – it's about six years old – I called out a service engineer to repair it. He replaced the programmer and I paid him on the spot. The machine soon broke down again and a neighbour of mine who looked at it found that the fault was merely a loose electrical connection which he tightened up with a screwdriver in no time at all. What action should I take?*

It may be difficult to prove that the programming unit

was not also faulty. If you kept the old unit, you could have it checked by an expert to see whether it need not have been changed. (This is one good reason for retaining components when repairs are done.) If you can show that the service engineer did unnecessary work and was careless in not identifying the fault correctly, he should give you your money back. Of course, even competent mechanics can make mistakes, and electrical faults may be difficult to diagnose. The engineer's responsibility is to carry out the service with reasonable care. Your case appears to be a strong one in view of the fact that your neighbour discovered the fault without much difficulty.

If the service engineer refuses to deal with your complaint, check to see whether one of the Codes of Practice may apply. These are the RETRA Code (see Q38), the Association of Manufacturers of Domestic Electrical Appliances (AMDEA) Code for Domestic Electrical Appliance Servicing, and the Electricity Boards' Code for Domestic Electrical Appliance Servicing. If he remains unhelpful, in the end you may have to sue him.

57 | *I've just had my shoes soled and heeled, but the workmanship is so poor that the shoes are now completely out of shape and no longer wearable. What is my position?*

The Supply of Goods and Services Act 1982 imposes two obligations on someone doing a repair like yours:

● to carry out the job with reasonable skill and care, and
● to use suitable materials of merchantable quality (see Q1).

Clearly your shoe repairer has broken the first obligation. Take the shoes back and ask for them to be put right free of charge. But if you have justifiably lost complete confidence in the shoe repairer, perhaps because it is a one-man business with no skilled person on the premises to rectify the fault, have them put right by another cobbler and claim the cost from the original repairer. If the shoes are now beyond repair, you should be entitled to compensation amounting to the second-hand value of the shoes and to have a refund of the repair charges which were wasted.

If your complaint is not resolved promptly, you may be able to take advantage of the Code of Practice for Shoe Repairs. Two trade associations subscribe to the Code, the National Association of Shoe Repair Factories and St Crispin's Boot Trades Association. Find out if your repairer is a member of one or other.

If he is, get in touch with the Association and ask it to intervene. Each has a conciliation service and, for a small fee, may obtain an independent test report to resolve the dispute. The Office of Fair Trading pamphlet *Shoes* explains the Code.

Hiring goods

58 | *If I hire equipment, am I protected regarding the quality and so on in the same way as if I'd bought it outright?*

Contracts of hire – often called rental or leasing agreements – are included in the Supply of Goods and Services Act 1982. The reason that legislation was required for cases of hire is that hire contracts fall outside the sale of goods legislation because the hirer (or 'bailee', to use the technical description) is entitled to the use and possession of the goods only during the hire period and will never become the owner of the goods under the terms of the agreement. (Where the agreement gives the hirer a right to buy the goods when the hire period expires, it is in law a hire-purchase agreement; see Q101.)

The provisions in the 1982 Act are based squarely on the comparable provisions in the Sale of Goods Act 1979 which covers the purchase of goods by consumers. The most important ones relate to description, quality and suitability. The comments on the related provisions discussed in Qs1 to 50 apply equally to hire contracts.

59 | *I agreed to hire a small cabin cruiser for a week's holiday on the Norfolk Broads. When I arrived at the boatyard, it was explained that due to overbooking the boatyard could not provide me with the boat I'd hired. However, the yard offered me a large, six-berth cruiser and then insisted on charging me the full rate for the larger boat. Was the boatyard correct?*

No. When you entered into the agreement to hire the small cruiser, a term was implied by the Supply of Goods and Services Act 1982 that the yard would supply a boat of that description for the agreed period. The error in overbooking boats of that type does not excuse the boatyard. You were entitled to treat the contract as at an end, hire a comparable boat elsewhere (if available) and claim from the original boatyard any additional cost over and above the agreed hire charge.

It is understandable that at a busy holiday period you took whatever was available rather than spoil

● *Supply of Goods and Services Act 1982*

This Act imposes the following duties on business suppliers of services where there is a contract between the supplier and the customer:

- to carry out the service with **reasonable care and skill** (Section 13)
- to carry out the service within a **reasonable time** where no time has been fixed (Section 14)
- to make a **reasonable charge** for the service where no charge has been agreed in advance (Section 15).

your holiday. In the circumstances you should not be out of pocket, as the boat firm is to blame, and you should have to pay only the lower charge for the smaller boat. You could even argue that you should be reimbursed some of your fuel costs as the smaller boat would have consumed less fuel. At the time, you should have made it absolutely clear that you were not content with the larger boat except on the basis that you paid the rate for the boat you hired. If you didn't, in agreeing to the larger boat you may have appeared to waive or excuse the breach of contract and to have given the impression that you would not be making a claim.

60 | *I hired a motor caravan in Manchester to take my wife and two children on a touring holiday in the West Country. I mentioned this to the car hire firm at the time. The vehicle turned out to be in a terrible state. The clutch failed while we were on our journey and we had to spend the night in a hotel while it was being repaired. Numerous other faults developed in the first few days and we seemed to spend most of our time calling in at garages to have them put right. The caravan was too unreliable to risk going as far as Devon and Cornwall and we spent the holiday at a caravan site in Somerset. Overall, the holiday proved a great disappointment and was certainly not the touring holiday we had planned. Can I get any compensation from the car hire firm?*

Indeed you can. The hire contract for the vehicle included an implied term that the vehicle was of merchantable quality (see Q1) and so would be roadworthy. This is bolstered by the implied term that it would be suitable for your particular purpose, namely touring in the West Country. The car hire firm broke these terms by providing a defective ve-

hicle and it is strictly liable for any losses you suffered which the firm could have foreseen when the contract was made.

Obviously the hire firm will have to reimburse the cost of the various repairs carried out during the holiday. But in addition to that it is important to remember that in recent years the courts have been willing to award damages to cover the cost of disappointment, upset, frustration and loss of enjoyment. Cases decided by the Court of Appeal show that these elements are particularly important in relation to holiday contracts. Presumably, your holiday was not a complete disaster, as you spent it in Somerset, but equally obviously there must have been substantial disappointment for all the members of your family in not travelling further. There are no clear guidelines on how much you could claim, but a figure of £100 or so would not be unreasonable and it could well be more. In addition, you can recover the hotel expenses for the night you could not sleep in the vehicle.

It was sensible to mention the purpose of the hire when you entered into the agreement, although in your case it was obvious that some sort of holiday was in prospect – people seldom hire motor caravans otherwise. The more information you give the supplier at the date of the contract, the more items of loss can be foreseen and then included when a claim is made.

61 | *I hired a cultivator from a garden centre, explaining that the soil on my land was heavy clay. Although the cultivator wasn't faulty, it wasn't powerful enough to turn over the soil and just got bogged down. The garden centre refuses to*

give me my money back, as there was nothing wrong with the equipment. Is it right to do so?

No. The garden centre should give you a full refund. The equipment was useless for your purpose, a purpose you made known to the garden centre when you entered into the contract of hire. So the supplier has broken the term, implied by the Supply of Goods and Services Act 1982, that the cultivator would be fit for your particular purpose. Nor will it help the supplier that he had no reason to believe that the machine was not powerful enough, as the obligation imposes strict liability on him.

It would be a different matter if the supplier had said that he wasn't sure whether the cultivator could cope with your soil conditions. In those circumstances it would be enough to supply a machine that worked properly in more friable soil, for you would be relying on yourself and not on the supplier as to its suitability for your special soil conditions.

62 | *Rental and hire contracts always seem to be set down in very detailed documents. Are these required by law?*

Yes. Regulations under the Consumer Credit Act 1974 specify detailed requirements that must be met by rental and hire companies when making agreements with consumers. (The name of the Act is misleading because it covers consumer hire as well as consumer credit.) Details of the hire terms must be included in the documents – for example, the amount of the rental and the period of hire – and certain information must be included explaining some of the hirer's statutory rights – for example, the hirer's right to terminate or cancel the agreement when appropriate.

63 | *I hired a van for the day to move some furniture. I pulled into a petrol station and, forgetting the height of the van, damaged the front of the cab and the roof on the forecourt canopy. The car hire firm claims that I'm responsible for the cost of repairing the van. Am I?*

Yes, you're responsible. When you hire goods you must return them at the end of the hire period in the same state as they were at the beginning, subject to fair wear and tear. The contract of hire will usually impose this liability on you. In any case, you will be liable for damage caused by your negligence.

Don't forget, though, that you would have taken out insurance on the van when you hired it. However, although the insurance will cover your liability

to third parties to comply with the Road Traffic Act 1972, it may not have been completely comprehensive and covered *all* damage to the van itself. Quite frequently there is a substantial excess to be borne by the hirer.

Finally, check the insurance policy on your own car. It may have an extension to its cover applying to other vehicles not owned by you.

Services

64 | *I took a suit to a dry cleaners and they lost it. Despite their enquiries they have no idea what happened to it. Will they have to buy me a new suit?*

The dry cleaners were under a duty to take reasonable care of the suit, as this is a contract for the supply of services covered by the Supply of Goods and Services Act 1982. In many cases it is difficult to prove that negligence has occurred. However, where as part of the service the supplier has your property in his possession there is a presumption that the supplier has been negligent if the property is lost or damaged without explanation. This appears to be your situation, and the cleaners will be responsible for the loss of your suit.

However, they will not necessarily have to buy you a *new* suit. Your compensation will be assessed on the value of the suit at the time it was lost, which is the second-hand value only. This legal rule is accurately explained in the Code of Practice drawn up by the Association of British Launderers and Cleaners (ABLC). The Code provides that 'both parties should take into account the depreciation, wear and tear which had occurred to the article prior to the loss or damage as this may affect the article's value in respect of which compensation is assessed'. The Code states that ABLC members should pay fair compensation where loss is due to the negligence of a member and sets out the Association's Customer Advisory Service under which free conciliation of a dispute is available. Telephone ABLC (address on page 509) to see whether the dry cleaners are members. The Code is explained in a free leaflet, *Launderers and Dry Cleaners*, published by the Office of Fair Trading.

65 | *The dry cleaners didn't lose a suit I'd taken in but said it had been stolen as part of a whole batch of clothes. Will they have to replace my suit?*

In these circumstances the cleaners would not be responsible for the loss, because they would have satisfied the duty of care imposed on them by the

Supply of Goods and Services Act 1982. A supplier of services is not under a strict liability and is not liable for loss or damage which don't result from carelessness.

This is where the ABLC Code of Practice (see Q64) has a great advantage over the law. It provides that an ABLC member should pay compensation for loss or damage caused by burglary or fire 'even though no negligence can be attributed to the member'. This generous provision does not apply where the article is covered by the customer's own insurance policy, so check your house contents policy to see whether the insurance cover extends to contents while away from the dwelling, as is frequently the case. If it does, claim on your house contents policy. If it does not, the cleaners should compensate you provided they are an ABLC member.

66 | *I've seen in dry cleaners and other places notices that say: 'We cannot accept responsibility for the loss of or damage to goods, however caused'. Are such notices effective in taking away any right to compensation if garments are lost or damaged?*

Unfortunately for the consumer, notices like these may protect suppliers. Exclusion clauses like this are subject to a 'reasonableness test' imposed by the Unfair Contract Terms Act 1977. If the clause is fair and reasonable between the parties, the supplier will be able to shelter behind it even though he may have been negligent. (This is in sharp contrast to the approach of the legislation when dealing with *goods*, where exemption clauses in consumer contracts are void and illegal; see Qs 42 to 45.)

Even so, you should not despair when confronted with a notice like this if you are prepared to take legal action. A number of decisions in the courts have shown that the courts are unwilling to uphold exclusion clauses where the customer has been in a weak bargaining position and unable to negotiate a better deal. And an important practical point is that the ABLC Code of Practice (see Q64) prohibits the use of clauses excluding or limiting liability, so you may prefer to do business with the Association's members to obtain this advantage.

67 | *Last month I went to a new hairdresser for a perm. I explained that my scalp was very sensitive and that only two years ago my hair had fallen out after a perm. I mentioned the name of a brand of perm solution which had been used with success by my last hairdresser. The salon owner said he could*

cope with my problems, but within a few days I had a bald patch on the top of my head. In the circumstances, could I expect to receive any compensation?

The hairdresser was providing a service and so should have used reasonable care and skill when giving you the perm. As the brand of perm solution which you mentioned had been used without ill effects on previous occasions, it seems that your new hairdresser failed to follow the instructions properly and applied the chemicals carelessly or used the wrong brand. Because of this, you will be entitled to compensation, and it will take account both of any pain suffered and of your upset at your unsightly appearance. This could easily exceed £100.

It is of course possible that there was something wrong with that batch of perm solution. Even so, the hairdresser would still be responsible, as he would be under a strict liability to supply materials suitable for your particular purpose bearing in mind your sensitive scalp (see Q9). Compensation would be assessed in the same way.

68 | *We recently moved into a new house. While carrying a wardrobe upstairs the furniture removers badly damaged a banister and the staircase wall. When we claimed the cost of repair and redecoration, they pointed to a clause in the contract limiting their liability for damages to £10. Is that their total liability?*

Probably not. There are two points to make. First, the removal men failed to carry out their removal service with reasonable care and skill, as they should under the Supply of Goods and Services Act 1982, so they should compensate you fully for the damage they caused. Second, you need to consider whether the limitation clause protects them. The Unfair Contract Terms Act 1977 regulates exemption and limitation clauses and allows the supplier to rely on them only if the supplier can prove that a particular clause is fair and reasonable. Bearing in mind that most removal firms use similar terms of trading and that the chances of your negotiating an individual improvement with the firm are slight, such a clause is unlikely to be upheld by the courts. It is also relevant that the furniture removers would almost certainly have an insurance policy covering their liability, and the cost of the insurance premiums would have been taken into account in pricing your job. This factor should also lead the courts to decide the matter in your favour. Do not be put off by the contract conditions, and see a solicitor if the removers persistently ignore your claim.

But a word of warning. If the removers offered you insurance against this risk which you refused to take advantage of, the courts might well take a different view; for the liability clause could be reasonable if you were in a position to protect yourselves with insurance.

69 | *While I was putting my car through an automatic car wash the water suddenly stopped but the brushes continued revolving and badly scratched the paintwork. The garage manager is refusing to pay the cost of a respray on the grounds that there was a large notice displayed on the coin box stating: 'The garage will not be responsible for damage to customers' cars, however caused.' Should the garage pay for the repair?*

You will first have to prove that the garage broke its duty to act with reasonable care when providing the service, so you will need to discover why the water stopped. If the cause of the breakdown in the car wash was that the garage had not had the equipment serviced and maintained properly, that would be evidence of negligence. The same would be true if someone had turned off the water by mistake while your car was going through. But if the garage was not to blame for the failure of the water supply, it would have no responsibility for the damage.

Assuming that you can prove negligence, your next problem is to surmount the barrier of the exemption clause in the notice. As the notice was in a prominent position where you should have been able to read it easily, you cannot deny that it was incorporated into the contract. Your only hope is to rely on the Unfair Contract Terms Act 1977. This will involve the garage in proving that in the circumstances the complete exclusion of liability was fair and reasonable. A similar case of damage caused by a car wash was heard in the county court; the court decided that such a clause was invalid. Although one county court decision is not binding on another county court, you ought to be able to negotiate a full settlement of your claim.

70 | *I wanted a tree in my back garden cut down. A man was recommended, and he came and quoted a favourable price. But when he cut down the tree, it fell the wrong way and demolished my greenhouse. I then found out that he's employed full time as a milkman and has just started his new line*

of business as a spare-time activity. Should he pay for the damage?

If someone offers his services in a particular field, he should have the skill and exercise the care of the ordinary competent man in that particular trade. It is no defence to say that it is a spare-time activity or that the business has only just started up. This is becoming increasingly common with people supplementing their wages in their spare time, or redundant employees entering new activities for which they have no training or experience. The fact that the job may be done more cheaply by such a person does not reduce the standard of competence which the customer should expect.

Because your 'cowboy' lumberjack broke his contractual duty of care, he is responsible for the cost of replacing the greenhouse. If he had been a full-time tree surgeon, doubtless he would have had appropriate insurance cover and your claim would have been paid without argument.

71 | *When I left my car in a busy city-centre car-park, the attendant asked me to leave my car keys with him so that he could move the cars around when customers came to collect them. When I collected my car, it had a large dent in the wing. The attendant refused to give any explanation for the damage. What is my legal position?*

This is another case where the supplier of a service has a duty to take reasonable care under the Supply of Goods and Services Act 1982. No doubt you suspect that the attendant caused the damage by carelessly parking your car. Although normally it is for the claimant to prove his case, yours is one of the exceptional situations where the supplier must *disprove* negligence. Cases like these arise where goods are left in the care of another person and only he is in a position to explain what has happened to them. In such a case the supplier will be liable, unless he can prove that the damage or loss occurred without his negligence. The owners of the car-park will be responsible for the full cost of repairing your car in the absence of a satisfactory explanation.

72 | *To cut down on heating costs I called in an engineer to install new controls on my central heating – a time clock and a thermostat. Since then the whole system has gone haywire, and an independent expert has said that the controls have been incorrectly fitted. Should I refuse to pay the engineer's bill?*

A contract for the supply and installation of new equipment is called by lawyers a contract for 'work and materials' (see Q52). The supplier has two obligations:

● to supply suitable materials, and
● to carry out the installation with reasonable care and skill (see Q57).

Apparently, in your case the controls were not faulty but had been connected up wrongly. The result of your heating engineer's incompetence is that he is in breach of contract and should pay the cost of any rewiring and other work necessary to fit the controls properly. If he is unwilling or unable to complete the job to put the system into full working order, you are entitled to call in someone else who is competent and deduct the charges of the second contractor from the heating engineer's bill by way of damages for breach of contract.

Your case shows the advantage of not paying in advance for work because, if anything goes wrong, the initiative has to be taken by the consumer, who is often reluctant to go to court. If you pay in arrears, then a sum can be deducted to cover whatever compensation is legally due.

73 | *A friend of mine who's a hi-fi fanatic tried to repair my record player when it developed a fault. Unfortunately, he connected up the wires incorrectly and the resultant short circuit caused a fire. The record player is now beyond repair. Is there anything I can do?*

No. The only thing you could expect from your friend is the standard of care of the ordinary, incompetent layman. It is very unlikely that you could prove a breach of that duty and so you appear to have no legal remedy.

74 | *Am I correct in thinking that when I buy a house with the assistance of a building society mortgage there is no need to have a separate survey done myself and that I can rely on the building society survey?*

You are clearly referring to an important court case of 1981 (*Yianni* v. *Edwin Evans*) in which a couple were buying a house for £15,000. When they applied to the Halifax Building Society for a £12,000 mortgage, the usual practice was followed of the building society having a survey of the house at the buyers' expense. This was done and the purchase and mortgage went through. Some time later the walls began to crack and expensive underpinning and repair work proved necessary. The High Court decided that although there was no contract between the buyers and the surveyor, since the surveyor had been instructed by the building society, nevertheless the surveyor owed a duty of care to the buyers. As that duty of care had been broken in this case, the surveyor was liable to compensate the buyers for the damage suffered.

Even so, you should remember that the survey undertaken for the building society is to discover whether the property will be adequate security for the amount of the loan. It is not a full structural survey and is not intended to deal in detail with the physical state of the building. There are still arguments in favour of house buyers continuing to commission their own separate survey. The Royal Institution of Chartered Surveyors has its own House Buyers Report and Valuation Scheme. And your building society may have its own scheme which allows you to top up its own valuation by paying an extra fee so that the survey covers the physical condition of the building in more detail; you also get a copy of this survey. See YOU AND YOUR HOME, Q163 for more details of house surveys.

Time and delivery

75 | *When I ordered a table from a furniture shop we agreed on a particular delivery date. What can I do if the table does not arrive on time?*

When the parties to a contract agree a delivery date, it is vital to discover whether that date is 'of the essence', which means that the delivery should take place precisely on the specified date. If delivery is delayed by even a day, the buyer is entitled to cancel the contract, treating the contract as ended because of the seller's breach of such a vital term. Although in commercial contracts between one businessman and another time provisions are impliedly of the essence, in consumer contracts there is no such implication.

Since in the case of your table there seem to be no special facts indicating that compliance with the delivery date was crucial, you cannot cancel the contract simply because the delivery date is not met.

Nevertheless, the date is not without significance. The seller has still broken the contract by not keeping to the date, even though precise compliance is less crucial than it would be if the date were of the essence. Although you cannot cancel the contract, you could recover compensation for any loss which would have been in the parties' minds when the agreement was made. It has to be admitted that in most consumer cases – and yours seems to be typical – the chance of any real loss being suffered as a result of late delivery is slender. But if you had bought a washing machine, say, and late delivery had caused you the expense of using a launderette meanwhile, such expense would be recoverable from the retailer.

Of course, you may have initially signed an order form which contained a clause stating that the shop disclaimed any responsibility for late delivery. In such a case the shop could rely on the disclaimer if it could show that the disclaimer was a reasonable exemption clause (see Q68).

76 | *If the table is not delivered on the agreed date, can I be kept waiting for ever without being able to do anything about it? What if I've paid a deposit? Surely I can get that back at least?*

You can do something to stimulate the seller into activity. Once the delivery date has passed, you can give notice, preferably in writing, to the seller imposing an ultimate time-limit. The period specified in the notice must be reasonable, say two or three weeks. If the seller has not delivered the goods by the deadline in the notice, you may terminate the agreement and recover your deposit.

77 | *What happens if I cancel an order because of delayed delivery and can find the same goods in other shops only at a higher price?*

This is an obvious case where the breach of contract by the seller has caused you loss and the seller should be responsible to you for the difference between the agreed contract price and the higher price paid elsewhere. The loss would be awarded by a court as damages for non-delivery.

On the other hand, if the price has dropped or remained the same, it would be pointless to make a claim against the seller, for although the seller has clearly broken the contract he will not have caused you any financial loss.

78 | *My husband and I bought a newly built house. We went to a carpet shop and explained that we wished the carpets to be laid before we moved in and gave them the removal date. They didn't turn up on time and we had to move in on to bare boards – we had completed the sale of our previous house that day and it was too late to make arrangements with any other carpet supplier. You can imagine the chaos when the carpets were laid a few days later while we were in occupation. Is there anything we can do?*

In this case the agreed time for laying the carpets was of the essence (see Q75). It was clear from the circumstances, which you explained when you placed the order, that it was important for the job to be done on time. It does not matter if the expression 'time to be of the essence' did not appear in any of the documents and was not mentioned by you. (Clearly, if that expression is written into the contract, the matter is beyond doubt.) When it became obvious that the work could not have been done on time, you would have been within your rights to rush off to another supplier who had the carpets in stock and have the job done immediately. In view of the urgency this would no doubt have cost you rather more, in which case the additional cost could have been claimed from the first carpet shop.

Although you cannot show any financial loss from the late completion of the work, clearly your family must have been harassed by the disruption when the carpets were actually laid all round you. To that

should be added the discomfort of the period when you were living on bare boards. The carpet supplier should compensate you for this vexation, as damages are recoverable nowadays in the courts for this type of loss. The precise amount is difficult to estimate and will depend on the length of the delay, the period of disruption while the work was in progress, and the number in your family upset by the whole affair. To expect £100-plus would not be unreasonable in some circumstances.

79 | *When I ordered double-glazing, the order form stated a delivery period of '10–12 weeks' and stated that 'time for delivery is not of the essence of the contract'. After 12 weeks nothing had happened. I waited another fortnight and then telephoned to cancel the order. The firm told me that the windows had been made and would be fitted the following week, and that if I did not take delivery it would keep the deposit and sue me for the balance of the price. Is that really the legal position?*

Yes, in effect, because time was expressly stated to be 'not of the essence'. And, anyway, there appear to be no special circumstances which made the delivery date vitally important to you. So although the company did not meet the delivery date, this did not entitle you to terminate the contract. You could have done so by giving the company reasonable notice imposing a deadline. For example, after you had telephoned you could have written a letter stating that unless the windows were supplied and fitted within two weeks at the latest you would treat the contract as repudiated by the company's breach and expect a refund of your deposit. But in the absence of a notice imposing a strict time-limit in that way, you were obliged to continue with the contract and let the double-glazing company complete the job.

Assuming that the windows were in fact ready for fitting the following week and you refused to let the work proceed, you would find yourself saddled with considerable expense. As the windows had been specially made for your house, it is unlikely that they could be sold to another customer and you would be liable for the total contract price less the small value of the glass and other materials left on the company's hands.

The moral is that if you wish a supplier to do the job on a particular date and to be able to cancel otherwise, you must ensure that the agreed date is seen to be of importance by stressing that performance must occur precisely on time, for example by saying that time is to be of the essence. Even if the supplier will

not amend his order form, an express oral undertaking by him to deliver on a particular date will be sufficient to make it an essential term.

80 | *I accepted a quotation from a local builder to erect an extension to my house nearly a year ago. Unfortunately, we didn't agree a starting date. Whenever I ring the builder to chase him, he tells me that he's busy with more work than he can cope with and that he will fit it in when he can. Is it entirely up to him to choose when to do my job, irrespective of my own wishes?*

Where no date has been agreed for work to be done (or goods to be delivered), the contract contains an implied term that it will be done within a reasonable time. In respect of contracts involving services like yours, the provision appears in the Supply of Goods and Services Act 1982. It is always a difficult question of fact what a reasonable time actually is in any particular case. But what is clear is that there is no excuse for the supplier to justify his delay on the grounds that he has taken on too much work. This is entirely a matter for him, as he should not undertake more than he can manage. It would certainly be reasonable to expect work to commence on any job within a few months. In spite of the long delay, you should not cancel the agreement at the drop of a hat. You should give him reasonable notice by setting a deadline – a month would seem long enough in your case. If nothing happens then, you will be released from the contract as a result of his breach. In strict theory you could then claim from the builder any additional cost of placing the building contract elsewhere, although few consumers bother to pursue that remedy.

81 | *I have a fairly old television set. The other day the picture disappeared, so I telephoned a television repairer who promised to call two days later. I took a day's holiday to wait for him but he failed to arrive. Will he have to compensate me for my wasted day?*

The television repairer certainly broke the agreement with you by not turning up on the specified day. But the problem is whether he is responsible for the wasted holiday, admittedly wasted through his fault. The general rule is that you can recover only those items of loss which both parties could have contemplated at the contract moment as being likely to result from any breach. Unless you told the repairer that you would have to take a day off work specially, he might have assumed that someone would have been at home anyway.

Why not point out the circumstances to him and ask him to make his delayed call in the evening or at a weekend when you will be there anyway? In the event, his breach of contract will have caused you no loss at all, since the job will have been done with only a day off work as planned. Of course, although this may mean his calling out of ordinary working hours, he should charge you no more than the normal rate which you would have paid had he come at the correct time. It will also help to discover whether he is a member of the Radio, Electrical and Television Retailers' Association (RETRA) (address on page 511). There are two provisions in the Association's Code of Practice which are relevant. First, an initial service call should be made within three working days after receiving the request; thus, a speedy visit is now the order of the day for you. Second, the retailer 'will endeavour to advise the customer, where practicable, of any change in call times' where an appointment has to be cancelled 'through circumstances beyond the normal running of the retailer's business'.

Draw these matters to the attention of the repairer and ask for some compensation, for example a free visit. If you are not satisfied with his answer, you could complain to the Association's conciliation service under the Code of Practice. The Office of Fair Trading leaflet *Electrical Goods* explains the various provisions of the Code.

82 | *After a collision my car was towed to a garage for repair, and the garage took eight weeks to do the job. I understand from an engineer that the job could have been completed in five weeks but that the garage was giving priority to manufacturers' warranty work and putting off doing my job. I hired a car while my own was off the road. Can I recover the hire charges from the garage?*

Under the Supply of Goods and Services Act 1982 the garage should have carried out the work 'within a reasonable time'. In your case five weeks seems to be that reasonable time in view of the expert evidence given to you. The extra three weeks' hire charges, therefore, were caused by the garage's delay and should be recoverable as damages for breach of contract. It is irrelevant that for commercial reasons the garage thought it best to give priority to defects in new cars. It would be a different matter if the garage's delay had been caused by something beyond its con-

trol, such as a shortage of spare parts, for which it could hardly be blamed.

83 | *A couple of months ago a set of encyclopaedias was delivered to me even though I hadn't ordered them. I've now received a letter threatening to sue me if I don't pay for them. What should I do?*

Nothing. This improper method of marketing was very common in the 1960s. It is now quite rare, since it was outlawed by the Unsolicited Goods and Services Act 1971. The Act has two sanctions, one civil and one criminal.

The civil sanction is that the recipient of the goods can treat them as an unconditional gift under certain conditions:

● he had not made any prior request for them
● they were sent to him in his private capacity
● he has not agreed to acquire them or agreed to return them.

As these conditions seem to be satisfied in your case, the goods will become yours at the end of six months from the date of receipt, provided you do not refuse to let the supplier take them away. They can become yours even more quickly if you send written notice to the supplier stating that the goods were unsolicited and giving your name and address; then after 30 days the goods are yours, unless you refuse to let the supplier take them away.

The trader has committed a criminal offence under the Act, which makes it illegal for him to claim payment or threaten legal proceedings, where the trader demands payment for unsolicited goods knowing that he has no right to payment. So don't pay. Hang on to the goods and in four more months they will belong to you.

Prices, charges and deposits

84 | *I saw a jacket in a shop window marked at £69. I tried one on in my size, liked it, and went to pay for it. The assistant charged me £89. I saw the manager and pointed out the price tag in the window, but he said that an assistant must have put the wrong label on the jacket. Reluctantly, I paid the higher price. Someone has told me I should have paid only the £69 specified on the price tag. Can I now recover the £20 difference?*

Probably not. As far as the civil law is concerned, the

placing of goods in a shop window does not oblige the shopkeeper to sell the goods to the customer at the specified price. The reason is that the shopkeeper is not offering to sell them to the public, but is inviting the public to come in to make an offer to buy them which the shopkeeper may accept or refuse as he thinks fit. The manager was entitled to refuse your offer of £69 for the jacket and to make the counter-offer of £89, which you decided to accept. There was thus a valid contract of sale at the price of £89. (Shops can even refuse to serve customers for no reason at all, although that tends to affect their good-will and turnover!)

However, it is possible that the owner of the shop committed a criminal offence under the Trade Descriptions Act 1968. The Act states that it is an offence to give an indication that goods exposed for sale are being offered at a lower price than that at which they are in fact being offered. The price tag certainly gave that impression. If you ask the Trading Standards Department of your local authority to investigate the matter, the shopkeeper may well think it appropriate to refund the £20. If the local authority decides to prosecute and obtains a conviction, you could ask the magistrates for compensation under the Powers of Criminal Courts Act 1973.

● *Consumer Protection Act 1987*

This Act, when later brought into force, will repeal the pricing provisions of the Trade Descriptions Act 1968 and the Price Marking (Bargain Offers) Order 1979. Both will be replaced by a less technical and detailed criminal offence relating to 'misleading prices'.

85 | *Why do some shops, when they mark down their prices, put up a notice that reads: 'The goods on display at reduced prices have not necessarily been sold at the higher price for a period of 28 days during the last six months'?*

The Trade Descriptions Act 1968 accounts for this long and cryptic formula. (Indeed, notices of this sort frequently refer to the Act.) The reason is that the Act makes it an offence for a trader to make false claims of a reduction from his previous price. An easy way round this rule would be for the trader to display the goods for only a day, or even a few hours, at the higher price and then to claim next day that he has reduced the price. The purpose of the 28-day/six-month provision is to ensure that the supplier has

offered them for a reasonably long continuous period (28 days minimum) during the comparatively recent past (the last six months). However, the Act does permit disclaimers such as the notice you mention to prevent shops from committing a criminal offence if they don't follow the 28-day/six-month provision.

86 | *I thought that recommended prices had been banned. So how can shops sell goods at prices discounted from the higher 'manufacturer's recommended price'?*

I'M NOT ASKING THE MANUFACTURER'S RECOMMENDED PRICE OF £500, I'M NOT ASKING £250, I'M NOT EVEN ASKING £50......FOR YOU... TODAY....TWO QUID!

There was a recommendation from the Office of Fair Trading that all manufacturers' recommended prices should be banned because they are frequently fixed at a very high level – sometimes called 'sky prices' – to enable retailers to cut prices heavily. That is only a recommendation. But the Price Marking (Bargain Offers) Order 1979 bans manufacturers' recommended prices on certain types of goods. These are beds and furniture, carpets, and electrical and electronic goods. If you see a claimed reduction from the MRP in relation to the banned goods – and carpet warehouses need to be watched – tell the Trading Standards Department of your local authority.

87 | *I have seen 'ASP' on beds and furniture. What do the letters mean?*

Those letters mean 'after sale price'. The Price Marking (Bargain Offers) Order 1979 allows traders to start off with a low price and to indicate that they propose to increase it later. The intention was to enable manufacturers when marketing a new product to stimulate sales by starting with an attractive low price for a period and in their advertisements to state that the price would be raised to the normal price – the after sale price – after the introductory offer.

88 | What has happened to price claims like 'Price elsewhere £120, our price £99'?

These are illegal under the Price Marking (Bargain Offers) Order 1979. The Order allows sellers to advertise that their prices are lower than elsewhere only provided they identify precisely their more expensive competitor, so nowadays you should only see notices like 'Bloggins' price £120, our price £99'.

89 | When I ordered a three-piece suite, the furniture store asked me for a £50 deposit which I paid. I was then made redundant and cancelled the order. The store refuses to return my deposit. Can it do that?

By cancelling the order you have broken the contract, as ultimately you should have taken delivery and paid the balance of the price. Where a deposit has been paid, the problem is to work out whether it was merely an advance payment towards the price or whether it was paid as a 'token of due performance' or 'earnest of faith' in the sense that the seller required a deposit as security to make the buyer have second thoughts before terminating the agreement.

It is likely that in a case like yours the deposit is taken as security, and the store is entitled to retain the deposit. In addition, strictly it is entitled to claim from you any loss of profit over and above the amount of the deposit, although fortunately most retailers do not pursue such claims.

90 | In October I ordered a carriage clock from a mail order catalogue, noting that the delivery period was six weeks, and paid for it in full by cheque. I intended to give the clock to my daughter as a Christmas present, so as the clock had not been delivered by the end of November I telephoned the company to enquire what had happened. It said that it had been inundated with orders and there would be some delay. I told the company that I wanted the clock in time for Christmas, otherwise I would have no use for it. It didn't arrive in time, so after Christmas I wrote cancelling the order and asking for my money back. The company refused to return my money, as the clock was then ready for despatch. What is my legal position?

The mail order company has broken the contract by not delivering the clock before Christmas. Although the original delivery period did not make time of the essence (see Q75), your telephone call at the end of November giving the company at least another three weeks was reasonable notice imposing a final time-limit expiring before Christmas. You are entitled to a complete refund, and if you bought a clock of broadly the same quality elsewhere which cost more than the mail order price, the mail order company should also reimburse you the additional cost.

If the company is a member of the Mail Order Traders' Association (address on page 510), you may use the complaints procedure set out in its Code of Practice. If a letter to the company setting out the grounds for your complaint has no effect, ask the Association to conciliate between you. This is a free service. If that does not resolve the difficulty, you can take advantage of the low-cost arbitration procedures arranged by the Association.

91 | I arranged for a building contractor to build an extension to my house and paid half the cost of the work in advance. Shortly after starting work the builder became insolvent. The liquidator of the company states that all the builder's assets will be used up in paying off his bank debts. What can I do about getting my money back?

This is the problem of making payments in stages for building work or, indeed, of making advance payments to any supplier. When the supplier goes bust, there is seldom enough money to pay off all his creditors in full. At best his creditors, who will include other customers in your position, will obtain a small dividend or percentage of the money due. You should really ensure that you make payments in stages only when work to the appropriate value has already been completed, unless you are absolutely sure that the builder will remain solvent.

It would be a different story if the builder had finished the job and been paid in full, and *then* had become insolvent before rectifying any defective work. If the builder were a member of a trade association such as the Federation of Master Builders (FMB) (address on page 509), this might help. For example, the FMB has a scheme called the National Register of Warranted Builders. If your builder were a member of the FMB *and* had joined the scheme *and* had registered your job under the scheme – unfortunately the scheme does not cover all work undertaken by members of the FMB – then you would be protected: the job would be finished at the expense of the scheme. The National Federation of Building Trade

Employers (address on page 511) also has a scheme of this type.

92 | I bought a set of mixer taps from a builders' merchants. When I went to the checkout to pay, the cashier added VAT to the price marked on the taps. Surely he was wrong to do so?

This problem is similar to the question relating to goods in a shop window (see Q84). As far as the law of contract is concerned, the cashier was entitled to refuse your offer to buy the goods at the marked price, as placing goods on a shelf is *not* an offer to the public to sell them at the marked price.

But at first sight an offence has been committed under the Trade Descriptions Act 1968, as you quite reasonably thought that you could buy the goods at the marked price. Obviously, it would be a different matter if the price label had clearly stated that VAT would be added or there were notices around the shop in prominent positions to the same effect. Incidentally, it is not enough to put up a notice of that sort over the cash till, since this information should be brought to the attention of the customer where the goods are on display. A complaint to your local authority's Trading Standards Department would help to knock this practice on the head.

93 | What's the difference between a quotation and an estimate?

There's no clear distinction, since the words have no well-settled legal meaning. When a price is quoted and the words 'quotation' or 'estimate' are used in that context, the vital question is: is the price, charge or fee mentioned in the quotation or estimate intended to fix precisely the financial liability of the customer (making it a quotation), or is it merely a rough-and-ready, if informed guide to the price level ultimately to be charged (making it an estimate)? In every case you have to try to give an objective answer to that difficult question.

Nevertheless, there is an increasing tendency to use the word 'quotation' to mean an offer to do the job at a fixed price, and the word 'estimate' to mean a guide as to the likely level of the final bill. For example, that is the way in which the words should be used according to the motor industry's Code of Practice: 'An estimate is a considered approximation of the likely cost involved, whereas a quotation constitutes a firm price for which the work will be done.' Thus, if a dispute arises as to the meaning of the word in relation to a car service or repair, the Code of Practice will provide a useful guideline, particularly if the

● Trading Standards Officers

They are employed by local authorities such as County Councils and work in the authorities' Trading Standards Departments or Consumer Protection Departments. They used to be known as Weights and Measures Inspectors before their duties were widely extended in the 1960s and 1970s by such legislation as the Trade Descriptions Act 1968.

The Officers deal with complaints from the public which suggest that a trader may have committed a *criminal* offence – for example, by selling bad food, giving short measures in pubs or petrol stations, or misdescribing facilities in package holiday brochures.

Some local authorities also give advice on consumer complaints about the poor quality of goods or services where no crime is suspected – for example, faulty electrical goods. In some areas there are Consumer Advice Centres which deal with similar matters and also give general shopping advice. They usually keep a stock of free pamphlets explaining Codes of Practice and consumer rights generally.

garage concerned is a member of the Motor Agents' Association (address on page 511).

In other contexts, the practical point is that the use of one word or another will not inevitably resolve the problem. Because of this, before you finalise a contract clarify with the supplier whether the proposed figure is meant to be your ultimate maximum liability or merely an informed forecast.

94 | Two months ago I ordered a new car. After some discussion, mainly about the amount of the discount, we agreed a purchase price of £7,800. The car is now ready for me to collect, but the garage tells me that it made a mistake with the recommended price when working out the discounted figure, as the salesman concerned was working from an outdated price list. I'm told I must pay another £400, as the later price list shows increases of slightly more than five per cent. Should I pay the extra?

No. There is clearly a fixed-price contract to sell the car to you for £7,800. It is unfortunate from the garage's point of view that it gave you an exceptionally low price because of its mistake, but unless you knew there was a mistake it has no legal effect. This type of subjective mistake by one of the parties, unknown to the other, is irrelevant. If the garage refuses to supply you with the car at the agreed price, you can buy the same model somewhere else in your area as cheaply as you can, and if the price is higher, claim the additional sum from the garage.

95 | *What happens if, when I buy a car, the manufacturer's recommended price rises between the time I place the order and the time I take delivery?*

In the absence of any special provision in the contract to cover this eventuality, the seller would still be bound by the original contract price. The law does not imply a term that if the price to the seller increases he may pass it on to the buyer.

This is a point to look out for when signing order forms for cars and other expensive items. If the order form provides that the seller may increase the price to take into account increases in the manufacturer's prices brought into effect prior to delivery, then that provision will be binding on the customer. If you do not like it, then strike out the clause – but not surreptitiously – in the hope that the garage will agree to your amendment.

96 | *I recently employed a decorator to paint the exterior of my house. When the job was finished, the bill was far higher than the figure on the quotation the decorator had given me before he started. When I queried the higher figure, he told me that the job had turned out to be more time-consuming than he had anticipated. How much should I pay?*

Assuming that the quotation was intended to be an offer by the decorator to do the entire job for the agreed figure and not merely a rough guide to the ultimate cost (see Q93), you should pay him only the amount in the original quotation. The decorator obviously made a bad deal by underestimating the amount of time and labour involved, and perhaps even the amount of materials to be used.

97 | *My drains became blocked over the week-end. I telephoned a company which specialises in clearing drains and it quoted me over the telephone a high call-out charge. To this was to be added travelling expenses at so much per mile. The company also stated that the call-out charge covered only 30 minutes' work on site and that an additional sum would be payable for each extra quarter of an hour (or part thereof) at a specified hourly rate. In the event it was a simple job that*

took only five minutes or so. I'm reluctant to pay the bill for the call-out charge, since on reflection it seems exorbitant. Can I legally object to it on the grounds that the charge is unreasonably high?

No. Although you appear to have made a bad bargain, there would be no power for any court to interfere. It is true that the Supply of Goods and Services Act 1982 implies a term in a contract for services that the customer will pay a reasonable charge, but this provision has no application where the charge has been agreed in advance.

The general point is that if you agree a fixed price for a job with a supplier who does no more or less than was agreed, he is entitled to recover the precise sum for the work done. It is irrelevant that the job is a larger or smaller one than the parties had expected.

98 | *One night a storm blew some slates off the roof and rainwater trickled in and damaged the ceiling of one of the bedrooms. I telephoned a building contractor next morning who came to repair the roof without delay. I've now received what I consider to be a very heavy bill for the work, bearing in mind the few hours he took to do the job. The contractor's attitude seems to be that he can charge what he likes, particularly as it was an urgent matter and considerable damage might have been caused if there had been any delay. Is he right?*

The contractor is wrong on this point. As no charge was specified when the agreement was made, the contractor may make only a reasonable charge in accordance with the Supply of Goods and Services Act 1982. The fact that it was an urgent matter for you and that the prompt repair may well have pre-

vented further damage does not justify the contractor increasing the charge except to take account of any disruption of his business caused by dropping everything else to help you out. A reasonable charge would be the same as the charge made by any roofing contractor in your area for an ordinary day-time job. Ask around other building contractors and send a cheque for what you consider to be the fair price.

99 | *I took my watch to be repaired at a local jeweller who gave me a rough estimate. When I went to collect it, I was charged more than double the estimate. As the assistant would not let me have the watch until I paid, I paid under protest. Is it too late to do anything about it?*

No, it's not too late, but you will probably have to take the jeweller to the county court to recover the excess charge. As there was no firm quotation, the jeweller is entitled to charge a reasonable figure in compliance with the Supply of Goods and Services Act 1982. Where an estimate is given, this gives a useful guide to what is a reasonable charge. If the trader tries to charge significantly more than the estimated figure, he will need to justify doing so. Has he had to do more work than was anticipated when he made his provisional assessment? Did more parts need replacing than had been expected? If not, the bill should bear a close resemblance to the original estimate.

A repairer is entitled to retain possession of goods until he has been paid for his services. But the jeweller should not have refused to hand over the goods when you were prepared to pay a fair charge. The only solution, short of giving in to his 'blackmail', would have been to sue him for the return of the watch, having tendered a reasonable sum to cover the repair. As it is, having paid too much you can sue him for the excess charge. You will have to decide whether this point of principle and the small amount involved justifies the trouble.

100 | *I had a boundary dispute with my neighbour, so I went to a solicitor who took up my case for me. After court proceedings the matter was resolved to my satisfaction, but when I received the solicitor's bill it was much higher than I had expected. How can I check whether it is justified?*

The basis of a professional man's charge should be the same as that for anyone else in business – the charge should be reasonable. If you think the fee was excessive (and you can always ask for an estimate before a solicitor acts on your behalf), contact a

senior partner of the firm – the names of the partners will be on the firm's notepaper – and ask for an explanation. If you are still not satisfied, you can ask the solicitors to have the bill checked, or 'taxed' as it is known, by the court. The solicitors must take the initiative. You need not pay until the court has approved the charges by this procedure.

Hire-purchase and credit

101 | *I appreciate that usually agreements do not need to be in writing, but is that true of hire-purchase agreements and other agreements involving credit?*

No. As long ago as 1938 legislation was introduced to protect people acquiring goods on hire-purchase. This was replaced by more extensive legislation in 1965, and this in its turn has been replaced by Regulations made under the Consumer Credit Act 1974.

The Regulations are very detailed, but a couple of points may be made. First, the agreement must be signed personally by the hirer, who is described in the Act as the 'debtor'. Second, the agreement must contain specified information such as the names and addresses of the parties, details of the goods, the cash price, the total purchase price to be paid by the debtor, the charge for the credit (broadly the amount of interest), and lastly the true or effective rate of interest (usually called the 'annual percentage rate' of charge, or APR; see Q104).

The Act also gives the debtor protection by specifying certain rights, such as a right of termination and in some cases a right of cancellation. These must be mentioned in the forms.

A failure to include all of these details does not stop you enforcing the agreement against the finance house or bank, although it may prevent them from enforcing it against you.

102 | *Does the Consumer Credit Act 1974 apply only to hire-purchase?*

No. The Act introduces a major extension of protection for consumers beyond the supply of goods on credit – hire-purchase, for example – to loan agreements and other credit transactions. From May 1985, when Regulations under the Act came into force, a bank or finance company which agrees to make you a personal loan will have to comply with the detailed documentation requirements of the Act. Quite frequently, such arrangements were made in a very informal way, so that the borrower was not always sure precisely what rates of interest were being charged. In future the debtor with a loan will generally (there are some exceptions) receive the same protection as someone taking goods on hire-purchase (see Q101).

It should be pointed out that some consumer credit agreements have been made exempt from the Act. The list of exempt agreements includes mortgages on land in favour of any building society or local authority, or in favour of specified mortgagees falling within certain categories, for example insurance companies or friendly societies. So in practice the vast majority of house purchase mortgages will not be regulated by the Act.

103 | Does the Consumer Credit Act 1974 apply whatever the circumstances of the loan or credit?

No. For most of the provisions to apply, as specified in Q101, the credit agreement must be 'regulated'. For this to happen two man requirements need to be satisfied. First, the amount of the credit (excluding interest) must not exceed £15,000. As an example, suppose that a consumer takes on hire-purchase a car with a cash price of £16,000. He trades in his old car for a part-exchange allowance of £4,000, or pays a deposit of £4,000. The balance of £12,000 plus interest of £3,000 is to be paid by instalments. The total price is £19,000 (cash price + interest). But the credit is only £12,000 – the total price of £19,000 less the interest of £3,000 and less also the deposit of £4,000. As the amount of credit does not exceed £15,000, the agreement is a regulated consumer credit agreement.

The second factor is that the consumer must be an 'individual'. Obviously this covers the individual private consumer. Perhaps more surprisingly, it also covers the sole proprietor of a business or a partnership. However, where the debtor is a company, the Act is irrelevant.

To sum up you ask yourself two questions: Does the amount of credit exceed £15,000, and is the borrower a company? If the answer to both these questions is no, the agreement is generally controlled by the 1974 Act (exceptionally some agreements – 'exempt' agreements – are taken outside the Act see Q102).

104 What do the letters 'APR' mean? I keep coming across them in advertisements for goods offered at hire-purchase rates.

They mean 'annual percentage rate'. The annual percentage rate of charge is the true, real or effective rate of interest to be paid by the consumer. The APR has to be displayed by creditors in their advertisements under the Advertisement and Quotation Regulations of the Consumer Credit Act 1974. This is to ensure that the consumer receives precise information about the cost of a prospective transaction.

Until the Regulations came into force it was common practice for creditors to specify flat rates of interest in their advertisements. So when a consumer saw goods advertised at a rate of interest of, say, 10 per cent per annum, he may not have realised that he would really be paying a true rate of interest of nearly 20 per cent per annum; for although his repayments would have been reducing the amount of capital outstanding, so that half way through the agreement almost half the original loan would have been repaid, he was still paying 10 per cent on the whole amount of the initial loan. The regulations introduced to the United Kingdom the North American concept of 'truth in lending'. The purpose of compelling creditors to indicate their true rates of interest is to enable prospective borrowers to see exactly the full amount of interest they will have to pay for credit.

The Regulations also entitle the consumer to a free written quotation of the creditor's typical terms.

105 | What procedure do I follow if I apply for credit or hire-purchase?

The Consumer Credit Act 1974 lays down rules that must be followed. The usual procedure is that the consumer signs a form applying for the credit facilities. This normally takes place at the bank or finance company or in the distributor's showroom, such as a garage, or at the shop. The applicant is given a copy of the form.

A period will then elapse during which the creditor checks on the creditworthiness of the applicant, for example by making enquiries at a credit reference agency (see Q120). If all seems well, the creditor will agree to make the advance, probably by sending the applicant a letter informing him of the fact. The agreement then takes effect; within seven days, the creditor must deliver to the applicant a second copy of the form. Where the application is signed by the consumer at home, the procedure is similar but the consumer has a right to cancel the agreement (see Q106).

106 | Last week a representative of a double-glazing firm called at my house at my request and gave me a detailed quotation for installing the double-glazing. As it was to be quite expensive, I

asked about credit terms. The salesman explained, I thought the terms reasonable and I signed there and then. On reflection I don't think that I can afford the repayments. Can I get out of the agreement now?

Normally a consumer cannot have a change of heart, when committed to an agreement, and get off scot free. Exceptionally, the Consumer Credit Act 1974 gives a debtor or hirer a right of cancellation where the agreement was signed at home and oral statements are made in the consumer's presence. This is a conscious attempt to combat the techniques of doorstep salesmen and to give the consumer the chance to cool off. The right of cancellation is certainly available in your case.

But you must act quickly. The 'cooling-off period' lasts for five clear days. There is a common misunderstanding about this period. It does not begin to run until the debtor has received the second copy of the agreement (see Q105). There are special rules about copies where the agreement is cancellable, and there are two main points to remember:

● Both copies of the agreement must mention the right of cancellation in addition to the other information.
● The second copy must be delivered by *post*. The count down to the fifth day of the cooling-off period does not begin until the debtor has *received* the second copy.

What you should do is check whether a copy has arrived through the post and, if so, search your

COULD I HAVE MY 'COOLING-OFF PERIOD' NOW, PLEASE?

memory to discover on which day it was delivered. You have five days, excluding the day of delivery, in which to cancel. For example, if the second copy was delivered to your home by the post office on Monday, you have until midnight on Saturday to cancel the agreement.

Cancellation is effected by giving written notice to the creditor or any intermediary who conducted the negotiation – in your case the salesman. It may be done by post, in which case it is effective as soon as the notice is posted. You should post a letter at once to the double-glazing company and note the time and date of posting This could be crucial. If the fifth day had already arrived and the last collection had been made by the post office, you would still not be too late provided you could prove that your letter was put into the post box before midnight. In those circumstances it would be useful to have a reliable witness with you at the time.

The effect of cancellation is to bring the agreement to an end and to absolve you from any future responsibility. If you have paid a deposit, that must be refunded to you.

107 | *An office equipment salesman has called at my office (I'm an accountant) and persuaded me to take a word processor on hire-purchase. Can I cancel the agreement?*

Assuming that the credit does not exceed £15,000 and that your business is not run as a limited company, the agreement is regulated (see Q103). Although the agreement was signed on your own trade premises, the fact that it is regulated means that you have the same rights regarding the cooling-off period and cancellation as an applicant who signed in his own home (see Q106). Cancellation is always available under these circumstances unless the agreement is signed at 'appropriate' trade premises, which means the premises of the creditor (or an intermediate negotiator such as a salesman).

108 | *Eighteen months ago I obtained a personal loan of £4,000 from a finance company to assist in buying a new car. It was repayable over a three-year period. I've now been left some money by a relative and wish to clear the debt. Can I insist on doing so?*

Yes. The Consumer Credit Act 1974 gives two related rights:

● a right for the debtor to pay off all amounts due at any time during the agreement, and
● a right to a rebate of the credit charges to take into

account the earlier receipt of the money by the creditor. The rebate is calculated in accordance with formulae set out in Regulations made under the Act.

You should write to the finance company asking them for a statement setting out the amount required to pay off the loan after taking into account the statutory rebate. The finance company is obliged to give you this statement free of charge.

109 | *I have a television set on hire-purchase at a total price of £270. I paid a deposit of £30. The balance is payable by instalments of £10 per month over two years. I paid two instalments on time but am behind with the third instalment, as my company is on short-time work. Can I stop paying the instalments if I return the set?*

You have a right to terminate the agreement at any time until the last instalment is due, so clearly you can stop payment and the company can recover the set. The Consumer Credit Act 1974 provides that on termination you must pay any instalment which is in arrears and also if that does not bring the total paid to date to one half of the total purchase price, an additional sum to raise your total payments to that level.

So far you have paid £50 (the deposit of £30 plus two payments of £10). You are £10 in arrears, which must be paid in any case. That makes £60 in all. As one half of the total price of £270 is £135, you will have to pay another £75. You terminate by giving written notice to the finance company. Having terminated, you must let the finance company take the set away. The end result will be that you will have had only a few months' use of the set for £135. It is not a cheap solution to your problem, but there may be no other way out.

110 | *I entered into a hire-purchase agreement nearly eight months ago for a dining-room suite. The cash price was £810, of which I paid £210 as a deposit. The balance, including the interest charges of £120, was payable over three years with monthly instalments of £20 each. I paid six instalments on time, but the seventh instalment is overdue. I've received a letter from the store telling me that unless I pay the overdue instalment within seven days it will terminate the hire-purchase agreement and repossess the furniture. What should I do?*

If you default on your instalment, the store will be able to take back the furniture provided it complies with the statutory procedures. Under a hire-purchase agreement the consumer does not become the owner of the goods until he has paid the final instalment and exercised his option to purchase the goods. Until then, whoever has provided the finance – the store in your case – retains the ownership in the goods.

However, there are special procedures in the Consumer Credit Act 1974 which give protection to the consumer in spite of his non-compliance with the agreement. First, the creditor should send the debtor a 'notice of default' informing him of his breach of contract, telling him what needs to be done to put the matter right and giving at least seven days in which to do so, and finally explaining the consequences of failing to do so. The store has apparently complied with this procedure by sending you the letter. Provided you pay £20 before the seven-day time-limit expires, all will be well – you will be treated as if you had not fallen behind with your payments.

111 | *But if I cannot pay the outstanding instalment, what will happen next? Will I finish up with nothing, although I have paid £330 towards the dining-room suite?*

Your continued failure to pay the overdue amount will result in the store's terminating the hire-purchase agreement. But it will be unable to 'snatch back' the suite for two reasons. First, you can refuse to permit the store's representatives to enter your house, and they are not allowed to force their way in. (There is no legal objection to their asking to collect their furniture. Then if you permit them to enter your premises, you will have no right to complain later.)

Second, the Consumer Credit Act 1974 contains special provisions to prevent 'snatch back' where goods are what are called in the Act 'protected'. The policy of the Act is to compel the creditor to go to court to recover the goods in cases where the consumer has paid a substantial part of the price. It is thought to be unfair that the consumer should throw away all the money paid to date merely because he may have got into temporary financial difficulty.

Goods become 'protected' where the debtor has paid one third or more of the total price. In your case the total price is £930, made up of the cash price of £810 and the interest of £120. So far you have paid the deposit of £210 and six instalments of £20 each, making £330. As you have paid at least a third of the total price, your dining-room suite is protected and the store must take you to court to recover it.

If you look at your copy of the hire-purchase agreement, you will see that it explains the provisions about protected goods and sets out the relevant figures. This is part of the information which must be given in the copies of the documents required under the Act.

112 | *If I fall into arrears with the hire-purchase instalments of the cost of my dining-room suite and the store demands repossession, wouldn't I be better off letting the store come and collect the suite if it can take me to court in any case?*

The store can bring proceedings in the county court to enforce its right to repossess the suite. But the court usually gives the debtor further time to pay, since the expectation of both parties at the commencement of the agreement was that the debtor would ultimately become the owner of the goods provided he paid the balance of the price. The way in which the court carries out this policy is to make a 'return order' which requires the debtor to return the goods to the creditor, but suspends the operation of the order on condition that the debtor pays the balance by instalments fixed by the court. For example, the court may reduce the amount of each instalment and in consequence extend the repayment period if this would assist a debtor with financial problems and enable the parties' intention to be carried out by the balance being paid in full in the end.

If you think that you can manage smaller instalments regularly, it would be sensible to make an offer to this effect to the store. If it refuses your offer and takes you to court, it is likely that the court will in any case make a suspended return order, as explained above.

Another possibility in your case, as the dining-room suite consists of a number of different pieces, is that the court will make a 'transfer order'. The effect of this is to split up the suite, so that the debtor must return some of it to the creditor and the ownership in the remainder is transferred to the debtor. There is an odd formula in the Consumer Credit Act 1974 which limits the value of the furniture which the court may transfer to the debtor. This ceiling is arrived at by adding up the sums paid so far and then deducting one third of the unpaid balance. In your case the calculation will be £330 − £600 ÷ 3 = £130. Depending on the prices of the table and chairs, the court would probably transfer the ownership to you of part of the suite valued at £130 and order you to return the rest to the store. That would be better than nothing, if you anticipate that even reduced instalments will be beyond your means.

113 | *I appreciate that the Consumer Credit Act 1974 gives protection to people who enter hire-purchase agreements and then fall into arrears with the payments. But what is to prevent the creditor ignoring the Act and repossessing the goods anyway?*

To flout the Act would be very expensive to the creditor, because the Act imposed a sanction whereby the creditor has to refund to the debtor all the money paid under the agreement – both the deposit and instalments – if he repossesses the goods. Because the wrongful repossession by the creditor kills the agreement once and for all, the end result is that the debtor has had the use of the goods until repossession free of charge. There is obviously considerable disadvantage to the creditor in not following the statutory provision strictly, as having hired out new goods the creditor then repossesses second-hand goods without a penny compensation for the depreciation and without earning anything from the debtor either.

The moral is that if you are falling behind with your payments and cannot make up the arrears, sit tight, refuse to allow the goods to be taken away and let the statutory procedure take its course.

114 | *My new car, which I bought on hire-purchase only last month, has developed a number of serious defects. I've complained to the garage where I bought it, but it's washed its hands of the affair and referred me to the HP company. I though the garage was responsible. What is the legal position?*

Technically, you are incorrect to say that you 'bought' the car from the garage. In law you have made no contract of sale with the garage.

Where a consumer obtains goods from a retailer or a distributor such as a garage, and the credit facilities are provided by a third party, such as a finance company, by way of hire-purchase, the legal sequence is as follows. The distributor sells the goods to the finance company and the finance company then lets them on hire-purchase to the consumer. The consumer's contractual relations are thus with the finance company, not with the retailer or distributor.

The agreement with the finance company falls outside the Sale of Goods Act 1979 because the consumer has not bought the goods. The two elements in a hire-purchase agreement are that

● the consumer has agreed to hire the goods and so

has the right to the use and possession of them during the period of the agreement (the 'hire element'), and
● the consumer is given the right to an option to purchase the goods when all the instalments have been paid and the period of the agreement has expired (the 'purchase element').

However, this does not mean that the consumer has no rights as regards defects in the goods. The Supply of Goods (Implied Terms) Act 1973 implies terms into a contract of hire-purchase virtually identical to the terms implied into a contract for the sale of goods. For example, there is an implied condition that the goods shall be of merchantable quality (see Q1). In your case the finance company has broken that implied condition, as the defects in the car indicate that it is not of the right quality or fit for its purpose. You are entitled to reject the car and obtain a refund of all your money from the HP company, and you will not have to pay any future instalments.

115 | *If my new car, bought on hire-purchase, were to develop serious faults, could I keep the car and claim the cost of repairs?*

Yes. You are not compelled to reject the car. If you prefer, you may have the defects repaired at the expense of the finance company, who will probably prefer that course of action. Doubtless the company will instruct the garage to carry out the repairs on that basis. Further, as you presumably received a guarantee with the car, the garage should be prepared to put right the defects on behalf of the manufacturer under the terms of the guarantee (see Q49).

However, there is a danger in allowing someone to undertake repairs. It is not inconceivable that the defects may be difficult or impossible to repair, or that another defect will reveal itself as soon as the first faults are cured. In the end you may get fed up with the car being repeatedly in the garage for repairs and may wish to reject it after all.

Although the hire-purchase legislation has no equivalent to the prejudicial 'acceptance' provision in the Sale of Goods Act 1979 (see Q34), there is a legal principle called 'affirmation' which applies even to hire-purchase cases. The effect is that the right to reject the goods will be lost if, knowing of the defects, you give the impression to the supplier that you are waiving your right to reject and will be content to receive compensation by way of having the vehicle repaired free of charge.

The way to leave your options open is to make it abundantly clear that you are prepared to allow repairs to take place only on the basis that if they are unsuccessful you will still be entitled to reject the car. The best way to do this is to send a letter to that effect to the finance company. This will provide useful evidence if court proceedings prove necessary.

116 | *As I was interested in acquiring a micro-computer for various home accounting purposes, I went to a computer centre and explained my requirements. The salesman recommended a particular model which he said would suit my purposes. As the cash price was in the region of £1,000, I asked for credit facilities. The salesman arranged a hire-purchase agreement with a finance company. Although the computer seems to work properly and hasn't broken down, it will not carry out the functions I need. The finance company takes the view that it is not responsible for the salesman's statements, as he was not authorised to make them on behalf of the finance company, and has no liability since the computer is not faulty. What is my position?*

The finance company's argument is unconvincing. It is true that generally retailers are in business on their own account, and this is true even of car dealers who are often described inaccurately as the manufacturer's 'main agents'. However, the Consumer Credit Act 1974 provides that an intermediary who conducts negotiations in relation to a consumer credit agreement should be deemed to be the agent of the creditor. Intermediaries of this sort are described in the Act as 'credit brokers'. Because of this, the salesman at the computer centre is treated as the agent of the finance company. As you made known to the salesman the particular purpose for which you required the computer, you were in a position equivalent to making known that purpose to the finance company. Because the goods have proved not to be fit for that purpose, the finance company has broken a condition implied by the Supply of Goods (Implied

Terms) Act 1973 (see QS 114 and 9). In addition, as the salesman expressly promised that the computer would be suitable, the finance company will be liable for breach of his express undertakings. You are therefore entitled to reject the computer and obtain a full refund, provided you are quick about it and do not affirm the contract (see Q115).

The discount shop will also be liable to you. Although there are no *implied* obligations imposed on the shop, the salesman's *express* undertaking would create a 'collateral contract' – a contract running side by side with the main agreement between yourself and the finance company – for breach of which you could recover damages. This liability will generally be useful only where the finance company has become insolvent and it is not usually of great importance.

117 | *I have replaced the windows in my house with new double-glazing units at a cost of £4,000. As I did not have sufficient cash, the representative of the double-glazing company produced a form and suggested that I apply for a personal loan to a finance company. In due course the loan was made. Now, the mechanism of the windows is faulty. I realise that I could make a claim against the double-glazing company, but the company has gone into liquidation. Is the finance company responsible?*

Yes, although you are correct in suggesting that the primary responsibility lies on the double-glazing company because of the obligations implied in a work and materials contract by the Supply of Goods and Services Act 1982 (see Q52). The finance company's responsibility stems from a very important provision in the Consumer Credit Act 1974. The effect of this provision (Section 75) is to make the creditor jointly liable with the supplier for breach of contract or misrepresentation. One crucial factor for this Section to apply is that there should be 'arrangements' between the supplier and the creditor, such as some business connection under which the supplier introduces business to the creditor.

The facts of your case give a clear indication of 'arrangements' between the double-glazing company and the finance company, as the supplier introduced you to the creditor and had application forms ready to hand. It follows that the finance company is responsible for the faults in the new windows and will have to bear the cost of rectifying them. Get in touch with the company and explain the situation, and stop making your repayments of the loan until the repairs have been made.

Your problem clearly illustrates the advantage of financing the purchase of goods or services through a personal loan from a lender connected with the supplier. You then have a double-barrelled shotgun to fire at the supplier or the creditor – they are both equally vulnerable.

118 | *If I had a bank loan to cover the cost of installing double-glazing, would I have the same protection as if I'd obtained a loan through a finance company?*

No. Unlike the position in Q117, in this case there would be no 'arrangements' or connection between the bank and the supplier. This link between the two is vital. It is irrelevant that the bank knows the purpose of the loan. Nor would it affect the issue if the double-glazing company had merely suggested that you go to your bank for a loan; for the suggestion would not arise from previous arrangements between your supplier and the bank.

In these circumstances you would have to continue to repay the loan to the bank. You would still have a claim against the double-glazing company. But this, of course, would be of little value if the company became insolvent and had insufficient assets to meet all its liabilities. Like all the other creditors of the company, you would have to hope for the best and see what dividend the liquidator would eventually pay to claimants like yourself.

119 | *I've bought a motor-cycle on hire-purchase. I was intending to sell it but I've been told by a friend that I can't do so until I've paid off all the instalments. Is that correct?*

Yes, your friend is right. The motor-cycle is still owned by the finance company, and it will not become your property until you have paid all the instalments and thus purchased it. Your only right at the moment is to use the motor-cycle.

No doubt your agreement is a regulated consumer credit agreement (see Q103), which means you have the right to settle the agreement early and to obtain a rebate on the interest charges to reflect the early repayment (see Q108). If you wish to do this you should write to the finance company to find out the settlement figure. Provided you pay that off, the motor-cycle will be yours to sell.

If you did not follow this procedure, you would have broken your contract with your buyer under the Sale of Goods Act 1979, and you would be liable to the finance company for wrongfully dealing with their property.

120 | Someone has told me that all finance houses have to be 'licensed'. What does this mean?

The Consumer Credit Act 1974 stipulates that certain types of business that deal with money must obtain a licence to carry out their business. The licensing system is operated by the Office of Fair Trading, and more than 100,000 licences have been issued.

Seven types of business need to be licensed under the Act. The two main ones are 'consumer credit businesses', such as banks, finance houses and moneylenders, and 'consumer hire businesses', such as television rental companies.

The five ancillary credit businesses that need licences are:

● credit-brokers, for example distributors, such as garages, who introduce prospective borrowers to prospective lenders
● debt-adjusters, who negotiate on behalf of debtors with creditors; these include solicitors and accountants
● debt counsellors, who advise debtors about their debts; these again include solicitors and accountants
● debt collectors
● credit reference agencies, who collect information on people to enable lenders and suppliers to check on creditworthiness.

● Office of Fair Trading

This is a government department staffed by civil servants (address on page 511). It was formed when the post of Director General of Fair Trading was created by the Fair Trading Act 1973.

The Office will *not* take up complaints from individual consumers about traders, but it does keep records of complaints received, including those passed on by Citizens Advice Bureaux and Trading Standards Departments. The overall picture thus obtained by the Office enables it to see whether particular traders or business sectors are indulging in unfair business practices and should be curbed.

Perhaps the Office's best-known function is the control of the licensing of finance houses and other businesses engaged in the credit and rental industries. This power comes from the Consumer Credit Act 1974.

The effect of such companies trading without a licence is twofold. First, it is a criminal offence; second, the civil consequence is that agreements made by the trader will generally be unenforceable against the borrower – an unlicensed moneylender will be unable to sue a borrower who fails to make repayments unless the Director General of Fair Trading makes an order allowing the agreement to be enforced against the borrower.

121 | I needed some money urgently, so I went to a moneylender who made me a loan at a very high rate of interest. As I was urgently in need of cash, I was in no position to argue. Do I have to pay the moneylender what I agreed?

Even if the moneylender is licensed (see Q120), you may be able to attack the agreement by claiming that it was an 'extortionate credit bargain'. The Consumer Credit Act 1974 gives the courts an extraordinarily wide power to reopen credit agreements so as to do justice between the parties. The power is available if the credit bargain is extortionate because the payments are grossly exorbitant or it otherwise grossly contravenes ordinary principles of fair dealing. The Act mentions a number of factors to be taken into account, including prevailing interest rates; the borrower's age, experience, business capacity, state of health and financial pressure upon him; and the degree of risk accepted by the creditor.

Sometimes high rates of interest can be justified because the debtor is a poor risk and can offer no security. It is worth your taking legal advice. For example, in one case the court decided that 48 per cent per annum was not exorbitant, as the borrower needed the money in a great hurry and the lender had no time to check the borrower's financial position and therefore accepted a high risk.

122 | My application for a personal loan from my bank has been refused. I suspect the reason is that the finance company registered me as a bad debtor after I withheld paying some hire-purchase payments until the car I'd bought was replaced. Can I find out from the bank if this is in fact the reason?

The right to privacy is an area covered by the Consumer Credit Act 1974. The Act entitles you to discover the name and address of any credit reference agency (see Q120) which the bank used in checking on your financial standing. You should make your request in writing within 28 days from the end of your negotiations with the bank about the loan; this will usually be the date when you were told that the loan would not be granted. The bank must then give you that information free of charge within seven days. You have the same right if a store or shop refuses you credit facilities.

123 | Can I obtain a copy of any file a credit reference agency may have on me?

The Consumer Credit Act 1974, and Regulations made under it, contains detailed provisions to enable a consumer to obtain a copy of his file and to correct erroneous entries in it. First write to the credit reference agency (see Q122) requesting a copy of your file and enclosing a fee of £1. The agency must send you a copy of the file within seven working days of the receipt of your request. At the same time the agency should give you a statement explaining your rights to correct inaccurate information.

If you consider an entry on your file to be incorrect and to your prejudice, you should ask the agency to remove or amend the entry. In 28 days the agency must notify you of the action taken, if any. If the entry has not been removed or satisfactorily amended, you have a further 28 days in which to send a notice of correction to be added to your file, but this must not exceed 200 words. Again within 28 days, the agency should notify you that it proposes to comply with your request by adding your notice to the file.

One exception to this right of correction occurs where the agency believes that it would be improper to publish the notice of correction because it is incorrect or 'unjustly defames any person, or is frivolous or scandalous, or is for any other reason unsuitable'. A dispute arising from the agency's refusal to amend the file is resolved by an application to the Office of Fair Trading, whom you would need to contact.

If the agency refuses to comply with these statutory obligations, it is committing a criminal offence.

124 | An incorrect entry on the file of a credit reference agency may have already prevented me from obtaining credit. The later correction of the entry will not affect past history. Will the agency do anything about this?

The Consumer Credit Act 1974 tackles this issue in the following way. Within 10 working days of notifying the consumer that an entry has been removed or that the consumer's notice of correction will be added to the file, the agency must contact everyone who was given the incorrect information during the six months before the consumer's original request for the amendment and must supply such persons with up-to-date information to disabuse them of their misapprehension.

125 | I consulted a credit-broker in the hope that he would be able to obtain a loan for me. He charged me a very substantial fee, which, although he was unsuccessful in getting me the loan, he refused to repay. Can he just keep the fee?

No. The solution to the problem is a simple one. The Consumer Credit Act 1974 allows a maximum fee of £3 to be charged where the credit-broker's efforts to obtain a loan are unsuccessful and do not result in a loan agreement within six months following the introduction of the consumer to a prospective lender. Any excess may be recovered from the broker, who may retain £3 only.

This provision is surprisingly little known. Report the broker to the Office of Fair Trading by letter in the hope that the broker's licence will be withdrawn if the malpractice continues.

The broker is entitled to keep the full fee when he successfully acquires a loan for a client.

Credit cards and cheques

126 | I bought a new washing machine and paid for it by credit card. I had the machine plumbed in immediately but it wouldn't work. Apparently the motor is defective and will need replacing. I asked the shop to collect the machine and give me my money back, but it refused. What can I do?

Your main line of attack is against the shop, which has broken the Sale of Goods Act 1979 by supplying goods which are not of merchantable quality (see Q1). You are entitled to reject the goods and obtain a full refund. As little time (see Q34) has passed since the goods were delivered to you, this remedy has not yet been lost.

It is quite likely that the washing machine is guaranteed by the manufacturer, and you may choose to take advantage of the guarantee (see Q49).

If neither remedy is open to you – because the shop continues to disregard your claim and the guarantee has just expired, say – in addition – and this is an important provision – you have a claim against the credit card company. Section 75 of the Consumer Credit Act 1974 makes the credit card company jointly liable with the supplier for breach of contract or misrepresentation provided there are 'arrangements' between the creditor and supplier (see Q117). It is almost certain that when a consumer uses a credit card to obtain goods or services, he can use it only where the supplier already has arrangements with the credit card company.

It is that link or connection between the credit card company and the shop in your case which makes the former liable, so you are entitled to a refund from the credit card company. The most straightforward way to obtain this is to deduct it from your next monthly account. This is quite proper because you owe them money on the account and they owe you the refund – you set off one against the other. And if you have not spent sufficient to offset it next month, you can do so at any time during the next six years, as debts do not become time-barred until then.

This advice is given on the assumption that your washing machine had a *cash* price of more than £100, as cheaper items are not covered by Section 75. Very expensive items are also excluded, with a cash price of more than £30,000.

127 | *If the door catch on my new washing machine had been faulty and then broken, flooding the kitchen with water, would the credit card company have had to pay for any damage?*

Strictly, yes. The liability of the credit card company is the same as the liability of the supplier. As the shop is responsible for any damage resulting from your buying a defective machine, so is the credit card company. If the shop won't help, don't bother to sue but get in touch with the credit card company.

However, there is some disagreement between the credit card companies and legal commentators about the precise effect of the Consumer Credit Act 1974 on credit cards first issued before 1 July 1977, when Section 75 of the Act came into force. Some credit card companies to which the Act applies (see Q128) take the view that even though those cards have since been renewed, the Section does not apply to them. The Office of Fair Trading takes the view that once the card has been renewed, the Section applies fully to each purchase subsequently made with it. Anyway, the credit card companies have reached a compromise whereby they accept liability on old cards up to the amount of the credit.

The effect in relation to your problem is that if you were using a card originally issued before 1 July 1977, the credit card company will be prepared to refund the amount of the credit – the cost of the washing machine – but may be unwilling to reimburse you for the damage resulting from the faulty machine.

128 | *Are all card companies liable if there's a breach of contract or misrepresentation between supplier and consumer?*

No. The unexpected effect of an Order passed pursuant to the Consumer Credit Act 1974 has been to exclude some cards from the Act's provisions but not others. Section 75 (see Q126) applies to *credit* cards where the user is entitled to repay the credit by instalments, as in the case of Access, Barclaycard and Trustcard. But if the cardholder has to settle the account for a period all at once by a single payment, Section 75 does not apply; this exempts from the Act, for example, American Express and Diners Club (usually called 'charge' cards).

129 | *Do cheque cards have the same effect on a bank's liability as credit cards do on the credit card companies'?*

No. The customer's use of a cheque card does not depend on there being 'arrangements' (see Q117) between the bank and the particular supplier. Cheque cards may be offered anywhere. The benefit of a cheque card to a trader is that the bank guarantees that cheques backed by the card will be paid up to an agreed limit, currently £50. So the trader may take such a cheque knowing that it will be met, even if the customer's account is overdrawn or the customer tries to stop payment.

The point is made clear by the Consumer Credit Act 1974. This states that arrangements are to be disregarded where the creditor undertakes to pay suppliers *generally*. In the case of credit cards the arrangements are made specifically with each supplier. Anyway, in most cases a cheque card will not be regulated by the Act at all because the element of 'credit' is missing.

130 | *If a shop refused to accept liability for selling me defective goods I'd bought with a credit card and I withheld my repayments to the credit card company, would the company simply refuse to renew my card when it expires?*

It could well do. Whenever a credit card is issued or renewed, the bank or issuing company makes an agreement with the customer to provide the credit facilities for the stated period, usually two years. There is no obligation on the bank to renew the agreement when it expires. (It is similar to insurance on property, such as cars, where at the end of each year the insurer states the terms on which he is prepared to renew the policy, if at all.) So you do indeed run the risk of prejudicing your future relationship by claiming your legal rights. That is true of making a claim against anybody in business; he or she may take umbrage and refuse to deal with you again and in law there's nothing you can do about it.

131 | I lost my wallet with my credit card in it. Will I have to pay if the finder or thief forges my signature in shops and goes on a spending spree?

You should notify the credit card company of the loss as soon as possible. The credit card agreement should contain the name, address and telephone number of the office you should contact. You will not be liable for any loss arising after that. But you must confirm any oral notice by giving written notice within the following seven days. If you are quick enough to contact the credit card company before the thief has had time to go shopping, you will have no liability at all. In any case, under the terms of the Consumer Credit Act 1974 you will be liable for no more than £50 even if you fail to notify the credit card company or the thief is quick off the mark.

132 | I wanted to pay for some groceries by cheque but the shop assistant refused to accept it even though I showed him my cheque card. Don't I have a right to pay by cheque if it's covered by a cheque card?

In common law, the obligation of a debtor such as a customer is to pay the debt in 'legal tender', which means cash. Legal tender has a specific meaning. Bank of England notes can be used for payment in any combination. There are limits to the amounts that coins can be used in payment; silver (cupronickel) coins exceeding 10p in value can be used for any amount up to £10; silver coins of 10p value or

less, amounts up to £5; copper or bronze, amounts up to 20p only. There is also a quaint rule, fortunately not applied in practice, that the debtor must offer the exact amount of legal tender; if he tenders a higher amount, he must not ask for change but should be content to leave the surplus with the creditor.

This means you cannot insist on anyone accepting a cheque instead of cash, even when it is backed by a cheque card. Nor, of course, can you insist on a credit card being accepted.

133 | What is the significance of a cheque card?

When a cheque is backed by a cheque card – or cheque guarantee card, to give it its more complete name – the bank guarantees payment up to a specified limit, currently £50, and a trader will be more ready to accept a cheque in payment with this guarantee than without it.

From the customer's point of view there is a major disadvantage in using a cheque card – he will be unable to stop the cheque. Normally a customer can countermand payment on a cheque – stop the payment – by instructing his bank not to pay the payee. (Of course, the customer then runs the risk of being sued by the payee for the amount of the cheque.) However, when a bank customer is issued with a cheque card he promises as part of the agreement not to countermand payment. The result is that although he may try to stop the cheque, the bank can ignore his instructions in this respect and pay just the same.

134 | I paid my telephone account by cheque. Although I had sufficient money in my account, the cheque bounced and was returned to British Telecom marked 'refer to drawer'. I'm very angry because it makes me look like a confidence trickster. Is the bank liable in any way?

The bank has clearly broken its contract with you. When you drew the cheque in favour of British Telecom, you were authorising and instructing the bank to pay the specified amount of money to it. As your account was in funds and you did not stop the cheque, the bank should have carried out your instructions.

The difficulty in your case will be in proving that the bank's breach of contract caused you loss. The decisions in the court show that damage to reputation can be assumed in the case of a businessman, but the corollary seems to be that a private customer could recover compensation only if actual loss could be proved. For example, if British Telecom had disconnected your telephone for non-payment of the

... ON THE OTHER HAND I COULD WRITE YOU OUT A CHEQUE.

account and you'd had to pay a reconnection charge, that charge would be recoverable from the bank as damages.

One would hope that at the very least the bank would write to British Telecom explaining the circumstances and admitting that the non-payment was the bank's fault. Banks have been known in these circumstances, while not admitting liability, to make some ex-gratia gift to the aggrieved customer – the manager taking him or her out for lunch, perhaps.

135 | *If I lost my cheque book, would I be liable if someone were to forge my signature?*

Not for a penny. When the customer's signature is forged, the cheque is invalid and the bank has to bear the total loss. You should, though, inform the bank as soon as the loss comes to your attention.

Even if you were carrying your cheque card with your cheque book and lost them both together, the bank could not debit your account for any amount written on a cheque with a forged signature. While the bank could argue that you were careless in not carrying them separately, the courts have not yet decided that such conduct amounts to carelessness and makes the customer liable.

The position would be different if you had been careless in filling in a cheque. A number of cases in the courts have shown that a customer owes a duty of care to his bank in drawing cheques on his account. You should not facilitate fraud by leaving blank spaces, and you should not leave room for the amount on the cheque to be altered and should complete the name of the payee.

Holidays and leisure

136 | *Early in the year I booked a week's summer holiday at a seaside hotel for my family and myself. There were no special booking conditions. After a very wet spring we decided to go abroad for some sunshine and I cancelled the hotel booking. The hotel proprietor is now threatening to sue me for the entire week's charges at the agreed inclusive rate. Can he do so?*

The hotel proprietor may be entitled to some compensation. It appears that you had made a firm booking, so that there was a binding agreement on both sides. It follows that your cancellation of the booking was in breach of the agreement.

Even so, it does not necessarily follow that you

must pay the proprietor any compensation. When you cancelled, he was under an obligation to try to relet the rooms and thereby to reduce his own loss. In law this is called the duty of 'mitigation'. If he did manage to let the rooms, then he will have been no worse off as a result of your cancellation and he would recover only nominal damages if he were foolish enough to take you to court. The result would be the same if he could have relet the rooms but did not bother to do so, but it will be for you to prove that he could have relet them, for example by showing that during the particular week there was a shortage of holiday accommodation in the area.

It is possible that, as in many seaside resorts, there was spare capacity in the area at the time and that the hotel had vacancies throughout the summer period. Even in those circumstances you are not responsible for the entire hotel charge because some reduction should be allowed for the savings made because of your absence – food and laundry costs, for example. With this in mind, an offer of a proportion of the hotel charges is likely to lead to the settlement of the dispute. It has been estimated that two-thirds constitutes the profit element; that should give you a guideline for your negotiation.

137 | *Would a hotel be entitled to charge me for the whole period booked (after I'd paid a deposit) if I had to cancel a family holiday as a result of illness in the family?*

No. There is a legal doctrine called 'frustration', which applies where the failure of one of the parties to carry out his obligations is caused by events beyond his control. The contract is terminated without any liability on either party in cases where it would be impossible or commercially pointless for the contract to continue in the changed circumstances. Illness is such an event. Although the family could go on holiday without the ill member of it, this would defeat the purpose of the holiday which was intended for the entire family.

Even though the contract may come to an end, so that you will not be liable to pay damages for any loss suffered by the hotel, the hotel is entitled to retain advance payments such as a deposit to cover any expenses incurred in carrying out the contract. The problem from the hotel's point of view is that it will be difficult to show that particular expenses – such as items of food – had already been bought in advance of your cancellation especially for you and your family. But if the deposit is not large you may think it reasonable for the hotel to keep it anyway.

138 | *If I pay a deposit when I book hotel accommodation, will the hotel keep the deposit should I have to cancel the booking?*

Yes. The hotelier would be entitled to keep the deposit, as it was paid as a form of security to ensure that cancellations were not made lightly and free of charge. If the loss from your cancellation exceeded the amount of the deposit, which is quite likely, the hotel proprietor could claim the additional loss from you.

Even if the hotel relets the rooms at the same rate, so that no loss is occasioned by your breaking the contract, the hotel can still keep the deposit because it was offered as a mark of good faith that the rooms would be yours for the period booked and that you would take them as agreed.

139 | *I telephoned to reserve a room at a hotel for the night, but when I arrived the hotel was full. The receptionist phoned around and was able to find accommodation for me in a much more luxurious and expensive hotel on the other side of town. I had to take a taxi to get there. Can I claim anything from the hotel that took my booking?*

Yes. The hotel broke the agreement with you by not keeping a room available. It was easily foreseeable that you would need accommodation elsewhere as a result. As no room was available in other hotels of the same price range and quality, in the circumstances you adopted the only course open to you by staying in a better hotel at a higher cost. This extra expense resulted directly from the original hotel's breach of contract and should be paid by them. The same is true of the taxi fare that would not have been incurred otherwise.

Write to the manager explaining the position. If that gets you nowhere and the hotel is part of a chain or group, write to the group's managing director.

140 | *When I wrote to reserve hotel accommodation for my family for our annual seaside holiday in the West Country, I particularly mentioned that I wanted rooms with a sea view. The hotel replied and confirmed the booking. When we arrived we found that we had been allocated rooms at the back overlooking the town. I protested, but was told that no other rooms were available and the receptionist emphasised that the hotel did not guarantee rooms with a sea view. Our holiday was considerably spoiled, as the weather was poor and much of our*

SEAVIEW HOTEL

time was spent looking out of the window at wet rooftops. What is our legal position?

It seems clear that you booked a room with a sea view rather than just a room. That term was clearly introduced by you when the agreement was made by the exchange of letters. The receptionist's remarks are irrelevant. The hotel broke its agreement with you and is liable to compensate you.

Fortunately there have been a series of cases in the last ten years or so awarding damages for upset, disappointment, frustration and injured feelings, and some of these have reached the Court of Appeal which has decided in the claimant's favour (see Q143).

You should write and demand compensation for the loss of enjoyment for both yourself and your wife and children (or get a solicitor to do so on your behalf). The hotel could have contemplated that if the weather were bad you would be using your room for much of the holiday. It is not possible to forecast the precise amount of compensation a court might award; something in the region of £200 might be a starting-point for negotiation.

141 | *I bought and paid for a package holiday through my local travel agent well ahead of my departure date. Then the tour operator was forced into liquidation because it was insolvent. Can I recover my fare from the tour operator or travel agent?*

Your chances of your getting anything from the tour operator are slim in the extreme. Probably all its assets will be dissipated in paying off its preferential creditors. Any surplus will be divided between the other creditors, which will include not only disappointed passengers like yourself, but the tour operator's unpaid trade suppliers like airlines. The best you can hope for is a small percentage of your fare back.

You can expect nothing at all from the travel agent. As it was acting on behalf of the tour operator, the resulting contract was made between yourself and the tour operator. Your only hope would be to bring a claim for fraud or negligence if you could prove that the travel agent knew or should have known that the tour operator was about to go bust.

Don't forget, though, the various trade bonding and insurance schemes. There is the Civil Aviation Authority's scheme to cover loss caused by the failure of a licensed package tour operator. To cover 'non-licensable' holidays (e.g. scheduled flights, rail, sea, coach) you may be able to look to the insurance cover provided by ABTA or the Tour Operators' Study Group.

142 | *Shortly before we were due to set off on a package holiday we received a letter from the tour operator stating that a surcharge would have to be paid. No explanation was given. We understood that the holiday price was fixed and had budgeted on that basis. Is there anything we can do?*

The strict legal position is that a surcharge should not be made unless the booking conditions allow for it. In the absence of such a clause the holiday price has been fixed and cannot be altered unilaterally by the tour operator. The operator's profit may be eroded if exchange rates deteriorate or the price of aviation fuel increases, but that is no excuse.

If the booking conditions contain a surcharge clause, you need to examine the Codes of Conduct of the Association of British Travel Agents (ABTA) (address on page 509), provided the tour operator is an ABTA member. The Office of Fair Trading leaflet *Package Holidays* explains the Codes. These Codes provide that 'Booking conditions (and/or brochures) shall prominently indicate the circumstances in which and the conditions on which surcharges may be made to clients'. Check the booking conditions to find out the circumstances in which it was agreed that surcharges could be made, then write to the tour operator asking for an explanation of the reason for the surcharge.

If the reason for the surcharge was a change in the rate of exchange, then the surcharge should not have been imposed later than 30 days before the date of departure. This rule applies to 'ground arrangements', which presumably means hotel costs. It is permissible to impose a surcharge closer to the date of departure as a result of increases in costs beyond the tour operator's control: the Codes particularly mention the cost of coach or aviation fuel.

If in your case the surcharge relates to a fluctuation in the rate of exchange, then it was too late to levy it and the tour operator has offended the Codes. Ask ABTA to conciliate.

You seem to have been unlucky. Many tour operators now guarantee their prices as fixed, or allow consumers to cancel their holidays if surcharges increase the price by more than a stated percentage. Some even give a refund if the rate of exchange improves. Before you book a holiday you should read the booking conditions carefully and then shop around to obtain the best deal.

143 | *I booked a holiday with a tour operator for myself and a friend. The brochure described the hotel as a 'superb five-star hotel, with excellent cuisine in first-class dining-room. Two heated swimming-pools. Each bedroom with terrace overlooking the sea. Nightly discotheque.' When we arrived we were put in a room at the rear, as all the rooms with a sea view had been allocated. The swimming-pools were empty; there was no discotheque; and the service was terrible as the staff were on strike. The operator denied liability because all these matters were beyond its control. Should I make a claim against the tour operator?*

The description of the hotel facilities in the travel brochure formed part of the contract between you and the tour operator. Although the failure to provide the facilities was the fault of the hotel, the tour operator is responsible for this; liability does not disappear by subcontracting the services.

You can seek compensation for upset, disappointment and loss of enjoyment. And although your friend was not a party to the contract, you will be able to recover compensation for him or her too (see Q144).

Don't be fobbed off with a few pounds. There are many cases where hundreds of pounds have been recovered, and one or two in which the damages exceeded £1,000 where larger groups than yours, usually family groups, had a disastrous time.

Of course, as always remember the ABTA Codes of Conduct (see Q142), assuming the tour operator is a member of the Association.

of the distress and disappointment caused you and your wife you will be entitled to substantial damages. You should get a solicitor to take up your case.

In some similar cases more than £1,000 has been awarded. For example, in a 1975 Court of Appeal case (*Jackson* v. *Horizon Holidays*) the claimant booked a four-week holiday for his family in Ceylon. Like you, he had particular requirements, although his taste for food was the opposite to yours. He asked for international cuisine, interconnecting rooms for the family, and separate bathrooms. In the event he was provided with bathrooms with showers but no baths (and fungus growing up the walls), and very distasteful food cooked in coconut oil. He was moved to another hotel but even that did not suit his requirements. Out of a holiday price of £1,200 he obtained £1,100 by way of damages. The case is also notable in that the Court awarded him damages to cover not only his own loss of enjoyment and disappointment but his family's too.

144 | *When I booked a holiday in Greece, I explained that I wanted a high-quality, traditional hotel serving Greek food and not a modern block with 'international' cuisine which could be anywhere in the world. I had the foresight to send the tour operator a covering letter with my booking form making my requirements clear. When my wife and I reached the hotel we discovered that, though traditional, it was little more than a scruffy flea-pit serving nauseating food. After one night we complained to the courier, who moved us to a modern block with international food served with bland sauces like wallpaper paste! The tour operator has refused to give us any compensation on the grounds that the price for a holiday in the modern hotel was higher, but we didn't have to pay the difference. Is there anything we can do?*

Recording your requirements in writing will be invaluable evidence if the dispute comes to court. The effect of stating your requirements when booking – and even oral statements are sufficient for this purpose – was to introduce express terms into the contract. If the tour operator could not meet your requirements, it should not have taken your booking and the operator must compensate you for not providing accommodation that met your needs. In view

145 | *I appreciate that if a tour operator does not provide a holiday that matches up to the description in the travel brochures, the customer may bring a legal action for breach of contract. But this may be expensive. Is there no other way of obtaining compensation?*

If the tour operator is a member of ABTA, then ask the Association for a copy of the Codes of Conduct (see Q142) and check to see whether the rules suggest that compensation is payable. If so, ask the Association to conciliate.

If it is the expense or complexity of civil proceedings which puts you off, you may wish to use the arbitration scheme operated by the Association, which is quite inexpensive (unless you are unwise enough to insist on an oral hearing as compared with a 'documents only' arbitration).

Another possibility is that your local authority's Trading Standards Department can be persuaded to bring a prosecution under the Trade Descriptions Act 1968 on the basis that the tour operator has knowingly or recklessly made a false statement about the provision of 'services, accommodation or facilities'.

For example, a prosecution was successful (in *R.* v. *Clarksons Holidays*) where the brochure stated that hotels were chosen for their cleanliness, good food and efficiency of service. It showed a picture of a modern hotel with a swimming-pool which turned out to be an artist's impression, as the hotel was still under construction at the time. It was still not finished when the holidaymakers arrived and the prosecution proved that it was never intended to be ready by then. The conviction was obtained because it could be proved that, when the brochure was published, the tour operator knew or should have known that the accommodation would not be available for the dates for which it was taking bookings.

But an offence will not be committed simply because facilities are not available when the holidaymakers reach the hotel, provided that the tour operator genuinely and for good reason believed at the time the brochure was published that it was accurate and that the accommodation would be available on the due date.

Why not leave these complications to the Trading Standards Officers? If they decide to prosecute and a conviction is obtained, you may be able to obtain compensation at the same hearing under the Powers of Criminal Courts Act 1973. Compensation could be awarded for any injury, loss or damage. In one case in 1974 Thompson Holidays had to pay £50 compensation for making a false statement in their brochure that a hotel had a night-club and swimming and paddling-pools. This method is cheap and painless, as all the work and expense are borne by your local authority. But you cannot be sure that it will wish to bring a prosecution rather than just give a warning.

---

146 | *When I arrived at my holiday hotel in Spain, the courier explained that it had been overbooked and that my friend and I had been switched to another hotel. Have we a right to be compensated because of the change in hotel?*

Not if the other hotel was as good or better than the one for which you were booked. Although technically the tour operator has broken the agreement with you, you would have suffered no loss as a result.

If the second hotel was inferior, then you will be entitled to compensation. This will cover two main elements. First, if the second hotel was less expensive, you should receive a repayment of part of the price to reflect this. Second, compensation will be payable for disappointment and loss of enjoyment (see Q144).

This problem is specifically dealt with in ABTA's Codes of Conduct (see Q142), which provide that if a hotel is overbooked and the tour operator does not know this before the holidaymaker departs, the holidaymaker should be offered reasonable compensation for 'disturbance' when the location or facilities of the alternative accommodation are inferior.

147 | *What would happen if a tour operator knows a hotel is oversubscribed before the people booked into it actually depart?*

The ABTA Codes of Conduct (see Q142) deal with this point too. The tour operator should immediately inform its customers and offer them the choice of an alternative holiday of at least comparable standard, or a full and prompt refund of all money paid if no such alternative is available.

Irrespective of the Codes, the customer is entitled to a full refund if, when he discovers that the tour operator cannot provide the promised holiday, he decides he is not prepared to accept an alternative.

148 | *I booked a spring holiday on one of the Greek islands. Two months before the departure date the tour operator informed me that the tour had been cancelled because of insufficient bookings. Has the tour operator a right to do that?*

No. Once a tour operator has entered into an agreement with you to provide you with a particular holiday on a particular date, it is bound by those arrangements. By informing you that it would not honour those arrangements, it was breaking the agreement even though the departure date had not arrived. You are entitled to a full refund of all money paid so far. Further, if it costs you more to book a similar holiday with another tour operator, the additional cost should be borne by the first one.

The ABTA Codes of Conduct (see Q142) provide that in a case like yours, where the cancellation takes place before the balance of the holiday price becomes due, the customer should be offered an alternative holiday of at least comparable standard or a prompt and full refund of all money paid. It may well be that the small print of your booking conditions contained a clause on similar terms to this provision in the Codes.

149 | *What if the tour operator cancels a holiday because it has insufficient bookings and does so only a week before we were due to depart?*

The strict legal position is the same as in Q149. However, the ABTA Codes of Conduct (see Q142) state categorically that 'a tour operator shall not cancel a tour . . . after the date when payment of the balance of the price becomes due'. But it does not say what happens if the tour operator wrongly does so. The answer for you would be to contact ABTA immediately in the hope that the Association can persuade the tour operator to comply with the Codes. (There are special provisions about cancellation where it is caused by 'hostilities, political unrest or other circumstances amounting to *force majeure*'; see Q154.)

150 | *I've booked a holiday abroad for the whole family and paid the usual deposit of 10 per cent. I now want to cancel the holiday, as unexpected repairs to my house have left me short of money. Do I have to pay the high cancellation charges mentioned in the booking conditions?*

The first point to realise is that you have no legal right to cancel in the circumstances apart from any such right given in the booking conditions. The basic position is that on cancellation you will be liable to the tour operator for its resulting losses. If the operator were able to resell your holiday, then its loss would be nil. If, on the other hand, the tour was not full in the end, you will be liable for the whole price of the holiday, less any expenses saved by the absence of your family on the plane and in the hotel; these might be comparatively small (see Q136).

If any cancellation fees are specified in the booking conditions, you might find it difficult to demonstrate that they are unreasonable. The question is whether the fees reflect a genuine attempt by the tour operator to estimate the likely loss resulting from cancellation by customers at various stages. If they are a genuine pre-estimate of loss, then you will have to pay them irrespective of whether or not your seats can be filled.

The only possible argument you would have against the cancellation fees is that they are a penalty in the sense that they are an unreasonably high figure put in to try to persuade customers to carry on with the agreement. If the clause is a penalty, it has no legal validity. But the consequence is that the tour operator could claim from you damages on the basis mentioned in the first paragraph, and you might find it cheaper to claim the benefit of the cancellation clause.

To sum up, you cannot cancel without expense to yourself. You will certainly lose the deposit. You will then either have to pay cancellation fees or, if you wish to allege that these are really a penalty, run the risk of paying damages. If substantial sums are involved, this is a case where it will pay you to seek expert advice.

151 | *I had a confirmed reservation on a scheduled flight. I checked in fairly late to be told that the flight was full and that I had been transferred to a later flight. I spent three uncomfortable hours in the packed departure lounge and reached my holiday destination late at night. Should I receive compensation?*

Airlines' practice of 'overbooking' has been very common. In a way it is understandable, as not infrequently passengers fail to take up reservations and the airlines are reluctant to fly with empty seats. Extra passengers are booked on the flight on the assumption that some will drop out. Occasionally the drop-out rate is low and passengers have to be transferred to another flight.

While this system makes economic sense for the airlines, it is not much solace to unlucky passengers like yourself. As you had a ticket for a particular flight, the airline should have carried you as agreed. Although you suffered no financial loss, except perhaps buying extra refreshments at the airport, you were clearly upset and frustrated and had your holiday somewhat spoilt. Damages may now be awarded in respect of these factors (see Q140), so you should receive compensation unless the booking conditions reasonably limit the airline's liability (see Q155).

It may help your case to bring the Trading Standards Department of your local authority into the picture. A criminal offence may have been committed under the Trade Descriptions Act 1968. The Act makes it an offence to make false statements with regard to the provision of 'any services, accommodation or facilities'. But the provider of the services will be convicted only if it can be shown that he knew the statement was false or made it recklessly. It is clear from an airline case decided by the House of Lords in 1975 that airlines commit an offence by indulging in the practice of overbooking, if when they confirm a reservation they fully intend to offload passengers should too many turn up for the flight. A trading standards officer may be prepared to intervene on your behalf.

If the local authority thinks it appropriate to prosecute and a conviction is obtained, you may ask for compensation under the Powers of Criminal Courts Act 1973 (see Q145).

152 | *I remember that when one airline collapsed considerable publicity was given to the advantages obtained by prospective passengers who had paid by credit card. What was the reason for this?*

This is another situation in which the Consumer Credit Act 1974 (Section 75) comes into play (see Qs 126 to 128). It will depend on what card was used. If, for example, a passenger had used Access or Barclaycard, the credit card company would be responsible for the airline's breach of contract in not transporting the passenger as agreed. As the passenger was entitled to a full refund from the airline, the passenger had the same rights against the credit card company. It can then be left to the credit card company to do its best to get its money back from the airline; the passengers are not out of pocket.

153 | *I live in Wales. I arranged a package holiday through a travel agent for my family (there are five of us). As the flight was from Heathrow in the morning, we travelled to London on the previous day and stayed overnight in a hotel. When we arrived at the airport the following morning, all flights to our destination had been disrupted because of a strike by air traffic controllers on the Continent. We milled around at the airport all day and, when it became clear that the strike would not be resolved immediately, free hotel accommodation was arranged for us. The following day the strike was over and we were able to start our holiday. We think that someone should pay us compensation for the inconvenience and the time lost. Who should we approach?*

Your claim should be made against the tour operator who put together the package holiday because your contract was made with the operator. As the company undertook to have you flown out on a particular date and failed to keep to that undertaking, it has broken the agreement. It is immaterial that the delayed flight was beyond its control. The operator is under a strict liability to do what it promised to do. It should pay you compensation for both the loss of the day's holiday and the upset and disappointment caused to you and your family by the disruption at

CARE FREE HOLIDAYS INC.

the airport. (However, it may have included in its booking conditions a clause limiting its liability to you; see Q155.)

There is no point in making a claim against either the travel agent or the airline. The travel agent merely made arrangements with you on behalf of the tour operator and is not responsible for the tour operator's breach of contract, as the travel agent was not a party to the agreement. The same is true of the airline, which was not in a contractual relationship with you. It is the tour operator's subcontractor for whom the tour operator bears responsibility to you.

If your claim against the tour operator is not resolved quickly and it is a member of ABTA, contact ABTA immediately (see Q142). The Codes of Conduct provide for a conciliation service and an inexpensive arbitration scheme.

Finally, check your holiday insurance policy carefully. It may well cover delayed departure, in which case you may not wish to pursue your claim against the tour operator.

154 | *My package holiday was delayed by an airline strike that looked as if it would be a long, drawn-out affair. From whom should I seek compensation, the airline or the tour operator?*

If on the departure date it seemed likely that there would be a very serious disruption of services, which might last for days or even weeks, your contract with the tour operator would terminate there and then. This is an example of the doctrine of 'frustration' under which agreements are terminated when it becomes impossible to perform them because of circumstances beyond the control of the parties.

The basic result is twofold. No claim would lie against the tour operator for breaking the agreement, but the consumer would be entitled to a refund. The latter is not as clear-cut as it sounds, though, as the tour operator will be entitled to retain out of advance payments – and the total holiday price would have been paid at that stage – sufficient to cover its expenses in making the holiday arrangements. In other words, any refund you get would depend on whether the tour operator could recover anything from the airline and the foreign hotel for the aircraft seats and hotel rooms reserved in advance.

These circumstances seem to be covered by the ABTA Codes of Conduct (see Q142), which include a paragraph relating to 'Alterations to tours, holidays or other travel arrangements'. This provides that 'as soon as material alterations become necessary', the tour operator shall offer the client a full refund of all money paid. That is the good part. But it goes on to state that the refund should be 'less reasonable expenses where the alteration is due to hostilities, political unrest or other circumstances amounting to *force majeure*'. As a strike would amount to *force majeure*, the tour operator could deduct reasonable expenses.

Here again it will be useful to contact ABTA to conciliate in the dispute if the tour operator is a member. And it will be crucial to check your insurance policy in view of the large sums involved in these circumstances. If the insurance company reimburses any loss to you, you can leave it to the insurance company to fight out any claim it may make against the tour operator.

155 | *A strike affecting our return flight from holiday delayed our departure from late at night to early the following morning, and as a result I missed a day's work. When I complained to the tour operator, I received a letter pointing out a clause in the booking conditions that excluded the company's responsibility for matters beyond its control. Must I accept this?*

A clause of this sort is controlled by the Unfair Contract Terms Act 1977, and clauses attempting to exclude or limit liability for breach of contract are subjected to a 'reasonableness' test. The tour operator will have to prove that in the circumstances the clause was a fair and reasonable one to be included in the contract.

Probably such a clause would be held to be unreasonable by a court if it attempted to exclude liability for *any* breach of contract; the clause would not then protect the tour operator and any claim you make for the loss of a day's pay is likely to succeed. It's a different matter, though, when the clause merely protects the tour operator for a breach of contract arising out of circumstances beyond its control, for example, a strike. Although such a clause must still survive the reasonableness test, it is arguable that it is not unfair in view of its limited scope and any claim you may make will probably not be accepted.

156 | *Newspapers have reported a number of bad accidents in which coaches have overturned and the passengers have been seriously injured. Are they entitled to compensation?*

The coach company via its driver is under an obligation to carry its passengers carefully and to employ drivers who are reasonably skilful. Any passengers injured in an accident in the United Kingdom will be entitled to recover damages for their personal injuries provided they can show that the coach drivers have been negligent. It will depend on the circumstances of the crashes.

For example, coach companies that turn a blind eye to their drivers driving for excessively long periods without a break are negligent in permitting this conduct to continue in circumstances where the drivers' sleepiness causes the accidents. The same will be true if the driver was travelling too fast in poor driving conditions. In contrast, if an accident were to occur when the coach driver was taking proper care, perhaps where someone else's negligence caused a collision, the coach company would have no responsibility for the injuries.

Coach travel is merely a special illustration of the general obligation imposed on carriers and others providing services to perform the service with reasonable care and skill.

157 | *I took some holiday photographs for developing and printing. When I went to collect them, the shop said they could not be found. No one had any idea what had happened to them. The shop said that it was merely an agent for the processing laboratory, whose terms of business limited the company's liability to the price of a new film. That is quite inadequate, as I shall never have that holiday again. Is there anything I can do?*

Though the shop acted as intermediary in the negotiation to begin with, if the film processing company cannot explain the loss of the film, the company will be liable to you for damages. The company has a duty of care in providing its services and, since it was in possession of your property, it will have to prove that it was careful.

Can the company rely on its exclusion clause? Unless it was drawn to your attention when you left the films at the shop, it will be irrelevant. So apparently you can ignore it, as it was mentioned only when you went to collect the film.

With regard to compensation, this is another of those situations where the courts have been prepared to award damages to cover upset, disappointment, distress and loss of enjoyment (see Q140). In a celebrated case on this in 1981 (*Woodman* v. *Photo Trade Processing*), a man, who had taken a film of 36 exposures at his friend's wedding as a wedding present, handed in the film for developing and printing to an electrical shop. The shop accepted the film as agents for the film processing company. Only 13 of the photographs were returned. The judge awarded £75 damages, including damages for injured feelings. Such a case (and other, similar ones) is a very useful precedent for your claim against the processing company.

158 | *My daughter's wedding reception was held at a hotel. Following the convention I paid the entire bill myself. The day after, a number of the guests and myself suffered from food poisoning. Can I obtain compensation from the hotel?*

Your first difficulty will be in proving that the food served at the wedding reception caused the food poisoning. Let us assume that you are able to obtain the necessary evidence, perhaps as the result of an investigation by the local authority's public health inspector.

First, your own position. As you made the contract with the hotel, you can make a claim against it for breach of contract. The hotel has supplied food not fit for human consumption and it is strictly liable to you under the Sale of Goods Act 1979 (the provision of a meal in a restaurant or hotel is a sale of goods). You will therefore recover compensation for your own illness.

The position of your guests is more difficult. As they made no contract with the hotel (see Q46), they cannot claim the benefit of the terms implied in a contract for the sale of goods by the 1979 Act. There has been the exceptional case in the courts where someone who had booked for a party was able to recover compensation for members of the party also, but it is by no means clear that this would cover your situation (see Q144).

Your guests would have to bring a claim under 'product liability' (see Q46). It would not be sufficient for them to prove that the food was unfit; they would also need to show that the hotel had been negligent. Yet the food poisoning may have been caused in spite of the care of the hotel, for example if it had used tainted ingredients that it had every reason to believe were fresh and wholesome. A useful tactic would be to contact your local authority to see whether an offence has been committed under the Food Act 1984. If a conviction is obtained, compensation may be awarded under the Powers of Criminal Courts Act 1973 (see Q145).

159 | *My wife and I went out for a meal recently and were horrified by the size of the bill, as each item cost more than the menu had specified. It turned out that VAT had not been included in the menu prices, and the waiter had also added on 12½ per cent for service. I refused to pay the bill unless these additional charges were deducted. Was I correct?*

Certainly. Your only commitment was to pay the menu prices for the food and drink. There is no implied obligation that VAT or service will be added. The customer can reasonably assume that these have been taken into account in calculating the prices, unless the contrary is made clear *before* he orders. Suppliers have no right to increase their charges or prices after the contract has been made, which in the case of a restaurant happens when an order is given by the customer and accepted by the waiter.

This assumption is supported by the Price Marking (Food and Drink on Premises) Order 1979, which requires restaurants to display their prices *inclusive of* VAT outside their premises or dining areas (strangely, not inside). This is in line with the general rule in the Finance Act 1972 that a price is to be treated as VAT-inclusive unless the contrary is stated.

You and the criminal law

Being searched

1 | *I hear that the police have been given new powers to stop and search people. What are my rights if I am stopped?*

A police officer has the power to search you, but only if he has reasonable grounds for suspecting that he will find on you controlled drugs or prohibited articles (stolen goods, offensive weapons, or articles to be used for burglary or theft). The officer has to identify himself, and if he is not in uniform he must produce evidence that he is a police officer. He must tell you what he is looking for and what grounds he has for his suspicions. He must also make a written record if practicable, on the spot or as soon as possible afterwards. This has to give details of the search and why it was carried out. In any event you must be told that you will be entitled to obtain a copy of the record if you want one. These records must be kept available for a year.

The officer can detain you for only so long as is reasonably required to carry out the search, and he is entitled to use force to carry it out if you resist. You are not obliged to submit to anything other than a cursory search in public, and in public places you cannot be required to remove any clothing other than an outer coat, jacket or gloves.

These are the only powers that the police have to force you to do anything in the street. Otherwise they

must arrest you, saying why you are under arrest, and take you to the police station.

2 | *Are these searches limited to the streets, or can they be carried out anywhere?*

The powers to search for prohibited articles apply in public areas to which people have ready access. This includes the inside of shops, cinemas, sports grounds and the common parts of blocks of flats or estates – walkways, corridors, stairs and lifts. It also includes open ground, even if privately owned. The power to search a person for drugs applies anywhere – even on private property.

3 | *What if I'm in a car; can the police search it?*

Yes. The police have the right to search vehicles in public places if, again, they have reasonable grounds, which must be explained, for suspecting that there are stolen or prohibited articles in the vehicle. They may also search anything in or on any vehicle. Again a written record has to be made if practicable and you are entitled to a copy.

They even have the right to search your car if you are not in it, but if it is unattended they must leave a notice stating that it has been searched and that compensation is available for any damage caused by the search.

Motoring

4 | *If I am driving my car, can the police compel me to stop?*

Yes. Uniformed police have always had a general power to stop vehicles, now contained in section 159 of the Road Traffic Act 1972. They can use this, for example, to check on traffic offences and vehicle licences, to establish census points, to warn drivers of hazards ahead, or possibly (though this has been disputed) to warn drivers that they may not travel towards a destination where a breach of the peace is feared (as in the 1984 miners' dispute).

5 | *Can the police use this power to set up road blocks whenever they like?*

Not quite. It depends on the purpose for which the road block is to be set up. For most purposes road blocks are unregulated and the police have in the past and can still set them up wherever and whenever they wish. But road blocks set up as part of criminal investigations are now regulated under the Police and Criminal Evidence Act 1984. If the block is to try to find a crime suspect or witness, or to check for someone planning a crime, it must be authorised by a police superintendent, except in urgent cases, when any police officer can authorise one. The crime in question has to be a serious one, in the category of 'serious arrestable offences' (see Q 1 2). Road blocks set up to apprehend escaped prisoners also have to be authorised.

These road blocks can be authorised for up to a week at a time and can last indefinitely, but need to be re-authorised every seven days.

If you are stopped in an authorised road block you have the right to obtain a written statement of its purpose. Oddly, if the road block was set up for some other purpose, not connected with criminal investigation, it does not have to be authorised, nor do you have any specific right to know why it was set up.

6 | I was stopped in my car the other evening and breathalysed. I'd been to a pub but I'd drunk only orange juice. Can the police stop people to breathalyse them?

In theory, no, random tests are not allowed. The policeman has to have 'reasonable cause' for believing that you had alcohol in your body, or that you had committed a traffic offence or that you had been involved in an accident. The mere fact that you had been to a pub shouldn't be enough. On the other hand, it's very difficult for the individual to prove that the policeman didn't have reasonable cause to stop him or her.

7 | Do I have to blow into the bag if I'm stopped and breathalysed?

Yes, otherwise you would be committing an offence. The policeman has to be in uniform, but otherwise all he has to do is ask. There used to be all sorts of loop-holes in the law, and people could escape prosecution if the policeman didn't follow a precise procedure or if the driver took a quick swig of alcohol from a convenient hip-flask. These loopholes have now been plugged. If the test proves positive the policeman will ask you to accompany him to the police station, and he is within his right to do so. At the station, you will be asked to take another breath test (or, in rare circumstances, give a specimen of blood or urine). There are different kinds of breath-test devices, some of which have come under criticism for not being accurate enough. Even if you share the doubts that have been expressed about these machines, it doesn't entitle you to refuse to take the test.

8 | If I'm convicted of drinking and driving, will I lose my driving licence?

Almost certainly. The penalty for driving while over the permitted alcohol limit is a maximum of six months' imprisonment and/or a fine of £2,000. Magistrates don't very often send such convicted drivers to prison, unless it was a particularly bad case or it wasn't the driver's first offence. For most people, the main punishment is the accompanying loss of their licence. The magistrates *must* disqualify a convicted drunk driver for a minimum of 12 months (except in very rare special circumstances), and most courts apply a sliding scale so that the higher the level of alcohol in the blood, the greater the period of disqualification – in the case of a first offender, in practice up to three years.

9 | How does the penalty points system work?

Quite simply, various driving offences are allocated penalty points according to their seriousness. For instance, reckless driving attracts 10 points, while parking a vehicle in a dangerous position, like on zig-zag lines, gets you three. When the driver has accumulated 12 points within three years, the magistrates *must* disqualify him from driving for at least six months. Of course, some offences, like driving with excess alcohol, lead to disqualification anyway, and the penalty points system won't apply in those cases

Being questioned in the street

10 | My son was walking home from a party late the other night when a policeman came up to him, asked him where he'd been and where he was going, and demanded to know his name and address. Have the police any right to do this without giving any reason?

Police officers do not need any special powers to speak to or question a person in the street, provided that they do not use any element of compulsion to make him remain or submit to a search. This does literally mean that no compulsion at all can be used, and even putting a hand on someone's arm to restrain him could put a police officer in the wrong. So while the police were within their rights to ask your son questions, he would have been within his rights to walk away and refuse to answer.

The police can only compel a person to remain if they have reasonable grounds for suspecting that he is carrying drugs or a prohibited article (stolen goods, offensive weapons, articles for use in theft or burglary) – in which case they have to give their reasons – or if they arrest him for an offence – in which case they must take him to a police station.

Arrest

11 | *What powers have the police got to arrest people without producing a warrant?*

Police officers can arrest people on reasonable suspicion that they have committed offences within a category of crimes called 'arrestable' offences. These are crimes which carry a maximum of over five years' imprisonment, and they include most theft and dishonesty offences and nearly all offences involving drugs, violence or deliberate property damage. There are some other offences which are also arrestable although the maximum imprisonment is less than five years: customs offences, violations of Official Secrets Acts, taking a vehicle, corruption offences, certain sexual offences and going equipped for stealing. This means that if an officer has a suspicion which is reasonable (he clearly does not have to have complete proof) that one of these offences has, at some time whenever in the past, been committed or attempted, he can arrest the person or people he suspects.

There are also some other offences where the police have an unrestricted power of arrest, even though the offences are not designated as 'arrestable'. These include public order offences (threatening, abusive or insulting words or behaviour, having an offensive weapon, wearing unlawful uniform), driving while drunk or disqualified, and desertion from the armed forces.

In the case of more minor offences which are neither arrestable nor carry these unrestricted powers of arrest, the normal practice is for the police to report offenders so that magistrates' court summonses can be sent to them. However, even for these offences the police have restricted powers of arrest if the suspected offender will not give his proper name and a satisfactory address – or if they believe that the person is likely to obstruct the highway, cause harm to himself or other people, or commit offences against public decency.

Anyone arrested must be told specifically that he is under arrest and what offence he has been arrested for, but he is not entitled necessarily to know what suspicions led the officer to make the arrest, as he is if stopped and searched (see Q1).

12 | *What is a 'serious arrestable offence'?*

This phrase is used in the Police and Criminal Evidence Act 1984 to define a category of crimes where the police have greater powers than usual.

Some arrestable offences are always serious: murder or manslaughter, rape and offences involving sexual violence, sex offences against children, and offences involving explosives, hostage-taking, kidnapping, hijacking, treason, and causing death by reckless driving.

Other arrestable offences are to be defined as serious only if they would have or are intended to have the following consequences:

● serious harm to the security of the State or to public order
● serious interference with the administration of justice or with the investigation of offences or of a particular offence
● the death of any person
● serious injury to any person
● substantial financial gain to any person
● serious financial loss to any person (loss is to be assessed from the point of view of the person suffering it).

It is the police officer concerned who is to determine whether the offence is a 'serious arrestable' one.

13 | *I have heard of people 'helping the police with their enquiries' at police stations and being kept there for long periods. Are the police entitled to hold these people?*

No. The police can only compel someone to remain at a police station by arresting them, and for this they must suspect on reasonable grounds that the person is guilty of an offence. Many people do go to police stations as witnesses or victims and are prepared to stay to help the police, but they cannot be forced to remain if they do not want to.

If the police decide that someone who is 'helping with enquiries' should not be allowed to leave, they must then, if they have the power to do so, place that person under arrest and inform him that he is no longer free to go. If they decide that the person should be treated as a suspect but not placed under arrest, they must caution the person, warning him that anything said can be used in evidence. They must also tell him that he is free to leave and that he may obtain legal advice.

14 | *What are my rights under arrest? Do I have to answer police questions?*

No. You have a right of silence, which means that you do not have to answer police questions if you do not want to. You cannot prevent them putting questions to you, but you can decide whether or not you are going to answer any or all of them. You must be cautioned, which means being told that you do not have to say anything, but that what you do say can be given in evidence before a court. This applies even to statements which a police officer does not write down, as he may remember what you said and later tell it to a court.

15 | What are my rights if I am taken to a police station under arrest?

Unless the offence for which you have been arrested is a 'serious arrestable offence' (see Q12), the position is as follows: when you arrive at a police station you must be seen by a custody officer who is responsible for your treatment while at the station. He must tell you why you are in custody, and inform you of your rights, giving you a written notice explaining them. These rights are the right not to be held incommunicado, the right to legal advice, and the right to consult the Code of Practice.

You are allowed to contact one person by telephone – although the police may listen in to the call. You can also ask the police to inform someone you know or who is likely to take an interest in you that you have been arrested. Whether anyone will be allowed in to see you is entirely up to the custody officer.

Your right to legal advice entitles you to consult a solicitor of your choice and to speak to him privately. If you do not know a solicitor, you should be given a list of available Duty Solicitors, who have their fees paid automatically under Legal Aid. If you have asked to see a solicitor, you should not be interviewed until he arrives (unless either you agree, or a superintendent certifies that the interview is urgent on account of risk of harm to persons or serious loss of property, or that the time the solicitor is likely to take in arriving would mean an unreasonable delay to the police investigation). If your solicitor does attend, you are entitled to have him with you when you are being questioned.

The Code of Practice sets out your rights and details the way you may be treated while in police custody. It also contains provisions about searches of property and identification procedures.

16 | How long can the police hold me at a police station?

Assuming that the offence you were arrested for is not a 'serious arrestable' one (see Q12), the maximum time you can be held before you must be released or charged is 24 hours.

If you are still in custody and have not been charged after six hours, an inspector not connected with the investigation of your offence is required to review the need for you to be held in custody. He must visit you (unless you are asleep) and listen to anything you or your solicitor or anyone on your behalf has to say. There must be another review if you are still in custody after 15 hours. If you are charged the custody officer must release you on bail unless he has grounds for believing that the name and address you have given are false, or that you should be detained for your own or someone else's protection, or that you would fail to appear in court, or might interfere with witnesses before the hearing.

If you are released without charge, this does not necessarily mean that no charges will follow later. You can be released on bail with a requirement to return to the station at some future date, but you cannot be held uncharged for more than 24 hours in total.

17 | What is the position if the police claim that the offence they suspect me of is a 'serious arrestable' one?

It is then possible for the police to hold you for longer and some of your rights can be suspended.

The maximum time for which you can be detained without a court's approval is then 36 hours. The decision to keep you beyond 24 hours has to be made by a police superintendent to whom you must be given an opportunity to speak. He may authorise the delay in your access to an outside person or to a solicitor if he has reasonable grounds for believing that such access would either lead to interference with or harm to evidence or physical harm to other people, or to the alerting of other suspects not yet arrested, or would hinder the recovery of property obtained as a result of the offence. These rights can be suspended only for as long as the police believe is necessary, but never longer than 36 hours – unless the offence is concerned with terrorism, in which case the delay can be 48 hours.

If the police still want to hold you longer than 36 hours, you must be taken to a magistrates' court. There will be a hearing where you can be represented by a solicitor under free Legal Aid. The magistrates can authorise you to be held for further periods of not more than 36 hours at a time, up to a maximum limit on detention before charge of 96 hours, or four days.

18 | *After I was arrested, a detective sergeant insisted on taking my fingerprints. Could I have refused to give them?*

Yes, but if you had refused to give them, the sergeant could have consulted a police superintendent, who can authorise fingerprints to be taken by force. He can also authorise the taking of prints from a suspect who has not been charged if it is thought that fingerprints will confirm or disprove his involvement in the offence, such as in a burglary where fingerprints had been found at the scene of the crime.

Otherwise an arrested person cannot have his fingerprints taken without his consent, and the consent must be given in writing to be effective. People must be told the reason why their fingerprints are required, and in the case of prints taken without consent the reason must be recorded.

Once a person has been convicted in court his fingerprints can be required if they have not been taken already.

19 | *What about destroying fingerprints if I am acquitted?*

You must be told of the provisions regarding destruction when your fingerprints are taken. If you are prosecuted and acquitted, or if you are not prosecuted at all, the prints and any copies must be destroyed, and, if you wish, you have the right to witness the destruction of the prints (if they have not already been destroyed). This applies whether the fingerprints were taken with your consent or without, and whether you were a suspect or merely a witness who gave his prints for elimination purposes.

Similar rules apply to any photographs taken of you while in police custody.

20 | *Can the police immediately search an arrested person as a matter of routine?*

No. They can only search people they have arrested if they have reasonable grounds for doing so. They must either believe that the person may be dangerous to himself or others, or that he has articles on him which he might use to escape or which might be evidence of a crime.

On the arrival of an arrested person at a police station, however, the position is that the custody officer has a duty to record all property that he has on him, and so he can authorise a search for this purpose if he considers it necessary. It can be carried out even if the person objects, and reasonable force can be used. The person carrying out the search must be of the same sex as the person searched.

21 | *What about intimate body searches and strip searches?*

Intimate searches of a person's body orifices (anus, rectum, vagina, mouth, etc.) can be authorised by a superintendent if he reasonably believes that the person may have concealed on him or her an article which could cause injury to himself or to others. Such a search is to be carried out by a doctor, nurse or midwife, unless the superintendent considers this impracticable, in which case a police officer of the same sex can do it.

Searches can similarly be authorised for Class A drugs (heroin, cocaine) but can only be carried out by medical personnel.

The provisions about intimate searches are set out in the Police and Criminal Evidence Act 1984. However, the Act says nothing about strip searches. The Code of Practice, on the other hand, says that strip searches should only take place if they are thought necessary by the custody officer to remove an article which an arrested person would not be allowed to keep.

22 | *I've heard about the right of citizen's arrest. Could I arrest someone I thought had committed an offence?*

Not necessarily. It depends on the offence and what you saw. A citizen's power of arrest is not quite as wide as that of the police, but a citizen can arrest someone whom he sees in the act of committing an arrestable offence (see Q12), or whom he reasonably believes to be in the act. So if you see someone who appears to be in the act of taking your car or deliberately damaging it (both arrestable offences) you could arrest that person.

Citizens also have a power to arrest a person reasonably suspected of being guilty of having (in the past) committed an arrestable offence, but only where such an offence has in fact taken place (and is not merely suspected of having taken place). So if you come on the scene after the event, you have to be certain that an offence has been committed. Provided it has, you can lawfully arrest someone who looks reasonably likely to have done it. For example, if you come back to your car and find it damaged and someone acting suspiciously near it, you would only be safe in arresting that person if your car had in fact not been damaged in an accident.

Police officers, on the other hand, can arrest people they suspect to be guilty of offences they suspect to have been committed, provided that in each case their suspicions are reasonable.

The citizen's power of arrest is used most frequently by store detectives, when they believe someone is shoplifting.

23 | *Suppose I saw someone who was just behaving in a threatening way to passers-by. That might not amount to an 'arrestable' offence. Surely I would be entitled to do something?*

Yes. As well as your right to arrest for arrestable offences, you also have the right (some would add the duty) to arrest for breaches of the peace. A breach of the peace takes place when a person is harmed or is in fear of being harmed through an assault or other disturbance, or where people are likely to be harmed. Every citizen who sees a breach of the peace, or thinks one is about to occur, has the right to take reasonable steps to make the person who is breaking the peace stop doing so – if necessary by arresting him.

24 | *Suppose I make an arrest as a citizen. What would I do with the person I'm arresting?*

If you arrest someone for an offence (as opposed to a breach of the peace) you should ensure that the police are called. If no one else will call the police you will have to try to take your prisoner to a police station. Alternatively you could go straight to a magistrates' court if one is open, since the law states that that is where a prisoner in the end has to be taken.

If you arrest someone for breach of the peace, you have no obligation to call the police or take your prisoner to court. You can simply release him when the danger of a breach of the peace has passed.

Suspected shoplifting

25 | *My mother was just leaving a department store when a man grabbed her arm, accused her of stealing a sweater, and asked her to go to his office. He turned out to be the manager. He'd made a mistake and later apologised. But did he have the right to detain and question her in the first place?*

If the manager genuinely believed that your mother was in the act of stealing the sweater, and had reasonable grounds for his belief, then he was entitled as a citizen to make an arrest, which is what in effect he did. If he had no reasonable grounds for his belief (say, if the sweater was obviously not one that could have come from the store), then he was not acting lawfully and he would have had no right to detain her, take her to the office or make her stay there. If this were so she could sue the store, claiming compensation for wrongful arrest. The amount of compensation she would be entitled to would depend on the length of time she had been detained and the degree of embarrassment caused to her.

Search of premises

26 | *The police arrested my husband at work, searched his office there and then came and searched our house. They had no search warrants but said an inspector had told them to carry out the searches. Was this legal?*

Quite possibly it was. The police have two quite distinct search powers after an arrest.

First, they can search the place where the arrested person was at the time of the arrest or immediately before it. They can only search for evidence of the offence for which the person was arrested, and they must have reasonable grounds for believing that there will be such evidence, but such a search does not need a warrant or any other authorisation. This gave the police the power to search your husband's office.

Secondly, the police do have a power to search the house or other premises belonging to an arrested person. The object of this kind of search can be to look either for evidence of the offence for which the arrest took place or for evidence of other similar or connected offences. Such a search does not need a warrant, but it must normally be authorised by a police inspector, who must record the object and the grounds of the search. However, if the arresting officer finds it necessary to the investigation to take the arrested person to the property to be searched direct before going to the station, he can carry out the search without the inspector's authorisation.

Whether the search of your home was legal will therefore depend on whether there were reasonable grounds for suspecting that there might be evidence of offences similar to or connected with the offence for which your husband was arrested.

27 | *Police officers came to my house saying that they wanted to arrest my brother for drugs. They had no arrest or search warrant. My brother sometimes stays with me but he was not there at the time. The police forced their way in and searched the whole house. They looked under floor-boards, in all the kitchen cupboards and in the bedrooms, but they did not find anything. Could I sue them for damages?*

Yes. Some of the search, at least, was illegal.

The legal part is that police officers can enter a house for the purpose of arresting a person they believe to be there whom they have power to arrest. Possession of drugs is an arrestable offence, so if they genuinely believed that your brother was in the house and they suspected him of possessing drugs, they could search the house for him.

But it is clear that the police were not just looking for your brother since it is unlikely he was hiding in a kitchen cupboard. They were obviously looking for drugs, and this they had no power to do without a search warrant. The right to enter to search for a wanted person without a warrant is strictly limited to the purpose of looking for that person. In this respect, therefore, the police were acting unlawfully and you could sue for compensation for the trespass, and then make a police complaint.

28 | *Police officers came to my house to search under a drugs warrant. They found the tiniest bit of cannabis. They also found some items of jewel-lery which they said could have been stolen. They took these away together with my address book and diary. Was this legal? Can I at least have my address book and diary back since I need them?*

Under a search warrant police can only search to the extent required for the purpose of the search, so, if they were clearly on a fishing expedition when they came across the jewellery, they were acting beyond their powers. However, this will not prevent them using the jewellery as evidence in court if it does turn out to be stolen. The police have the power to retain it for as long as is necessary to establish whether or not it does belong to anyone else. But if they do not return it after a reasonable period you can ask a magistrates' court to order that it should be returned by applying under the Police (Property) Act 1897.

As far as your address book and diary are concerned, the police would probably claim that they are evidence in relation to the drugs. There is a power for the police, while executing a search warrant, to seize items they reasonably believe to be evidence of offences. You are, however, entitled to demand access to your belongings, and in the case of documents you are entitled to photocopy them, provided that the officer in charge does not believe that this would prejudice the investigation.

Being bound over

29 | *I read of someone who was arrested for breach of the peace, taken to court, and wound up in prison for a week. Is this usual?*

No. If a person arrested for breach of the peace is brought to court, he is there not to be fined or impri-soned or dealt with as other accused people are. He is there to be 'bound over'. The evidence against him must be given, and he has a chance to defend himself in the usual way. If the court finds the evidence proved, it can then order him to be bound over 'to keep the peace and be of good behaviour'. This means he has to sign a recognisance for a certain sum – that is agreeing in effect to forfeit that sum if he should not keep the peace within the period stated. But if he refuses to sign to be bound over, the court can sen-tence him to up to six months' imprisonment.

The person you read about must have refused to be bound over.

30 | *My sister and I went on a peaceful demonst-ration. However, she was arrested and I went to court to give evidence for her. At the end of the case the magistrates decided that not only should she be bound over but that I should be as well. As I was only in court as a witness and went there voluntar-ily, was this right?*

As long as you were given a chance to object to the binding over, it may be legal. Magistrates have the right to bind over any person appearing before them, whether as a party to proceedings or as a witness. But as you were just a witness you should have been warned by the magistrates that they were proposing to order a bind-over and given an opportunity to state why that might be unfair or inappropriate. The magistrates must be satisfied before making a bind-over that there is a risk that the person might break the peace, and this can be evidenced by his previous conduct, or even by his behaviour in court.

A person bound over has a right of appeal to the Crown Court. The Crown Court (see page 476) must rehear the case and decide if the circumstances justify it.

Complaining about the police

31 | *I recently joined a peaceful demonstration against nuclear weapons. There was a scuffle near me and, although I wasn't involved, a policeman started manhandling me and dragged me to the police van. He was extremely offensive, called me names, swore violently and threatened to put me away if I didn't shut up. I was never charged, and I now want to lay a complaint against him. How do I go about it?*

You can make a complaint at any police station, orally or in writing; or you could send it in a letter or have a friend or adviser (such as a solicitor) send it in for you.

It is best to put as much detail as you can remember in the complaint – including if possible the officer's number or any identifying features. The complaint will be investigated by a senior police officer, and you will be informed of the outcome. Since what you have alleged amounts to criminal conduct on the part of the officer, the decision on whether he will be charged will be made by the Director of Public Prosecutions. If your complaint only referred to the swearing and abusive behaviour (not criminal conduct) then the question of whether the officer should be disciplined would be referred to

the Police Complaints Authority (unless the chief constable decided first to initiate disciplinary proceedings).

It may also be worth sending a copy of your complaint to the Police Complaints Authority direct. They have power to supervise the investigation of complaints if they think that they are serious enough to justify it.

Alibis

32 | *I was drinking with a friend on my birthday. Apparently the police have now charged him with a crime which took place at the time he was with me, and I have received a letter from his solicitor asking me to be a witness. I have been in trouble with the police in the past, and don't much want to have dealings with them. Will they be involved?*

They will certainly be eventually. But if you want to help your friend you should co-operate with his solicitor as soon as possible. You should tell him about your previous involvement with the police as he will need to know.

The law requires that the police be told in advance of the trial of the names and addresses of alibi witnesses, and it is therefore quite possible that a police officer will want to see you to confirm your evidence. If you are worried about this, tell the solicitor and ask him or her to be present.

33 | *A friend of mine is in trouble with the police and has asked me to cover for him if the police ask me questions. I know he is guilty of quite a serious crime, but do not want to see him arrested. What is my position if the police come round to see me? I don't want to be involved. Do I have to answer their questions, and if so must I tell them the truth?*

In general no one has to answer police questions or help with police enquiries. The only exception to this rule concerns terrorist activities; if you have information about terrorism you commit an offence by not telling the police.

You must decide whether you will talk to the police or not, and you would be within your rights to decide not to help them. If that is your decision, it would probably be wise to have someone else present when you see them. Remember that from their point of view your non-cooperation may seem suspicious and could lead them to believe that you were involved yourself; they might then even arrest you.

It must be your decision alone to decide not to talk. It is an offence to demand or accept anything from your friend in return for keeping quiet.

On the other hand, if you do talk you must not actively mislead the police. It is an offence to commit an act with intent to impede someone's arrest or prosecution, if you know that person is guilty of a serious crime.

Giving evidence

34 | *I was interviewed by the police to give evidence as a witness. I made a written statement, but foolishly I included something which was not true. Could I be charged with perjury?*

Theoretically you could. Statements taken by police are not under oath, but they contain a declaration that the persons making them will be liable to prosecution if anything is stated which the person knows to be false or does not believe to be true. But this only applies if the statement is tendered in evidence, so if there has been no court hearing yet you could not be charged. It is best to tell the police as soon as possible – very few people are charged with perjury and the police and the courts are likely to take a more lenient view if you tell them swiftly.

35 | *I was in a pub when a fight broke out. I saw how it started and what happened. One man was hurt and the police arrested and charged two others with assault. The police say I am a witness and must make a statement. Do I have to?*

You have no legal obligation to give a statement to the police or to anyone else, but if you were a witness to matters on which people are going to have to face trial, you may have a public duty to give evidence. If you do not volunteer, you may be summoned to attend court to give evidence at the trial either by the prosecution or by the defence, but it is unlikely (though possible) that either side will do this unless they know in advance your version of events.

If you are brought to court to give evidence, you must do so and must tell the truth, otherwise you could be in trouble for contempt of court or perjury.

Surety

36 | *I have been asked if I would stand surety for a friend who has been arrested. What does this involve?*

If you agree to be a surety you will be asked to stand for a certain sum of money. You do not have to produce the money in cash immediately; you merely have to agree to forfeit that sum should your friend fail to turn up in court. You may be asked how you would raise the money if you had to.

You have to decide whether you trust your friend enough not to let you down. If at any time you think he is going to run off, you can ask to be relieved of your duty and the police may then arrest him.

If he does let you down, it is not automatic that you will have to forfeit the whole sum. There will be a court hearing at which you will be given the opportunity to explain your situation. You may have to give evidence of your finances, and of the effort you made to ensure that your friend did not abscond. The court may then let you off all or part of the sum.

Money ordered to be forfeited is treated like a fine: if you do not pay, you could eventually face imprisonment.

Naturally it is an offence for your friend to advance you the money or for you to accept any cash from him in return for standing surety.

Bail

37 | *I understand that people who are released on bail don't normally have to produce cash bail before they can be released. But I read of someone who was required to deposit £1,000 before the court would let him out on bail. Was this legal, and if so why don't courts do this more often?*

The Bail Act 1976 prohibits cash deposits except in relation to people unlikely to remain in the country. This is normally used only in the case of foreigners whose home and family are abroad, and who will have to go back home during the period of their release on bail. If a person living here was genuinely thought likely to abscond abroad, the court would probably not grant bail at all and would keep him in custody. Alternatively, he could be released on bail on condition that he surrendered his passport to the police.

See also CHILDREN, Q70.

Jury service

38 | *A colleague of mine at work was called for jury service and found it disastrously inconvenient both for his work and for his private life. Could he have got out of it?*

Not necessarily. People summoned for jury service

are legally obliged to attend unless they are disqualified, not eligible, or entitled to be excused.

People disqualified are those with criminal convictions – those who have at some time been sentenced to five years' imprisonment, or in the previous ten years have served any part of a prison or custodial sentence or community service order, or in the previous five years have been placed on probation.

People not eligible are the mentally ill, the clergy (ministers of religion, nuns and monks), the judiciary (judges and JPS) and others concerned with the administration of justice (lawyers, police officers and people working in courts, prisons, etc.) and everyone over the age of 65.

People entitled to be excused are MPS, members of the armed forces, and people in the medical profession (doctors, dentists, nurses, midwives, vets and chemists).

However, jury summoning officers have the discretion to excuse other people for any other good reason, such as poor health, disability or standing holiday arrangements, so if you think you have grounds to be let off it is worth asking.

39 | How long does jury service last? What about loss of earnings and expenses?

Normally two weeks. Most trials last only a few days and so jurors often try two or more cases during their time. Sometimes, however, jurors will have to serve on a long case. Although the lawyers involved can usually tell roughly how long the case will last, their estimates are sometimes wrong. Some cases can last two or even three months.

If your employer will not pay you while you are on jury service, or you are self-employed, you are entitled to claim for loss of earnings. If you serve for the normal two weeks, the maximum you can claim is £21 per day (if you lose that much). If you serve longer, you can claim up to £42 per day from the eleventh day onwards. You can also claim for travelling, subsistence (necessary meals while you are away from home) and in some cases for a child-minder.

The legal system

How the system works

Every society needs a body of rules or laws to regulate the behaviour of its citizens. The more complex the society grows, the more complex those rules need to be. In a small community, where everybody is known to everybody else, accepted norms of conduct can be enforced by social pressures rather than by formal sanctions, but in large societies these have to be replaced by formal structures, which together we call law.

We have to ban certain types of conduct in the public interest, enforcing the bans with punishments that can be inflicted on transgressors. These are what we call crimes, and they are regulated in this country by the criminal courts, which can mete out punishments such as imprisonment and fines. Wrong-doers are mainly brought before the courts through instruments of the state, especially the police force and government departments such as Customs and Excise, although the private citizen does have the right to bring a private prosecution, too.

Other types of behaviour which are not formally proscribed by the criminal law may constitute civil wrongs. Here the rights of one individual have been infringed by another and the law allows the injured party to bring a claim for compensation. They most commonly involve a 'tort', which is a harmful act such as negligence (on which most claims for damages for personal injuries are based), or trespass to land, or a breach of contract, such as selling defective goods or failing to repay a debt.

The civil law developed from simple beginnings but has had to become more complex. In a free society the citizen must have rights in relation to the state as well as in relation to other people and so must be able to challenge the demands which the state makes on him or her. For example, the law has to give the state a right to levy taxation, but the taxpayer must be able to challenge the state in circumstances where he considers that the law is being wrongly applied and a tax incorrectly claimed.

As society changes the law may have to be changed with it for social and political reasons. For example, the right of a landlord to end a tenancy without giving good reason has been abolished in recent years as it was widely felt to be more important that people should enjoy security of tenure of their homes than that landlords should exercise absolute jurisdiction over who lived in their property.

Where does the law come from?

The two main sources of our law are Acts of Parliament and judge-made law, otherwise known as 'judicial precedent'.

Usually about 70 Acts of Parliament are passed each year. Many are purely political in character, and do not really affect the mass of the population at all. One government puts through an Act to nationalise an industry and the next passes another to reverse the process. Many others are purely technical, affecting only a tiny minority of the population and going virtually unnoticed by the media. Others are economic, most notably the Finance Act, which gives legal effect to the Budget tax proposals. But some do affect the law as it touches the ordinary citizen, such as the recent changes in divorce law and the powers of the police.

Often an Act of Parliament does not itself specify all the provisions of a new law. It may give a minister or some other person or group a power to make regulations in a process known as delegated legislation. This allows detailed law to be made and changed without going back to Parliament for close scrutiny each time, enabling the person delegated to put the flesh on the skeleton provided by the Act. Examples of these include most local by-laws and the 'construction and use regulations' governing motor vehicles.

Interpretation of Acts of Parliament is the function of the courts. If a person, or a government department, claims that an Act means one thing and someone else maintains that it means another, it is for a court to decide which is right. The loser may still disagree, in which case there can be an appeal, on occasions up to the highest court in the land, which is the House of Lords.

Once the legal process has put a construction on an Act, the interpretation is binding, not only on the parties involved but in any subsequent cases where the same point of law applies. The government is no more exempt than a private individual, unless it changes the law by a new Act or regulation. The meaning given to the words by the court in question will be binding on any lower court, so a decision of the House of Lords binds all other courts. The Court of Appeal being the next senior court, its decisions are binding on all lower courts, and the decision of a High Court judge is binding on the county courts and magistrates' courts.

Occasionally a novel point of law arises which is not covered by an Act of Parliament. Recently, for example, two victims of motor accidents claimed damages for matters in which there was no precedent. One man claimed that he had been turned into a sexual offender by his injuries and sought compensation for having been imprisoned as a result. The other said that his marriage had broken up as a result of his injuries and claimed damages to compensate him for the maintenance he was now having to pay. Both cases succeeded. In deciding that compensation can be awarded for these types of loss the courts have made new law; lower courts are now bound by those decisions in any similar cases unless and until a higher court rules otherwise.

This judge-made law is sometimes referred to as the common law. It has been in existence for centuries, and much of our law has been fashioned by it, including most of the modern law of tort and contract.

The courts

The courts of law in England and Wales have developed like the law itself in a piecemeal fashion over 900 years or so. As society and the law have grown more complex the functions of the courts have had to develop to keep up with changing needs. In typical English fashion our system is the product of evolution rather than drastic restructuring, and we are left with a patchwork rather than a nice neat pyramid of seniority among the courts.

Even though they are not exclusive, since some courts, notably the magistrates' court, can deal with both types of case, the courts can be divided into two groups: those which deal with criminal cases, involving the trial and punishment of offenders against the criminal law, and those which deal with civil cases, involving disputes between individuals or between individuals and the state.

THE CIVIL COURTS
There are three courts to which civil cases can be taken, and the choice of which depends on the nature and sometimes the size of the case.

THE MAGISTRATES' COURT
Although the magistrates' court is often seen in the public mind as a purely criminal court, and indeed some people still refer to it as 'the police court', it does have some civil jurisdiction. For the most part it is concerned with matrimonial and family cases, involving applications for maintenance by deserted wives and by the mothers of illegitimate children, custody and access disputes, domestic violence cases and adoption.

The 'domestic court', as it is known, sits in private to decide matrimonial and family cases. The magistrates hearing such cases are experienced JPs who have received special training in this type of work. Other cases with which the court can deal concern licensing for the sale of liquor, applications by residents to change street names, and other miscellaneous matters of that sort. Magistrates' courts have no power to decide claims for damages for injuries, nor to enforce ordinary debts, nor to deal with property disputes. (For the structure and personnel of the magistrates' courts, see page 479.)

THE COUNTY COURT
The county courts were created in the last century to provide convenient local justice in the smaller civil cases which had previously had to go to the High Court. Despite their title, they have nothing to do with geographic counties. There are some 300 altogether in England and Wales.

A county court today has an enormously wide range of functions. It is impossible to list them all, but they include the following:

- claims for debts and damages for tort and breach of contract of up to £5,000
- undefended divorce cases
- claims affecting maintenance, domestic violence, custody, matrimonial property and other matters on breakdown of a marriage and between cohabitees
- bankruptcy (other than in the London area)
- actions by building societies and other lenders to get possession of property when mortgages are in arrears
- landlord and tenant disputes, including claims by landlords to evict tenants
- actions to evict squatters
- disputes over wills and trusts.

In some of these cases a county court can only hear the case if the property involved is below a certain value, or, in the case of premises, below a certain rateable value.

The judges who sit in a county court are called circuit judges, the same level as those who sit in the Crown Court – indeed the same judges often sit in both courts. Most judges were formerly practising barristers, but a few were previously solicitors. In court they are addressed as 'Your Honour' and they are referred to as 'His or Her Honour Judge So-and-so'. They have three main functions in a county court: first, to try cases which cannot be heard by the registrar (see below), second, to pronounce decrees of divorce and to deal with some other matrimonial cases such as applications for injunctions to ban domestic violence and custody disputes, and, third, to hear appeals from decisions of the registrar.

Other legal decisions – the majority in fact – in a county court are taken by registrars. They are judicial officers, like judges, empowered to try cases, make orders and give judgments. They were formerly practising solicitors rather than barristers. Their work also falls into three main categories. First, they take most of the decisions in ordinary civil cases for debts and damages apart from the trial itself, dealing with any preliminary hearings necessary to prepare a case for trial, including deciding if necessary whether there is a triable defence, and make orders for the enforcement of judgments. Second, they do virtually all the work in matrimonial cases except those parts described above; they decide in most cases whether a divorce can be granted, from reading through papers sent in by the parties, and they make the orders for maintenance and decide what is to happen to the home and other assets. Third, in disputed claims for debts and damages where the amount involved does not exceed £1,000, they can try the case. In practice most such claims are dealt with by arbitration (see page 501, Q18).

THE HIGH COURT

The High Court handles the largest range of cases in civil law and those of the greatest value and importance. Whereas a county court can usually only award damages or give judgment on debts up to £5,000, the jurisdiction of the High Court is unlimited, and it can and does decide cases worth millions of pounds. Although the High Court is most commonly associated with the Law Courts in the Strand in London, it has offices, called district registries, in large provincial towns, and cases can be tried by High Court judges sitting outside London.

The High Court is divided into three 'divisions', each specialising in different types of case and each with judges assigned to it.

The Chancery Division is almost entirely concerned with 'lawyers' law'. It specialises in property disputes of one kind or another, including titles to land, trusts, company law, mortgages and wills. It is also often referred to as the 'court of construction' because it will normally hear cases on questions arising solely on the meaning of a document or the legality of a particular step under the constitution of an institution.

The Family Division, as its name suggests, hears the difficult and complicated cases involving family law, such as divorce, contested custody and financial disputes between husband and wife, and other disputes between spouses or cohabitees, or involving the welfare of children.

One of the Family Division's functions is to exercise jurisdiction over wards of court, that is children under the age of 18 who have been placed under the control of the High Court. Anyone who can show a proper 'interest' in the child, not just a parent or relative, can make a child a ward by filing application papers at a court office, and then all matters affecting the child are subject to the direction of the court. Particular use is made of this procedure where a child has been snatched and is likely to be taken abroad, as the court can act rapidly to prevent his or her removal.

The largest of the three divisions is the Queen's Bench Division and it has the broadest range of work. One could say that it does the types of work the other divisions do not. Most of its cases are general civil claims for debts and damages, contract disputes, accident claims and the like, but it has specialist courts within it such as the Commercial Court, which, as its name suggests, exists to try substantial commercial disputes between trading concerns, and the Admiralty Court, which deals with shipping cases. This division also has a special Divisional Court which protects the rights of the individual. It sits with one or two judges, and usually hears short cases which do not involve the calling of evidence. It is here that the ancient remedy of Habeas Corpus can be sought, which is a means of challenging detention by the police, immigration authorities, or any other person or body holding someone against his will. The court will demand to know by what right the person is being detained and can order his release. The Divisional Court of the Queen's Bench Division also hears most appeals from magistrates' courts on points of law and can make orders controlling the lower courts.

The Queen's Bench Division is the division of the High Court which hears cases on points of criminal law as well.

High Court judges, addressed in court as 'My Lord' or 'My Lady', and referred to as 'Mr Justice So-and-So' or 'Mrs Justice So-and-So', are drawn exclusively from among the ranks of barristers. Before appointment they will normally have been senior and very able Queen's Counsel (see page 483). Although each will be assigned to a particular division of the High Court, and may well specialise in particular subjects, they can sit in any division and have the power to deal with any type of case.

Apart from the judges themselves, the High Court has other judicial officers with functions similar to those of a county court registrar. Out of London the district registrar may deal with cases in any division. In London each division has its own officers, known as masters in the Queen's Bench and Chancery Divisions and as registrars in the Family Division. Though litigants themselves may come before a Family Division registrar, who can hear financial and property disputes on divorce, it is usually only lawyers who appear before masters, as their main function is to hear technical applications in the preparation of a case prior to its trial before a judge.

APPEALS IN CIVIL CASES

Appeals from a decision of a magistrates' court usually go to the High Court by a procedure called 'case stated'. The magistrates must 'state a case' saying why they did what they did, and the Divisional Court of the Queen's Bench Division will usually either uphold them or send the case back to be reheard giving a direction on the law to be applied. In licensing cases and in affiliation cases – claims for maintenance brought by the mother of an illegitimate child against the father – some appeals go to the Crown Court.

A person who wants to appeal against the decision of a judge, whether in a county court or in the High Court, must usually go to the Court of Appeal. That court is the second highest in the land, and it consists of two or three judges known as Lords Justices of Appeal, most of whom have been promoted from High Court judges. Sometimes, however, High Court judges will sit in the court. One can leapfrog the Court of Appeal and appeal direct from the High Court to the House of Lords, but this is rare.

The House of Lords is the final court to which one can appeal. There is no right in itself to go to that court, and permission must be given by the House itself or by the lower court whose decision you want to challenge. The court is not the entire House of Lords, but consists of former High Court judges usually promoted from the Court of Appeal and known as the Lords of Appeal in Ordinary. They sit in private at Westminster.

The High Court, Court of Appeal and House of Lords are sometimes collectively called the Supreme Court.

THE CRIMINAL COURTS

The magistrates' courts and the Crown Court between them hear all criminal cases, other than some appeals. All cases begin in the magistrates' court, and over 90 per cent are dealt with completely there. Many minor offences, especially road traffic

cases, can only be heard in a magistrates' court, there being no right to trial in the Crown Court for them. The most serious crimes, however, such as murder, rape and robbery, cannot be tried by the magistrates and the case must be transferred or 'committed' by them to the Crown Court. For a large number of offences of middling seriousness, such as simple thefts and the more serious traffic cases like reckless driving, the person charged has the choice of which court to have the case tried in.

THE MAGISTRATES' COURT

The office of magistrate, or 'justice of the peace', dates back over 600 years, from the time when the forerunners of the modern JP were a sort of primitive police force. The magistrates' court of today is a local court providing justice in less serious cases, and acting as a filter through which graver cases pass on their way to the Crown Court. The proceedings are relatively informal.

Most magistrates are lay people appointed by the Lord Chancellor from among respected members of the local community. They are unpaid and part-time. For most cases two or three sit on the bench together and their job is to pass sentence on those who plead guilty, and to decide whether the prosecution has proved its case where the accused has pleaded not guilty, and then pass sentence. Although they receive some basic training in the law, they rely on the clerk to the justices, or one of his or her legally qualified assistants, to give them advice on questions of law and on the extent of their powers. The decisions and sentences as such are theirs.

In London and other big cities full-time legally qualified magistrates known as stipendiary magistrates sit, usually singly, to deal with cases. The best-known court where this happens is at Bow Street in central London, the senior magistrates' court.

Prosecutions of juveniles – persons aged under 17 – will always be dealt with by magistrates sitting in private in a juvenile court, unless the juvenile is jointly charged with an adult or is charged with an offence of causing death or some other very serious offence.

THE CROWN COURT

The Crown Court ranks as part of the Supreme Court. Most large towns have a Crown Court centre and one such is the Central Criminal Court, or the Old Bailey as it is better known, in London.

The judges who sit in the Crown Court may be either High Court judges, who deal with the gravest offences such as murder, or circuit judges, who take the less serious ones. Sometimes experienced barristers or solicitors sit as part-time judges and are known as recorders or assistant recorders. If the accused person pleads guilty, the judge will simply have to pass sentence, but if he or she pleads not guilty the judge, unlike a magistrate, cannot decide the question of guilt; that is for a jury of twelve ordinary people drawn at random from the community to decide. When the accused has the choice of having his case heard at a magistrates' court or the Crown Court, he is in effect being given the option of being tried by a jury.

The judge is concerned with matters of law while the jury is there to decide questions of fact. The judge presides over the course of the trial, rather like an umpire, and may have to decide questions of law during the case – whether a particular piece of evidence can be admitted, for example – and he or she will sum up the case to the jury and direct the members of it on matters of the law. The jury listens to the evidence from the witnesses, the arguments of the lawyers and the directions on the law from the judge, and then retires to a private room to decide on its verdict. If that verdict is one of guilty, the judge will pass sentence.

The procedure in the Crown Court is very formal. The judge wears a wig and robes, as do the barristers appearing for the prosecution and the defence. Solicitors can only rarely appear as advocates.

OTHER COURTS

CORONERS' COURTS

Coroners' courts do not exist to try issues or disputes, but to hold inquiries or 'inquests', mainly into cases of sudden or unexplained deaths, and deaths in prison or police custody. The coroner, usually a qualified lawyer or doctor, often sits with a jury.

Inquests are also held to decide whether finds of gold and silver are 'treasure trove', and hence the property of the Crown.

THE EUROPEAN COURT OF JUSTICE

This is the Court of the European Economic Com-

munity sitting in Luxembourg. It decides questions of Community law, and its judgments in that area are superior to those of the House of Lords. In practice, it has been concerned only with commercial and business matters, and not matters directly affecting the individual.

TRIBUNALS

Outside the structure of the courts themselves there exists another system of bodies to which certain types of dispute may, and in most cases must, be taken. These are the various tribunals, usually consisting of a legally qualified chairperson sitting with relevant lay experts, who decide specialist questions, sometimes between individuals but more commonly between an individual and the government or a government department.

There are over 50 of them, but some of the most important are:

● the General Commissioners of Inland Revenue, who adjudicate on some tax appeals
● the Social Security Appeal Tribunals, which decide questions of benefit entitlement
● the Rent Tribunals, which decide among other things the 'fair rent' for a dwelling
● the Industrial Tribunals, which deal with cases of redundancy and unfair dismissal.

Where a tribunal exists to deal with a particular type of question or claim, a court cannot generally deal with it instead. In many cases a person dissatisfied with a tribunal's decision must appeal to a higher tribunal with a right to go on to the courts only if a point of law is involved.

Many tribunals sit locally, and each has its own simple procedure. Most provide explanatory leaflets and forms for making and opposing applications.

In most cases you will not be able to have a lawyer to present your case unless you can pay privately, or someone else, such as a trade union, provides one. This is because Legal Aid is not generally available (see page 495). You can get help from a Citizens Advice Bureau, and a solicitor can advise and assist you in preparing your case under the Green Form Scheme if you qualify financially.

The criminal process

The basic rules by which someone suspected of having committed a criminal offence is brought to court and tried are the same whether the offence involved is a minor one not usually regarded as criminal conduct at all, such as a traffic offence, or a major one such as murder or treason.

Prosecutions

Until 1986 most prosecutions were brought by the police. They investigated the crime, they decided who to prosecute and on what charges, and often they appeared in court to conduct the prosecution.

Now, there is a division of responsibilities. The police still investigate the crime and come to an initial conclusion that there is a case against a particular suspect. But whether or not to prosecute, and for what, is now in the hands of the Crown Prosecution Service (CPS), made up of lawyers who weigh up the evidence gathered by the police. And the police no longer present cases in court. That task, too, has been taken over by the CPS.

Broadly speaking, the more difficult or sensitive the alleged offence, the higher up in the CPS structure the decision to prosecute will be made, with the Director of Public Prosecutions at the summit. In exceptional cases – such as those involving national security – the final decision will be made by the Attorney-General.

Certain government departments have retained the power to prosecute in their particular areas of responsibility, for instance the Inland Revenue, Customs and Excise and the Department of Trade. Local authorities, too, can prosecute, for weights and measures and food hygiene offences, for example.

Private prosecutions can be brought by any member of the public or other body subject to the Director of Public Prosecutions' right to take over – or to stop – any such prosecution, but with two exceptions they are very rare. The first exception is in the case of shoplifting, where it is usually the store that prosecutes for theft, and the second is where a charitable organisation prosecutes, the RSPCA, for example, for suffering caused to an animal.

Even where the CPS or the DPP believe that they have a good case and are likely to secure a conviction, they are not obliged to prosecute, and sometimes they may decide not to in the public interest. Juveniles and elderly people who have admitted to minor offences are often formally cautioned at a police station instead of being brought to trial.

How cases start

The wheels of a prosecution can start to turn in one of three ways. First, the police may apply to a magistrate for a warrant for the arrest of a person they suspect of having committed a crime. He or she will then be arrested and brought before the magistrates' court. Despite the impression given by many detective novels and films, this is quite a rare procedure. Second, the person may be charged by the police at a police station with an offence. He or she will usually have been arrested without a warrant, the police believing on reasonable grounds that he or she had committed the offence. They may take the person before a magistrates' court to be remanded (see below) or they may grant him or her bail to appear at the court on a later date. This is the way in which most of the more serious offences are dealt with. The third way of bringing a case, that used in the less serious ones including traffic offences, is for a police officer or other prosecutor to 'lay an information' before a magistrate or the clerk to the justices. This is usually just a matter of form-filling and the court will issue a summons ordering the person to whom it is addressed to attend the court on a particular day. In many traffic cases offenders will in fact be told they need not attend if they intend to plead guilty – this can be done by post – and that if they intend to plead not guilty the case will be adjourned to a later date.

Bail pending trial

In the most serious cases the police will usually keep suspects in custody after they have been charged. They have to take them before the magistrates' court asking for a remand in custody within 24 hours of their being charged, or 48 at weekends. The magistrates can remand in custody for up to only eight days at a time, and unless the person consents to later remand hearings being made in his or her absence, he or she will be brought back to the court each week until the case itself is tried by the magistrates or until they commit the accused to the Crown Court.

Bail, that is to say the right to remain free pending a court appearance, is not necessary where a summons has been issued but it is where a person charged with a serious offence is to be released. The police can grant bail themselves in most cases but, if they refuse, the person can apply for it to the magistrates' court before which he or she is brought. It must be granted unless he or she is likely to abscond, commit further offences while on bail, interfere with witnesses, or needs to be in custody for his or her own protection. The magistrates can impose conditions on bail, such as regular reporting to a police station or the surrender of a passport, and they may require sureties, which are sums of money pledged by a person other than the person charged and which may be forfeited if the defendant fails to reappear at court. If the magistrates refuse bail, as they may do especially where the police object for one of the reasons above, a further application can be made to a judge.

Cases in a magistrates' court

If you have to appear before a magistrates' court the proceedings will probably go much as follows.

You may have a solicitor or barrister to present your case, in which case he or she will do most of the talking. When you arrive at court you should meet your lawyer, if you have one, and report to the usher, who will tell you where to wait until your case is called. When that happens you will go into court, which is in public, and there you will see the magistrates sitting on a raised 'bench' with the clerk in front of them, and lawyers, police, probation officers, press and other people also sitting in court. In less serious cases, especially outside London, you will not usually have to go into the dock, but will sit in one of the seats in the main part of the court.

When you have answered to your name, the clerk will read out the charge and ask if you understand it. If the case is one, such as theft or reckless driving, where you have a right to be tried by a jury at the Crown Court, he or she will tell you of that right and ask whether you want to exercise it or be tried by the magistrates; you will be told that if you are convicted and the magistrates think that the sentence should be more than they can impose (six months' imprisonment and/or a fine of up to £2,000 in most cases) you can be sent to the Crown Court for sentence. If you say that you want to be tried by the magistrates, you will be asked whether you plead guilty or not guilty.

If you plead guilty, as most people do, the only question for the court is the sentence you should receive. The crown prosecutor will summarise the facts of the case to the court and will tell the magistrates of any other recent convictions you have. Your or your solicitor or barrister can now make a speech 'in mitigation', that is to say, trying to get off as lightly as you can. In this you can explain why you did what you did and express your regret for an act which was wholly out of character, an isolated lapse in a blameless driving lifetime, or whatever the facts may be, and, where a fine is likely, you should give short details of what you earn and pay out. In some cases there may be a social enquiry report about the offender from the probation service, or the court may adjourn the case for one to be prepared. This gives background information to help the court decide what to do in a difficult case. The magistrates may retire to their private room to decide on the sentence and they may call in their clerk for legal advice. More commonly, they put their heads together and talk quietly without leaving the bench, and announce what the sentence is to be. They may also order you to make a payment towards the costs of the prosecution.

If you plead not guilty, the court will have to try the case. A rather unsatisfactory feature of the magistrates' court is that in some cases you have no right to see the statements of the prosecution witnesses, nor to know the detail of the case against you, although you should have a pretty shrewd idea of what it is.

The prosecutor will open the case by outlining the facts to the court, and he or she will then call the first witness, who will take the oath, swearing to tell the truth, and be taken through what is called the 'evidence in chief'. This usually means repeating what is in the statement made to the police. Then you or your lawyer can 'cross-examine' him or her, asking your own questions, challenging the truth or reliability of the evidence given, putting your own version of events, and so on. Other prosecution witnesses follow in the same way.

Once the prosecution case is finished, you can give evidence yourself and call other witnesses as the prosecution did. You are not forced to give evidence yourself, but it is usually advisable to do so. If you do, and you have a solicitor, he or she will take you through your evidence in chief, basing the questions on the statement you gave to him or her. Your solicitor cannot ask leading questions, or to put it another way, cannot put words into your mouth. The prosecutor will then cross-examine you, challenging what you say where it differed from the evidence of the prosecution witnesses. Any other witnesses you want to call will give their evidence in the same way. If someone you want to call as a witness refuses to come, you can get a witness summons from the court ordering them to do so; you should, of course, do so before the hearing. However, in practice the reluctant witness is often not a good one to call.

Once the evidence from both sides has been given, you or your solicitor or barrister can make a closing address to the court to argue that on the basis of the evidence given you should not be convicted. The magistrates will then retire if necessary to consider their decision, asking the clerk for any legal advice they want, and the chairperson will announce whether or not they find the case proved.

If they find the case proved they will now have to consider the sentence in the same way as for a guilty plea.

Cases going to the Crown Court

STAGE 1: THE COMMITTAL

Cases rarely go direct to the Crown Court. By far the majority have to pass through the magistrates' court by the process of committal. This acts as a filter to ensure that only cases where there appears to be a case to answer proceed, and also to enable arrangements for bail, legal aid and the attendance of prosecution witnesses to be made.

In most cases the committal is little more than a formality, provided that the accused person is legally represented and consents to the process. The prosecution provides the defence solicitors with copies of the statements made by witnesses to the police, and, if they can see that there is a case to answer, even though their client denies the charge, the committal will be automatic. The whole thing takes about five minutes.

The defence may, however, decide to test the strength of the prosecution case, or to find out more about it, by asking for what is often called an 'old style' committal, which means that all or most of the prosecution witnesses have to give their evidence aloud before the magistrates, whose clerk writes down what is said. The defence can cross-examine them, and may be able to convince the magistrates that in the light of the evidence given there is, in fact, no case to answer. This, however, is fairly rare, and the magistrates will usually decide that it is justified to send the case for trial.

Whichever type of committal takes place, the press cannot publish anything about the case other than the barest particulars, unless the person charged asks for these reporting restrictions to be lifted, which few people do. Also, in neither case is the defence under any obligation to give or reveal any of its evidence, either now or at any time before the trial itself, other than particulars of an alibi.

STAGE 2: THE TRIAL

Although all trials follow their own course, the following is a summary of the normal procedure in a Crown Court trial.

The Crown Court is far more formal than a magistrates' court. The judge and the barristers are robed and wear wigs, and the prosecution is brought in the name of the Crown ('*Regina*'). The person charged will usually have to sit in the dock except when giving evidence, and he or she will be flanked by prison officers in uniform.

The first step is the reading by the clerk of the court of the indictment, the formal document containing the charges, and the defendant is asked to plead guilty or not guilty to it. If he or she pleads guilty, the procedure followed is very similar to that in the magistrates' court already described (see page 479). The prosecution gives particulars of the offence and any recent convictions, the defence makes a plea in mitigation, and the judge passes sentence, often after reading a social enquiry report.

If the defendant pleads not guilty, there will be a trial to decide his or her guilt, and a jury will be 'empanelled'. Each potential juror is called into the jury box and swears an oath to try the case and give a true verdict. The defence may 'challenge', or object to, a particular juror – it can have up to three people excluded from the jury without giving a reason (though this will soon change if the government's proposal to abolish the defendant's right to challenge jurors becomes law, as is likely). The prosecution too can ask a juror to 'stand by' – in effect, a challenge. And both sides can challenge 'for cause' – for a particular reason.

The jury is told what the charge is and the prosecuting barrister outlines the case. He or she then calls the witnesses, one by one, asking them to give their evidence; each can be cross-examined by the defence. The defence witnesses are called, give their evidence and can be cross-examined by the prosecution in the same way. The defendant may also give evidence and if so he or she can be cross-examined, but is not obliged to give evidence at all. Although the defence barrister may address the jury before calling his or her evidence, this is not often done. Instead, once the evidence for both sides has been given both barristers make closing speeches, the prosecution going first and the defence having the last word.

The judge then sums up, and his or her job is to summarise the evidence and each side's case to the jury, to direct it on the law which applies to the crime in question, and in particular to explain that it is for the Crown to prove guilt, not the defence to prove innocence, and that to return a verdict of guilty the jury must be satisfied 'beyond all reasonable doubt'.

The jury now retires to consider its verdict, which it does in secret. It has to try to reach a unanimous verdict, but if the members have not agreed after a period which is usually at least two hours, the judge may call them back in to court and tell them that he or she will accept the verdict of a majority of at least 10 of them.

Once the jury has reached its verdict, it returns to the court and one of them, the foreman, announces it. If it is not guilty the defendant is discharged and is free to go. If it is guilty the judge passes sentence.

Proof of guilt

The rule that the prosecution must prove guilt beyond all reasonable doubt stands as the cornerstone of our system of criminal justice. Unless the accused person admits the crime, it is for the prosecution to prove its case; it is not for the defendant to prove his or her innocence, although obviously he or she may try to do so. Once the prosecution has called its evidence, whether in the magistrates' court or in the Crown Court, the defence can make a submission that there is no case to answer – in other words, saying that the evidence given, even if it is all true, does not make up the offence charged (in the Crown Court this is a matter for the judge to decide, and the jury is not present at the time) or it can call no evidence of its own and simply say to the court that the Crown evidence should not be believed. The defendant need not go into the witness box to give evidence and risk cross-examination; he or she can keep silent. Apart from a few technical defences, such as insanity, all the burden of proof rests with the prosecution.

A further important consideration reinforces this rule. The police often get on to the track of a criminal because he or she has committed similar crimes in the past, and this one fits his or her way of working. Useful though it might be to the prosecution to give evidence about past offences suggesting guilt of this one, they cannot do so. A person's past convictions cannot be given in evidence by the prosecution; the only exception is if the defendant 'throws away the shield' such as by falsely claiming to have none.

The standard of proof – proof beyond all reasonable doubt – is very high. It is not enough for the magistrates or a jury to think that the prosecution's case is more probable than not; they must be satisfied so that they are sure the person is guilty as charged before they can convict.

Sentences

One crime – murder – carries only one sentence, that of life imprisonment. This is a sentence of no fixed length which allows the Home Secretary of the day to release the prisoner on licence at whatever time seems to him appropriate. It may be after a few years only for a 'domestic' murderer, or thirty or more for a man who shoots a police officer. When sentencing the judge can only make a recommendation as to the minimum length of detention.

For most offences, however, the law lays down maximum sentences only, and may give different ones for magistrates' and Crown Courts. The maximums are rarely imposed: few burglars get the 14 years which the court could inflict. The court must look at each case on its merits and balance the factors of punishment, deterrence and the protection of society with the reform and rehabilitation of the offender.

Immediate prison sentences are avoided wherever possible if the court can impose some other penalty. Prison sentences may be completely suspended so that the offender will only serve it if he or she offends again, or a sentence can be immediate in part with the balance held suspended.

Fines can be imposed for less serious offences, and community service orders made requiring the person to perform a set number of hours in such service. Probation orders are not sentences as such, but place the offender under the supervision of a probation officer for a period of time, usually two years, and conditions can be imposed as to hospital treatment and where the person shall live. If he or she reoffends during the period of the probation order the person can be sentenced for both offences. The court can decide that none of these is necessary and give an absolute or conditional discharge.

In many cases offenders before the court on one charge ask it to 'take into account' other offences which the person admits but with which he or she has not been charged; this often occurs with thieves and burglars. It means that this sentence may be heavier, but that a prosecution for the other offences is most unlikely to take place; the slate is wiped clean, so to speak.

The court has other powers at its disposal and it can make other orders. Commonly in traffic cases penalty points will be endorsed on a driving licence and a person may be disqualified from driving. Property, such as the instruments of crime or illegal drugs, may be ordered to be forfeited or destroyed. There are various provisions giving the courts powers to make sure that criminals do not keep the financial fruits of their crimes.

Legal costs of a defendant who is acquitted

The courts have a general power to order the costs of a person who is acquitted to be paid out of central (government) funds. Costs are not usually awarded where the person charged acted so as to bring suspicion on himself or herself, or was acquitted on a legal technicality.

Seeking legal advice

It is not easy to find out the law for yourself. Although some law books, and copies of Acts of Parliament, can be found in most public libraries, they are difficult to understand and it can be hard to find what you are looking for. Law books are usually written for lawyers or law students and use technical terms and their indexes are not usually designed for the lay person to use. Books written for lay people can be very useful, but the law changes, sometimes very rapidly, and they get out of date. It may be dangerous to rely on them too heavily.

The obvious person to take a legal problem to is a solicitor. You may be eligible for Legal Advice and Assistance (see page 490) to get advice and help, and if you have a case which may go to court you may get Legal Aid (see page 490). Many solicitors also operate a £5 interview scheme, under which you can have up to half an hour's advice for a flat fee of £5.

If you do not want to go to a solicitor, at any rate initially, there are other places you can turn to for advice. The Citizens Advice Bureaux can help with most types of problem, and indeed many have solicitors who hold free advice sessions. If a Citizens Advice Bureau cannot help you itself it will usually be able to pass you on to someone else who can.

Alternatively, depending on the sort of problem you have and where you live, there may be other places to go. Most large cities have Law Centres where free advice can be given on a wide range of problems. A consumer problem over defective goods can be taken to the local authority trading standards department or a consumer advice centre for help and advice, and the housing or social services departments help with housing and other problems. If you have a problem arising out of the use of a motor vehicle, an accident for example, and you belong to the AA or RAC, you can ask their legal department for advice and help.

Solicitors and barristers

The English legal profession is unusual in being divided into two branches, solicitors and barristers. Many people think that barristers are solicitors who have been 'promoted', or they see the distinction between the two branches as being similar to the split in the medical profession between general practitioners and specialists. Neither of these beliefs is true. In particular, although some lawyers transfer from one branch to the other (and it is a two-way traffic), the training and qualifications of each are quite separate and distinct. Although most members of both sides start with a degree in law, they undergo different exams and further training.

Members of both branches can and do specialise in one or more areas of the law, particularly in fields such as tax, commercial and company law, shipping and so on. This is especially the case with solicitors in the City of London.

Barristers

Two particular features distinguish the barrister from the solicitor. First, only barristers have the right to appear as advocates before a jury in the Crown Court, and before the High Court, the Court of Appeal and the House of Lords. Second, you cannot as a client go direct to a barrister; you have to go through a solicitor who selects and 'instructs' the barrister for you.

There are three main situations where your solicitor will instruct a barrister. First, if you have a case which is going to be tried in a court in which the solicitor cannot appear, he will 'brief' a barrister to represent you – a brief is the set of papers giving the barrister the information he needs to conduct the case, including the statements of witnesses and other documents. Second, although the solicitor may have the right to appear as an advocate in the court in question – for example, in the county court or the magistrates' court – it may be preferable to be represented by a barrister, because of the difficulty of the case or its importance to you, or because the solicitor does not do advocacy work, or simply because it may be cheaper to employ a barrister rather than a solicitor, especially when the case is to be tried some distance from his office. Third, the solicitor may decide to get the help of a specialist barrister when he or she does not know the answer to a particular problem or wants a second opinion. For example, barristers who specialise in personal injury claims are often asked to give an opinion about the proper amount of damages to claim or accept. In addition, solicitors often ask barristers to prepare the formal documents which are needed in court cases.

Barristers practise as individuals, although a dozen or so usually share offices known as 'chambers'. In these they also share the library, typing facilities and the services of the clerk. Some chambers specialise in particular areas of the law, but most are general, dealing with crime, divorce, accident claims and other general litigation often collectively called 'common law work'. Most solicitors have their own favourite chambers to which they send most of their cases, and individual barristers whom they prefer to use for particular types of case. The more experienced a barrister becomes, the higher the fees he or she can command, so solicitors assess the 'weight' of a case and approach a barrister of appropriate expertise.

Barristers are divided into two tiers, junior barristers and Queen's Counsel – also known as QCs or 'silks' (from the silk gowns they wear). A successful junior barrister can apply to the Lord Chancellor to become a QC or to 'take silk', normally after 15 years or so of practice, but not every applicant succeeds, and QCs form only the top 10 per cent or so of the profession. By convention in most cases in which a QC appears, he will be accompanied in court by a junior barrister, whose fee must also be paid.

All barristers belong to one of the four ancient Inns of Court in London – the Inner and Middle Temples, Lincoln's Inn and Gray's Inn. Many of them have their chambers here, but more and more chambers are being established in the provinces.

Barristers are also referred to as 'members of the Bar', the expression 'the Bar' often being used to refer to the whole of that branch of the legal profession. It comes from the ceremony of 'calling to the Bar' at which each new entrant formally becomes a barrister. The ceremonies take place at each of the four Inns of Court. Originally there was a bar in court rooms, rather like a church chancel rail, at which only barristers would stand to plead cases.

The governing body of the Bar is the Senate of the Inns of Court. It decides policy and is responsible for the disciplinary tribunal. The Bar also elects a body known as the Bar Council, which sets standards of professional conduct and ethics, and generally represents its members' interests. The four Inns and the Bar Council have representatives on the Senate.

Solicitors

Although some solicitors work alone as sole practitioners, the majority practice in partnerships. A few in London have upwards of 50 partners, but these are mainly specialist firms dealing with commercial law. Most consist of two to 10 partners and aim to provide a general practice service to their clients; they will deal with the complete range of work that comes their way, and call in a barrister or another expert for specialist advice if necessary.

Solicitors divide their work into 'contentious' business, or litigation, involving court cases such as criminal work, divorce, injury claims, and so on, and 'non-contentious' business, such as conveyancing and probate. The latter accounts for more than two thirds of the average firm's work.

The increasing complexity of the law and the need to streamline for greater efficiency has led most solicitors to specialise to a greater or lesser extent. Although the firm as a whole may provide a complete general practice service, you may well find that the partner who dealt with your will or conveyancing will hand you over to another partner if you get into trouble with the police or are involved in a dispute which looks like going to court.

People sometimes think solicitors spend all their time in the office dealing with papers while barristers spend theirs in court. This is not so. Some barristers rarely appear in court, and many solicitors who deal with litigation will be in court more than they are behind their desks. Most advocacy in the magistrates' court (which is where the bulk of criminal cases start and finish) and much of that in the county court is conducted entirely by solicitors.

When you go to a solicitor's office, the person you see may not be a partner in the firm or even a qualified solicitor as most partnerships employ people at different levels of qualification. When solicitors first qualify they usually work for another solicitor or firm as a salaried employee; such a person is called an 'assistant solicitor' and, outside London, will usually expect to become a partner in two to five years after qualification.

After passing the rigorous Law Society examinations and completing their formal training, trainee solicitors, or 'articled clerks' as they used to be more commonly known, put into practice what they have learned during an apprenticeship known as 'articles'. This usually lasts two years. Most firms also have at least one legal executive on their staff. They have been fairly described as the non-commissioned officers of the profession and are the modern equivalent of the old-fashioned managing clerk. However, their numbers are declining as their work is increasingly taken over by assistant solicitors. Legal executives generally handle the more straightforward and routine work, such as house conveyancing and probate and some types of litigation, divorce in particular.

Although your case may not be dealt with by a partner, you can always insist on seeing one. In most firms there is pretty close supervision of what the non-partners are doing and they go to a partner for help and advice if need be. The protection afforded to clients against negligence or fraud is just the same whoever is handling your file.

The solicitors' professional body is the Law Society. It deals with their qualification, regulates professional standards and practice, and deals with complaints and matters of discipline. In particular it organises a compensation fund for the victims of fraud by solicitors or their staffs and a block insurance policy which provides cover for professional negligence and which extends to all firms.

Although solicitors are now able to advertise the work they do and the sort of charges they make, the best way to find one to suit you, especially for matters outside the general run of conveyancing and probate, is by personal recommendation from friends or relatives, preferably people who have had the same sort of case as yours. A trade union official may be able to put you in touch with a solicitor he or she knows is experienced in employment problems or accidents at work, and your insurance company may recommend a solicitor to deal with road accident cases. Clubs for the divorced and separated know from their members which lawyers are good for divorce and marriage problems.

Citizens Advice Bureaux, libraries and the courts maintain lists of local practitioners which indicate the types of work they do.

Complaints against lawyers

If you think you have a justifiable complaint against a lawyer the first point to consider is which of the three main types of complaint you have. The first is where you think that your lawyer, whether a solicitor or a barrister, has been negligent – that is to say that he or she has given you wrong advice or failed to do something and as a result of that mistake you have suffered a loss. In that case you are looking for compensation, money to replace what you have lost. The second type of complaint is about a breach of professional etiquette – for instance if your lawyer has failed to keep your affairs confidential, or has insulted you or will not tell you what is happening on your case. With solicitors there can be a third type of problem, over the amount of their fees or interest on your money they have been holding, and these problems are subject to special procedures which are discussed later (see page 487).

NEGLIGENCE CLAIMS

If a solicitor or barrister has made a mistake which causes you to lose money, then you may have a claim. 'May' is the operative word, however, because it will be necessary to show that he or she failed to exercise the standard of care in dealing with your case that one would expect of a reasonably competent professional person. An error of judgment is not necessarily negligence, and you will not get compensation for poor advocacy, as barristers are immune from claims for negligence in court, as almost certainly are solicitors too.

Most negligence claims are fairly clear cut because the omission or error is obvious. The law is full of time limits, especially for starting court proceedings to make certain types of claim, and one of the commonest types of claims against solicitors is for failing to notice that a time limit is about to expire, with the result that the client's rights are forfeited.

In common with the disciplinary bodies of other professions, the Law Society (for solicitors) and the Bar Council (for barristers) will not try negligence claims and award compensation. You have to take legal action and that will mean taking legal advice to find out whether you have a case. If you have, it is most unlikely to go to court as most cases are settled and paid by negotiation. All solicitors and most barristers have professional negligence insurance policies.

Where your claim is against a solicitor you may think you will have trouble finding one to help you take proceedings against another. It is true that solicitors are sometimes reluctant to take legal action against colleagues in the same locality, but they will usually make arrangements for you to see an experienced solicitor some little distance away whose independence can be trusted.

If you are in doubt about which solicitor you should first go to, you should take your problem to a Citizens Advice Bureau, and, if you cannot find a solicitor to help you, you should write to either the Solicitors' Complaints Bureau (see below) or your local Law Society whose address you can get from the Bureau, and ask to be put in touch with a member of the Law Society's negligence panel for a free initial interview.

In practice, a solicitor who knows that he or she has been negligent will normally tell the client and try to put the matter right without involving the client in any additional expense. In the case of time-limits these can sometimes be overridden by the court, and the solicitor would then almost certainly try to get this done.

OTHER COMPLAINTS AGAINST SOLICITORS

If you have a complaint against your solicitor, the first step will nearly always be to take it up with him or her face to face. Most complaints about solicitors arise from a lack of communication rather than anything more serious. For example, you may think your solicitor is being very slow attending to your case when in fact he or she is waiting for a letter or a report or a search from someone else. But if you are not reassured, ask for an appointment with the senior partner in the firm; he or she may be able to sort things out.

If your complaint is serious you will have to take it to the Law Society, the governing body of the solicitors' profession. The Society has recently created an independent body, the Solicitors' Complaints Bureau, to deal with complaints. The majority of the members of its Investigation Committee are lay persons.

Your first step should be to write to the Bureau (address on page 512) with brief details, adding in your letter an authority for your solicitor to disclose to it details of your case so they can look at the file and get answers to their questions.

Although the Bureau cannot award you compensation for losses caused by negligence as explained above, and nor can it tell your solicitor how to handle your case if he or she is acting properly, in cases of shoddy work it can order it to be put right at the solicitor's own expense where this is possible or have the bill reduced. It may be that what appear to be unreasonable delays or an improper holding on to your file when you change solicitors are in fact justified, and you may get only an explanation from the Bureau. But at least you will have the reassurance that your complaint has been impartially investigated.

In the gravest cases, where the solicitor appears to be guilty of 'conduct unbefitting' a member of his profession – dishonesty, not keeping a client's affairs confidential, persistent delays in answering letters and dealing with cases, and so on – the Bureau may refer the case to the Solicitors' Disciplinary Tribunal, where he or she may be reprimanded, fined, temporarily suspended from practice or even 'struck off' and prevented from practising.

Different rules apply if your complaint is about the

size of the bill you have been sent. You should always speak to your solicitor first to see if you can get it reduced, or to give him or her the opportunity to satisfy you that the charge is justified for the work done. If not, you have two ways of challenging the bill. If the work did not involve a court case you can demand that your solicitor obtains a 'remuneration certificate' from the Law Society. This means that he or she will have to send the file to the society where it will be examined by a panel of experienced solicitors, together with your comments. They will issue a certificate stating whether or not the bill is fair and reasonable, and they can reduce it. The panel cannot increase a bill, and there is no charge to the client.

In both court work and other cases, you have the right to have your solicitor's bill independently vetted by the court, and where court proceedings have been issued – even if the case did not actually go to a court hearing – you will have to do this, as the Law Society cannot then act. A senior officer of the court will examine the work done and the amount charged, and can reduce the bill. However, unless the bill is reduced by at least a fifth you will pay the costs of this procedure.

If you have not paid your solicitor, before he or she can sue you the solicitor must inform you in writing of these provisions. You then have a month to follow them up if you want.

If you think that your solicitor should pay you interest on money of yours that he or she has held for some time – say, because you were abroad for a while after the sale of some property and asked for the money to be held pending your return – you should again speak to him or her first. If you do not get satisfaction, you can demand that your solicitor obtains from the Law Society a certificate as to how much interest, if any, is due to you. In practice, if the circumstances are such that interest ought in fairness to be paid to you, your solicitor will put your money into a separate deposit account for you. If this is not done a sum in lieu must be paid out of the solicitor's own pocket. The guidelines are that sums of £500 and over which are likely to be held for at least two months should be invested, although it is accepted that larger sums could attract appreciable interest even if they are likely to be held for a shorter time. These rules do not usually apply to deposits held in conveyancing transactions.

THE LAY OBSERVER

The 'Lay Observer' is an independent watchdog over the Law Society's complaints machinery, but he cannot intervene directly to get any form of redress from an individual solicitor. His job is to monitor the Law Society's own conduct in the handling of complaints, and to ask the Society to reconsider any complaint where he disagrees with the action taken.

OTHER COMPLAINTS AGAINST BARRISTERS

Complaints against barristers are far fewer than those against solicitors, largely because there are far fewer of them and they do not have the same regular contact with the client and continuous conduct of the case. In most cases a complaint will be made by the solicitor involved rather than the client. It should usually first be taken to the head of the barrister's chambers.

If the matter is serious or unresolved a complaint may be made to the Bar Council. Write giving particulars of the barrister concerned, the solicitors in the case, the court number if it is a court case, and details of the complaint and anyone else who can provide further information. The professional conduct committee of the Bar Council will have any necessary investigation made and it can, if necessary, refer the matter to the disciplinary committee of the senate of the Inns of Court for a hearing. The barrister may be reprimanded or in a very grave case disbarred or suspended. As with the Law Society, neither the council nor the committee can award you compensation, though the disciplinary committee can order a barrister to repay or forgo his fees if he has acted improperly. For compensation you must take legal action if you think you have a case.

Legal costs

Solicitors' charges

Solicitors in private practice are self-employed people, running their businesses either alone or in partnership with others. They earn their living from the fees they receive. Like anyone in business on his or her own account they must bring in enough fees to pay their office rent, staff wages and other overheads, and be left with enough to live on. At the same time the amount charged to each client must be reasonable in the light of the work done.

'Scale fees' laid down by law, which set rates determined by one fixed element, such as determining the charge for conveyancing solely according to the price of the land concerned, have all but disappeared, and solicitors' bills now are costed to produce a result which is fair and reasonable to the solicitor and the client. Slightly different rules apply to different types of work, but for conveyancing and other general 'non-contentious business' – that is to say most legal work apart from cases which actually go to court – the relevant factors laid down by law for determining fees include the complexity of the matter, or the difficulty or novelty of the question raised; the skill, labour, specialised knowledge and responsibility involved; the time spent on the business; the number and importance of the documents prepared or perused; the place where and the circumstances in which the business or any part of it is transacted; the amount or value of any property involved; and whether any land involved is registered land.

You would therefore expect to pay more for having a difficult or intricate matter handled than a straightforward one, or for a matter where particular expertise is called for and where the solicitor bears responsibility for large sums of money. With property you have to pay more for work involving expensive items, such as conveying an expensive house or winding up a large estate, than for cheap ones, even though the work involved may be pretty much the same, and you also have to pay more when your solicitor conveys land that depends on title deeds rather than a registered title guaranteed by the state, as the work is less simple. You also pay more if your solicitor has to travel, is called out at night, or has to drop everything to deal with an emergency.

But the most important factor is usually the time spent. Most firms operate a fairly sophisticated system of time costing, which involves knowing how much it costs to run the firm per working hour just to cover overheads. Detailed records are kept of all time spent on each client's behalf on interviews, preparing documents, making phone calls, and so on, and when the bill is prepared the cost of that time is calculated before the other factors are considered in working out the final amount.

However, time is not the sole guide. It would not be fair for a slow and inefficient lawyer to charge more than a quick and efficient one. Equally, a specialist in a particular type of case may spend less time on a piece of work than someone who has to look everything up. All the above factors are weighed and balanced in arriving at a fair price.

Another factor to consider is that a firm in the City of London, or some other expensive area, is likely to have to charge more for a job than one in a small country town, simply because of the much higher overheads they have to pay for rent and staff wages.

PROFIT COSTS AND DISBURSEMENTS

The solicitor's own charges are known as the 'profit costs', although they are not all profits, as overheads have to be paid out of them. They are subject to Value Added Tax. Most bills also include further items called 'disbursements'. These are amounts which the solicitor has to pay in order to deal with the matter in hand. This money does not go into the solicitor's pocket but to third parties. A typical bill for the purchase of a £50,000 house with registered title is given on page 488. Although it totals £1210.30, only £500 is income for the solicitor's firm. The rest is paid to the local authority, with whom the search has to be made, to the Land Registry, to have the buyer registered as the new owner, to the Inland Revenue because stamp duty is a tax, and to Customs and Excise for VAT. None of these can be avoided.

Most types of work involve disbursements. In probate matters there will be such items as probate registry fees and valuers' fees, and in a claim for damages after a road accident there may be doctors' fees for medical reports, court fees to issue a writ, barristers' fees for their work, and so on.

AGREED FEES AND ESTIMATES

As with any other trade or profession you are quite free to shop around to see who will do the job you want for the lowest cost; solicitors are no exception. In particular, with house conveyancing being so competitive these days, clients often contact a number of solicitors to find out what the charges will be. Even if you intend to go to the solicitor you have always used in the past it is sensible to know at the outset how much the bill is likely to be.

MESSRS ROSS & CROMARTY
SOLICITORS
9/10 NORTH STREET
SOUTHWOOD

AB/CD.

DR. to Mr and Mrs J.J.Citizen.

To Professional Charges in acting for you
in connection with your purchase of
Vine Cottage, Melchester, at the price of £50,000.

To include taking instructions, considering
and approving draft contract, raising enquiries
before contract with the Vendors' solicitors,
exchanging contracts, investigating title
and raising requisitions, preparing and
engrossing Transfer and completing the purchase.

Also to include the making of all necessary
searches and all attendances on you.

Fee			500.00
ADD:			
VAT			75.00
Disbursements:			
Local search fees	12.30		
Land Registry fees	123.00		
Stamp duty	500.00		635.30
			1210.30

With compliments

As with most trades or professions, it is possible to ask for a quote or an estimate, the first being binding and the second no more than an indication of the likely amount. Solicitors can agree to do a particular piece of work for a fixed quoted price, called an agreed fee. Whether a solicitor is prepared to agree a fee depends mainly on the type of work involved, because once the fee is agreed that is all he or she can charge regardless of how difficult and time-consuming the case may turn out to be. For that reason it would not be right for a solicitor to agree a fee in a personal injury claim, for example, because no one knows how quickly it will be settled, if at all, or whether it will go to a trial. On the other hand, you might be able to agree a fee for a solicitor to represent you on a careless driving charge at a particular magistrates' court on a particular day. Some solicitors will also agree a fee for conveyancing.

More commonly, however, solicitors will be prepared to give an estimate of their likely charges only on the assumption that the matter goes as expected with no surprise complications. For conveyancing, the Law Society supplies solicitors with special printed forms on which a written estimate can be given. In many other types of work, especially litigation, it will not be possible for the solicitor to give any real estimate at all, because of the complete uncertainty of how things will go.

Costs in litigation

The subject of legal costs in litigation cases – dealing with disputes in court – is one of the most difficult for clients to understand. Solicitors often imagine that their clients know the rules and do not explain them, and clients very rarely ask about them in good time. The basic rules concerning costs are in fact quite clear.

First, the solicitor must be paid for his or her work, whether the case is won or lost. An English solicitor, unlike lawyers in some American states, cannot agree to be paid only if the case is successful and then to receive a percentage of the damages. Such 'contingency fees', as they are known, are not allowed by the Law Society.

Second, a solicitor has a duty to tell the client if he or she seems to be eligible for Legal Aid and, if so, to see that he or she can apply for it. This rule applies even if the solicitor in question does not do Legal Aid work; the client can go to another one who does.

Third, unless the client is legally aided or the fees are being paid by an insurance company or trade union or similar organisation, the client is personally liable to pay the solicitor's bill, no matter whether the case is won or lost, and whether or not any order for 'party and party' costs (see below) is made against the loser.

Finally, a solicitor need not wait until the end of the case to deliver a bill or ask for money. Unless the client is legally aided he or she can ask for what amount to 'stage payments', either by delivering interim bills, or by asking for money 'generally on account of costs'. If the client does not pay as requested, the solicitor is entitled to stop acting. These payments are customary and sensible, since the client knows from them roughly what the case is costing as it goes along and can call a halt to it without leaving a large unpaid bill at the end.

In other words, unless the Legal Aid Fund or some other body is financing the case for you, you are going to be paying your solicitor for all the work done for you and expenses incurred, such as court fees and barristers' fees, whether or not your case succeeds, and that is so if you are bringing the claim yourself or fighting one brought by someone else against you.

At the end of a civil case that has gone to court, the judge or registrar will usually order the loser to pay the winner's costs. This is called an order for costs 'as between party and party'. Unfortunately for the winner, this does not always mean quite what he or she may think. It may not mean that the winner will get from the loser the full amount he has had to pay his own lawyers. The court will in due course vet a detailed bill prepared by the winner's solicitors under a process known as 'taxation' (although it has nothing to do with the Inland Revenue). The taxing officer will allow the winner only to claim 'a reasonable amount in respect of all costs reasonably incurred', and it is for the winner to prove reasonableness, not the loser to prove unreasonableness. So if you take a straightforward case to an expensive specialist lawyer, or you get two medical reports when only one was reasonable, or if you insist on seeing your solicitor twice on a point that one phone call could have sorted out, you may end up paying yourself for these 'luxuries', as they are sometimes called. Though the winner may think it unfair that he has to pay for making doubly sure that he would win, from the loser's point of view it is certainly fair.

In some matrimonial cases at present things are even tighter for the winner. The loser may be ordered to pay only whatever costs were 'necessary for the attainment of justice' with the emphasis very much on the word 'necessary'. Since in such cases the costs paid to the lawyers come out of the family's assets rather than simply reducing a damages claim, it is more than ever necessary to ask your solicitor exactly how costs will affect your case, not just at the start but at regular intervals as the case goes along.

The result of this is that the difference between what the winning claimant pays his or her own lawyer and what is received by way of party and party costs from the loser must come out of the debt or damages recovered, or, if the case was not about cash, then it will have cost the winner money to enforce his or her rights.

If a claim is settled by negotiation, as many are, it will usually include agreed terms about costs. Sometimes, especially in accident claims, the insurance company concerned will agree to pay the claimant's costs in full, or a fixed amount towards them.

If a case such as a debt claim ends shortly after a writ or county court summons is issued – either because the debtor pays or he or she has no defence so judgment can be obtained without a trial – the law lays down certain fixed figures for legal costs. These are simply added to the debt to avoid the need for a taxation.

In a county court there are a number of special rules about party and party costs. First, if a claim for no more than £500 is dealt with by arbitration, the general rule is that no legal costs for the hearing can be allowed at all. This is to withdraw the deterrent effect of a heavy order for costs against the loser. You can hire a lawyer if you want, but it will be entirely at your own expense. This is explained in the section on small claims. Second, there are limits to what can be awarded for the various steps in cases which are not taken by arbitration, depending on the value of the case itself. You may not get as much from the loser of a small case as you would had the case been larger, even though your lawyer has done the same amount of work.

If you decide to handle your own case as a litigant in person, you will not have a solicitor's bill to pay, but you may be able to get an order for costs against the loser anyway. At the moment the law allows you to claim up to £2 per hour spent over the case, or rather more – up to two thirds of what a solicitor would have cost – if you have actually suffered financial loss by handling the claim yourself.

Where one or both parties are legally aided, rather special and different rules apply, limiting the amount which a legally aided loser can be ordered to pay towards the winner's costs. These are explained in the section on Legal Aid.

The rules described above give the general position about costs, but like nearly all legal rules they are subject to exceptions. You should always think about costs in any dispute you may be involved in and ask your solicitor what the final position is likely to be.

Legal Aid

The modern Legal Aid system dates from 1950. It came into existence to ensure that no one is denied legal help that they genuinely need because they cannot afford the fees. The government provides the money out of the public purse, from a source called the Legal Aid Fund. There is no national legal service. Work for legally aided clients is done by solicitors and barristers in private practice, and they act in the same way as they would for a fee-paying client, except that their bills are paid out of the Fund.

Responsibility for the day-to-day administration of Legal Aid rests with the Legal Aid department of the Law Society. Since all legal work on Legal Aid is done by solicitors or by barristers instructed by solicitors it is convenient and efficient that the Society, as the professional body for English and Welsh solicitors, should run Legal Aid. The Legal Aid department, with a headquarters staff in London and area offices around the country, is separate from the general functions of the Law Society, and operates under closely worded Acts of Parliament and detailed legal regulations, as one would expect where large sums of public expenditure are involved. The types of work which can be undertaken under the system and the financial eligibility limits are laid down by Parliament and the Lord Chancellor's department.

Although we usually speak of the Legal Aid system as if there were only one system covering all types of work, there are in fact three separate schemes:

● the Legal Advice and Assistance Scheme, otherwise known as the 'Green Form Scheme', which exists to provide legal help of almost any kind up to a usual maximum cost of £50
● Civil Legal Aid, which enables a Legal Aid certificate to be granted to cover the cost of making or defending a civil claim – for example, damages for injuries after a traffic accident or maintenance on the breakdown of a marriage
● Criminal Legal Aid, which provides for paying lawyers to represent a person before the courts charged with a criminal offence.

Each scheme has its own detailed rules, but they have in common the fact that the person of modest means will have financial help with legal fees. Sometimes there is nothing for the person to pay, and the help will be completely free. In other cases the applicant's means are such that he or she can be expected to pay a contribution to the cost, and will be required to do so.

The Legal Advice and Assistance Scheme (the 'Green Form Scheme')

1 | *What types of work does Legal Advice and Assistance cover?*

This scheme is intended to cover help of almost any kind from a solicitor. The solicitor can give advice, write letters, negotiate, prepare documents, and other kinds of work. It does not matter what field of law is involved: divorce and marriage breakdown, an accident at work or on the road, hire purchase and other consumer claims, redundancy and other employment problems, housing and tenancy difficulties, and so on. Although most of the cases where the scheme is used involve a dispute of one kind or another, it can be used where there is none at all. It could be used to meet the fees for making a will or to prepare an agreement, for example.

There are, however, a few limits on what can be done.

First, it does not, subject to four important exceptions (see Q5), enable the solicitor to appear in court or in a tribunal as an advocate, or to conduct a court case. For that the client has to apply for a Legal Aid certificate in a civil case, or a Legal Aid order in a criminal case. The solicitor can, however, use the Green Form Scheme to give preliminary advice in such a case and to take the early steps, including helping his client to apply for a certificate or order.

Second, other than in some divorce cases, the amount of work cannot exceed a cost of £50, unless the solicitor applies to the Legal Aid office for authority to do more. An extension will usually be granted where a small amount of further work will be needed to see an end to the matter, or where higher expenditure is justified – for example, to get the help of a barrister to advise or to call in a technical expert to report. In many cases where more money has to be spent, especially where there is a dispute, the client will have to apply for a Legal Aid certificate.

Third, the scheme only applies to questions of English law. It does not cover Scottish law or the law of any other country.

2 | *How do I apply for Advice and Assistance?*

Through your solicitor. He or she will ask you some questions about your income, savings and dependants and then check the figures you give against a chart called a 'key card' to see whether you qualify, and what, if any, contribution you will have to make.

If you want to go ahead you should sign the form – the Green Form itself – which the solicitor completes. There is no question of your having to fill in detailed forms or having your means assessed and investigated.

3 | *How do I qualify financially for Advice and Assistance?*

This depends on your savings and income, including your spouse's, unless you are separated from each other or are in dispute – if you are seeing the solicitor about a divorce or maintenance claim, for example. The figures quoted are current at the time of writing, but they are increased every year.

Any cash, savings or investments you have will have to be declared, as well as any property you own which is of substantial value, such as jewellery; but you can omit the value of your home and household effects, your clothing and trade tools, and the value of an item which is the subject of your seeking legal advice. What is left is your disposable capital. If you have no dependants you qualify if it is no more than £825; with one dependant you qualify if no more than £1,025, with two £1,145. Add £60 each for any further dependants.

Unless you are ineligible because your savings exceed these figures, your income is also taken into account. If you draw Supplementary Benefit or Family Income Supplement you will be eligible. If not, your solicitor will ask for your income for the previous week, and will deduct from it

- income tax and National Insurance contributions
- maintenance, if any, paid out to a divorced spouse, for example
- £29.70 for your husband or wife, unless you are separated
- an allowance for each of your dependants of £13 for a child under 11, £19.50 for a child between 11 and 15, £23.45 for a child between 16 and 18 and £30.45 for an older dependant.

What is left is your 'disposable income'. If it is no more than £54 you will get free Advice and Assistance. If it exceeds £118 you will not be eligible at all. If it is between those figures you will be liable to pay a contribution to the solicitor of between £5 and £64 computed on a sliding scale. Your solicitor may agree to accept it in instalments.

If your contribution exceeds £50, the normal initial maximum value of work that can be done under the scheme, your solicitor will only ask for the excess to be paid if an extension is sought.

If the cost of the work done is less than your contribution, your solicitor will refund the balance to you. If the cost is more than your contribution he or she will claim the extra from a Legal Aid office, subject to the clawback described in Q4.

The advantage of the scheme is that if you are financially eligible you know at the outset what the maximum cost will be. If you are liable to pay a contribution you could finish up paying for all the work yourself, where little work needs to be done, but if it turns out to be more expensive your contribution is the most you pay.

4 | *Suppose my solicitor helps me to claim some money or property, or helps me to resist a claim. Do I have to pay any more?*

Yes, you may do. If money or property is 'recovered or preserved' as a result of work done under the Green Form Scheme, and is worth more than your contribution, your solicitor must use it to pay his or her bill.

Suppose you see your solicitor about a debt you are owed of £500. He or she writes some letters to the debtor and the debt is paid. The solicitor's fees are £30. If you had no contribution to pay the solicitor would collect his or her £30 from the £500, leaving you with £470. If your contribution had been £10, the solicitor would take the remaining £20 from the £500, leaving you with £480. In other words, the net result to you would be the same if you had not been helped under the scheme. The reason for this is that it would be unfair to make the state pay when you have been successful.

But this clawback (technically called a 'charge') does not always apply. Maintenance payments, or up to £2,500 of capital or property recovered or preserved in a matrimonial case, are completely exempt, as are some state benefits. Your solicitor can also ask the Legal Aid office for permission not to enforce the clawback where it would cause hardship or would be difficult to make because of the nature of the property concerned. It would cause hardship if, in the example above, the debt itself was only £30 or so and the creditor was poor, and it would be difficult to enforce the clawback if the property in dispute were a pet animal. In these cases the Legal Aid Fund would meet the whole bill, less any contribution from the applicant.

5 | *When can a solicitor appear as an advocate under the Green Form Scheme?*

There are four situations when a solicitor can appear as an advocate and be paid under the scheme. The system is called 'assistance by way of representation', or 'ABWOR' for short.

The first is in domestic proceedings in a magistrates' court. These are usually proceedings between husband and wife, or ex-spouses, or the parents of a child where the claim is over such matters as maintenance, custody and access to a child, or protection from domestic violence. In these cases the client will consult the solicitor at his or her office in the usual way, and, if the case is going to court, the solicitor can apply to a Legal Aid office for approval for ABWOR. The client does not have to complete long forms and have his or her means assessed, and no further contribution is payable beyond that originally assessed under the Green Form. Yet the solicitor will be paid the full amount of his or her charges, less the client's contribution, if any, so the normal £50 initial limit disappears.

The second is in care proceedings in the juvenile court, where the parents wish to be represented, perhaps to oppose a local authority application for an order placing the child in care. The same sort of application for approval for ABWOR will be made with the same effects.

The third is best known in connection with Duty Solicitor Schemes in magistrates' courts. The court may request a solicitor who is present within the precincts of the court to represent a person who is before the court, or approve a proposal by such a solicitor that he or she should do so. The usual limit of £50 still applies in such a case, as do the rules about eligibility and contributions. This device is mainly used in criminal cases where a person is brought before the court for the first time and has no lawyer; prompt advice can be given and, if necessary, an application can be made for bail and a Legal Aid order to conduct the defence. It can also be used in a county court.

None of the Legal Aid schemes provide general cover for cases before tribunals, but ABWOR is available to enable a person to be represented before a Mental Health Review Tribunal, which decides whether a patient confined to a mental hospital should be released. The application to the Legal Aid office is made in much the same way as for magistrates' domestic proceedings.

6 | *How is the Green Form Scheme used in connection with court cases?*

Where a case is going to court, the Green Form Scheme has little part to play. It is used mainly to provide early advice and help, including making an application for a Legal Aid certificate in a civil claim, or a Legal Aid order in a criminal case. The certificate or order will cover the cost of the trial and preparing the case. In civil cases, in particular, the Green Form is used to assemble enough of the case to justify the grant of the certificate.

Where assistance by way of representation is available the Green Form Scheme, of which ABWOR is just a development, applies throughout.

Although the Green Form Scheme itself does not cover having a solicitor to conduct a case as an advocate, he or she may nonetheless help a client conduct his or her own case in person, by helping to prepare court documents, collecting evidence, writing lists of questions to ask witnesses, and preparing statements to read to the court. A special use of this device is made in connection with undefended divorce. Similar use of it can be made in claims in a county court for less than £500 (see page 501).

Civil Legal Aid

7 | *I am making a civil claim which could finish up in court. Can I get Legal Aid?*

For you to get a Legal Aid Certificate a number of conditions have to be satisfied:

● you must be financially eligible (see Q9)
● your case must not be on the list of excluded types, of which the most important are claims for libel or slander
● you must have reasonable grounds for taking the proceedings (or defending or being a party to a case if someone else is making a claim against you); in other words you must have a reasonably strong case
● it must be reasonable to grant you Legal Aid – it would not be reasonable if you were trying to claim money from a person who obviously hasn't got any and who is not insured, or where the claim itself is trivial. It would also not be reasonable to grant Legal Aid in a case which does not need a lawyer, such as a small claim going to arbitration in a county court.

8 | *How do I apply for a Legal Aid certificate? Who do I apply to?*

The application is made to a Legal Aid office of the Law Society, and is made through your solicitor, who will help you to fill in an application form. The forms differ slightly depending on whether your case is a matrimonial dispute or something else, but each consists of two main parts, a statement of your case, and a statement of your means.

The statement of your case will normally be prepared by your solicitor; it should cover all the facts needed to show that you have a good case and that it is reasonable to grant you a certificate. The solicitor may attach other documents to it, such as copies of letters written about the case, or statements of witnesses.

The statement of your means provides the basic information about your finances to see whether you appear eligible financially.

You will sign the form, and your solicitor will send it to the Legal Aid office for you.

When you make the application your solicitor will hand you a leaflet explaining how Legal Aid affects you. You should read it through carefully and ask about anything that is not clear.

9 | *How do I qualify financially for Legal Aid? Will I have to pay a contribution?*

Deciding whether you qualify financially is a job for the Department of Health and Social Security, who will establish your 'disposable capital' and your 'disposable income'. You have to qualify on both counts. The financial statement you signed will be detached from your Legal Aid application form and sent to them. The assessment is usually done by post, but you may be asked to go for an interview. They may want to see financial records such as your bank statements, pass books and business accounts, and to ask you questions about the value of your assets. Unless you are separated, or the case is a dispute between the two of you (such as a claim for maintenance), your spouse's means are counted as part of yours.

The financial limits are changed every year, and those referred to below are current probably only until April 1988.

Your disposable capital is all your assets except the value of your home, your furniture, clothes and tools of trade, and the value of any property which is the subject of the claim itself (if any). If it exceeds £4,850 you will not get Legal Aid, unless your case will be very expensive, and if it does not exceed £3,000 you will not have to pay a contribution out of capital at all. If it is between those two you will have to pay a contribution. This can be the whole amount over £3,000, but may be less if your case is unlikely to cost that much.

Your disposable income is based on a close estimate of your income and outgoings for the following 12 months. The DHSS takes your gross income and deducts outgoings such as income tax, National Insurance, pension and trade union contributions, rent or mortgage payments and the cost of travel to work.

Fixed allowances are deducted for your spouse, children and other dependants.

If your disposable income is over £5,585 you do not qualify. If it is below £2,325 you will not have to pay a contribution out of income, and between those figures a contribution will be required. You will normally have to pay any capital contribution in one go if you accept the offer of a certificate, but an income contribution is usually paid by 12 monthly instalments.

If your income or savings increase or decrease within the 12 months after your application (sometimes longer), you may be reassessed, and you must tell the Legal Aid office of any changes.

The DHSS tells the Legal Aid office the maximum contribution you can be asked to pay. That office decides what your actual contribution is to be, based on the likely cost of the case. It may be less than the maximum.

10 | *Who decides whether my case deserves Legal Aid?*

It is obviously necessary to have some machinery to filter out those cases on which public money should not be spent because they are too weak or because the claim or defence is not worth making. Broadly speaking, the position is that in cases which are clearly strong and reasonable the certificate can be granted by one of the senior members of a Legal Aid office staff. He or she will be a solicitor employed full time to deal with Legal Aid applications. If he or she is in doubt, the case is referred to a special committee of practising solicitors and barristers.

11 | *I'm told it takes weeks to get a Legal Aid certificate. What happens if my case is very urgent?*

You are right; it does take some time for a Legal Aid certificate to be granted. The average is six to eight weeks, most of the time being taken up by the assessment of the applicant's means. If your case is very urgent and needs immediate action your solicitor will help you to apply for an emergency certificate, which can be granted without a detailed financial investigation. Your solicitor will ask you to sign an extra application form in addition to the normal one, and, provided that you seem to qualify financially for Legal Aid and the Legal Aid office agrees that you need immediate help, an emergency certificate will be granted. Sometimes cases are so urgent that cover is given over the telephone leaving the paperwork to follow by post.

Income from all sources before deduction of income tax, National Insurance contribution and rent

	Maximum permitting free Legal Aid	Minimum which makes applicant ineligible for Legal Aid
	Gross income (Including child benefit)	Gross income (Including child benefit)
1) Single person	£4,501 (£86.55 pw)	£9,736 (£187.23 pw)
2) Married couple	£6,476 (£124.53 pw)	£11,570 (£222.50 pw)
3) Married couple with 1 child aged 6	£7,320 (£140.77 pw)	£12,414 (£238.73 pw)
4) Married couple 2 children aged 4 and 8	£8,164 (£157.00 pw)	£13,258 (£254.96 pw)
5) Married couple 3 children aged 4, 8 and 13	£9,537 (£183.40 pw)	£14,631 (£281.36 pw)
6) Married couple 4 children aged 4, 8, 13 & 15	£10,909 (£209.78 pw)	£16,004 (£307.77 pw)
7) Married man apart from wife, paying court order of £1,200 per annum	£6,010 (£115.57 pw)	£11,104 (£213.53 pw)
8) Single parent with 2 children aged 4 and 8	£5,474 (£105.27 pw)	£10,709 (£205.94 pw)
9) Single parent with 3 children aged 4, 8 and 13	£6,987 (£134.36 pw)	£12,082 (£232.34 pw)

NOTES

The examples in this table are intended to be illustrative only and are based on the following assumptions:

1) the appropriate allowances for income tax and National Insurance contributions will be given;
2) an allowance for rent or its equivalent of £1,300 (£25 a week): NB If housing costs exceed £1,300 per annum then the gross income amounts shown above would be increased by approximately £145 for each £100 of housing cost: and
3) that in examples 2–6 only the husband has earnings.

The emergency certificate is only temporary and you will still need to proceed with your application for a normal one. If when your means are assessed it turns out that you do not qualify for Legal Aid, you will have to pay to the Law Society the full amount of your solicitor's costs.

Typical cases where this procedure is used include domestic violence injunctions, unlawful evictions of tenants and potential kidnapping of children by a parent who has lost custody.

12 | *What will happen about costs if I win my case? Will I get my contribution back? Will I have to pay any more costs?*

At the end of the case your solicitor's and barrister's fees will be paid to them out of the Legal Aid Fund. The amount they get will normally have been decided by a senior official at the court where you brought your case, to whom your solicitor submits a detailed bill. The court will also usually have ordered your opponent to pay your 'party and party' costs, but the amount will usually be less than your lawyers' total fees as paid by the Fund. Those party and party costs, if your opponent actually pays them, will be paid into the Fund, and the Legal Aid office can now see how your account stands.

If the amount paid into the Fund, consisting of your contribution plus any party and party costs paid by your opponent, is more than the Fund has paid out to your lawyers, you will get all or part of your contribution back. For example, if you contribute £400 to the costs, and your opponent is ordered to pay £1,200, but the total legal fees are only £1,300, then £300 will be paid back to you.

If, on the other hand, the Legal Aid Fund has paid out more to your lawyers than it takes in by way of your contribution and party and party costs paid by your opponent, it will have a deficiency, and, if you have 'recovered or preserved' any money or property as a result of the work done, the Fund has what is called 'the statutory charge' over the money or property in question. This means that you will have to make good the Fund's deficiency out of it.

As an example, suppose you have sued your employer after an accident at work, and the court awards you £10,000 damages. Your lawyers' fees are £2,000 and your employer pays £1,200 party and party costs. Your contribution to legal aid was £200. Then the Fund pays your lawyers £2,000. It receives your contribution of £200 and £1,200 from your employer, making a total of £1,400. It therefore has a deficiency of £600. Since you have 'recovered' damages of £10,000 the statutory charge operates to deduct the £600 from them, so you get £9,400 net. Allowing for the £200 contribution the case has cost you £800. Had the claim been about a piece of property rather than cash, the £600 would generally be paid when it comes to be sold.

Unlike the position under the Green Form Scheme (see Q4) the Law Society has no power to agree not to enforce the charge in cases of hardship.

The charge may seem unfair, but it has always been part of the philosophy behind Legal Aid that it is an indemnity scheme, not just a free or contributory one like the National Health Service. A legally aided litigant who wins is put in the same position as a fee-paying client. If you had paid your own lawyers privately instead of being legally aided, you would have paid them £2,000 and this would come out of the total of £11,200 you get from the case, leaving you in the same final position.

If you win a claim for damages, the charge is unlikely to cause great hardship. In matrimonial cases, however, where the charge operates against assets of the family concerned, it can create nasty and unexpected problems.

13 | *What happens about costs if I lose my case?*

If you lose your case, and recover or preserve nothing, you will be in a much better position than a person who is paying his or her lawyers privately. The Legal Aid fund will pay all your legal costs; you will have paid your contribution and will not be required to pay any more.

The court usually orders the losing party to pay the winner's costs, and if the loser is not legally aided there is no limit to what they might be; the fact that he or she has little or no money is not taken into account. People have been made bankrupt by the amount of those costs. However, if you lose a court case as a legally aided person, the court can only order you to pay whatever is a reasonable amount for you to pay. In deciding how much that should be the court will look at the financial positions of both parties and your conduct in connection with the case. Often the court will decide that you should pay to the winner only an amount equal to your original contribution of Legal Aid, although that is not an inflexible rule and it could be more.

14 | *My neighbour has got Legal Aid to sue me over a boundary dispute. I don't qualify for Legal Aid; where does that leave me? I'm sure he hasn't got a case. Will I get my costs back if I win?*

Let's take the point about the strength of his case first. If he had no case worth arguing it was most unlikely he would have been granted Legal Aid. He need not have shown a cast iron case, but there must be something to it, and you should have another word with your solicitor about it.

As far as costs are concerned, you will have to bear the costs of your own solicitor and your barrister, if you have one, and your solicitor is likely to ask you to provide money on account of these costs as the case goes along. Your neighbour is relieved of that and only has to pay his contribution to Legal Aid.

If you win the case you may be in difficulties getting any of your costs back from your neighbour. Because he is legally aided, the court cannot order him to pay more than whatever is a reasonable amount for him to find, taking into account your means and his, among other things (see Q13). It may be very little. You can, however, try to get an order that the Legal Aid Fund should pay towards your costs. As you were not legally aided and an assisted person brought a case against you and lost, the court could make such an order if you would otherwise suffer severe financial hardship. This rule would not apply, however, if you, as the fee-paying party, had started the case, and slightly different rules apply if the case goes to an appeal.

15 | *Can Legal Aid be granted for cases going before tribunals instead of courts?*

Generally, no. Legal Aid cannot usually be granted to cover the cost of tribunal cases. This is because in most of them it is not really necessary to have a lawyer.

A Legal Aid certificate can, however, be granted for cases in the Lands Tribunal and the Employment Appeals Tribunal as these both hear cases which can involve tricky points of law for which a lawyer is

needed. In addition 'assistance by way of representation' can be granted for cases before a Mental
Health Review Tribunal (see Q5).

In any other case, Legal Aid is not available for the
case itself, although the Green Form Scheme will
enable you to get help from a solicitor in preparing
the case, drafting documents, and deciding on the
points to make and the questions to ask witnesses. He
or she can even come along to the hearing at the
tribunal and 'advise and assist' you there, but it will
only be possible for him or her to tell you what to do
or say; the solicitor cannot appear as an advocate.
The main problem here is that the £50 initial limit on
such help will not cover much of the solicitor's time,
and some of that amount will have been used up in
time spent with you in his office.

Criminal Legal Aid

Just as Legal Aid may be provided for a person involved in a civil claim, so it is available for a person
charged with a criminal offence. Lawyers will be paid
to represent him or her out of public moneys if he or
she cannot afford to pay privately. This Aid is commonly given: 95 per cent of Crown Court cases are
legally aided.

There are two main differences from Civil Legal
Aid. First, the application for a Legal Aid order is
made to the court rather than to the Law Society. It is
usually made to a magistrates' court, as that is where
the case is to come first, and the Aid can cover the
hearings there and later in the Crown Court, if
necessary. Secondly, it does not matter if the applicant does not have a worthwhile defence, or indeed
any defence; a person who admits a serious crime can
be given Legal Aid to be represented in court when he
or she comes up for sentence.

The law says that Legal Aid should be granted
where it is in the interests of justice to do so, provided
that the applicant's means are such that he or she
genuinely requires it.

The criteria the magistrates' court should follow
were laid down a few years ago by a committee
chaired by a High Court judge who later became Lord
Chief Justice. The most important is that it should
normally grant Legal Aid wherever there is a serious
risk of the defendant losing his or her liberty, job or
reputation. Other factors include the complexity of
the case and any language difficulties he or she may
have.

Depending on his or her means, the applicant may
have to pay a contribution, out of income or capital.
The contribution, if any, is fixed at the time the order
is made, but is subject to review if his or her circumstances change. Broadly speaking, if the applicant
has disposable capital worth over £3,000, such as
savings, investments and valuable items of property,
other than the home and its ordinary furniture and
fittings, the whole of the excess can be taken as the
contribution to the costs. If, for example, your disposable capital is worth £3,250, then £250 can be taken
as your contribution. Contributions out of income
are payable by instalments over six months, the
amount depending on the applicant's disposable income. This is the average weekly income over that
period after deducting tax and National Insurance
contributions, travel costs to work, housing costs and
so on, and fixed allowances (50 per cent over Supplementary Benefit scale rates) for dependants. If the
sum is no more than £42 per week there will be no
contribution from income, but if it is more the
amounts payable – basically, one quarter of any
surplus – will be ascertained from a sliding scale.
These figures are current until November 1984 and
are reviewed each year.

If contributions are not duly paid Legal Aid can be
withdrawn, and, if the amount paid exceeds the
actual amount of costs paid to the lawyers at the end
of the case, the balance will be repaid.

If you do not have a solicitor at the time of arrest
and charge at a police station, then, if you qualify
financially for Legal Aid, the Green form Scheme
applies (see Q1); only the application is handled at a
police station.

Suing for damages

Motoring accidents

1 | *I was quite badly hurt a few weeks ago in a motor accident. It was clearly the other driver's fault, and I'm going to put in a claim against his insurance. What losses can I claim for?*

You will have suffered two kinds of financial loss. Your car was probably damaged at the time of the accident, and you may also have suffered damage to your clothes and other property. These can be claimed, insofar as they are not paid by your own insurer, as they may be if you have comprehensive insurance.

But you will also have suffered losses subsequent to the accident. You may have lost income through being off work. If you had to stay in hospital your family will have had the expense of visiting you, and if you were an outpatient you will have had to pay for your journeys to and from the hospital. Bills for private nursing or other private treatment may have been incurred, and other members of your family may have lost time from work to look after you. Your family may have had to hire another car while yours was off the road. These and any similar items can be calculated exactly and will be payable.

However, there may also be future losses to compensate for. It may be some months before you can go back to work. You may even be so badly injured that you will never work again, or find that you can only do a lighter and less well-paid job. There may be continuing treatment and expenses ahead. These future losses can also be claimed for, but because the future is always uncertain they cannot be calculated precisely. The way they are assessed is by calculating a 'net annual loss' based on the medical and other evidence and applying a 'multiplier' to it based on your age and likely period of disability. As the losses are in the future the net annual loss can take account of likely increases in income, so that, for example, a medical student who is disabled would be treated as having a doctor's income from some future date. However, the multiplier is rarely more than 15 even for a young person, to take account of the fact that a lifetime's income is being received at once rather than month by month over the years.

2 | *In working out the sum to claim, must I give credit for tax savings, benefits received, and so on?*

Yes. You are being compensated for your losses and any savings made or income now received as a result of the accident must be set off against them.

Tax refunds under the PAYE system must be deducted, and the fact that you will pay less tax on a reduced income is relevant to working out the net annual loss. If an employer has paid sick pay during absence from work, this will reduce the loss of earnings claim, unless it was paid on the basis that it would be repayable out of damages to be received. State benefits are taken into account in different ways. Supplementary Benefit and unemployment benefits are deducted in full. Others are not deducted at all, and one half of sickness, invalidity and disablement benefits received or likely to be received in the first five years will be deducted. Any sums received under private insurance arrangements are ignored.

3 | *How much will I get?*

That will depend on how seriously injured you are and what your losses are. Obviously a high-earning young person whose livelihood is taken away will have a much larger claim than a person near retirement on a modest income. What is a small injury to one person may be a disaster to another. A solicitor or accountant who loses a finger will lose little income compared with a pianist or surgeon who suffers the same injury. The damages would reflect this.

4 | *What else can I claim?*

Apart from actual and future financial losses, compensation can also be claimed for what lawyers call 'pain and suffering' and 'loss of amenity'.

'Pain and suffering' is easy to understand. Damages can be claimed for the pain of the original injury, the pain of past and future medical treatment, and residual pain, which may be short term or continue for life. 'Loss of amenity' is the inability to lead a full and active life, which may be temporary, such as missing a season of football, or permanent, where a disability will deprive the victim of one or some of his pleasures for the rest of his life.

These two are separate heads of damage and one can exist without the other. Nevertheless, they are usually compensated by a single sum, the size of which depends on the degree and length of the suffering and the extent to which the fullness of life has been reduced in the individual case.

5 | *Can I claim more compensation later if my condition gets worse?*

As a result of a recent change in the law, yes. If you accept compensation or you are awarded damages at a trial you can now come back for more. At the trial the judge can award 'provisional damages', leaving the door open to a further application should the condition get worse. This will be especially important in 'whiplash' neck injuries and others where doctors find it very difficult to say with any certainty what the future holds for the victim and where it may be many years before the full effects show themselves.

6 | How long will I have to wait for my case to be settled?

This is the most difficult question to answer, because it all depends on the facts of your case. There are always two aspects to be dealt with before a claim can be settled, or finally tried by a judge if necessary.

The first is what lawyers call 'liability'. Fault or blame for the accident must be established to make one party liable to pay compensation to the other. This is usually straightforward – for example one car pulled out of a side road or overtook on a bend – but sometimes the two drivers tell quite different stories, such as each of them claiming that he had a green traffic light. One must be wrong and yet neither side will settle.

Lawyers call the second aspect 'quantum' – the amount of damages payable. This turns largely on what the doctors say. Compensation can be assessed once there has been a recovery, or when they know exactly what the long-term effects will be, but not until then. Sometimes the doctors disagree; the insurance company's doctors might find the injuries less serious than the claimant's, or they might maintain that the claimant is malingering.

A substantial dispute on liability or quantum will usually mean the case going to trial on one or both aspects, unless the parties agree to split the difference. Fortunately for all concerned, few cases end that way. Where there is no continuing disability, the majority end by settlement shortly after the final medical reports.

7 | My claim is going to court, and I've been told that it could take ages. I desperately need money. Can I get at least some of it now?

Being injured is bad enough, but having to wait a long time for any compensation, with the whole family perhaps living on state benefits, can cause very grave hardship. A few years ago the law was changed to enable some claimants to get what is called an 'interim payment', which is an advance payment on account of the damages they are eventually likely to receive.

Where court action has been started, the court can usually order such a payment if you can show that the defendant has admitted liability or that you are likely to win the case and be awarded substantial damages. The defendant might challenge your entire case, or might claim that your damages will not be substantial because of contributory negligence on your part (see Q9) or a counterclaim of his, so your case has to be good and strong.

The amount will be what the court thinks is a reasonable proportion of what you will finally get, and it would probably cover your out-of-pocket expenses and loss of pay to date, plus a proportion of your other damages. You would strengthen your case here by showing particular needs; a person in a wheelchair might ask for the cost of adapting his home or moving to a bungalow, and the cost of an adapted car.

Insurance companies sometimes make interim payments voluntarily without the need to apply to the court, especially in respect of property damage.

8 | My young daughter was with me in the car, and was also injured. Can she claim for herself?

As a person who has suffered injuries she is entitled to damages from whoever caused them – the other driver or you, or both of you if you were each partly at fault. Even if the accident was all the other driver's fault, you could be partly liable if you failed to take proper care for her safety, by strapping her in her child seat, for example.

Do not be surprised if your solicitor says that another solicitor should advise on her claim. There can often be a conflict of interests between a driver and his or her passenger injured in the same accident, even if they are related, and one solicitor cannot act for both. Yours may well suggest that your husband or wife sees another firm about your daughter's claim.

Since she is under 18, she cannot handle her own claim or sue. An adult with no other interest in the case must do so for her as her 'next friend'. Any proposed settlement of her claim must usually have the approval of the court, and any damages received will be invested under its direction.

9 | The other driver's insurers are claiming that the accident was partly my fault. How does this affect the damages?

There are two aspects to this. Fault on your part can affect the amount you can recover from the other driver by way of damages, and it can also make you liable to pay part of that person's losses. If you were partly at fault for the accident happening, or if your lack of care for your own safety meant that either you suffered injuries you would not otherwise have suffered or they were made more serious, then you have been 'contributorily negligent' and your damages will be reduced as a result.

Negligence contributing to the accident itself is easy enough to understand. Failure to take care for one's own safety these days usually means not wearing a seat belt. The guideline figures here are that if no injuries would have been suffered had a belt been worn the damages are cut by 25 per cent, and if they would have been less serious the reduction is 15 per cent. If not wearing the belt made no difference at all, there will be no reduction.

If you were partly at fault for the accident, you (or rather your insurers, one would hope) will be liable to pay part of the damage suffered by the other driver. If you and the other driver were equally to blame, and on a full liability basis your damages are £50,000 and the other driver's £500, then he is liable to pay you £25,000 and you are liable to pay him £250.

10 | *The owner of the car responsible for the accident wasn't complying with the terms of his insurance policy. Can his insurers refuse to pay my claim?*

This is a rather complicated question, and there is no short answer. The broad position is as follows.

First, the insurers can refuse to pay out anything at all if at the time of the accident the vehicle was being driven by an unauthorised person (for example, the policy-holder's son, when the policy covers only him and his spouse) or if it was being driven for an unauthorised purpose (for example, for business use, when the policy covers only social use). In either case what happened was outside the terms of the policy, and the driver is completely uninsured under it.

Second, they can refuse to pay for property damage, to your car for example, if he failed to comply with the terms of the policy. Examples would include overloading the car, or failing to report the accident to the company within the period fixed by the policy.

As far as your claim for damages for your personal injuries is concerned, provided that the driver and use were authorised, they cannot generally refuse to pay despite his failure to comply with the policy terms. The same applies to damages for causing death. In respect of damages for death and personal injuries the insurers must pay any judgment obtained provided notice is given to them when the action in court is begun. They can only avoid liability if they can show that the policy itself was obtained by fraud or misrepresentation.

11 | *The other car didn't stop and can't be traced. Does that mean I get no damages?*

As the person who caused the accident cannot be found he cannot be sued, no matter how strong your case, so you will not get anything from him. Unless you have comprehensive motor insurance, you will have to pay for the repair to your own car and other property damage out of your own pocket. But you will get compensation for your personal injuries. The Motor Insurers Bureau (address on page 511), an association of the motor insurance companies, has agreed with the Department of Transport to pay compensation for personal injuries and death arising from the use of a motor vehicle where the driver is untraced, but who would, if traced, be liable to pay damages. The amount is the same as that which a court would award, the claim being negotiated and paid by a member company of the Bureau. If agreement cannot be reached a QC arbitrates. To be eligible for the compensation you must apply to the Bureau within three years of the accident.

12 | *The other driver wasn't insured and has no assets to meet any damages. Is there any way I can get anything?*

Unless you have comprehensive insurance you will yourself have to foot the bill for the repairs to your own car and other property. However, your personal injury damages will be paid by the Motor Insurers Bureau (see Q11). Under an agreement with the Department of Transport they will meet the amount of any court judgment for personal injuries or death arising out of the use of a motor vehicle if it is not paid by the defendant within seven days. Notice must have been given to the Bureau within seven days of the start of the action if it was plain at the outset that there was no insurance. If it appeared then that the other driver was insured, but it was subsequently discovered that he was not, the Bureau will still pay provided that the company which appeared originally to be covering the claim was given notice.

If the other driver did have sufficient assets, it would be worth suing him, and you might win an enforceable judgment.

13 | *Can I myself handle a claim for damages in a motoring accident, or do I need a solicitor?*

If you are claiming damages for personal injuries, you should certainly see a solicitor. Medical and other evidence will need to be collected and weighed, and the damages will have to be assessed as to what is a reasonable figure (see Q1). The lay person cannot really be expected to be able to do that.

If the claim is for only a small amount of damage to property, say the cost of repairs to a car after a slight bump in traffic, where the garage bill and a couple of more expensive estimates is all there is to the question of amount, then you might do it yourself perhaps with some advice from your solicitor or insurance brokers. You may find that your insurance brokers will deal with such a claim for you even though you do not have comprehensive insurance, and it is worth asking.

A practical point is that the other driver and his insurers may take a letter from a solicitor or from brokers rather more seriously than one from an aggrieved car-owner in person, who may or may not know what he or she is talking about.

If the claim is for less than £500, it can be taken to the county court if need be and tried under arbitration (see Q18).

14 | *Before I bought my house a few months ago I hired a surveyor to report. He said it was sound, but since we moved in we have found dry rot and other serious defects. I feel sure I must have a case against him and would like to sue him. How do I set about it? How will the case proceed?*

You should see a solicitor straight away; this is not the sort of case you can handle yourself, and it is likely to be much too big to be dealt with as a small claim (see Q16). Your solicitor will advise you about Legal Aid and help you to apply for it if you qualify financially (see page 490).

Whether you will win your claim depends mainly on whether you can prove that the surveyor was negligent, that is to say that he failed to come up to what lawyers call the 'standard of care' of a reasonably competent person in his profession. To prove that you would need to prove that he did not make the proper tests, did not look for the right things, or did not draw the right conclusions from what he saw in the way a competent professional person would. To get your proof you would have to call in another surveyor, perhaps two or more, to say what they would have done. You may find that the defects would not have been visible without the surveyor's damaging the property in his searches in a way the vendor would not allow.

It will also be necessary to look carefully at what you agreed with the surveyor he was to do; was it to be a full detailed survey, or something more in the nature of a valuation? You should examine the correspondence with him, the contract (if there was one) and the report itself as these could make it clear that certain things were outside the scope of his commission, and you may not then be able to claim for them.

If you seem to have a case, it is unlikely that it will have to be fought out in court. Nearly all professional people carry insurance cover against negligence claims, and yours would be passed to his insurers who would negotiate it and pay whatever damages are due in the same way as happens with traffic accidents. You would probably not even have to issue a writ, unless your solicitor thought it was necessary to put tactical pressure on the other side. However, if they refused to settle, the case would have to go to court, which would almost certainly be the High Court.

15 | *I was putting some boxes on a shelf at work when the ladder I was standing on broke. I fell and hurt my back quite badly. Do I have a claim for damages against my employer?*

Yes. The law places various duties on employers to look after the safety of their employees, and if those duties are broken an injured worker can sue for damages. In particular, an employer must provide a safe system of work and safe equipment. Having said that, you must take reasonable care for your own safety, and if you did not and the accident was partly your own fault you may have your claim cut. Did you know, for example, that the ladder was old and dangerous?

You should see a solicitor as soon as you can; claims for personal injuries are not the sort of thing you should try to handle on your own. If you belong to a trade union, it may provide a solicitor for you, or at least recommend a good one who specialises in your sort of case. The union may meet the fees, and, if not, your solicitor will help you apply for Legal Aid if you qualify financially (see page 490).

Your case will proceed in very much the same way as a traffic accident claim. Your employer should be insured and his insurance company will handle the claim. They will probably pay your damages after negotiation without the need to go to court. The damages you get will depend on how serious your injuries are and what financial losses you have incurred. You will be able to claim for the same sort of things as the victim of a road crash: compensation for pain and suffering, loss of earnings, extra costs and loss of amenity, if you cannot enjoy as full a life after the injury as before.

Small claims

16 | *I've heard people talk about a 'Small Claims Court'. What is a 'small claim'?*

A small claim is one for a sum of money of no more than £500. This might be an unpaid debt, the cost of repairs to a car damaged in an accident, the price of defective goods, and so on. The county court has a special procedure for dealing with disputed cases of up to that amount, disposing of them by way of an informal arbitration procedure rather than a formal trial.

The object is to enable simple disputes not involving much money to be brought to court and handled by the parties themselves without the expense of hiring lawyers. Indeed, lawyers are actively discouraged in that, if you do decide to get a solicitor to conduct the case for you, you will have to pay all his charges yourself even if you win, because the court cannot generally make orders for the loser to pay the winner's legal costs, other than a small amount for issuing the summons and the costs of enforcing the judgment (see Q25). This rule also removes the deterrent from a person who is worried that if he takes action and fails he will be faced with a crippling bill for the other party's costs.

Where the claim is for something instead of or in addition to money, such as an injunction or a declaration about a land boundary, the small claims procedure cannot be used, and there will have to be a trial in the usual way.

17 | *A pedestrian walked out in front of my car and made me drive into a wall. The damage to my car cost £550 to repair, for which I'm not insured. I know the pedestrian has the money to pay me, but he won't do so. Should I sue him? What will happen if he defends the claim, since it's over £500?*

If you want your money and he will not pay up, you will have to sue him. On the face of it he was negligent in walking out in front of you when it was not safe to do so and you have suffered loss, so you have a case. You have the usual two choices: putting the claim in the hands of your solicitor or taking steps yourself, perhaps with the preliminary advice and help of a solicitor.

The first step is to write a letter telling the pedestrian that if he does not pay within a week you will issue a county court summons. You can write that letter yourself or you can get your solicitor to do it, which may carry more weight and persuade him to pay. If he does not pay, a summons will have to be issued.

Because your claim is for more than £500 it is too large to be referred automatically to arbitration (see Q16) if it is disputed, so if he defends it there would normally be a formal trial, and orders for costs could be made. You would probably find it necessary, although it is not compulsory, to have a solicitor at the trial because the strict rules of evidence and other technical rules apply. You could apply for Legal Aid but, even if you win, the statutory charge (see page 495) could claw back a lot of your damages to repay the Legal Aid Fund. Privately paid legal fees would also cost you money, win or lose.

You might then consider suing for £500 instead of the full amount; that way, if he does defend the claim it will be referred automatically to arbitration, and since your case is quite simple you could handle it yourself. If you lose you will not face a large bill for his costs.

Whether you decide to sue for the full amount or just £500, he may pay when he gets the summons or you may be able to get a judgment without a trial or arbitration at all if he admits the claim or does not put in a defence within 14 days of the summons being served.

Even if you do sue for £550 and he defends, it is not always the case that there must be a trial rather than an arbitration. You and he could agree that the case should be arbitrated despite its size, and you could agree that a term of the arbitration should be that no orders for costs would be made. Alternatively, you could decide to abandon the top £50 of your claim later, so as to bring it back within the automatic arbitration limit.

Taken all round, you would probably be best advised to sue for £500 only; that way you know exactly where you stand.

18 | *What's the difference between a trial and an arbitration?*

Both types of hearing involve a court, in the shape of the judge or the registrar, hearing evidence from both sides to the dispute and reaching a decision on the issues. The effect of both will be an order that one party is to pay money to the other, that order being enforceable if the sum due is not paid. The main differences lie in the procedure adopted at the hearing and the existence of some technical rules of evidence at a trial which do not apply to an arbitration.

Procedure at a trial is formal. The lawyers wear gowns. Witnesses give evidence standing in a witness box with restrictions preventing 'leading questions' being asked by the advocate who called that witness. There is a prescribed order of stages, which the court must follow rather than taking the initiative itself and adopting the role of an inquisitor. There are also rules which need to be observed and steps taken before the trial even begins if certain types of evidence can be admitted at all, especially where documents are to be put before the court or conversations repeated to try to satisfy the court that what was written or said is true.

At an arbitration things are very different. It will not take place in a traditional courtroom, but in a large office, and no one wears robes. Although each witness will swear an oath before giving evidence, everyone sits around a table and the process is more like a discussion than a trial. The arbitrator can decide how to proceed, and he or she will normally take an active part and ask questions, often putting a point to each party alternately rather than going all through one person's case and then the other's.

The terms of the arbitration provide that the strict rules of evidence do not apply, so that documents and the contents of conversations can be put in evidence without observing the usual formalities. You can ask 'leading questions' of any witnesses you have called.

19 | *Do all small claims go to arbitration?*

Only contested cases go to arbitration. There is no need for a hearing if the claim is settled beforehand, or if the defendant offers no defence (most debt cases end this way). Most contested small claims are dealt with by arbitration in the county court. However, if the case is exceptionally complicated, if there is a question of fraud, or if the arbitration could cause injustice to an unrepresented person, the court will direct that the case should go for formal trial. If this happens, the 'no legal costs' rule does not apply and Legal Aid may be granted because of the need for the parties to be legally represented.

20 | *I have a claim against a car-dealer who made various statements about a car he was selling me that were not true. As there are no strict rules of evidence at an arbitration, do I need to call witnesses?*

First of all, in preparing a case for arbitration, you must realise that if you are suing it is up to you to prove your case. That is to say, you must prove to the arbitrator that your claim is justified; it is not for the other party to disprove it. The arbitrator will need to be satisfied about what the car-dealer said, and if it is your word against the dealer's you might or might not be believed. If you have a friend who can give evidence in person corroborating or confirming your word, your case will be stronger. A letter or written statement from the friend repeating the words will be less convincing, but better than nothing. Oral evidence is always the best, and though a witness you want to attend can expect you to pay any expenses or loss he or she may incur in coming to court, if you win your case the other party can be ordered to reimburse you up to certain limits.

21 | *Can I appeal against the arbitrator's decision?*

The right to appeal against an arbitrator's decision is very limited, and whatever findings of fact he or she makes cannot be challenged. You can have the decision set aside only if there was a clear mistake of law, or if the arbitration was improperly conducted. Such cases are very rare.

22 | *I think I may have to bring a small claim in the county court. What should I do first?*

The first thing to do is to read two booklets, both available free from your local county court. They are called *Small Claims in the County Court – How to sue and defend actions without a solicitor* and *Enforcing Money Judgments in the County Court – How to obtain payment without a solicitor*. The first explains the procedure for bringing a claim (or defending one) and includes all the stages and steps to be taken to get a judgment. Because the other party may not pay even though you have a judgment, you may have to enforce it and the second booklet explains how. Both include specimen letters and other documents you will find useful.

You should also obtain from the court office a copy of the current list of court fees. Even though you may not use a solicitor and have no legal costs, court fees have to be paid and can be quite substantial, especially if you are going to have to enforce a judgment. Weigh up the cost involved, bearing in mind that you may not get all your money back. As a boldly printed warning in *Small Claims in the County Court* says, 'The principal purpose of this guide is to tell you how to sue in the county court. Whether it is worth your while to do so is another matter. There is little satisfaction to be gained from winning an action if your opponent has no money to pay the judgment debt. You should consider this question very carefully before you start proceedings.'

23 | *I feel worried about handling the case myself. Can I get Legal Aid to have a solicitor conduct a small claim for me?*

The answer is generally no. Because the procedure is simple and designed to allow a lay person to handle his or her own case (see Q16), a lawyer advocate is not necessary and Legal Aid will not be available.

However, if you need legal advice or help and cannot afford to pay for it, a solicitor can advise and assist you under the Green Form Scheme (see page 490). This will include help in completing any of the forms you find difficult and getting your case ready for the arbitration if necessary. Although you will have to present your own case, the solicitor will be able to tell you what to say and will prepare the questions you will need to ask the other party.

24 | *What are the main stages in a small claim?*

The main stages are illustrated by the chart on the right.

You (or your solicitor) will prepare the request for issue of the summons using a form supplied by the court office, and two copies of the 'particulars of claim', the formal document setting out what you are claiming and why. These are taken or sent to the court with the fee.

The court prepares the summons and serves it, that is, sends it to the defendant (the person against whom you are claiming), with a copy of the particulars of claim, and a court form called the form of 'admission, defence and counterclaim'.

The summons tells the defendant that:

● if he or she does nothing within 14 days from service, you can request judgment to be entered against him or her;
● if he or she pays to the court the full amount of the claim, including the fees and costs shown on the summons, within 14 days, the action will be 'stayed';
● if he or she wants to defend your claim and/or make a counterclaim against you, or if he or she wants to admit the claim, perhaps asking for time to pay by instalments which he or she offers, the form of admission, defence and counterclaim should be completed accordingly and returned to the court within the 14-day period.

The court will have informed you of the date of service of the summons, so that you can request judgment if nothing happens within 14 days, and it

---

Stages in a county court action

1) P (plaintiff) takes or sends to the court:
Request for Summons
Particulars of Claim
Fee

2) Court Office:
Prepares and serves summons and other papers on D (defendant)
Notifies P

3) D receives from court:
Summons
Copy Particulars of Claim
Form of Admission, Defence and Counterclaim

4a) D may do nothing within 14 days:
4b) P requests the court to enter judgment 'in default'

5a) *or* D may defend the claim:
5b) The court refers the claim to arbitration and notifies P and D

6a) *or* D may pay the whole amount claimed:
6b) The court sends the money to P and the action is ended

7a) *or* D may admit the claim:
7b) P requests the court to enter judgment

8a) *or* D may admit the claim but ask for time to pay by offering instalments:
8b) If P accepts the instalments offered, P requests the court to enter judgment accordingly
8c) If P does not accept the instalments offered the court fixes a 'disposal' hearing when it will decide them

---

will send you any money received from the defendant or a copy of the form of admission, defence and counterclaim if he or she returns it.

Unless he or she is defending or counterclaiming you will be able to enter judgment, and the only need for a court hearing will be if you think an offer to pay by instalments is unacceptable.

If there is a defence or counterclaim the court will fix a date for an arbitration, or for a preliminary hearing to isolate the issues, which is the practice in a few courts. If, because of the counterclaim, the amount in dispute exceeds £500, the court will fix a hearing called a 'pre-trial review' when the registrar will consider the case and give directions about how it is going to be dealt with.

Enforcement

25 | *I've obtained a judgment, but the defendant still won't pay. What do I do next?*

You will now have to consider enforcing the judgment, that is to say taking further court proceedings intended to get your money. The procedure is explained in the booklet *Enforcing Money Judgments in the County Court* (see Q22). The court will do nothing at all on its own initiative and it is up to you to choose a method of enforcement to do the job. There are various methods which can be used to compel payment, such as by forcibly selling up property, emptying a bank or other account, or getting deductions made from your debtor's pay. The key to successful enforcement is to find out what assets there are and to select a method of enforcement which will get at them.

You may know something about your debtor's assets already. If your claim is for repairs to his car or house, you know that he has a car or a house, or at any rate did have. If you sold him something which has not been paid for, where is it? Traders often ask debtors' employees what they know about the debtor from conversations about hobbies and interests, or things they have noticed when working at the debtor's premises, such as boats or cameras. Bounced cheques have an account number on them, so you know details of the account.

The problem is that a general belief is not good enough, because you need to know detail – for example, whether any assets are owned by the debtor and not hired, like a video recorder, or leased, like business equipment, or borrowed or leased from a landlord. The best thing to do is to apply to the court for the 'oral examination of a judgment debtor', which means that he will have to attend court to be questioned on oath about his means. He will be asked first to supply a written statement, but if you do not find that adequate you can ask for a hearing and go along armed with a list of the detailed questions you want to ask. Get as much detail as you can. Ask where each piece of property is and who owns it, and where each account is, getting account numbers and balances. The more thorough you are, the more likely you are to get your money.

26 | *What are the most common methods of enforcement?*

The two most common are 'attachment of earnings' and 'execution against goods'. Attachment of earnings enforces payment from the wages or salary of an employed (as opposed to self-employed) person. The employers are obliged to make specified deductions from pay week by week or month by month and pay it to the court. The order fixes the normal deductions, subject to leaving the debtor with a protected minimum figure so that he or she cannot be reduced below subsistence level.

Execution against goods is the seizure by the court bailiff of the debtor's goods, which can then be sold at auction to pay the debt. Only the debtor's own goods can be taken, not items on hire purchase or property belonging to someone else. Some property cannot be seized, including clothes, bedding and trade tools up to a certain value. The property will not be taken and sold at once; the debtor will be given some time to pay and the goods are left with him or her, although they must not be disposed of. Often the debtor will try very hard to pay to avoid the sale, and may apply to stay the execution, promising to pay by instalments. It is important to give the court as much information about the property as you can – what goods there are and where they are. Remember, however, that second-hand goods may not fetch much at auction, and after paying transport and sale costs you could finish up with little in the end. Again, think hard before going ahead.

27 | *What are the other methods available? What assets will they reach?*

There are several less common methods: a 'charging order' on land, 'garnishee proceedings', and 'receivers'.

If the debtor owns land of any kind, either alone or jointly with someone else, a charging order on land can be sought with the object of having it sold to pay the judgment debt. The property will usually be an owner-occupied home or business premises. The court is not obliged to make this order, and it must look at all the circumstances before making a decision, in particular the size of the debt and the value of the property. A person's home would be unlikely to be sold up to pay a small debt, which could be enforced in some other way.

Garnishee proceedings are taken to intercept moneys that are due to the debtor. One can garnishee a trade or other debt payable to one's own debtor, but more commonly it is used as a way of getting hold of moneys in a bank or building society account. Such an account must be in the sole name of the judgment debtor, not in joint names. The order first freezes the account, and then orders the bank or building society to pay to the court enough from it to cover the debt. Two practical tips are: first, be ready after an oral examination to go ahead with this immediately before the debtor has the chance to empty the account, and second, in the case of a bank account, find out the day of the month on which a salary is paid in, so the account can be garnished the next day when there is some money in it.

When none of the other methods of enforcement will get at a particular asset, the court can appoint a receiver and give him or her whatever powers are needed to enforce the judgment. Examples of these powers are: reaching the surrender value of insurance policies, business profits, interests under trusts, rents of tenanted property, money in a joint bank or building society account, and so on.

Although charging orders on land and garnishee proceedings against a bank account are explained in the booklet on enforcing judgments in the county court, they are much more complicated than attachment of earnings and execution against goods, and most people would be well advised to leave them to solicitors.

28 | *Does imprisonment for debt still exist?*

No. Imprisonment for ordinary civil debts was abolished in the early 1970s, although it still exists in respect of unpaid maintenance in matrimonial cases and unpaid taxes. The only risk an ordinary debtor runs of going to prison is when he or she fails to comply with an order of the court, in which case he or she can be committed to prison for contempt. Failing to attend an oral examination is an example (see Q25).

Addresses and index

Addresses

Action for the Victims of Medical Accidents
135 Stockwell Road
London SW9 9TN
01-403 4744

Advisory Centre for Education (ACE)
18 Victoria Park Square
London E2 9PB
01-980 4596

Advisory, Conciliation & Arbitration Service (ACAS)
HEAD OFFICE
11–12 St James's Square
London SW1Y 4LA
01-210 3600

Age Concern
Bernard Sunley House
60 Pitcairn Road
Mitcham Surrey CR4 3LL
01-640 5431

Association of British Launderers & Cleaners Ltd
Lancaster Gate House
319 Pinner Road
Harrow Middlesex HA1 4HX
01-863 7755

Association of British Travel Agents (ABTA)
55–57 Newman Street
London W1P 4AH
01-637 2444

Association of Manufacturers of Domestic Electrical Appliances (AMDEA)
Leicester House
8 Leicester Street
London WC2H 7BN
01-437 0678

Automobile Association
Fanum House Basingstoke
Hampshire RG21 2EA
Basingstoke (0256) 20123

Birth Centre
55 Dartmouth Park Hill
London NW5 1SL
01-267 3006

British Agencies for Adoption and Fostering (BAAF)
11 Southwark Street
London SE1 1RQ
01-407 8800

British Homoeopathic Association
27a Devonshire Street
London W1N 1RJ
01-935 2163

British Medical Acupuncture Society
67–69 Chancery Lane
London WC2 1AF
(written enquiries only)

British Overseas Trade Board
1–19 Victoria Street
London SW1H 0ET
01-215 7877

British Pregnancy Advisory Service
7 Belgrave Road London SW1 9HD
01-222 0985

Chartered Institute of Arbitrators
75 Canon Street London EC4N 5BH
01-236 8761

Child Poverty Action Group
Fourth floor
1–5 Bath Street London EC1V 9PY
01-253 3406

Children's Legal Centre
20 Compton Terrace London N1 2UN
01-359 6251

Commission for Racial Equality
Elliot House 10–12 Allington Street
London SW1E 5EH
01-828 7022

Companies House
55–71 City Road London EC1Y 1BB
01-253 9393

Companies Registration Office
Companies House Crown Way
Maindy Cardiff CF4 3UZ
Cardiff (0222) 388588

Court of Protection
Staffordshire House 25 Store Street
London WC1E 7BP
01-636 6877

Department of Education and Science
Elizabeth House 39 York Road
London SE1 7PH
01-934 9000

Department of Health and Social Security
Alexander Fleming House
Elephant and Castle London SE1 6BY
01-407 5522

Department of Health and Social Security
North Fylde Central Offices
Norcross Blackpool FY5 3TA
Blackpool (0253) 856123

(DHSS war pensioners and aids and appliances branch)

Department of Trade and Industry
1–19 Victoria Street
London SW1H 0ET
01-215 7877

Direct Selling Association
44 Russell Square London WC1B 4JP
01-580 8433

Disability Alliance Educational and Research Association
25 Denmark Street London WC2H 8NJ
01-240 0806

Education Otherwise
25 Common Lane
Hemmingford Abbot
Cambridgeshire TE18 9AN

Equal Opportunities Commission
1 Bedford Street London WC2E 9HD
01-379 6323

Equal Opportunities Commission
Overseas House Quay Street
Manchester M3 3HN
061-833 9244

Export Credits Guarantee Department
PO Box 272 Export House
50 Ludgate Hill
London EC4M 7HY
01-382 7000

Families Anonymous
88 Caledonian Road London N1 9DN
01-278 8805

Family Division of the High Court (Divorce Registry, Probate Registry)
Somerset House Strand
London WC2R 1LB
01-936 6000

Family Rights Group
8 Manor Gardens Holloway Road
London N7 6LA
01-272 7308

Federation of Master Builders
33 John Street London WC1N 2BB
01-242 7583

Footwear Distributors' Federation
Commonwealth House
1–19 New Oxford Street
London WC1A 1PA
01-404 0955

General Medical Council
44 Hallam Street London WIN 6AE
01-580 7642

General Register Office (Births, Deaths and Marriages)
St Catherines House
10 Kingsway London WC2B 6JP
01-242 0262

Glass and Glazing Federation
44–48 Borough High Street
London SE1 1XB
01-403 7177

Health Service Commissioner (Ombudsman) for England
Church House Great Smith Street
London SW1P 3BW
01-212 7676

Health Service Commissioner (Ombudsman) for Wales
Fourth Floor Pearl Assurance House
Greyfriars Road Cardiff CF1 3AG
Cardiff (0222) 394621

Home Office
Immigration and Nationality Department
Lunar House Wellesley Road
Croydon Surrey CR9 2BY
01-686 0688

The Housing Corporation
149 Tottenham Court Road
London W1P 0BN
01-387 9466

Incorporated Society of Valuers and Auctioneers
3 Cadogan Gate London SW1X 0AS
01-235 2282

Industrial Tribunals (Central Office for England and Wales)
93 Ebury Bridge Road
London SW1W 8RB
01-730 9161

Institute for Complementary Medicine
21 Portland Place London W1N 3HF
01-636 9543

Joint Council for the Welfare of Immigrants (JCWI)
115 Old Street London EC1V 9JR
01-251 8706

Land Registry
Lincolns Inn Fields
London WC2A 3PH
01-405 3488

Land Registry, District
Birkenhead (Cheshire, Merseyside)
Old Market House

Hamilton Street Birkenhead
Merseyside L41 5FL
051-647 2377

Croydon (Greater London south of Thames)
Sunley House Bedford Park
Croydon CR9 3LE
01-686 8833

Durham (Cleveland, Cumbria, Durham, Humberside, Northumberland, North Yorks, Tyne and Wear)
Southfield House Southfield Way
Durham DH1 5TR
Durham (0385) 66151

Gloucester (Berks, Gloucs, Oxon, Warwicks, W. Midlands)
Twyver House Bruton Way
Gloucester GL1 1DQ
Gloucester (0452) 28666

Harrow (Greater London north of Thames exc. Barking and Dagenham, Havering, Newham, Redbridge and Waltham Forest)
Lyon House Lyon Road Harrow
Middlesex HA1 2EU
01-427 8811

Lytham (Gtr Manchester, Lancs)
Birkenhead House East Beach
Lytham St Annes Lancs FY8 5AB
Lytham (0253) 736999

Nottingham (Derbys, Notts, South Yorks, Staffs, West Yorks)
Chalfont Drive Nottingham NG8 3RN
Nottingham (0602) 291166

Peterborough (Cambs, Leics, Lincs, Norfolk, Northants, Suffolk)
Aragon Court Northminster Road
Peterborough PE1 1XN
Peterborough (0733) 46048

Plymouth (Avon, Cornwall, Devon, Dorset, Som, Wilts)
Plumer House Tailyour Road
Crownhill Plymouth PL6 5HY
Plymouth (0752) 701234

Stevenage (London boroughs of Barking and Dagenham, Havering, Newham, Redbridge and Waltham Forest, Beds, Bucks, Essex, Herts)
Brickdale House Danestrete
Stevenage Herts SG1 1XG
Stevenage (0438) 313003

Swansea (Wales, Hereford and Worcs, Salop)
Ty Bryn Glas High Street
Swansea SA1 1PW
Swansea (0792) 476677

Tunbridge Wells (East Sussex, Kent, Surrey)
Curtis House Hawkenbury

Tunbridge Wells Kent TN2 5AQ
Tunbridge Wells (0892) 510015

Weymouth (Hants, Isle of Wight, West Sussex)
1 Cumberland Drive
Weymouth Dorset DT4 9TT
Weymouth (03057) 76161

Lands Tribunal
48–49 Chancery Lane
London WC2A 1JR
01-936 7200

Law Society, The
113 Chancery Lane
London WC2A 1PL
01-242 1222

Legal Action Group
242-4 Pentonville Road
London N1 9UN
01-833 2931

Local Government Ombudsmen Commissioners for Local Administration
(Greater London, South-East, South-West, W Midlands, East Anglia)
21 Queen Anne's Gate
London SW1H 9BU
01-222 5622
(North and E Midlands)
29 Castlegate York YO1 1RN
York (0904) 30151
(Wales)
Derwen House Court Road Bridgend
Mid Glamorgan CF31 1BN
Bridgend (0656) 61325

Mail Order Publishers, Association of
1 New Burlington Street
London W1X 1FD
01-437 0706

Mail Order Traders' Association of Great Britain
25 Castle Street
Liverpool L2 4TD
051-236 7581

The Maternity Alliance
59–61 Camden High Street
London NW1 7JL
01-388 6337

MENCAP (The Royal Society for Mentally Handicapped Children and Adults)
123 Golden Lane London EC1Y 0RT
01-253 9433

Mental Health Act Commission (MHAC) and Mental Health Review Tribunals (MHRT)
Cressington House
249 St Mary's Road
Garston Liverpool L19 0NF

051-427 2061 (MHAC)
051-494 0095 (MHRT)

Floors 1 and 2
Hepburn House Marsham Street
London SW1P 4HW
01-211 8858/4946

Government Buildings
Spur A, Block 5 Chalfont Drive
Western Boulevard
Nottingham NG8 3RZ
Nottingham (0602) 293409 (MHAC)
Nottingham (0602) 294222 (MHRT)

(MHRT)
2nd Floor
New Crown Buildings
Cathays Park Cardiff CF1 3NQ
Cardiff (0222) 825111

MIND (National Association for
Mental Health)
22 Harley Street London W1N 2ED
01-637 0741

Motor Agents' Association
201 Great Portland Street
London W1N 6AB
01-580 9122

Motor Insurers Bureau
New Garden House
78 Hatton Garden
London EC1N 8JQ
01-242 0033

Narcotics Anonymous
PO Box 417 London SW10 0TP
01-351 6794

National Association for the
Childless
318 Summer Lane Newtown
Birmingham B19 3RL
021-359 2113

National Association for Gifted
Children
1 South Audley Street
London W1Y 5DQ
01-499 1188

National Association for the
Welfare of Children in Hospital
Argyll House 29–31 Euston Road
London NW1 2SO
01-833 2041

National Association of Estate
Agents
Arbon House 21 Jury Street
Warwick CV34 4EH
Warwick (0926) 496800

National Association of Funeral
Directors
57 Doughty Street
London WC1N 2NE
01-242 9388

National Association of Retail
Furnishers
3 Berners Street London W1P 4JP

National Association of Shoe
Repair Factories
82 Borough High Street
London SE1 1LL

National Association of Voluntary
Hostels
33 Long Acre London WC2E 9LA
01-240 3222

National Association of Widows
c/o Stafford District Voluntary Service
Centre
Chell Road Stafford ST16 2QA
Staffordshire
Stafford (0785) 45465

National Association of Young
People in Care (NAYPIC)
Salem House 28A Manor Row
Bradford EO1 4QU
Bradford (0274) 728484

National Childbirth Trust
9 Queensborough Terrace
London W2 3TB
01-221 3833

National Council for Civil Liberties
(NCCL)
21 Tabard Street London SE1 4LA
01-403 3888

National Council for One-Parent
Families
255 Kentish Town Road
London NW5 2LX
01-267 1361

National Federation of Building
Trade Employers
82 New Cavendish Street
London W1M 8AD
01-580 5588

National Foster Care Association
Francis House Francis Street
London SW1P 1DE
01-828 6266

National Pharmaceutical Associ-
ation
Mallinson House
40–42 St Peters Street
St Albans Herts AL1 3NT
St Albans (0727) 32161

National Society for the Prevention of Cruelty to Children
(NSPCC)
67 Saffron Hill London EC1N 8RS
01-242 1626

Office of Fair Trading
Field House
15–25 Bream's Buildings
London EC4A 1PR
01-242 2858

Consumer Credit Licensing Branch
Government Buildings
Bromyard Avenue
Acton London W3 7BB
01-743 5566

Patients Association
Room 33 18 Charing Cross Road
London WC2H 0HR
01-240 0671

Post Office Users Council for
Wales
1st Floor Caradog House
St Andrews Place Cardiff CF1 3BE
Cardiff (0222) 374028

Post Office Users' National
Council
Waterloo Bridge House
Waterloo Road London SE1 8UA
01-928 9458

Pregnancy Advisory Service
11–13 Charlotte Street
London W1P 1HD
01-637 8962

Radio, Electrical & Television
Retailers' Association (RETRA)
RETRA House
57–61 Newington Causeway
London SE1 6BE
01-403 1463

Release
169 Commercial Street
London E1 6BW
01-377 5905

Royal Automobile Club
RAC House Lansdowne Road
Croydon CR9 2JA
01-686 2525

Royal Institution of Chartered
Surveyors (RICS)
12 Great George Street
Parliament Square
London SW1P 3AD
01-222 7000

Society of Master Shoe Repairers
St Crispin's House
21 Station Road Desborough
Northamptonshire NN14 2SA
Kettering (0536) 760374

Society to Support Home Confine-
ments
Lydgate Lydgate Lane
Wolsingham Bishop Auckland
Durham DL13 3HA
Bishop Auckland (0388) 582044

The Solicitors' Complaints Bureau
Portland House Stag Place
London SW1E 5BW
01-834 2288

The Standing Conference on Drug
Abuse
1-4 Hatton Place London EC1N 8ND
01-430 2341/2

United Kingdom Council for Overseas Student Affairs (UKCOSA)
60 Westbourne Grove
London W2 5SH
01-229 9268/9

United Kingdom Immigrants
Advisory Service (UKIAS)
PO Box 132 London WC2E 7LR

Youthaid
9 Poland Street London W1V 3DG
01-439 8523

Index

Entries in capitals refer to major sections. The first figure indicates the page reference, followed by the question number, as in 41:1 (page 41, Question 1). Figures in italics indicate boxed descriptions.